D1368136

THE
UNITED STATES
GOVERNMENT
INTERNET
MANUAL

2007

THE
UNITED STATES
GOVERNMENT
INTERNET
MANUAL

2007

Edited by Peggy Garvin, MLS

BERNAN PRESS
Lanham, MD

ISBN: 978-1-59888-073-1

ISSN: 1547-2892

Cover Photo of the U.S. Capitol: comstock.com.

Composed and printed by Automated Graphic Systems, Inc., White Plains, MD, on acid-free paper that meets the American National Standards Institute Z39-48 standard.

2008 2007   4 3 2 1

BERNAN PRESS
4611-F Assembly Drive
Lanham, MD 20706
800-274-4447
email: info@bernan.com
www.bernanpress.com

Contents

Chapter 9: Energy

Chapter 10: Engineering and Technology

Chapter 11: Environment and Nature

Chapter 12: Government and Politics

Chapter 13: Health and Safety

Chapter 20: Transportation

Appendixes

Indexes

About the Editor

Peggy Garvin is an information consultant and the editor of *The United States Government Internet Manual*, published by Bernan Press. She writes a monthly column about government information online for the Web magazine LLRX.com, and is also author of *Real World Research Skills*, published by TheCapitol.Net. Peggy has trained librarians, public policy analysts, U.S. congressional staff, and other Washington professionals on using government Internet resources. Her 20-year career includes work in reference and electronic resource management with both the Library of Congress Congressional Research Service and the private sector in Washington, DC. Peggy chairs the Government Information Division of the Special Libraries Association and is a member of the American Libraries Association and the Association of Independent Information Professionals. She earned her Bachelor of Arts degree in American History from the University of Virginia and her Master of Library Science degree from the Syracuse University School of Information Studies.

Preface

The fourth edition of *The United States Government Internet Manual* is your research guide to federal government information on the World Wide Web. Designed as a complement to the official *United States Government Manual*, this book is written to help you locate and understand government information. Substantive descriptions, government organization charts, and multiple indexes assist you in finding valuable data and information that usually remains hidden in the "deep Web."

The *Manual* features entries for over 2,000 government information Web sites organized by topic for easy browsing. Web site descriptions typically include information about the sponsoring agency, notes on the useful or unique aspects of the site, and lists of some of the major government publications hosted on the site. A one-page "Quick Guide," which can be found inside this book's front cover, lists major federal agencies and the leading online library, data source, and finding aid sites with their Web addresses. Organization charts for the federal government, the U.S. Congress, and each Cabinet-level department are also presented with Web addresses. An appendix lists Web addresses for individual members of Congress and congressional committees. Multiple indexes in the back of the book help you locate Web sites by agency, site name, subject, and government publication. A separate index lists Web sites with full or substantial Spanish-language versions.

Production of the *Manual* is the work of a small team. I would like to thank the following members of the Bernan Press editorial and production departments for their efforts: publisher Kenneth E. Lawrence, managing editor Katherine A. DeBrandt, staff editor Shana Hertz, production team leader Jo A. Wilson, and Bernan's IT staff.

In introducing this fourth edition of *The United States Government Internet Manual*, I would also like to thank the keepers of the Web sites listed in this book for the services they provide.

Peggy Garvin, MLS
Editor

Introduction

The United States Government Internet Manual is a researcher's guide to federal government information on the World Wide Web. The United States government has long been known as a prolific publisher. Now, most of its publishing activity takes place online. Citizens and researchers around the globe can turn to the World Wide Web for access to laws, regulations, maps, consumer health tips, satellite images, medical and scientific research, education resources, military history, foreign policy, grants and contract opportunities, financial data, and statistics of every kind—all published in digital formats on U.S. federal government Web sites. The federal government has also moved beyond static Web publications to provide e-government services and online tools for interactive information analysis.

The explosion of government information on the Internet has many positive aspects for researchers. Information that once had to be purchased and delivered by mail, such as copies of the *Federal Register*, can now be accessed online quickly and usually at no charge. Much of the government information online is free of copyright restrictions; it can now be copied and distributed easily in its electronic form. Information and services that previously could be obtained only during government working hours or library hours have become available online at almost any time, on any day, and independent of physical location.

As more information is created in electronic format with no printed equivalents, however, weaknesses in the current state of online government information have become evident. Primary concerns for researchers, libraries, and governments include authentication, cataloging, permanent access, and long-term preservation. Current government initiatives addressing aspects of these challenges include:

- National Archives and Records Administration Electronic Records Archives. The goal of this project is to create a system that will authentically preserve and provide access to any kind of electronic record, free from dependency on any specific hardware or software. For more information, see <http://www.archives.gov/era/>.

- National Digital Information Infrastructure and Preservation Program (NDI-IPP). A collaborative effort led by the Library of Congress, the Digital Preservation program brings a national focus to the policy, standards, and technical components necessary to preserve digital content of all types. For more information, see <http://www.digitalpreservation.gov/>.

- The Government Printing Office Future Digital Information System (FDsys). FDsys will serve as the next generation system for organizing, authenticating, preserving, and providing access to federal government documents online. The system will handle all documents within the scope of the Federal Depository Library Program for both printed documents and documents that exist only in digital format. It will also handle text and multimedia formats. For more information, see <http://www.gpo.gov/projects/fdsys.htm>.

Finding Government Information on the Web

A report by the California Digital Library on Web-based government information summarized its review of government Web sites this way:

> In general, the domain of Web-based government information is hard to define, constantly expanding, and highly volatile. In addition, Web-based government information is generally marked by a high degree of format diversity (ranging from text, to images, to databases), genre diversity (including publications, documents, and databases) and opacity (a high percentage of the content is hidden in the deep Web).[1]

The California Digital Library report notes that government information is not neatly confined to the .gov or .mil Internet domains. Some government and quasi-government sites have Web addresses ending in .fed.us, .edu, .org, and even .com. The report also notes that much government information is "hidden in the deep Web." The phrase "the deep Web" refers to content on the Internet that cannot be indexed by search engines for various reasons. Recent articles[2] have quoted Google executive J. L. Needham as stating that roughly 20 to 40 percent of the content at agency Web sites cannot be indexed by Google (and, presumably, other search engines).

These characteristics make finding Web-based government information difficult. Research aids are needed. But why publish a printed directory to online information? *The United States Government Internet Manual* presents some key advantages. It provides the *context* that an alphabetical list of agency links or the mixed results of a search engine do not. It zeroes in on resources of research value and identifies noteworthy resources within large sites.

Search engines are most helpful when a researcher knows that certain information exists somewhere on the Web and can construct a search that produces the desired Web site within the first few pages of the search results. Even then, information may be missed because search engine databases cannot and do not find everything on the Internet. The *Manual* offers overlapping approaches to *browsing* for government information, helping researchers discover resources they may not have realized were available or quickly locate resources that are difficult to describe in a keyword search.

This fourth edition of the *Manual* adds numerous new sites and updates content descriptions and publications listings. It also acknowledges the need of many libraries for pointers toward information available in Spanish. This edition includes an index to government Web sites that have a full or substantial Spanish-language version. In addition, individual site descriptions note any content available in Spanish or other foreign languages. Overall, the book's focus remains on researchers, from the elementary school teacher looking for educational materials to the engineer looking for technical standards.

---

[1] University of California. California Digital Library. "Web-based Government Information: Evaluating Solutions for Capture, Curation, and Preservation (November 2003.) <http://www.cdlib.org/programs/Web-based_archiving_mellon_Final.pdf>, page 5. (Accessed December 14, 2006.)

[2] Jackson, Joab. "Google Wants You." (November 20, 2006). <http://www.gcn.com/print/25_33/42593-1.html>. (Accessed December 14, 2006); and Pulliam, Daniel. "Google Seeks Better Access to Government Information." (October 25, 2006). http://www.govexec.com/dailyfed/1006/102506p1.htm>. (Accessed December 14, 2006.)

Scope

The United States Government Internet Manual focuses on United States federal government information and services accessible via the Internet. The majority of the Web sites described in this book are the products of federal government agencies. The book also includes sites from interagency groups, federal advisory boards and commissions, private organizations established by congressional legislation, and quasi-governmental organizations, as well as sites produced by outside organizations with federal agency sponsorship or partnerships. In addition, it covers selected sites created by nongovernmental organizations to help researchers find federal government information, such as the University of Michigan Documents Center and the privately run National Security Archive.

Each entry typically represents one Web site. In some cases, complementary or companion sites are described in the same entry. The term "site" is used loosely to describe a block of information, data, and/or services found at the provided Web address. Due to the networked nature of the Web, it is often difficult to define where one Web site ends and another begins. We have taken a practical approach in this book by defining sites to be those identifiable blocks of Web pages that serve a research, reference, promotional, or educational purpose. Some Web databases, publications, or services that might be considered part of a larger site are given their own entry when they are of high research or reference value.

Web sites included in the *Manual* span a broad range of subjects and serve an equally broad range of audiences. A sampling of sites representative of this breadth includes the Abraham Lincoln Bicentennial Commission, Biomass Research, Census 2010, The National Trails System, Nutrition.gov, science.gov, TradeStats Express, and the United States Supreme Court. The government Web sites in this publication have been selected and annotated because they meet the research and reference needs of citizens, consumers, businesses, librarians, teachers, scientists, students, and others.

For the most part, only sites that do not require payment or registration, or otherwise limit public access, are included. All exceptions have been noted. Some sites are publicly accessible but block portions of their content; where significant, this has been noted as well.

Organization

The inside cover of this book features a "Quick Guide to Primary Government Web Sites and Finding Aids." The Quick Guide has Web addresses for frequently used government information sites and the entry number for each site's listing in the *Manual*.

The *Manual's* table of contents provides a starting point for browsing Web sites by topic. The table of contents shows the starting page numbers for the 20 subject-oriented chapters and the sub-topic breakdown within those chapters.

The *Manual's* prefatory pages include U.S. government organization charts. Charts are provided for each of the Cabinet-level departments or agencies, the United States Congress, and for an overview of the United States government. The charts are based on similar organization charts in the government document *The United States Government Manual* (Washington, DC: Government Printing Office) and from organization charts provided on some of the departments' Web sites. The charts are annotated with Web addresses for each organizational component when available. These organization charts are not intended to represent the complete or formal organization of government entities, but rather to provide an alternative approach to finding government Web sources.

The main section of the book presents entries describing individual government information Web sites. These are divided into 20 subject-oriented chapters. Arranged alphabetically, chapters are further divided by sub-topic. Each chapter begins with a note about the scope of the chapter. The first chapter, Finding Aids, describes a selection of Web sites designed to help researchers find government information. These sites typically cut across many subject areas. The sections covering libraries and kids' pages also cut across many subject areas.

Individual entries are organized as follows:

Entry Number: Each record starts with an entry number. The entry numbers are used in all of the indexes to refer back to specific records.

Site Name: Directly following the entry number is a site name or title for the resource. Determining the site name of an Internet source is not as easy as finding the title of a book. For the purposes of this work, the editor has used several sources to identify the site name, including agency press releases referring to the site, the name given to the site in the HTML <title> tag, or the initial heading or graphic. Because names of Web sites are subject to ambiguity or change and do not always uniquely identify a site, they represent just one way of referring to a resource. The Web address (also referred to as a Uniform Resource Locator or URL) is the best way to uniquely identify a resource, although even this can change.

Primary URL: The Web address or URL indicates the location that should be entered in your Web browser to retrieve the Web site.

Alternate URL: For Web sites with several valid addresses or significant complementary Web sites, additional URLs are listed in the Alternate URL field. The site description often explains the utility of the alternate URL.

Sponsors: This section identifies the lead organization that produces the site. Sponsors are most often federal government agencies, but commercial, educational, and nonprofit organizations will also be listed here when they host or sponsor a specific resource. Most of the government agencies listed are United States federal agencies, so "United States" has usually been dropped from the start of the sponsoring agency names (unless it is an integral part of the name). For government agencies, the sponsor name in the entries usually includes a full or partial organizational hierarchy, such as "Agriculture Department — Economic Research Service." In some cases, the full hierarchy has been collapsed. Consult *The United States Government Manual*, <http://www.gpoaccess.gov/gmanual/>, or other resources for official organizational information.

Description: The resource description explains a site's organization, principal features, menu items, and significant links. For many agencies, a brief description of the agency's mission is included to help explain the site's subject coverage. The description may mention significant publications available on the site and which sections of the site include online documents. If the site has content available in languages other than English, that is noted. The utility of the site, its ease of use, and the potential audience may be evaluated as well; this usually can be found in the last paragraph of the description.

Subjects: The subject terms describe the primary focus of the resource. Some of the subject terms contain subheadings that more accurately represent the topic. The subject headings are included in the Master Index. (The book's table of contents, with subject-oriented chapters and chapter subsections, can also be used to find material by topic.)

Publications: This section lists the selected publications available from the Web site. The types of publications listed include important titles, series, or periodicals, but not every available publication is listed. The Superintendent of

Documents (SuDoc) number at the end of most of the titles is used by the Federal Depository Library Program to identify and often to shelve print publications from the Government Printing Office. The SuDoc numbers are useful for finding online counterparts of print publications in a Federal Depository Library collection, as well as for tracking down older print counterparts of online publications. The root SuDoc number is most often used, rather than the full SuDocs for each individual item. Selected publications without SuDoc numbers are also included in this field. The Publication Index provides access to the entries containing listed publications by publication title.

Two appendixes at the end of the book list the Web addresses for members of the House and Senate and for the congressional committees in both chambers.

At the back of the book, the *Manual* features four indexes:

The **Sponsor Name/Site Name Index** lists entries by their sponsoring department or organization, using the top level of the organizational hierarchy. For example, entries from the Internal Revenue Service are listed under "Treasury Department," along with sites from other Treasury agencies and bureaus. Excluded from this index are entries for the Web sites of members of Congress and the individual congressional committees.

The **Publication Index** lists government publications referenced in the individual entries. They are in alphabetical order and include the Superintendent of Documents number (SuDoc) if available.

The **Spanish Web Site Index** lists sites that have full or substantial versions available in Spanish. Many government Web sites carry some publications or pages in Spanish, and individual entries in the *Manual* note what type of non-English material is available at each site. The Spanish Web Site Index is limited to those sites with substantial Spanish-language versions.

The **Master Index** is a combined index of entries by subject, sponsor name (at the agency, bureau, division, or department level), and site name. Excluded from this index are entries for the Web sites of members of Congress and the individual congressional committees.

How to Use this Book

If Looking For ...	Check ...
Major department or agency Web site	• Quick Guide, inside cover • U.S. Government Organization Charts
Web sites on a topic	• Table of Contents, with chapters and chapter subtopics • Master Index
Web site sponsored by a particular agency or organization	• Sponsor/Site Name Index
A major government publication that might be online	•Publication Index
Web site for which you know the name, but not the Web address	• Master Index

What to Watch for in 2007

Each year, new government Web sites are being developed and are scheduled to come online after this book goes to press. A sample of the noteworthy developments is provided here.

The Department of the Interior's **Bureau of Indian Affairs (BIA) Web site** remains affected by the ongoing *Cobell v. Kempthorne* litigation in the U.S. District Court for the District of Columbia. The BIA site currently carries the following message: "The BIA Web site as well as the BIA mail servers have been made temporarily unavailable due to the *Cobell* litigation. Please continue to check from time to time. We have no estimate on when authorization will be given to reactivate these sites." The Department of Justice maintains a Web page on the topic at <http://www.usdoj.gov/civil/cases/cobell/>. The Blackfeet Reservation Development Fund maintains an informative site for the plaintiff at <http://www.indiantrust.com/>.

The **Federal Funding Accountability and Transparency Act of 2006** (Public Law 109-282) directs the Office of Management and Budget (OMB) to ensure that, by January 2008, the federal government provides public access to a single, searchable Web site that reports federal awards (grants, loans, cooperative agreements) and expenditures. For future announcements about the system, check the OMB press releases at <http://www.whitehouse.gov/omb/pubpress/>.

FirstGov, <http://www.firstgov.gov>, is planning to launch a video service to provide centralized, public access to the government's online video libraries.

The Government Printing Office (GPO) is moving forward with a major re-engineering of its pioneer **GPO Access** (<http://www.gpoaccess.gov/>) Web site. The project is currently called FDsys, short for Future Digital System. Background information is available on the project Web site at <http://www.gpo.gov/projects/fdsys.htm>. Updates on the project are posted to the FDsys blog at <http://fdsys.blogspot.com/>.

In 2006, the **Library of Congress** launched a beta test version of a new site search engine, which can be found at <http://www.loc.gov/search/new/>. For the first time, users can search many of the Library of Congress's popular Web collections from a single search box. This site will be enhanced in 2007 to allow users to search additional repositories.

The Department of Energy is planning to upgrade its **science.gov** Web site (<http://www.science.gov/>) to version 4.0. The new version will include such features as the ability to send search results via e-mail to an individual or to a listserv, to sort results by date, and to focus search results by searching within the results of an initial search.

In 2007, the Library of Congress will launch several new features on the **THOMAS** legislative information Web site, <http://thomas.loc.gov>. New features will potentially include the ability to search all documents types simultaneously, to search all Congresses from a single search box, and to perform guided searches for legislative materials.

What Can You Find at Agency Web Sites?

Federal departments and agencies vary widely in the amount and type of information they provide online, but some standard content can typically be found at these sites. A list of the type of content or features one can often (but not always) find at federal agency sites is in the following list.

(Agencies are required to provide certain content on their Web sites, such as Freedom of Information Act information. The list below is not limited to required content. See the Laws, Regulations, and Policies section of the Webcontent.gov site, <http://www.firstgov.gov/webcontent/>, for further information on requirements.)

- Advisory council information

- Agency history

- Agency leadership biographies

- Agency leadership speeches and congressional testimony

- Budget, annual report, and strategic plan

- Business opportunities in the areas of agency acquisitions, contracting, and technology transfer programs

- Databases related to the regulatory, research, education, or outreach mission of the agency

- Education resources, career information, and pages designed for kids

- Email form for submitting comments or questions

- Employment, fellowships, or internship opportunities

- Forms for program applications, regulatory requirements, or other purposes (Many sites have automated their program application or regulatory filing processes.)

(Continued on next page)

(Continued from page xxii)

- Freedom of Information Act (FOIA) information and copies of popular documents previously requested via FOIA

- Frequently Asked Questions (FAQs) section on programs or services

- Grants information

- Laws and regulations under which the agency operates or which they are responsible for enforcing

- Legal or administrative decisions, rulings, or guidance issued by the agency

- Links to nongovernment Web sites on topics relevant to the agency's work

- Links to related federal and, occasionally, state and tribal agencies

- Links to the Web pages for the departments, divisions, or regional offices of the agency

- News services, including email alerts, RSS news feeds[3], online video, podcasts and webcasts

- Official publications or catalogs of publications

- Press releases, media kits, fact·sheets, and digital photos related to agency operations

- Program descriptions

- Program information or publications in Spanish or additional languages

- Site search feature and site index or map

- Statistics on programs or populations served

---

[3]RSS stands for Really Simple Syndication; the acronym is always used in place of the full term. For more information about RSS and government RSS news feeds, see <http://www.firstgov.gov/Topics/Reference_Shelf/Libraries/RSS_Library/What_Is_RSS.shtml>.

Organization Charts

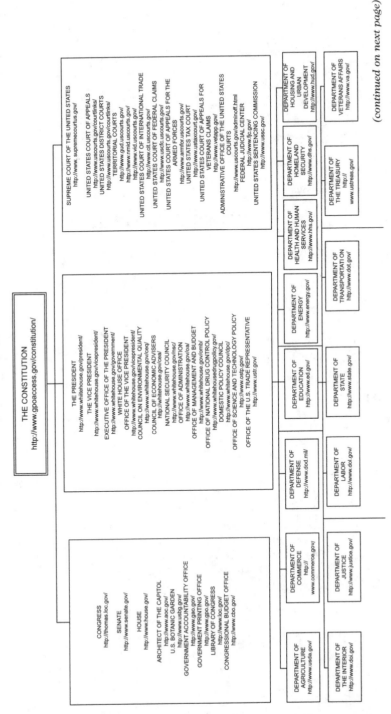

The United States Government
http://www.firstgov.gov

THE CONSTITUTION
http://www.gpoaccess.gov/constitution/

CONGRESS
http://thomas.loc.gov/
SENATE
http://www.senate.gov/
HOUSE
http://www.house.gov/
ARCHITECT OF THE CAPITOL
http://www.aoc.gov/
U.S. BOTANIC GARDEN
http://www.usbg.gov/
GOVERNMENT ACCOUNTABILITY OFFICE
http://www.gao.gov/
GOVERNMENT PRINTING OFFICE
http://www.gpo.gov/
LIBRARY OF CONGRESS
http://www.loc.gov/
CONGRESSIONAL BUDGET OFFICE
http://www.cbo.gov/

THE PRESIDENT
http://www.whitehouse.gov/president/
THE VICE PRESIDENT
http://www.whitehouse.gov/vicepresident/
EXECUTIVE OFFICE OF THE PRESIDENT
http://www.whitehouse.gov/government/
WHITE HOUSE OFFICE
OFFICE OF THE VICE PRESIDENT
http://www.whitehouse.gov/vicepresident/
COUNCIL ON ENVIRONMENTAL QUALITY
http://www.whitehouse.gov/ceq/
COUNCIL OF ECONOMIC ADVISERS
http://www.whitehouse.gov/cea/
NATIONAL SECURITY COUNCIL
http://www.whitehouse.gov/nsc/
OFFICE OF ADMINISTRATION
http://www.whitehouse.gov/oa/
OFFICE OF MANAGEMENT AND BUDGET
http://www.whitehouse.gov/omb/
OFFICE OF NATIONAL DRUG CONTROL POLICY
http://www.whitehousedrugpolicy.gov/
DOMESTIC POLICY COUNCIL
http://www.whitehouse.gov/dpc/
OFFICE OF SCIENCE AND TECHNOLOGY POLICY
http://www.ostp.gov/
OFFICE OF THE U.S. TRADE REPRESENTATIVE
http://www.ustr.gov/

SUPREME COURT OF THE UNITED STATES
http://www. supremecourtus.gov/
UNITED STATES COURT OF APPEALS
http://www.uscourts.gov/courtlinks/
UNITED STATES DISTRICT COURTS
http://www.uscourts.gov/courtlinks/
TERRITORIAL COURTS
http://www.gud.uscourts.gov/
http://www.nmid.uscourts.gov/
http://www.vid.uscourts.gov/
UNITED STATES COURT OF INTERNATIONAL TRADE
http://www.cit.uscourts.gov/
UNITED STATES COURT OF FEDERAL CLAIMS
http://www.uscfc.uscourts.gov/
UNITED STATES COURT OF APPEALS FOR THE
ARMED FORCES
http://www.armfor.uscourts.gov/
UNITED STATES TAX COURT
http://www.ustaxcourt.gov/
UNITED STATES COURT OF APPEALS FOR
VETERANS CLAIMS
http://www.vetapp.gov/
ADMINISTRATIVE OFFICE OF THE UNITED STATES
COURTS
http://www.uscourts.gov/adminoff.html
FEDERAL JUDICIAL CENTER
http://www.fjc.gov/
UNITED STATES SENTENCING COMMISSION
http://www.ussc.gov/

DEPARTMENT OF
AGRICULTURE
http://www.usda.gov/

DEPARTMENT OF
THE INTERIOR
http://www.doi.gov/

DEPARTMENT OF
COMMERCE
http://
www.commerce.gov/

DEPARTMENT OF
JUSTICE
http://www.justice.gov/

DEPARTMENT OF
DEFENSE
http://www.dod.mil/

DEPARTMENT OF
LABOR
http://www.dol.gov/

DEPARTMENT OF
EDUCATION
http://www.ed.gov/

DEPARTMENT OF
STATE
http://www.state.gov/

DEPARTMENT OF
ENERGY
http://www.energy.gov/

DEPARTMENT OF
TRANSPORTATION
http://www.dot.gov/

DEPARTMENT OF
HEALTH AND HUMAN
SERVICES
http://www.hhs.gov/

DEPARTMENT OF
HOMELAND
SECURITY
http://www.dhs.gov/

DEPARTMENT OF
THE TREASURY
http://
www.ustreas.gov/

DEPARTMENT OF
HOUSING AND
URBAN
DEVELOPMENT
http://www.hud.gov/

DEPARTMENT OF
VETERANS AFFAIRS
http://www.va.gov/

(continued on next page)

The United States Government—*continued*
http://www.firstgov.gov

INDEPENDENT ESTABLISHMENTS AND GOVERNMENT CORPORATIONS

AFRICAN DEVELOPMENT FOUNDATION
http://www.adf.gov/
BROADCASTING BOARD OF GOVERNORS
http://www.bbg.gov/
CENTRAL INTELLIGENCE AGENCY
http://www.cia.gov/
COMMODITY FUTURES TRADING COMMISSION
http://www.cftc.gov/
CONSUMER PRODUCT SAFETY COMMISSION
http://www.cpsc.gov/
CORPORATION FOR NATIONAL AND COMMUNITY SERVICE
http://www.cns.gov/
DEFENSE NUCLEAR FACILITIES SAFETY BOARD
http://www.dnfsb.gov/
ENVIRONMENTAL PROTECTION AGENCY
http://www.epa.gov/
EQUAL EMPLOYMENT OPPORTUNITY COMMISSION
http://www.eeoc.gov/
EXPORT-IMPORT BANK OF THE U.S.
http://www.exim.gov/
FARM CREDIT ADMINISTRATION
http://www.fca.gov/
FEDERAL COMMUNICATIONS COMMISSION
http://www.fcc.gov/
FEDERAL DEPOSIT INSURANCE CORPORATION
http://www.fdic.gov/
FEDERAL ELECTION COMMISSION
http://www.fec.gov/
FEDERAL HOUSING FINANCE BOARD
http://www.fhfb.gov/
FEDERAL LABOR RELATIONS AUTHORITY
http://www.flra.gov/
FEDERAL MARITIME COMMISSION
http://www.fmc.gov/
FEDERAL MEDIATION AND CONCILIATION SERVICE
http://www.fmcs.gov/
FEDERAL MINE SAFETY AND HEALTH REVIEW COMMISSION
http://www.fmshrc.gov/

FEDERAL RESERVE SYSTEM
http://www.federalreserve.gov/
FEDERAL RETIREMENT THRIFT INVESTMENT BOARD
http://www.frtib.gov/
FEDERAL TRADE COMMISSION
http://www.ftc.gov/
GENERAL SERVICES ADMINISTRATION
http://www.gsa.gov/
INTER-AMERICAN FOUNDATION
http://www.iaf.gov/
MERIT SYSTEMS PROTECTION BOARD
http://www.mspb.gov/
NATIONAL AERONAUTICS AND SPACE ADMINISTRATION
http://www.nasa.gov/
NATIONAL ARCHIVES AND RECORDS ADMINISTRATI ON
http://www.archives.gov/
NATIONAL CAPITAL PLANNING COMMISSION
http://www.ncpc.gov/
NATIONAL CREDIT UNION ADMINISTRATION
http://www.ncua.gov/
NATIONAL FOUNDATION ON THE ARTS AND THE HUMANITIES
http://www.arts.gov/
NATIONAL LABOR RELATIONS BOARD
http://www.nlrb.gov/
NATIONAL MEDIATION BOARD
http://www.nmb.gov/
NATIONAL RAILROAD PASSENGER CORPORATION (AMTRAK)
http://www.amtrak.com/
NATIONAL SCIENCE FOUNDATION
http://www.nsf.gov/
NATIONAL TRANSPORTATION SAFETY BOARD
http://www.ntsb.gov/
NUCLEAR REGULATORY COMMISSION
http://www.nrc.gov/
OCCUPATIONAL SAFETY AND HEALTH REVIEW COMMISSION
http://www.oshrc.gov/
OFFICE OF THE DIRECTOR OF NATIONAL INTELLIGENCE
http://www.dni.gov/

OFFICE OF GOVERNMENT ETHICS
http://www.usoge.gov/
OFFICE OF PERSONNEL MANAGEMENT
http://www.opm.gov/
OFFICE OF SPECIAL COUNSEL
http://www.osc.gov/
OFFICE OF THE DIRECTOR OF NATIONAL INTELLIGENCE
http://www.dni.gov/
OVERSEAS PRIVATE INVESTMENT CORPORATION
http://www.opic.gov/
PEACE CORPS
http://www.peacecorps.gov/
PENSION BENEFIT GUARANTY CORPORATION
http://www.pbgc.gov/
POSTAL RATE COMMISSION
http://www.prc.gov/
RAILROAD RETIREMENT BOARD
http://www.rrb.gov/default.asp
SECURITIES AND EXCHANGE COMMISSION
http://www.sec.gov/
SELECTIVE SERVICE SYSTEM
http://www.sss.gov/
SMALL BUSINESS ADMINISTRATION
http://www.sba.gov/
SOCIAL SECURITY ADMINISTRATION
http://www.socialsecurity.gov/
TENNESSEE VALLEY AUTHORITY
http://www.tva.gov/
TRADE AND DEVELOPMENT AGENCY
http://www.tda.gov/
U.S. AGENCY FOR INTERNATIONAL DEVELOPMENT
http://www.usaid.gov/
U.S. COMMISSION ON CIVIL RIGHTS
http://www.usccr.gov/
U.S. INTERNATIONAL TRADE COMMISSION
http://www.usitc.gov/
U.S. POSTAL SERVICE
http://www.usps.com

Legislative Branch

House of Representatives
http://www.house.gov

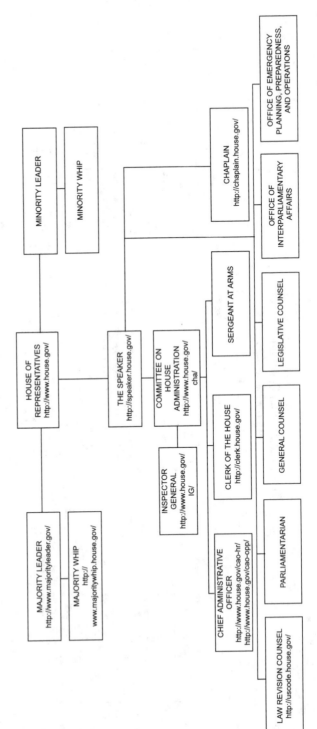

(continued on next page)

Legislative Branch—*continued*

Senate*
http://www.senate.gov

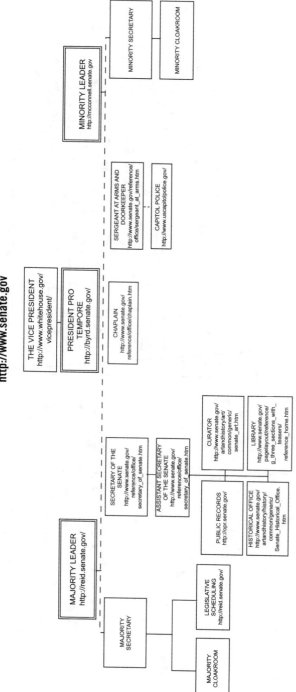

THE VICE PRESIDENT
http://www.whitehouse.gov/
vicepresident/

PRESIDENT PRO
TEMPORE
http://byrd.senate.gov/

CHAPLAIN
http://www.senate.gov/
reference/office/chaplain.htm

MINORITY LEADER
http://mcconnell.senate.gov

MINORITY SECRETARY

MINORITY CLOAKROOM

SERGEANT AT ARMS AND
DOORKEEPER
http://www.senate.gov/reference/
office/sergeant_at_arms.htm

CAPITOL POLICE
http://www.uscapitolpolice.gov/

MAJORITY LEADER
http://reid.senate.gov/

MAJORITY
SECRETARY

MAJORITY
CLOAKROOM

LEGISLATIVE
SCHEDULING
http://reid.senate.gov/

SECRETARY OF THE
SENATE
http://www.senate.gov/
reference/office/
secretary_of_senate.htm

ASSISTANT SECRETARY
OF THE SENATE
http://www.senate.gov/
reference/office/
secretary_of_senate.htm

CURATOR
http://www.senate.gov/
artandhistory/art/
common/generic/
senate_art.htm

LIBRARY
http://www.senate.gov/
pagelayout/reference/
g_three_sections_with_
teasers/
reference_home.htm

PUBLIC RECORDS
http://lopr.senate.gov/

HISTORICAL OFFICE
http://www.senate.gov/
artandhistory/history/
common/generic/
Senate_Historical_Office.
htm

* Many Senate offices do not have their own Web sites and are not included in this chart.

Department of Agriculture
http://www.usda.gov

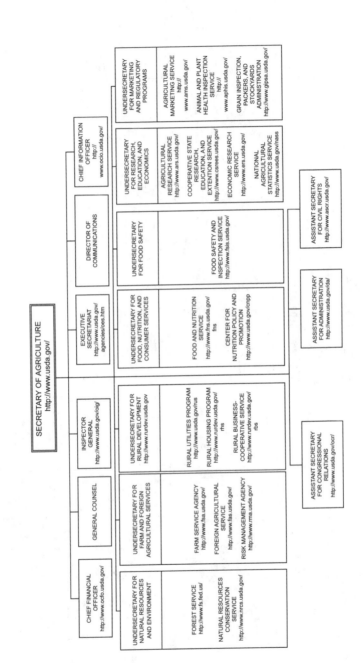

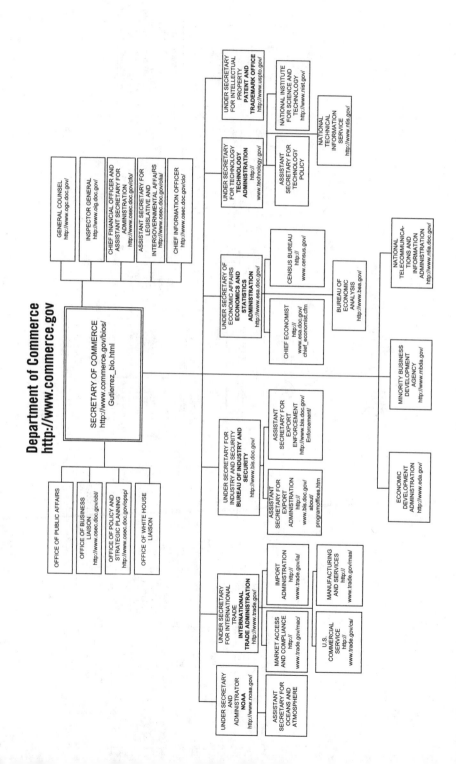

Department of Commerce
http://www.commerce.gov

SECRETARY OF COMMERCE
http://www.commerce.gov/bios/
Gutierrez_bio.html

GENERAL COUNSEL
http://www.ogc.doc.gov/

INSPECTOR GENERAL
http://www.oig.doc.gov/

CHIEF FINANCIAL OFFICER AND
ASSISTANT SECRETARY FOR
ADMINISTRATION
http://www.osec.doc.gov/cfo/

ASSISTANT SECRETARY FOR
LEGISLATIVE AND
INTERGOVERNMENTAL AFFAIRS
http://www.osec.doc.gov/olia/

CHIEF INFORMATION OFFICER
http://www.osec.doc.gov/cio/

OFFICE OF PUBLIC AFFAIRS

OFFICE OF BUSINESS
LIAISON
http://www.osec.doc.gov/obl/

OFFICE OF POLICY AND
STRATEGIC PLANNING
http://www.osec.doc.gov/opsp/

OFFICE OF WHITE HOUSE
LIAISON

UNDER SECRETARY
FOR INTELLECTUAL
PROPERTY
**PATENT AND
TRADEMARK OFFICE**
http://www.uspto.gov/

UNDER SECRETARY
FOR TECHNOLOGY
**TECHNOLOGY
ADMINISTRATION**
http://
www.technology.gov/

ASSISTANT
SECRETARY FOR
TECHNOLOGY
POLICY

NATIONAL INSTITUTE
FOR SCIENCE AND
TECHNOLOGY
http://www.nist.gov/

NATIONAL
TECHNICAL
INFORMATION
SERVICE
http://www.ntis.gov/

UNDER SECRETARY OF
ECONOMIC AFFAIRS AND
**ECONOMICS AND
STATISTICS
ADMINISTRATION**
http://www.esa.doc.gov/

CHIEF ECONOMIST
http://
www.esa.doc.gov/
chief_economist.cfm

CENSUS BUREAU
http://
www.census.gov/

BUREAU OF
ECONOMIC
ANALYSIS
http://www.bea.gov/

NATIONAL
TELECOMMUNICA-
TIONS AND
INFORMATION
ADMINISTRATION
http://www.ntia.doc.gov/

UNDER SECRETARY FOR
INDUSTRY AND SECURITY
**BUREAU OF INDUSTRY AND
SECURITY**
http://www.bis.doc.gov/

ASSISTANT
SECRETARY FOR
EXPORT
ADMINISTRATION
http://
www.bis.doc.gov/
about/
programoffices.htm

ASSISTANT
SECRETARY FOR
EXPORT
ENFORCEMENT
http://www.bis.doc.gov/
Enforcement/

MINORITY BUSINESS
DEVELOPMENT
AGENCY
http://www.mbda.gov/

ECONOMIC
DEVELOPMENT
ADMINISTRATION
http://www.eda.gov/

UNDER SECRETARY
FOR INTERNATIONAL
TRADE
**INTERNATIONAL
TRADE ADMINISTRATION**
http://www.trade.gov/

IMPORT
ADMINISTRATION
http://
www.trade.gov/ia/

MARKET ACCESS
AND COMPLIANCE
http://
www.trade.gov/mac/

MANUFACTURING
AND SERVICES
http://
www.trade.gov/mas/

U.S.
COMMERCIAL
SERVICE
http://
www.trade.gov/cs/

UNDER SECRETARY
AND
ADMINISTRATOR
NOAA
http://www.noaa.gov/

ASSISTANT
SECRETARY FOR
OCEANS AND
ATMOSPHERE

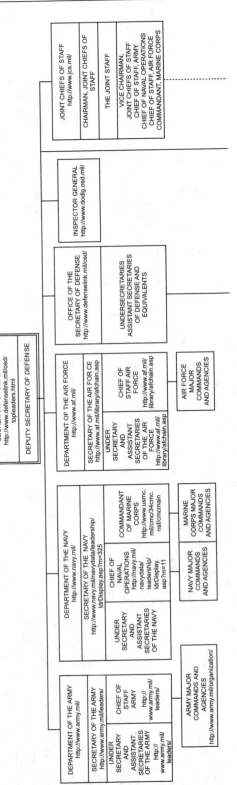

Department of Defense
http://www.defense.gov

(continued on next page)

Department of Defense—*continued*
http://www.defense.gov

DOD FIELD ACTIVITIES

AMERICAN FORCES INFORMATION SERVICE
http://www.dod.mil/afis/
DEFENSE POW/MP OFFICE
http://www.dtic.mil/dpmo
DEFENSE TECHNICAL INFORMATION CENTER
http://www.dtic.mil/dtic/index.html
DEFENSE TECHNOLOGY SECURITY ADMINISTRATION
http://www.dod.mil/policy/sections/policy_officers/dtsa/index.html
DEPARTMENT OF DEFENSE EDUCATION ACTIVITY
http://www.dodea.edu/
DEPARTMENT OF DEFENSE HUMAN RESOURCES
ACTIVITY
http://www.dhra.osd.mil/
TRICARE MANAGEMENT ACTIVITY
http://www.tricare.mil/
WASHINGTON HEADQUARTERS SERVICES
http://www.whs.pentagon.mil/

DEFENSE AGENCIES

DEFENSE ADVANCED RESEARCH PROJECTS AGEN CY
http://www.darpa.mil/
DEFENSE COMMISSARY AGENCY
http://www.commissaries.com/
DEFENSE CONTRACT AUDIT AGENCY
http://www.dcaa.mil/
DEFENSE CONTRACT MANAGEMENT AGENCY
http://www.dcma.mil/
DEFENSE FINANCE AND ACCOUNTING SERVICE
http://www.dod.mil/dfas/
DEFENSE INFORMATION SYSTEMS AGENCY
http://www.disa.mil/
DEFENSE INTELLIGENCE AGENCY
http://www.dia.mil/
DEFENSE LEGAL SERVICES AGENCY
http://www.dod.mil/dodgc/
DEFENSE LOGISTICS AGENCY
http://www.dla.mil/
DEFENSE SECURITY COOPERATION AGENCY
http://www.dsca.osd.mil/
DEFENSE SECURITY SERVICE
http://www.dss.mil/
DEFENSE THREAT REDUCTION AGENCY
http://www.dtra.mil/
MISSILE DEFENSE AGENCY
http://www.mda.mil/
NATIONAL GEOSPATIAL-INTELLIGENCE AGENCY
http://www.nga.mil/
NATIONAL SECURITY AGENCY/CENTRAL SECURITY SERVICE
http://www.nsa.gov/
PENTAGON FORCE PROTECTION AGENCY
http://www.pfpa.mil/

COMBATANT COMMANDS

CENTRAL COMMAND
http://www.centcom.mil/
EUROPEAN COMMAND
http://www.eucom.mil/
JOINT FORCES COMMAND
http://www.jfcom.mil/
NORTHERN COMMAND
http://www.northcom.mil/
PACIFIC COMMAND
http://www.pacom.mil/
SOUTHERN COMMAND
http://www.southcom.mil/
SPECIAL OPERATIONS COMMAND
http://www.socom.mil/
STRATEGIC COMMAND
http://www.stratcom.mil/
TRANSPORTATION COMMAND
http://www.transcom.mil/

Department of Education
http://www.ed.gov

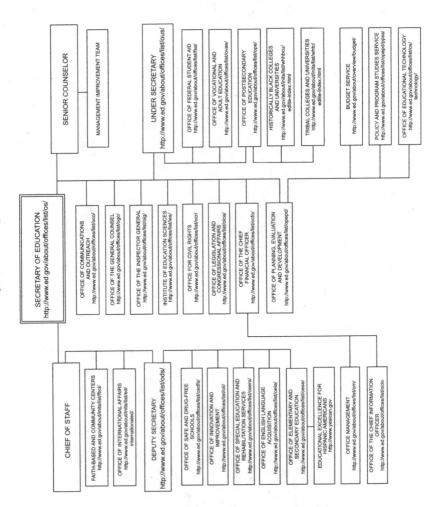

Department of Energy
http://www.energy.gov

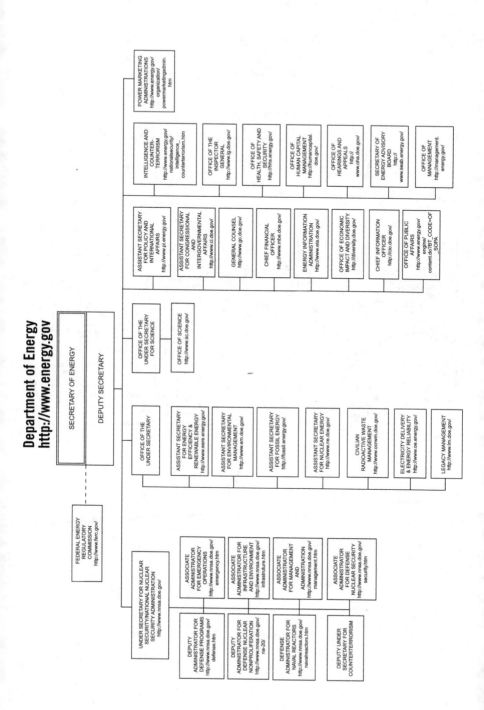

SECRETARY OF ENERGY

DEPUTY SECRETARY

FEDERAL ENERGY REGULATORY COMMISSION
http://www.ferc.gov/

UNDER SECRETARY FOR NUCLEAR SECURITY/NATIONAL NUCLEAR SECURITY ADMINISTRATION
http://www.nnsa.doe.gov/

DEPUTY ADMINISTRATOR FOR DEFENSE PROGRAMS
http://www.nnsa.doe.gov/defense.htm

ASSOCIATE ADMINISTRATOR FOR EMERGENCY OPERATIONS
http://www.nnsa.doe.gov/emergency.htm

DEPUTY ADMINISTRATOR FOR DEFENSE NUCLEAR NONPROLIFERATION
http://www.nnsa.doe.gov/na-20/

ASSOCIATE ADMINISTRATOR FOR INFRASTRUCTURE AND ENVIRONMENT
http://www.nnsa.doe.gov/infrastruture.htm

DEPUTY ADMINISTRATOR FOR NAVAL REACTORS
http://www.nnsa.doe.gov/navalreactors.htm

ASSOCIATE ADMINISTRATOR FOR MANAGEMENT AND ADMINISTRATION
http://www.nnsa.doe.gov/management.htm

DEPUTY UNDER SECRETARY FOR COUNTERTERRORISM

ASSOCIATE ADMINISTRATOR FOR DEFENSE NUCLEAR SECURITY
http://www.nnsa.doe.gov/security.htm

OFFICE OF THE UNDER SECRETARY

ASSISTANT SECRETARY FOR ENERGY EFFICIENCY & RENEWABLE ENERGY
http://www.eere.energy.gov/

ASSISTANT SECRETARY FOR ENVIRONMENTAL MANAGEMENT
http://www.em.doe.gov/

ASSISTANT SECRETARY FOR FOSSIL ENERGY
http://fossil.energy.gov/

ASSISTANT SECRETARY FOR NUCLEAR ENERGY
http://www.ne.doe.gov/

CIVILIAN RADIOACTIVE WASTE MANAGEMENT
http://www.ocrwm.doe.gov/

ELECTRICITY DELIVERY & ENERGY RELIABILITY
http://www.oe.energy.gov/

LEGACY MANAGEMENT
http://www.lm.doe.gov/

OFFICE OF THE UNDER SECRETARY FOR SCIENCE

OFFICE OF SCIENCE
http://www.sc.doe.gov/

ASSISTANT SECRETARY FOR POLICY AND INTERNATIONAL AFFAIRS
http://www.pi.energy.gov/

ASSISTANT SECRETARY FOR CONGRESSIONAL AND INTERGOVERNMENTAL AFFAIRS
http://www.ci.doe.gov/

GENERAL COUNSEL
http://www.gc.doe.gov/

CHIEF FINANCIAL OFFICER
http://www.mbe.doe.gov/

ENERGY INFORMATION ADMINISTRATION
http://www.eia.doe.gov/

OFFICE OF ECONOMIC IMPACT AND DIVERSITY
http://diversity.doe.gov/

CHIEF INFORMATION OFFICER
http://cio.doe

OFFICE OF PUBLIC AFFAIRS
http://www.energy.gov/engine/content.do?BT_CODE=OF_SOPA

INTELLIGENCE AND COUNTER-TERRORISM
http://www.energy.gov/nationalsecurity/intelligence_counterterrorism.htm

OFFICE OF THE INSPECTOR GENERAL
http://www.ig.doe.gov/

OFFICE OF HEALTH, SAFETY AND SECURITY
http://hss.energy.gov/

OFFICE OF HUMAN CAPITAL MANAGEMENT
http://humancapital.doe.gov/

OFFICE OF HEARINGS AND APPEALS
http://www.oha.doe.gov/

SECRETARY OF ENERGY ADVISORY BOARD
http://www.seab.energy.gov/

OFFICE OF MANAGEMENT
http://management.energy/gov/

POWER MARKETING ADMINISTRATIONS
http://www.energy.gov/organization/powermarketingadmin.htm

Environmental Protection Agency
http://www.epa.gov

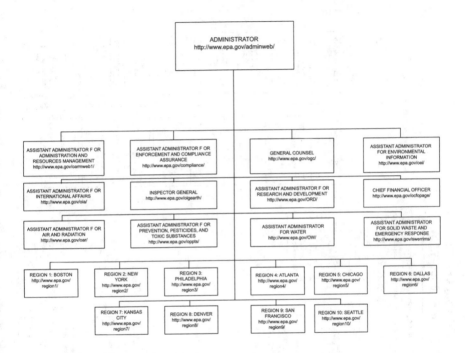

Department of Health and Human Services
http://www.hhs.gov

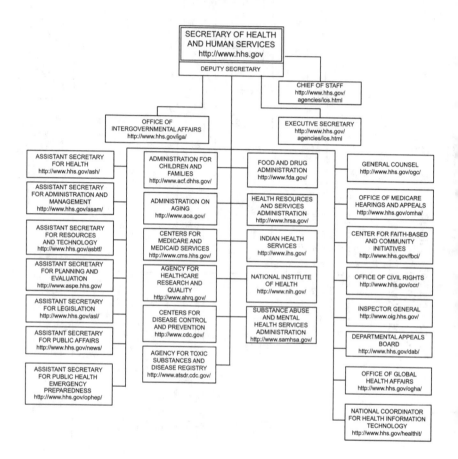

Department of Homeland Security
http://www.dhs.gov

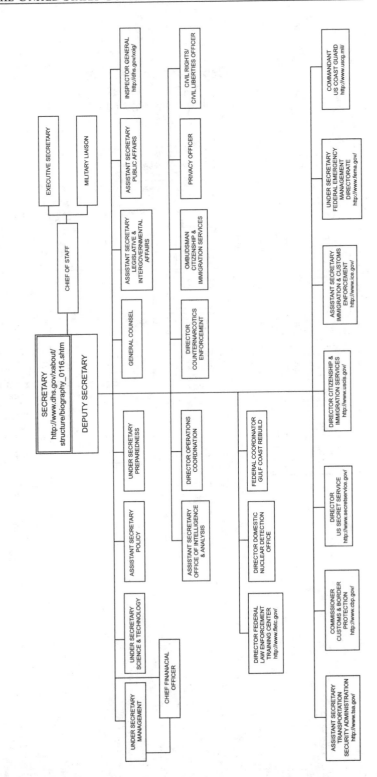

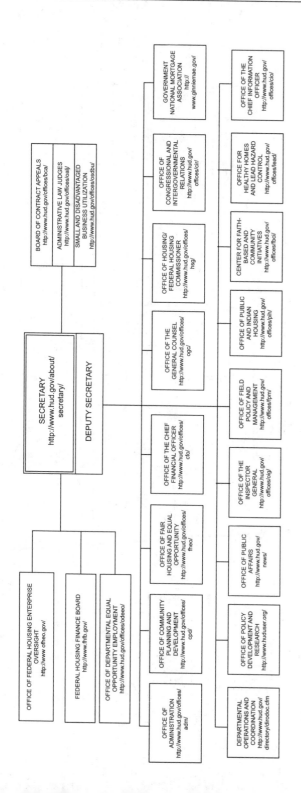

Department of Housing and Urban Development
http://www.hud.gov

SECRETARY
http://www.hud.gov/about/secretary/

DEPUTY SECRETARY

BOARD OF CONTRACT APPEALS
http://www.hud.gov/offices/bcaI/

ADMINISTRATIVE LAW JUDGES
http://www.hud.gov/offices/oalj/

SMALL AND DISADVANTAGED BUSINESS UTILIZATION
http://www.hud.gov/offices/osdbu/

OFFICE OF FEDERAL HOUSING ENTERPRISE OVERSIGHT
http://www.ofheo.gov/

FEDERAL HOUSING FINANCE BOARD
http://www.fhfb.gov/

OFFICE OF DEPARTMENTAL EQUAL OPPORTUNITY EMPLOYMENT
http://www.hud.gov/offices/odeeo/

OFFICE OF ADMINISTRATION
http://www.hud.gov/offices/adm/

OFFICE OF COMMUNITY PLANNING AND DEVELOPMENT
http://www.hud.gov/offices/cpd/

OFFICE OF FAIR HOUSING AND EQUAL OPPORTUNITY
http://www.hud.gov/offices/fheo/

OFFICE OF THE CHIEF FINANCIAL OFFICER
http://www.hud.gov/offices/cfo/

DEPARTMENTAL OPERATIONS AND COORDINATION
http://www.hud.gov/directory/dirodoc.cfm

OFFICE OF POLICY DEVELOPMENT AND RESEARCH
http://www.huduser.org/

OFFICE OF PUBLIC AFFAIRS
http://www.hud.gov/news/

OFFICE OF THE INSPECTOR GENERAL
http://www.hud.gov/offices/oig/

OFFICE OF FIELD POLICY AND MANAGEMENT
http://www.hud.gov/offices/fpm/

OFFICE OF THE GENERAL COUNSEL
http://www.hud.gov/offices/ogc/

OFFICE OF HOUSING/FEDERAL HOUSING COMMISSIONER
http://www.hud.gov/offices/hsg/

OFFICE OF CONGRESSIONAL AND INTERGOVERNMENTAL RELATIONS
http://www.hud.gov/offices/cir/

GOVERNMENT NATIONAL MORTGAGE ASSOCIATION
http://www.ginniemae.gov/

OFFICE OF PUBLIC AND INDIAN HOUSING
http://www.hud.gov/offices/pih/

CENTER FOR FAITH-BASED AND COMMUNITY INITIATIVES
http://www.hud.gov/offices/fbci/

OFFICE FOR HEALTHY HOMES AND LEAD HAZARD CONTROL
http://www.hud.gov/offices/lead/

OFFICE OF THE CHIEF INFORMATION OFFICER
http://www.hud.gov/offices/cio/

Department of the Interior
http://www.doi.gov

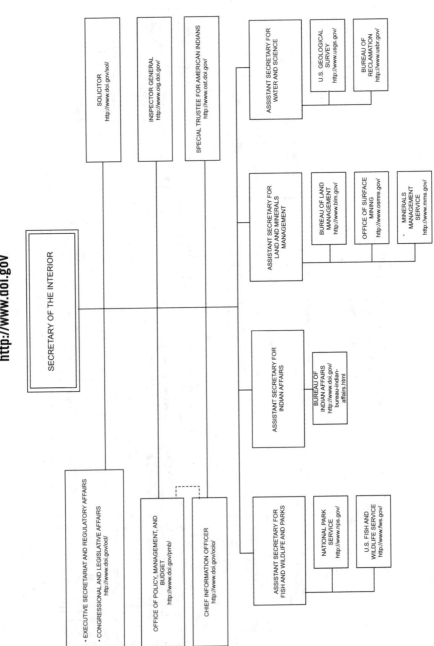

Department of Justice
http://www.justice.gov

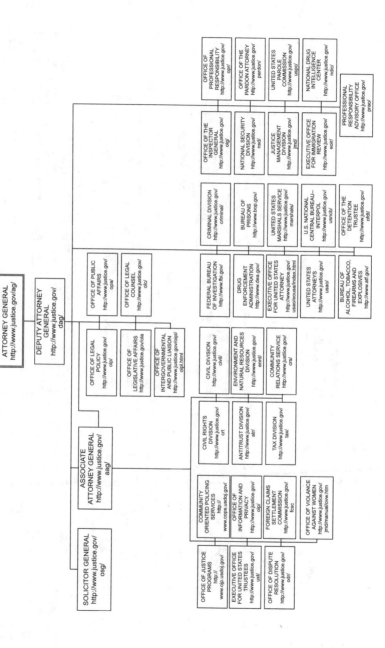

ATTORNEY GENERAL
http://www.justice.gov/ag/

DEPUTY ATTORNEY GENERAL
http://www.justice.gov/dag/

SOLICITOR GENERAL
http://www.justice.gov/osg/

ASSOCIATE ATTORNEY GENERAL
http://www.justice.gov/asg/

OFFICE OF PUBLIC AFFAIRS
http://www.justice.gov/opa/

OFFICE OF LEGAL COUNSEL
http://www.justice.gov/olc/

OFFICE OF LEGAL POLICY
http://www.justice.gov/olp/

OFFICE OF LEGISLATIVE AFFAIRS
http://www.justice.gov/ola

OFFICE OF INTERGOVERNMENTAL AND PUBLIC LIAISON
http://www.justice.gov/opl/opl.html

CIVIL DIVISION
http://www.justice.gov/civil

ENVIRONMENT AND NATURAL RESOURCES DIVISION
http://www.justice.gov/enrd/

COMMUNITY RELATIONS SERVICE
http://www.justice.gov/crs

CIVIL RIGHTS DIVISION
http://www.justice.gov/crt

ANTITRUST DIVISION
http://www.justice.gov/atr/

TAX DIVISION
http://www.justice.gov/tax/

COMMUNITY ORIENTED POLICING SERVICES
http://www.cops.usdoj.gov/

OFFICE OF INFORMATION AND PRIVACY
http://www.justice.gov/oip/

FOREIGN CLAIMS SETTLEMENT COMMISSION
http://www.justice.gov/fcsc

OFFICE OF VIOLENCE AGAINST WOMEN
http://www.justice.gov/jmd/manual/ovw.htm

OFFICE OF JUSTICE PROGRAMS
http://www.ojp.usdoj.gov/

EXECUTIVE OFFICE FOR UNITED STATES TRUSTEES
http://www.justice.gov/ust/

OFFICE OF DISPUTE RESOLUTION
http://www.justice.gov/odr/

FEDERAL BUREAU OF INVESTIGATION
http://www.fbi.gov/

DRUG ENFORCEMENT ADMINISTRATION
http://www.dea.gov/

EXECUTIVE OFFICE FOR UNITED STATES ATTORNEY
http://www.justice.gov/usao/eousa/index.html

UNITED STATES ATTORNEYS
http://www.justice.gov/usao/

BUREAU OF ALCOHOL, TOBACCO, FIREARMS AND EXPLOSIVES
http://www.atf.gov/

CRIMINAL DIVISION
http://www.justice.gov/criminal/

BUREAU OF PRISONS
http://www.bop.gov/

UNITED STATES MARSHALS SERVICE
http://www.justice.gov/marshals/

U.S. NATIONAL CENTRAL BUREAU-INTERPOL
http://www.justice.gov/usncb/

OFFICE OF THE DETENTION TRUSTEE
http://www.justice.gov/ofdt/

OFFICE OF THE INSPECTOR GENERAL
http://www.justice.gov/oig/

NATIONAL SECURITY DIVISION
http://www.justice.gov/nsd/

JUSTICE MANAGEMENT DIVISION
http://www.justice.gov/jmd/

EXECUTIVE OFFICE FOR IMMIGRATION REVIEW
http://www.justice.gov/eoir/

OFFICE OF PROFESSIONAL RESPONSIBILITY
http://www.justice.gov/opr/

OFFICE OF THE PARDON ATTORNEY
http://www.justice.gov/pardon/

UNITED STATES PAROLE COMMISSION
http://www.justice.gov/uspc/

NATIONAL DRUG INTELLIGENCE CENTER
http://www.justice.gov/ndic/

PROFESSIONAL RESPONSIBILITY ADVISORY OFFICE
http://www.justice.gov/prao/

Department of Labor
http://www.dol.gov

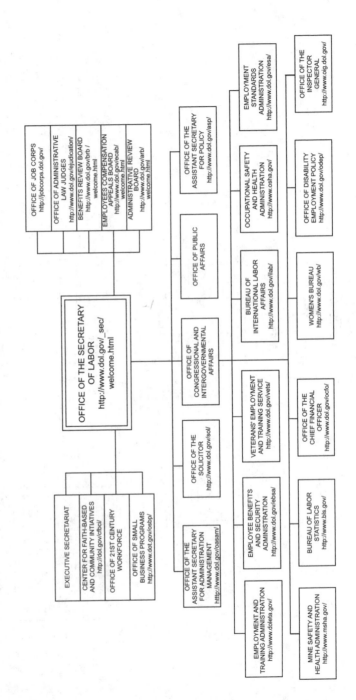

Department of Transportation
http://www.dot.gov

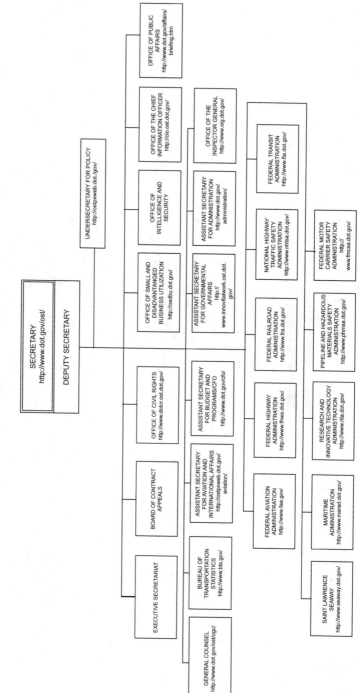

SECRETARY
http://www.dot.gov/ost/

DEPUTY SECRETARY

UNDERSECRETARY FOR POLICY
http://ostpxweb.dot./gov/

OFFICE OF PUBLIC AFFAIRS
http://www.dot.gov/affairs/briefing.htm

OFFICE OF THE CHIEF INFORMATION OFFICER
http://cio.ost.dot.gov/

OFFICE OF THE INSPECTOR GENERAL
http://www.oig.dot.gov/

OFFICE OF INTELLIGENCE AND SECURITY

OFFICE OF SMALL AND DISADVANTAGED BUSINESS UTILIZATION
http://osdbu.dot.gov/

ASSISTANT SECRETARY FOR ADMINISTRATION
http://www.dot.gov/administration/

ASSISTANT SECRETARY FOR GOVERNMENTAL AFFAIRS
http://www.innov8atwork.ost.dot.gov/

OFFICE OF CIVIL RIGHTS
http://www.dotcr.ost.dot.gov/

ASSISTANT SECRETARY FOR BUDGET AND PROGRAMS/CFO
http://www.dot.gov/cfo/

BOARD OF CONTRACT APPEALS

ASSISTANT SECRETARY FOR AVIATION AND INTERNATIONAL AFFAIRS
http://ostpxweb.dot.gov/aviation/

EXECUTIVE SECRETARIAT

BUREAU OF TRANSPORTATION STATISTICS
http://www.bts.gov/

GENERAL COUNSEL
http://www.dot.gov/ost/ogc/

FEDERAL TRANSIT ADMINISTRATION
http://www.fta.dot.gov/

NATIONAL HIGHWAY TRAFFIC SAFETY ADMINISTRATION
http://www.nhtsa.dot.gov/

FEDERAL MOTOR CARRIER SAFETY ADMINISTRATION
http://www.fmcsa.dot.gov/

FEDERAL RAILROAD ADMINISTRATION
http://www.fra.dot.gov/

PIPELINE AND HAZARDOUS MATERIALS SAFETY ADMINISTRATION
http://www.phmsa.dot.gov/

FEDERAL HIGHWAY ADMINISTRATION
http://www.fhwa.dot.gov/

RESEARCH AND INNOVATIVE TECHNOLOGY ADMINISTRATION
http://www.rita.dot.gov/

FEDERAL AVIATION ADMINISTRATION
http://www.faa.gov/

MARITIME ADMINISTRATION
http://www.marad.dot.gov/

SAINT LAWRENCE SEAWAY
http://www.seaway.dot.gov/

Department of State
http://www.state.gov

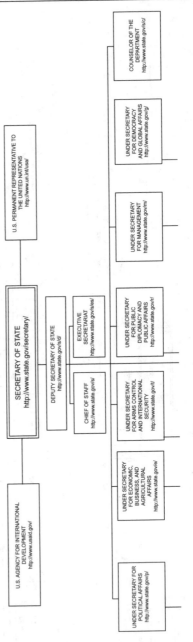

(continued on next page)

Department of State—*continued*

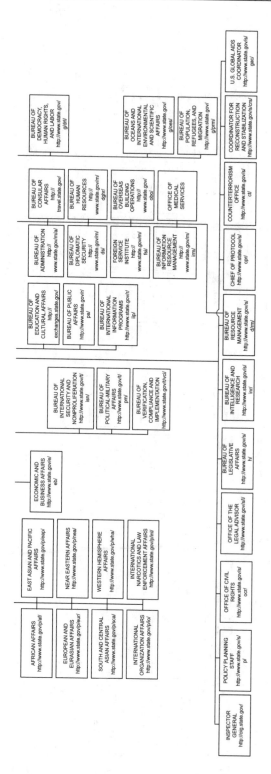

Department of the Treasury
http://www.treasury.gov

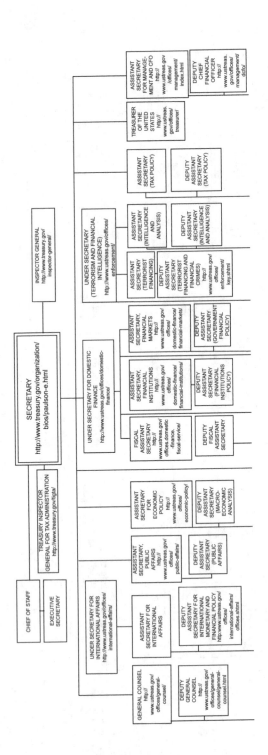

(continued on next page)

Department of the Treasury—*continued*

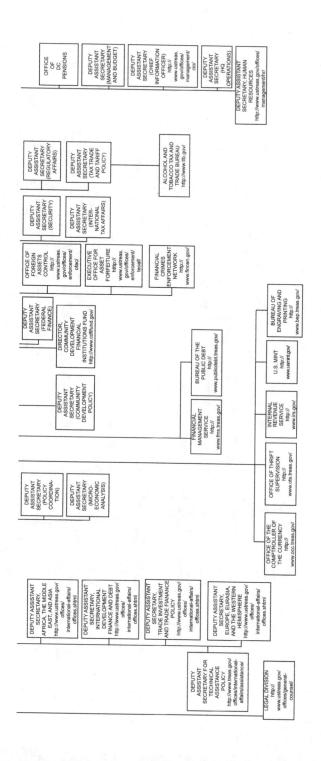

Department of Veterans Affairs
http://www.va.gov

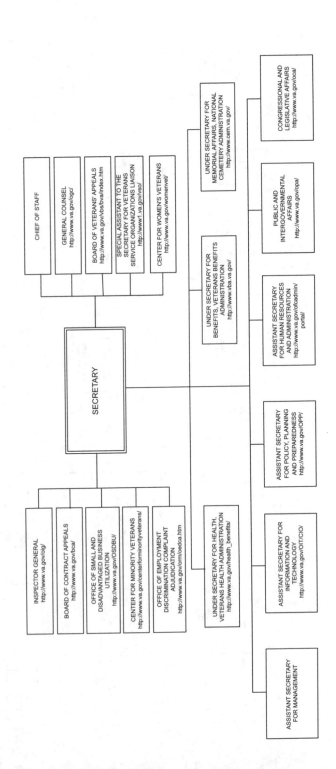

CHAPTER 1

Finding Aids

The Web sites described in this chapter are specifically designed to help users find United States federal government information. These sites organize access to government grants, forms, press releases, publications, statistics, and other resources. When searching for government information, these finding aids can be much more effective tools than general search engines.

The two subsections of this chapter describe finding aids developed by the U.S. government and finding aids developed by nongovernment organizations.

Government Sources

1. Catalog of U.S. Government Publications
http://catalog.gpo.gov/
Sponsor(s): Government Printing Office (GPO) — Superintendent of Documents
Description: The online Catalog of U.S. Government Publications (CGP) is a catalog of both print and electronic government publications from the legislative, executive, and judicial branches of the U.S. government. The catalog records cover government publications cataloged from 1976 onward. The records provide bibliographic information and link to a copy of the cited publication if one is available online.

Use the advanced search option to take full advantage of the CGP's features, such as limiting searches by year, format, or special collection within the catalog.

The CGP is the online version of the *Monthly Catalog of United States Government Publications* printed catalog and constitutes the National Bibliography of U.S. Government Publications. The CGP is not a sales catalog. Sales publications can be found in the online GPO U.S. Government Bookstore, ⟨http://bookstore.gpo.gov⟩.
Subjects: Government Publications; Publication Catalogs

2. Federal Telephone Directories
http://www.info.gov/phone.htm
Alternate URL(s): http://www.pueblo.gsa.gov/call/phone.htm
Sponsor(s): General Services Administration (GSA)
Description: This section of the National Contact Center Web site features direct links to telephone directories for cabinet agencies, independent agencies, commissions, members of Congress, and federal toll-free hotline numbers.
Subjects: Federal Government; Directories

3. FedStats
http://www.fedstats.gov/
Sponsor(s): Federal Interagency Council on Statistical Policy
Description: The FedStats Web site was established so that users could access statistics from over 100 federal agencies without having to know which agency makes the data available. FedStats is a portal. For the most part, it points to statistical information that is maintained and updated by federal agencies on their own Web servers.

The site is arranged in two main sections, Links to Statistics and Links to Statistical Agencies. Links to statistics are organized in several ways: Topic Links A to Z; MapStats (statistical profiles of states, counties, and congressional or federal judicial districts); Statistics by Geography; Statistical Reference Shelf; and a keyword search. Agency links are listed alphabetically and by subject. In addition, FedStats links to statistical agency news releases, federal statistical policy documents, and to some of the major interactive data tools offered at federal agency Web sites.

FedStats is a central starting point for finding government statistics. The fact that the site points to the originating agency server rather than duplicating statistics at its own site reduces the likelihood of getting out-of-date numbers from this intermediary. Once an originating agency has been identified, however, researchers may want to search that site directly to be certain not to miss new or supplemental information.

Subjects: Statistics; Finding Aids

4. FedWorld

`http://www.fedworld.gov/`
Sponsor(s): Commerce Department — Technology Administration (TA) — National Technical Information Service (NTIS)
Description: FedWorld is a government information gateway managed by the National Technical Information Service (NTIS). It links to other government online resources and to NTIS-developed resources described elsewhere in this directory. FedWorld features a finding aid called Top Government Web Sites, and a link to search the FirstGov site. It also links to the NTIS catalog of government research and development publications, a federal jobs database, archived IRS forms and publications, and a directory of government science and technology Web resources.

Although FedWorld was a federal Web pioneer, it now includes a rather eclectic selection of resources. Nevertheless, several of the individual tools — such as SciTechResources.gov — are particularly helpful and are described elsewhere in this directory.

Subjects: Government Information

5. FirstGov

`http://www.firstgov.gov/`
Sponsor(s): General Services Administration (GSA)
Description: Labeled "the U.S. Government's Official Web Portal," FirstGov is an executive branch initiative offering multiple routes to government information on the Internet. FirstGov links are most prominently organized by audience: citizens, business and nonprofits, federal employees, and other governments. Links for citizens include Find Government Benefits, Change Your Address, Get or Renew a Passport, and Apply for Government Grants. Other sections of FirstGov organize government information by topic, such as Consumer Guides and Voting and Elections. A Reference section links to sites with federal forms, data and statistics, and laws and regulations.

FirstGov also has quick links to agency Web sites, for users who already know which agency provides the information they need. The section organized by agency includes links to federal, state, local, and tribal government organizations. A special FirstGov Internet search engine searches both federal and state government Web sites.

FirstGov does an excellent job of serving multiple audiences and helping many people find basic government information faster. The design is particularly well suited for browsing and finding information and services when it is not known which agency is responsible. In addition, FirstGov dramatically improved its search engine in 2006. The advanced search option allows users to limit to just federal Web sites or to specific states. The results display has advanced features, such as sorting results by agency and displaying Web page hits in a preview window.

Subjects: Government Information; Finding Aids
Publications: *FirstGov*, GS 1.40:

6. FirstGov en español

http://www.firstgov.gov/Espanol/
Alternate URL(s): http://www.espanol.gov/
Sponsor(s): General Services Administration (GSA)
Description: This Spanish-language Web site is not a word-for-word translation of the English-language FirstGov site; instead, it is customized for those more likely to use it. Sections for recent immigrants and for foreign visitors are featured on the home page, for example. The search engine allows users to search for words in Spanish and retrieve federal and state government Web results that are in Spanish. Users can also complete some government transactions online in Spanish.
Subjects: Finding Aids

7. Forms.gov: Federal Forms Catalog

http://www.fedforms.gov/
Sponsor(s): General Services Administration (GSA)
Description: This portal site has been set up to provide "one-stop shopping" for forms commonly needed for federal government services. Users can locate forms by form number, agency name, or form name. Links go directly to the page at the agency Web site where the forms are available.

Forms.gov is most helpful to users who know the name or number of a form but do not know the agency. When the agency is known, it may be best to go directly to that agency's site. Agencies may have new instructions or new forms elsewhere at their site. Forms.gov has a large collection of forms, but does not include all forms from all agencies.
Subjects: Government Forms

8. Government News and FirstGov Media

http://www.firstgov.gov/Topics/Reference_Shelf/News.shtml
Sponsor(s): General Services Administration (GSA)
Description: This section of the FirstGov site proves several useful compilations, including links to agency press releases, e-mail newsletters, podcasts, and RSS newsfeeds.

Each compilation is not necessarily complete. If specific agencies are of strong interest to you, check the agency Web sites directly to find any additional news sources they may provide.
Subjects: Finding Aids; News Services

9. GPO Access Online Resources

http://www.gpoaccess.gov/databases.html
Sponsor(s): Government Printing Office (GPO) — Superintendent of Documents
Description: Numerous databases and online publications available from the GPO Access Web site offer a wealth of legislative, regulatory, reference, and other government information. This page provides an A-Z index of links to all GPO Access resources. In addition, it offers options to search across multiple databases or to see the links grouped by branch of government.

Core online resources include the *Congressional Directory, Congressional Record, Code of Federal Regulations, Federal Register, Public and Private Laws, Public Papers of the Presidents, U.S. Government Manual, United States Code,* and *Weekly Compilation of Presidential Documents.*

GPO Access databases use the WAIS search engine, which may produce unexpected results for the inexperienced user. Also, search capabilities vary from database to database, in part because of the variety of databases offered. See the "helpful hints" sections linked from individual database search pages for suggestions on constructing an effective search in that database. GPO is planning to make improvements to its search technology in 2007 and 2008.

Subjects: Government Publications
Publications: *Budget of the United States Government*, PREX 2.8:
Calendar of United States House of Representatives and History of Legislation, Y 1.2/2:
Code of Federal Regulations, AE 2.106/3:
Congressional Bills, Y 1.6:
Congressional Directory, Y 4.P 93/1:1/
Congressional Pictorial Directory, Y 4.P 93/1:1 P/
Congressional Record, X 1.1/A:
Congressional Record (Full-text, Daily Digest, Index), X 1.1/A:
Davis-Bacon Wage Determinations, L 36.211/2:
Decisions of the Comptroller General, GA 1.5/A-2:
Deschler's Precedents of the United States House of Representatives, Y 1.1/2:
Economic Indicators, Y 4.EC 7:EC 7/
Economic Report of the President, Pr 42.9:
Federal Register, AE 2.106:
GAO Reports, GA 1.5/A:
Hinds' Precedents of the House of Representatives
House Bills, Y 1.4/6:
House Documents, Y 1.1/7:
House Journal, X JH:
House Reports, Y 1.1/8:
House Rules and Manual, Y 1.2:R 86/2/
LSA, List of CFR Sections Affected, AE 2.106/2:
Privacy Act Issuances Compilation, AE 2.106/4-2:
Public Papers of the President, AE 2.114:
Senate Bills, Y 1.4/1:
Senate Calendar of Business (daily), Y 1.3/3:
Senate Documents, Y 1.1/3:
Senate Manual, Y 1.1/3:
Senate Reports, Y 1.1/5:
U.S. Constitution, Analysis and Interpretation, Y 1.1/2:
U.S. Public Laws, AE 2.110:
United States Code, Y 1.2/5:
United States Government Manual, AE 2.108/2:
United States Statutes at Large, GS 4.111
Weekly Compilation of Presidential Documents, AE 2.109:

10. Grants.gov
http://www.grants.gov/
Sponsor(s): Health and Human Services Department
Description: Grants.gov is the federal government portal for finding and applying for competitive grant opportunities from federal grant-making agencies. Users can search the full text of grants and refine searches by limiting to certain agencies, topics, dates, or type of grant. Applications can be downloaded and completed offline. Completed grant application packages can then be submitted online. In addition to using the grants search feature, researchers can subscribe to receive e-mail notification of grant opportunities in their areas of interest. The site also has guides to writing grant proposals and finding grants from many sources. Grants.gov issues a quarterly newsletter, *Succeed*.
Subjects: Grants; Finding Aids
Publications: *Succeed*

11. Registry of U.S. Government Publication Digitization Projects
http://www.gpoaccess.gov/legacy/registry/
Sponsor(s): Government Printing Office (GPO)
Description: The Registry of U.S. Government Publication Digitization Projects describes and links to online collections of digitized U.S. government publications. The collections are from government agencies, universities, and other institutions.
Subjects: Government Publications

12. U.S. Blue Pages
http://www.usbluepages.gov/
Sponsor(s): General Services Administration (GSA)
Description: The U.S. Blue Pages program is responsible for creating both this site and the printed blue pages sections of local telephone directories. Listings of federal telephone numbers can be searched geographically (by state, city, or area code) and by keyword. The About section explains the U.S. Blue Pages project. The Directories section provides free, public access to download the directory in its entirety.

Search features at this site involve a few quirks. For example, one must first select a state in order to browse and select from the list in the Agency or Service field. Searchers will want to review the search tips provided directly below the search boxes.
Subjects: Government Services; Directories

13. U.S. Government News and Press Release Gateway
http://www.pueblo.gsa.gov/call/pressreleases.htm
Sponsor(s): General Services Administration (GSA)
Description: Part of the Federal Citizen Information Center, this site organizes links to government agency press releases on the Internet. Sites are organized by executive, legislative, or judicial branch of government. The links lead, in most cases, directly to the page of the agency Web site where press releases or other newsletters are made available.
Subjects: Government Publications

14. U.S. Government Photos and Multimedia
http://www.firstgov.gov/Topics/Graphics.shtml
Sponsor(s): General Services Administration (GSA)
Description: Part of the FirstGov Web site, this resource provides direct links to collections of graphics and photos on federal agency Web sites. Access is by agency or photo collection name. As stated on the site, many but not all of these graphics are freely available for use in the public domain; check the specific disclaimers posted at each source.

This is a useful compilation of links since image collections are scattered across many federal agency Web sites. Common collection themes include science, nature, medicine, space, and U.S. history. There is no subject index, but the FirstGov Internet search engine can be used to search for images on federal, state, and local government Web sites.
Subjects: Photography; Finding Aids

15. Where to Find Military Information
http://www.nps.edu/Library/Research/SubjectGuides/Military%20
Resources/Military%20Information/MilitaryInformationEssay.html
Sponsor(s): Navy — Naval Postgraduate School (NPS)
Description: This guide from the Dudley Knox Library at the Naval Postgraduate School provides a detailed index to frequently requested military information on the Web. Links are organized under broad subject categories, such as Budget, Equipment,

and History. Rather than using the long URL above, the site can also be reached by going to the more general guide at ⟨http://www.nps.edu/Library/Research/Subject-Guides/⟩ and selecting "Military Information" in the Military Resources section. Other guides in the Military Resources section may also be of assistance.
Subjects: Military Information

Other Sources

16. CyberCemetery
http://govinfo.library.unt.edu/
Sponsor(s): University of North Texas Libraries
Description: The stated goal of the CyberCemetery is to provide "permanent public access to the Web sites and publications of defunct U.S. government agencies and commissions." The CyberCemetery is operated under a partnership with the U.S. Government Printing Office. Links to the archived sites are organized by branch of government, by date of the office's expiration, and by name. The sites can also be searched by keyword. Archived sites include those of the Coalition Provisional Authority for Iraq, the National Commission on Terrorist Attacks Upon the United States, and the National Partnership for Reinventing Government.

The policies, processes, and technologies for systematic archiving of electronic government information — and for providing access to and preservation of that information — are being actively developed by federal agencies. In the meantime, the CyberCemetery is providing a commendable service to researchers with straightforward access to resources that might otherwise be lost.
Subjects: Government Information

17. Government Document Brochures and Pamphlets
http://libweb.lib.buffalo.edu/cts/GovDocBP/
Sponsor(s): University of Buffalo. Library
Description: This site links to online government brochures and pamphlets, including some that have been digitized by the University of Buffalo Libraries. The pamphlets cover subjects ranging from home improvement to national security, and the site includes a section for government pamphlets in Spanish. Pamphlets are arranged by broad subject category. The advanced search capability enables searching on a combination of title, keyword, category, date, or language.
Subjects: Government Publications; Finding Aids

18. Government Information en Español
http://library.stmarytx.edu/acadlib/doc/spannew.htm
Sponsor(s): University of St. Mary's. Library.
Description: This compilation of links to Spanish-language material on federal government Web sites is conveniently organized by topic. The Web site itself is in Spanish, with parenthetical English-language translations of federal agency names. The site is maintained by the government documents library section of St. Mary's University in San Antonio.
Subjects: Finding Aids

19. Government Periodicals
http://library.louisville.edu/government/periodicals/periodall.html
Sponsor(s): University of Louisville. Ekstrom Library
Description: This university library site offers a list of links to U.S. government bulletins, journals, and other periodicals. Links to the periodicals on government

Web sites are arranged alphabetically by title. Each of the periodical links is supplemented with a list of links on related topics.

This Web site's simple interface provides quick access to hundreds of government periodicals online. Note that the site is not comprehensive, but it can help to quickly locate a title.

Subjects: Government Publications; Finding Aids

20. LSU Libraries Federal Agencies Directory

http://www.lib.lsu.edu/gov/fedgov.html

Sponsor(s): Louisiana State University. Library

Description: This finding aid is the product of a partnership between Louisiana State University and the Government Printing Office's Federal Depository Library Program. The site has an unannotated list of links to federal government Web sites. The list can be searched and displayed in several ways: alphabetically, hierarchically, by a word search, or by browsing categories such as Executive, Judicial, or Legislative. Not every level of an organization may be displayed hierarchically; the site also recommends checking the parent agency's Web site for further levels and offices.

The FAQ, or Frequently Asked Questions, section is actually a subject guide to selected popular government Web sites. Featured subject categories include Grants and Funding, Military Records, and Jobs.

Subjects: Federal Government; Finding Aids

21. University of Michigan Documents Center

http://www.lib.umich.edu/govdocs/

Sponsor(s): University of Michigan. Library

Description: This extensive compilation of Web links is maintained at the University of Michigan Library's Document Center. Links are organized into divisions including Federal, Foreign Governments, International, Local, and State. Special sections focus on Documents in the News, Political Science, and Statistical Resources on the Web. The resources themselves include government, nonprofit, and commercial Web sites related to government and political information. Because a primary audience is the University, cited resources also include some only available to the University of Michigan campus.

This site is one of the more comprehensive online finding aids for government and political information on the Internet. Links do not lead only to government sources, and they appear to be selected and annotated based on frequently asked reference questions.

Subjects: Government Information; Finding Aids

CHAPTER 2
Agriculture, Fishing, and Forestry

This chapter describes Web sites that cover agricultural practices, science, marketing, statistics, and related areas. Web sites concerning food and nutrition can be found in the Health and Safety chapter. This chapter also includes Web sites about fishing (or aquaculture) and forestry; additional resources on fish and forests can be found in the Environment and Nature chapter.

Subsections in this chapter are Agriculture, Fishing, and Forestry.

Agriculture

22. AGRICOLA
http://agricola.nal.usda.gov/
Sponsor(s): Agriculture Department (USDA) — National Agricultural Library (NAL)
Description: AGRICOLA, also called the NAL Catalog, is a large bibliographic database covering literature from all areas of agriculture and related fields. It indexes journal articles, short reports, book chapters, and other materials. The database was created in 1970 but also contains content from prior years. Users of AGRICOLA on the Web can also search the book collection of the National Agricultural Library (NAL) separately or in combination with AGRICOLA. Cited materials are not available online in full-text format through AGRICOLA. This Web site describes document delivery options; most remote users will need to find the materials through their local libraries.

Due to its quality, size, scope, and historical coverage, AGRICOLA is a key resource for conducting literature searches on any topic related to agriculture.
Subjects: Agriculture Information; Databases

23. Agricultural Marketing Service
http://www.ams.usda.gov/
Sponsor(s): Agriculture Department (USDA) — Agricultural Marketing Service (AMS)
Description: AMS supports the marketing, testing, regulation, and efficient transportation of agricultural commodities. AMS issues marketing orders that establish basic minimum prices for commodities. The agency also runs the National Organic Program, and its Web site links to a related Department of Agriculture Web site on that topic.

The AMS site covers its programs concerning cotton, dairy, poultry, fruit and vegetable, livestock and seed, science and technology, tobacco, transportation and marketing, and civil rights (ensuring agency compliance with federal laws). Additional sections cover commodity pricing news, farmers markets, the National Organic Program, federal rulemaking developments, and AMS services in the global marketplace. The site's search engine allows users to search the entire site or to limit a search to a section, such as the Dairy or Poultry program sections.

The AMS Web site provides essential data for users concerned with the domestic agriculture sector. The site is designed to provide quick access to the key pricing and statistical information available in such releases as the *Market News Reports*.
Subjects: Agricultural Commodities; Food Safety
Publications: *Daily Spot Cotton Quotations*, A 88.11/4:
Dairy Market Statistics, Annual Summary, A 88.14/13:
Dairy Plants Surveyed and Approved for USDA Grading Service, A 88.14/12:
Food Purchase Reports & Invitations to Bid, A 88.67:

Grain Transportation Report, A 88.68:
Items of Interest in Seed Control, A 88.63:
Market News Reports, A 88.66:
National Farmers Market Directory, A 88.69/2:
National Weekly Pricing Report, A 88.71:
Ocean Freight Rate Bulletin, A 88.70
Pesticide Data Program Annual Summary, A 88.60:
Plant Variety Protection Database, A 88.52/2:
PlantBook (Voluntary Poultry and Egg Grading and Certification Services Directory), A 88.15/23:
Standards for (Fruits, Vegetables, etc.) (irregular), A 88.6/2:
Weekly Cotton Market Review, A 88.11/2:

24. Agricultural Outlook Archives
http://usda.mannlib.cornell.edu/MannUsda/
viewDocumentInfo.do?documentId=1483
Sponsor(s): Cornell University — Mann Library
Description: *Agricultural Outlook*, a primary source for the Department of Agriculture's farm and food price forecasts, ceased publication in December 2002. This site has archival issues of the magazine going back to 1995. It also links to the USDA Economic Research Service publications that took over from *Agricultural Outlook*. The archived magazine issues have data on individual commodities, the general economy, U.S. farm trade, farm income, production expenses, input use, prices received and paid, per capita food consumption, and other related topics.
Subjects: Agricultural Economics; Agriculture — Statistics
Publications: *Agricultural Outlook*, A 93.10/2:

25. Agricultural Research Service
http://www.ars.usda.gov/
Sponsor(s): Agriculture Department (USDA) — Agricultural Research Service (ARS)
Description: ARS leads the Department of Agriculture's research projects in agriculture, nutrition, technology, and the environment. The ARS Web site presents information about its national research programs in four major areas: Nutrition and Food Safety and Quality, Animal Production and Protection, Natural Resources and Sustainable Agricultural Systems, and Crop Production and Protection.

In the Products and Services section, the site links to educational resources, ARS publications (including *Agricultural Research* magazine articles back to January 1996), and the TEKTRAN database of pre-publication notices of recent ARS research results. This section also provides software and datasets of interest to scientists working in agricultural research areas. in the News and Events section, the site has fact sheets, press releases, video programs, and an image gallery with digital photographs of crops, produce, plants, and insects. The site also has a Spanish-language version available.

The ARS Web site will primarily be of interest to agricultural researchers and research institutions, although it also contains materials that may be of interest to food and science reporters and teachers and students.
Subjects: Agricultural Research
Publications: *Agricultural Research*, A 77.12:
Food & Nutrition Research Briefs (irregular), A 77.518:
Healthy Animals, A 77.519:
TEKTRAN: Technology Transfer Automated Retrieval System, A 77.518/2:
USDA National Nutrient Database for Standard Reference, A 77.715:

26. Agriculture Network Information Center (AgNIC)
http://www.agnic.org/

Sponsor(s): Agriculture Department (USDA) — National Agricultural Library (NAL)
Description: AgNIC links to agricultural information on the Internet as selected by the National Agricultural Library, land-grant universities, and other institutions. AgNIC is a distributed network that provides access to agriculture-related information, subject area experts, and other resources. From the AgNIC Web site's home page, users can perform a simple search of the information database or browse its contents by subject. A calendar of events lists conferences, meetings, and seminars in various agricultural fields.
Subjects: Agriculture Information

27. Alternative Farming Systems Information Center (AFSIC)
http://www.nal.usda.gov/afsic/

Sponsor(s): Agriculture Department (USDA) — National Agricultural Library (NAL)
Description: AFSIC covers alternative cropping systems (such as sustainable, organic, low-input, biodynamic, and regenerative agriculture), alternative crops, and new uses for traditional crops. Its Web site includes bibliographies, guides, database links, and conference news. Special sections focus on aquaculture, agriculture funding resources, and historic Department of Agriculture publications related to organic agriculture.
Subjects: Aquaculture; Farms and Farming

28. Amber Waves
http://www.ers.usda.gov/Amberwaves/

Sponsor(s): Agriculture Department (USDA) — Economic Research Service (ERS)
Description: *Amber Waves*, a Department of Agriculture magazine, began publication in February 2003, replacing *Agricultural Outlook*, *FoodReview*, and *Rural America*. The magazine includes feature articles with information and economic analysis about food, farms, natural resources, and rural community issues. An Indicators section provides data and charts on crop and livestock cash receipts, farm household income, agricultural imports and exports, food spending, and other related topics. *Amber Waves* is published five times a year. A print version is available by paid subscription, but issues can be downloaded for free from the Web site. The free online version adds articles and updates in advance of the printed issues.
Subjects: Agricultural Economics
Publications: *Amber Waves*, A 93.62:

29. Animal and Plant Health Inspection Service
http://www.aphis.usda.gov/

Sponsor(s): Agriculture Department (USDA) — Animal and Plant Health Inspection Service (APHIS)
Description: APHIS's mission is to protect the animal and plant resources of the United States from agricultural pests and diseases. Major sections of its Web site cover animal health, plant health, biotechnology regulation, wildlife damage management, animal welfare, and importing and exporting concerns. Quick links on the site's main page lead to information about reporting a pest or disease, permits for import and interstate movement of plants and animals, and veterinarian accreditation.
Subjects: Agriculture — Regulations; Animals — Regulations; Plants — Regulations; Veterinary Medicine
Publications: *APHIS Fact Sheets*, A 101.31:
APHIS Technical Reports, A 101.30:

30. Beltsville Agricultural Research Center (BARC)
http://www.ba.ars.usda.gov/
Sponsor(s): Agriculture Department (USDA) — Agricultural Research Service (ARS)
Description: BARC encompasses research from a variety of agricultural science disciplines. Its Web site describes research coming out of BARC's many laboratories. Major sections include Animal and Natural Resources, Human Nutrition, Plant Sciences, and the National Arboretum. A Products and Services section includes searchable databases and online datasets and models.
Subjects: Agricultural Research; Nutrition — Research; Plants — Research

31. Carl Hayden Bee Research Center
http://gears.tucson.ars.ag.gov/
Sponsor(s): Agriculture Department (USDA) — Agricultural Research Service (ARS)
Description: The mission of the Carl Hayden Bee Research Center is "solving problems associated with the transport and introduction of honey bee colonies for crop pollination. Our research is directed at honey bee nutrition, Varroa mites, Africanization of European honey bees, and crop pollination" (from the Web site). The Web site's Research section includes information about advanced research projects and dealing with bee stings.
Subjects: Beekeeping; Entomology

32. Center for Veterinary Medicine
http://www.fda.gov/cvm/
Sponsor(s): Health and Human Services Department — Food and Drug Administration (FDA) — Center for Veterinary Medicine (CVM)
Description: CVM regulates the manufacture and distribution of drugs and feed additives intended for animals. Its Web site features sections including Animal Feeds, Antimicrobial Resistance, Biotechnology, BSE (Bovine Spongiform Encephalopathy or "mad cow disease"), the "Green Book" (the *FDA Approved Animal Drug List*), the Minor Use and Minor Species Animal Health Act, and Guidance Documents. The site also carries the *FDA Veterinarian* newsletter. Some publications are available in Spanish.
Subjects: Veterinary Medicine
Publications: *FDA and the Veterinarian*, HE 20.4402:F 73/
FDA Veterinarian, HE 20.4410:

33. Cooperative State Research, Education, and Extension Service (CSREES)
http://www.csrees.usda.gov/
Sponsor(s): Agriculture Department (USDA) — Cooperative State Research, Education, and Extension Service (CSREES)
Description: CSREES supports agricultural research, education, and extension programs in the Land-Grant University System and other organizations. Its Web site organizes information about funding and activities into major topical program areas, including Agriculture and Food Biosecurity, Biotechnology and Genomics, Economics and Commerce, Education, and Pest Management. Further information about grants and other opportunities can be found in the Funding Opportunities and Business with CSREES sections. The Quick Links section includes a directory of state and national CSREES partners.
   This site is an excellent gateway to research and education information about many agricultural subjects.
Subjects: Agricultural Education — Grants; Agricultural Research — Grants; Extension Services

Publications: *CSREES — Update,* A 94.20:
Family Economics News, A 94.28:
Plant Sciences Update, A 94.27:
Small Farm Digest, A 94.23:

34. Crop Explorer

http://www.pecad.fas.usda.gov/cropexplorer/

Sponsor(s): Agriculture Department (USDA) — Foreign Agricultural Service (FAS)
Description: Crop Explorer is an interactive Web tool for mapping global crop condition information, based on satellite imagery and weather data. For major crop-growing areas around the world, Crop Explorer displays thematic maps of conditions such as precipitation, temperature, and soil moisture. The site also provides frequently updated satellite data and imagery, regional growing season profiles, and narrative reports.

Crop Explorer is designed to assist in forecasting production, supply, demand, and food assistance needs. The site has a well-designed interface and a rich library of current data.

Subjects: Agriculture — International

35. Economic Research Service

http://www.ers.usda.gov/

Sponsor(s): Agriculture Department (USDA) — Economic Research Service (ERS)
Description: ERS produces key economic indicators and detailed data on the economics of food, farming, natural resources, and rural development. The ERS Web site provides multiple ways of accessing its information by topic. According to the site, its Briefing Rooms offer "an in-depth discussion synthesizing ERS research and the economic issues that frame the analysis" for topics such as agricultural biotechnology, farm labor, farm and commodity policy, rural economies, and food prices and spending. The Browse by Subject section links to a fuller array of topics; it lists publications, datasets, and Briefing Rooms related to each of these topic. Researchers can also browse by farm commodity or by U.S. regions and states , as well as by a selection of foreign countries and world regions. The New Releases calendar on the home page includes an option that allows users to be notified automatically of new ERS data and publications, either by e-mail or RSS feed.

The Publications section contains all of the agency's publications from 1996 onward; these are searchable by title, topic, or date. The ERS Outlook Reports provide analysis and data on production, consumption, international trade, and prices received for key agricultural commodities.

ERS is a key resource for data and analysis on the agricultural economy. Its Web site provides excellent, multiple approaches to discovering this information.

Subjects: Agricultural Economics; Agriculture — Statistics; Rural Development — Statistics
Publications: *Amber Waves,* A 93.62:
Aquaculture Outlook, A 93.55:
Cotton and Wool Outlook, A 93.24/2:
Feed Outlook, A 93.11/2:
Floriculture and Nursery Crops Outlook, A 93.29/2-3:
Foreign Agricultural Trade of the United States, A 93.17/7:
Fruit and Tree Nuts Outlook and Yearbook, A 93.12/3:
Livestock, Dairy, and Poultry Outlook, A 93.46/3:
Oil Crops Outlook, A 93.23/2:
Retail Scanner Prices for Meat, A 93.2:
Rice Outlook, A 93.11/3:
Sugar and Sweeteners Outlook, A 93.31/3:
Tobacco Outlook, A 93.25:

U.S. Agricultural Trade Update, A 93.17/7-5:
Vegetables and Melons Outlook, A 93.12/2:
Wheat Outlook, A 93.11:

36. Extension Disaster Education Network (EDEN)
http://www.agctr.lsu.edu/eden/
Sponsor(s): Agriculture Department (USDA) — Cooperative State Research, Education, and Extension Service (CSREES)
Description: EDEN links agricultural extension services across the United States and promotes the use and sharing of resources to reduce the impact of disasters. Its Web site provides current news and background information about disaster preparedness, recovery, and mitigation. The Issues section contains briefings and resources on agrosecurity, avian flu, pandemic flu, children and disasters, and other topics. A directory of EDEN delegates is also available.
Subjects: Disasters and Emergencies; Extension Services

37. Farm Credit Administration
http://www.fca.gov/
Sponsor(s): Farm Credit Administration (FCA)
Description: FCA is an independent agency responsible for enforcement and regulation of the Farm Credit System (FCS), which includes the Federal Agricultural Mortgage Corporation (Farmer Mac). The FCA Web site features detailed information about the agency, the FCA board, and leading officials. The FCS Institutions section of the site includes a directory of these lending institutions, which specialize in providing credit and related services to farmers, ranchers, and producers and harvesters of aquatic products. The Legal Info section includes the *FCA Handbook*, which contains FCA regulations and statutes and summaries of selected legal opinions prepared by the FCA's Office of General Counsel.
Subjects: Farm Loan Programs
Publications: *Annual Performance Plan, Farm Credit Administration*, FCA 1.2:
Performance and Accountability Report, Farm Credit Administration, FCA 1.1/4:

38. Farm Service Agency Online
http://www.fsa.usda.gov/pas/
Sponsor(s): Agriculture Department (USDA) — Farm Service Agency (FSA)
Description: FSA assists farmers in income stabilization, resource conservation, credit services, and disaster recovery. The home page of its Web site presents important program dates and quick links to information of interest to citizens and industry. A sidebar on the home page provides access to much of the information on the site. The Services/Programs section includes subsections on Farm Loans, Price Supports, Environmental Compliance, and Disaster Assistance. Other menu items include FSA regional office directories and links to information resources (such as fact sheets, online forms, and agency communications to Congress).
    This Web site provides much information to its constituents. Its detailed subsections pull together resources to address many concerns of the American farmer.
Subjects: Conservation (Natural Resources); Disaster Assistance; Farm Loan Programs
Publications: *FSA Commodity Fact Sheets*, A 112.15:

39. FAS Online
http://ffas.usda.gov/
Sponsor(s): Agriculture Department (USDA) — Foreign Agricultural Service (FAS)
Description: FAS represents U.S. interests in foreign markets. Its Web site includes information about countries, commodities, trade policy and negotiations, export

programs, exporter assistance, buying U.S. products, import programs, and the 2007 Farm Bill. News releases, reports, fact sheets, congressional testimony, *Federal Register* notices, and featured reports are available in the Newsroom section. The FAS Offices section links to the Web pages for FAS overseas posts and to specialized FAS division pages.

Subjects: Agricultural Trade

Publications: *Cotton: World Markets and Trade*, A 67.18:FC
Dairy Monthly Imports, A 67.18:FD-MI
Dairy: World Markets and Trade, A 67.18:FD
Export Assistance, Food Aid, and Market Development Programs, A 67.46:
FAS Worldwide, A 67.7/3:
Grain: World Markets and Trade, A 67.18:FG
Livestock & Poultry: World Markets and Trade, A 67.18:FL&P
Monthly Summary of Export Credit Guarantee Program Activity, A 67.47:
Oilseeds: World Markets and Trade, A 67.18:FOP
Sugar: World Markets and Trade, A 67.18:FS
Tobacco: World Markets and Trade, A 67.18:FT
Tropical Products: World Markets and Trade, A 67.18:FTROP
U.S. Export Sales Report, A 67.40:
U.S. Planting Seed Trade, A 67.18/3:
Wood Products: International Trade and Foreign Markets, A 67.18:WP
World Agricultural Production, A 67.18:WAP
World Horticultural Trade and U.S. Export Opportunities, A 67.18:FHORT

40. Grain Inspection, Packers, and Stockyards Administration (GIPSA)

http://www.gipsa.usda.gov/

Sponsor(s): Agriculture Department (USDA) — Grain Inspection, Packers, and Stockyards Administration (GIPSA)

Description: GIPSA facilitates the marketing of grains, livestock, poultry, and meat for the overall benefit of consumers and U.S. agriculture. The GIPSA Web site features services provided by the Federal Grain Inspection Service and information about the Packers and Stockyards Programs. Target audiences for the site include grain inspectors, domestic grain marketers, international governments and customers, livestock producers, and poultry growers. The Markets and Trade section includes the annual *Packers and Stockyards Statistical Report* and links to the Department of Agriculture's Agriculture Marketing Service for grain and feed market news. Most GIPSA publications are listed in the News and Events section.

Subjects: Grains — Regulations; Livestock — Regulations

Publications: *Annual Report of the Grain Inspection, Packers and Stockyards Administration*, A 113.1:
Assessments of the Cattle and Hog Industries
Grain Inspection Handbook, A 113.8:
Official United States Standards for Beans, A 113.10/3:
Official United States Standards for Grain, A 113.10:
Official United States Standards for Rice, A 113.10/2:
Official United States Standards for Whole Dry Peas, Split Peas and Lentils, A 113.10/4:
Packers and Stockyards Statistical Report, A 113.15:
U.S. Grain Exports: Quality Report, A 104.12/2-3:

41. GrainGenes

http://wheat.pw.usda.gov/

Sponsor(s): Agriculture Department (USDA) — Agricultural Research Service (ARS)

Description: GrainGenes is a genetic database for Triticeae, oats, and sugarcane. Access to the data is available through an alphabetical browse feature (by category and name) and by a variety of keyword searches. The site also has information about related news, projects, data, publications, and other resources.

The GrainGenes database contains a substantial amount of genetic information and many links to other genome databases. The interactive and collaborative capabilities of the Internet are used to good advantage, as researchers can submit data for entry into the database and browse through data that has already been included.

Subjects: Germplasms; Grains — Research; Plant Genetics

42. Green Book

`http://www.fda.gov/cvm/Green_Book/greenbook.html`

Sponsor(s): Health and Human Services Department — Food and Drug Administration (FDA) — Center for Veterinary Medicine (CVM)

Description: *FDA Approved Animal Drug Products*, known as the "Green Book," is available online in searchable form. The printed publication is issued annually, with monthly updates. The online book includes FDA Approved Animal Drug Database files that support production of the book, all chapters of the printed book itself, and a searchable archive of monthly updates dating back to 2001.

This is a useful database for veterinarians and anyone interested in official FDA information about specific animal drugs.

Subjects: Veterinary Medicine
Publications: *FDA Approved Animal Drug Products*, HE 20.4411:

43. Joint Agricultural Weather Facility (JAWF)

`http://www.usda.gov/oce/weather/`

Sponsor(s): Commerce Department — National Oceanic and Atmospheric Administration (NOAA); Agriculture Department (USDA) — World Agricultural Outlook Board

Description: JAWF collects global weather and agricultural information to determine the impact of growing season weather conditions on international crops and livestock production prospects. The JAWF Web site features U.S. Agricultural Weather Highlights, Major World Crop Areas and Climatic Profiles, and the *Weekly Weather and Crop Bulletin*.

Subjects: Agriculture — International; Weather
Publications: *Weekly Weather and Crop Bulletin*, C 55.209:

44. Journal of Extension

`http://www.joe.org/`

Sponsor(s): Agriculture Department (USDA) — Cooperative State Research, Education, and Extension Service (CSREES)

Description: The *Journal of Extension (JOE)*, a peer-reviewed journal for Extension Service personnel, is published six times a year and only in electronic format. The print version ceased publication in 1994. Issues from 1963 through the present are available and searchable online. Issues prior to 1984 are available in PDF format; those published in 1984 onward are available in HTML format.

JOE is an easy-to-use online journal, with supplemental material about the journal, its peer review procedures, and usage statistics.

Subjects: Extension Services
Publications: *Journal of Extension*

45. National Agricultural Library Digital Repository

`http://naldr.nal.usda.gov/`

Sponsor(s): Agriculture Department (USDA) — National Agricultural Library (NAL)

Description: The National Agricultural Library Digital Repository (NALDR) is a collection of digitized agriculture documents from past years. The collection can be

browsed or searched by keyword. It comprises over 2,000 digitized volumes, including the *Yearbook of the U.S. Department of Agriculture* series for selected years between 1894 and 1992.
Subjects: Agriculture Information

46. National Agricultural Statistics Service (NASS)
http://www.nass.usda.gov/
Sponsor(s): Agriculture Department (USDA) — National Agricultural Statistics Service (NASS)
Description: NASS publishes a broad range of state and national statistics on crops, livestock, and farming. Its Web site's sidebar allows users to browse NASS data by the following topics: Crops and Plants, Economic (land values, prices paid by farmers, and more), Environmental, and Livestock and Animals. The site has searchable data from the *Census of Agriculture*, which is conducted every five years. The Data and Statistics section features the QuickStats database for searching national, state, and local data by commodity, state, and year. The Surveys section explains, in detail, what data NASS collects and where it is published. The Publications section includes NASS reports, newsletters, and the annually published *Agricultural Statistics*. The Newsroom section provides NASS statistical reports and news releases, which can be delivered as an RSS feed. Broadcast reports on crop production are online in MP3 audio format.
   This site, in combination with the Department of Agriculture's Economics and Statistics System hosted by Cornell University, provides a substantial number of agricultural and crop-related statistical publications.
Subjects: Crop Production — Statistics; Farms and Farming — Statistics; Livestock — Statistics
Publications: *Agricultural Prices*, A 92.16:
Agricultural Statistics, A 1.47:
Census of Agriculture, A 92.53:
Census of Agriculture (Vol. 2, Subject Series), A 92.54:
Census of Agriculture, State and County Data, Geographic Area Series, Volume 1 (U.S. Summary), A 92.53/51:
Farm Labor, A 92.12:

47. National Agriculture Compliance Assistance Center
http://www.epa.gov/agriculture/
Sponsor(s): Environmental Protection Agency (EPA)
Description: The National Agriculture Compliance Assistance Center, or Ag Center, offers information about environmental regulatory compliance for the agricultural community. The information is organized by agricultural sector, such as crops, forestry, or animals. Topics include agricultural waste, aquaculture, and fertilizers.
Subjects: Environmental Law; Farms and Farming — Regulations

48. National Agriculture Safety Database (NASD)
http://www.cdc.gov/nasd/
Sponsor(s): Health and Human Services Department — Centers for Disease Control and Prevention (CDC) — National Institute of Occupational Safety and Health (NIOSH)
Description: NASD is an online clearinghouse for a diverse array of materials related to agricultural health, safety, and injury prevention. The database can be searched by keyword, topic, or state name. Its long list of topics includes chemicals/pesticides, hearing conservation, lightning, personal protective equipment, and supervising for safety. Safety videos are available for online viewing. Many brochures are also available in Spanish.

NASD provides easy access to practical guides that may also be of use to nonfarm industries. Due to the diversity of these materials, users may want to check the source and date provided at the bottom of each document.

Subjects: Farms and Farming; Safety

49. National Animal Identification System (NAIS)

http://animalid.aphis.usda.gov/nais/

Sponsor(s): Agriculture Department (USDA) — Animal and Plant Health Inspection Service (APHIS)

Description: NAIS is a cooperative and currently voluntary program to standardize and expand animal identification practices for all livestock species and poultry. NAIS will eventually provide a record of a diseased or exposed animal's movements in order to help contain the spread of animal-borne disease. The NAIS Web site provides background information about the program and details about the program's Animal Identification Number and Premises Identification Number systems. The Newsroom section contains press releases, fact sheets, webcasts, and other program materials.

Subjects: Animals — Regulations

50. National Arboretum

http://www.usna.usda.gov/

Sponsor(s): Agriculture Department (USDA) — Agricultural Research Service (ARS)

Description: The National Arboretum's Web site is more than an online brochure for the nation's official garden in Washington, DC. The site provides information of interest to the general gardening public, including horticultural facts, pest management, new hybrid plant releases, lists of state trees and flowers, and a plant hardiness map depicting the lowest expected temperatures in the United States. Information for researchers includes a directory of National Arboretum scientists and their specialties, as well as background on the Woody Landscape Plant Germplasm Repository. The site also presents the usual information for visitors, such as introductions to exhibits, an interactive map of the grounds, and calendars of blooms and educational events.

This well-designed site is a useful resource for serious nonprofessional gardeners and plant enthusiasts.

Subjects: Gardening and Landscaping; Trees

Publications: *Arboretum Plant Introduction and Winners (fact sheets)*, A 77.38/2: *USNA News and Notes*

51. National Center for Agricultural Law

http://www.nationalaglawcenter.org/

Sponsor(s): University of Arkansas. School of Law

Description: The National Center for Agricultural Law is funded by the Department of Agriculture and operated by the University of Arkansas School of Law. The center conducts original research into areas of food and agricultural law. Its Web site presents this research alongside research material from other sources. A series of Reading Room sections organizes information by topic, including biotechnology, country of origin labeling, marketing orders, and international agricultural trade. Each Reading Room category links to related major laws, regulations, case law, legal research, and government publications. Other highlights on the site include an agricultural policy glossary, legislative histories for past Farm Bills, general reference links, and digests of federal regulations and court cases concerning agricultural law.

The National Center for Agricultural Law site is an excellent starting point for legal, legislative, and government documents research on agricultural policy topics.

Subjects: Agriculture — Laws

52. National Genetic Resources Program
http://www.ars-grin.gov/
Sponsor(s): Agriculture Department (USDA) — Agricultural Research Service (ARS)
Description: The National Genetic Resources Program is responsible for acquiring, characterizing, preserving, documenting, and distributing scientific information about germplasms of all lifeforms important for food and agricultural production. Its Web site includes a link to the Germplasm Resources Information Network, which has germplasm information about plants, animals, microbes, and invertebrates within the National Genetic Resources Program. Each of the germplasm databases varies in terms of scope and access points. The four databases available are the National Plant Germplasm System, the National Animal Germplasm Program, the National Microbial Germplasm Program, and the National Invertebrate Genetic Resources Program. Information from the National Genetic Resources Advisory Council (NGRAC) is also available.

This site will primarily be of interest to users researching the germplasm of plants and animals.
Subjects: Germplasms; Plant Genetics

53. National Organic Program
http://www.ams.usda.gov/nop/
Sponsor(s): Agriculture Department (USDA) — Agricultural Marketing Service (AMS)
Description: This Web site presents Department of Agriculture regulations and policies concerning growing, labeling, and marketing farm produce as organic. A Questions and Answers section addresses the definition of organic produce, production requirements, certification, and the national list of allowed and prohibited substances. It also has a section on the National Organic Standards Board.

This informative site should be of practical benefit to producers, retailers, and consumers of organic food.
Subjects: Food — Regulations

54. National Plant Data Center (NPDC)
http://npdc.usda.gov/
Sponsor(s): Agriculture Department (USDA) — Natural Resources Conservation Service (NRCS)
Description: NPDC focuses its resources on the acquisition, development, integration, quality control, dissemination, and access of plant information. Its Web site features the fully searchable PLANTS database and detailed fact sheets on selected trees and plants. Special sections focus on endangered and threatened plants, invasive species, and culturally significant plants. The site also has general information about NPDC and its activities.
Subjects: Plants
Publications: *PLANTS database*, A 57.80:

55. Office of Public Health and Science (OPHS)
http://www.fsis.usda.gov/About_FSIS/OPHS/index.asp
Sponsor(s): Agriculture Department (USDA) — Food Safety and Inspection Service (FSIS)
Description: OPHS provides scientific analysis and recommendations on public health and science topics of concern to FSIS. The OPHS Web site describes the agency's major departments and programs, including the Food Emergency Response Network, the Human Health Sciences Division, and the Microbiology Division. It also links to a directory of the FSIS Regulatory Field Services Laboratories.
Subjects: Food Safety — Research

56. PLANTS National Database
http://plants.usda.gov/
Sponsor(s): Agriculture Department (USDA) — Natural Resources Conservation Service (NRCS)
Description: The PLANTS National Database features standardized information about the plants found in the United States and its territories. It includes names of plants, checklists, automated tools, identification information, species abstracts, distributional data, crop information, plant symbols, plant growth data, plant materials information, plant links, and references. In addition, the database can generate reports such as lists of endangered and threatened plants, invasive and noxious plants, wetlands plants, and state-specific lists of plants.
　This database is an excellent source for verifying plant names and other plant information.
Subjects: Plants; Databases
Publications: *PLANTS database*, A 57.80:

57. PS&D Online
http://www.fas.usda.gov/psd/
Sponsor(s): Agriculture Department (USDA) — Foreign Agricultural Service (FAS)
Description: The Production, Supply and Distribution (PS&D) online database has current and historical Department of Agriculture data on production, supply, and distribution of agricultural commodities for the United States and selected producing and consuming countries. The site offers predefined tables and the opportunity to download the raw data in comma-separated value format. Users can also perform custom queries by searching for a specific commodity, type of statistic, country, and year.
Subjects: Agricultural Commodities — Statistics

58. Risk Management Agency
http://www.rma.usda.gov/
Sponsor(s): Agriculture Department (USDA) — Risk Management Agency (RMA)
Description: RMA manages the Federal Crop Insurance Corporation (FCIC) and other risk management programs for agricultural producers. Its Web site describes crop insurance policies, reinsurance agreements, and pilot programs. It provides a directory of RMA field offices and guides to locating insurance agents companies. RMA State Profiles section shows the availability of insurance plans by crop, pilot programs, and 15-year crop insurance history. Information produced by RMA is available in the Publications, Data, and News sections.
Subjects: Crop Insurance; Disaster Assistance
Publications: *Crop Insurance Handbook*, A 62.58/2:
Crop Insurance Manager's Bulletins, A 112.17:

59. Rural and Agricultural Transportation
http://ntl.bts.gov/ruraltransport/
Sponsor(s): Agriculture Department (USDA)Transportation Department
Description: This Web site brings together information from the federal government and other organizations concerning the transportation of agricultural commodities and freight and rural passengers. The Rural Transport Toolbox section identifies federal agency programs concerned with the topic.
Subjects: Agricultural Commodities; Rural Development

60. SOILS
http://soils.usda.gov/

Sponsor(s): Agriculture Department (USDA) — Natural Resources Conservation Service (NRCS)

Description: The SOILS Web site is part of the National Cooperative Soil Survey, a cooperative federal-state-academic project. The site has a broad range of scientific, applied, and educational information about soils. The centerpiece of the site is the Soil Survey, which has survey maps, soil characterization data, and soil climate data. The Soil Data Mart enables the downloading of tabular and spatial soil data. Other major sections provide images of soil, information about soil use, classification standards, current research topics, and resources for teachers and students.

Subjects: Soil Surveys

Publications: *Field Book for Describing and Sampling Soils*, A 57.2:
Keys to Soil Taxonomy, A 57.2:
National Soil Survey Handbook, A 57.6/2:
Soil Taxonomy, A 1.76:

61. State Fact Sheets from USDA/ERS
http://www.ers.usda.gov/StateFacts/

Sponsor(s): Agriculture Department (USDA) — Economic Research Service (ERS)

Description: The State Fact Sheets Web site contains basic demographic and farm statistics for each state. The same statistics are also available for the United States as a whole and include population, employment, income, farm characteristics, top agriculture commodities, top agriculture exports, and farm financial indicators. Data come from six different government sources and are updated as new information becomes available.

This is a simple service for basic demographic and agricultural profiles of the states. Researchers looking for more detailed data can click on the links provided throughout each fact sheet to consult more extensive data tables. Agency contacts are also provided.

Subjects: Farms and Farming — Statistics

62. United States Department of Agriculture
http://www.usda.gov/

Sponsor(s): Agriculture Department (USDA)

Description: The main Department of Agriculture Web site provides efficient and uncluttered access to department information. The front page of the site contains current news, event announcements, quick task-based links (such as find a form and find current food recalls), information about administration initiatives, and a feature to browse site contents by subject area. Major topical sections include: Agriculture, Education and Outreach, Food and Nutrition, Marketing and Trade, Natural Resources, Rural and Community Development, and Research and Science.

As the umbrella site for a large department, the Department of Agriculture site provides a page of links to the Web sites for its agencies, services, and programs. The site also features a Spanish-language version, which contains news, program information, and educational material.

This is a well-organized site with a simple, consistent interface. It serves as a gateway to the organization of the department and its major programs and publications. The Web sites of the department's component agencies have been redesigned to follow the standard format of this main site.

Subjects: Agriculture

Publications: *Agriculture Fact Book*, A 1.38/2:
Performance and Accountability Report for FY . . ., A 1.1:

63. USDA Economics and Statistics System
http://usda.mannlib.cornell.edu/

Sponsor(s): Cornell University — Mann Library

Description: This Web site features a collection of nearly 300 reports and data sets from Department of Agriculture economics agencies, including the Economic Research Service, the National Agricultural Statistics Service, and the World Agricultural Outlook Board. It includes current and historical data and reports on national food and agricultural developments; it also forecasts the effects of changing conditions and policies on domestic and international agriculture.

Users may search the entire database or a combination of its components for reports or datasets. They may also browse by topic, with available topics including agricultural baseline projections; farm sector economics; field crops; food; inputs, technology, and weather; international agriculture; land, water, and conservation; livestock, dairy, and poultry; rural affairs; specialty agriculture; and trade issues. In addition, information may be browsed alphabetically by agency through the links at the top of the home page.

Materials cover both U.S. and international agricultural topics. Most reports are presented as PDF or ASCII text files. Most datasets are in spreadsheet format and include time-series data that are updated annually. The Calendar section organizes reports and datasets by expected release date, and users can sign up to receive selected reports when they are released.

While some of these reports are available in full from Department of Agriculture Web sites, the value of this Cornell University Web site lies in its standard interface, centralized access, and historical back files.

Subjects: Agriculture — Statistics; Agriculture Information

64. USDA On Line Photography Center
http://www.usda.gov/oc/photo/opchomea.htm

Sponsor(s): Agriculture Department (USDA) — Office of Communications

Description: The USDA On Line Photography Center creates and collects photography that depicts general agriculture, health, economics, resource conservation, forestry, and other programs administered by the department's component agencies. Collections include farm animals, food markets, and forest fire fighting. This Web site has an extensive, annotated collection of such photos in JPEG format. In addition to the contemporary photos, the site includes a selection of photos from the Farm Security Administration (FSA) photograph collection of the late 1930s and early 1940s.

Subjects: Agriculture Information; Photography

65. Water Quality Information Center
http://www.nal.usda.gov/wqic/

Sponsor(s): Agriculture Department (USDA) — National Agricultural Library (NAL)

Description: The Water Quality Information Center Web site compiles links to Internet resources concerning water supply and water quality in relation to agriculture. Resources include Web sites, conference reports, journal articles, and other online publications, which mostly come from government and academic sources. The site links to water-related databases and has numerous bibliographies on such topics as conservation buffers, drainage, nutrient management, and wetlands. The site also has educational materials, tools, and guides.

Subjects: Agricultural Waste; Farms and Farming; Water

66. World Agricultural Outlook Board (WAOB)

http://www.usda.gov/oce/commodity/

Sponsor(s): Agriculture Department (USDA) — World Agricultural Outlook Board
Description: WAOB coordinates analysis from many Department of Agriculture agencies to produce a monthly *World Agricultural Supply and Demand Estimates* report, and it houses the Joint Agricultural Weather Facility. This Web page, part of the larger Department of Agriculture Office of the Chief Economist Web site, provides information about the WAOB and copies of its publications.
Subjects: Agricultural Economics — International
Publications: *USDA Agricultural Baseline Projections to . . .*, A 93.44:
World Agricultural Supply and Demand Estimates, A 93.29/3:

Fishing

67. Aquaculture Information Center

http://www.lib.noaa.gov/docaqua/frontpage.htm

Sponsor(s): Commerce Department — National Oceanic and Atmospheric Administration (NOAA) — National Environmental Satellite, Data, and Information Service (NESDIS)
Description: This Web site acts as a portal to other aquaculture-related Web sites. Links are organized under such topics as statistics, laws and regulatory information, electronic newsletters, and aquaculture issues bibliographies. The site also links to aquaculture education resources and to related programs from the Department of Commerce and international partners.
Subjects: Aquaculture

68. Atlantic States Marine Fisheries Commission (ASMFC)

http://www.asmfc.org/

Sponsor(s): Atlantic States Marine Fisheries Commission
Description: The ASMFC, a group made up of the 15 Atlantic coastal states, was formed by an interstate compact approved by Congress. These states work together through ASMFC to manage the Atlantic fisheries. The ASMFC Web site includes news, research and statistics, law enforcement compliance reports, links to other fisheries organizations, and information about pending actions open for public input.
Subjects: Fisheries

69. Census of Aquaculture 2005

http://www.nass.usda.gov/Census_of_Agriculture/2002/Aquaculture/

Sponsor(s): Agriculture Department (USDA) — National Agricultural Statistics Service (NASS)
Description: The 2005 Census of Aquaculture provides data on the aquaculture industry, covering production methods, surface water acres and sources, sales, aquaculture employment and payroll, and other topics. The report is online in PDF and text formats, with tables also available in comma-separated value format. This is the second such census; the first was conducted in 1998.
Subjects: Aquaculture — Statistics

70. Fisheries Information System

http://www.st.nmfs.gov/fis/

Sponsor(s): Commerce Department — National Oceanic and Atmospheric Administration (NOAA) — National Marine Fisheries

Description: NOAA's Fisheries Information System program was established to improve data collection and management nationwide for commercial and recreational fisheries statistics. This Web site describes the proposed system, which was under development at the time of this writing. It also links to existing sources for national and regional fishery statistics.

Subjects: Fisheries — Statistics

71. Fishing

http://fishing.fws.gov/

Sponsor(s): Interior Department — Fish and Wildlife Service (FWS)

Description: The FWS Web site, Fishing, focuses on recreational fishing. The site provides information about the agency's work to improve fisheries and links to other organizations that provide information for recreational fishers. It features national and state fishing statistics from the *National Survey of Fishing, Hunting, and Wildlife-Associated Recreation* and hunting and fishing license statistics back to 1975.

Subjects: Fishing

Publications: *National Survey of Fishing, Hunting, and Wildlife-Associated Recreation,* I 49.98:

72. Gulf States Marine Fisheries Commission

http://www.gsmfc.org/

Sponsor(s): Gulf States Marine Fisheries Commission (GSMFC)

Description: GSMFC is a Congress-authorized organization made up of the five Gulf of Mexico states (Texas, Louisiana, Mississippi, Alabama, and Florida). Its Web site includes sections with information about programs, publications, meetings, regulations, invasive species, and toxic blooms.

Subjects: Fisheries

73. NOAA Fisheries — National Marine Fisheries Service

http://www.nmfs.noaa.gov/

Sponsor(s): Commerce Department — National Oceanic and Atmospheric Administration (NOAA) — National Marine Fisheries

Description: The National Marine Fisheries Service is the component of NOAA charged with conserving, protecting, and managing living marine resources. Each major section of the site links to program information from NOAA divisions. The Sustaining Fisheries section covers domestic and international fisheries, highly migratory species, and seafood inspection. The Protecting Marine Species section discusses endangered species, marine mammal conservation, and coral reefs. The Conserving Marine Habitat section links to NOAA divisions with responsibilities in that area. The Science and Technology section includes fisheries statistics and economic information, along with reports on the work of NOAA Fisheries science centers and research vessels. The Law Enforcement section describes the work of NOAA Fisheries special agents and enforcement officers.

The Media Center section has press releases and allows users to sign up for the free FishNews e-mail service. Other sections of the site provide information about grants, legislation, permits, and international cooperation relating to marine resources. Publications can be found on each NOAA division Web page.

Although it sports an uncluttered and fun look (with fish graphics and a search function that says "Go Fish!"), the NOAA Fisheries site contains broad and deep coverage of its topics. Users can easily navigate the NOAA divisions to find science, research, statistics, regulations, and other information related to NOAA's marine resources activities.

Subjects: Fisheries; Marine Mammals
Publications: *Fisheries of the United States,* C 55.309/2-2:
Fishery Bulletin, C 55.313:
Fishery Market News, C 55.318:
Imports and Exports of Fishery Products, Annual Summary, C 55.309/2-10:
Our Living Oceans, Annual Report on the Status of U.S. Living Marine Resources,
   C 55.1/2:

74. Northwest Fisheries Science Center (NWFSC)
http://www.nwfsc.noaa.gov/
Sponsor(s): Commerce Department — National Oceanic and Atmospheric Administration (NOAA) — National Marine Fisheries
Description: NWFSC is a NOAA Fisheries research center. Its Web site describes the center's research and includes publications, a fisheries science glossary, killer whale image library, and other information resources.
   This site has a wide variety of research information, primarily in the Publications, Resources, and Library sections.
Subjects: Fisheries

75. Pacific States Marine Fisheries Commission
http://www.psmfc.org/
Sponsor(s): Pacific States Marine Fisheries Commission (PSMFC)
Description: PSMFC, authorized by Congress in 1947, is one of three interstate commissions dedicated to resolving fishery issues. It serves as a forum for discussion of fishery issues in California, Oregon, Washington, Idaho, and Alaska. Its Web site has information about current projects, events, grants and contracts, workshop proceedings, and links to fisheries data projects.
Subjects: Fisheries

76. Your Guide to Fishing on National Wildlife Refuges
http://www.fws.gov/refuges/FishingGuide/
Sponsor(s): Interior Department — Fish and Wildlife Service (FWS)
Description: This interactive online guide displays wildlife refuge information by state and by type of fish available. The Special Features section includes tips about catch and release, invasive aquatic species, and other topics.
Subjects: Fishing
Publications: *Your Guide to Fishing on National Wildlife Refuges,* I 49.6/2:

Forestry

77. Ecosystem Management Coordination
http://www.fs.fed.us/emc/
Sponsor(s): Agriculture Department (USDA) — Forest Service (USFS)
Description: The Ecosystem Management Coordination (EMC) Office is concerned with information and analysis to support Forest Service planning. Its Web site includes information about the Forest Service's environmental appeals and litigation, information related to the National Environmental Protection Act and Environmental Impact Statements, and planning documents related to the National Forest Management Act.
Subjects: Environmental Law; Forests — Policy

78. Forest Service
http://www.fs.fed.us/
Sponsor(s): Agriculture Department (USDA) — Forest Service (USFS)
Description: The Forest Service manages public lands in national forests and grasslands. Its Web site includes the following sections: Employment, Fire and Aviation, Maps and Brochures, Passes and Permits, Recreational Activities, Safety, Research and Development, and State and Private Forestry. The Publications section includes the full-text versions of USFS directives, manuals, handbooks, and other publications. The Projects and Policies section highlights proposed regulatory and policy initiatives and links to the Schedule of Proposed Actions "that will soon begin or are currently undergoing environmental analysis and documentation" (from the Web site).

The Research and Development section has databases of research publications and offers links to six regional research stations and to the International Institute of Tropical Forestry in Puerto Rico. Each regional research station provides publications and more in-depth research information about local forestry topics.

The State and Private Forestry section concerns Forest Service assistance to landowners, state governments, and other communities and institutions. Topics covered include tribal relations, sustainable development, conservation education, and urban forestry.

The site is well organized with a substantial amount of information about the agency, its component forests, and publications.
Subjects: Forestry
Publications: *Fire Management Today (formerly Fire Management Notes)*, A 13.32:
Global Leaflet, A 13.153:
Land Areas of the National Forest System, A 13.10:
U.S. Forest Facts and Historical Trends, A 13.2:F 76/
Wildland Waters, A 13.110/19:

79. Forestry
http://www.nrcs.usda.gov/technical/forestry.html
Sponsor(s): Agriculture Department (USDA) — Natural Resources Conservation Service (NRCS)
Description: This Web page serves as a central point for links to the Department of Agriculture and other federal agencies that provide information about forestry. Linked resources include Department of Agriculture publications and manuals, maps, and economic models.
Subjects: Forestry

80. Healthy Forests Initiative (HFI)
http://www.healthyforests.gov/
Sponsor(s): Interior Department
Description: HFI was created by the Bush administration to encompass information about regulatory and legislative changes in the management of national forests. Its Web site provides information about HFI policies, project status, contracting opportunities, and research. It also includes HFI activity reports for each state.
Subjects: Forests — Policy

81. National Symbols Program
http://www.symbols.gov/
Sponsor(s): Agriculture Department (USDA) — Forest Service (USFS)
Description: The National Symbols Program controls the use of such symbols as Smokey the Bear and Woodsy Owl. These symbols can only be used by approved

customers for educational purposes. This Web site explains the allowed usages of the symbols and describes available products and educational tools.
Subjects: Environmental Education

82. USDA National Agroforestry Center
http://www.unl.edu/nac/
Sponsor(s): Agriculture Department (USDA)
Description: Agroforestry combines forestry, agriculture, land conservation, and sustainable development practices. The National Agroforestry Center (NAC) conducts research into agroforestry practices, provides tools and training, and disseminates information about agroforestry. Its Web site provides NAC publications, guides, educational display materials, and links to related Web sites. Special topics include riparian forest buffers, silvopasture, and forest farming. The site also provides a blog with conservation news and an agroforestry image library.
Subjects: Forestry — Research
Publications: *Agroforestry Notes*, A 13.164/2:
Inside Agroforestry, A 13.164:
Working Trees, A 13.2:

CHAPTER 3
Business and Economics

The federal government regulates and supports U.S. businesses and monitors and influences the national economy. These roles drive much of the business and economic information published by the government; this information has long been an important, authoritative source of industry and finance data. While this chapter has broad coverage, it does not feature labor-related information (which can be found in the Employment chapter) or government finance and taxation (which can be found in the Government and Politics chapter).

Subsections in this chapter are Business and Industry, Consumer Information, Economics, Federal Reserve System, Finance, International Trade, and Money.

Business and Industry

83. Alcohol and Tobacco Tax and Trade Bureau
http://www.ttb.gov/
Sponsor(s): Treasury Department — Alcohol and Tobacco Tax and Trade Bureau (TTB)
Description: TTB was created by the Homeland Security Act of 2002, which moved the law enforcement functions of the Bureau of Alcohol, Tobacco, and Firearms (ATF) from the Department of the Treasury to the Department of Justice. The act established TTB to manage the ATF functions that remained at Treasury Department. TTB administers and enforces the federal laws and tax code provisions related to the production and taxation of alcohol and tobacco products. The bureau also collects all excise tax on the manufacture of firearms and ammunition.

The TTB Web site includes tax and fee schedules, services for the regulated industries, and legal and regulatory information. An extensive Frequently Asked Questions section addresses such topics as starting a business to import tobacco, the federal and state excise taxes imposed on alcohol, and the legality of selling home-produced wine. The site also has information about American viticultural areas, labeling requirements for organic alcoholic beverages, and alcohol import requirements.
Subjects: Guns — Regulations; Taxation; Tobacco — Regulations; Alcohol — Regulations
Publications: *Monthly Statistical Release—Beer*, T 70.9/4:
Monthly Statistical Release—Wines, T 70.9/5:

84. Baldrige National Quality Program (BNQP)
http://www.quality.nist.gov/
Sponsor(s): Commerce Department — Technology Administration (TA) — National Institute of Standards and Technology (NIST)
Description: The Malcolm Baldrige National Quality Award, sponsored by the Department of Commerce, is the centerpiece of BNQP. This award recognizes performance excellence and focuses on an organization's overall performance management system. The award is presented in five categories: manufacturing, service, small business, education, and health care.

The BNQP Web site presents detailed information about the award, the award process, performance criteria, past winners, and the Foundation for the Malcolm Baldrige National Quality Award. The site also has information about the Quest for Excellence, the official conference of the Baldrige Award.
Subjects: Business Management — Awards and Honors

85. Business.gov

http://www.business.gov/

Sponsor(s): Small Business Administration (SBA)

Description: Business.gov provides one-stop access to business-related information and services from numerous federal agencies, including the SBA. The Business.gov Web site emphasizes access to regulatory and legal compliance information. Users can select a business topic (such as finance or information security) or an industry (such as transportation or construction) to find federal compliance and business assistance information. The site has a separate tool for finding state-level compliance information, as well as a directory of federal agency contacts for compliance assistance information.

This easy-to-navigate site is an excellent starting point and source of information for businesses searching for government assistance, regulations, forms, and guidance.

Subjects: Business Information; Small Business

86. Center for Veterans Enterprise

http://www.vetbiz.gov/

Sponsor(s): Veterans Affairs Department

Description: The Center for Veterans Enterprise works to promote veteran-owned businesses. Its Web site includes information about starting a business and promotes special networking, marketing, and mentoring opportunities for veterans. It also has a database of veteran-owned businesses that have registered with the site.

Subjects: Small Business; Veterans

87. Committee on Foreign Investments in the United States

http://www.ustreas.gov/offices/international-affairs/exon-florio/

Sponsor(s): Committee on Foreign Investments in the United States (CFIUS)

Description: CFIUS, an interagency committee chaired by the Secretary of the Treasury, reviews notices of foreign acquisitions of U.S. companies and may investigate on behalf of the president if such acquisitions could threaten national security. This Department of the Treasury Web page provides a description of CFIUS's role in implementing the Exon-Florio provision in the Omnibus Trade and Competitiveness Act of 1988; it also describes the provision. In early 2006, the site also carried announcements concerning the controversial committee decision regarding Dubai Ports World's proposed takeover of terminal operations at a number of U.S. ports.

Subjects: Companies and Enterprises — Regulations; National Security

88. Department of Commerce

http://www.commerce.gov/

Sponsor(s): Commerce Department

Description: The Department of Commerce Web site is an excellent starting point for finding government information related to the world of business. The site also provides population totals, weather forecasts, and the time of day—as the Census Bureau, the National Weather Service, and the National Institute of Standards and Technology all fall under the jurisdiction of the Commerce Department.

The components of the department are listed and linked in the About Commerce—Department of Commerce Officials section. Other information is grouped into four main categories. The Free Trade section has links to trade opportunities, compliance information, and export regulations. The Innovation section provides links to offices that deal with technology, telecommunications, patents and trademarks, weather, and coastal and marine resources issues. The Economic Growth section includes information about economic analysis, economic development, and grants and contracting opportunities. The International Outreach section has information about trade missions. The site's home page also features news, the latest economic indicator releases, and a link to a Spanish-language version of the page.

The site provides easy access by topic to the many other Commerce Department online information sources.

Subjects: Business Information; International Trade
Publications: *Budget and Annual Performance Plan of the U.S. Department of Commerce*, C 1.1/8:

89. E-Stats: Measuring the Electronic Economy
http://www.census.gov/eos/www/ebusiness614.htm
Sponsor(s): Commerce Department — Economics and Statistics Administration (ESA) — Census Bureau
Description: E-Stats is a central clearinghouse for reports and data from the Census Bureau that define and measure electronic commerce across multiple economic sectors. The E-Stats Web site has quarterly reports on online retail sales and annual reports comparing e-commerce sales to total sales.
Subjects: Electronic Commerce — Statistics

90. Federal Trade Commission
http://www.ftc.gov/
Sponsor(s): Federal Trade Commission (FTC)
Description: The FTC enforces federal antitrust and consumer protection laws. Its Web site contains resources for antitrust law practitioners and researchers in the Antitrust and Competition section. Documents provided include related economics research papers, antitrust guidelines, pre-merger notifications under the Hart-Scott-Rodino Act, and antitrust case filings. The Formal Actions section includes FTC advisory opinions, FTC rules, public comments on proposed regulations, commission and staff reports, and other documents. In 2006, the FTC brought Commission decisions going back to 1969 online. The Legal section has FTC amicus briefs and the litigation status report.

On the consumer side, the FTC site offers many fact sheets and guides, an online complaint form, and links to federal consumer Web sites, including Consumer.gov, Econsumer.gov, and the online Do Not Call Registry. The site's home page also links to a Spanish-language page about the FTC's fraud prevention work and its Hispanic Outreach initiative.

The Economics Resources section includes FTC Economic Reports, issue papers, conference presentations, and information about competition in the health care industry. The site also has a special section on FTC privacy initiatives.

This Web site serves a valuable public function by presenting clear, fresh, and timely information. The multiple ways to access information ensure that both consumers and antitrust researchers will be able to find what they need.

Subjects: Business — Regulations; Consumer Information
Publications: *A Guide to the Federal Trade Commission*, FT 1.8/2:
For Consumers: Consumer Alerts, FT 1.32/4:

91. Manufacturing, Mining, and Construction Statistics
http://www.census.gov/mcd/
Sponsor(s): Commerce Department — Economics and Statistics Administration (ESA) — Census Bureau
Description: This Census Bureau gateway Web site compiles all census-related information about manufacturing, mining, and construction into one page. Data primarily come from the *Annual Survey of Manufactures*, *Current Industrial Reports*,

and the *Economic Census*, although information from other programs is also available. Construction statistics include new residential construction, sales, and building permits. The Manufacturing section includes the latest releases on manufacturers' shipments, inventories, and orders.

Subjects: Construction Industry — Statistics; Manufacturing — Statistics; Mining — Statistics

Publications: *Annual Survey of Manufactures*, C 3.24/9
Current Industrial Reports, Manufacturing Profiles, C 3.158/4:
Manufacturers' Shipments, Inventories, and Orders, C 3.158:

92. Minority Business Development Agency

http://www.mbda.gov/

Sponsor(s): Commerce Department — Minority Business Development Agency (MBDA)

Description: MBDA's mission is to promote the growth and competitiveness of minority business enterprises (MBEs) of all sizes. The agency funds business development centers throughout the United States to assist MBEs. The MBDA Web site has agency news and events, a directory of regional offices, and background information about federal contracting and about starting, financing, and managing a business. Publications are available under the Publications and Research link, which is located under the title banner on the site's home page. The publication *The State of Minority Business* is released every five years; the most current report is based on 2002 data.

The site also offers a variety of online business tools that can be used after setting up a free account. Tools include a contract referral system, an interactive business plan writer, and online forums.

Subjects: Minority-Owned Businesses
Publications: *The State of Minority Business*, C 1.102:

93. NAICS—North American Industry Classification System

http://www.census.gov/epcd/www/naics.html

Sponsor(s): Commerce Department — Economics and Statistics Administration (ESA) — Census Bureau

Description: NAICS is the official industry classification system used by U.S. statistical agencies. Adopted in 1997, NAICS replaced the Standard Industrial Classification (SIC) codes that had been used in government reports since the 1930s. This Web site is the central location for NAICS news and documentation. It includes information about the 2002 edition of the *NAICS Manual* and its subsequent updates and has cross-walks between the SIC codes and editions of NAICS. A NAICS Search section allows keyword and NAICS code number searching of the 1997 and 2002 editions of the *NAICS Manual*, with links to display the code's hierarchy and description. A section called Ask Dr. NAICS includes an e-mail contact and answers to frequently asked NAICS-related questions.

The NAICS Web site enables quick code look-ups and is particularly helpful for updates on NAICS implementation.

Subjects: Industries

94. National Women's Business Council

http://www.nwbc.gov/

Sponsor(s): National Women's Business Council

Description: The National Women's Business Council is a federal advisory council that provides advice and policy recommendations to the president, Congress, and the Small Business Administration on issues relevant to female business owners. Its Web site features news, reports, and referrals to business mentoring programs.

The Publications section includes fact sheets, statistics, and analysis pertaining to women and entrepreneurship.
Subjects: Women-Owned Businesses

95. NTIS Business Collection
http://www.ntis.gov/products/families/business.asp?loc=4-3-1
Sponsor(s): Commerce Department
Description: This National Technical Information Service (NTIS) bookstore Web site provides a database of business-related publications from the government, selected nonprofit organizations, and commercial publishers. The collection can be searched by broad topic or by keyword, and items are available for purchase from NTIS.
Subjects: Business Information; Government Publications

96. Office of Small Business Development Centers
http://www.sba.gov/SBDC/
Sponsor(s): Small Business Administration (SBA)
Description: Small Business Development Centers (SBDCs) provide management assistance to small businesses in local communities across the United States. This Web site explains the role of these centers and provides a state-by-state roster of all SBDCs. The site also features a Spanish-language version.
Subjects: Small Business

97. Online Women's Business Center
http://www.onlinewbc.gov/
Sponsor(s): Small Business Administration (SBA)
Description: This Web site is designed to provide resources for women in business, including information about starting a new business and operating in the global marketplace. It includes a nationwide directory of women's business centers and has sections on starting, financing, and managing a business.

This site serves as a limited gateway to information of general interest to women business owners.
Subjects: Women-Owned Businesses

98. Patent and Trademark Office
http://www.uspto.gov/
Sponsor(s): Commerce Department — Patent and Trademark Office (PTO)
Description: The home page of the PTO Web site provides quick links for searching about, checking the status of, and filing for patents and trademarks. Patents issued since 1976 are available in full-text format; those issued since 1790 are in full-image format. Published patent applications are online for March 2001 and onward. TESS, a database of pending, registered, and dead federal trademarks, is also available through the site.

In addition to the databases, this site has a tremendous amount of information about the agency, patent and trademark law and procedures, international intellectual property issues, the patent classification system, resources for inventors, and more.

Consistent interfaces for the Patents, Trademarks, and How To Guides sections help readers find information on this information-dense site. The alphabetical site index is another useful resource.
Subjects: Intellectual Property; Patent Law; Trademarks
Publications: *Basic Facts About Registering a Trademark*, C 21.2:R 26/
Cassis Currents Newsletter, C 21.31/12:
Electronic Official Gazette: Patents, C 21.5:

General Information Concerning Patents, C 21.26/2:
Index to the U.S. Patent Classification, C 21.12/2:
List of Patent Classification Definitions (database), C 21.3/2:
Manual of Patent Classification, C 21.12:
Manual of Patent Examining Procedure, C 21.15:
Patent Public Advisory Committee Annual Report, C 21.1/4:
Products and Services Catalog, C 21.30:
Trademark Official Gazette, C 21.5/4:
Trademark Public Advisory Committee Annual Report, C 21.1/3:
U.S. Patent Applications Database, C 21.31/17:

99. Patent and Trademark Office Electronic Business Center

http://www.uspto.gov/ebc/indexebc.html
Sponsor(s): Commerce Department — Patent and Trademark Office (PTO)
Description: The Electronic Business Center Web site links to the online services provided by the PTO. These include the patent and trademarks databases, online document ordering services, and electronic filing systems. The site also has an interface for managing deposit accounts with the PTO.
Subjects: Patent Law; Trademarks; Databases

100. SBA Office of Advocacy

http://www.sba.gov/advo/
Sponsor(s): Small Business Administration (SBA)
Description: The SBA Office of Advocacy Web site states that the office was created to "protect, strengthen and effectively represent the nation's small businesses within the federal government's legislative and rule-making processes." The office provides regulatory alerts, notices of documents published in the *Federal Register* and open for comment that may significantly affect small businesses, and information about laws and legislation affecting small businesses. The Research and Statistics section includes a full array of statistics on small business and the small business economy, as well as research papers on topics such as small business finance and the impact of regulatory costs on small firms. The State Activities section reports on the office's Small Business Regulatory Flexibility Initiative.
Subjects: Business Statistics; Small Business — Regulations
Publications: *Small Business Advocate*, SBA 1.51:
Small Business Economic Indicators, SBA 1.1/2-2:
State Small Business Profiles, SBA 1.50:
The Small Business Economy, SBA 1.1/2:

101. Small Business Administration (SBA)

http://www.sba.gov/
Sponsor(s): Small Business Administration (SBA)
Description: The SBA Web site's Services section provides links to information about SBA financial assistance, grants, contracting opportunities, counseling, training, and other topics. The Tools section of the site contains publications, forms, statistics, and information about laws and regulations. The site also features a planner for small businesses and directory of local SBA offices and mentoring resources. A link in the upper right corner leads to a Spanish-language version of the site.
Subjects: Small Business
Publications: *Annual Report of the Chief Counsel for Advocacy on Implementation of the Regulatory Flexibility Act*, SBA 1.1/5:
Forms, SBA 1.40:
Small Business Advocate, SBA 1.51:
Small Business Economic Indicators, SBA 1.1/2-2:

Small Business Lending in the United States, SBA 1.52:
State Small Business Profiles, SBA 1.50:
The Small Business Economy, SBA 1.1/2:

102. StopFakes.Gov/Small Business
http://www.stopfakes.gov/smallbusiness/
Alternate URL(s): http://www.uspto.gov/smallbusiness/
Sponsor(s): Commerce Department — Patent and Trademark Office (PTO)
Description: This Web site is part of the PTO campaign to educate small businesses about the effects of piracy, counterfeiting, and theft of intellectual property. It includes basic information about patents, trademarks, and the government's anti-piracy campaign. The Download Materials section has a fact sheet on small business and intellectual property theft.
Subjects: Intellectual Property; Small Business

103. U.S. Industry and Trade Outlook News
http://www.outlook.gov/
Sponsor(s): Commerce Department — International Trade Administration (ITA)
Description: The Department of Commerce is planning an Internet-only version of its classic business reference publication, *U.S. Industry and Trade Outlook*. This book was last published in 2000, and the department has been working on an online version ever since. (The online version is still in development at the time of this writing.) This Web site provides status information on the project and refers users to other Commerce Department Web pages, which can provide meaningful industry data in the meantime.

This project has been in the planning stages for many years. At this time, the status page does not discuss a target launch date.
Subjects: Industries — Statistics
Publications: *U.S. Industry and Trade Outlook*, C 61.48:

104. Women-21.gov
http://www.women-21.gov/
Sponsor(s): Labor Department; Small Business Administration (SBA)
Description: The Women-21.gov Web site is described as a "one-stop federal resource for targeted information, registration for online programs, and networking opportunities to help women entrepreneurs navigate the ever-changing business world." The site features a calendar of relevant events, news items, helpful articles, and a Tool and Tips section with links that provide information about topics such as access to capital, affordable health care, and labor law.
Subjects: Women-Owned Businesses

105. WomenBiz.gov
http://www.womenbiz.gov/
Sponsor(s): National Women's Business Council
Description: This government gateway Web site compiles and links to information for women-owned businesses planning to sell products and services to the federal government. The site features government contracts news and a section that describes the "5 steps to government contracting."
Subjects: Government Procurement; Women-Owned Businesses

Consumer Information

106. Aviation Consumer Protection Division
http://airconsumer.ost.dot.gov/
Sponsor(s): Transportation Department
Description: The Aviation Consumer Protection Division of the Department of Transportation receives the general public's complaints about airline consumer issues and works with the aviation industry to improve compliance with consumer protection requirements. The Web site's Air Travel Problems and Complaints section explains how to file a complaint and includes an e-mail address and other filing options. The Air Travel Consumer Report section has monthly statistics on flight delays, mishandled baggage, and other complaint areas. The Service Cessations section has chronological and detailed information about airlines that have ceased flight operations. The Travel Tips and Publications section has consumer information about topics such as travel with animals and charter flights. The site includes an HTML version of the publication *Fly Rights: A Consumer Guide to Air Travel*.
Subjects: Airlines; Consumer Information
Publications: *Fly Rights: A Consumer Guide to Air Travel*, TD 1.8:F 67/

107. Consumer Action Website
http://www.consumeraction.gov/
Sponsor(s): General Services Administration (GSA)
Description: This Web site is an online version of the *Consumer Action Handbook*, which is also available in print or in PDF format online. The site offers basic consumer advice on topics such as cars, insurance, credit, and utilities. The Resources Directory section provides an extensive directory of addresses, phone numbers, and Web sites for corporations, state and county consumer protection agencies, state insurance regulators, national consumer organizations, and other useful groups.
Subjects: Consumer Information

108. Consumer Information Security
http://www.ftc.gov/bcp/conline/edcams/infosecurity/
Sponsor(s): Federal Trade Commission (FTC) — Bureau of Consumer Protection
Description: This Web site contains practical information for consumers and businesses on computer security and safeguarding personal information. The Consumer Information section includes online pamphlets about spyware, online shopping, spam, privacy, children's online privacy, and identity theft. The Resources section provides links to related Web sites for more information, and the For Kids section is designed especially for children. Parts of the Web site, including the kids' section and a selection of the consumer guides, are available in Spanish.
Subjects: Consumer Information; Identity Theft; Privacy

109. Consumer Product Safety Commission
http://cpsc.gov/
Sponsor(s): Consumer Product Safety Commission (CPSC)
Description: CPSC develops and enforces standards to reduce the risk of injury or death from consumer products. The CPSC Web site highlights recent product recall news, which is available as an RSS feed, podcast, or downloadable MP3 file. It also has an online file of previous recall announcements organized by date, product category, and company. The CPSC Publications section provides links

to consumer guidance pamphlets and notices in HTML or PDF formats. All announcements and some publications are available in Spanish.

Other resources on the site include the National Electronic Injury Surveillance System (NEISS) database of emergency hospital visits involving an injury associated with consumer products; regulations, laws, and information for manufacturers, importers, distributors, and retailers; and industry guidance.

This is a useful site for consumers, who can use it to report defective consumer products and check to see which products have been recalled. Consumers may also wish to visit the federal government's Recalls.gov Web site.

Subjects: Product Recalls; Product Safety
Publications: *Annual Report*, Y 3.C 76/3:1
Consumer Product Safety Review (quarterly), Y 3.C 76/3:28
CPSC Public Calendar, Y 3.C 76/3:26

110. Consumer Sentinel

http://www.consumer.gov/sentinel/
Sponsor(s): Federal Trade Commission (FTC)
Description: The FTC's Consumer Sentinel Web site provides information about consumer fraud and an online form for reporting fraud complaints. The Fraud Trends section includes national, state, and local statistics on fraud and identity theft complaints.
Subjects: Fraud

111. Consumer.gov

http://www.consumer.gov/
Sponsor(s): Federal Trade Commission (FTC)
Description: This FirstGov.gov for Consumers gateway Web site provides links to consumer information from numerous government agencies. Major topical sections include Food, Product Safety (recalls), Health, Home and Community (emergency preparedness, home heating, mortgages), Money, Transportation, Children, Careers and Education, and Technology. Consumer news headlines and popular topics, such as identity theft, telemarketing, and privacy information, are featured on the main page.

Rumors circulate quickly around the Internet, but Consumer.gov is an authoritative source for reliable information about scams, product recalls, and reporting consumer fraud.
Subjects: Consumer Information; Finding Aids

112. EConsumer.gov

http://www.econsumer.gov/
Sponsor(s): Federal Trade Commission (FTC)
Description: The EConsumer.gov Web site is a collaborative effort of 20 nations; the FTC is primarily in charge of the participation of the United States. The site was developed in response to the international nature of Internet fraud. It provides general information about consumer protection in of the all countries that belong to the International Consumer Protection Enforcement Network (ICPEN), contact information for consumer protection authorities in those countries, and an online complaint form. In the Complaint Trends section, the site provides statistics about the nature of the complaints received through EConsumer.gov. The site can be viewed in English, Spanish, German, French, Korean, and Polish.
Subjects: Fraud

113. FCC Consumer and Governmental Affairs Bureau
http://www.fcc.gov/cgb/
Sponsor(s): Federal Communications Commission (FCC) — Consumer and Governmental Affairs Bureau
Description: The FCC Consumer and Governmental Affairs Bureau (CGB) informs consumers on telecommunications issues and works with other government agencies at all levels to formulate telecommunications policy. The CGB Web site carries news, regulatory announcements, fact sheets, and consumer alerts on topics such as voice over Internet protocol (VoIP), charges on phone bills, broadband Internet access, and the regulation of indecency and obscenity on broadcasts. The Inquiries and Complaints section features a quarterly press release that contains statistics on the types of consumer inquiries and complaints received by the bureau.

This site provides clear answers for common consumer questions and alerts users to telephone, broadcast, and Internet scams. It also helps explain the consumer side of a wide range of technologies, such as wireless phones and digital television.
Subjects: Consumer Information; Telecommunications; Telephone Service

114. FDA Consumer Magazine
http://www.fda.gov/fdac/
Sponsor(s): Health and Human Services Department — Food and Drug Administration (FDA)
Description: *FDA Consumer* magazine provides information and advice for the general public. The magazine reports on health tips and fads, FDA activities, and safety information about food, drugs, medical devices, cosmetics, and other products regulated by the agency. The full copies are online for 1995 forward; for 1989 to 1994, selected articles are online.

FDA has done a great public service by putting these practical and timely publications online. Access would be improved with the addition of an e-mail or RSS newsfeed subscription. Print subscriptions are available for a fee through the Government Printing Office.
Subjects: Consumer Information; Health Products

115. FTC for the Consumer
http://www.ftc.gov/ftc/consumer.htm
Sponsor(s): Federal Trade Commission (FTC) — Bureau of Consumer Protection
Description: This Web site features over 100 full-text pamphlets from FTC with advice for consumers and businesses from the Federal Trade Commission. These publications are online versions of *Facts for Consumers* and are categorized into sections, such as Automobiles; At Home; Credit; Investments; Diet, Health, and Fitness; Identity Theft; Telephone Services; and Scholarships and Employment Services. Pamphlets are available in text and PDF formats; a few are available as audio files. If the FTC has a public education campaign on a particular topic, the applicable link leads to the education campaign site rather than to the online pamphlet. The site also offers online ordering of the printed pamphlets.

Although brief, these consumer and business information brochures can be excellent resources for users.
Subjects: Consumer Information
Publications: *Facts for Consumers*, FT 1.32:

116. Mymoney.gov
http://www.mymoney.gov/
Sponsor(s): Financial Literacy and Education Commission
Description: Aimed at the individual consumer, this Web site provides tips on financial planning, credit, saving, home ownership, retirement, and other personal

finance topics. A Spanish-language version is also available. The site is sponsored by Financial Literacy and Education Commission, an interagency organization.
Subjects: Personal Finance

117. National Do Not Call Registry
http://www.donotcall.gov/
Sponsor(s): Federal Trade Commission (FTC)
Description: The National Do Not Call Registry is managed by FTC and allows individuals to block most telemarketing calls to their phones. Consumers can use this Web site to register their phone numbers or file complaints about violations of the "do not call" rules. The site also has a Spanish-language version.
This site is clearly written and easy to use.
Subjects: Telemarketing — Regulations

118. OnGuard Online
http://onguardonline.gov/
Sponsor(s): Federal Trade Commission (FTC)
Description: OnGuard Online presents practical tips for securing personal computers and personal information. Topics covered on its Web site include spyware, wireless security, online scams, and teaching kids about online safety. The File a Complaint section directs users to appropriate agencies. The Resources section provides a computer security glossary, videos and tutorials, and interactive educational activities. A Spanish-language version is also available.
Subjects: Computer Security

119. Privacy Initiatives
http://www.ftc.gov/privacy/
Sponsor(s): Federal Trade Commission (FTC)
Description: This FTC Web site focuses on educating consumers and businesses about the importance of personal information privacy and what the FTC is doing to help make private information more secure. Major sections of this site are Unfairness and Deception, Financial Privacy, Credit Reporting, and Children's Privacy. Each section provides information about laws and regulations, enforcement, consumer education, business guidance, FTC testimony and reports, and news of current developments.
Subjects: Privacy

120. Publications from Pueblo
http://www.pueblo.gsa.gov/
Sponsor(s): General Services Administration (GSA)
Description: This Federal Citizen Information Center Web site provides numerous consumer-oriented resources on a variety of topics. It is essentially an online version of the well-known *Consumer Information Catalog*. Unlike the print catalog, which simply lists the various federally produced free consumer publications, this site includes the full-text versions of many of the publications. It also provides news updates concerning product recalls, scams, and fraudulent schemes. Print copies of the consumer publications can be ordered online or via phone, fax, or mail.
This site is a treasure trove for consumer information. By providing the full texts of the publications themselves, users have a much easier time browsing the publications.
Subjects: Consumer Information
Publications: *Consumer Focus*, GS 11.9/3-2:
Consumer Information Catalog, GS 11.9:

121. Recalls.gov

http://www.recalls.gov/

Sponsor(s): Consumer Product Safety Commission (CPSC)

Description: Recalls.gov is a central interagency source for information about product recalls and safety alerts. Information about recalls is organized into several sections: Consumer Products, Motor Vehicles, Boats, Food, Medicine, Cosmetics, and Environmental Products (pesticides and auto emissions equipment). Participating agencies include the Coast Guard, the Consumer Product Safety Commission, the Environmental Protection Agency, the Food and Drug Administration, the National Highway Traffic Safety Administration, and the Department of Agriculture.

Despite the "one-stop" goals of the site, Recalls.gov does not integrate product recall information into a single stream. Each product category page merely directs the recall information available on separate agency Web sites. The most integrated information is available in the Recent Recalls section, which offers a one-page view of six separate windows linking to each agency's product recall press releases.

Subjects: Product Recalls

122. SPAM

http://www.ftc.gov/bcp/conline/edcams/spam/

Sponsor(s): Federal Trade Commission (FTC) — Bureau of Consumer Protection

Description: This Web site is designed for consumers and businesses concerned about e-mail scams and unwanted junk e-mail. It includes tips for limiting spam and protecting private information. The site also features laws and regulations related to unsolicited e-mail, a compliance guide for businesses, FTC reports on the topic, and a resources page linking to other Web sites about e-mail spam.

This site is a good basic introduction to junk e-mail and e-mail scams, and serves as a central location for FTC reports and regulations on the topic. It has a Spanish-language section, but this section's coverage is limited to translations of several consumer guides.

Subjects: Fraud; E-mail

Economics

123. ALFRED®: Archival Federal Reserve Economic Data

http://alfred.stlouisfed.org/

Sponsor(s): Federal Reserve — Federal Reserve Bank of St. Louis

Description: ALFRED® is a database of economic data that allows researchers to analyze historical decisions that were made based on the data that were available at the time (prior to revisions and updates). "Vintage" data sets, as they are called on ALFRED®, can be downloaded as compressed spreadsheets or as tab-delimited text files. Over 2,000 data sets are organized into 11 categories, including Consumer Price Indexes, Gross Domestic Product, Interest Rates, Business/Fiscal (such as wages, federal debt, industrial production), Reserves and Monetary Base, and Trade.

ALFRED® is intended for academic professionals and other advanced economics researchers.

Subjects: Economic Statistics

124. Bureau of Economic Analysis

http://www.bea.gov/

Sponsor(s): Commerce Department — Economics and Statistics Administration (ESA) — Bureau of Economic Analysis (BEA)

Description: BEA produces the data for the U.S. national income and product accounts (NIPAs), which feature estimates of gross domestic product (GDP) and related measures of the national economy. The latest figures for these key economic measures appear in a sidebar on the home page of the BEA Web site. The sidebar also includes an Overview of the U.S. Economy section, which contains a summary report on leading indicators.

BEA organizes links to its data under National, International, Regional, and Industry sections. Data cover the topics of personal income, balance of payments, gross state product, GDP by industry, and other economic measures. Reports and data tables are available in a mix of HTML, PDF, and spreadsheet formats. The site offers the *Survey of Current Business* journal online in PDF format going back to 1994; selected *Survey* articles from 1987 to 1993 are also online. In addition, BEA has started an online Digital Library section for "seminal documents related to the history of the U.S. national economic accounts" (from the Web site).

The BEA Web site presents important national economic statistics, with multiple access points and several convenient downloading options.
Subjects: Economic Statistics; National Accounts — Statistics
Publications: *National Income and Product Accounts*, C 59.11/5-3:
Survey of Current Business, C 59.11:

125. Census Bureau Economic Programs
http://www.census.gov/econ/www/
Sponsor(s): Commerce Department — Economics and Statistics Administration (ESA) — Census Bureau
Description: This Web page provides a central access point for economic data from a variety of Census Bureau programs. It has quick links to publications including the *Economic Census*, *Statistics of U.S. Business*, *County Business Patterns*, *Annual Survey of Manufactures*, *Annual Capital Expenditures Data*, and *Monthly Retail Sales and Inventories*. The site's sidebar organizes links to Census Bureau data by sector (such as construction) and by topic (such as companies, small business, poverty, and historic data). It also provides links to economic data at other government agency Web sites.

The Economic Programs Web page offers both an introduction to and easy finding tool for economic data from the Census Bureau.
Subjects: Economic Statistics

126. Economic Census 2002
http://www.census.gov/econ/census02/
Sponsor(s): Commerce Department — Economics and Statistics Administration (ESA) — Census Bureau
Description: Every five years, the Economic Census profiles the U.S. economy from the national to the local level. This census tabulates the number of business establishments (or companies), number of employees, payroll, and measures of output (such as sales and receipts); data are reported by industry sector and by geography. This census also surveys business owner characteristics, such as race, age, and education. Data and reports from the Economic Census are available from this Web site and via the Census Bureau's American FactFinder (described elsewhere in this book; see the Master Index).

Economic Census data have applications for market research, business planning, and economic policy. The Census Bureau uses an online guide and series of online slide presentations to make the data accessible and understandable.
Subjects: Economic Statistics; Industries — Statistics
Publications: *Guide to the Economic Census*, C 3.253/4:

127. Economic Indicators
http://www.gpoaccess.gov/indicators/
Sponsor(s): Council of Economic Advisers (CEA)
Description: The monthly publication *Economic Indicators* is prepared by the CEA for Congress's Joint Economic Committee. *Economic Indicators* is hosted online by the Government Printing Office Access system. Analyzed indicators include gross domestic product (GDP), sources of personal income, unemployment rates, productivity, producer prices, consumer prices, federal receipts and outlays, and more. Issues of *Economic Indicators* can be searched online from 1995 onward, and browsed from 1998 onward. Each issue is available in text and PDF formats. *Economic Indicators* is a convenient compilation for reference use. However, as it is a monthly publication, researchers should check elsewhere to see if an indicator has recently been updated. *Economic Indicators* notes the source of each indicator and makes it easy for users to check the Web site of the issuing agency, such as the Bureau of Labor Statistics. Researchers will also want to consult the Economic Indicators.gov site described elsewhere in this chapter. The Federal Reserve's FRASER Web site has *Economic Indicators* back to 1948. FRASER is described elsewhere in this publication.
Subjects: Economic Statistics
Publications: *Economic Indicators*, Y 4.EC 7:

128. Economic Indicators.gov
http://www.economicindicators.gov/
Sponsor(s): Commerce Department — Economics and Statistics Administration (ESA)
Description: Economic Indicators.gov is a gateway to current economic statistics from the Bureau of Economic Analysis (BEA) and the Census Bureau. For each economic indicator, the Web site provides information about the agency source, release frequency, and scheduled hour of release, as well as a direct link to the agency's current news release. The site also has a monthly calendar of release dates and a free subscription service, which will automatically send out selected indicator announcements by e-mail (registration is required). A Spanish-language version of the site is available, although the agency news releases are only available in English.
Subjects: Economic Statistics

129. Economic Statistics Briefing Room
http://www.whitehouse.gov/fsbr/esbr.html
Sponsor(s): White House
Description: Hosted by the White House Web site, the Economic Statistics Briefing Room provides easy access to current federal economic indicators in eight broad categories: Employment, Income, International, Money, Output, Prices, Production, and Transportation. The site posts brief summaries of the most recent indicators and links to the agency sites for further information.
Subjects: Economic Statistics

130. Economics and Statistics Administration
http://www.esa.doc.gov/
Sponsor(s): Commerce Department — Economics and Statistics Administration (ESA)
Description: ESA delivers economic data, analyses, and forecasts. Its Web site provides information about the organization and its leadership. The site's top menu bar links to information from its better-known component agencies, including the Census Bureau, the Bureau of Economic Analysis, and STAT-USA. ESA periodi-

cally conducts its own studies, and these are available for 1995 to present in the Reports section. The Economic Links section has an annotated list of government, academic, and commercial Web sites that provide economic information.
Subjects: Economics

131. FRASER—Federal Reserve Archival System for Economic Research
http://fraser.stlouisfed.org/
Sponsor(s): Federal Reserve — Federal Reserve Bank of St. Louis
Description: FRASER® provides copies of historical economic statistical publications and releases in PDF format. Key documents include *All-Bank Statistics, United States, 1896–1955*, which was published by the Federal Reserve Board of Governors in 1959, and the Fed's *Banking and Monetary Statistics* for the periods 1914–1941 and 1941–1970. Other statistical series include the *Annual Statistical Digest* (1970–2000), *Productivity and Costs* (1985–2003), and the *Business Statistics* supplement to the *Survey of Current Business* (1932–1965). The site also carries digitized documents reflecting the Fed's history, such as excerpts from the Open Market Investment Committee and its successor for the 1923–1931 period.

By providing resources that were previously only available in printed form, FRASER helps researchers compile uninterrupted historical data series. FRASER also allows researchers to obtain data as they were reported in preliminary, revised, and final releases.
Subjects: Banking — Statistics; Economic Statistics

132. FRED—Economic Data
http://research.stlouisfed.org/fred2/
Sponsor(s): Federal Reserve — Federal Reserve Bank of St. Louis
Description: FRED—Federal Reserve Economic Data—is a database of U.S. economic data available as time series. (The database was named FRED II for a time because it is a successor to an older version of the database.) FRED data can be downloaded in spreadsheet or text formats or viewed as charts. The system has over 3,000 time series. Data series are grouped under topical headings such as Banking, Exchange Rates, Interest Rates, Consumer Price Indexes, Producer Price Indexes, and Monetary Aggregates. In addition to topical browsing, FRED offers keyword searching of series titles. Data updates are posted in reverse chronological order as a current awareness service.
Subjects: Economic Statistics

133. Liber8™ Economic Information Portal
http://liber8.stlouisfed.org/
Sponsor(s): Federal Reserve — Federal Reserve Bank of St. Louis
Description: The full subtitle of the Liber8™ Web site is "An Economic Information Portal for Librarians and Students." The site links to recent economic research, the latest economic indicators, and other useful economics-oriented Web sites. Each of the site's categories is divided into International, National, and Regional information sections. Most of the links access resources from the Federal Reserve Web sites or other government Web sites; some link to educational or commercial Web sites. The site also includes the International Economic Statistics (IES) database maintained by the St. Louis Fed's Research Library.

Liber8™ provides an uncluttered interface that links to a carefully selected and organized set of Web resources. It should be of assistance to anyone unsure of where to begin researching economic conditions.
Subjects: Economic Conditions — Research

134. Office of Economic Policy

http://www.ustreas.gov/offices/economic-policy/index.html

Sponsor(s): Treasury Department — Office of Economic Policy

Description: The Department of the Treasury's Office of Economic Policy analyzes domestic and international economic issues and the financial markets. The office's Web site includes economic policy reports, reports on key economic indicators and the monthly schedule for their release, and annual reports of Total Taxable Resources (TTR). It also contains the Social Security Trustees Report and the Medicare Trust Funds Trustees Report, which the office prepares for the secretary of the treasury.

Subjects: Economic Policy

Publications: *Annual Report of the Board of Trustees of the Federal Old-Age and Survivors Insurance and Disability Insurance Trust Funds*, SSA 1.1/4: *Annual Report of the Boards of Trustees of the Federal Hospital Insurance and Federal Supplementary Medical Insurance Trust Funds*, Y 1.1/7:

135. Quarterly Services Survey (QSS)

http://www.census.gov/indicator/qss/QSS.html

Sponsor(s): Commerce Department — Economics and Statistics Administration (ESA) — Census Bureau

Description: The Census Bureau's QSS provides information about total operating revenue for service industry sectors. QSS, which began in 2004, is the Census Bureau's newest economic indicator. It covers the sectors of information; professional, scientific, and technical services; administrative and support and waste management and remediation services; and hospitals and nursing and residential care facilities. The QSS Web site has current and past quarterly releases in PDF format, with supporting tables available in spreadsheet format. The *Annual Revision of Quarterly Services Estimates* is also in PDF.

Subjects: Service Industries — Statistics

Publications: *Annual Revision of Quarterly Services Estimates*

136. Regional Economic Conditions (RECON)

http://www2.fdic.gov/recon/

Sponsor(s): Federal Deposit Insurance Corporation (FDIC)

Description: RECON provides standard reports, graphs, and maps depicting economic conditions and their changes over time at the state, county, and metropolitan statistical area (MSA) levels. Data cover employment and job growth, housing and construction, commercial real estate activity, and banking conditions. RECON is updated eight times a year. A tutorial is available at the site.

Subjects: Economic Conditions

137. STAT-USA/Internet

http://www.stat-usa.gov/

Sponsor(s): Commerce Department — Economics and Statistics Administration (ESA)

Description: Unlike most of the resources described in this directory, STAT-USA is a fee-based subscription service. However, free subscriptions are available for federal depository libraries. The goal of STAT-USA is to provide a central access point for economic, business, and international trade information produced by the U.S. government. Its principal offerings are the State of the Nation database and the information contained in the GLOBUS & NTDB (National Trade Data Bank) section. The State of the Nation database provides access to current and historical economic and financial releases and economic data. The GLOBUS & NTDB section has current and historical trade-related releases, international market research, trade opportunities, country analyses, and access to the files from the full National Trade Data Bank.

STAT-USA is a large, important collection of statistics and business-related, full-text publications. While a significant portion of the data available here is freely accessible from other sites, the ease of access and the unique resources available may make a STAT-USA subscription worth considering for individuals and organizations with a frequent need for this type of information.

Subjects: Economic Statistics; Databases

Federal Reserve System

138. Board of Governors of the Federal Reserve System

http://www.federalreserve.gov/

Sponsor(s): Federal Reserve — Board of Governors

Description: The Federal Reserve, the central bank of the United States, hosts this Web site, which includes sections on the Federal Reserve System, Monetary Policy, Banking Regulation, Community Development, Payment Services to Banks, Economic Research and Data, and Consumer Financial Education.

In the Monetary Policy section, the site has information about the Federal Open Market Committee, which announces targets for the federal funds rate. The Monetary Policy section also links to the Fed's *Summary of Commentary on Current Economic Conditions by Federal Reserve District*, commonly known as the *Beige Book*. The Publications and Education Resources section includes articles from the *Federal Reserve Bulletin*, bank supervision manuals, and news releases and historical data for interest rates, foreign exchange rates, consumer credit, and other related topics.

This Web site offers a substantial body of information and statistics from the Board of Governors of the Federal Reserve System. It serves as a good starting point for users seeking information about the system as a whole. However, valuable data are also available from the individual Federal Reserve Banks. One limitation of this main site is that its links to the member bank Web sites are several clicks away, in the About the Fed section.

Subjects: Banking Regulation; Monetary Policy

Publications: *Annual Report*, FR 1.1:

Federal Reserve Bulletin

Summary of Commentary on Current Economic Conditions (Beige Book)

139. Fed in Print

http://www.frbsf.org/publications/fedinprint/

Sponsor(s): Federal Reserve — Federal Reserve Bank of San Francisco

Description: Fed in Print is an index to Federal Reserve economic research. Sponsored by the Federal Reserve Bank of San Francisco, it covers Federal Reserve publications from all of the system's banks. The search form supports keyword, title, author, bank, publication year, and publication name searches.

Subjects: Economics — Research; Databases

140. Federal Reserve Bank of Atlanta

http://www.frbatlanta.org/

Sponsor(s): Federal Reserve — Federal Reserve Bank of Atlanta

Description: The Federal Reserve Bank of Atlanta encompasses banking institutions in the Sixth Federal Reserve District, which is made up of Alabama, Florida, and Georgia, as well as parts of Louisiana, Mississippi, and Tennessee. The main sections of the Atlanta Fed's Web site are About the Fed (including information about the Atlanta Fed and the Federal Reserve System), Banking Information, Services for Financial Institutions, Community Development, Consumer Information, Economic Research and Data, News and Events, and Publications. The Publications section includes the quarterly magazine *EconSouth*, which focuses on the economy of the Southeast region.

Subjects: Banking Regulation; Monetary Policy
Publications: *EconSouth*

141. Federal Reserve Bank of Boston

http://www.bos.frb.org/

Sponsor(s): Federal Reserve — Federal Reserve Bank of Boston
Description: The Federal Reserve Bank of Boston serves the First Federal Reserve District, which includes the six New England states: Connecticut (excluding Fairfield County), Massachusetts, Maine, New Hampshire, Rhode Island, and Vermont. Along with full information from the Federal Reserve System, the Boston Fed's Web site features a New England Spotlight section with links of local economic interest. Local information include the Web site for the Federal Reserve Banks' New England Public Policy Center; the monthly *New England Economic Indicators* publication; banking, economic, and government finance profiles for the region; and a link to the educational New England Economic Adventure Web site. Online publications include *Bank Notes*, *Regional Review*, and *New England Economic Review*.

This site is an excellent resource for New England economic reports, and also has a wealth of educational resources for teachers.

Subjects: Banking Regulation; Monetary Policy
Publications: *Bank Notes*
New England Economic Indicators
New England Economic Review
Regional Review

142. Federal Reserve Bank of Chicago

http://www.chicagofed.org/

Sponsor(s): Federal Reserve — Federal Reserve Bank of Chicago
Description: The Federal Reserve Bank of Chicago's Web site features a wide range of banking information for the Seventh Federal Reserve District, which comprises all of Iowa and most of Illinois, Indiana, Michigan, and Wisconsin. The main sections of the site include Banking Information, Economic Research and Data, Services for Financial Institutions, Community Development, Education Resources, and Consumer Information. The Consumer Information section has a database comparing banking products and services throughout the Midwest. Online periodicals include *AgLetter*, *Chicago Fed Letter*, and *Economic Perspectives*. A blog on the Midwest economy can be found in the Economic Research and Data section.

Subjects: Banking Regulation; Monetary Policy
Publications: *AgLetter*
Chicago Fed Letter
Economic Perspectives

143. Federal Reserve Bank of Cleveland

http://www.clevelandfed.org/

Sponsor(s): Federal Reserve — Federal Reserve Bank of Cleveland
Description: This Web site serves the Fourth Federal Reserve District, which is made up of Ohio, western Pennsylvania, eastern Kentucky, and the northern panhandle of West Virginia. The Regional Research and Data section provides statistics and commentary about the region's economic trends. The Publications section

includes the *Fourth District Conditions* journal. A special section called Inflation Central tracks and analyzes research, data, and publications concerning inflation.
Subjects: Banking Regulation; Monetary Policy
Publications: *Fourth District Conditions*

144. Federal Reserve Bank of Dallas

http://www.dallasfed.org/

Sponsor(s): Federal Reserve — Federal Reserve Bank of Dallas
Description: The Federal Reserve Bank of Dallas covers the 11th Federal Reserve District, which includes Texas, northern Louisiana, and southern New Mexico. It has branches in El Paso, San Antonio, and Houston. Its Web site features a Spanish-language section called Entrada, and the section for the bank's Center for Latin American Economics (CLAE) research institute is available in both English and Spanish. Regional economic data is available in both the Economic Research and Economic Data sections, including the DataBasics introduction to Texas economic indicators. The Publications and Resources page features periodicals including *Houston Business*, *Southwest Economy*, and *Business Frontier* (El Paso).

The Dallas Fed Web site is a good resource for information about economic factors affecting the 11th District, such as the impacts of the oil industry and trade with Mexico.
Subjects: Banking Regulation; Monetary Policy
Publications: *Banking and Community Perspectives*
Business Frontier (El Paso)
Houston Business
Southwest Economy

145. Federal Reserve Bank of Kansas City

http://www.kc.frb.org/

Sponsor(s): Federal Reserve — Federal Reserve Bank of Kansas City
Description: This Web site serves the 10th Federal Reserve District, which comprises Colorado, Kansas, Nebraska, Oklahoma, Wyoming, northern New Mexico, and western Missouri. The main sections of the site include Financial Services, Banking Information, Community Development, Consumer Information, Economic Research, Payments System Research, and Publications and Education Resources. The site also links to the Center for the Study of Rural America, a research institute created by the Kansas City Fed.
Subjects: Banking Regulation; Monetary Policy

146. Federal Reserve Bank of Minneapolis

http://woodrow.mpls.frb.fed.us/

Sponsor(s): Federal Reserve — Federal Reserve Bank of Minneapolis
Description: This Web site features a variety of resources for the Ninth Federal Reserve District, which includes Montana, North Dakota, South Dakota, Minnesota, the Upper Peninsula of Michigan, and northwestern Wisconsin. Economic data is available for the United States with a focus on the Ninth District states. The site has a searchable database called BancSearch with financial data for each of the banks in the Ninth District. Publications online include the *fedgazette* and *The Region*.

Well organized and easy to navigate, this site is a rich resource for nationwide banking information and for region specific information.
Subjects: Banking Regulation; Monetary Policy
Publications: *fedgazette*
The Region

147. Federal Reserve Bank of New York

http://www.ny.frb.org/

Sponsor(s): Federal Reserve — Federal Reserve Bank of New York
Description: The New York Federal Reserve Bank is responsible for the Second District: New York State, the 12 northern counties of New Jersey, and Fairfield County in Connecticut. Research and data on the geographical region can be found throughout the site, but are most readily available in the Research and Regional Outreach section. Second District publications include *Current Issues in Economics and Finance*, *Second District Highlights*, and *Upstate New York Regional Review*.

In addition to the regional economic research and data, highlights of this Web site include a rich Education section and numerous RSS feeds for news, events, and research topics.
Subjects: Banking Regulation; Monetary Policy
Publications: *Current Issues in Economics and Finance*
Second District Highlights
Upstate New York Regional Review

148. Federal Reserve Bank of Philadelphia

http://www.phil.frb.org/

Sponsor(s): Federal Reserve — Federal Reserve Bank of Philadelphia
Description: The Federal Reserve Bank of Philadelphia is responsible for eastern Pennsylvania, southern New Jersey, and the state of Delaware. It features a special Payment Cards Center (PCC), which focuses on "credit cards, debit cards, smart cards, stored-value cards, and similar payment vehicles." The PCC includes pertinent studies, legislative information, and consumer information. Other sections of the site include Economic Research; Consumer Information; Community Development; Supervision, Regulation, and Credit; Economic Education; Services for Financial Institutions; and Financial and Regulatory Reporting. The Publications page includes the Annual Report, Circular Letters, Consumer Booklets, and Research Publications subsections.

The PCC provides information useful at a national level. The current and diverse resources from the PCC should be of interest to consumers, policymakers, academics, and others.
Subjects: Banking Regulation; Consumer Credit — Research; Monetary Policy

149. Federal Reserve Bank of Richmond

http://www.rich.frb.org/

Sponsor(s): Federal Reserve — Federal Reserve Bank of Richmond
Description: The Federal Reserve Bank of Richmond serves the Fifth Federal Reserve District—which includes the District of Columbia, Maryland, Virginia, North Carolina, South Carolina, and most of West Virginia. Its Web site features Research, Banking Resources, Financial Services, Community Affairs, Educational Info, and News and Speeches sections. Regional data can be found in both the Research section and in the online magazine *Region Focus*. The site also contains a virtual tour of the Fifth District's Money Museum, in the Educational Info section.
Subjects: Banking Regulation; Monetary Policy
Publications: *Region Focus*

150. Federal Reserve Bank of San Francisco

http://www.frbsf.org/

Sponsor(s): Federal Reserve — Federal Reserve Bank of San Francisco
Description: This Web site serves the 12th Federal Reserve District, which comprises the states of Alaska, Arizona, California, Hawaii, Idaho, Nevada, Oregon, Utah, and Washington, as well as the territories of American Samoa, Guam, and the

Northern Mariana Islands. The San Francisco Federal Reserve Bank Web site features these sections: About the Fed, News and Events, Economic Research and Data, Publications, Educational Resources, Community Development, Consumer Information, Banking Information, and Services for Financial Institutions. Publications on the site include research papers from the affiliated Center for Pacific Basin Monetary and Economic Studies. Education resources include *Econ Ed and the Fed*, an Ask Dr. Econ section, and an online American Currency Exhibit with images and history of money.

Subjects: Banking Regulation; Monetary Policy
Publications: *Econ and the Fed*

151. Federal Reserve Bank of St. Louis
http://www.stls.frb.org/

Sponsor(s): Federal Reserve — Federal Reserve Bank of St. Louis
Description: The Federal Reserve Bank of St. Louis represents the Eighth Federal Reserve District, which comprises all of Arkansas and portions of Illinois, Indiana, Kentucky, Mississippi, Missouri, and Tennessee. Its Web site includes sections entitled Banking Information, Community Development, Consumer Information, Economic Research, Education Resources, News and Events, Publications, and Services for Financial Services. The Economic Research section provides easy access to over 2,500 U.S. economic time series through the FRED® system. Another database, FRASER®, provides historical economic statistical publications. Under Publications, the site offers PDF copies of the *Federal Reserve Bank of St. Louis Review* going back to 1967 and *The Regional Economist* going back to 1996.

Along with ALFRED®—an archival database—the St. Louis Fed's FRED® and FRASER® databases and other online services are described in separate entries in this chapter.

The innovative resources in the Economic Research section make the St. Louis Fed Web site one of the more interesting regional sites for national-level research.
Subjects: Banking Regulation; Monetary Policy
Publications: *Federal Reserve Bank of St. Louis Review*
The Regional Economist

152. Federal Reserve Education
http://www.federalreserveeducation.org/FRED/

Sponsor(s): Federal Reserve
Description: This Web site organizes links to the many educational resources made available by the Federal Reserve Banks. Sections provide both teacher resources (classroom activities, curriculum packages, and teacher workshops) and personal financial education information (Web sites about credit, mortgages, interest rates, and more). The site highlights educational publications and videos from the Fed and links to other Web sites related to economic education. An interactive section called "Fed 101" describes the Fed's history, structure, and responsibilities.

This Federal Reserve Web site does an excellent job of compiling numerous educational resources from a variety of sources and putting them together under a helpful interface. Many of the resources are aimed at teachers, but the site is also useful for anyone who wants to learn more about the Fed or finance.
Subjects: Economics; Educational Resources

153. Federal Reserve System Publications Catalog
http://www.ny.frb.org/publications/frame1.cfm

Sponsor(s): Federal Reserve — Federal Reserve Bank of New York
Description: This Web site presents a comprehensive guide and online ordering facility for all publications and materials available from the Federal Reserve System. Most items are free of charge, and many are available in PDF format.

Publications are organized into sections by topic, with sections including Banking System, Community Development, Economics, Federal Reserve System, Financial Markets and Instruments, International Economics, Financial Education, Money, and Payment Systems. Journal subscriptions from each Fed district are also available. The catalog may be searched by keyword, audience type, Federal Reserve Bank location, and media type.

Subjects: Banking; Monetary Policy; Publication Catalogs

154. National Information Center—Federal Reserve System

`http://www.ffiec.gov/nicpubweb/nicweb/nichome.aspx`

Sponsor(s): Federal Reserve — Board of Governors

Description: This Web site describes the National Income Center (NIC) database as a "central data repository containing information about U.S. banking organizations and their domestic and foreign affiliates, as well as information about foreign banking organizations located in the United States." For the institutions it covers, NIC has information about corporate hierarchy, mergers, acquisitions, name changes, financial reports, and other related topics. The database can be searched by institution name and location. The advanced search field allows searches by institution type, and contains a link that allows users to search for U.S. branches of foreign banking organizations. In addition, NIC has lists and information about the nation's top 50 bank holding companies.

Subjects: Banking; Databases

Finance

155. Commodity Futures Trading Commission

`http://www.cftc.gov/cftc/cftchome.htm`

Sponsor(s): Commodity Futures Trading Commission (CFTC)

Description: CFTC is an independent agency regulating commodity futures and options markets in the United States. The CFTC Web site features sections entitled Commitments of Traders, Customer Protection, Exchanges and Products, Market Oversight, Before You Trade, Market Oversight, Law and Regulation, Reports and Publications, and How to Register. The Commitments of Traders section includes *Commitments of Traders in Futures* reports in a compressed, comma-delimited format for loading into a spreadsheet. Both the long form and short form data reports are available. Some reports are available back to 1986.

The About the CFTC section includes an online video, CFTC organization chart, and links to the commissioners' biographies. The Web site also has a glossary of futures industry terminology and links to related sites such as the exchanges designated by the CFTC as contract markets and derivatives clearing organizations registered with the CFTC.

Subjects: Securities and Investments — Regulations

Publications: *Annual Report/Commodity Futures Trading Commission*, Y 3.C 73/5:1/

Commitments of Traders in Futures, Y 3.C 73/5:9-3/

156. Comptroller of the Currency—Administrator of National Banks

`http://www.occ.treas.gov/`

Sponsor(s): Treasury Department — Comptroller of the Currency (OCC)

Description: An independent bureau of the Department of the Treasury, OCC charters, regulates, and supervises all national banks and supervises the federal branches and agencies of foreign banks. The OCC Web site features information about banking regulations, community development investments of national banks, consumer rights, and electronic banking, and other topics. The Issuances section consists of advisory letters, alerts, and *OCC Bulletins*. The Legal section contains a database of formal enforcement actions. The Public Information section explains how to find information on the Web about individual topics such as financial literacy and Native American banking.

Subjects: Banking Regulation
Publications: *Economic Working Papers*, T 12.22:
OCC Advisory Letters, T 12.23:
OCC Alerts, T 12.21:
OCC Bulletins, T 12.20:
Problem Bank Identification, Rehabilitation and Resolution: A Guide to Examiners, T 12.2:
Quarterly Journal, Comptroller of the Currency, T 12.18:

157. EDGAR—SEC Filings and Forms
http://www.sec.gov/edgarhp.htm
Sponsor(s): Securities and Exchange Commission (SEC)
Description: The EDGAR database performs automated collection and indexing of submissions by companies and others required by law to file forms with the SEC. The filings provide information about company finances, management, legal proceedings, and more. The EDGAR Search page includes options for finding companies and their current associated filings, browsing the latest filings, and searching archived EDGAR documents. In 2006, the SEC added the capability to search the full text of filings. SEC also added a Mutual Fund Search and Variable Insurance Products Search in 2006. The EDGAR Web site includes a tutorial, a guide to SEC filings, and detailed information about the database content.

The filings available through EDGAR are a standard source of information about publicly traded companies. Many researchers supplement EDGAR with commercial, for-fee database subscriptions that provide the same data, but with enhanced search and report features. There are also free commercial Web sites for EDGAR filings, such as SEC Info at http://www.secinfo.com/.
Subjects: Companies and Enterprises; Databases

158. Federal Deposit Insurance Corporation
http://www.fdic.gov/
Sponsor(s): Federal Deposit Insurance Corporation (FDIC)
Description: The FDIC was created during the Great Depression to insure deposits in banks and thrift institutions in the United States. Major topical sections of the FDIC Web site are Deposit Insurance, Consumer Protection, Industry Analysis (which includes statistics and a bank directory), Regulations and Examinations, and Asset Sales (from failed banks). The site organizes content by audience, with separate pages for bankers, consumers, analysts, and investors; there is also a link to the limited Spanish-language material available on the site. FDIC publications are linked from several sections, including News and Events. The site also has over 20 specialized e-mail alert services, which offer updated bank data, consumer news, research publications news, and other news releases.

The FDIC Web site's offerings will be appealing to both professionals and the consumers. For professionals, the detailed statistics and various full-text reports provide opportunities for research into banking trends and specific institutions. For consumers, the site offers advice, referrals to rating services, and statistics on individual institutions.
Subjects: Banking Regulation
Publications: *Annual Report*, Y 3.F 31/21-3:1/
FDIC Banking Review, Y 3.F 31/8:
FDIC Consumer News, Y 3.F 31/8:24/

FDIC Quarterly Banking Profile, Y 3.F 31/8:29/
FDIC Statistics on Banking, Y 3.F 31/8:1-4/
Financial Institution Letters, Y 3.F 31/8:34
Historical Statistics on Banking, Y 3.F 31/8:26/
Merger Decisions, 3.F 31/8:1-3/

159. Federal Financial Institutions Examination Council
http://www.ffiec.gov/
Sponsor(s): Federal Financial Institutions Examination Council (FFIEC)
Description: According to its Web site, the FFIEC is "a formal interagency body empowered to prescribe uniform principles, standards, and report forms for the federal examination of financial institutions by the Board of Governors of the Federal Reserve System, the Federal Deposit Insurance Corporation, the National Credit Union Administration, the Office of the Comptroller of the Currency, and the Office of Thrift Supervision and to make recommendations to promote uniformity in the supervision of financial institutions." In addition to links to the other agencies, this site contains informational sections including Information About the FFIEC, Press Releases, Reports, Reporting Forms, Handbooks and Catalogues, Enforcement Actions and Orders, and On-line Information Systems. The site also links to detailed information about the Home Mortgage Disclosure Act and the Community Reinvestment Act.
Subjects: Banking Regulation
Publications: *Annual Report*, Y 3.F 49:1/
HMDA Aggregate Reports, FR 1.63/54:
HMDA Disclosure Reports, FR 1.63/55:

160. Joint Board for the Enrollment of Actuaries
http://www.irs.gov/taxpros/actuaries/
Sponsor(s): Treasury Department — Internal Revenue Service (IRS)
Description: The Joint Board for the Enrollment of Actuaries sets the qualification standards and certification process for individuals who perform actuarial services as required under the Employee Retirement Income Security Act of 1974 (ERISA). Its Web site provides information about the board and its qualification and renewal processes.
Subjects: Finance — Regulations

161. MSB.gov
http://www.msb.gov/
Sponsor(s): Treasury Department
Description: Money Services Businesses (MSBs) are nonbank financial institutions defined as such for purposes of the Bank Secrecy Act. This Web site provides a definition of MSBs, regulatory guidance, forms, news, and background information.
Subjects: Finance — Regulations

162. National Credit Union Administration
http://www.ncua.gov/
Sponsor(s): National Credit Union Administration (NCUA)
Description: NCUA is an independent federal agency that supervises and insures credit unions. The NCUA Web site offers pages tailored to its two main audiences, with pages entitled Resources for Credit Unions and Resources for Consumers. The section for credit unions includes manuals and forms, information about the National Credit Union Share Insurance Fund (NCUSIF), and guidance on implementing information technology. The section for consumers includes a searchable directory of credit unions and an online Consumer Complaint Center.

Documents available from the NCUA Web site include relevant laws, rules, and regulations; statistical reports; and *NCUA Letters to Credit Unions*.
Subjects: Credit Unions — Regulations
Publications: *Accounting Manual for Federal Credit Unions*, NCU 1.8:
Annual Report of the National Credit Union Administration, NCU 1.1:
Mid-Year Statistics for Federally Insured Credit Unions, NCU 1.9/3:
NCUA Credit Union Directory, NCU 1.16:
NCUA Letters to Credit Unions, NCU 1.19:
NCUA Year End Statistics for Federally Insured Credit Unions, NCU 1.9/2:
Regulatory Alert, NCU 1.6/2:
Your Insured Funds, NCU 1.2:F96/

163. Office of Domestic Finance

http://www.ustreas.gov/offices/domestic-finance/index.html
Sponsor(s): Treasury Department — Office of Domestic Finance
Description: The Office of Domestic Finance has broad policy and oversight roles in areas relating to financial institutions, financial markets, and government finance. Programs and offices managed by the Office of Domestic Finance include the Bureau of the Public Debt, Student Loan Marketing Association (SLMA) oversight, and the Terrorism Risk Insurance Program. The office's Web site provides detailed descriptions of the programs within the Office of Domestic Finance and offers links to associated boards, commissions, bureaus, and resources.
Subjects: Finance — Policy

164. Office of Thrift Supervision

http://www.ots.treas.gov/
Sponsor(s): Treasury Department — Office of Thrift Supervision (OTS)
Description: OTS is the primary regulator of all federal and many state-chartered thrift institutions, including savings banks and savings and loan associations. Its Web site includes the necessary filing forms for thrift institutions and a section for legal and regulatory guidance. The Data and Research section contains information about the industry's financial performance, searchable databases of institutions and holding companies, and related papers and statistical information. The site also has databases for searching enforcement actions and Community Reinvestment Act ratings. OTS links to the FDIC Web site for its database of *Thrift Financial Reports*. The OTS site features consumer educational publications on home equity loans and predatory lending. Most other publications concern regulatory guidance for thrift institutions.
　　Researchers should use the Quick Navigation links—an alphabetical site index—to get an overview of the information offered on this site.
Subjects: Savings and Loan Institutions; Thrift Institutions

165. Securities and Exchange Commission

http://www.sec.gov/
Sponsor(s): Securities and Exchange Commission (SEC)
Description: The SEC, which is led by five presidentially appointed commissioners, regulates the securities markets. The SEC Web site features both financial information for investors and information for the securities industry that it oversees. A major offering is the EDGAR (Electronic Data Gathering, Analysis, and Retrieval System) database of company information, which is described elsewhere in this chapter. Other sections of the site include Investor Information, Regulatory Actions, Staff Interpretations, News and Public Statements, Litigation, and SEC Divisions. Information is also arranged by audience, with offerings especially for accountants, broker dealers, EDGAR filers, funds and advisers, municipal markets, and small businesses.

Links to publications are scattered throughout the site. The *SEC Annual Report* is located under the About the SEC section, while the *SEC News Digest* is accessible from the News and Public Statements page. The Investor Information section contains the bulk of the online titles. Investor Information has consumer education materials; some material is available in Spanish. The SEC also provides webcasts of its open meetings, forums, and other public events.
Subjects: Securities and Investments — Regulations
Publications: *Annual Report*, SE 1.1:
Final Report of the SEC Government-Business Forum on Small Business Capital Formation, SE 1.35/2:
SEC Rules of Practice
SEC Special Studies, SE 1.38:
Securities and Exchange Commission News Digest (daily), SE 1.25/12:

166. Treasury International Capital System
http://www.treas.gov/tic/
Sponsor(s): Treasury Department
Description: The Treasury International Capital (TIC) System tracks the flow of investment funds between U.S. residents and foreign residents. Various data are released on a monthly, quarterly, and annual basis, and are available from this site. The site features an FAQ and a TIC user guide.
Subjects: International Finance — Statistics
Publications: *Foreign Portfolio Holdings of U.S. Securities*

International Trade

167. AESDirect
http://www.aesdirect.gov/
Sponsor(s): Commerce Department — Economics and Statistics Administration (ESA) — Census Bureau
Description: AESDirect (Automated Export System Direct) allows shippers to electronically file Shipper's Export Declarations (SEDs) with the Census Bureau. Its Web site offers an online tour, registration information, and instructions for use. It also provides information about the AESDirect interface with third-party Internet application developers. The data collected are used by the Census Bureau to compile trade statistics.
Subjects: Exports — Regulations; Shipper's Export Declarations

168. African Growth and Opportunity Act (AGOA)
http://www.agoa.gov/
Sponsor(s): Commerce Department — International Trade Administration (ITA)
Description: AGOA implementation is designed to offer incentives for African nations to maintain open economies and free market practices. Under the act, eligible Sub-Saharan African countries may export certain products to the United States with no import duty. The AGOA Web site describes the original legislation, Public Law 106-200, and its subsequent amendments. The site includes AGOA reports to Congress, lists of eligible countries and products, African trade statistics, and information from the AGOA trade forums.
Subjects: Trade Agreements; Africa

169. BISNIS: Business Information Service for the Newly Independent States

http://www.bisnis.doc.gov/

Sponsor(s): Commerce Department — International Trade Administration (ITA)

Description: BISNIS is a resource center for those involved in doing business with Russia and the other states of the former Soviet Union. Its Web site has sections for Country Reports, Industry Reports, Leads, Events, Sources of Finance, and the *BISNIS Bulletin*. Users may register to receive industry reports and country reports by e-mail.

BISNIS is a useful resource for businesses and individuals seeking more information about trade with Russia and business opportunities in that region.

Subjects: Emerging Markets; International Business; Eurasia

Publications: *BISNIS Bulletin*, C 61.42:

BISNIS Search for Partners, C 61.42/2:

170. Bureau of Industry and Security

http://bxa.doc.gov/

Sponsor(s): Commerce Department — Bureau of Industry and Security (BIS)

Description: BIS regulates the export of sensitive goods, such as weapons technologies and encryption software and regulates exports to certain countries in accordance with U.S. policy. BIS also enforces U.S. antiboycott laws, the Fastener Quality Act, and the reporting provisions of the Chemical Weapons Convention. Prior to April 2002, BIS was known as the Bureau of Export Administration.

The BIS Web site links to major regulations, export licensing guidelines, news, and training courses on export restrictions. The primary audience for the site is the U.S. exporter community. The Policies and Regulations section has a link to the Export Administration Bureau regulations hosted at the GPO Access Web site and information about countries that come under special export restrictions. It explains restrictions on the export of high-performance computers and on U.S. participation in other countries' boycotts. The site also provides information about the multilateral Wassenaar Arrangement on Export Controls for Conventional Arms and Dual-Use Goods and Technologies. Other sections discuss licensing, regulatory compliance, enforcement (with a list of major cases), and the Defense Industrial Base programs.

While geared toward the practical needs of exporters, the BIS Web site is also a good source for general research on U.S. export controls.

Subjects: Exports — Regulations

Publications: *Export Administration Regulations*, C 63.23:

171. China Business Information Center

http://www.export.gov/china/

Sponsor(s): Commerce Department — International Trade Administration (ITA)

Description: The China Business Information Center Web site provides information for U.S. companies seeking to do business with China. It provides information about American Trading Centers in China, trade policy initiatives, and China's business laws and regulations. The site also has sections on trade leads, trade events, industry sectors with the best prospects, and links to other useful sites.

Subjects: Exports; China

172. Commercial News USA

http://www.thinkglobal.us/

Sponsor(s): Commerce Department — International Trade Administration (ITA)

Description: This Web site is the online version of *Commercial News USA*, an official export magazine of the Department of Commerce. The magazine and Web site are designed to assist importers around the world in their efforts to locate the desired American products and services.

Although an official publication of the Commerce Department, this magazine is managed by a private company and accepts advertising. Access is free, but users must register to receive a password.

Subjects: Exports
Publications: *Commercial News USA*, C 61.10:

173. Committee for the Implementation of Textile Agreements (CITA)

`http://otexa.ita.doc.gov/cita.htm`
Sponsor(s): Committee for the Implementation of Textile Agreements (CITA)
Description: CITA is an interagency committee responsible for taking actions to comply with and ensure compliance with the international textile agreements to which the United States is a party. CITA is chaired by the Department of Commerce and receives staff assistance by the Office of Textiles and Apparel. The CITA Web site consists of a very brief description of the committee's role.

Subjects: Textile Industry; Trade Agreements

174. Customs and Border Protection Bureau

`http://www.cbp.gov/`
Sponsor(s): Homeland Security Department — Customs and Border Protection Bureau
Description: CBP was created as part of the Department of Homeland Security. Its responsibilities lie in areas previously covered by the Customs Service, the Immigration and Naturalization Service, and the Animal and Plant Health Inspection Service. Major sections of CBP's Web site include Import, Export, Travel, and Border Security (including the Border Patrol, which is described in a separate entry in this publication). A secondary tier on the site's menu bar includes quick links to information about ports and contracting and pages with links to forms, publications, and legal information. Online databases include the Customs Rulings Online Search System (CROSS) and the Intellectual Property Rights Search (IPRS); both databases can be found in the Legal section.

The Import section includes cargo policies, information about customs brokers, and a searchable database of antidumping and countervailing duty messages. The Export section has export documents and license rules and information about lists of "blocked, denied, and debarred persons" (from the Web site). The Travel section features information about current border wait times, restricted or prohibited goods, and travel alerts. The Frequent Traveler section covers the Secure Electronic Network for Travelers Rapid Inspection (SENTRI) program, the United States-Canada NEXUS program, and the U.S. Visitor and Immigrant Status Indicator Technology (US-VISIT) program.

The CBP Web site employs multiple approaches to navigation, including a site map, two levels of search engines, several levels of menus, and a context-sensitive "see also" list in the right sidebar. The site includes a colorful two-page "Tips for Using the Website" brochure that clearly explains these navigation features. It also provides RSS feeds for its regularly updated information, and was one of the earliest government sites to use RSS so widely.

Subjects: Customs (Trade); International Borders; Law Enforcement
Publications: *CBP Today*, HS 4.115:
Customs and Border Protection Today, HS 4.115:
Foreign Trade Zones Manual, HS 4.108:
Importing into the United States, T 17.17:
Know Before You Go, T 17.2:

175. DataWeb—USITC Interactive Tariff and Trade Database
http://dataweb.usitc.gov/
Sponsor(s): International Trade Commission (ITC)
Description: DataWeb is a tariff and trade database designed by the U.S. International Trade Commission (USITC). The data comes from the Census Bureau, the Customs Service, and the ITC itself. The system is free of charge but requires registration. DataWeb offers a number of options for specifying commodity level and country or country groupings. The site has online sort capabilities that report options include downloading to a spreadsheet format. DataWeb also generates prepared summary tables for commonly requested information, such as U.S. trade by geographic regions and by partner country. A separate Tariff Database presents tariff treatment information and links to trade data.

DataWeb is a flexible and relatively sophisticated system for U.S. trade data. Users may need to run through the search and display options several times to master all the system's capabilities. For regular trade and tariff data users, DataWeb can be a very useful tool. New users may first wish to see if the site's prepared trade data tables can answer their questions.
Subjects: Trade Statistics; Databases

176. Defense Technology Security Administration
http://www.dod.mil/policy/sections/policy_offices/dtsa/
index.html
Sponsor(s): Defense Department — Defense Technology Security Administration (DTSA)
Description: DTSA's primary mission is to preserve critical U.S. military technological advantages through control of technology exports and technical exchanges. The Web site has sections describing the work of DTSA's Licensing, Policy, Space, and Technology Directorates.
Subjects: Arms Control; Exports — Regulations; Military Technology

177. Directorate of Defense Trade Controls (DDTC)
http://pmdtc.org/
Sponsor(s): State Department — Defense Trade Controls Directorate
Description: The DDTC Web site provides information about the rules governing U.S. exports of defense materials and services. For manufacturers, exporters, and brokers of defense articles, the site has sections such as Register Your Company, Licensing, and Get Forms. The D-Trade system handles electronic defense export authorization requests. The Reference Library section has text versions of relevant laws and regulations, a Country Embargo Reference Chart, and other defense trade documents. The site carries the Section 655 Annual Military Assistance Reports, which list the defense goods and services authorized as direct commercial sales to each foreign country from 1999 to the present. The site also lists the direct commercial sales that, by law, must be reported to Congress.
Subjects: Exports — Regulations

178. Doing Business in International Markets
http://www.state.gov/e/eb/cba/
Sponsor(s): State Department — Economic and Business Affairs Bureau
Description: The Office of Commercial and Business Affairs within the Department of State's Economic and Business Affairs Bureau sponsors this page of links to State Department international business information. It includes a Frequently Asked Questions section about doing business abroad and information about how the State Department facilitates business overseas.
Subjects: International Business

179. Export Administration Regulations
http://www.access.gpo.gov/bis/
Sponsor(s): Commerce Department — Bureau of Industry and Security (BIS)
Description: This is the online version of the loose-leaf subscription service for *Export Administration Regulations*, which features a compilation of official regulations and policies governing the export licensing of commodities and technical data. Each section is marked with the date of its last update. Regulations are in PDF, ASCII, and WordPerfect (R) format. The online version also includes the text of rules published in the *Federal Register* from 1996 onward that affect the *Export Administration Regulations*.
Subjects: Exports — Regulations
Publications: *Export Administration Regulations*, C 63.25/2:

180. Export.Gov
http://www.export.gov/
Sponsor(s): Commerce Department — International Trade Administration (ITA)
Description: Export.Gov is a portal for information relevant to U.S. exporters. The site covers export basics, trade leads, trade events, export finance, market research, trade data, and trade problems (such as trade barriers and unfair practices). The market research section includes a step-by-step guide for researching markets using government Web sites and other resources. The site also includes webcasts and webinars on export topics.

As with other subject-oriented government Web portals, this Web site provides one-stop access to resources available from a variety of government agencies. While it is intended for those in the export business, it also serves as a useful entry point and reference resource for international trade researchers.
Subjects: Exports

181. Export.Gov/Iraq
http://www.export.gov/iraq/
Sponsor(s): Commerce Department — Iraq Investment and Reconstruction Task Force (IIRTF)
Description: IIRTF assists companies that are pursuing reconstruction and other business opportunities in Iraq. This Web site provides information about Iraqi economic development, business climate, and market opportunities. It includes a set of links to relevant Web sites from the U.S. and Iraqi governments, Iraqi financial and business organizations, and international organizations.
Subjects: Exports; Iraq

182. ExportControl.org
http://www.exportcontrol.org/
Alternate URL(s): http://www.state.gov/t/isn/export/ecc/20779.htm
Sponsor(s): State Department — Nonproliferation Bureau
Description: ExportControl.org is sponsored by the Export Control and Related Border Security Assistance program (EXBS), a U.S. government interagency program designed to help other countries improve their export control systems. The site has an overview of the U.S. export control program and describes its best practices. The Resource Links section directs users to information from the European Union, nongovernmental organizations, and other sources. The program is managed by the Department of State's Bureau of International Security and Nonproliferation. More information about the program is available at the alternate URL listed above.
Subjects: Arms Control; Exports — Regulations

183. Export-Import Bank of the United States

http://www.exim.gov/

Sponsor(s): Export-Import Bank of the United States

Description: The Export-Import Bank offers export financing for U.S. businesses. The Products and Policies section of its Web site provides information about the bank's working capital financing, export credit insurance, loan guarantees, and direct loans. Application forms and instructions on applying are included with the information. Users should also look in the Apply section, where more services are listed. The Apply section contains reference material, such as the Country Limitation Schedule, which indicates where the bank puts restrictions on financing. The site also features sections for specific audiences, including small business, U.S. exporters, and lenders.

Subjects: Finance; International Trade

Publications: *Annual Report/Export-Import Bank of the United States*, Y 3.EX 7/3:1/ *Ex-Im Bank News*, Y 3.EX 7/3:14/

184. Foreign Trade Statistics

http://www.census.gov/foreign-trade/www/index.html

Sponsor(s): Commerce Department — Economics and Statistics Administration (ESA) — Census Bureau

Description: The Foreign Trade Division (FTD) of the Census Bureau manages two major statistical programs: the Automated Export System (AES), which captures shipping data, and the compilation and reporting of trade statistics. The AES portion of the Web site will primarily be of interest to exporters participating in the program. Foreign trade data, which appears in the Statistics section, appeals to a much broader range of interests. The Statistics section also features reports on individual country balance of trade and products traded with the United States, a monthly list of the top trading partners with the United States, state export data, and historic trade balance data going back to 1960. In the Press Releases section, current and past issues of the *FT900*—the major monthly update of U.S. trade in goods and services—are available. Exhibits, or data announced in the *FT900* release, are available in PDF, text, or spreadsheet formats.

Subjects: Trade Statistics

Publications: *Imports of Steel Products*, C 3.164:900-A/ *U.S. International Trade in Goods and Services, FT900*, C 3.164:900/

185. Import Administration (IA)

http://ia.ita.doc.gov/

Sponsor(s): Commerce Department — International Trade Administration (ITA) — Import Administration

Description: IA enforces laws and agreements to prevent unfairly traded imports. Its Web site provides IA documents on anti-dumping and countervailing duties reviews and determinations. Major programs and offices within IA have their own sections on the site; sections include Foreign-Trade Zones Board, Steel Import Monitoring and Analysis, Subsidies Enforcement, and Trade Remedy Compliance.

The IA Web site is closely integrated with the larger ITA Web site, Trade.gov, which causes the IA content to be overshadowed by the rest of the site. To fully explore what IA has to offer, use the menu in the right-hand column and scroll down to view information after it expands. Under the Additional Information section, for example, the Decisions and Data subsection has important case information but can easily be missed without taking the steps described above.

Subjects: Trade Laws and Regulations

Publications: *Policy Bulletin*

186. International Trade Administration
http://www.trade.gov/
Alternate URL(s): http://www.ita.doc.gov/
Sponsor(s): Commerce Department — International Trade Administration (ITA)
Description: ITA promotes U.S. exports and U.S. companies seeking to export. Most information about the agency is included in the About Us and ITA Organization sections of its Web site. The site features prominent links to ITA's component agencies: the U.S. Commercial Service, Manufacturing and Services, Market Access and Compliance, and the Import Administration. It also contains a Frequently Asked Questions section about exporting and links to the major publications, programs, and Department of Commerce Web sites that promote exports.
Subjects: International Trade
Publications: *Energy and Environmental Export News*
Export Programs Guide, C 61.8:
International Trade Update

187. International Trade Commission
http://www.usitc.gov/
Sponsor(s): International Trade Commission (ITC)
Description: ITC is an independent federal agency that examines unfair trade practices and the impact of imports on U.S. industries. The ITC Web site's Trade Remedy Investigations section includes major case news and documents regarding antidumping and countervailing duty investigations, intellectual property investigations (called "section 337" investigations), and "global safeguard" investigations. The Industry and Economic Analysis section contains detailed reports on products, services, and regions and a link to DataWeb, ITC's international trade statistics and U.S. tariff database. The Tariff Information Center includes the *Harmonized Tariff Schedule of the United States (HTS)*, which describes all goods in trade for duty, quota, and statistical purposes. *HTS* is online in PDF and database formats.
   The availability of the tariff schedules and the DataWeb statistical tool makes this an important resource for international trade information.
Subjects: International Trade
Publications: *Harmonized Tariff Schedule of the United States, Annotated for Statistical Reporting Purposes*, ITC 1.10:
Industry Trade and Technology Review, ITC 1.33/2:
International Economic Review (monthly), ITC 1.29:

188. Manufacturing and Services
http://www.ita.doc.gov/td/td_home/tdhome.html
Sponsor(s): Commerce Department — International Trade Administration (ITA)
Description: Manufacturing and Services, a division of ITA, offers services to promote U.S. exports and has special expertise in U.S. industry sectors. Its Web site contains pages for over 15 sectors, such as Forest Products and Metals, and each sector page provides links to industry trade associations, statistics, and information about industry-specific export programs and issues.
Subjects: Exports

189. Market Access and Compliance
http://www.mac.doc.gov/
Sponsor(s): Commerce Department — International Trade Administration (ITA) — Market Access and Compliance
Description: MAC "identifies and overcomes trade barriers, resolves trade policy issues, and ensures that our trading partners fully meet their obligations under

our trade agreements" (from the Web site). The About MAC section of the site has an organizational chart, links to regional offices, and links to MAC programs such as the Special American Business Internship Training (SABIT) program for Eurasia.

Like other ITA Web sites, the main page of the MAC Web site follows a standard ITA template. However, pages at the secondary level are arranged differently, making navigation at this level somewhat confusing.

Subjects: Exports; Trade Laws and Regulations

190. Middle East and North Africa Business Information Center
http://www.export.gov/middleeast/
Sponsor(s): Commerce Department — International Trade Administration (ITA)
Description: The Middle East and North Africa Business Information Center (MENA-BIC) Web site provides information to assist U.S. companies doing business in that region. Sections include Country Information, Industry Information, Trade Leads, Trade Events, Assisting U.S. Exporters, and Key Links for Middle East Business.
Subjects: Exports; Middle East

191. Notify U.S.
http://www.nist.gov/notifyus
Alternate URL(s): http://tsapps.nist.gov/notifyus/data/index/index.cfm
Sponsor(s): Commerce Department — Technology Administration (TA) — National Institute of Standards and Technology (NIST)
Description: This free e-mail subscription service offers U.S. entities (citizens, industries, and organizations) an opportunity to review and comment on proposed foreign technical regulations that may affect their businesses and their business' access to international markets. The U.S. receives notice of these proposed regulations as a member of the World Trade Organization.
Subjects: Exports — Regulations

192. Office of Textiles and Apparel
http://otexa.ita.doc.gov/
Sponsor(s): Commerce Department — International Trade Administration (ITA)
Description: The Office of Textiles and Apparel (OTEXA) Web site provides information about exporting U.S.-made textiles and apparel products. Primary sections include Trade Data, Trade Agreements, and *Federal Register* Notices. The Reference section includes the *Harmonized Tariff Schedule of the United States* for textiles and textile articles. Export Advantage is a special section of the site. It features links to textile market reports, a database of U.S. suppliers and overseas buyers, and country-specific information about topics such as import tariffs, apparel size standards, and labeling requirements.
Subjects: Exports; Textile Industry
Publications: *Harmonized Tariff Schedule of the United States*
Major Shippers Report, C 61.53:
U.S. Exports of Textile and Apparel Products, C 61.50:
U.S. Imports of Textile and Apparel Products, C 61.52:
U.S. Textile and Apparel Category System, C 61.54:

193. Office of the United States Trade Representative
http://www.ustr.gov/
Sponsor(s): Trade Representative (USTR)
Description: The Office of the United States Trade Representative (USTR) is responsible for developing and coordinating U.S. international trade, commodity, and

direct investment policy and for overseeing trade negotiations with other countries. This Web site presents information about negotiations, treaties, and issues in sections organized by trade agreement and by world region. The Trade Sector section organizes information by topic, such as intellectual property, labor, and environment. The WTO section has fact sheets, *Federal Register* notices, other material relating to the United States and the World Trade Organization, and a link to the U.S. Mission in Geneva (where the USTR maintains an office). The Document Library section, which is accessible from the USTR home page, provides easy access to transcripts, speeches, reports, fact sheets, and other material.

The USTR Web site provides a starting point for research on U.S. international trade policies, agreements, and disputes. The World Regions section, which compiles relevant documents by region, may be particularly helpful.

Subjects: International Trade — Policy
Publications: *National Trade Estimate Report on Foreign Trade Barriers*, PREX 9.10:
Trade Policy Agenda and Annual Report of the President of the United States on the Trade Agreements Program, PREX 9.11:

194. Office of Trade and Industry Information
http://www.ita.doc.gov/td/industry/otea/
Sponsor(s): Commerce Department — International Trade Administration (ITA)
Description: The Office of Trade and Industry Information (OTII) prepares and publishes data, research, and analysis on trade and investment issues to support U.S. trade promotion and trade policy. Its Web site links to a wealth of trade data, including *U.S. Foreign Trade Highlights*, the TradeStats Express database (including state-level export data), and the Exporter database of export activities for U.S. small- and medium-sized enterprises. The Trade Data Basics section provides a guide to trade statistics.
Subjects: Trade Statistics
Publications: *Monthly Trade Update*, C 61.46:
Small & Medium-Sized Exporting Companies: A Statistical Handbook
U.S. Foreign Trade Highlights, C 61.28/2:

195. Overseas Private Investment Corporation (OPIC)
http://www.opic.gov/
Sponsor(s): Overseas Private Investment Corporation
Description: OPIC is an independent U.S. government agency that assists U.S. companies investing in emerging economies around the world. For these companies, OPIC provides financing, political risk insurance, and investment funds. Its Web site has sections describing each of these services. The Publications section includes reports on OPIC activities in specific regions and countries.
Subjects: International Business; International Economic Development
Publications: *Annual Report/Overseas Private Investment Corporation*, OP 1.1:
OPICNews, OP 1.10:

196. Special American Business Internship Training Program (SABIT)
http://www.mac.doc.gov/sabit/
Sponsor(s): Commerce Department — International Trade Administration (ITA) — Market Access and Compliance
Description: The SABIT program assists U.S. companies and organizations working in Eurasian countries by funding training programs for managers and scientists from that region. The program is intended to facilitate U.S.-Eurasian business partnerships. Its Web site describes the program and links to a Russian SABIT Web site.
Subjects: Emerging Markets; Eurasia

197. StopFakes.Gov
http://www.stopfakes.gov/
Sponsor(s): Commerce Department
Description: StopFakes.Gov is a product of the government's Strategy Targeting Organized Piracy (STOP!) campaign against the piracy and counterfeiting of U.S. goods. Its Web site describes the campaign, provides resources for assistance, and includes links to relevant information at the Web sites of the U.S. Patent and Trademark Office (PTO), Office of the U.S. Trade Representative, Customs and Border Protection, and other U.S. government agencies. Country-specific intellectual property rights toolkits are available for Brazil, China, Korea, Malaysia, Mexico, Russia, and Taiwan.

This Web site is particularly helpful, as it brings together intellectual property information distributed across the Web sites of many agencies.
Subjects: Intellectual Property; International Trade — Laws

198. Trade Compliance Center (TCC)
http://www.tcc.mac.doc.gov/
Sponsor(s): Commerce Department — International Trade Administration (ITA)
Description: TCC monitors foreign compliance with trade agreements and helps U.S. businesses overcome unfair trade practices. The TCC Web site features the following sections: Report a Barrier, Trade Agreements, Technical Regulation Updates, Country Market Research, Bribery, and News.

The Trade Agreements section links leads to the TCC's Trade and Related Agreements Database (TARA). TARA covers active, binding agreements between the United States and its trading partners concerning manufactured products and services (excluding agriculture). TCC's exporter's guides, available on the same page as TARA, have concise explanations for a variety of trade agreements.
Subjects: Trade Agreements; Trade Laws and Regulations
Publications: *Addressing the Challenges of International Bribery and Fair Competition*, C 61.2:IN
National Trade Estimate Report on Foreign Trade Barriers, PREX 9.10:

199. Trade Information Center
http://www.trade.gov/td/tic/
Alternate URL(s): http://www.ita.doc.gov/td/tic/
Sponsor(s): Commerce Department — International Trade Administration (ITA)
Description: The Department of Commerce's Trade Information Center links to federal export assistance programs and country and regional market information. Its sections include Answers to Your Export Questions, Country Information, Tariff and Tax Information, Export Resources, Trade Offices Nationwide, Trade Events, and Industry Information. The Export Resources section contains links to various publications, including the *National Export Directory*.
Subjects: Exports; Market Research — International
Publications: *A Basic Guide to Exporting*, C 61.8:EX 7/3/
Export Programs Guide, C 61.8:EX 7/8/
National Export Directory, C 61.44:

200. TradeStats Express
http://tse.export.gov/
Sponsor(s): Commerce Department — International Trade Administration (ITA)
Description: TradeStats Express™ delivers annual U.S. trade data in the form of basic world maps, pie charts, and data tables. Its Web site is divided into sections for National Trade Data and State Export Data. For national trade, users can find

U.S. exports, imports, and trade balances for all countries for a given commodity, or they can find data on all products traded between the U.S. and another country. For state exports, users can find data on a state's or U.S. region's exports to one or all countries or world regions, or they can view a state-by-state profile of U.S. exports to a given country.

TradeStats meets its goal of being easy to use. However, the trade data are complex enough that users should review the manual available via the Help link.
Subjects: International Trade — Statistics

201. U.S.-Israel Science and Technology Commission (USISTC)
http://www.usistc.org
Alternate URL(s): http://www.ta.doc.gov/International/MideastAfrica/Israel/USISTC.html
Sponsor(s): Commerce Department — Technology Administration (TA)
Description: USISTC promotes cooperation between the high-tech sectors in the United States and Israel to help create jobs and stimulate economic growth in both countries through the awarding of grants. The commission is co-chaired by the U.S. secretary of commerce and the Israeli minister of industry and trade. The alternate URL links to the Department of Commerce's description of the commission.
Subjects: Technology — International; Israel

202. United States Trade and Development Agency
http://www.tda.gov/
Sponsor(s): U.S. Trade and Development Agency (USTDA)
Description: USTDA is an independent federal agency that provides assistance to developing countries for economic and infrastructure improvements and promotes opportunities for U.S. businesses abroad. This Web site has information about USTDA projects by world region and by industry sector. It also provides information about contracting with the agency.
Subjects: International Business; International Economic Development

Money

203. Advanced Counterfeit Deterrence
http://www.treasury.gov/offices/domestic-finance/acd/
Sponsor(s): Treasury Department — Office of Domestic Finance
Description: The Advanced Counterfeit Deterrence Steering Committee works to prevent the problem of counterfeit currency and makes decisions on counterfeit-deterrent currency design. Its Web site provides information on the program, currency design updates, and what people can do if they suspect a counterfeit note or have information about counterfeiting activity.
Subjects: Counterfeiting

204. Bureau of Engraving and Printing (BEP)
http://www.bep.treas.gov/
Sponsor(s): Treasury Department — Bureau of Engraving and Printing
Description: BEP's Web site features the following sections: About the Bureau, Locations and Tours, Procurement, the BEP Store (which sells collectible products and souvenirs), and Classroom (with links to educational materials). Other sections provide information about the redesigned U.S. paper currency, counterfeit deterrence, money history and trivia, and what to do with damaged currency; the site

also contains information for collectors. A Spanish-language version of the site is also available.

This Web site is particularly strong in its education and outreach efforts.
Subjects: Money

205. Foreign Exchange Rates
http://www.federalreserve.gov/releases/G5/
Alternate URL(s): http://www.federalreserve.gov/releases/h10/update/
Sponsor(s): Federal Reserve — Board of Governors
Description: The first URL above links to the *Federal Reserve Statistical Release G.5*, a monthly report of the average exchange rates for the previous month and comparable figures for earlier months. The alternate URL links to the *Federal Reserve Statistical Release H.10* for daily and weekly data on foreign exchange rates. Both the daily and monthly releases are based on noon buying rates in New York for cable transfers payable in the listed currencies. The monthly releases are available from June 1996 onward. Daily averages are available from 1971 onward.

The Federal Reserve releases do not include rates for all countries and may not be as current as some of the nongovernment online sources for daily exchange rates.
Subjects: Exchange Rates
Publications: *Foreign Exchange Rates*, FR 1.32/2:

206. United States Mint
http://www.usmint.gov/
Sponsor(s): Treasury Department — United States Mint
Description: The United States Mint produces and distributes United States coins, protects national gold and silver assets, and produces and sells platinum, gold, and silver bullion coins. In the About Us section, the Mint's Web site has information about its current work, its history, its regional facilities, and the Mint Police, as well as biographies of its sculptor-engravers. The Key Topics section has quick links to popular topics such as the state quarters and the golden dollar coin. An online store sells commemoratives, medals, and other Mint products. The Consumer Awareness section has links to information about coin promotions, counterfeiting, and investing. It also includes a section with information for businesses interested in selling coin products. The site has an online virtual tour of the Mint and information about on-site tours at its Denver and Philadelphia facilities.
Subjects: Coins; Money
Publications: *Annual Report of the Director of the United States Mint*, T 28.1:
United States Mint Strategic Plan, T 28.2:

CHAPTER 4
Culture and Recreation

Culture, for the purposes of this chapter, can be broadly defined to include the arts, humanities, and preservation of human heritage. The federal government has various roles in each of these areas and in the promotion of recreational opportunities on federal lands. Many of the Web sites in this chapter are designed for the general public; others — particularly some of the federal libraries listed in the Libraries section — are for a far more limited and specialized audience. The federal library listings cover all subject areas, from the humanities to the sciences and engineering.

Subsections in this chapter are Arts, Culture, History, Libraries, Museums, Recreation, and Reference.

Arts

207. Indian Arts and Crafts Board
http://www.doi.gov/iacb/
Sponsor(s): Interior Department
Description: The Indian Arts and Crafts Board enforces the legal requirements that products advertised as "Indian made" must indeed be made by Indians. The board also promotes Indian arts and crafts and operates three regional museums. Its Web site includes an online version of the *Source Directory of American Indian and Alaska Native Owned and Operated Arts and Crafts Businesses.*
Subjects: Arts; American Indians
Publications: *Source Directory of American Indian and Alaska Native Owned and Operated Arts and Crafts Businesses,* I 1.84/3:

208. National Endowment for the Arts
http://www.arts.gov/
Alternate URL(s): http://arts.endow.gov/
Sponsor(s): National Endowment for the Arts (NEA)
Description: NEA is an independent federal agency that promotes and provides funding for the arts and arts education. Its Web site has information on how to apply for a grant and lists recent grant recipients. It also provides a fact sheet and a list of recipients of NEA's Jazz Master Fellowships, National Heritage Fellowships, and National Medal of Arts honors program. An NEA Partners section lists state and regional arts organizations. The Newsroom section contains press releases, fact sheets, and NEA's bimonthly newsletter, *NEA ARTS.*
Subjects: Arts — Grants
Publications: *Before and After Disasters: Federal Funding for Cultural Institutions,* HS 5.102:
NEA Annual Report, NF 2.1:
NEA ARTS, NF 2.18:

209. National Film Preservation Board
http://www.loc.gov/film/
Sponsor(s): Library of Congress
Description: The National Film Preservation Board serves as a public advisory group to the Librarian of Congress on matters related to motion picture preservation. According to its Web site, the board assists the Librarian each year in selecting

titles of "cultural, historical or aesthetic significance" to add to the National Film Registry. The Library of Congress then works to ensure that these films are preserved. The board's Web site includes title lists of selections dating back to 1989. The site also links to the National Film Preservation Foundation (with which it is associated) and to international film archive Web sites.

Subjects: Movies — History

210. Poetry and Literature Center of the Library of Congress

http://www.loc.gov/poetry/

Sponsor(s): Library of Congress

Description: The Poetry and Literature Center is the home of the Poet Laureate Consultant in Poetry, who is named by the Librarian of Congress. The center also administers the Rebekah Johnson Bobbitt National Prize for Poetry and the Witter Bynner fellowships for poets. This Web site offers webcasts of poetry readings at the Library of Congress and further information about the center.

Subjects: Writing

211. President's Committee on the Arts and the Humanities

http://www.pcah.gov/

Sponsor(s): President's Committee on the Arts and the Humanities

Description: The President's Committee on the Arts and the Humanities works to demonstrate the value of the arts and humanities and to stimulate increased private investment in these fields. It also supports the National Medal of Arts and the National Humanities Medals. Its Web site has information about its programs, publications, and membership.

Subjects: Arts; Humanities

212. U.S. Commission of Fine Arts

http://www.cfa.gov/

Sponsor(s): U.S. Commission of Fine Arts

Description: The U.S. Commission of Fine Arts is an independent agency that advises the federal government and the District of Columbia governments on matters of art and architecture that affect the appearance of the nation's capital. Its Web site includes the legislative and regulatory history of the commission, public meeting agendas and minutes, and information about the National Capital Arts and Cultural Affairs program.

Subjects: Architecture; Public Buildings

Culture

213. American Folklife Center

http://www.loc.gov/folklife/

Sponsor(s): Library of Congress — American Folklife Center

Description: The Library of Congress's American Folklife Center is charged with preserving and presenting American folklife. The center is responsible for the Library's Archive of Folk Culture, a repository for American folk music. Its Web site offers a number of online collections; featured projects include the Veterans History Project, StoryCorps, the Alan Lomax Collection, and the Save Our Sounds recorded sound preservation project. Many of the center's publications are available on the site, which also features an extensive list of links to Internet resources for ethnographic studies.

The A to Z Index is particularly useful for discovering the full scope of this site.

Subjects: Folklife Studies; Music

Publications: *A Teacher's Guide to Folklife Resources*, LC 39.9:
Folklife and Fieldwork, LC 39.9:
Folklife Center News, LC 39.10:
Folklife Sourcebook, LC 39.9:

214. Archeology Program
http://www.cr.nps.gov/archeology/
Sponsor(s): Interior Department — National Park Service (NPS)
Description: The NPS Archeology Program Web site has information about archeological investigations at national parks and links to NPS regional archeological centers and offices. The site also carries the *National Park Service Archeology Guide* on responsible management of archeological resources under the stewardship of the National Park Service. The site also provides information about federal archeology and archeology programs nationwide.
Subjects: Archeology
Publications: *National Park Service Archeology Guide*

215. Corporation for Public Broadcasting (CPB)
http://www.cpb.org/
Sponsor(s): Corporation for Public Broadcasting (CPB)
Description: CPB is a private, nonprofit corporation that was created by Congress in 1967. It receives partial funding through annual congressional appropriations and, in turn, funds public television and radio programming. The About CPB section of this Web site includes a history of the organization, leadership profiles, CPB's annual reports to Congress, and financial information. The Programs and Projects section has a directory of CPB-funded programs for television, radio, and the Web.
Subjects: Broadcasting

216. Cultural Heritage, Paleontological Resources and Tribal Consultation on the Public Lands
http://www.blm.gov/heritage/
Sponsor(s): Interior Department — Bureau of Land Management (BLM)
Description: This is the Web site for the BLM's Cultural and Fossil Resources and Tribal Consultation Group. The site has sections on historic preservation laws and initiatives, tribal consultation, heritage education resources (including project archeology), and fossil resources on BLM-managed public lands.
Subjects: Archeology; Public Lands
Publications: *America's Priceless Heritage: Cultural and Fossil Resources on Public Lands*, I 53.2:

217. Heritage Preservation Services
http://www.cr.nps.gov/hps/
Sponsor(s): Interior Department — National Park Service (NPS)
Description: HPS helps local communities identify, evaluate, protect, and preserve historic properties. Its Web site describes HPS programs, including the American Battlefield Protection Program, the Federal Historic Preservation Tax Incentives, and the Historic Surplus Property Program.
Subjects: Historic Preservation; Historic Sites

218. Institute of Museum and Library Services
http://www.imls.gov/
Sponsor(s): Institute of Museum and Library Services (IMLS)
Description: IMLS is an independent federal agency that provides funding in support of all types of museums, libraries, and archives. Its Web site has sections for IMLS

Grant Applicants, Grant Reviewers, and Grant Recipients. The Project Profiles section highlights IMLS-funded projects. The site also has an RSS feed with news and publications updates.

Those users seeking funding for public museums and libraries should be sure to browse this site, as the informatoin about the availability and type of past awards can help inform future applicants.

Subjects: Libraries — Grants; Museums — Grants
Publications: *Conservation Assessment Program, Grant Application and Information*, NF 4.2:
Museum Assessment Program, Grant Application and Information, NF 4.11:
National Leadership Grants, Grant Application and Guidelines, NF 4.11/2:
Primary Source, NF 4.15/2:

219. International Cultural Property Protection
http://exchanges.state.gov/culprop/
Sponsor(s): State Department — Educational and Cultural Affairs Bureau
Description: The Department of State's Office of Cultural Property supports U.S. compliance with laws and international agreements regarding the import, export, and transfer of ownership of cultural property. The office and its Web site are primarily concerned with the Convention on Cultural Property Implementation Act (Public Law 97-446). The site explains import restrictions and identifies U.S. and international agreements concerning the looting and destruction of archaeological sites and the theft of cultural property. An Image Database section shows photos of the types of artifacts that are subject to import restrictions. There are selected links to Spanish-language information, most of which is related to objects and agreements concerning Central and South American nations.
Subjects: Archeology; Cultural Artifacts

220. John W. Kluge Center at the Library of Congress
http://www.loc.gov/loc/kluge/
Sponsor(s): Library of Congress
Description: The Kluge Center hosts humanities scholars at the Library of Congress and presents the international John W. Kluge Prize in the Human Sciences. The center offers Kluge Chairs to selected accomplished scholars in such areas as world cultures, American law and governance, and modern culture. The Web site has information on the Kluge Chairs, fellowships and grants, the Kluge Prize, resident scholars, and the Scholars' Council.
Subjects: Fellowships; Humanities — Awards and Honors

221. Moving Image Collections
http://mic.loc.gov/
Sponsor(s): Library of Congress
Description: The Moving Image Collections (MIC) Web site provides a catalog of moving images from the Library of Congress and other collections around the world, as well as a directory of moving image archives. The site links to portals for the general public, archivists, and science educators; these portals provide information about topics such as film preservation, organizing film exhibitions, and using moving images in the classroom.
Subjects: Movies

222. National Archeological Database (NADB)

`http://www.cr.nps.gov/archeology/TOOLS/nadb.htm`
Sponsor(s): Interior Department — National Park Service (NPS)University of Arkansas. Center for Advanced Spatial Technologies
Description: The NADB online system is maintained through a cooperative agreement between the National Parks Service and the Center for Advanced Spatial Technologies (CAST) at the University of Arkansas. NADB has three components. The Reports section includes references to over 350,000 reports on archeological planning and investigation. The Permits section contains a database of permits issued by the Department of the Interior under the Antiquities Act of 1906 and the Archaeological Resource Protection Act (ARPA) of 1979. The MAPS (Multiple Attribute Presentation System) section is a graphical application that contains a variety of maps in GIS format. These maps show the national distribution of cultural and environmental resources across the United States at the state and county levels.
Subjects: Archeology; Databases

223. National Capital Planning Commission

`http://www.ncpc.gov/`
Sponsor(s): National Capital Planning Commission (NCPC)
Description: NCPC coordinates all planning activities for federal land and buildings in the National Capital Region, which includes Washington, D.C., and surrounding communities in Maryland and Virginia. The NCPC Web site features information about the commission in the following sections: About the NCPC, Commission Meeting Information, Planning Initiatives, Commission Actions, and Publications and Press Releases. Additionally, the Information for Submitting Agencies section provides guidelines for submitting proposals and offers a calendar of submission deadlines.
Subjects: Public Buildings; District of Columbia
Publications: *Designing for Security in the Nation's Capital*, NC 2.2:
Extending the Legacy: Planning America's Capital for the 21st Century, NC 2.2:
General Guidelines and Submission Requirements, NC 2.2:
NCPC Quarterly (National Capital Planning Commission Newsletter), NC 2.11/2:

224. National Center for Preservation Technology and Training (NCPTT)

`http://www.ncptt.nps.gov/`
Sponsor(s): Interior Department — National Park Service (NPS)
Description: As part of the National Park Service, NCPTT is concerned with the art and science of preservation in areas such as archeology and historic architecture. The center's grants program focuses on the training, technology, and basic research aspects of preservation and conservation. Major sections of its Web site are Archeology and Collections, Architecture and Engineering, Historic Landscapes, Materials Research, and Heritage Education. The products catalog has links to PDF copies of many NCPTT reports and allows users to order up to five reports online for free.

NCPTT provides rich information for preservation technology professionals. The Heritage Education section will be of interest to teachers.
Subjects: Historic Preservation
Publications: *NCPTT (National Center for Preservation Training and Technology) Notes*, I 29.136:

225. National Endowment for the Humanities

http://www.neh.gov/

Sponsor(s): National Endowment for the Humanities (NEH)

Description: According to its Web site, "NEH is an independent grant-making agency of the United States government that supports research, education, preservation, and public programs in the humanities." The Apply for a Grant section on agency's Web site has application forms, deadlines, and guidelines. The News and Publications section includes press releases, lists of new grants recipients, and articles from *Humanities* magazine. The About NEH section includes a staff directory, budget information, links to the State Humanities Councils, and information about the Jefferson Lecture in the Humanities and the National Humanities Medals.

Subjects: Grants; Humanities

Publications: *Humanities*, NF 3.11:

226. National NAGPRA

http://www.cr.nps.gov/nagpra/

Sponsor(s): Interior Department — National Park Service (NPS)

Description: As part of the NPS's National Center for Cultural Resources, National NAGPRA develops regulations and guidance for implementing the Native American Graves Protection and Repatriation Act (NAGPRA). National NAGPRA also provide training and grants. Its Web site is a resource for information on the act, which delineates a process for museums and Federal agencies to return certain Native American cultural items. The site has information for tribes, agencies, museums, the public, and the press. It links to the Native American Consultation Database, which identifies consultation contacts for Indian tribes, Alaska Native villages and corporations, and Native Hawaiian organizations.

Subjects: Cultural Artifacts; American Indians

227. National Recording Preservation Board

http://www.loc.gov/rr/record/nrpb/

Sponsor(s): Library of Congress

Description: According to its Web site, National Recording Preservation Board advises the Librarian of Congress on the selection of "culturally, historically, or aesthetically important" sound recordings to be added to the National Recording Registry. These selections may include music, non-music, spoken word, or broadcast sound. The Web site includes information about the registry and the board's preservation planning work. It also links to Web sites for sound archives and useful information about audio preservation.

Subjects: Archives; Music

228. Preserve America

http://www.preserveamerica.gov/

Sponsor(s): White House

Description: Preserve America is a White House initiative launched by First Lady Laura Bush and developed together with the Department of the Interior, the Department of Commerce, and the Advisory Council on Historic Preservation. The initiative is intended to encourage federal agencies to better carry out the integration of heritage preservation and economic development, to bolster local heritage preservation efforts, and to promote intergovernmental and public-private partnerships to help accomplish these goals. This Web site presents the executive order establishing Preserve America, an application for communities to be designated Preserve America Communities, and information on the Preserve America Presidential Awards.

Subjects: Historic Preservation

229. Smithsonian Center for Folklife and Cultural Heritage
http://www.folklife.si.edu/
Sponsor(s): Smithsonian Institution
Description: On its Web site, the Smithsonian Center for Folklife and Cultural Heritage describes its mission of preserving "contemporary grassroots cultures in the United States and abroad." The site has information about the center's major endeavors, including the annual Folklife Festival and Smithsonian Folkways Recordings (including a searchable catalogue of the recordings). Other topics provide information about the center's publications, archives, educational materials, and collections.
Subjects: Folklife Studies

230. Smithsonian Institution
http://www.si.edu/
Sponsor(s): Smithsonian Institution
Description: The main Smithsonian Institution Web site links to all other Smithsonian museum sites and to information about the Smithsonian's research facilities, archives, and other centers. The site includes information about the history of the Smithsonian, hours and locations of the Smithsonian museums, and links to Smithsonian affiliate museums across the United States. From the Visitor Information section, there are links to Smithsonian guides in German, Spanish, Japanese, Arabic, and other languages. Two sections that may be particularly helpful for researchers are listed in fine print in the top right-hand corner of the site: About Smithsonian and Websites A-Z, an extensive index of Smithsonian Web sites.
This Web site provides an excellent overview of the Smithsonian's component institutes and programs.
Subjects: Museums
Publications: *Annual Report, Smithsonian Institution*, SI 1.1:
Inside Smithsonian Research, SI 1.50:
Smithsonian (Web magazine), SI 1.45:
Smithsonian Opportunities for Research and Study, SI 1.44:

231. Smithsonian Institution Research Information System (SIRIS)
http://www.siris.si.edu
Sponsor(s): Smithsonian Institution
Description: SIRIS provides quick links to the specialized databases and information resources that are located on the many Smithsonian Institution Web sites. The resources are grouped by category into the following categories: Smithsonian Libraries; Archival, Manuscript, and Photographic Collections; Smithsonian American Art Museum Research Databases; Specialized Research Bibliographies; and History of the Smithsonian.
Subjects: Museums; Databases

232. Smithsonian Magazine
http://www.smithsonianmag.si.edu/
Description: This online version of the *Smithsonian Magazine* includes the table of contents, columns, and articles and images from the print version. Articles are accompanied by links to additional sources and relevant archived articles.
Subjects: Culture and Recreation
Publications: *Smithsonian Magazine*

History

233. Abraham Lincoln Bicentennial Commission
http://www.lincolnbicentennial.gov/
Sponsor(s): Abraham Lincoln Bicentennial Commission
Description: The Abraham Lincoln Bicentennial Commission is planning the commemoration of the 200th birthday of Abraham Lincoln, with events planned from February 2008 to February 2010. This Web site provides information about Lincoln, the Bicentennial Commission, and events planned to date.
Subjects: Presidency — History

234. Access to Archival Databases (AAD)
http://www.archives.gov/aad/
Sponsor(s): National Archives and Records Administration (NARA)
Description: AAD provides the public with access to a selection of historic databases and other electronic records maintained by the National Archives. This site includes nearly 85 million historic electronic records created by more than 30 federal agencies. The electronic records vary widely in subject matter, but all of them identify specific persons, geographic areas, organizations, or dates — making them useful as finding aids. Information includes several files on Korean War casualties and prisoners of war, the Japanese-American Internee File for 1942–1946, the Work Stoppages Historical File for 1953–1981, and a data file of Records for Passengers Who Arrived at the Port of New York During the Irish Famine 1848–1851.

First-time users should consult the Getting Started Guide for instructions on how to search AAD and for an explanation of what records are included in AAD. The records in AAD represent only a small fraction of the electronic records holdings of the National Archives. For the most part, AAD does not include digitally scanned images of paper records and other non-electronic records.
Subjects: Archives; Databases

235. Advisory Council on Historic Preservation (ACHP)
http://www.achp.gov/
Sponsor(s): Advisory Council on Historic Preservation
Description: ACHP is an independent federal agency and the major policy adviser to the federal government in the field of historic preservation. The Web site contains an overview of the National Historic Preservation Program, including directories of federal, state, and tribal preservation officers and preservation-related Web sites. The site also has the full text of the Section 106 regulations, *Protection of Historic Properties*, from the *Code of Federal Regulations*.
Subjects: Historic Preservation
Publications: *Federal Historic Preservation Case Law, 1966–2000*, Y 3.H 62:
Protecting Historic Properties: A Citizen's Guide to Section 106 Review, Y 3.H 62:8/

236. American Battle Monuments Commission
http://www.abmc.gov/
Sponsor(s): American Battle Monuments Commission (ABMC)
Description: AMBC is an independent federal agency responsible for commemorating the services of the U.S. armed force at places where they have served since 1917. AMBC administers cemeteries on foreign soil and memorials both in the United States and abroad. Its Web site has databases of servicemembers interred at the American World War I and World War II cemeteries overseas; the missing in

action from World War I and World War II, who are memorialized on Tablets of the Missing within these cemeteries and on three memorials in the United States; and servicemembers killed during the Korean War.

Subjects: Monuments and Landmarks; Veterans' Cemeteries
Publications: *American Battle Monuments Commission Annual Report,* Y 3.AM 3:1/

237. American Memory
http://memory.loc.gov/
Sponsor(s): Library of Congress
Description: The Library of Congress's American Memory Web site provides online versions of distinctive, historical Americana materials from the library's collections. These include digitized photographs, manuscripts, rare books, maps, recorded sound, and moving pictures. The diverse collections include Civil War photographs, the papers of Thomas Jefferson, nineteenth century American sheet music, and late eighteenth century maps of North America. The collections can be accessed in a number of ways; methods include browsing by topic, historical time period, or the material's original format type. The site also provides a section for teachers (the Learning Page), which has guides on using primary source materials in the classroom.
Subjects: Digital Libraries; History

238. Heritage Documentation Programs
http://www.cr.nps.gov/hdp/
Alternate URL(s): http://lcweb2.loc.gov/ammem/hhhtml/
Sponsor(s): Interior Department — National Park Service (NPS)
Description: Heritage Documentation Programs administers HABS (Historic American Buildings Survey) and companion programs HAER (Historic American Engineering Record), HALS (Historic American Landscapes Survey), and CRGIS (Cultural Resources Geographic Information Systems). In the Collections section, its Web site links to the database of the program's architectural, engineering, and landscape documentation at the Library of Congress, which can be found at the alternate URL provided above. The site also carries the standards and guidelines for its historical documentation drawings.
Subjects: Architecture — History; Civil Engineering — History

239. History & Culture
http://www.cr.nps.gov/
Sponsor(s): Interior Department — National Park Service (NPS)
Description: The History & Culture Web site links to the cultural information available in the NPS component Web sites and publications. It includes databases, grants listings, museum directories, and more. The Grants section has information on grants, tax credits, and other programs to encourage preservation of cultural resources. The site also includes sections for teachers and kids. The About Our Program section has an alphabetical index of the resources online, from the American Battlefield Protection Program to the Tribal Preservation Program.

The History & Culture Web site is a useful and well-designed portal for exploring the wide range of resources available through the National Parks Service. Several of its resources are described in separate entries in this section.
Subjects: Historic Sites; National Parks and Reserves — History

240. History of Social Security
http://www.ssa.gov/history/
Sponsor(s): Social Security Administration (SSA)
Description: The History of Social Security Web site provides extensive information and documentation on both SSA and the Social Security Program. It includes transcripts and audio files of presidential statements and conversations, oral history interviews, legislative history documents, as well as a photo gallery, chronology, and other resources.
Subjects: Social Security — History

241. JFK Assassination Records
http://www.archives.gov/research/jfk/
Sponsor(s): National Archives and Records Administration (NARA)
Description: The President John F. Kennedy Assassination Records Collection Act (Public Law 102-526) requires that all records related to his 1963 assassination be housed in a single NARA collection. This Web site provides descriptions and finding aids for the physical collection of records, which can be viewed in NARA's College Park, MD, research rooms. Online finding aids include the Assassination Records Collection Register, which lists all of the records in the collection at the general series level, and the JFK Assassination Collection Database, which is an index of many of the documents in the collection.
Subjects: Archives; President — History

242. MINERVA
http://www.loc.gov/minerva/
Sponsor(s): Library of Congress
Description: MINERVA is an acronym for Mapping the Internet Electronic Resources Virtual Archive. This Library of Congress online project has selected, saved, and cataloged historical information that previously appeared exclusively on Web sites and might otherwise have been lost to future researchers. Current online collections are built around events such as the September 11, 2001, terrorist attacks and the national elections of 2000. The site also includes reports and presentations on the project.
Subjects: Digital Libraries; World Wide Web — History

243. National Historical Publications and Records Commission
http://www.archives.gov/nhprc/
Sponsor(s): National Archives and Records Administration (NARA) — National Historical Publications and Records Commission (NHPRC)
Description: NHPRC is a NARA grant-making affiliate whose purpose is to help identify, preserve, and provide public access to records, photographs, and other materials that document American history. Its Web site has directories of commission members, staff, and state coordinators. There is also information about the projects funded by the commission and how to apply for and administer a grant.
Subjects: Archives — Grants
Publications: *Annotation, The Newsletter of the National Historical Publications and Records Commission*, AE 1.114/2:

244. National Park Service History
http://www.cr.nps.gov/history/index.asp
Sponsor(s): Interior Department — National Park Service (NPS)
Description: This Web site provides historical background on the NPS and on individual parks. It lists NPS Web sites by historical theme, such as the Civil War and

Hispanic ethnic heritage. The Web site also covers NPS's Maritime Heritage Program.

Subjects: National Parks and Reserves — History

245. National Register of Historic Places

http://www.cr.nps.gov/nr/

Sponsor(s): Interior Department — National Park Service (NPS)

Description: On its Web site, the National Register of Historic Places describes itself as "the nation's official list of cultural resources worthy of preservation." The site provides information about how to get a property listed on the National Register and links to thematic Web sites on teaching about and traveling to historic places. It also links to the National Register Information System (NRIS), a database of places listed in or determined eligible for the National Register of Historic Places.

Subjects: Historic Sites

246. Naval Historical Center

http://www.history.navy.mil/

Sponsor(s): Navy — Naval Historical Center

Description: The Naval Historical Center manages the Navy Department Library, 12 U.S. Navy museums, art collections, archives, and an underwater archaeology program. Its Web site contains numerous online collections, exhibits, publications, and guides to information on U.S. Navy history and traditions. It also links to the Web sites for many of the naval museums. The FOIA Reading Room section, linked at the bottom of the main page, includes documents on popular topics such as the 1941 Pearl Harbor attack and Navy policy on submerged aircraft and shipwrecks. Most content can be found in these sections: Frequently Asked Questions, Online Resources, Publications, Research and Collections, For Fleet and Veterans, and Wars and Conflicts. It can be difficult to anticipate what information will be found in which section; researchers may need to browse each one.

While there is not a great depth of online historical material here, the broad scope of the collection and the references to print resources make this an excellent starting point for historical information about the U.S. Navy.

Subjects: Military History

Publications: *Cruise Books of the United States Navy in World War II: A Bibliography*, D 221.17:2

Historical Manuscripts in the Navy Department Library: A Catalog, D 221.17:3

Naval Aviation News, D 202.9:

The Reestablishment of the Navy, 1787-1801 Historical Overview and Select Bibliography, D 221.17:4

The Spanish-American War: Historical Overview and Select Bibliography, D 221.17:5

United States Naval History: A Bibliography, D 221.17:1

247. Our Documents

http://www.ourdocuments.gov/

Sponsor(s): National Archives and Records Administration (NARA)

Description: Our Documents is an educational outreach project sponsored by the National Archives, the USA Freedom Corps, and several private organizations, including National History Day and the History Channel. The Web site provides copies of and background information about the "100 Milestone Documents," which were selected by the National Archives. These include the Declaration of Independence, the Bill of Rights, constitutional amendments, the Emancipation Proclamation, the Gettysburg Address, the Manhattan Project Notebook, the Marshall Plan, *Brown v. Board of Education*, the Civil Rights Act, the Voting Rights Act, and more. The documents are intended to serve as topics of educational and historical outreach activities. The site includes a Tools for Educators section and a section with news of the events and activities that make up the Our Documents project.

Subjects: Government Publications — History

248. State-Level Casualty Lists from Vietnam and Korean Conflict

http://www.archives.gov/research/vietnam-war/casualty-lists/

Sponsor(s): National Archives and Records Administration (NARA)

Description: The National Archives Center for Electronic Records has indexed the records for U.S. military casualties from the Korean War and the Vietnam War by the state "home of record" for the servicemember. In addition to providing free online access to these lists, the page describes how to order copies of the databases. For the Korean War, the database includes records for persons who died as a result of hostilities during the 1950–1957 period, including those who died while missing or captured. For Vietnam, the database includes records for persons who died during the 1956–1998 period as a result of hostile or nonhostile occurrences in the Southeast Asian Combat Area, including those who died while missing or captured.

Subjects: Korean War; Vietnam War

249. The American Civil War

http://cwar.nps.gov/civilwar/

Sponsor(s): Interior Department — National Park Service (NPS)

Description: The NPS has designed this Web site in anticipation of the sesquicentennial anniversary of the American Civil War, which will be observed from 2011–2015. It covers the 70-plus parks in the NPS and includes information about resources related to the history of the Civil War, programs related to protection of historic battlefields, and other topics.

Subjects: Civil War (United States); National Parks and Reserves — History

250. U.S. Army Center of Military History

http://www.army.mil/cmh-pg/

Sponsor(s): Army — Center of Military History (CMH)

Description: The CMH site offers full-text military history books, documents, and a museum display of army art. The majority of the collection can be found under the Online Bookshelves section. The Force Structure and Unit History section features the *Army Lineage Series*. The Frequently Asked Questions section addresses questions such as finding official unit records, and provides brief background information on "frequently researched topics," such as the integration of the U.S. army and the origin of the 21-gun salute. The site has a Medal of Honor citations list and a directory of Army museums. It also features a series of guides about researching military history, including information on oral history techniques, and a separate section about the history of military history.

Subjects: Military History

Publications: *Publications of the United States Army Center of Military History*, D 114.10:

251. Veterans History Project

http://www.loc.gov/vets/

Sponsor(s): Library of Congress — American Folklife Center

Description: The Veterans History Project collects, presents, and preserves firsthand accounts from veterans of World War I, World War II, the Korean War, the Vietnam War, the Persian Gulf War, and the current conflicts in Afghanistan and Iraq. The accounts include letters, photographs, and oral histories in audio and video formats. Records describing the collections can be searched in a database and many digitized collections can be viewed or heard online. The site also includes information on how to submit veterans' stories to the collection.

Subjects: Veterans — History

252. Vietnam-Era Prisoner-of-War/Missing-in-Action Database
`http://lcweb2.loc.gov/pow/powhome.html`
Sponsor(s): Library of Congress — Federal Research Division (FRD)
Description: This database indexes government documents related to U.S. military personnel that were listed as unaccounted for in Southeast Asia during American involvement in Vietnam. The title of the collection is "Correlated and Uncorrelated Information Relating to Missing Americans in Southeast Asia." The database does not contain full-text documents, but the site explains how the actual documents can be obtained.

Subjects: Prisoners of War; Databases

Libraries

253. AFIT Academic Library
`http://www.afit.edu/library/`
Sponsor(s): Air Force — Air Force Institute of Technology (AFIT)
Description: The AFIT Library Web site offers public access to its online library catalog. The site's Subject Guides to Web Resources section has links to information on a wide variety of topics.

Subjects: Scientific and Technical Information

254. Air Force Research Laboratory (AFRL) Technical Library
`http://www.afrl.af.mil/wrslibrary/`
Sponsor(s): Air Force — Air Force Research Laboratory
Description: The AFRL Technical Library serves the personnel at Wright-Patterson Air Force Base in Ohio. Many of the services on its Web site are restricted to authorized users.

Subjects: Scientific and Technical Information

255. Air University Library and Press
`http://www.au.af.mil/au/aul/lane.htm`
Sponsor(s): Air Force — Air University
Description: Many of the resources available through the Air University (AU) Library Web site are restricted to AU users. However, the site provides public access to Internet bibliographies compiled by the library staff about topics such as asymmetric warfare and weapons of mass destruction. The site also links to the *Air University Library Index to Military Periodicals*.

Although many sections of the site are open only to authorized users, other researchers will find the publicly accessible bibliographies, links to electronic journals and news sources, and the index of periodicals to be of benefit.

Subjects: Military Information; Bibliographies
Publications: *Air University Library Index to Military Periodicals*, D 301.26/2:

256. Alfred M. Gray Marine Corps Research Center
http://www.mcu.usmc.mil/MCRCweb/index.htm
Sponsor(s): Marine Corps
Description: The Gray Research Center includes the library and research archives of the Marine Corps University, also called "The Library of the Marine Corps." Its Web site contains descriptive information and finding aids for the collections. In the Library Resources section, the Doctrinal Publications and Hot Documents subsections link to the full text of reports. Under Research Guides, the site offers a wide variety of bibliographies on topics related to the military and warfare.
Subjects: Marine Corps — Research

257. ALIC Archives Library Information Center
http://www.archives.gov/research_room/alic/
Sponsor(s): National Archives and Records Administration (NARA)
Description: ALIC serves National Archives staff and researchers on-site as well as online. The ALIC Web site links to the center's collection catalog and to full-text NARA publications online. The Reference at Your Desk section is designed for archivists but will be of use to others as well; links lead to information about records management, African-American history, genealogy, and military history. Bibliographies include *Holocaust-Era Assets* and *Selected Resources on the Civil War*. Some commercial databases linked on the ALIC page are only available to staff or on-site researchers.
Subjects: Archives — Research; Genealogy

258. Center for the Book in the Library of Congress
http://www.loc.gov/loc/cfbook/
Sponsor(s): Library of Congress
Description: The Center for the Book promotes books, reading, libraries, and literacy. It is affiliated with the state book centers that conduct local activities for the same purpose. Its Web site has information about the center's themes and projects, literary events (including the National Book Festival), publications, and affiliate programs.
Subjects: Literacy; Reading

259. Combined Arms Research Library
http://cgsc.leavenworth.army.mil/CARL/
Sponsor(s): Army — Command and General Staff College (CGSC)
Description: The Combined Arms Research Library (CARL) is described on its Web site as "a comprehensive military science research center supporting the Army Command and General Staff College." The site's Digital Library section has several digitized and indexed collections, such as the WWII Operations and General Military History collection. The CARL News and Information Feed section contains an alert service for new reports and information sources of interest.
Subjects: Military Information

260. Department of the Interior Library
http://library.doi.gov/
Sponsor(s): Interior Department
Description: The Department of the Interior Library Web site includes descriptive information about the library and its services and collections. In the DOI Information section, the site has useful indexes to DOI component Web sites by topic, such as agency histories, online publications, and management reports.
Subjects: Public Lands — Research

261. Depository Library Council
http://www.access.gpo.gov/su_docs/fdlp/council/
Sponsor(s): Government Printing Office (GPO) — Depository Library Council (DLC)
Description: DLC advises the Public Printer on policy matters concerning the Federal Depository Library Program. This site includes the following sections: About the Council, Congressional Testimony, Council Meeting Sites, Members of Council, Reports and Publications, Recommendations and Responses, and Minutes of Meetings.
Subjects: Federal Depository Library Program

262. EPA Libraries
http://www.epa.gov/natlibra/
Sponsor(s): Environmental Protection Agency (EPA)
Description: This site links to EPA libraries and provides access to the Online Library System (OLS) union catalog. The OLS index includes several special collections: the National Service Center for Environmental Publications, the Environmental Financing Information Network, the National Enforcement Training Institute, and the GroundWater Ecosystems Restoration Database.

   The EPA began closing a number of its libraries at its Washington, DC, headquarters and EPA regional offices in 2006. The situation remains in flux at the time of this writing.
Subjects: Environmental Protection — Research

263. ERDC: Professional Library Services
http://itl.erdc.usace.army.mil/library/
Sponsor(s): Army — Army Corps of Engineers — Engineer Research and Development Center (ERDC)
Description: The ERDC Library Web site provides access to its online catalog, ERDC online publications, and the Cold Regions Science and Technology bibliography.
Subjects: Civil Engineering — Research

264. FBI Library
http://fbilibrary.fbiacademy.edu/
Sponsor(s): Justice Department — Federal Bureau of Investigation (FBI)
Description: The FBI Library at the FBI Academy has a Web site with the online library catalog, bibliographies on over 60 law enforcement topics, and links to related Web sites.
Subjects: Law Enforcement — Research

265. FDLP Desktop
http://www.access.gpo.gov/su_docs/fdlp/
Sponsor(s): Government Printing Office (GPO) — Superintendent of Documents
Description: To facilitate public access to federal government information, GPO's Federal Depository Library Program (FDLP) provides print and electronic government publications to over 1,000 designated depository libraries throughout the country. The FDLP Desktop Web site has detailed news and information about the system's operations.

   The audience for much of the information on this site is limited to those people who staff and manage depository libraries. Some links may be of interest to users researching access to government information or making extensive use of the depository system.
Subjects: Federal Depository Library Program

Publications: *Administrative Notes* (monthly), GP 3.16/3-2:
Administrative Notes Technical Supplement, GP 3.16/3-3:
Federal Depository Library Directory, GP 3.36/2:

266. Federal Bureau of Prisons Library
http://bop.library.net/
Sponsor(s): Justice Department — Federal Bureau of Prisons
Description: This Web site is primarily a Web interface for the library catalog. The site also includes a description of the library, a periodicals list, and a video list.
Subjects: Prisons — Research

267. Federal Library and Information Center Committee
http://www.loc.gov/flicc/
Sponsor(s): Library of Congress — Federal Library and Information Center Committee (FLICC)
Description: FLICC and FEDLINK provide service and guidance to federal libraries and information centers. This Web site features the following sections: Education and Training, Federal Library Resources, Account Management, Information for Vendors, and Contracting/Vendor Products and Services. Separate links to FLICC and FEDLINK provide more information from each of these offices.
Subjects: Libraries
Publications: *FEDLINK (Federal Library and Information Network) Technical Notes*, LC 1.32/5:
FLICC Newsletter, LC 1.32:

268. Fermilab Information Resources Department
http://lss.fnal.gov/ird/index.html
Sponsor(s): Energy Department — Fermi National Accelerator Laboratory
Description: The Fermilab Library Web site features access to its online catalog and to full-text documents and preprints from the lab. It links to two resources from the Stanford Linear Accelerator Center: the SPIRES High Energy Physics database and the SLAC Library's list of free journals.
Subjects: Physics — Research; Preprints

269. Glenn Technical Library
http://grctechlib.grc.nasa.gov/
Sponsor(s): National Aeronautics and Space Administration (NASA) — Glenn Research Center
Description: The NASA Glenn Research Center Technical Library Web site features sections such as Who We Are, What We Do, and Collections We Have. A section called Where You Can Go lists Web sites on science, aviation, and engineering topics that have been evaluated by the Glenn Research Center Library.
Subjects: Aerospace Engineering — Research

270. Goddard Library
http://library.gsfc.nasa.gov/public/
Sponsor(s): National Aeronautics and Space Administration (NASA) — Goddard Space Flight Center (GSFC)
Description: The Goddard Space Flight Center Library's Extranet is the public version of the library's Web site. It features links to publicly available Web resources, such as technical reports, image databases, and the library's online catalog.
Subjects: Scientific and Technical Information

271. GOVDOC-L [e-mail list]
http://govdoc-l.org/
Sponsor(s): Duke University. Perkins Library
Description: This is the oldest, and still the primary, e-mail list for government documents librarians. While it is neither hosted nor sponsored by the federal government, the discussions, questions, and announcements relate directly to government information and the practice of government documents librarianship.

Previously, the Government Printing Office used GOVDOC-L for its official announcements to depository libraries. GPO now has its own announcements list, called GPO-FDLP-L.

Subjects: Federal Depository Library Program; E-mail Lists

272. Library of Congress
http://www.loc.gov/
Sponsor(s): Library of Congress
Description: As the largest library in the world, it is only fitting that the Library of Congress Web site should be one of the most extensive and information-packed governmental library Web sites. Its American Memory section, with scanned images, movies, audio files, and other reproductions of historic documents, is a leading example of the how the Internet is being used to make rare collections available to the public. The site's Exhibitions section has digital versions of major library exhibitions dating back to 1993. Another major section, the Global Gateway, emphasizes the international nature of the Library's collection and staff expertise. A section called "Resources For. . ." organizes information by audience, including researchers, librarians, teachers, publishers, visitors, and kids and families. The section for researchers includes links to the Web sites for the library's special reading rooms, such as the Hispanic Reading Room, Science Reference Services, and the Recorded Sound Reference Center.

The main Library of Congress online catalog contains approximately 14 million records representing books, serials, computer files, manuscripts, cartographic materials, music, sound recordings, and visual materials. The library also has an online catalog for its special Prints and Photographs and Recorded Sound collections.

The library site also links to the legislative information service THOMAS and to the Copyright Office. These and other specialized sections are described in more detail elsewhere in this publication.

While the Web site offers only a very small fraction of the material available at the library itself, it does provide a significant collection of free online material as well as detailed information about the library's collections and services. This is a large, growing site that offers substantial resources of interest to librarians, historical researchers, publishers, lawyers, Congress, and the general public.

Subjects: Digital Libraries; Libraries; United States — History
Publications: *American Memory Digital Collections*, LC 1.54/3:
Area Handbook Series, D 101.22:550
Bibliographic Products and Services, LC 30.27/2:
CONSER LINE, LC 30.22/2:
FEDLINK (Federal Library and Information Network) Technical Notes, LC 1.32/5:
Handbook of Federal Librarianship, LC 1.32/6-2:
LC Cataloging Newsline, LC 9.16:
LC Science Tracer Bullet, LC 33.10:
Library of Congress Classification, Additions and Changes, (weekly) LC 26.9/2:
Library of Congress Information Bulletin, LC 1.18:

Library of Congress Subject Headings Weekly List, LC 26.7/2-3:
NewsNet, LC 3.4/3:
Thomas: Legislative Information on the Internet, LC 1.54/2:

273. Library of Congress Listservs
http://lcweb.loc.gov/flicc/listsrvs.html
Sponsor(s): Library of Congress
Description: The Library of Congress hosts a number of e-mail listservs on its Web site. The URL above provides information about several lists, including FEDLIB: Federal Librarians Discussion List; FEDCAT-L: FEDLINK Cataloging Peer Council; FEDLIBIT: Federal Librarians Information Technology Discussion; FEDREF-L: Federal Reference Librarians' Discussion List; and OCLCFED: FEDLINK OCLC Members List. Most of these lists will primarily be of interest to federal government librarians, but FEDREF-L will be of interest to the entire government documents librarian community.
Subjects: Libraries; E-mail Lists
Publications: *CONSERline*
LC Cataloging Newsline, LC 9.16:

274. Library Statistics Program
http://nces.ed.gov/surveys/libraries/
Sponsor(s): Education Department — Institute of Education Sciences — National Center for Education Statistics (NCES)
Description: NCES publishes data on public, academic, and school libraries and state library agencies. Statistics and publications on this Web site are divided into those categories. The Data Tools section (under the Library Statistics Program heading) features a searchable directory of public libraries and tools to produce statistical reports comparing academic libraries and public libraries with others of those types.
Subjects: Libraries — Statistics

275. LLNL Library
http://www.llnl.gov/library/
Sponsor(s): Energy Department — Lawrence Livermore National Laboratory (LLNL)
Description: This LLNL Library Web site features Web-based online catalogs and descriptions of its services and collections. LLNL-authored, unclassified technical reports are available in the Reports Search section. The site also features links to major LLNL online publications.
Subjects: Scientific and Technical Information; Weapons Research
Publications: *Science Technology Review*, E 1.53:

276. Locate a Federal Depository Library
http://www.gpoaccess.gov/libraries.html
Sponsor(s): Government Printing Office (GPO) — Superintendent of Documents
Description: Use a clickable map of the United States and U.S. commonwealths and territories to find federal depository libraries by location. Users can also see a list of all depositories or search the listings by state, area code, or congressional district. The site also links to information about the Federal Depository Library Program.
Subjects: Federal Depository Library Program
Publications: *A Directory of U.S. Government Depository Libraries*, Y 4.P 93/1-10:

277. Los Alamos National Laboratory Research Library
http://library.lanl.gov/
Sponsor(s): Energy Department — Los Alamos National Laboratory (LANL)
Description: The general public can search the LANL Library catalog, but most resources on this Web site are restricted to authorized LANL users. At the bottom of the main page, the Research Library staff publications and presentations will interest users involved in information technology and digital libraries.
Subjects: Scientific and Technical Information

278. MERLN (Military Educational Research Library Network)
http://merln.ndu.edu/
Sponsor(s): Defense Department — National Defense University (NDU)
Description: MERLN is a Web site compendium of military education libraries that cooperate in collecting, organizing, and sharing educational resources. The site's Digital Collection section features military education research materials digitized by MERLN participants. The Military Policy Awareness Links (MiPALS) are Web bibliographies on such topics as Afghanistan and North Korea. The Publications section provides a convenient collection of annotated links to journals and publications available from MERLN member sites.
Subjects: Military Information

279. NARA Locations Nationwide
http://www.archives.gov/locations/
Sponsor(s): National Archives and Records Administration (NARA)
Description: The National Archives operates research facilities across the United States, including NARA regional facilities and presidential libraries. This Web site provides collections and location information for each facility. The NARA regional facilities typically offer genealogy resources, federal agency records from the region, and federal courts records including bankruptcy cases. NARA Presidential Libraries are described in a separate entry in this section.
Subjects: Archives; Genealogy — Research

280. NASA Langley Research Center Technical Library
http://library.larc.nasa.gov/Public/
Sponsor(s): National Aeronautics and Space Administration (NASA) — Langley Research Center (LaRC)
Description: The NASA Langley Research Center Technical Library has created this page for public use; it excludes material available only to staff and authorized users. The site includes a Virtual Reference Shelf section and a Technical Reports section. The Technical Reports section links to the Aeronautics and Space Access Page Technical Report Server, the Langley Technical Report Server, and the NASA Technical Report Server.
Subjects: Scientific and Technical Information

281. National Agricultural Library
http://www.nalusda.gov/
Sponsor(s): Agriculture Department (USDA) — National Agricultural Library (NAL)
Description: NAL is a major source for national and international agricultural information. The NAL Web site acts as a gateway to the library's resources and associated institutions. Primary sections include NAL Catalog, NAL Collections, Information Centers, and NAL Services. The NAL Catalog, also known as AGRICOLA, is an extensive database of published agriculture information. The NAL Collections section includes the National Agricultural Library Digital Repository (NALDR) of publications either digitized by NAL or through NAL's partnerships with other

institutions. The Information Centers section links to specialized resources ranging from the Alternative Farming Systems Information Center to the Water Quality
Information Center; each of these centers are described in separate entries in
this publication. The Web site also links to the *NAL Agricultural Thesaurus*, an
online vocabulary look-up tool for agricultural and biological terms.

This site can be used as an excellent starting point for finding agricultural
information. The site helpfully organizes its many resources by topic, such as
Animals and Livestock, Food and Nutrition, and Rural and Community Development.

Subjects: Agriculture Information; Libraries
Publications: *Animal Welfare Information Center Bulletin*, A 17.27/2:
List of Journals Indexed in AGRICOLA, A 17.18/5:
NAL Agricultural Thesaurus
National Agriculture Library Annual Report, A 17.1:

282. National Commission on Libraries and Information Science

http://www.nclis.gov/

Sponsor(s): National Commission on Libraries and Information Science (NCLIS)
Description: NCLIS is an independent federal government agency charged with advising the executive and legislative branches on national library and information
policies and plans. NCLIS reports and other works are in the Information Policy
section of this Web site. NCLIS information about public library statistics is
available in the Statistics and Surveys section. The About NCLIS section has
information about commissioners, meetings, and the budget.
Subjects: Information Policy; Libraries — Policy

283. National Defense University Library

http://www.ndu.edu/Library/

Sponsor(s): Defense Department — National Defense University (NDU)
Description: The NDU Library resources available online include the library catalog
and digitized collections focusing on Fort McNair history, special commission
reports on national defense, and related topics.
Subjects: Military Information

284. National Library of Education

http://ies.ed.gov/ncee/projects/nat_ed_library.asp

Sponsor(s): Education Department — National Library of Education (NLE)
Description: The NLE's one-page Web site states that NLE "serves as the federal
government's primary resource center for education information." The library,
located in Washington, DC, is open for public use. NLE staff also respond to phone,
Internet, fax and mail inquires.

This single Web page of text does little to help constituents do their own
education research. The site only describes NLE's collections and services. There
are no links out to education information resources.
Subjects: Education Research

285. National Library of Medicine

http://www.nlm.nih.gov/

Sponsor(s): National Institutes of Health (NIH) — National Library of Medicine
(NLM)
Description: As a leading center for health sciences information, NLM offers a wealth
of resources through its Web site. The site's home page provides quick links to
major NLM databases — such as PubMed and MedlinePlus — and to sections
customized for NLM client groups: the general public, health care professionals,

researchers, librarians, and publishers. Each customized section acts as a portal to relevant news, databases, publications, and specialized NLM Web resources. The site map helps to show the full scope of the Web site's content. It organizes links under the following headings: Health Information, Library Catalog and Services (includes NLM publications), History of Medicine, Online Exhibitions and Digital Projects, Human Genome Resources, Biomedical Research and Informatics (which the includes UMLS/Unified Medical Language System), Environmental Health and Toxicology, About the NLM, Grants and Funding, Training and Outreach, Network of Medical Libraries, and Health Services Research and Public Health.

The NLM Web site is a gateway to the various programs and information resources offered by the library. Many of the specific Web resources created by NLM are described elsewhere in this publication.

Subjects: Libraries; Medical Information
Publications: *Current Bibliographies in Medicine*, HE 20.3615/2:
List of Journals Indexed for MEDLINE, HE 20.3612/4:
List of Serials Indexed for Online Users (annual), HE 20.3618/2:
Medical Subject Headings, HE 20.3612/3-8:
National Library of Medicine Classification, HE 20.3602:
National Library of Medicine Fact Sheet, HE 20.3621:
National Library of Medicine Programs and Services, HE 20.3601:
NLM LOCATORplus, HE 20.3626:
NLM Newsline, HE 20.3619:
NLM Technical Bulletin (monthly), HE 20.3603/2:

286. National Library Services for the Blind and Physically Handicapped (NLS)

http://www.loc.gov/nls/
Sponsor(s): Library of Congress — National Library Services for the Blind and Physically Handicapped (NLS)
Description: NLS administers a free library program that circulates Braille and recorded materials to eligible borrowers through a network of cooperating libraries. The Learn section of its Web site has information on how NLS works. The following section, Find Books and Magazines in Braille or Audio, includes the online catalog of Braille and audio books, the *Braille Book Review* and other bibliographies. The NLS Publications section includes NLS fact sheets, bibliographies, circulars, and directories of libraries and resources related to reading material for the blind and physically handicapped. It also includes information on digital talking books and Web-Braille.

The NLS site is designed for text-based browsers, such as Lynx, that are frequently used by blind readers. See the About This Site section for more information.

Subjects: Libraries; Vision Disorders
Publications: *Braille Book Review*, LC 19.9:
For Younger Readers, Braille and Talking Books, LC 19.11/2:
Magazines in Special Media, LC 19.11/2-2:
News (NLS), LC 19.13:
Talking Book Topics, LC 19.10:
Update (NLS), LC 19.13/2:

287. National Network of Libraries of Medicine (NN/LM)

http://nnlm.gov/

Sponsor(s): National Institutes of Health (NIH) — National Library of Medicine (NLM)

Description: NN/LM is coordinated by NLM with the goal of improving access to medical information for both health professionals and the public. Its Web site has information about NN/LM services and a directory of the more than 5,000 member libraries. It features materials on teaching health literacy, evaluating medical information on the Internet, working with Spanish-speakers, and related consumer health education topics.

Librarians and health educators are the intended audiences for much of the information on this site. General public users interested in medical libraries and information systems may also find helpful material.

Subjects: Libraries; Medical Information

288. National Radio Astronomy Observatory Library

http://www.nrao.edu/library/

Sponsor(s): National Science Foundation (NSF) — National Radio Astronomy Observatory (NRAO)

Description: This Web site features the library's catalog and the RAPs database of published papers and preprints for staff and visitor works. Some sections of the site are restricted to NRAO staff.

Subjects: Astronomy — Research; Preprints

289. National Transportation Library (NTL)

http://ntl.bts.gov/

Sponsor(s): Transportation Department — Bureau of Transportation Statistics (BTS)

Description: NTL serves federal, state, and local governments. Its collection is entirely electronic. Resources available on its Web site include the NTL catalog, the TranStats transportation statistics database, the Transportation Research Thesaurus, and the cooperatively-produced TRIS Online database of published transportation literature. The Reference Sources section includes links to major transportation information sites and a directory of government and private transportation libraries in the United States and Canada.

Subjects: Transportation — Research

290. Navy Department Library

http://www.history.navy.mil/library/

Sponsor(s): Navy — Department of the Navy

Description: The Navy Department Library traces it beginnings to a request from President John Adams in 1800. The library's current Web site provides online access to its catalog of resources on the U.S. Navy and bibliographies on naval history. The Special Collections section includes selected images from its historical collections, such as Navy uniform regulations from 1797 to 1943. The site also has research guides on such topics as Navy cruise books and Navy documents at the National Archives.

Subjects: Navy — History

291. NCAR Library

http://www.ucar.edu/library/

Sponsor(s): National Science Foundation (NSF)

Description: The National Center for Atmospheric Research (NCAR) Library Web site includes its online catalog and information about the library and its services.

Many of the featured databases are agency subscriptions that are restricted to authorized users.

Subjects: Atmospheric Sciences — Research

292. NIEHS Library

http://library.niehs.nih.gov/

Sponsor(s): National Institutes of Health (NIH) — National Institute of Environmental Health Sciences (NIEHS)

Description: The NIEHS Library serves the scientific and administrative staff of NIEHS, but also provides limited services to the public. Publicly accessible resources on its Web site include the Research Links and Consumer Health Links sections.

Subjects: Health and Safety — Research

293. NIH Library Online

http://nihlibrary.nih.gov/

Sponsor(s): National Institutes of Health (NIH)

Description: The NIH Library Online Web site features information about the library and services. Most information is restricted to authorized users.

Subjects: Medical Information

294. Nimitz Library

http://www.nadn.navy.mil/Library/

Sponsor(s): Navy — United States Naval Academy (USNA)

Description: The Nimitz Library Web site features information about the library and its services. Sections that may be of use to those not enrolled at the Naval Academy include Research Guides by Subject and Electronic Reference Shelf. The online "Reading List for Life" lists books recommended by faculty on a wide range of topics, such as astronomy, engineering, literature, history, physics, and sociology.

Subjects: Engineering Research

295. NIST Virtual Library

http://nvl.nist.gov/

Sponsor(s): Commerce Department — Technology Administration (TA) — National Institute of Standards and Technology (NIST)

Description: Beyond general information about the library and its services, the NIST Virtual Library Web site offers its online catalog, standards information, and subject guides. While many resources on the site are restricted to NIST staff, the subject guides are — for the most part — available to the public. They link to Internet resources on such topics as chemistry, engineering, and physics.

Subjects: Scientific and Technical Information

Publications: *Journal of Research of the National Institute of Standards and Technology,* C 13.22:

296. NOAA Central Library

http://www.lib.noaa.gov/

Sponsor(s): Commerce Department — National Oceanic and Atmospheric Administration (NOAA)

Description: The NOAA Central Library Web site features WINDandSea, a directory of over 1,000 links to Web sites concerned with oceanic and atmospheric issues. The site also includes NOAALINC, the online library catalog, and NOAA Browser, a directory of links to over 500 NOAA science, policy, and administrative Web

sites. The NOAA Library and Information Network section provides links to NOAA libraries by state.
Subjects: Atmospheric Sciences — Research; Oceanography — Research

297. NOAA Seattle Regional Library
http://www.wrclib.noaa.gov/lib/
Sponsor(s): Commerce Department — National Oceanic and Atmospheric Administration (NOAA)
Description: This regional NOAA library serves NOAA agencies in the West. Basic library information, such as hours, policies, and services, are provided, along with access to the online catalog, charts and maps, and links to NOAA's many environmental databases.
Subjects: Atmospheric Sciences — Research

298. Northwest and Alaska Fisheries Science Centers Library
http://lib.nwfsc.noaa.gov/
Sponsor(s): Commerce Department — National Oceanic and Atmospheric Administration (NOAA) — National Marine Fisheries
Description: This library supports the centers and field stations located in the Pacific Northwest and Alaska that serve NOAA's National Marine Fisheries Service (NMFS). Its Web site has several directories of links, covering such topics as fisheries and charts, with an emphasis on the Pacific region.
Subjects: Fisheries — Research

299. Patent and Trademark Depository Library Program
http://www.uspto.gov/go/ptdl/
Sponsor(s): Commerce Department — Patent and Trademark Office (PTO)
Description: The PTO designates qualified libraries throughout the country to act as Patent and Trademark Depository Libraries. These libraries receive printed materials and electronic access from the PTO to better assist users in the general public who are in need of patent and trademark information. This Web site describes the program's operations, provides links to depository and partner library Web sites, and lists the core publications and databases available through these libraries.
Subjects: Libraries; Patent Law; Trademarks

300. Presidential Libraries
http://www.archives.gov/presidential-libraries/
Sponsor(s): National Archives and Records Administration (NARA) — Presidential Libraries Office
Description: This National Archives Web page provides general information about the presidential libraries system and guides for doing research in presidential materials. Links to each of the presidential libraries Web sites are provided. The libraries in the system are the George Bush Library, the Carter Library, the Clinton Library, the Eisenhower Library, the Ford Library, the Hoover Library, the Johnson Library, the Kennedy Library, the Nixon Presidential Materials Staff, the Reagan Library, the Roosevelt Library, and the Truman Library.
Subjects: Presidential Documents

301. Ralph J. Bunche Library
http://www.state.gov/m/a/ls/
Sponsor(s): State Department
Description: This Web site offers a description of the main Department of State library. Its mission is to support the research needs of State Department personnel,

and it offers few services to the public. The site calls the State Department's library "the oldest Federal Government library. . .founded by the first Secretary of State, Thomas Jefferson in 1789."
Subjects: Foreign Policy — Research

302. Ruth H. Hooker Research Library InfoWeb
http://library.nrl.navy.mil/
Sponsor(s): Navy — Naval Research Laboratory (NRL)
Description: The Naval Research Laboratory library focuses on such topics as chemistry, meteorology, oceanography, physics, and space sciences, in support of the laboratory's staff. While some sections of its Web site are restricted to staff, the online catalog is publicly available. In the Find Any Book section, the catalog covers the library's books, journals, and unclassified reports. Both public Web and restricted-access resources on numerous science and general topics are linked in the Browse by Subject and Resources by Format sections.
Subjects: Engineering Research

303. Scientific Library, National Cancer Institute — Frederick
http://www-library.ncifcrf.gov/
Sponsor(s): National Institutes of Health (NIH) — National Cancer Institute (NCI)
Description: The Scientific Library's Web site offers public access to its online catalog and a selected list of links to Internet resources. These resources relate to biomedicine, bioterrorism, chemistry, veterinary science, patents, and other related topics.
Subjects: Medical Information

304. Smithsonian Institution Libraries
http://www.sil.si.edu/
Sponsor(s): Smithsonian Institution
Description: This is the principal starting point for information about the various Smithsonian Institution libraries. Sections include Exhibitions, Digital Library, Libraries, Special Collections, Research and Internships, and Giving to the Libraries. The Digital Library section is a gateway to everything from annual reports and fact sheets to the library catalog and bibliographies. Many of the online resources are included in the site's Galaxy of Knowledge section, which features collections in science, industry, art, and American history.
Subjects: Libraries

305. U.S. Geological Survey Library
http://library.usgs.gov/
Sponsor(s): Interior Department — U.S. Geological Survey (USGS)
Description: Established in 1879, the USGS Library's Web site "is now the largest library for earth sciences in the world" (from the Web site). The site links to many of the USGS online research resources, including the USGS Publications Warehouse, and maintains links to online resources on mapping and geography. It also provides online copies of the *USGS Enterprise Web Thesaurus* and the *U.S. Geological Survey Library Classification System*.
Subjects: Geology — Research; Maps and Mapping
Publications: *U.S. Geological Survey Library Classification System*, I 19.3:2010

306. United States Naval Observatory Library
http://www.usno.navy.mil/library/
Sponsor(s): Navy — Naval Observatory (USNO)
Description: This site provides access to the USNO Library's online catalog and collection of historical photos. It also has historical photos of the library, dating back to the 1890s. The Astronomical Resources section provides links to selected Web sites.
Subjects: Astronomy — Research

307. USACE Library Program
http://www.usace.army.mil/library/
Sponsor(s): Army — Army Corps of Engineers
Description: The U.S. Army Corps of Engineers Library Program Web site features an online union catalog for the Army Corps of Engineers libraries and a directory of participating libraries.
Subjects: Civil Engineering — Research

308. USAID Library
http://library.info.usaid.gov/
Sponsor(s): Agency for International Development (USAID)
Description: The USAID Library is concerned with agency information and information about the topic of sustainable development. Its Web site offers the library catalog, the Development Experience Clearinghouse, and a guide to conducting research on past USAID activities.
Subjects: International Economic Development — Research

309. Wirtz Labor Library
http://www.dol.gov/oasam/library/
Sponsor(s): Labor Department
Description: The Department of Labor's Wirtz Labor Library has a Web site with information about labor, law, and the library's special collections. The site has an online catalog and an extensive list of links for further labor-related research. The Law Library section features a "Law Tip of the Week," available online or by free e-mail subscription. The Internet Bibliographies section provides links to resources for commemorative occasions, such as African American History Month, Labor Day, and Hispanic Heritage Month.
Subjects: Libraries; Employment Law

Museums

310. Anacostia Community Museum
http://anacostia.si.edu/
Sponsor(s): Smithsonian Institution
Description: The Smithsonian Institution's Anacostia Community Museum focuses on the history and culture of the African American community and family. It is located in the historic Washington, DC, neighborhood of Anacostia, the former home of abolitionist Frederick Douglass. The museum's Web site has information on visiting, exhibits, events, and Anacostia history. Its On-line Academy section presents expert information on African American historical materials.

Previously, the museum was called the Anacostia Museum and Center for African American History and Culture. The name was changed in 2006 to distin-

guish it from the Smithsonian's planned National Museum of African American History and Culture.
Subjects: History; Museums

311. Cooper Hewitt, National Design Museum
http://ndm.si.edu/
Sponsor(s): Smithsonian Institution
Description: The Cooper-Hewitt, in New York City, concentrates on historic and contemporary design. Its Web site has information on the museum, its education programs, and the annual National Design Awards.
Subjects: Arts — Awards and Honors; Museums

312. Hill Aerospace Museum
http://www.hill.af.mil/museum/
Sponsor(s): Air Force — Hill Aerospace Museum
Description: Located at Hill Air Force Base in Utah, the Hill Aerospace Museum collection includes a wide variety of military aircraft and missiles, assorted munitions and weapons, ground vehicles associated with aircraft and missiles, and thousands of other historical artifacts. Its Web site provides information about visiting, museum activities and exhibits, and base history.
Subjects: Aviation — History

313. National Air and Space Museum
http://www.nasm.si.edu/
Sponsor(s): Smithsonian Institution
Description: The National Air and Space Museum offers information about the museum and its programs, including the Steven F. Udvar-Hazy Center, which provides and exhibition hangar, theater, and classrooms. This Web site features a visitor guide and information about the museum's collections, educational programs, research, events, and membership.
Subjects: Aviation; Museums

314. National Gallery of Art
http://www.nga.gov/
Sponsor(s): National Gallery of Art (NGA)
Description: On the NGA Web site, the Planning a Visit section includes information about location and the gallery's hours, as well as maps and information about how the NGA is organized and funded. The Collection section offers searches of the collections by author, title, or subject; searches can also be limited to items for which online images are available. An Online Tour section provides more than 50 online tours, organized by theme or artist. The Resources section covers a broad scope, with links to information on the Arts Research Library (with online catalog), the Center for Advanced Study in the Visual Arts, curatorial records, the gallery's archives, the Slide Library, and press materials including news of current exhibitions and recent acquisitions.
Subjects: Museums; Visual Arts

315. National Museum of African American History and Culture
http://www.nmaahc.si.edu/
Sponsor(s): Smithsonian Institution
Description: Authorized by law in 2003, the National Museum of African American History and Culture is now in the planning stages. Its Web site has information about the museum's goals, leadership, funding, and planning.
Subjects: African Americans — History; Museums

316. National Museum of African Art
http://www.nmafa.si.edu/
Sponsor(s): Smithsonian Institution
Description: The National Museum of African Art Web site has information about its exhibits, programs, collections, library, and archives. The Research section has a collections catalog that can be browsed visually or searched by a variety of criteria. The Radio Africa section has African music from the Smithsonian Institution and art discussions available as podcasts. The site also has a section of activities for children.
   This is a colorful, multimedia site that makes use of high quality photographs, sound, and images.
Subjects: Museums; Visual Arts; Africa

317. National Museum of American History
http://americanhistory.si.edu/
Sponsor(s): Smithsonian Institution
Description: The National Museum of American History provides images, online exhibits, and research information related to American history. Educational resources are available in the Kids and Educators sections. The museum itself will be closed from fall 2006 to summer 2008 for renovation; the site has information about the project status.
Subjects: Museums; United States — History

318. National Museum of Health and Medicine
http://nmhm.washingtondc.museum/
Sponsor(s): Defense Department — Armed Forces Institute of Pathology (AFIP)
Description: The National Museum of Health and Medicine's main focus is on American military medicine. Its collections include anatomical specimens and medical devices, many of which are from the Civil War era (when the museum was established). This Web site has online guides to the museum's collections and photographs of many of its exhibits.
Subjects: Medicine and Medical Devices — History; Museums

319. National Museum of Natural History
http://www.mnh.si.edu/
Sponsor(s): Smithsonian Institution
Description: This Web site presents information about the National Museum of Natural History's exhibits, collections, programs, and research. The Information Desk section has facts for visitors. The Research and Collections section features a collections database, bibliographies, and links to Department of Science Web sites for anthropology, botany, entomology, mineral sciences, paleobiology, and zoology. The site also has information about the museum's new educational Ocean Initiative.
Subjects: Museums; Natural History

320. National Museum of the American Indian (NMAI)
http://www.nmai.si.edu/
Sponsor(s): Smithsonian Institution
Description: This Web site describes the three Smithsonian NMAI facilities: the George Gustav Heye Center in New York City; the Cultural Resources Center in Suitland, MD; and NMAI on the National Mall in Washington, DC. Major sections include Visitor Information, Exhibitions, Events, Outreach, Education, and Collections.
Subjects: Museums; American Indians

321. National Postal Museum
http://www.si.edu/postal/
Sponsor(s): Smithsonian Institution
Description: The National Postal Museum is funded by the U.S. Postal Service, the Smithsonian Institution's federal appropriation, and private gifts. The museum's collections include stamps, vehicles used to transport the mail, mailboxes, postage meters, and greeting cards. Major sections of its Web site include Exhibits, Collection, Educators, Stamp Collecting, and the Activity Zone (for both kids and adults).
Subjects: Postage Stamps; Postal Service — History

322. Naval Undersea Museum
http://naval.undersea.museum/
Sponsor(s): Navy — Naval Sea Systems Command (NAVSEA)
Description: The Naval Undersea Museum in northwest Washington State presents submarines, torpedoes, diving equipment, and other artifacts related to naval undersea history, science, and operations. This Web site includes online exhibits, photos of the collection, and information about visiting the museum. The museum library's catalog is also available online.
Subjects: Museums; Underwater Warfare — History

323. Smithsonian American Art Museum (SAAM)
http://americanart.si.edu/
Sponsor(s): Smithsonian Institution
Description: This Web site features images of hundreds of works of art and information about current exhibits and events. Featured sections include Search Collections, Art Information Resources, Photo Study Collections, and Researching Your Art. An Ask Joan of Art section addresses public inquiries about American art.

The SAAM site also has information about the Renwick Gallery, which specializes in American crafts and decorative arts.
Subjects: Arts; Museums
Publications: *American Art*

324. United States Botanic Garden
http://www.usbg.gov/
Sponsor(s): Congress — Architect of the Capitol
Description: The United States Botanic Garden Web site has information about its gardens, production facility, and conservatory on the National Mall. The site offers visitor information, a virtual tour, and a description of the Botanic Garden's plant collections and work in plant conservation.
Subjects: Botany

325. United States Holocaust Memorial Museum
http://www.ushmm.org/
Sponsor(s): United States Holocaust Memorial Council
Description: The United States Holocaust Memorial Museum became an independent establishment of the United States government under Public Law 106-292. The museum's Web site provides information about the museum and resources on Holocaust education, research, and history. It features a *Holocaust Encyclopedia* in English, French, and Spanish. The Conscience section discusses contemporary genocide and related acts of organized violence.
Subjects: Museums; War Crimes — History

Recreation

326. Corps Lakes Gateway

http://corpslakes.usace.army.mil/visitors/
Alternate URL(s): http://www.corpslakes.us/
Sponsor(s): Army — Army Corps of Engineers
Description: Corps Lakes Gateway describes outdoor recreation opportunities at lakes managed by the Army Corps of Engineers. The site has a clickable U.S. map for finding Corps lakes and information about them.
Subjects: Lakes; Outdoor Recreation

327. Forest Service National Avalanche Center

http://www.fsavalanche.org/
Sponsor(s): Agriculture Department (USDA) — Forest Service (USFS)
Description: This Forest Service site provides avalanche awareness information and interactive guides for snowmobilers, skiers, snowboarders, snowshoers and others exploring the steep and snowy backcountry. It also links to the regional avalanche center Web sites for reports on local conditions.
Subjects: Outdoor Recreation

328. Hunting

http://hunting.fws.gov/
Sponsor(s): Interior Department — Fish and Wildlife Service (FWS)
Description: While the hunting of wildlife within state boundaries is largely the concern of state fish and wildlife agencies, the U.S. Fish and Wildlife Service is ultimately responsible for regulating migratory bird hunting nationwide. This Web site has answers to frequently asked questions about migratory bird hunting.
Subjects: Outdoor Recreation

329. National Park Service

http://www.nps.gov/
Sponsor(s): Interior Department — National Park Service (NPS)
Description: The official NPS Web site is the primary source for information about America's national parks. It includes information about national memorials, national battlefields, national seashores, national historic sites, and other related sites. The Parks and Recreation section links to information on each of the NPS locations by name, state, or interest (such as fossils, fishing, or battlefields). Individual parks have their own Web pages, which contain printable travel guides, maps, and background information. The History and Culture section describes significant people, places, and events associated with the national parks. It offers learning programs and information about historic preservation grants. The Nature and Science section covers natural resources data and publications; major topics are air, biology, geology, natural sounds, and water. The Nature and Science section also has an Explore Topics sidebar, which links to coverage of current issues, laws, regulations, policy, guidance, and publications. The Interpretation and Education section focuses on teacher resources.

With its broad approach to the resources and heritage of the national parks system, the NPS Web site is relevant for many audiences, including travelers, scientists, history buffs, and teachers.
Subjects: Historic Preservation; National Parks and Reserves
Publications: *Conserve O Gram*, I 29.100:
CRM (Cultural Resources Management), I 29.86/2:
National Park Statistical Abstract, I 29.114:

National Register Information System, I 29.76/4:
National Register of Historic Places Bulletins, I 29.76/3:
Natural Resource Year in Review, I 29.1/4:
Park Science, Resource Management Bulletin (quarterly), I 29.3/4:
Preservation Briefs, I 29.84:
Yellowstone Center for Resources (annual), I 29.138/2:
Yellowstone Wolf Project Annual Report, I 29.138:

330. National Scenic Byways Program
http://www.byways.org/
Sponsor(s): Transportation Department — Federal Highway Administration (FHWA)
Description: The Department of Transportation has designated certain roads as National Scenic Byways, or All-American Roads, based on their archaeological, cultural, historic, natural, recreational, and scenic qualities. This Web site provides information about the National Scenic Byways Program and each of the designated roads or byways. It offers maps and descriptions of noteworthy sites along the routes.
Subjects: Highways and Roads

331. National Trails System
http://www.nps.gov/ncrc/programs/nts/
Sponsor(s): Interior Department — National Park Service (NPS)
Description: The National Trails System is a network of scenic, historic, and recreational trails administered by the Department of the Interior and the Department of Agriculture in partnership with other agencies and organizations. Its Web site includes a trail system map, information about designating national scenic and national historic trails, and a link to the nonprofit Partnership for the National Trails System organization's Web site.
Subjects: Outdoor Recreation

332. National Zoological Park
http://natzoo.si.edu/
Sponsor(s): Smithsonian Institution
Description: The National Zoo's Web site features information for visitors and pictures and information about the animals. The Giant Pandas section (under the Animals heading) has PandaCams, a panda photo gallery, and giant panda facts. The Education section includes subsections on Classroom Resources, Teacher Workshops, Wildlife Careers, and Professional Training Courses. A section entitled Conservation and Science: The Hidden Zoo has information about zoological medicine, land and aquatic ecosystems, and endangered species science.
Subjects: Animals; Conservation Biology; Zoos

333. Presidio Trust
http://www.presidio.gov/
Sponsor(s): Presidio Trust
Description: The Presidio, a former U.S. Army installation in San Francisco, is now a National Historic Landmark District. It is managed by the Presidio Trust, a federal agency established by Congress in 1996. This Web site provides information about the management of the Presidio and visiting the park.
Subjects: Historic Sites

334. Recreation Maps
http://www.recreationmaps.gov/
Sponsor(s): General Services Administration (GSA)
Description: The Recreation Maps Web site has a database of recreation locations that can be searched by activity and geographic area. Maps of the desired locations can be customized to show features such as highways and federal land type (e.g., National Forest or National Preserve).
Subjects: Maps and Mapping; Outdoor Recreation

335. Recreation.gov
http://www.recreation.gov/
Sponsor(s): General Services Administration (GSA)
Description: Recreation.gov is designed to be a central source of recreation information from federal and local land management agencies. Users can find recreation locations by state or activity (such as boating, camping, fishing, or hiking). Recreation location information includes phone numbers, addresses, URLs, descriptions of activities, and types of recreational opportunities at that site. Recreation.gov also links to state recreation and tourism information, reservations information, federal recreation pass program information, and recreation maps.
Subjects: Outdoor Recreation

336. ReserveUSA.com
http://www.reserveusa.com/
Sponsor(s): Army — Army Corps of Engineers; Interior Department — National Park Service (NPS)
Description: The National Recreation Reservation Service offers reservation services for USDA Forest Service, Army Corps of Engineers, National Park Service, Bureau of Land Management, and Bureau of Reclamation outdoor recreation facilities and activities. Facility information typically includes reservation options, a park map, and information about services and amenities.

337. U.S. Air Force Entertainment Liaison
http://www.airforcehollywood.af.mil/
Sponsor(s): Air Force
Description: The U.S. Air Force Entertainment Liaison provides information and assistance to those planning movies and television programs with Air Force themes or segments. This Web site provides a description of their services and examples of projects on which they have consulted.
Subjects: Movies

338. U.S. National Parks Reservation Service
http://reservations.nps.gov/
Sponsor(s): Interior Department — National Park Service (NPS)
Description: This is the official Web site for making reservations at and checking availability of National Park campgrounds and tours. Not all NPS campgrounds and tours are available via this system, but the reservation service allows online booking and reservations for available sites.
Subjects: National Parks and Reserves

339. USDA Forest Service Recreational Activities
http://www.fs.fed.us/recreation/
Sponsor(s): Agriculture Department (USDA) — Forest Service (USFS)
Description: The Forest Service offers this Web site as an overview of the recreational opportunities and the guidelines for the use of national forests and grasslands.

The forests and grasslands can be found by using a clickable map or by browsing by state or site name. Other sections provide information about passes, permits, and travel advisories.

Subjects: National Forests

340. USGS Recreation

`http://recreation.usgs.gov/`

Sponsor(s): Interior Department — U.S. Geological Survey (USGS)

Description: This Web site is subtitled "Your Science Gateway for Safe and Vital Enjoyment of the Outdoors." It serves as a portal to USGS and other government information relevant to outdoor activities. Sections include Nature Watching/ Exploration, Boating, Camping, Climbing, Fishing, Hiking/Biking, and Hunting. Resources include maps, weather data, bird checklists, tide predictions, safety tips, and educational information about geology.

Subjects: Outdoor Recreation

Reference

341. Geographic Names Information System

`http://geonames.usgs.gov/domestic/`

Sponsor(s): Interior Department — U.S. Geological Survey (USGS)

Description: The Geographic Names Information System (GNIS) database has federally recognized names of physical and cultural geographic features in the United States and its territories. Geographic features are defined broadly and include populated places, as well as airports, cemeteries, mines, lakes, rivers, streams, schools, beaches, and parks. For each feature, GNIS provides coordinates, state and county, and feature type. The site includes the FIPS55 database, which contains the Federal Information Processing Standard (FIPS) data processing codes for named populated places, primary county divisions, and other locational entities of the United States and areas under the jurisdiction of the United States.

Subjects: Geography; Reference

342. Official U.S. Time

`http://www.time.gov/`

Sponsor(s): Commerce Department — Technology Administration (TA) — National Institute of Standards and Technology (NIST); Navy — Naval Observatory (USNO)

Description: This Web site provides the current time in all U.S. time zones, including the time zones for the U.S. Pacific territories. The Time Exhibits section of the site links to educational sites about time, clocks, daylight savings time, and calendars.

Subjects: Time

343. Plain Language

`http://www.plainlanguage.gov/`

Sponsor(s): Chief Information Officers Council

Description: The Plain Language Web site focuses on improving communications from the federal government to the public. The idea is to use "plain language" that can be understood at first reading. The intended audience is government agencies. The site includes relevant examples, guidelines, and resources. It is hosted by the Federal Aviation Administration and sponsored by the Web Content Management Working Group of the Interagency Committee on Government Information (ICGI).

While this is intended for government writers, other writers will also find it to be a useful reference as well.
Subjects: Writing — Policy
Publications: *Writing User-Friendly Documents*

344. Popular Baby Names
http://www.socialsecurity.gov/OACT/babynames/
Sponsor(s): Social Security Administration (SSA)
Description: This database of trends in baby names is compiled from names listed on Social Security card applications. Users can search for the most popular baby names by year and by state, track the popularity of a name over time, or look up popular names for twins.
Subjects: Families

345. Social Security Death Index
http://www.ntis.gov/products/pages/ssa-death-master.asp
Sponsor(s): Commerce Department — Technology Administration (TA) — National Technical Information Service (NTIS); Social Security Administration (SSA)
Description: The Social Security Death Index database has basic information on deceased persons who possessed Social Security numbers and whose deaths have been reported to the Social Security Administration. Records include name, Social Security number, dates of birth and death, and ZIP code of last residence. NTIS makes the database available through a paid online subscription or purchase of file downloads. This Web site describes the Death Master File and subscription options in detail.
   The Death Master File is available for free from various online services and at many libraries. An example is the Search for Ancestors section on the Family-Search Web site, which is managed by the Church of Latter-Day Saints and is available at ⟨http://www.familysearch.org/⟩.
Subjects: Genealogy; Social Security; Databases

CHAPTER 5

Defense and Intelligence

The national defense, homeland security, and intelligence operations of the United States are all represented to varying degrees on the Internet. The Department of Defense and the nation's armed forces, in particular, maintain numerous publicly accessible Web sites. These sites cover topics ranging from current military operations, to advanced research, to daily contracts and acquisitions matters. Researchers may also wish to check the International Relations chapter for information about arms treaties, or the Education chapter for information about the educational activities managed by the Defense Department and the armed forces.

Subsections in this chapter are Armed Forces, Defense Operations, Defense Research, Homeland Security, Intelligence, and Military Morale and Welfare.

Armed Forces

346. Air and Space Power Chronicles
http://www.airpower.maxwell.af.mil/
Sponsor(s): Air Force
Description: *Air and Space Power Journal*, the focus of this Web site, is an Air Force magazine that works to promote professional dialogue and development among military airmen. This site also carries *Chronicles Online Journal* (an online companion to *Air and Space Power Journal*). Current issues of *Aerospace Power Journal* are available in HTML and PDF formats. Archival issues back to 1967 are available in HTML format. Archival issues of *Air University Review*, which preceded the journals, are indexed and available online for 1971 through 1987.

Versions of *Air and Space Power Journal* in Arabic, French, Portuguese, and Spanish are also available at this site.
Subjects: Air Force
Publications: *Air and Space Power Journal*, D 301.26/24:
Air University Review, D 301.26:
Chronicles Online Journal

347. Air Combat Command
http://www.acc.af.mil/
Sponsor(s): Air Force — Air Combat Command (ACC)
Description: ACC, headquartered at Langley Air Force Base in Virginia, provides air combat forces for the Unified Combatant Commands. Its Web site has a Units section with links to each ACC subordinate unit and a Library section with leadership information. Other sections provide news, photos, and art (including images of official shields and aircraft).
Subjects: Military Aircraft

348. Air Education and Training Command
http://www.aetc.af.mil/
Sponsor(s): Air Force — Air Education and Training Command (AETC)
Description: AETC is responsible for Air Force programs in military, technical, and flight training, as well as education programs at many levels, including programs for security assistance, medical and dental, and officer development. This Web site provides information on Air Force career opportunities, tuition assistance,

the GI Bill, basic military training, technical training, and flying training. It also links to the Air Force Academy, Air Force ROTC, and Community College of the Air Force.
Subjects: Military Training and Education

349. Air Force Cyberspace Command
http://www.8af.acc.af.mil/
Sponsor(s): Air Force
Description: The Secretary of the Air Force designated the 8th Air Force as the new Cyberspace Command in November 2006. The 8th Air Force Web site began to carry news of the new command as this book was going to press.
Subjects: Air Force; Military Computing

350. Air Force Inspection Agency
http://afia.kirtland.af.mil/
Sponsor(s): Air Force — Air Force Inspection Agency (AFIA)
Description: AFIA's mission is to provide Air Force senior leaders with independent assessments of mission capability, health care, and resource management. The agency conducts management reviews and health inspections and provides guidance and information for Air Force commanders, inspectors general, and inspectors. The AFIA site has information about the history and organization of the agency. The Air Force Inspector General's magazine, *TIG Brief*, is described but not available to the public online.
Subjects: Inspectors General

351. Air Force Link — Official Web Site of the U.S. Air Force
http://www.af.mil/
Sponsor(s): Air Force
Description: The emphasis of this central Air Force Web site is on current news. Along with a wealth of articles, the site provides Air Force TV and radio programs and has sections for Air Force photos and art. In addition to current news, a Heritage section describes major milestones from the past and includes feature articles and illustrations.

One of the most useful parts of the site is the Sites section, which links to Air Force base Web sites and sites for major commands. The Library section has a wealth of links to Air Force magazines and base newspapers, biographies of Air Force leaders, and fact sheets on aircraft. The Careers section provides personnel information for enlisted servicemembers, officers, civilians, and retirees.

This is the first place to look for Air Force information. The site is well organized, offers substantial information content, and is easy to navigate.
Subjects: Air Force
Publications: *Air Force News*, D 301.122:
Air Force Policy Letter Digest, D 301.120:
Airman, D 301.60:
Report of Air Force Research Regarding the Roswell Incident, D 301.2:R 73/2/
United States Air Force Posture Statement, D 301.1/3:

352. Air Force Personnel Center
http://ask.afpc.randolph.af.mil/
Sponsor(s): Air Force — Air Force Personnel Center (AFPC)
Description: The AFPC Web site serves as a portal to information for and about military and civilian Air Force personnel. Topics include career planning, retire-

ment, personnel statistics and demographics, and family support services. Not all sections of the site can be accessed by the public.

Subjects: Air Force; Civilian Defense Employees

353. Air Force Reserve Command

http://www.afrc.af.mil/

Sponsor(s): Air Force — Air Force Reserve (AFRES)

Description: The Air Force Reserve Command Web site features news, leadership biographies, fact sheets, weapon systems, and unit information. The Join section links to the official recruiting page. The Library section's Employer Resources subsection links to the Web site for the National Committee for Employer Support of the Guard and Reserve.

Subjects: Military Reserves

Publications: *Air Force Reserve Handbook for Congress*
Citizen Airman, D 301.8:

354. Air Force Space Command

http://www.afspc.af.mil/

Sponsor(s): Air Force — Air Force Space Command

Description: The Air Force Space Command Web site has current news and links to the various command newspapers online. The site also has a directory of unit locations and a Library section that provides leadership biographies and other reference information. The online *Air Force Space Command Almanac* provides an overview of the command's history and operations.

Subjects: Air Force; Rockets

Publications: *Air Force Space Command Almanac*
High Frontier, D 301.130:

355. Air Mobility Command

http://www.amc.af.mil/

Sponsor(s): Air Force — Air Mobility Command (AMC)

Description: AMC's mission is to provide airlift, air refueling, special air mission, and aeromedical evacuation for U.S. forces. Its public Web site provides current news, links to base newspapers, and biographies of AMC leadership. The Library section features a tally of AMC support for Operation Enduring Freedom and Operation Iraqi Freedom, including the total number of missions flown and troops moved. The Library section also features fact sheets, history, photos, information on "space available" travel on AMC flights, and airlifts for non-Defense goods and personnel.

Subjects: Airlifts; Military Logistics

356. Airforce.com

http://www.airforce.com/

Sponsor(s): Air Force

Description: This Air Force recruitment Web site offers information for prospective recruits at all levels. An Education section includes links to the Air Force Academy and Reserve Office Training Corps Web sites. A version of the recruitment site is also available in Spanish.

Subjects: Military Recruiting

357. Army and Army Reserves Recruiting
http://www.goarmy.com/
Sponsor(s): ArmyArmy — Army Reserves (USAR)
Description: Established as a recruitment site for both the Army and the Army Reserves, this Web site features information likely to be of interest to prospective members. It includes sections on careers, benefits, and soldier life, with an extra section for parents. The site also offers a Spanish-language online chat for questions.
Subjects: Military Recruiting

358. Army Public Affairs
http://www4.army.mil/ocpa/menu.php
Sponsor(s): Army
Description: The Army Public Affairs Web site is replete with links to general Army information, Army community relations news, Army online news publications, and other resources for the news media. The site features current headlines from the Army News Service and provides many links to other Army sites.
Subjects: Army

359. Army Publishing Directorate
http://www.apd.army.mil
Sponsor(s): Army — Army Publishing Agency (USAPA)
Description: The Publishing Directorate is the Army's agency for publishing and distributing information products. Its Web site features electronic forms and publications, ordering information, and administrative news. The Official Army Publications Sites section links to a multitude of resources for Army documents.
Subjects: Military Publishing

360. Assistant Chief of Staff for Installation Management (ACSIM)
http://www.hqda.army.mil/acsimweb/homepage.shtml
Sponsor(s): Army
Description: ACSIM is the Army's proponent for military bases and the soldiers, civilians, and families who live on them. The Organizational Links section includes BRAC (Base Realignment and Closure), CFSC (Community and Family Support Center), and Facilities and Housing subsections. The Functional Links section covers Army real property and congressional actions (tracking military spending bills and related legislation). The References section includes an index of the Web site's topics.
Subjects: Military Bases and Installations

361. Assistant Secretary of the Army for Acquisition, Logistics, and Technology
https://webportal.saalt.army.mil/
Sponsor(s): Army
Description: This Web site is a central location for regulations, policies, and other documentation for the Army Acquisition Community. It links to leadership information, news, and resources. Some links are restricted to authorized users.
Subjects: Military Procurement
Publications: *Army AL&T Magazine*, D 101.52/3:

362. Bureau of Naval Personnel

http://www.npc.navy.mil/channels

Sponsor(s): Navy — Naval Personnel Bureau

Description: The Bureau of Naval Personnel Web site serves current officers and enlisted personnel by providing information about pay, benefits, career progression, and quality of life services. It also includes information for retirees. The Reference Library section provides Navy personnel forms, manuals, and regulations, as well as links to various publications, such as *Link-Perspective* for Navy professionals and *Shift Colors* for retirees.

The site will primarily be of interest to people in the Navy. Some sections are only open to authorized, registered users.

Subjects: Defense Administration

Publications: *LINK Magazine,* D 208.19/2:

Shift Colors, The Newsletter for Navy Retirees, D 208.12/3-2:

363. Center for Army Lessons Learned (CALL)

http://call.army.mil/

Sponsor(s): Army — Center for Army Lessons Learned (CALL)

Description: According to its Web site, CALL's mission is to "collect and analyze data from a variety of current and historical sources, including Army operations and training events, and produces lessons for military commanders, staff, and students. CALL disseminates these lessons and other research materials via a variety of print and electronic media, including this Web site." Public versions of the CALL database and the CALL thesaurus are available. CALL also has its own search engine for the ".mil" domain.

Subjects: Military Information

Publications: *Center for Army Lessons Learned,* D 101.22/25:

364. DefendAMERICA

http://www.defendamerica.mil/

Sponsor(s): Defense Department

Description: The DefendAMERICA Web site was set up after the September 11, 2001, terrorist attacks to carry news of the U.S. military's efforts to fight global terrorism. Using a news format, the site features current articles and photos, along with audio and video files. Special news sections include Iraq, Afghanistan, and the War on Terrorism.

Subjects: Military Operations; Terrorism; Afghanistan ; Iraq

365. Headquarters Air Force Materiel Command

http://www.afmc.af.mil/

Sponsor(s): Air Force — Air Force Materiel Command (AFMC)

Description: Headquartered at Wright-Patterson Air Force Base, AFMC equips and supplies the Air Force through supply management, depot maintenance, systems testing and evaluation, information services, and combat support. The AFMC Web site has current news and background on the command's organization and programs. The Units section links to AFMC field operating agencies, air logistics centers, test centers, laboratories, and other establishments. The Library section includes fact sheets, speeches, and links to unit newspapers.

Subjects: Military Logistics; Military Supplies

366. Headquarters Air Reserve Personnel Center

http://arpc.afrc.af.mil/

Sponsor(s): Air Force — Air Force Reserve (AFRES)

Description: The AFRES Personnel Center Web site has information about assignments, mobilization, family assistance, decorations, retirement, separations and discharges, benefits for reservists, and other related topics.

Subjects: Military Reserves

367. Headquarters Marine Corps (HQMC)

http://www.hqmc.usmc.mil/

Sponsor(s): Marine Corps

Description: This Web site offers links to the Marine Corps Headquarters agencies and offices and provides biographies for active, retired, and deceased officers. It also provides links to Marine Corps units and publications. Access to some sections may require registration.

Subjects: Marine Corps

368. Joint Chiefs of Staff — JCS Link

http://www.dtic.mil/jcs/

Sponsor(s): Defense Department — Joint Chiefs of Staff

Description: The JCS Link Web site provides information about the chairman of the Joint Chiefs of Staff, the Joint Chiefs, Joint Staff, and the combatant commands. It also provides links to news, JCS speeches, and historical information with biographies of former chairmen.

Subjects: Military Leadership

Publications: *Joint Electronic Library*, D 5.21:

369. Joint Forces Command

http://www.jfcom.mil/

Sponsor(s): Defense Department — Joint Forces Command

Description: The Joint Forces Command has responsibility for strategic issues, the training of joint forces, and the integration of U.S. military capabilities. Headquartered in Norfolk, VA, they are one of nine unified commands in the Department of Defense. Its Web site provides information on their mission, operations, and component forces.

Subjects: Unified Combatant Commands

370. Marine Forces Reserves

http://www.marforres.usmc.mil/

Sponsor(s): Marine Corps — Marine Forces Reserves (MFR)

Description: The MFR Web site links to headquarters information and to major subordinate commands and support units. The headquarters section includes leadership biographies, policy letters and guidance, and information about each of the directorates and special staff, such as the chaplain, band, and Public Affairs Office.

Subjects: Marine Corps

Publications: *Continental Marine*, D 214.23:

371. Marines

http://www.marines.com/

Sponsor(s): Marine Corps

Description: This Web site is the Marine Corps recruiting site. It offers a Flash presentation and an HTML alternative format. It also provides a form for requesting additional information about the Marine Corps and a section with information

for parents and advisers. For a general information Web site about the Marines see the official Marine Corps Web site at ⟨http://www.usmc.mil⟩.
Subjects: Marine Corps; Military Recruiting

372. Military Publications and Manuals
http://www.ntis.gov/products/families/military.asp?loc=4-3-4
Sponsor(s): Commerce Department — Technology Administration (TA) — National Technical Information Service (NTIS)
Description: This Web site provides a searchable catalog of Army technical manuals (TMs), field manuals (FMs), Army regulations (ARs), technical bulletins (TBs), and similar publications. The site does not link to copies of the publications; instead, it provides information about purchasing them through NTIS.
Subjects: Military Information

373. Naval Sea Systems Command — NAVSEA
http://www.navsea.navy.mil/
Sponsor(s): Navy — Naval Sea Systems Command (NAVSEA)
Description: The Naval Sea Systems Command develops, acquires, modernizes, and maintains affordable ships, ordnance, and systems for the Navy. The NAVSEA Web site features sections including News, Programs, Innovations, About NAVSEA, and a directory of NAVSEA Commands. It also provides an image and video gallery.
Subjects: Military Ships; Military Technology

374. Naval Undersea Warfare Center (NUWC)
http://www.nuwc.navy.mil/
Sponsor(s): Navy
Description: NUWC is the Navy's research, development, testing, engineering, and fleet support center for submarines, weapons associated with undersea warfare, and other underwater systems. Its Web site features links to the sites for its divisions in Keyport, WA, and Newport, RI; these sites provide more information on the center's activities. Other sections include Leadership, History, Strategy, and Events. The History section discusses the history of the Navy in Rhode Island.
Subjects: Submarines; Underwater Warfare

375. Navy Blue Angels
http://www.blueangels.navy.mil/
Sponsor(s): Navy
Description: This Web site provides information about the choreographed flying of the Navy's Blue Angels squadron, including biographies of the squadron's officers and enlisted team. The site also features information about the show schedule, practice schedule, how to apply to be on the squadron, as well as a long list of frequently asked questions. The Multimedia section includes photos and computer screensavers. The site itself opens with audio and video displays. A toggle for turning the sound off can be found in the lower right corner of the screen.
Subjects: Military Aircraft; Navy

376. Navy Reserve
http://navyreserve.navy.mil/
Sponsor(s): Navy — Naval Reserve Forces
Description: The Web site for the Commander of the Navy Reserve Force includes current news, a command map, and a summary of its mission and history. The site also provides issues of the *Navy Reservist* magazine from the current year.
Subjects: Military Reserves
Publications: *The Navy Reservist*

377. Navy.com
http://www.navy.com/
Alternate URL(s): http://www.elnavy.com/
Sponsor(s): Navy
Description: This is the primary Navy recruiting site. The Careers and Jobs section covers the many fields of specialty for officers or the enlisted. The alternate URL points to a similar site designed for Hispanic Americans; it has English and Spanish versions.

The Careers section should be particularly helpful to users interested in joining the Navy or the armed services.
Subjects: Military Recruiting

378. Redstone Arsenal
http://www.garrison.redstone.army.mil/
Sponsor(s): Army — Redstone Arsenal
Description: The Redstone Arsenal in Alabama is the home of the U.S. Army Aviation and Missile Command (AMCOM) and the Space and Missile Defense Command. This Web site has news and information about these and other units at Redstone. Redstone played an early role in U.S. rocket research and Cold War activities. The History section has substantial historical information on that era, including videos of early rockets and a biography of Wernher Von Braun, who worked at Redstone in the 1950s.
Subjects: Army Bases; Missile Defense; Rockets — History

379. SMC Link, Los Angeles Air Force Base
http://www.losangeles.af.mil/
Sponsor(s): Air Force — Air Force Space and Missile Systems Center
Description: As part of the Air Force Space Command, the Los Angeles-based Space and Missile Systems Center (SMC) manages the acquisitions programs for military satellites and space systems. Organizations at the base include the Military Satellite Communications Systems Wing, the Space Development and Test Wing, and the 61st Air Base Wing. The Public Affairs section has SMC news releases, fact sheets on satellites and launch vehicles, leadership biographies, and the base newspaper, *Astro News*.
Subjects: Air Force Bases; Space Technology

380. Space and Naval Warfare Systems Command
http://enterprise.spawar.navy.mil/
Sponsor(s): Navy — Space and Naval Warfare Systems Command (SPAWAR)
Description: SPAWAR's mission is to develop and maintain integrated command, control, communications, computer, intelligence, and surveillance systems. Major sections of its Web site describe the command, its business opportunities (contract announcements, small business research grants, and foreign military sales), and its products and services. A Reference Library section includes leadership biographies, manuals, handbooks, and technical papers.
Subjects: Military Technology

381. Special Operations Command
http://www.socom.mil/
Sponsor(s): Defense Department
Description: The U.S. Special Operations Command (USSOCOM) Web site presents the command's mission and current news. It provides links to the component

special operations commands from the Army, Navy, and Air Force, and to the Joint Special Operations University.
Subjects: Unified Combatant Commands
Publications: *Capstone Concept for Special Operations*

382. The National Guard
http://www.ngb.army.mil/
Sponsor(s): National Guard Bureau
Description: The National Guard Web site provides news and information about the National Guard Bureau, its leadership, and Joint Staff organization. The Media section has speeches, fact sheets, and officer biographies. The Resources section includes links to each state's Web sites for the National Guard.
Subjects: National Guard
Publications: *The On Guard*

383. The United States Air Force Band
http://www.usafband.com/
Sponsor(s): Air Force — Air Force Bands
Description: The Air Force Band site includes concert and broadcast schedules, and information on recordings and how to request a performance. A history section summarizes the band's progress from 1941 forward.
Subjects: Military Bands

384. The United States Army
http://www.army.mil/
Sponsor(s): Army
Description: This is the central Web site for the Army. The site links to Army news services and leadership biographies. The Organization section connects users to major commands and units; it also links to installations and facilities including airfields, barracks, forts, libraries, medical centers, proving grounds, schools, and more. The References section links to Army publications, forms, and libraries. Other sections include Career Management and Well-Being. The Army A-Z section provides an alphabetical listing of Army Web sites.

This well-designed and well-organized site should be one of the first stopping points for anyone seeking information about the Army, its bases, or related news. It is also a good resource for those in active service, the reserves, or retired from the Army.
Subjects: Army

385. Today's Military
http://www.todaysmilitary.com/
Sponsor(s): Defense Department
Description: Today's Military is an overall guide to the benefits of joining U.S. armed forces. A Military Careers section has information about more than 4,000 possible job paths possible for officers and enlisted servicemembers.
Subjects: Military Recruiting
Publications: *Military Careers: A Guide to Military Occupations and Selected Military Career Paths*, D 1.6/15:

386. U.S. Air Force Bands Program

http://www.af.mil/library/band/

Alternate URL(s): http://www.usafband.com/

Sponsor(s): Air Force — Air Force Bands

Description: Part of the Air Force Link site, these Web pages provide extensive background information on the Air Force Bands, including the Air National Guard Bands. They also feature audition information and sound files. The site at the alternate URL above provides additional information and photographs.

Subjects: Military Bands; Music

387. U.S. Army Bands

http://bands.army.mil/

Sponsor(s): Army — Army Bands

Description: The Army Bands' Web site has links to the various bands, news, history, and performance schedules. The Music section includes the lyrics of the official Army song and music for the Army bugle calls.

Subjects: Military Bands; Music

388. U.S. Army Combat Readiness Center

https://crc.army.mil/home/

Sponsor(s): Army — Army Safety Center

Description: Formerly known as the Army Safety Program, the Combat Readiness Center defines itself as the Army's "focal point for analyzing accident, serious incident, and combat loss reports, identifying lessons learned and tactics, techniques, and procedures (TTPs) to mitigate and prevent future losses," according to its Web site. The site contains statistics and reports on military fatalities and accidents. Other sections include News, Safety Guidance, and Training Information.

Subjects: Military Operations; Safety

389. U.S. Army Signal Center and Fort Gordon

http://www.gordon.army.mil/usascfg/

Sponsor(s): Army — Army Signal Command

Description: This Web site describes the mission and organization of the Army Signal Center in Fort Gordon, GA. The center is the home base of the Signal Regiment, which manages Army information and communications technology and systems worldwide. The latest online edition of the *Army Communicator, Voice of the Signal Corps* is available in the Regiment heading. Sections of the site that are part of the Army Knowledge Online (AKO) portal are not open to the general public.

Subjects: Military Technology

Publications: *Army Communicator, Voice of the Signal Corps,* D 111.14:

390. U.S. Navy

http://www.navy.mil/

Sponsor(s): Navy

Description: The official Web site of the Navy has news, leadership biographies, and links to the numerous other Navy Web sites. The Fact File section connects users to fact sheets on Navy aircraft, weapons, submarines, surface ships, and various Navy forces. The Our Ships section has information about each class of ship. Speeches and congressional testimony by Navy leadership are also available on the site.

Subjects: Navy

Publications: *All Hands* (monthly), D 207.17:

391. U.S. Pacific Command

http://www.pacom.mil/
Sponsor(s): Defense Department — Pacific Command
Description: The U.S. Pacific Command (USPACCOM) is one of nine Unified Combatant Commands assigned to oversee operational control of U.S. combat forces. Headquartered in Hawaii, the command's geographic area of responsibility is the Asia-Pacific region, including China, Russia, Japan, India, the Philippines, and North and South Korea. The Web site includes command news and leadership information.
Subjects: Unified Combatant Commands; Asia

392. United States Army Publications

http://www.army.mil/publications/
Sponsor(s): Army — Army Publishing Agency (USAPA)
Description: This Web site features *Soldiers*, the Army's official magazine. PDF versions of the magazine are online back to 2002. Some content from 2001 is also online. The site also has a Professional Writing Collection section that showcases articles from other professional journals relevant to the Army.
Subjects: Army
Publications: *Soldiers*, D 101.12:

393. United States Army Reserve

http://www.army.mil/usar/
Sponsor(s): Army — Army Reserves (USAR)
Description: The USAR Web site describes the Reserve's mission, history, current news, leadership, capabilities, and organization. The Capabilities section covers reservist training and the type of watercraft, aircraft, and land-based equipment utilized. The site also links to information for families and employers of reservists, and to the Reserve recruitment site. The For Soldiers section includes online access to the *Army Reserve Magazine*.

This site is fairy easy to use, but lacks both a search engine and a site map.
Subjects: Military Reserves
Publications: *Army Reserve Magazine*, D 101.43:

394. United States Central Command

http://www.centcom.mil/
Sponsor(s): Defense Department — Central Command
Description: The United States Central Command (USCENTCOM) is one of nine Unified Combatant Commands assigned operational control of U.S. combat forces. Its area of responsibility spans a region from the Horn of Africa to Central Asia and includes Iraq and Afghanistan. At this time, its Web site has extensive information about the Iraq and Afghanistan operations. The site also provides news, photos, video, and command history.
Subjects: Unified Combatant Commands; Iraq

395. United States Coast Guard

http://www.uscg.mil/
Sponsor(s): Homeland Security Department — Coast Guard
Description: The United States Coast Guard is part of the Department of Homeland Security, but in wartime or when directed by the president, it operates under the Secretary of the Navy. The breadth of information on the Coast Guard's Web site reflects its multiple roles. Its mission includes national defense and homeland security, as well as maritime search and rescue, International Ice Patrol operations, polar and domestic waterway icebreaking, bridge administration, aids to

navigation, recreational boating safety, vessel traffic management, at-sea enforcement of living marine resource laws and treaty obligations, and at-sea drug and illegal migrant interdiction. All of these topics are covered on the Web site.

Major sections of the site include News, Careers, Units, Missions, Leaders, Library, and Multimedia. In the About Us section, the USCG has fact sheets on Coast Guard aircraft, cutters, and boats. It also contains a History subsection with information on lighthouses, the Coast Guard Museum, historic photographs, and more. The Units section links to each of the regional Coast Guard districts. The Library section contains Coast Guard magazines, newsletters, forms, and directives.

Subjects: Coast Guard; Homeland Security
Publications: *Coast Guard Directives System*, TD 5.8:D 62
Coast Guard Magazine, TD 5.3/11
Marine Safety Manual, TD 5.8:SA 1/2/
Navigation and Vessel Inspection Circulars, TD 5.4/2:
The Reservist, TD 5.14:

396. United States European Command
http://www.eucom.mil/
Sponsor(s): Defense Department — European Command
Description: The United States European Command is a unified combatant command headquartered in Stuttgart, Germany. The territory covered by the European Command extends from the North Cape of Norway, through the waters of the Baltic and Mediterranean seas, across most of Europe, through parts of the Middle East, and to the Cape of Good Hope in South Africa. The Command's Web site has news releases, information about major operations, and a directory of headquarters leadership.
Subjects: Unified Combatant Commands

397. United States Marine Corps (USMC)
http://www.usmc.mil/
Sponsor(s): Marine Corps
Description: The official USMC Web site focuses on current news, featuring articles written by Marines and accompanied by photographs. Major sections provide information about the USMC Headquarters, links to individual units' Web pages, USMC news services, and publications. The site also connects users to other USMC sites of interest on careers, quality of life issues, and education.

For those people not serving in the Marines, this site is best used for its news, leadership biographies, and links to the individual units' Web sites.
Subjects: Marine Corps
Publications: *Concepts and Programs*, D 214.27:
Marines (monthly), D 214.24:

398. United States Navy Band
http://www.navyband.navy.mil/
Sponsor(s): Navy — Navy Band
Description: The Navy Band's Web site has information about each of the Navy's bands and ensembles. The site includes concert schedules, a discography, history, resources for music educators, and the *fanfare* newsletter. The site also has information on the Navy Hymn and the Navy Service Song, "Anchors Aweigh."
Subjects: Military Bands; Music

399. United States Northern Command

http://www.northcom.mil/

Sponsor(s): Defense Department — Northern Command

Description: The United States Northern Command (USNORTHCOM) was established in 2002 to counter threats and aggression aimed at the United States and its territories. The command's geographic area of responsibility includes North America, Puerto Rico, the U.S. Virgin Islands, and their respective air, land, and sea approaches. The command's Web site provides news and leadership information. The Educational section includes information about homeland defense for students and teachers.

Subjects: Homeland Security; Unified Combatant Commands

400. United States Southern Command

http://www.southcom.mil/home/

Sponsor(s): Defense Department — Southern Command

Description: The United States Southern Command (USSOUTHCOM), one of the nine Unified Combatant Commands, is headquartered in Miami. Its area of responsibility includes Latin America south of Mexico, the waters adjacent to Central and South America, the Caribbean Sea, Caribbean nations and territories, the Gulf of Mexico, and a portion of the Atlantic Ocean. The command's Web site includes information about its mission, activities, and components (which include the Joint Task Force Guantanamo in Cuba).

Subjects: Unified Combatant Commands

401. United States Strategic Command

http://www.stratcom.mil/

Sponsor(s): Defense Department — Strategic Command

Description: United States Strategic Command (USSTRATCOM) is one of the nine Unified Combatant Commands. USSTRATCOM has responsibility for missions in the areas of Space Operations; Information Operations; Integrated Missile Defense; Global Command and Control; Intelligence, Surveillance, and Reconnaissance; Global Strike; and Strategic Deterrence. Its Web site has information about the command's organization and leadership. The Resources section provides fact sheets on missile systems, military space forces, and strategic computer and communications networks.

Subjects: Unified Combatant Commands; Missile Defense

402. United States Transportation Command

http://www.transcom.mil/

Sponsor(s): Defense Department — Transportation Command

Description: According to its Web site, the mission of the United States Transportation Command (TRANSCOM) is "to provide air, land, and sea transportation for the Department of Defense in time of peace and time of war" (from the Web site). The site has information on TRANSCOM's organization, leadership, news, and history. The Publications section includes the Defense Transportation Regulations.

Subjects: Airlifts; Military Logistics; Unified Combatant Commands

Defense Operations

403. ACQWeb
http://www.acq.osd.mil/
Sponsor(s): Defense Department — Office of the Under Secretary of Defense for Acquisition, Technology, and Logistics
Description: ACQWeb is the official Web site for the Office of the Under Secretary of Defense for Acquisition, Technology, and Logistics (AT&L). According to the site, the office advises the Secretary of Defense "on all matters pertaining to the Department of Defense's acquisition process, research, and development; advanced technology; test and evaluation; production; logistics; military construction; procurement; economic security; and atomic energy." The AT&L Archives section has the full text of the Under Secretary's press releases, speeches, and testimony before Congress. The Office Navigator page presents a large menu of AT&L component offices and featured Web sites.

ACQWeb is a central Web site for Department of Defense personnel involved in acquisitions work. It will also be relevant to those contracting with the department.
Subjects: Defense Administration; Military Procurement

404. Air Force Link BRAC 2005
http://www.af.mil/brac/
Sponsor(s): Air Force
Description: The Air Force Base Realignment and Closure (BRAC) Web site includes state-by-state detail on affected bases and facilities. It also has BRAC news and related material. For more information about BRAC, see the entry for Base Realignment and Closure 2005 elsewhere in this chapter.
Subjects: Air Force; Military Bases and Installations

405. Army Financial Management
http://www.asafm.army.mil/
Sponsor(s): Army
Description: Manuals, documents, and other information about Army accounting and financial management practice make up the bulk of this site. Sections include Army Budget, Financial Operations, and Cost and Economics. The Army Budget section contains detailed materials on the current fiscal year and a table that provides organized access to budget documents from previous years.

The primary target audience for this fairly technical site is Army's budget and resource management staff.
Subjects: Army; Defense Administration
Publications: *Cost and Economic Analysis Program*, D 101.9:
Department of the Army Justification of Estimates, D 101.2:J 98/
Resource Management Magazine, D 101.89:
The Army Budget, D 101.121:

406. Base Realignment and Closure 2005
http://www.dod.mil/brac/
Sponsor(s): Defense Base Closure and Realignment Commission
Description: This Web site reports on the implementation of recommendations from the 2005 Defense Base Realignment and Closure (BRAC) Commission. The site includes news, documents, and reports from prior BRAC rounds. Many of the documents are in ZIP format and must be downloaded before opening.
Subjects: Military Bases and Installations
Publications: *2005 Defense Base Closure and Realignment Commission Report*

407. Defense Information Systems Agency
http://www.disa.mil/
Sponsor(s): Defense Department — Defense Information Systems Agency (DISA)
Description: DISA develops information technology systems for the military. On its Web site, the About DISA section describes the agency's mission areas: communications, combat support computing, information assurance, joint command and control, and joint interoperability support. About DISA also covers the agency's history, organization, and current news. The site has the full text of the *DSN Telephone Directory*. (Defense Switched Network, or DSN, is used for voice communications between Department of Defense offices.) The DISA Publications section of the site is blocked to all but those using .gov and .mil domains.
Subjects: Military Computing; Communications Technology

408. Defense Logistics Agency
http://www.dla.mil/
Sponsor(s): Defense Department — Defense Logistics Agency (DLA)
Description: DLA is the central supply and distribution agency for the military; it provides goods such as weapons parts, fuel, uniforms, food rations, and medical supplies. Major sections of the Web site include Business Opportunities, Information Technology, and Corporate Headquarters. The About DLA section includes a fact sheet, brochure, video, DLA acronym list, and other information about the agency.
Subjects: Military Logistics
Publications: *Defense Logistics Agency Handbooks, DLAH*, D 7.6/7:
Defense Logistics Agency Manuals, DLAM, D 7.6/8:
Defense Logistics Agency Regulations, DLAR, D 7.6/6:
Defense Standardization Program Journal, D 1.88:
DLAPS Publications, D 7.41:

409. Defense Nuclear Facilities Safety Board (DNFSB)
http://www.dnfsb.gov/
Sponsor(s): Defense Nuclear Facilities Safety Board
Description: DNFSB is responsible for independent, external safety oversight of the Department of Energy (DOE) nuclear weapons complex. Its Web site offers information about the Board's members and organizational structure. The Public Documents section organizes DNFSB documents by type, with subsections including Recommendations and Technical Reports. An interactive map on the site's home page provides access to the same documents by DOE nuclear site name. The Public Documents section also includes annual reports to Congress and public hearings information.
Subjects: Nuclear Weapons
Publications: *Annual Report to Congress (Defense Nuclear Facilities Safety Board)*, Y 3.D 36/3:1
DNFSB Site Representatives Weekly Activities Report, Y 3.D 36/3:11
DNFSB Staff Issue Reports, Y 3.D 36/3:12
DNFSB Technical Reports, Y 3.D 36/3:9
Recommendations of the DNFSB, Y 3.D 36/3:10

410. Defense Prisoner of War/Missing Personnel Office
http://www.dtic.mil/dpmo/
Sponsor(s): Defense Department — Defense Prisoner of War/Missing Personnel Office (DPMO)
Description: The DPMO Web site covers the federal government's efforts to account for missing persons from all wars. News releases on the site, covering 1996 to

present, document the office's activities, agreements, and major events, as well as announcements when a soldier's remains are identified. The site includes policies, archival research results, and DNA identification procedures. It features lists reported from missing personnel databases from the Cold War, Vietnam, and Korea. The site also has information about family support and National POW/MIA Recognition Day.

Subjects: Prisoners of War

411. Defense Procurement and Acquisition Policy (DPAP)

http://www.acq.osd.mil/dpap/

Sponsor(s): Defense Department — Office of the Under Secretary of Defense for Acquisition, Technology, and Logistics

Description: Part of the Department of Defense, DPAP is concerned with policy and with training the acquisitions work force. The Web site links to DPAP directorates, including the Defense Acquisition Regulations Service and the Defense Acquisition University. The Policy Vault section has acquisition policy documents available for dissemination to the public.

Subjects: Government Procurement

412. Defense Security Service

http://www.dss.mil/

Sponsor(s): Defense Department — Defense Security Service (DSS)

Description: DSS conducts personnel security investigations and operates programs in industrial security and security training. The DSS Web site describes its programs, including the National Industrial Security and Facility Security Clearance program, the Counterintelligence program, the Information Assurance program, and the DSS Academy. Documents from the site can be found in the Security Library section.

Much of the information at this site is for DSS customers, which are federal agencies as well as private industry and universities carrying out government contracts or conducting research and development.

Subjects: Military Intelligence; National Security

413. Defense Supply Center, Columbus (DSCC)

http://www.dscc.dla.mil/

Sponsor(s): Defense Department — Defense Logistics Agency (DLA)

Description: DSCC, a Department of Defense procurement and supply center, offers information about military procurement and about buying from and selling to the center. The site links to the DSCC Internet Bid Board System (DIBBS) and to the DoD (Electronic Mall) EMALL system.

This site will primarily be of interest to those in the Defense Department procurement business.

Subjects: Military Procurement

414. Department of Defense

http://www.defenselink.mil/

Alternate URL(s): http://www.dod.mil/

Sponsor(s): Defense Department

Description: The official Department of Defense Web site features current armed forces news, leadership biographies and speeches, and various items of current interest. News on the site comes from the Armed Forces Press Service and the Pentagon Channel broadcasts. In the Press Resources section, the site provides press advisories and news briefing slides and transcripts. The Websites section organizes links to the numerous DoD sites alphabetically and by category.

The Publications section links to military regulations and forms and a selection of DoD reports, as well as major publications from other agencies, such as the Department of State's *Background Notes*.

This site is an excellent starting point for users looking for U.S. military Web sites or current DoD news, but it does not offer much direct access to DoD publications.

Subjects: Military Information; Finding Aids
Publications: *Defense Almanac*, D 2.15/3:
Final Report of the Independent Panel to Review DoD Detention Operations, D 1.2:D 48/2/FINAL
National Defense Strategy of the United States of America, D 1.2:
National Military Strategy of the United States of America, D 5.2:
Quadrennial Defense Review Report, D 1.2:

415. Department of Defense Network Information Center
http://www.nic.mil/
Sponsor(s): Defense Department — Defense Information Systems Agency (DISA)
Description: The Department of Defense Network Information Center (NIC) is responsible for the Defense Information Systems Network (DISN) and other DoD sponsored networks. The NIC Web site includes a basic description of what the center does.

This Web site is an essential point of contact for any U.S. military organization that desires to establish or expand its Internet presence. Most information cannot be accessed by the public, and all users must consent to monitoring in order to access the site.
Subjects: Military Computing

416. Department of Defense Single Stock Point for Specifications, Standards, and Related Publications
http://dodssp.daps.dla.mil/
Sponsor(s): Defense Department — Defense Automated Printing Service (DAPS)
Description: This Web site provides access to information about military specifications and standards. It includes PDF versions of the Department of Defense's *Index of Specifications and Standards* (DoDISS). Authorized users can link to the Acquisition Streamlining and Standardization Information System (ASSIST) database, a management and research tool which includes DoDISS and other military specifications and standards documents. Other sections include a Procurement Gateway, the Technical Manual Publish-on-Demand System (TMPODS), the Navy Electronic Directives System (NEDS), and Navy Forms Online.
Subjects: Standards and Specifications

417. Departmental Representative to the DNFSB
http://www.deprep.org/
Alternate URL(s): http://www.hss.energy.gov/DepRep/
Sponsor(s): Energy Department
Description: This is the Web site for the Department of Energy's representative to the Defense Nuclear Facilities Safety Board (DNFSB), which is concerned with public health and safety issues at the department's nuclear facilities. The site includes information about the DNFSB and the Office of the Representative, as well as copies of public documents. Additional descriptive information is available at the alternate URL.
Subjects: Nuclear Weapons

418. Document Automation and Production Service
http://www.daps.dla.mil/
Sponsor(s): Defense Department — Defense Logistics Agency (DLA)
Description: DLA's Document Automation and Production Service provides professional printing, copying, duplicating, scanning, imaging, and Internet services to the Department of Defense. This Web site describes its products and services.
Subjects: Military Publishing; Printing

419. DoD 101: Introduction to the United States Department of Defense
http://www.defenselink.mil/pubs/dod101/
Sponsor(s): Defense Department
Description: The U.S. military service branches are older than the nation, but the Department of Defense was not established in its current form until 1949. This public relations Web site explains the department's history, structure, and operations with a minimum of technical language. The site is set up like a slide presentation and can be viewed in several different formats, including outline HTML, PDF, and PowerPoint.
Subjects: Military Forces

420. DoD Dictionary of Military Terms
http://www.dtic.mil/doctrine/jel/doddict/
Sponsor(s): Defense Department — Joint Chiefs of Staff
Description: This is the online version of the *DOD Dictionary of Military and Associated Terms*. It provides brief explanations of terms such as "prearranged fire" and "reserved obstacles." The site also links to the Joint Acronyms and Abbreviations list, which links from acronym of terms to their full names.
Subjects: Military Information; Reference
Publications: *Department of Defense Dictionary of Military and Associated Terms*, D 5.12:

421. DoD Personnel and Procurement Statistics
http://siadapp.dior.whs.mil/
Sponsor(s): Defense Department — Statistical Information Analysis Division
Description: The Personnel section of this Web site includes current military and civilian defense personnel and military casualty statistics, with some statistical reports available back to 1995. The *Selected Manpower Statistics* and *Civilian Manpower Statistics* have historical data going back to 1950. The Procurement section has detailed reports on procurement actions for each branch of the military. Under Procurement, the Historical Statistics subsection offers lists of the 100 companies receiving the largest dollar volume of prime contract awards for 1996 to the present. Historical procurement data is available for downloading in compressed format for 1966 forward. This Defense office and its Web site were formerly known as the Directorate for Information Operations and Reports (DIOR).
   This site has a simple interface but provides few guides to understanding the data itself. Also, the subsection headings may not always be helpful. For example, users should look at the Publications subsection of Personnel in addition to the Military and Civilian sections to see all available reports.
Subjects: Military Forces — Statistics; Military Procurement — Statistics
Publications: *100 Companies Receiving The Largest Dollar Volume of Prime Contract Awards*, D 1.57:
100 Contractors Receiving The Largest Dollar Volume of Prime Contract Awards for RDT&E, Fiscal Year, D 1.57/2:
Atlas/State Data Abstract for the U.S. and Selected Areas, D 1.58/4:

Catalog of DIOR Reports, Department of Defense, D 1.33/4:
Civilian Manpower Statistics, D 1.61/2:
Companies Participating in the Department of Defense Subcontracting Program, D 1.57/9:
Distribution of Personnel by State and by Selected Locations, D 1.61/5:
Selected Manpower Statistics, Fiscal Year. . ., D 1.61/4:
Worldwide Manpower Distribution by Geographical Area (quarterly), D 1.61/3:
Worldwide U.S. Active Duty Military Personnel Casualties, D 1.61/6:

422. DoD Web Sites

http://www.dod.mil/sites/
Sponsor(s): Defense Department
Description: This page provides an alphabetical index to many of the Department of Defense's public Web sites. The home page has a selective list of about 40 of the most frequently used sites. Click on an individual letter to view the complete site listings.

   Since the Defense Department has so many Web sites, this can be a useful finding aid.
Subjects: Military Information; Finding Aids

423. DoN Acquisition One Source

http://www.acquisition.navy.mil
Sponsor(s): Navy
Description: DoN Acquisition One Source provides acquisitions news, policy, regulations, and other information of interest to the Navy acquisitions and procurement community.
Subjects: Military Procurement
Publications: *ABM (Acquisition & Business Management) Online*, D 201.44:

424. DTRALink

http://www.dtra.mil/
Sponsor(s): Defense Department — Defense Threat Reduction Agency (DTRA)
Description: DTRA addresses the threat of weapons of mass destruction (chemical, biological, radiological, nuclear, and high explosives) with combat support, technology development, threat control, and threat reduction. DTRALink provides background information on the agency and its work. The News Media section includes fact sheets, news releases, and publications. The site also has information on the Nuclear Test Personnel Review to assist veterans who received doses of radiation while participating in U.S. atmospheric nuclear tests during the Cold War era.
Subjects: National Defense; Radiation Exposure

425. MDA LINK

http://www.mda.mil/
Sponsor(s): Defense Department — Missile Defense Agency (MDA)
Description: MDA is charged with developing an integrated missile defense system. The Ballistic Missile Defense Organization (BMDO) became the MDA in 2002, elevating the organization to agency status. MDA Link, the agency's Web site, explains the basics of missile defense. Other sections provide budget information, a glossary, and a guide to doing business with MDA. The News/Resources section includes images and videos of missile defense systems, fact sheets, and congressional testimony.
Subjects: Missile Defense
Publications: *MDA TechUpdate*

426. National Nuclear Security Administration (NNSA)

http://www.nnsa.doe.gov/

Sponsor(s): Energy Department — National Nuclear Security Administration

Description: NNSA, a semi-autonomous agency within the Department of Energy, officially began operations on March 1, 2000. Its mission is to carry out the national security responsibilities of the Department of Energy, including maintenance of nuclear weapons, promotion of international nuclear safety and nonproliferation, and management of the naval nuclear propulsion program. The Defense Programs section of the NNSA Web site covers the Stockpile Stewardship Program. A separate section provides information from and about the NNSA Office of Defense Nuclear Nonproliferation. The Reading Room section includes congressional testimony, reports, budget information, and policy letters.

Subjects: Nuclear Weapons

Publications: *NNSA News*

427. Navy BRAC Program Management Office

http://www.bracpmo.navy.mil/

Sponsor(s): Navy

Description: The Navy Web site for the 2005 round of base closures has sections with information about major base closures, major base realignments, Navy Reserve Center closures, surplus property notices, BRAC maps, and prior BRAC rounds.

Subjects: Military Bases and Installations; Navy

428. Office of the Under Secretary of Defense (Comptroller)

http://www.dod.mil/comptroller/

Sponsor(s): Defense Department — Office of the Under Secretary of Defense (Comptroller)

Description: The Comptroller's page provides an extensive set of Department of Defense budget documents and, in the Defense Budget Execution section, a database of budget reprogramming actions. Other sections cover financial regulation and financial management topics, such as reimbursement rates and guidance on unsolicited donations or gifts.

Subjects: Defense Administration

429. Overseas Basing Commission

http://www.obc.gov/

Sponsor(s): Overseas Basing Commission

Description: The full name of the Overseas Basing Commission is the United States Congress Commission on Review of Overseas Military Facility Structure of the United States. It is an independent commission charged with making recommendations to Congress and to the president regarding overseas military facilities. Its Web site includes the commission's August 2005 report, along with information about the commission and its hearings, congressional statements, and press releases.

   This site has also been archived by the University of North Texas Libraries CyberCemetery Web site.

Subjects: Military Bases and Installations

430. Pentagon Force Protection Agency

http://www.pfpa.mil/

Sponsor(s): Defense Department — Police Force Protection Agency (PFPA)

Description: PFPA is responsible for security at the Pentagon and other Department of Defense facilities and activities in the Washington, DC, area. It performs stan-

dard police work and criminal investigations and is also concerned with terrorist, chemical, biological, and nuclear threats. The PFPA Web site has basic information about the agency, its component organizations, and employment opportunities.
Subjects: Homeland Security; Police

431. Pentagon Renovation Program
http://renovation.pentagon.mil/
Sponsor(s): Defense Department
Description: Even before the September 11, 2001, terrorist attack on the Pentagon, a massive renovation program for the building was underway. This Web site is a central point for information about the renovation. It includes a Contractor Opportunities section and *The Renovator* newsletter, which reports on construction progress. The site also links to information about the Pentagon Memorial for those who died in the terrorist attack.
Subjects: Military Bases and Installations
Publications: *The Renovator*

432. Selective Service System
http://www.sss.gov/
Sponsor(s): Selective Service System (SSS)
Description: The SSS Web site features information about the agency and the military draft and can be used to register online or check a registration. The site includes sections such as About the Agency, the History/Records section, Publications, Registration Information, What Happens in a Draft, and Fast Facts. History/Records includes historical draft statistics, a guide to requesting archival records of draft registrants, and a general history of the draft in the United States. The Publications section contains current and past editions of the agency's *Annual Report to Congress, Selective Service System* and back issues of the newsletter *The Register*.
Subjects: Military Draft
Publications: *Annual Report to Congress, Selective Service System*, Y 3.SE 4:1
The Register, Y 3.SE 4:27/

433. Special Inspector General for Iraq Reconstruction
http://www.sigir.mil/
Sponsor(s): Defense DepartmentState Department
Description: The Special Inspector General for Iraq Reconstruction (SIGIR) is a temporary federal agency providing auditing and investigatory oversight of funds intended for Iraq reconstruction programs. Its Web site has background information about the office and carries the SIGIR publications, audit reports, and project assessment reports. The Newsroom section provides further information on the role of the SIGIR. A significant amount of content, including some reports, is also available in Arabic.
Subjects: Iraq
Publications: *Special Inspector General for Iraq Reconstruction Quarterly Report to Congress*

434. U.S. Army Base Realignment and Closure (BRAC) Office
http://www.army.mil/BRAC/
Sponsor(s): Army
Description: This Web site covers the impact of the 2005 BRAC recommendations for the Army. It includes Army and Department of Defense reports and special sections on the environmental, budget, and real estate aspects of BRAC.
Subjects: Army; Military Bases and Installations

Defense Research

435. Air Force Office of Scientific Research (AFOSR)
http://www.afosr.af.mil/
Sponsor(s): Air Force
Description: AFOSR directs the Air Force's basic research program, with research concerning aerospace and materials sciences, chemistry and life sciences, mathematics and information sciences, and physics and electronics. Its Web site includes current research news and thorough descriptions of projects in each research area. The site also has information about AFOSR education outreach, assistantships, and awards programs.
Subjects: Military Research Laboratories

436. Air Force Research Laboratory (AFRL)
http://www.afrl.af.mil/
Sponsor(s): Air Force — Air Force Research Laboratory
Description: AFRL conducts basic and applied research to improve the Air Force fighting capabilities. Its directorates include air vehicles, directed energy, human effectiveness, information, materials and manufacturing, munitions, propulsion, sensors, and space vehicles. Each directorate has a page with more information. The Business Info section has information on technology transfer and announcements of opportunities. The site also has a map of AFRL locations and an organization chart.
Subjects: Military Research Laboratories
Publications: *AFRL Newsletter*

437. Air University Library Index to Military Periodicals
http://www.dtic.mil/dtic/aulimp/
Sponsor(s): Air Force — Air University
Description: The Air University Library Index to Military Periodicals is a Web site database of citations to journal, magazine, and trade paper articles on the topics of defense and aeronautics. The index goes back to 1988 and can be searched by author, subject, article title, journal title, and date range. Search results do not link to the full-text versions of the articles, but the Air University Library provides a list of indexed periodicals with online editions.
Subjects: Databases; Defense Research
Publications: *Air University Library Index to Military Periodicals*, D 301.26/2:

438. Army Research Laboratory (ARL)
http://www.arl.army.mil/
Sponsor(s): Army — Army Materiel Command
Description: ARL's Web site provides information about its organization, research, and funding opportunities. ARL's research directorates include computational and information science, sensors and electron devices, survivability and lethality analysis, weapons and materials research, human research and engineering, and vehicle technology. Research and Analysis Programs include robotics, precision guided missiles, tactical communications, and battlefield weather research. Each is described in more detail at the Web site. A separate section provides information about doing business with ARL.
Subjects: Military Computing; Military Research Laboratories; Weapons Research

439. Center for Terrorism Studies
http://c21.maxwell.af.mil/cts-home.htm
Sponsor(s): Air Force — Maxwell Air Force Base
Description: The Center for Terrorism Studies is part of the Air National Guard Conflict 21 effort, which conducts research and education related to homeland security, proliferation of weapons of mass destruction, and future conflict scenarios. Its Web site is a portal to a wide array of Internet resources. Topics covered include law, doctrine, and policy; theory and research; psychology; terrorist financing; international resources; and state and local resources.

This portal is useful for bringing together reports and Web sites that cover many aspects of terrorism studies. The site includes current information but, at this time, many of the referenced documents are from the 2002–2005 time period.
Subjects: Terrorism

440. Chemical and Biological Defense Information Analysis Center
http://www.cbiac.apgea.army.mil/
Sponsor(s): Defense Department — Chemical and Biological Defense Information Analysis Center (CBIAC)
Description: CBIAC, a Defense Information Analysis Center, was established to be the Department of Defense's focal point for Chemical, Biological, Radiological and Nuclear (CBRN) scientific and technical information. Access to many of the products and services on the CBIAC Web site is limited to Defense and other government agencies and their approved contractors. The Related Links section includes some publicly accessible resources, such as Web sites, news stories, and journal articles related to the CBIAC research focus.
Subjects: Biological Warfare; Chemical Warfare; Information Analysis Centers

441. Combating Terrorism Center at West Point
http://www.ctc.usma.edu/
Sponsor(s): Army — United States Military Academy (USMA)
Description: The Combating Terrorism Center conducts education, research, and policy analysis on such topics as terrorism, counterterrorism, homeland security, and weapons of mass destruction. Its Web site includes staff publications and links to related academic, think tank, and government Web sites.
Subjects: Terrorism — Research

442. Defense Advanced Research Projects Agency
http://www.darpa.mil/
Sponsor(s): Defense Department — Defense Advanced Research Projects Agency (DARPA)
Description: DARPA, founded in 1958 as the Advanced Research Projects Agency (ARPA), manages research and development to promote the technological superiority of the U.S. military. The DARPA Web site features an overview and history of the agency, with links to the Web sites of its component offices. The Doing Business with DARPA and Solicitations sections provide information about contracts and grants processes. A special Web section called DARPA Legacy highlights DARPA-sponsored technologies that have transitioned to successful products.
Subjects: Military Technology — Research

443. Defense Science Board (DSB)
http://www.acq.osd.mil/dsb/
Sponsor(s): Defense Department — Office of the Under Secretary of Defense for Acquisition, Technology, and Logistics
Description: As stated on its Web site, the Defense Science Board (DSB) was established to advise the Department of Defense's leadership on "matters relating to science, technology, research, engineering, manufacturing, acquisition process, and other matters that are of special interest to the Department of Defense." DSB accomplishes much of its work through special task forces. Its Web site lists current task forces and their missions and has PDF copies of past task force reports.
Subjects: Military Technology; Defense Research
Publications: *DSB Newsletter*, D 1.107/2:

444. Defense Technical Information Center
http://www.dtic.mil/dtic/index.html
Alternate URL(s): http://stinet.dtic.mil/
Sponsor(s): Defense Department — Defense Technical Information Center (DTIC)
Description: DTIC is the Department of Defense's central distribution point for technical defense-related information. It offers the Defense community, including contractors and DoD-funded researchers, a broad range of services for locating and delivering technical reports, research summaries, summaries of independent research and development, and other relevant publications. Access to many services on this site is restricted to registered users. Publicly accessible resources are provided via DTIC's Public STINET Web site (located at the alternate URL listed above).

The Products and Services section describes the range of DTIC's offerings. A section called DTIC From A to Z provides a quick index of links to DTIC offices and online products. Full information on eligible user groups and the registration process is available in the Registration section.

For defense contractors, researchers, and defense personnel, this should be the first site to visit when searching for defense technical material. Non-registered researchers should look through the linked Public STINET site.
Subjects: Scientific and Technical Information
Publications: *DTIC Digest*, D 10.11:
DTIC Review, D 10.11/2:1/1
Products and Services Catalog, D 10.12:P 94/

445. DoD Biometrics
http://www.biometrics.dod.mil
Sponsor(s): Army — Biometrics Management Office
Description: DoD Biometrics is the central Web site for information about research, testing, standards development, collaboration, and other work in support of Department of Defense biometrics applications. Biometrics consists of the tools to verify the identity of an individual based on distinct and measurable physiological characteristics, such as fingerprints. The Web site has information about the program and about biometrics, including a basic tutorial, glossary, and news stories on the topic.
Subjects: Biometrics — Research
Publications: *Biometric Bulletin*

446. DoD High Performance Computing Modernization Program
http://www.hpcmo.hpc.mil/

Sponsor(s): Defense Department — High Performance Computing Modernization Program (HPCMP)

Description: HPCMP provides supercomputer services, high-speed network communications, and computational science expertise for the research, development, and test activities of the Department of Defense laboratories and test centers. Its Web site provides information about the program and related high-performance computing activities.

While focusing on military HPC, this site will be of interest to others in the HPC community.

Subjects: High-Performance Computing; Military Computing

Publications: *High Performance Computing Modernization Program Annual Report*

447. Foreign Military Studies Office
http://fmso.leavenworth.army.mil/

Sponsor(s): Army — Foreign Military Studies Office (FMSO)

Description: According to its Web site, FMSO "conducts analytical programs focused on emerging and asymmetric threats, regional military and security developments, and other issues." Many of the FMSO analytical products are available online, organized by country, world region, and topic. In 2006, FMSO had made available a public collection of digitized "unclassified documents and media captured during Operation Iraqi Freedom" (from the Web site); these documents were later taken down due to security concerns.

Subjects: Military Intelligence; Defense Research

448. Information Analysis Centers
http://iac.dtic.mil/

Sponsor(s): Defense Department — Defense Technical Information Center (DTIC)

Description: This site provides a central directory for home pages of the Department of Defense and other military Information Analysis Centers (IACs). The IACs establish databases of historical, technical, scientific, and other data and information on a variety of technical topics. Information collections include unclassified, limited distribution, and classified information. The IACs also provide analytical tools such as models and simulations. Most of the home pages of the IACs describe the databases that they maintain, although they rarely provide public access.

The IACs include: Advanced Materials, Manufacturing and Testing; Chemical and Biological Defense; Chemical Propulsion; Data and Analysis Center for Software; Human Systems Integration; Information Assurance Technology; Modeling and Simulation; Military Sensing; Reliability; Survivability/Vulnerability; Weapon Systems Technology; Airfields, Pavements, and Mobility; Coastal Engineering; Cold Regions Science and Technology; Concrete Technology; Defense Threat Reduction; Environment; Hydraulic Engineering; Shock and Vibration; and Soil Mechanics.

Most of the resources from the IACs will only be of interest to the defense community due to the access restrictions. However, there are a few databases that have unclassified material available.

Subjects: Information Analysis Centers; Military Information; Scientific and Technical Information

449. Information Assurance Technology Analysis Center
http://iac.dtic.mil/iatac/
Sponsor(s): Defense Department — Information Assurance Technology Analysis Center (IATAC)
Description: IATAC is charged with gathering information on information assurance technologies, system vulnerabilities, research and development, and models, while providing analyses to support the development and implementation of effective defenses against information warfare attacks. Its Web site includes Products, Services, and Resources sections. The Resources section links to government, military, commercial, and academic Web sites on the topics of information security and intelligence.
Subjects: Computer Security; Electronic Warfare; Information Analysis Centers

450. Institute for National Strategic Studies (INSS)
http://www.ndu.edu/inss/
Sponsor(s): Defense Department — National Defense University (NDU)
Description: INSS conducts policy research and analysis for senior U.S. military decision-makers and for decision-makers in the executive branch and in Congress. INSS includes the National Strategic Gaming Center. This Web site has information on the INSS, its research themes, publications, and symposia.
Subjects: Defense Research
Publications: *Joint Force Quarterly*, D 5.20:
McNair Papers, D 5.416:
Strategic Forum, Institute for National Strategic Studies, D 5.417:

451. Los Alamos National Security
http://www.lanl.gov/natlsecurity/
Sponsor(s): Energy Department — Los Alamos National Laboratory (LANL)
Description: As stated on its Web site, "the mission of Los Alamos National Laboratory is national security." This site highlights the research being done at LANL about the U.S. nuclear weapons stockpile and threat reduction. The Threat Reduction section of the site discusses battlefield technologies and biothreats.
Subjects: National Security — Research; Nuclear Weapons — Research

452. Modeling and Simulation Information Analysis Center
http://www.msiac.dmso.mil/
Sponsor(s): Defense Department — Modeling and Simulation Information Analysis Center (MSIAC)
Description: Featuring information about MSIAC's services and products, this site offers sections including Modeling and Simulation (M&S) FAQs, *M&S Journal Online*, and links to other modeling and simulation Web sites.
Subjects: Information Analysis Centers; Military Computing
Publications: *M&S Journal Online*

453. Naval Research Laboratory
http://www.nrl.navy.mil/
Sponsor(s): Navy — Naval Research Laboratory (NRL)
Description: This is the main page for the many directorates and divisions of NRL. The laboratory's research focus is broad, covering scientific areas within the realm of sea, sky, and space. Major research areas include oceanography and atmospheric science, ocean acoustics, marine meteorology and geosciences, remote oceanic and atmospheric sensing, and space technology. NRL also has a Nanoscience Institute. The Web site includes the sections About NRL, Accomplishments, Research, Doing Business with NRL, News Room, and Field Sites. Fellowships and

student opportunities are described in the Accept the Challenge section. The search section has a word search feature and also provides links to NRL's component Web sites. Publications can be found in the News Room section.
Subjects: Navy — Research; Research Laboratories
Publications: *NRL Fact Book*, D 201.17/3:
NRL Review, D 210.17/2:

454. SCAMPI — Staff College Automated Military Periodicals Index
http://www.dtic.mil/dtic/scampi/
Sponsor(s): Defense Department — National Defense University (NDU)
Description: SCAMPI indexes roughly 100 defense-related magazines and journals, such as *Joint Force Quarterly* and *Seapower*, from 1996 to the present.
Subjects: Military Information
Publications: *Joint Force Quarterly*
Seapower

455. SENSIAC: Military Sensing Information Analysis Center
http://www.sensiac.gatech.edu/
Sponsor(s): Defense Department — Defense Technical Information Center (DTIC)
Description: SENSIAC focuses on sensing technologies for military use, such as infrared sensors, laser systems, radar, underwater acoustics, and seismic sensors. Only the most general information is available free of charge on this Web site.
Subjects: Military Technology — Research

456. Survivability/Vulnerability Information Analysis Center
http://iac.dtic.mil/surviac/
Sponsor(s): Defense Department — Survivability/Vulnerability Information Analysis Center (SURVIAC)
Description: SURVIAC is a Department of Defense information analysis center concerned with nonnuclear survivability/vulnerability data, information, methodologies, models, and analysis related to U.S. and foreign aeronautical and surface systems. Access to most of SURVIAC's databases and technical libraries is restricted, but the *Aircraft Survivability* and *SURVIAC Bulletin* periodicals are freely available free of charge in the Libraries, Databases, & Publications section.
Subjects: Information Analysis Centers; Weapons Systems — Research
Publications: *Aircraft Survivability*
SURVIAC Bulletin

457. U.S. Army Medical Research Institute of Infectious Diseases (USAMRIID)
http://www.usamriid.army.mil/
Sponsor(s): Army — Army Medical Command
Description: USAMRIID researches and develops medical solutions to protect troops from biological threats. Its Web site has information about the institute's achievements, current news, and technology transfer opportunities. The Scientific Publications section provides a bibliography of staff-authored journal articles. The Reference Materials section includes downloadable copies of textbooks and manuals.
Subjects: Bioterrorism; Military Medicine
Publications: *Defense Against Toxin Weapons*, D 101.2:
Medical Management of Biological Casualties Handbook, D 101.6/5:
Textbook of Military Medicine: Medical Aspects of Chemical & Biological Warfare

458. USAF Counterproliferation Center (CPC)
http://www.au.af.mil/au/awc/awcgate/awc-cps.htm
Sponsor(s): Air Force — Air University
Description: Hosted by Air University, the CPC conducts counterproliferation research and education for the Air Force. Its Web site serves as a portal to military, civilian government, and private sources of online information related to weapons of mass destruction. The main page links to general counterproliferation policy papers, publications, conferences, documents, and laws. Specific subject-oriented pages link to online resources on nuclear weapons, biological warfare, chemical weapons, terrorism, treaties, and other related topics.

This large portal takes a disciplined approach to explaining counterproliferation doctrine and organizing links to numerous valuable Web sites from a variety of sources. Researchers seeking official documents on the topic may wish to make this their first stop online.
Subjects: Arms Control; Weapons Research

459. Weapons Systems Technology Information Analysis Center (WSTIAC)
http://wstiac.alionscience.com/
Sponsor(s): Defense Department — Weapons Systems Technology Information Analysis Center (WSTIAC)
Description: WSTIAC is the defense community's central information service for advanced technologies research relevant to weapons systems. Most of the products and services described on the site are restricted to authorized users.
Subjects: Information Analysis Centers; Weapons Research

Homeland Security

460. Center for Homeland Defense and Security
http://www.chds.us/
Sponsor(s): Navy — Naval Postgraduate School (NPS)
Description: NPS's Center for Homeland Defense & Security (CHDS) provides educational programs for government and military leaders. Its Web site describes the center and links to related resources on the Internet. According to the site, the center's online Homeland Security Digital Library section is open to "all homeland security policy planners, strategists, researchers, scholars, managers, and first responders." Eligible users must register for access. The center's new *Homeland Security Affairs* journal is also available on the site.
Subjects: Homeland Security — Research; Military Training and Education
Publications: *Homeland Security Affairs*

461. Civil Air Patrol
http://www.cap.gov/
Sponsor(s): Air Force — Civil Air Patrol (CAP)
Description: CAP flies U.S. inland search and rescue missions and supports disaster relief, humanitarian assistance efforts, drug interdiction, and the U.S. Air Force homeland defense. Its Web site describes these core operations and CAP aerospace education and cadet programs. It also provides information about joining CAP or becoming a corporate partner. The News section has press releases, the annual report to Congress, and the online magazine *Civil Air Patrol Volunteer*.
Subjects: Civil Air Patrol
Publications: *Civil Air Patrol Volunteer*

462. Department of Homeland Security

http://www.dhs.gov/

Sponsor(s): Homeland Security Department

Description: The Department of Homeland Security was formed in January 2003 by consolidating many existing agencies and agency divisions whose missions relate to domestic defense. The DHS Web site organizes information into thematic sections: Information Sharing and Analysis; Prevention and Protection; Preparedness and Response; Research; Commerce and Trade; Travel Security and Procedures; and Immigration. Each of these sections has current news, publications, grants, laws, program links, and background information. Links to the free-standing Web sites of component agencies, such as the Transportation Security Administration, are usually included in these sections. A complete list of links to component agencies and offices is provided in the section About DHS, along with budget information, major reports, and leadership biographies.

Information is also organized for specific audiences: citizens, first responders, businesses, and governments (including grants information). A separate section, Open for Business, has DHS procurement information. The bottom of the home page lists quick links to selected DHS pages under the themes of Secure and Open Borders, Preparedness, and About the Department.

DHS redesigned its Web site in October 2006. The new design, while very similar to the previous, provides some additional paths to information. Researchers may also want to check the Web sites of DHS component agencies for detailed information. Many DHS component agencies are described elsewhere in this publication.

Subjects: Homeland Security

Publications: *National Response Plan*, HS 1.2:

463. FBI National Security Branch

http://www.fbi.gov/hq/nsb/nsb.htm

Sponsor(s): Justice Department — Federal Bureau of Investigation (FBI)

Description: The FBI National Security Branch (NSB) was established in 2005 to combine the bureau's counterterrorism, counterintelligence, and intelligence resources. The NSB Web site has news and background information about the branch. It also links to the Web pages for the NSB Counterterrorism Division, Counterintelligence Division, Directorate of Intelligence, and Weapons of Mass Destruction Directorate. The Counterterrorism Division page has information about the Terrorism Screening Center, including frequently asked questions about the consolidated terrorist watch list. The Counterintelligence Division page includes information about the Awareness of National Security Issues and Response (ANSIR) program, which disseminates unclassified national security threat and warning information to U.S. corporations, law enforcement, and government agencies.

Subjects: Homeland Security; Terrorism

464. Homeland Security Advanced Research Projects Agency — SBIR Program

http://www.hsarpasbir.com/

Sponsor(s): Homeland Security Department — Homeland Security Advanced Research Projects Agency (HSARPA)

Description: The Homeland Security Advanced Research Projects Agency (HSARPA) participates in the federal government's Small Business Innovation Research (SBIR) grant program. This official Web site presents information about solicitations, proposal review, and awards. (The Small Business Administration has addi-

tional information about the SBIR program on its Web site — in a section entitled SBIR and STTR Programs and Awards — described elsewhere in this book.)
Subjects: Homeland Security — Research

465. Homeland Security Advisory Council
http://www.dhs.gov/xinfoshare/committees/editorial_0331.shtm
Sponsor(s): Homeland Security Department
Description: The Homeland Security Advisory Council provides advice and recommendations to the secretary of homeland security. The council includes members from state and local government, academia, and the private sector. Its Web site contains member information, press releases, and meeting minutes.
Subjects: Homeland Security

466. Homeland Security Organization
http://www.llnl.gov/hso/
Sponsor(s): Energy Department — Lawrence Livermore National Laboratory (LLNL)
Description: The Homeland Security Organization at Lawrence Livermore National Laboratory maintains this Web site, which describes the organization's structure, goals, and programs. Program areas include Chemical and Biological Countermeasures, Nuclear and Radiological Countermeasures, and Information Analysis and Infrastructure Protection.
Subjects: Defense Research

467. Homeland Security SAFETY Act
http://www.safetyact.gov
Sponsor(s): Homeland Security Department
Description: The SAFETY Act, part of the Homeland Security Act of 2002 (Public Law 107-296), provides liability protections for sellers of qualified anti-terrorism products. This Web site provides information about the legislation and applications for the SAFETY Act Designation or Certification for products.
Subjects: Business — Regulations

468. Integrated Deepwater System (IDS)
http://www.uscg.mil/deepwater/
Sponsor(s): Homeland Security Department — Coast Guard
Description: The Coast Guard's IDS Program is a large acquisitions program intended to upgrade ships, aircraft, information systems, and logistics capabilities for deepwater — rather than coastal or inland — missions. Deepwater is defined on the IDS Web site as "beyond the normal operating range of single-crewed shore-based small boats." The site tracks the status of the program and provides links to congressional activity and published reports. The Domains section has information about the new cutters and aircraft that are part of the program.
Subjects: Homeland Security; Military Aircraft; Military Ships

469. Los Alamos Center for Homeland Security
http://www.lanl.gov/orgs/chs/
Sponsor(s): Energy Department — Los Alamos National Laboratory (LANL)
Description: The Los Alamos Center for Homeland Security applies LANL expertise in advanced research and technology to issues of homeland defense. Its Web site describes the center's work in the areas of borders, information, and infrastructure protection; chemical and biological threat reduction; and radiological and nuclear threat reduction.
Subjects: Defense Research

470. National Commission on Terrorist Attacks Upon the United States
http://www.9-11commission.gov/
Alternate URL(s): http://govinfo.library.unt.edu/911/
Sponsor(s): National Commission on Terrorist Attacks Upon the United States
Description: The National Commission on Terrorist Attacks Upon the United States — also known as the 9-11 Commission — was an independent, bipartisan commission charged with investigating the September 11, 2001, terrorist attacks. The 9-11 Commission issued its final public report in July 2004 and closed in August 2004. Documents at the site include the final report, video and transcript archives of the 12 public hearings, and staff monographs on terrorist financing and terrorist travel. The Press section includes photos and press releases.

This site is archived and will not be updated further. It has been kept online in its archived state by the National Archives and Records Administration and was still online at the time of this writing. The 9-11 Commission site has also been archived at the University of North Texas Libraries' CyberCemetery Web site (located at the alternate URL listed above).

Subjects: Homeland Security; Terrorism

Publications: *9/11 and Terrorist Travel: Staff Report of the National Commission on Terrorist Attacks*, Y 3.2:T 27/2/T 69

Eighth Public Hearing of the National Commission on Terrorist Attacks Upon the United States (March 23-24, 2004), Y 3.2:

Eleventh Public Hearing of the National Commission on Terrorist Attacks Upon the United States (May 18-19, 2004), Y 3.2:

Hearing of the National Commission on Terrorist Attacks Upon the United States (May 22-23, 2003), Y 3.2:

Hearing of the National Commission on Terrorist Attacks Upon the United States: Fourth Public Hearing, Intelligence and the War on Terrorism (October 14, 2003), Y 3.2:

Hearing of the National Commission on Terrorist Attacks Upon the United States: Subject, Private-Public Sector Partnerships for Emergency Preparedness (November 19, 2003), Y 3.2:

Hearing of the National Commission on Terrorist Attacks Upon the United States: Subject, Sixth Public Hearing (December 8, 2003), Y 3.2:

Hearing of the National Commission on Terrorist Attacks Upon the United States: Terrorism, Al Qaeda, and the Muslim World (July 9, 2003), Y 3.2:

Hearing of the National Commission on Terrorist Attacks Upon the United States: Witness, Dr. Condoleezza Rice (April 8, 2004), Y 3.2:

Monograph on Terrorist Financing: Staff Report to the Commission, Y 3.2:T 27/2/F 49

National Commission on Terrorist Attacks Upon the United States: Public Hearing (April 1, 2003), Y 3.2:

National Commission on Terrorist Attacks Upon the United States: Public Hearing (March 31, 2003), Y 3.2:

Seventh Public Hearing of the National Commission on Terrorist Attacks Upon the United States: Subject — Borders, Transportation and Managing Risks (January 26-27, 2004), Y 3.2:

Tenth Public Hearing of the National Commission on Terrorist Attacks Upon the United States (April 13-14, 2004), Y 3.2:

The 9/11 Commission Report. Executive Summary., Y 3.2:T 27/2/FINAL/EXEC.SUM

The 9/11 Commission Report: Final Report of the National Commission on Terrorist Attacks, Y 3.2:T 27/2/FINAL

Twelfth Public Hearing of the National Commission on Terrorist Attacks Upon the United States (June 16-17, 2004), Y 3.2:

471. Ready.gov

http://www.ready.gov/

Alternate URL(s): http://www.listo.gov/

Sponsor(s): Homeland Security Department

Description: The Ready.gov Web site provides advice on preparing for potential terrorist attacks or other emergencies. Advice is divided into sections for America (citizens), businesses, and kids. The America section includes advice for seniors, people with disabilities and special needs, and people with pets. Checklists and brochures can be downloaded in PDF format.

A Spanish-language version of the site is available at the alternate URL listed above.

Subjects: Disaster Preparedness; Homeland Security

472. Rewards for Justice

http://www.rewardsforjustice.net/

Sponsor(s): State Department — Diplomatic Security Bureau

Description: This Web site promotes awareness of the Department of State's monetary awards program for information that assists in countering acts of international terrorism against the United States. The site includes photos and information about the most wanted terrorists. An Acts of Terror section catalogs international terrorist incidents in which crimes were committed against U.S. citizens or property. Information about the rewards program is available in over 10 languages, including Spanish, French, Arabic, Russian, German, Farsi, and Pashtu.

Clearly designed to reach a more international audience than most U.S. government Web sites, Rewards for Justice also offers an RSS/XML feed and a podcast for announcements of new reward offers.

Subjects: Terrorism

473. Transportation Security Administration (TSA)

http://www.tsa.gov/

Sponsor(s): Homeland Security Department — Transportation Security Administration (TSA)

Description: TSA was established within the Department of Transportation in response to the terrorist attacks of September 11, 2001; it has since been transferred to the Department of Homeland Security. The agency has responsibility for transportation security nationwide. The TSA Web site provides information about its mission, organization, and operations. The Our Travelers section includes lists of items prohibited in carry-on or checked luggage, tips for travelers with disabilities or medical conditions, and information about security by mode of transport (air, rail, mass transit, etc.). The Research Center section covers a variety of topics, including the Aviation Security Advisory Committee, FOIA, civil rights and privacy issues, security fees, and security laws and regulations.

Subjects: Aviation Safety; Transportation Security

Publications: *Criminal Acts Against Civil Aviation*, TD 4.811:

474. U.S. Commission on National Security/21st Century

http://govinfo.library.unt.edu/nssg/index.html

Sponsor(s): Commission on National Security/21st Century (USCNS/21)

Description: The U.S. Commission on National Security/21st Century, also known as the Hart-Rudman Commission, was a bipartisan, independent advisory commission charged with thinking comprehensively and creatively about how the United States should provide for its national security during the first quarter of the twenty-first century. The commission issued its final report in February 2001. Its Web site has been archived by the University of North Texas Libraries Government

Documents Department. (As part of the Federal Depository Library Program, the UNT Libraries and Government Printing Office created a partnership to provide permanent public access to the Web sites and publications of defunct U.S. government agencies and commissions.)

The site featured three debate forums: Institutional Redesign, Securing the National Homeland, and Recapitalizing America's Science and Education. Other sections include About Us, Reports, and News. The commission's final report is available in PDF format.

After the tragic events of September 11, 2001, the commission's final report became an important reference document about security issues in the United States pertaining to terrorism. Fortunately, UNT Libraries has been able to archive the report, and the entire Web site is preserved exactly as it appeared when it was taken offline in 2004.

Subjects: National Security — Policy
Publications: *Road Map for National Security: Imperative for Change: The Phase III Report of the U.S. Commission on National Security/21st Century*, PR 43.2:SE 1/R 53/FINAL

475. United States Secret Service

http://www.secretservice.gov/
Sponsor(s): Homeland Security Department — Secret Service
Description: The United States Secret Service was transferred in 2003 from the Department of the Treasury, where it was founded in 1865, to the Department of Homeland Security. On the Web site, the Protection and Investigations sections describe the Secret Service's role in protecting the president, vice president, former U.S. presidents, visiting foreign dignitaries, and other leaders, as well as its role in investigating counterfeiting and other financial crimes. Under Investigations, the Know Your Money subsection provides details on how to detect counterfeit currency and guard against forgery loss. The Secret Service's National Threat Assessment Center provides reports on assessing threats against computer networks, public figures, schools, and the judiciary. Other sections cover Secret Service history, most wanted fugitives, employment information, and the field office directory.

Although the Secret Service does not discuss details of its security operations, its Web site is designed to give clear answers to many of the questions the public might have. The FAQ section answers such questions as "Who is the Secret Service authorized to protect?" and "How long do former presidents receive Secret Service protection after they leave office?" A Kid's FAQ section answers such questions as "Do I have to be good at math to be an agent?"

Subjects: Counterfeiting; Homeland Security; Law Enforcement

Intelligence

476. Air Intelligence Agency

http://aia.lackland.af.mil/
Sponsor(s): Air Force — Air Intelligence Agency (AIA)
Description: The Air Force Air Intelligence Agency, headquartered at Lackland Air Force Base in Texas, provides basic organizational and career information on its Web site. The Products and Services section features AIA publications and forms, FOIA information, and the online edition of *Spokesman* magazine.

Subjects: Intelligence Agencies; Military Intelligence
Publications: *Spokesman Magazine*, D 301.124:

477. Bureau of Intelligence and Research (INR)

http://www.state.gov/s/inr/

Sponsor(s): State Department

Description: The Department of State's Bureau of Intelligence and Research (INR) analyzes intelligence to support U.S. diplomacy. INR is a member of the U.S. intelligence community. Its Web site provides information about the Title VIII grants program supporting advanced research, language, and graduate training programs conducted by U.S.-based organizations. The site also has INR's Independent States in the World and Dependencies and Areas of Special Sovereignty lists, which give the department's official short and long names and Federal Information Processing Standard (FIPS) codes for the recognized independent countries and dependencies of the world.

Subjects: Intelligence; Language Education — Grants

478. Central Intelligence Agency

http://www.cia.gov/

Sponsor(s): Central Intelligence Agency (CIA)

Description: The CIA Web site has information about the agency, its directorates and centers, CIA careers, press releases, speeches and testimony, and a CIA Homepage for Kids section. Other sections include a Virtual Tour of the CIA, Frequently Asked Questions, and the CIA Museum. Full text, bibliographic, and order information for CIA maps and publications is available under the Library and Reference section, through the Publications link. The full-text versions of two major reference publications, *The World Factbook* and *Chiefs of State and Cabinet Members of Foreign Governments*, can be found online. In addition, the *Factbook on Intelligence* contains information about the history, structure, and operations of the CIA. The Press Room section of the site links to selected CIA reports from 1997 to present.

    The Directorate of Intelligence, Directorate of Science and Technology, and Office of General Counsel have sections describing their work and emphasizing CIA career opportunities. Other component sections include the Center for the Study of Intelligence, the Office of Military Affairs, and the Office of Public Affairs. The site also links to the Web sites for the Director of National Intelligence and the National Intelligence Council.

    The availability of *The World Factbook* and *Chiefs of State and Cabinet Members of Foreign Governments* makes the CIA Web site an important reference source.

Subjects: Foreign Countries; Intelligence Agencies

Publications: *Center for the Study of Intelligence (General Publications)*, PREX 3.17:
Center for the Study of Intelligence (Monographs), PREX 3.18:
Chiefs of State and Cabinet Members of Foreign Governments, PREX 3.11/2:
Comprehensive Report of the Special Advisor to the DCI on Iraq's WMD, PREX 3.2:
Factbook on Intelligence, PREX 3.2:
Studies in Intelligence, PREX 3.19:
The World Factbook, PREX 3.15/2:

479. CIA Electronic Reading Room

http://www.foia.cia.gov/

Sponsor(s): Central Intelligence Agency (CIA)

Description: This is the CIA's public gateway for access to agency documents through the Freedom of Information Act (FOIA) and the Electronic Freedom of Information Act. The centerpiece is a searchable database of records that have been created since 1940 and released or declassified under FOIA since November 1996. Users can search the full texts of the documents. A Frequently Requested Records section has the full text of a small set of frequently requested documents such as "UFOs: Fact or Fiction?"; the "Bay of Pigs Report"; and Vietnam POW/MIA documents. It also provides links to the 25 most-requested over the previous month. Under Special Collections, the site identifies declassified documents collections at Princeton University and the National Archives, and describes the CIA's Historical Review Program to review and declassify historically significant information. The Your Rights section identifies the laws governing the release of documents.

The CIA Electronic Reading Room will answer the basic questions a researcher may have about FOIA and other access to declassified documents from the CIA. Researchers may also want to check the Web site of the private National Security Archive group, which maintains a repository of declassified documents obtained through FOIA.

Subjects: Declassified Documents; Freedom of Information Act; Intelligence

480. Commission on the Intelligence Capabilities of the United States Regarding Weapons of Mass Destruction (WMD Commission)
http://www.wmd.gov/
Alternate URL(s): http://govinfo.library.unt.edu/wmd/
Sponsor(s): Commission on the Intelligence Capabilities of the United States Regarding Weapons of Mass Destruction
Description: The WMD Commission closed its offices in May 2005 after making its final report. Its Web site is still available at the primary URL listed above at the time of this writing. The site has also been archived at the University of North Texas Libraries' CyberCemetery, at the alternate URL above. The site includes the final report and information about the WMD Commission and its members.
Subjects: Intelligence Agencies
Publications: *The Commission on the Intelligence Capabilities of the United States Regarding Weapons of Mass Destruction Report to the President of the United States*

481. Defense Intelligence Agency
http://www.dia.mil/
Sponsor(s): Defense Department — Defense Intelligence Agency (DIA)
Description: DIA provides military intelligence to warfighters, defense planners, and defense and national security policymakers. Its Web site has information about DIA's organization and history, and employment and contracting opportunities with the agency. The DIA's Joint Military Intelligence College has its own section on the site. The Public Affairs section includes a FOIA archive with records on such topics as Pan Am Flight 103, poisonous snakes, and Soviet parapsychology research. The site also has an extensive image library and military art collection.
Subjects: Intelligence Agencies; Military Intelligence

482. In-Q-Tel
http://in-q-tel.com/
Sponsor(s): In-Q-Tel
Description: In-Q-Tel is a private, nonprofit enterprise funded by the CIA. It was established to help apply new commercial information technologies to intelligence and analysis. The In-Q-Tel Web site has information about the organization's history, mission, and leadership. The Technologies section gives an overview of In-Q-Tel's focus in the areas of software, infrastructure (security and semiconductors), and materials sciences (biotechnology and nanotechnology).
Subjects: Information Technology; Intelligence

483. Marine Corps Intelligence Department
http://hqinet001.hqmc.usmc.mil/dirint/mcrip/
Sponsor(s): Marine Corps
Description: The Marine Corps Intelligence Department is part of the U.S. intelligence community. The department's Web site has basic information about its mission, functions, and organization.
Subjects: Military Intelligence

484. National Counterterrorism Center
http://www.nctc.gov/
Sponsor(s): Office of the Director of National Intelligence
Description: The National Counterterrorism Center (NCTC) serves as the nation's central point for integrating and analyzing intelligence pertaining to terrorism and counterterrorism. The NCTC site provides background information about the agency and its role.
Subjects: Terrorism

485. National Geospatial-Intelligence Agency
http://www.nga.mil/
Sponsor(s): Defense Department — National Geospatial-Intelligence Agency (NGA)
Description: NGA, formerly known as the National Imagery and Mapping Agency (NIMA), is an intelligence and combat support agency with expertise in cartography, geospatial analysis, imagery analysis, geodesy, and related disciplines. NIMA was formed in 1996 and the agency was renamed in late 2003. The Products and Services section of its Web site has instructions on ordering agency publications that are in the public domain; publications are not available from a single source and are not directly available from the agency. Another feature is the Raster Roam tool, which provides public access to view and download imagery, maps, digital elevation data, and other geographic information produced by the federal government and commercial vendors. The Products and Services section also leads to the agency's divisional home pages and the public domain information, databases, and software it offers. Divisions include Geospatial Sciences, Aeronautical Information, and Maritime Safety Information. Specific links include the GEOnet Names Server (NGA database of foreign geographic feature names) and the National Center for Geospatial Intelligence Standards.

Although much of NGA's work product is classified and restricted to authorized users, the Web site does have information to share with the geospatial sciences community, particularly in its Products and Services section.
Subjects: Maps and Mapping; Military Intelligence
Publications: *Foreign Names Information Bulletin*, I 33.3/2:
GEOnet Names Server (database), D 5.319/2:
Notice to Mariners, D 5.315:
Pathfinder: The Geospatial Intelligence Magazine

486. National Intelligence Council
http://www.dni.gov/nic/
Sponsor(s): Office of the Director of National Intelligence
Description: The National Intelligence Council (NIC) reports to the Office of Director of National Intelligence on matters of mid-term and long-term strategic thinking. The NIC Web site has information about its history, mission, and organization. Its primary product is the Estimate, or forward-looking assessment. The Declassified NIC Publications section highlights past National Intelligence Estimates for Vietnam and China. In this same section, the Other Publications link points to

the searchable NIC collection of declassified documents at the CIA FOIA Electronic Reading Room.
Subjects: Intelligence Agencies
Publications: *Mapping the Global Future*, PREX 3.21:

487. National Reconnaissance Office
http://www.nro.gov/
Sponsor(s): Defense Department — National Reconnaissance Office (NRO)
Description: As part of the U.S. intelligence community, the NRO designs, builds, and operates the nation's reconnaissance satellites. The Web site provides an agency overview, press releases, and contracting information. One section is dedicated to information, photos, and videos about Corona, the first photo reconnaissance satellite system.
Subjects: Intelligence Agencies

488. National Security Agency
http://www.nsa.gov/
Sponsor(s): Defense Department — National Security Agency (NSA)
Description: Specializing in cryptology, NSA works to protect U.S. information systems security and to produce foreign intelligence. The Web site's About NSA section includes leadership biographies, answers to frequently asked questions, overviews of the Information Assurance and Signal Intelligence fields, and links to information on the National Cryptologic Museum and National Cryptologic Memorial. A History section provides brochures and photos about NSA history. The Research section includes published staff work, technology transfer information, and a feature on security-enhanced Linux. The Public Info section links to press releases, congressional testimony, Freedom of Information Act (FOIA) releases, and information from NSA's own declassification initiatives.
Subjects: Cryptography and Encryption; Intelligence Agencies

489. National Security Archive
http://www.gwu.edu/~nsarchiv/
Sponsor(s): National Security Archive
Description: The National Security Archive is a private, independent research institute and library located at George Washington University in Washington, DC. Despite the official-sounding name, it is not a government agency. The archive collects and publishes declassified documents acquired through the Freedom of Information Act (FOIA). Only a fraction of the archive's holdings are online; nevertheless, the online offerings are significant.

The archive has an online collection called the "September 11th Sourcebooks," with public and declassified documents on such topics as U.S. terrorism policy, the Soviet war in Afghanistan, and the hunt for Osama bin Laden. This and other online collections can be found in the collection of Electronic Briefing Books under the Documents heading. They cover such topics as Cold War events, CIA involvement in Latin America, nuclear history, government secrecy, and U.S. intelligence agencies.

The National Security Archive provides a valuable research service offline, with its archive of declassified U.S. documents obtained through FOIA and its own print and microform publications. The online collections meet some popular information needs and present documents with contextual commentary identifying the people and events related to the documents.
Subjects: Declassified Documents; Foreign Policy — Research; Freedom of Information Act

490. Office of Intelligence Policy and Review

http://www.justice.gov/oipr/

Sponsor(s): Justice Department — Office of Intelligence Policy and Review
Description: Among its other duties, the Office of Intelligence Policy and Review prepares and files all applications for electronic surveillance and physical search under the Foreign Intelligence Surveillance Act of 1978. Most information on the site is found in the FOIA electronic reading room section. The"Annual Foreign Surveillance Act Report to Congress," typically a one-page letter, provides a count of the requests to conduct electronic surveillance or physical searches under the Foreign Intelligence Surveillance Act.
Subjects: Intelligence — Laws

491. Office of Naval Intelligence (ONI)

http://www.nmic.navy.mil/

Sponsor(s): Navy — Naval Intelligence Office
Description: This Web site has basic information about ONI and its employment opportunities. The History section, under the About Us heading, provides a brief illustrated history of ONI since its founding in 1882.
Subjects: Intelligence Agencies; Military Intelligence

492. Office of the Director of National Intelligence

http://www.dni.gov/

Sponsor(s): Office of the Director of National Intelligence
Description: The Office of the Director of National Intelligence (ODNI) was established by the Intelligence Reform and Terrorism Prevention Act of 2004 (Public Law 108-458), following a recommendation of the 9-11 Commission. The director is the principal adviser to the president on intelligence, separate from the CIA. The Web site includes an interactive organization chart and sections on major ODNI organizations, including the Information Sharing Environment, the National Counterterrorism Center, the National Intelligence Council, and the National Counterintelligence Executive.
Subjects: Intelligence Agencies
Publications: *National Intelligence Strategy of the United States of America,* PREX 28.2:

493. Office of the National Counterintelligence Executive

http://www.ncix.gov/

Sponsor(s): Office of the National Counterintelligence Executive
Description: The National Counterintelligence Executive is appointed by the president and is charged with improving the performance of U.S. counterintelligence efforts. This Web site has information about the office, its mission, and organization. The site offers a four-volume reader on the evolution of U.S. counterintelligence in PDF format, beginning with the American Revolutionary War. Under Publications, the site provides the text of counterintelligence laws and booklets with advice about economic espionage and protecting oneself while traveling abroad. The site also links to information about the National Counterintelligence Institute, which was begun in 2006.
Subjects: Intelligence Agencies
Publications: *National Counterintelligence Strategy of the United States,* Y 3.C 83/2:15/

494. Open Source Center
http://www.opensource.gov/
Sponsor(s): Central Intelligence Agency (CIA) — Open Source Center (OSC)
Description: The Open Source Center Web site is only available to registered, qualified government and military users. It provides English translations of news and information from a wide array of unclassified international sources. The Open Source Center was established as part of the CIA in late 2005; it absorbed the Foreign Broadcast Information Service (FBIS), which previously published English translations of foreign broadcasts and printed news.
Subjects: Intelligence — International; News Services

495. OpenNet
http://www.osti.gov/opennet/
Sponsor(s): Energy Department — Nuclear and National Security Information Office
Description: The Department of Energy's OpenNet database consists of references to government documents declassified (or never classified) and made publicly available after October 1, 1994. The documents concern nuclear weapons testing, studies of the effects of radiation, and related activities of the U.S. and other governments. The site's Advanced Search function includes the ability to search full-text documents, as well as limit searches by declassification status, document location, and other factors. The main page of the Web site links to the Department's *Report on Inadvertent Releases of Restricted Data and Formerly Restricted Data under Executive Order 12958* (as presented to Congress) and other Department of Energy Openness Initiative products.
Subjects: Declassified Documents; Nuclear Weapons — History
Publications: *Report on Inadvertent Releases of Restricted Data and Formerly Restricted Data under Executive Order 12958*, E 1.143:

496. U.S. Army Intelligence and Security Command (INSCOM)
http://www.inscom.army.mil/
Sponsor(s): Army — Army Intelligence and Security Command
Description: INSCOM collects battlefield intelligence and has responsibilities in the areas of counterintelligence and force protection, electronic warfare, and information warfare. The central INSCOM Web site links to its organizational components and field Web sites.
Subjects: Military Intelligence
Publications: *INSCOM Journal*, D 101.85:

497. United States Intelligence Community
http://www.intelligence.gov/
Sponsor(s): Office of the Director of National Intelligence
Description: This Web site provides a unified face to the collection of agencies and offices referred to as the U.S. intelligence community. The site explains the IC's structure, goals, and membership. It also has a recruitment page for those interested in careers in intelligence.
Subjects: Intelligence Agencies

498. University of Military Intelligence
http://www.universityofmilitaryintelligence.us/
Sponsor(s): Army — Army Intelligence Center
Description: Part of the United States Army Intelligence Center, the University of Military Intelligence maintains a Web site with information about its training

and related resources. The site also features the quarterly *Military Intelligence Professional Bulletin (MIPB)*.
Subjects: Military Intelligence
Publications: *Military Intelligence Professional Bulletin*, D 101.84:

Military Morale and Welfare

499. Air Force Crossroads
http://www.afcrossroads.com/
Sponsor(s): Air Force
Description: Air Force Crossroads is the official community Web site of the U.S. Air Force. The site offers a multitude of links to information important to Air Force family members on topics such as casualty and loss, Department of Defense installations, education, employment, family separation and readiness, finances, and relocation.
Subjects: Military Morale and Welfare

500. Air Force Medical Service
http://airforcemedicine.afms.mil/
Sponsor(s): Air Force — Air Force Medical Service
Description: The Air Force Medical Service Web site has basic information about the service and Air Force medical facilities. The Public Affairs section includes the newsletter of the Air Force Surgeon General, *Newswire*.
Subjects: Air Force; Military Medicine
Publications: *Newswire*

501. America Supports You
http://americasupportsyou.mil/
Sponsor(s): Defense Department
Description: America Supports You highlights stories of citizens expressing support for the U.S. troops. It includes an online form for sending message to the troops, and posts both the messages and responses from the troops.
Subjects: Military Morale and Welfare

502. Arlington National Cemetery
http://www.arlingtoncemetery.org
Sponsor(s): Arlington National Cemetery
Description: The official Web site for Arlington National Cemetery is organized into the following sections: Visitor Information, Funeral Information, Ceremonies, Historical Information, and Photo Gallery. The site is rich in historical information about such topics as famous memorials, lists of famous individuals buried at Arlington, the origins of "Taps" and the 21-gun salute, and the history of the Tomb of the Unknowns. The Photo Gallery section includes photographs of military burial ceremonies. The Funeral Information section provides information about eligibility requirements for interment or inurnment at Arlington.

While it may not be obvious from the simple and uncluttered home page, this site is rich in information. Researchers looking for historic information are advised to look in both the Visitor Information and Ceremonies sections, as well as in the Historic Information section. There is a site map to aid in exploration, but no search engine.
Subjects: Military History; Veterans' Cemeteries

503. Armed Forces Retirement Home
http://www.afrh.gov/
Sponsor(s): Armed Forces Retirement Home (AFRH)
Description: The Armed Forces Retirement Home (AFRH) consists of two campuses, one in Washington, DC, and one in Gulfport, MS. The Gulfport campus was damaged by Hurricane Katrina and has been closed since then. The site has information about both facilities.
Subjects: Veterans

504. Army and Air Force Exchange Service
http://www.aafes.com/
Sponsor(s): Defense Department — Army and Air Force Exchange Service (AAFES)
Description: AAFES serves active duty military members, retirees, reservists, and their dependents by providing goods and services through a corporation and central store that sell a wide range of consumer products. While AAFES's physical facilities are located on military bases, its online presence provides access to its services to any eligible person with Internet access. The AAFES Web site includes online shopping, store locations, job openings, and information about AAFES, with most sections open only to authorized users. It also has an option for sending gift certificates or prepaid phone cards to deployed troops.

This site caters to the active and retired military community authorized to shop at Army and Air Force Exchanges. Others may find useful information in the About AAFES section, which explains the history and operations of the military base exchanges and provides information for suppliers or manufacturers wanting to do business with AAFES.
Subjects: Military Morale and Welfare

505. Department of Defense Education Activity (DoDEA)
http://www.dodea.edu/
Sponsor(s): Defense Department — Department of Defense Education Activity
Description: This is the official Internet presence of the K–12 schools operated by the Department of Defense, which are located overseas and in the United States. The DoDEA Web site features school directories and profiles, school enrollment data, and standardized achievement test scores. Employment information can be found in the Human Resources section.
Subjects: Elementary and Secondary Education; Military Morale and Welfare

506. Department of Veterans Affairs (VA)
http://www.va.gov/
Sponsor(s): Veterans Affairs Department
Description: The VA Web site features a variety of sections useful to veterans and those helping veterans claim benefits. It has a directory of VA facilities and offices nationwide and a section for applying for benefits online. Major sections include Health Care, Benefits (Pension, Education, Home Loans, Survivors' Benefits, and more), Burials and Memorials, Board of Veterans' Appeals, VA Jobs, and Business Opportunities.

This site should prove useful to veterans and people involved in assisting them. Using the site map will help to uncover all of the available information.
Subjects: Veterans
Publications: *Federal Benefits for Veterans and Dependents*, VA 1.19; *Geographic Distribution of VA Expenditures*, VA 1.2/11;

507. EDUGATE

https://ca.dtic.mil/edugate/

Sponsor(s): Defense Department

Description: This Web site provides general information on educational programs sponsored in whole or in part by the Department of Defense; it also provides informational resources for teachers. The site was originally intended to include only programs in the sciences, mathematics, and engineering, but it has expanded in scope to include all DoD-supported educational programs. Nevertheless, most listed programs fall within the original scope. Programs include summer internships, tuition assistance, and more.

This is an excellent resource for finding educational materials and links to DoD educational resources at all educational levels.

Subjects: Military Training and Education

508. Employer Support of the Guard and Reserve

http://www.esgr.mil/

Sponsor(s): Defense Department — Office of the Secretary of Defense

Description: The National Committee for Employer Support of the Guard and Reserve (ESGR) works to facilitate the relationship between Reserve component members and their civilian employers. The Reserve is defined as all National Guard members and Reserve forces from all branches of the military. This Web site has information about the Uniformed Services Employment and Reemployment Rights Act (USERRA), ESGR incentive programs for employers, and local employer support volunteers. It also provides tips and facts sheets for both employers and for members of the Reserve forces.

Subjects: Labor-Management Relations; Military Reserves; National Guard

509. LIFELines

http://www.lifelines.navy.mil/

Sponsor(s): Marine CorpsNavy

Description: The Navy and Marine Corps sponsor this portal to quality of life information for military personnel. The site links to information about housing, education, combat stress, family life, financial management, health insurance, relocation, and transition assistance, and other related topics.

Subjects: Military Morale and Welfare

510. Military Sentinel

http://www.consumer.gov/military/

Sponsor(s): Defense DepartmentFederal Trade Commission (FTC)

Description: Military Sentinel is a cooperative project between the FTC and the Department of Defense to provideconsumer protection advice for members of the armed forces and their families. To file a consumer complaint, users should click on the seal representing their service branch.

Subjects: Consumer Information; Military Morale and Welfare

511. Military Teens on the Move (MTOM)

http://www.dod.mil/mtom/

Sponsor(s): Defense Department — Military Assistance Program

Description: MTOM gives military adolescents tips on dealing with their parents' military career and relocations. The site also has a section called MTOM For Kids, which addresses moving and relocation issues for younger children.

Subjects: Adolescents; Military Morale and Welfare

512. MilitaryHOMEFRONT

http://www.militaryhomefront.dod.mil/

Sponsor(s): Defense Department

Description: MilitaryHOMEFRONT is the official Department of Defense Web site for military quality of life information and services. Topics include financial assistance, family life, housing, health, and education. It has three audience-specific sections: Troops and Families, Leadership, and Service Providers. On the site's home page, the QOL (Quality of Life) Resources section includes a military community directory with state-by-state and overseas listings of military family support centers. The Reports section includes the *1st Quadrennial Quality of Life Review Report to Congress*.

Subjects: Military Morale and Welfare

513. Navy Environmental Health Center

http://www-nehc.med.navy.mil/

Sponsor(s): Navy — Navy Environmental Health Center

Description: The Navy Environmental Health Center aims to ensure Navy and Marine Corps readiness through leadership in the prevention of disease and the promotion of health. The site links to the center's directorates and field activities. Although much of the site is designed for a Navy audience, some pages provide health information of general interest.

Subjects: Preventive Health Care; Military Medicine

514. Navy Medicine Online Portal

http://navymedicine.med.navy.mil/

Sponsor(s): Navy — Medicine and Surgery Bureau

Description: The Navy Bureau of Medicine and Surgery provides health care to active duty Navy and Marine Corps members, retired servicemembers, and their families. This site primarily provides information and services for those working in the Navy medical system and for the sailors they serve. The site also carries the texts of Navy Medicine Policies and Navy Medicine Directives.

Subjects: Military Medicine

515. Safeguarding the Rights of Servicemembers and Veterans

http://www.servicemembers.gov/

Sponsor(s): Justice Department — Civil Rights Division

Description: This Web site explains the major laws that support the rights of veterans and military servicemembers: the Uniformed Services Employment and Reemployment Rights Act (USERRA), the Uniformed and Overseas Citizen Absentee Voting Act (UOCAVA), and the Servicemembers Civil Relief Act (SCRA). The site has information about filing claims, recent cases, and frequently asked questions. It also provides referrals to related resources.

Subjects: Military Forces; Veterans

516. SportsLink

http://dod.mil/armedforcessports/

Sponsor(s): Defense Department — Armed Forces Sports Council (AFSC)

Description: This central Web site for sports activities in the military features a calendar of armed forces championship competitions and sections for each included sport.

Subjects: Military Morale and Welfare; Sports

517. Veterans Benefits Administration
http://www.vba.va.gov/
Sponsor(s): Veterans Affairs Department — Veterans Benefits Administration (VBA)
Description: The VBA Web site is part of the larger Department of Veterans Affairs (VA) Web site. It displays the same side menu bar as the VA site, followed by specific VBA menu items. VBA offers Benefits Fact Sheets, in English and Spanish, covering such topics as service-connected disabilities, home loans, and insurance. The site has forms and applications, links to regional VA office Web sites, and a section on survivors' benefits. The Reports and Surveys section includes the *VBA Annual Benefits Report* and results from customer and employee satisfaction surveys.
Subjects: Veterans
Publications: *VBA Annual Benefits Report*

518. White House Commission on Remembrance
http://www.remember.gov/
Sponsor(s): White House Commission on the National Moment of Remembrance
Description: The White House Commission on the National Moment of Remembrance was established by Congress to honor active U.S. troops, U.S. troops who have died in service, and citizens killed as the result of acts of terrorism. Its Web site has information about the commission and its activities. A section called Toll of Terrorism provides background information about such events as the Oklahoma City bombing, the *USS Cole* incident, and September 11, 2001 terrorist attacks.
Subjects: Military Forces; Terrorism

CHAPTER 6
Demographics and Sociology

Much of the statistical information about the U.S. population comes from the Department of Commerce's Census Bureau. This chapter includes Census Bureau Web sites presenting demographic data, Web sites from other agencies that produce demographic data, and sites from academic institutions that play a role in making Census data available on the Internet. Information on other types of federal government statistics, such as education statistics, can be found in the relevant subject chapters, such as the Education chapter.

Subsections in this chapter are Census and Statistics and Demographic Groups.

Census and Statistics

519. American Community Survey (ACS)
http://www.census.gov/acs/www/
Sponsor(s): Commerce Department — Economics and Statistics Administration (ESA) — Census Bureau
Description: The Census Bureau's American Community Survey (ACS) is part of a revised Census strategy. ACS gathers selected sample data on demographics, housing, and social and economic information every year. It will replace the current Census of Population and Housing long form sample data in 2010 (but not the short form distributed to all U.S. households). The goal of the program is to provide governments with data that are more timely than the data from the decennial census in order to help administer federal programs, distribute funding, and plan future projects. This Web site describes ACS's goals, methodology, data release schedule, products, and other details.

This site points to the ACS data, which is integrated into the Census Bureau's American FactFinder interface. The site also has information about how to use the data and announcements of new ACS products. Basic information about ACS is provided in Spanish, Vietnamese, and other languages.

This site provides a wealth of background information about the relatively new ACS and about the transition from the long form data.
Subjects: Census Techniques
Publications: *American Community Survey*, C 3.297:

520. American FactFinder
http://factfinder.census.gov/
Sponsor(s): Commerce Department — Economics and Statistics Administration (ESA) — Census Bureau
Description: American FactFinder is a major Census Bureau effort to help the public retrieve, print, and download the Census Bureau's data. Users do not have to know the names or details of individual datasets; instead, they can select options from sections including People, Housing, and Business and Government. Each of these topical sections can be searched by geographic area to display a menu of available data tables and thematic maps.

The Data Sets section of American FactFinder is designed for more advanced users, although it is still straightforward and menu-driven. Users can select between the decennial census, the American Community Survey, the Economic Census and annual economic surveys, and annual population estimates. Each data set page offers appropriate options for creating customized tables, comparisons, and thematic maps.

The Maps section provides direct access to tools for reference and thematic maps. The Reference Shelf section links to the PDF versions of popular printed Census publications and to other Census Web pages appropriate for the average user.

American FactFinder accesses enough data and has enough functionality to make it the first and last stop for many users, especially those looking for population and housing statistics in the form of basic tables and geographic comparisons.

Subjects: Census; Economic Statistics; Population Statistics

521. Census 2000 Gateway

http://www.census.gov/main/www/cen2000.html

Sponsor(s): Commerce Department — Economics and Statistics Administration (ESA) — Census Bureau

Description: As its name implies, the Census 2000 Gateway Web site is a starting point for finding products, datasets, news, documentation, and other information relating to the latest decennial census of population and housing. There are three main approaches to the data itself. The American FactFinder section provides tables and maps of Census 2000 data for all geographies, from the nation as a whole to the block level. The State and County Quick Facts section has summaries of the most requested data for states and counties. The Data Highlights section links to a variety of information at the state, county, and place level, including American FactFinder tables and maps, FTP access to data sets, technical documentation, news releases, state data center contacts, redistricting data, and other related statistics. Other data reports include rankings and comparisons, briefs and special reports, and selected historical census data.

The Census Gateway also has Census Bureau operations information, the Census Store, PDF copies of the short and long form questionnaires, and contact information for bureau subject experts and state and local resource centers. A Census in Schools section includes teaching resources and lesson plans.

Subjects: Census; Population Statistics

522. Census 2010

http://www.census.gov/2010census/

Sponsor(s): Commerce Department — Economics and Statistics Administration (ESA) — Census Bureau

Description: The Census Bureau has launched a Web site for the 2010 decennial census. At this early stage, the site consists largely of job news related to the 2010 effort and information on opportunities for communities to get involved. The site also has general information on the decennial census.

Subjects: Census

523. Census Bureau

http://www.census.gov/

Sponsor(s): Commerce Department — Economics and Statistics Administration (ESA) — Census Bureau

Description: The Census Bureau home page offers multiple routes to the wide variety of information from and about the bureau. Major categories include Census 2000, People and Households, Business and Industry, Geography, Newsroom, and Special Topics. The Publications section and Subjects A to Z index provide other avenues to the data. The Data Tools section links to Internet data tools, software, databases, and the American FactFinder (described elsewhere in this chapter). Information about the Census Bureau itself is provided in the sections About the Bureau, Regional Offices, and Doing Business With Us sections.

Overall, the Census Bureau Web site offers one of the largest collections of readily accessible statistical data and recent statistical press releases on the

Internet. This should be one of the first sites checked by users for demographic and economic statistics.

Subjects: Census; Economic Statistics; Population Statistics
Publications: *American FactFinder,* C 3.300:
American Housing Survey, H-150, C 3.215/19:
America's Families and Living Arrangements, C 3.186/17-2:
Annual Benchmark Report for Retail Trade, C 3.138/3-8:
Annual Benchmark Report for Wholesale Trade, C 3.133/5:
Annual Capital Expenditures, C 3.289:
Annual Survey of Manufactures, C 3.24/9
Census Brief, C 3.205/8:
Census of Construction Industries: Geographic Area Series, C 3.245/7:
Census of Governments, C 3.145/4:
Census of Transportation, Communications, and Utilities, C 3.292:
Census Product Update, C 3.163/7-2:
Consolidated Federal Funds Report, C 3.266/3:
Construction Reports: Housing Completions, C22, C 3.215/13:
Construction Reports: Housing Units Authorized by Building Permits, C40, C 3.215/4:
Construction Reports: New One-Family Homes Sold and For Sale, C25, C 3.215/9:
Construction Reports: Value of Construction Put in Place, C30, C 3.215/3:
County Business Patterns, United States, C 3.204/3-1:
Current Business Reports, Service Annual Survey, C 3.138/3-4:
Current Business Reports: Annual Survey of Communications Services, C 3.138/3-6:
Current Business Reports: Monthly Retail Trade Sales & Inventories, C 3.138/3:
Current Business Reports: Monthly Wholesale Trade, C 3.133:
Current Housing Reports, C 3.215:
Current Industrial Reports, C 3.158:
Current Population Reports, Consumer Income, C 3.186:P-60/
Current Population Reports, Population Characteristics, C 3.186:P-20/
Current Population Reports, Special Studies, C 3.186:P-23/
Economic Census, C 3.277/3:
Federal Expenditures by State, C 3.266:
Government Finance and Employment Classification Manual, C 3.6/2:F 49/6/
Guide to Foreign Trade Statistics, C 3.6/2:F 76
Housing Vacancies and Homeownership Survey, C 3.294:
International Briefs (IB) Series, C 3.205/9:
Measuring America: the Decennial Censuses from 1790 to 2000, C 3.2:
News Releases, Census Bureau, C 3.295:
Population Profile of the United States, C 3.186/8:
Public Elementary-Secondary Education Finances, C 3.191/2-10:
Quarterly Employee Retirement, C 3.242:
Quarterly Financial Report for Manufacturing, Mining and Trade Corporations, C 3.267:
Quarterly Tax Survey, C 3.145/6:
School Enrollment Social and Economic Characteristics, C 3.186/12:
State and Metropolitan Area Data Book, C 3.134/5:
State Government Tax Collection Data by State, C 3.191/2-8:
Statistical Abstract of the United States, C 3.134:
Survey of Minority-Owned Business Enterprises, C 3.258:
Telephone Contacts for Data Users, C 3.238/5:
The Hispanic Population in the United States, C 3.186/14-2:
U.S. Trade with Puerto Rico and U.S. Possessions, FT-895, C 3.164:895/
Voting and Registration in the Election of. . ., C 3.186/3-2:

We the People. . .(series), C 3.205/8-3:
We, the Americans . . . (series), C 3.2:AM 3/
Women-Owned Businesses, C 3.250:

524. Census Bureau Regional Offices
http://www.census.gov/field/www/
Sponsor(s): Commerce Department — Economics and Statistics Administration (ESA) — Census Bureau
Description: This Web site uses a clickable image map and alternative text list to link to the Web sites of the Census Bureau's 12 regional offices of the Census Bureau. Each office's page provides local contact information, employment opportunities, and information about regional resources.
Subjects: Census

525. Census Monitoring Board
http://govinfo.library.unt.edu/cmb/cmbp/
Alternate URL(s): http://govinfo.library.unt.edu/cmb/cmbc/
Sponsor(s): Census Monitoring Board
Description: The Census Monitoring Board was an eight-member bipartisan oversight board that was created in 1997 to monitor all aspects of the 2000 decennial census and report its findings to Congress. Four board members were appointed by the president, two by the House of Representatives, and two by the Senate. The presidential and congressional appointees created separate Web sites and filed separate reports. Much of the material on these sites concerns the issue of statistical adjustment for possible undercounts. Both sites have been archived at the University of North Texas Libraries CyberCemetery Web site. The presidential appointees maintained the site given here as the primary URL. The alternate URL is for the congressional appointees' site.
Subjects: Census Techniques

526. Census State Data Center Program
http://www.census.gov/sdc/www/
Sponsor(s): Commerce Department — Economics and Statistics Administration (ESA) — Census Bureau
Description: This Web site provides basic contact information for the Census Data Center in each state, along with an overview of services available at each center. It also links to related sites, such as the State Data Center and Business Industry Data Center network.
Subjects: Census

527. County and City Data Book (at Geostat)
http://fisher.lib.virginia.edu/collections/stats/ccdb/
Sponsor(s): University of Virginia Library
Description: The Census Bureau's *County and City Data Book* series presents statistical tables for all U.S. counties, all U.S. cities with 25,000 or more people, and all U.S. places of 2,500 or more people. This Web site, from the University of Virginia Library's Geospatial and Statistical Data Center, offers access to data from the 1988, 1994, and 2000 editions of the *County and City Data Book*. Initial access is by city, state, county, or place data. The 1994 and 2000 editions also include rankings and source notes. After choosing the geographic level, the user can select which of the more than 200 available variables should be displayed. Variables cover such areas as demographics, housing, income and poverty, wholesale and retail trade, and government employment and expenditures. The results

can be displayed in HTML or as a comma-delimited file (available via anonymous FTP).

The site also has historical city, county, and state data for 1944 to 1983. This data can be used to build custom tables online, but it is not available for download.

The *County and City Data Book* is available online in PDF format from the Census Bureau Web site. The Geostat version has much more functionality, as it allows users to select and manipulate data and to customize reports. The next edition of the *Data Book* will be dated 2006 and should be available on both the Geostat and Census Web sites.

Subjects: Population Statistics
Publications: *County and City Data Book*, C 3.134/2:C 83/2/

528. Fast Facts for Congress
http://fastfacts.census.gov/
Sponsor(s): Commerce Department — Economics and Statistics Administration (ESA) — Census Bureau
Description: This Web site was designed for use by members of Congress and their staff, but it is available to the general public. The site's emphasis is on access to Census Bureau data by congressional district, by state and by other local geographies. Searches by congressional district locate basic population, housing, and economic statistics with the data mapped to the district boundaries. The home page also links to congressional district maps and other popular Census Bureau products.
Subjects: Congressional Districts — Statistics

529. Historical Census Browser
http://fisher.lib.virginia.edu/collections/stats/histcensus/
Sponsor(s): Inter-University Consortium for Political and Social Research (ICPSR); University of Virginia Library
Description: The Historical Census Data Browser has statistics from each of the decennial census reports from 1790 to 1960. The data on this Web site come from datasets created by ICPSR and taken from the U.S. decennial censuses and other sources. Coverage is available for all existing counties and states during the 1790–1960 period. Subject coverage includes population and a variety of other criteria, depending on which date is chosen.

This is one of the few sites that provide historical U.S. census data. The forms-based interface is easy to use and the generated HTML output is easy to browse. The tables automatically generate sums when relevant; there are also options to sort and graph the data once it is initially displayed. Users who need to do more complex manipulations of the data will be referred to ICPSR for access to the original data sets. Researchers may also want to consult the Census Bureau's Selected Historical Decennial Census Population and Housing Counts Web page, also described in this chapter. This page provides historical background and scanned copies of historical Census Bureau documents.
Subjects: Census; Databases

530. International Programs Center (IPC)
http://www.census.gov/ipc/www/
Sponsor(s): Commerce Department — Economics and Statistics Administration (ESA) — Census Bureau
Description: IPC, part of the Census Bureau's Population Division, offers a variety of international population statistics at its site. The World Population section features the World POPClock with a second-by-second simulation of the world's population growth, along with a calculation of world births, deaths, and natural increase for the current year expressed per year, month, day, hour, minute, and

second. The site also has a table of census dates for countries of the world from 1945 to 2014.

The IPC produces two databases: the International Data Base and the HIV/AIDS Surveillance Database. Each can be downloaded and run on a local computer, but the site also offers summary tables from each database that are extensive enough to meet many reference needs. Additionally, the site describes the center and its work, and offers some software applications and a training program schedule.

This is a useful site for those interested in demographics beyond the United States.

Subjects: Vital Statistics — International

531. IPUMS USA

http://usa.ipums.org/usa/

Sponsor(s): University of Minnesota — Minnesota Population Center

Description: The Integrated Public Use Microdata Series (IPUMS) consists of census microdata for social and economic research. It is a project of the University of Minnesota that is partially funded by the National Science Foundation and National Institutes of Health. IPUMS USA offers population and household data from the U.S. decennial census from 1850 to 2000. Users can download data by either extracting custom files or downloading entire data sets. IPUMS is free but registration is required before extracting data.

The IPUMS tools may be the most useful to expert researchers running statistical studies using sample data. The data cannot be browsed online and extracted files are very large.

Subjects: Census

532. POPClocks

http://www.census.gov/main/www/popclock.html

Sponsor(s): Commerce Department — Economics and Statistics Administration (ESA) — Census Bureau

Description: Two population clocks, or POPClocks, give up-to-the-minute estimates of the population. The United States POPClock estimates the resident population of the United States at the current minute and gives the criteria for how the estimate is derived; historical estimates and documentation are also available. The World POPClock estimates the world's population at the current minute, lists monthly estimates for the next year, links to other world population information and POPClocks, and provides notes on the estimates. The Census Bureau also provides an RSS feed for daily updates on the U.S. or world populations.

The POPClocks are useful for demonstrating the rate of change in the U.S. and world populations. However, before citing the estimates, users should read the documentation on how those estimates are reached and revised.

Subjects: Population Statistics

533. Selected Historical Decennial Census Counts

http://www.census.gov/population/www/censusdata/hiscendata.html

Sponsor(s): Commerce Department — Economics and Statistics Administration (ESA) — Census Bureau

Description: The full title of this Web page is "Selected Historical Decennial Census Population and Housing Counts." It compiles links to past census data. The actual decennial reports are online in PDF format for every decade from 1790 through 2000, along with corresponding historical notes. The page also links to tabulations of data items across the years. For example, it links to a table comparing urban and rural populations for 1790 through 1990 and to historical census statistics on the foreign-born population for 1850 through 1990. Histories and question-naires from past censuses are also provided.

Researchers may also wish to consult the University of Virginia's Historical Census Browser, which is described elsewhere in this chapter. This page presents data from each census from 1790 to 1960.

Subjects: Census — History; Population Statistics

Publications: *Historical Census Statistics on the Foreign-born Population of the United States: 1850-1900,* C 3.223/27:

Historical Statistics of the United States: Colonial Times to 1970, C 3.2:

Measuring America: the Decennial Censuses from 1790 to 2000, C 3.2:

534. State and County QuickFacts

http://quickfacts.census.gov/qfd/

Sponsor(s): Commerce Department — Economics and Statistics Administration (ESA) — Census Bureau

Description: State and County QuickFacts offers simple access to frequently requested national, state, and county data from various Census Bureau programs. Users can choose a state from a list or from the clickable U.S. map and then select a county or city. Information at each geographic level is presented for three topics: people, business, and geography. At the state level, statistics are given for the state versus the country as a whole; at the county and city levels, county and city statistics are compared to the statewide numbers. Each state and county data table also has a link to more data sets for that location. The additional data sets include historical population counts, congressional district statistics, and tables from the American Community Survey, Economic Census, County Business Patterns, and the *Consolidated Federal Funds Reports,* among other resources.

This site serves as both a quick reference tool and a resource locator. By clicking on the information icon next to each data heading, users link to a page that presents the source, definition, scope, and methodology for that heading, along with a list of relevant links.

Subjects: Census; Population Statistics

535. Statistical Abstract of the United States

http://www.census.gov/compendia/statab/

Sponsor(s): Commerce Department — Economics and Statistics Administration (ESA) — Census Bureau

Description: Published since 1878, the *Statistical Abstract of the United States* is a core reference tool with current and historical statistics on the U.S. population, health, education, workforce, government finances, elections, energy, income, prices, and other related topics; these data are presented in a series of tables. Its Web site features the current version and digitized copies of editions going back to 1878. For the current edition, the site features both a PDF version of the publication and tables in spreadsheet format. The main page also links to related valuable resources, including a guide to sources used for the book, links to sources of federal agency statistical reports, and links to state-level equivalents to the *Statistical Abstract of the United States.*

Historical editions of the publication have been scanned into PDF format. The Earlier Editions section of the site also links to *Historical Statistics of the United States: Colonial Times to 1970* from the Census Bureau.

The *Statistical Abstract* has long been a research staple because of the data it provides and the fact that each statistical table includes a citation to the source of the data (thus identifying likely sources for more information on the topic). The online version retains those attributes as a PDF file that is equivalent to the print version. Aside from the addition of the spreadsheets, the PDF version does not have many more advantages over the print version, although it does provide

ready access to the content for users who do not have the print edition at hand. The addition of the digitized back issues makes this site an essential reference tool.
Subjects: Social Indicators — Statistics; United States — Statistics
Publications: *Historical Statistics of the United States: Colonial Times to 1970,* C 3.2:
Statistical Abstract of the United States, C 3.134:

536. TheDataWeb
http://www.thedataweb.org/
Sponsor(s): Commerce Department — Economics and Statistics Administration (ESA) — Census Bureau
Description: TheDataWeb, a cooperative effort of the Census Bureau and the Centers for Disease Control and Prevention, includes diverse data sets and the software tools needed to browse, manipulate, and analyze the data. Data sets currently available include the American Community Survey, the American Housing Survey, the Consumer Expenditure Survey, the Current Population Survey, the National Health and Nutrition Examination Survey, and the Survey of Income and Program Participation. DataFerrett, a companion to TheDataWeb, enables users to extract needed variables, construct tables, and create charts or graphs. The site includes a tutorial and a users' guide.
Subjects: Social Science Research — Statistics

537. TIGER Page
http://www.census.gov/geo/www/tiger/
Sponsor(s): Commerce Department — Economics and Statistics Administration (ESA) — Census Bureau
Description: TIGER (Topologically Integrated Geographic Encoding and Referencing system) is the name given to the Census Bureau's digital mapping system for decennial census and other data. The TIGER home page offers TIGER-based digital geographic products, documentation and metadata, and information about the system. The TIGER/Line files are the primary public product created from the data in the TIGER database. The files comprise a database of geographic features, such as roads, railroads, and rivers. They can be used with the mapping or geographic information system (GIS) software that can import TIGER/Line files.
    The TIGER Page is the central place to check for updates to the TIGER/Line files and related products. Explanatory material is available for both the newcomer and the experienced community of digital geographic data users.
Subjects: Census Mapping; Geographic Information Systems (GIS)

Demographic Groups

538. AgingStats.Gov
http://www.agingstats.gov
Sponsor(s): Federal Interagency Forum on Aging-Related Statistics
Description: The Federal Interagency Forum on Aging-Related Statistics is made up of 13 federal agencies that produce or use statistics on aging. Their Web site, AgingStats.gov, is a finding aid for these statistics. The site links directly to aging-related statistics on its members' Web sites, including relevant data at the Census Bureau, the Department of Veterans Affairs, the National Center for Health Statistics, and the Social Security Administration. A Subject Area Contact List for Federal Statistics section provides the names, area of expertise, and contact information for federal agency experts. The Forum section produces its own

publications, including *Older Americans: Key Indicators of Well-Being*. This publication is online in HTML and PDF formats.

Subjects: Senior Citizens — Statistics

Publications: *Older Americans: Key Indicators of Well-Being*, HE 20.3852:

539. ChildStats.gov

http://www.childstats.gov/

Sponsor(s): Federal Interagency Forum on Child and Family Statistics

Description: This Web site provides access to federal and state statistics and reports on children and their families, including population and family characteristics, economic security, health, behavior and social environment, and education. The Federal Interagency Forum on Child and Family Statistics offers several reports on the site, the most prominent of which is the annual *America's Children: Key National Indicators of Well-Being*. The International section links to reports from other sources that have comparative international statistics for various indicators of children's well-being.

Subjects: Child Welfare — Statistics

Publications: *America's Children in Brief: Key National Indicators of Well-Being*, PR 42.8:

America's Children: Key National Indicators of Well-Being, PR 43.8:

540. Veteran Data and Information

http://www.va.gov/vetdata/

Sponsor(s): Veterans Affairs Department

Description: The Veteran Data and Information Web page links to demographic information about veterans and program information about the Department of Veterans Affairs. Sections include Census 2000, Demographics, Health Care, Trends, Veterans Affairs Expenditures and Workload, and Survey Results (from the National Survey of Veterans).

Subjects: Veterans — Statistics

Publications: *National Survey of Veterans (NSV): Final Report*, VA 1.2:

CHAPTER 7
Education

The Department of Education is naturally the leader in publishing federal government education information on the Internet. This chapter includes many of the online resources made available by the Education Department, but also includes information about military education activities, federally sponsored scholarships, and some education-related social service programs. The Kids' Pages section of this chapter includes over 40 Web sites designed for a younger audience that cover a wide variety of subject areas.

Subsections in this chapter are Adult Education, Curriculum, Early Childhood Education, Education Funding, Education Policy, Education Research and Statistics, Educational Technology, Elementary and Secondary Education, Higher Education, International Education, Kids' Pages, and Teaching.

Adult Education

541. DANTES — Defense Activity for Non-Traditional Education Support
http://www.dantes.doded.mil/
Sponsor(s): Defense Department
Description: DANTES provides support for the off-duty, voluntary education programs of the Department of Defense. Its Web site has information about certification programs, counselor support, distance learning, and tuition assistance. It also has a section about the Troops-to-Teachers program, which assists military personnel interested in beginning a second career as public school teacher.
Subjects: Military Training and Education
Publications: *DANTES External Degree Catalog*, D 1.33/7:
DANTES Independent Study Catalog, D 1.33/7-2:

542. Interagency Coordinating Group for Adult Literacy
http://www.ed.gov/about/bdscomm/list/icgae/edlite-index.html
Sponsor(s): Education Department
Description: This interagency group was established in 2006 to improve the investment in and outcomes for adult education. The Web site includes a database of federal funding sources for adult literacy education and a directory of foundations likely to fund adult literacy projects.
Subjects: Adult Education; Literacy

543. Literacy Information and Communication System (LINCS)
http://www.nifl.gov/lincs/
Sponsor(s): National Institute for Literacy (NIFL)
Description: NIFL and its partners sponsor this Web site as a gateway to adult education and literacy resources on the Internet. The site has information about grants and funding, literacy job openings, events, discussion lists, Web sites, statistics, and resources for teachers and students. The site also features America's Literacy Directory, a database of local adult education programs that can be searched by town or ZIP code.
Subjects: Adult Education; Literacy

544. National Audiovisual Center (NAC)
http://www.ntis.gov/products/nac/
Sponsor(s): Commerce Department — Technology Administration (TA) — National Technical Information Service (NTIS)
Description: NAC manages a catalog of over 9,000 training and education materials on video, audiocassette, CD-ROM, and other types of media. The products are available for sale. The Web site features an online "screening room," with clips from the most popular videos available for purchase. Major topics covered by the collection include language training, law enforcement, health, and safety.
Subjects: Educational Resources; Vocational Education

545. National Institute for Literacy (NIFL)
http://www.nifl.gov/
Sponsor(s): National Institute for Literacy (NIFL)
Description: NIFL promotes literacy efforts, coordinates literacy services and policy, and serves as a resource for adult education and literacy programs. The NIFL Web site provides a section on grants and contracts, information on programs and services, and publications about teaching reading. The Facts and Statistics section compiles literacy data from numerous studies.
Subjects: Literacy

546. Office of Vocational and Adult Education, Department of Education
http://www.ed.gov/about/offices/list/ovae/index.html
Sponsor(s): Education Department — Vocational and Adult Education Office
Description: This site provides information about the Office of Vocational and Adult Education programs, grants, events, legislation, and resources concerning the fields of adult education and vocational education. Key sections are High Schools, Career and Technical Education, Community Colleges, and Adult Literacy and Education.
Subjects: Adult Education; Vocational Education

547. USDA Graduate School
http://grad.usda.gov/
Sponsor(s): Agriculture Department (USDA) — Graduate School, USDA
Description: The Graduate School, USDA is a continuing education institution offering career-related courses to federal workers and the public. The Web site has the current course catalog and information on faculty and certification programs.
Subjects: Adult Education

Curriculum

548. Agriculture in the Classroom
http://www.agclassroom.org/
Sponsor(s): Agriculture Department (USDA) — Cooperative State Research, Education, and Extension Service (CSREES)
Description: The USDA's Agriculture in the Classroom program coordinates state education programs designed to teach children about the role of agriculture in the economy and in society. The site includes a directory of the state programs, information from regional consortiums, and teacher resources. It also has Kid's Zone and Teen Scene sections.
Subjects: Agricultural Education

549. ArtsEdge: The National Arts and Education Information Network

http://artsedge.kennedy-center.org/

Sponsor(s): Kennedy Center for the Performing ArtsNational Endowment for the Arts (NEA)

Description: ArtsEdge, from the Kennedy Center, is a major arts resource for educators and students. The site includes lesson plans and content standards for grades K–12. ArtsEdge highlights articles, reports, and organizations related to arts education. The site also features an arts education advocacy section.

This well-designed site should be a primary stopping point for people involved in arts education.

Subjects: Arts Education

550. BLM Learning Landscapes

http://www.blm.gov/education/

Sponsor(s): Interior Department — Bureau of Land Management (BLM)

Description: This BLM Web site has information and activities for students and teachers. The Teachers' section has information about field programs (mostly in western states), Web sites, resources, and classroom activities. The site's Curriculum Connections correlates BLM classroom activities to National Science Education Standards and National Geography Standards. Online resources for teachers and learners cover such areas as archeology, geology, paleontology, American history, wildlife, and energy.

Subjects: Environmental Education; Science Education

551. Census in Schools

http://www.census.gov/dmd/www/teachers.html

Sponsor(s): Commerce Department — Economics and Statistics Administration (ESA) — Census Bureau

Description: The Census in Schools program provides K–12 teaching materials, workshops for educators, and other outreach activities. Its Web site includes teaching kits and reference materials, primarily about the decennial census.

Subjects: Census; Social Studies Education

552. Directorate for Education and Human Resources — NSF

http://www.nsf.gov/dir/index.jsp?org=ehr

Sponsor(s): National Science Foundation (NSF)

Description: The Directorate for Education and Human Resources (EHR) provides leadership in the effort to improve science, mathematics, engineering, and technology education in the United States. Its Web site includes links to descriptions of the EHR divisions and the types of projects they sponsor: the Division of Graduate Education (DGE); the Division of Undergraduate Education (DUE); the Experimental Program to Stimulate Competitive Research (EPSCoR); and the Division of Elementary, Secondary and Informal Education (ESIE). The Publications category includes selected full-text documents. The Funding Opportunities section has announcements for opportunities sponsored by directorate and interagency groups.

This site will be of assistance to science and engineering students and educators at all levels who are interested in pursuing grants or scholarships.

Subjects: Science Education — Grants

553. EDSITEment
http://edsitement.neh.gov/
Sponsor(s): National Endowment for the Humanities (NEH)
Description: The EDSITEment tag line is "the best of the humanities on the Web." It provides a cataloged selection of lesson plans built around high-quality, freely accessible material available on the Internet. The lesson plans are organized into sections for Art and Culture, Literature and Language Arts, Foreign Language, and History and Social Studies. Each detailed lesson plan is labeled with the appropriate grade level, subject area, time required, and skills taught. The site is sponsored by a partnership between the National Endowment for the Humanities, the MarcoPolo Foundation, and Verizon.

EDSITEment provides quality resources on a well-designed and attractive Web site.
Subjects: Lesson Plans; Humanities

554. GLOBE Program
http://www.globe.gov/
Sponsor(s): National Aeronautics and Space Administration (NASA)
Description: The Global Learning and Observations to Benefit the Environment (GLOBE) program is designed to promote science education at the primary and secondary school levels. GLOBE is funded by NASA and the National Science Foundation, supported by the Department of State, and implemented through a cooperative agreement between NASA, the University Corporation for Atmospheric Research in Boulder, CO, and Colorado State University in Fort Collins, CO. The GLOBE program's primary objective is to involve students in taking environmental measurements. Schools in more than 95 countries have submitted thousands of data reports based on observations by GLOBE student scientists. The data is accessible to anyone, and there is information on how new schools can register to be included in the program. The site also has a teacher's guide and schedule of teacher workshops. Much of the content is available in Spanish and other non-English languages.

With participating schools from all over the world, this kind of collaborative project demonstrates how the Internet can be used in a K–12 environment. In addition, this Web site is well designed and makes navigation easy even for those not familiar with the program.
Subjects: Environmental Protection; Science Education

555. Learning Page of the Library of Congress
http://lcweb2.loc.gov/ammem/ndlpedu/
Sponsor(s): Library of Congress
Description: Designed for the educational community, this site helps students and teachers find relevant materials within the National Digital Library collection on the Library of Congress Web pages, with particular emphasis on the American Memory project. The Web site features sections such as Lesson Plans, Features and Activities, and Professional Development.
Subjects: Educational Technology; Lesson Plans; Social Studies Education

556. NASA Education
http://education.nasa.gov/home/
Sponsor(s): National Aeronautics and Space Administration (NASA) — Education Office
Description: The NASA Education Web site provides information about the education programs that NASA offers to K–12 educators and students as well as to undergraduate and graduate students and faculty at universities. News and resources are

divided into sections including Elementary and Secondary Education, Higher Education, and Informal Education. The section on Elementary and Secondary School programs has information on Educator Astronauts and the NASA Explorer Schools program. Under the NASA Education Offices heading, the site links to the individual Web sites of NASA education programs, NASA Flight and Research Centers, and each of NASA's directorates.

Subjects: Science Education

557. NOAA Education Resources

http://www.education.noaa.gov/

Sponsor(s): Commerce Department — National Oceanic and Atmospheric Administration (NOAA)

Description: The NOAA Education site has materials for teachers covering weather, climate change, oceans and coasts, weather satellites, and space environments. The Primarily for Students section has educational resources and other information color-coded for K–5 grades, 6–12 grades, and higher education students. The Cool Sites for Everyone section highlights NOAA Web sites covering a variety of topics.

Subjects: Environmental Education

558. NSF Classroom Resources

http://www.nsf.gov/news/classroom/

Sponsor(s): National Science Foundation (NSF)

Description: The NSF provides organized links to classroom resources on the Internet. The Web site describes its intended audience as "classroom teachers, their students, and students' families." Links are organized into science topics such as biology, computing, environment, mathematics, and physics. The linked sites are from a variety of educational organizations and institutions.

Subjects: Science Education

559. Office of English Language Acquisition

http://www.ed.gov/about/offices/list/oela/

Sponsor(s): Education Department — English Language Acquisition Office

Description: The full title of this office is the Office of English Language Acquisition, Language Enhancement, and Academic Achievement for Limited English Proficient Students (OELA). OELA administers Title III of the No Child Left Behind Act (Public Law 107-110) on Language Instruction for Limited English Proficient and Immigrant Students. It also administers a state formula grant program. The site has program information and technical assistance for those applying for Title III grants. It also links to the National Clearinghouse for English Language Acquisition and Language Instruction Educational Programs (NCELA), which is funded by the Department of Education.

Subjects: Language Education — Grants

560. USGS and Science Education

http://www.usgs.gov/education/

Sponsor(s): Interior Department — U.S. Geological Survey (USGS)

Description: The USGS education Web site covers topics of concern to USGS scientists: geography, geology, biology, and water resources. Educational resources are organized for grades K–6, grades 7–12, and undergraduate education. One section aligns USGS and other Web resources with an established list of science and social science curriculum standards for California. The site also covers USGS careers, internships, and post-doctoral fellowships.

The USGS site content spans a number of categories, including general information about science education, links to science education Web sites, specific resources developed at USGS, and information on USGS involvement with the promotion of science education.

Subjects: Science Education; Kids' Pages

Early Childhood Education

561. Head Start Bureau

http://www.acf.hhs.gov/programs/hsb/

Sponsor(s): Health and Human Services Department — Administration for Children and Families (ACF) — Head Start Bureau

Description: Head Start is a child development program that serves low-income children and their families. The Programs and Services section describes specific programs such as Early Head Start and the American Indian-Alaska Native Program Branch. The site has sections for grant information and a link to the Head Start Information and Publication Center online. A Research/Statistics section has further links to publications and data on the program. The Budget/Policy section covers program reauthorization, administration policy initiatives, and statistical fact sheets.

The site provides quick access to a breadth of information about the program for its clients and partners, as well as convenient links for the policy researcher. There is no search engine at the site; those looking for very specific Head Start resources or programs may wish to use the Site Map.

Subjects: Early Childhood Education

Publications: *Head Start Bulletin*, HE 23.1103:

562. National Child Care Information Center (NCCIC)

http://nccic.org/

Sponsor(s): Health and Human Services Department — Administration for Children and Families (ACF) — Child Care Bureau

Description: NCCIC is a national clearinghouse and technical assistance center for parents, early education professionals, governments, researchers, and the general public. The site has background information and an extensive section of links on topics such as licensing regulations, childcare as a business, federal policy, child development, literacy, and school readiness. The State Information section has profiles of childcare in each individual state. Some information is available in Spanish.

Subjects: Child Care

Education Funding

563. Federal Cyber Service: Scholarship for Service

http://www.sfs.opm.gov/

Sponsor(s): Office of Personnel Management (OPM)

Description: OPM's Scholarship for Service program funds the education expenses of graduate and undergraduate students in information assurance fields in exchange for an obligation to work for the federal government for an agreed-upon term. The program is designed to strengthen the federal government's expertise in information assurance (the security of computer and communication networks

and the information they carry). This Web site has further details on the program and a list of participating higher education institutions.
Subjects: Computer Science; Scholarships

564. Federal School Code Search Page
http://www.fafsa.ed.gov/fotw0607/fslookup.htm
Sponsor(s): Education Department — Postsecondary Education Office
Description: This site provides searchable access to the federal Title IV School Codes required on many financial aid forms.
Subjects: Financial Aid to Students
Publications: *Federal School Code List*, ED 1.92/2:

565. Free Application for Federal Student Aid (FAFSA)
http://www.fafsa.ed.gov/
Sponsor(s): Education Department — Federal Student Aid Office
Description: FAFSA on the Web makes it possible to apply online for federal financial aid for college. The FAFSA renewal application may also be completed online. The site provides guidance on applying for aid, the application process, and deadlines. Some instructions are also provided in Spanish.
Subjects: Financial Aid to Students

566. GI Bill Website
http://www.gibill.va.gov/
Sponsor(s): Veterans Affairs Department
Description: The GI Bill site provides information on the range of education benefits for active duty and reserve servicemembers, veterans, survivors, and dependents. Information on the programs is available in the sections Education Benefits, Information for Benefit Recipients, and Questions and Answers. The site also has a section for school officials working with beneficiaries.

The site has a history of the original GI Bill, the Servicemembers' Readjustment Act of 1944, which preceded the current program.
Subjects: Military Training and Education; Veterans

567. Information for Financial Aid Professionals (IFAP)
http://ifap.ed.gov/
Sponsor(s): Education Department — Federal Student Aid Office
Description: IFAP is an electronic library for financial aid professionals containing publications, regulations, and guidance regarding the administration of the Title IV Federal Student Aid (FSA) Programs. This site features technical documentation, online tools, worksheets, and schedules related to the programs.
Subjects: Financial Aid to Students
Publications: *Direct Loan Bulletin*, ED 1.40/6:
Federal Student Financial Aid Handbook, ED 1.45/4:
High School Counselor's Handbook, ED 1.45:

568. Student Aid on the Web
http://studentaid.ed.gov/
Sponsor(s): Education Department — Federal Student Aid Office
Description: This site is a portal and service center for federal student aid information and programs. It begins with information about preparing for, choosing, applying to, and attending a college. Other sections contain facts about funding your education and repaying student loans. The site links to the Free Application for Student Aid (FAFSA) online.
Subjects: Education Funding; Student Loans

569. Tax Benefits for Education
http://www.irs.gov/publications/p970/
Sponsor(s): Treasury Department — Internal Revenue Service (IRS)
Description: This Web page has the full text of Publication 970, *Tax Benefits for Education*. The publication outlines the tax deductions and benefits available to those saving for or paying education costs. Most benefits concern higher education.
Subjects: Education Funding; Taxation
Publications: *Tax Benefits for Education*, T 22.44/2:

Education Policy

570. ED.gov — U.S. Department of Education
http://www.ed.gov/
Sponsor(s): Education Department
Description: The Education Department Web site features current news and links to information on the No Child Left Behind program, Pandemic Flu Preparedness, and other high-profile initiatives. The top menu of the site's home page directs users to information by audience: Students (financial aid, homework help), Parents (encouraging reading, college planning), Teachers (how to become a teacher, finding teaching jobs), and Administrators (guidance on the No Child Left Behind Act, policy information). The site also organizes its content into several Information Centers: Grants and Contracts, Financial Aid, Research and Statistics, Policy, and Programs. In addition, it has an A-Z index and a site map.

The About ED section has a directory of offices, budget and appropriations information, and press releases. Publications are available through the linked ED Pubs Web site and the ERIC (Education Resources Information Center) database. Some information is available in Spanish.
Subjects: Education — Policy; Educational Resources; Financial Aid to Students
Publications: *Annual Accountability Report*, ED 1.1/6:
Grant Award Actions Database, ED 1.83:
Helping Your Child Succeed in School, ED 1.302:C 43/
Helping Your Child with Homework, ED 1.302:C 43/
U.S. Department of Education Strategic Plan, 2002-2007, ED 1.2:

571. No Child Left Behind
http://www.nclb.gov/
Alternate URL(s): http://www.nochildleftbehind.gov/
Sponsor(s): Education Department
Description: This Department of Education Web site is dedicated to information about Public Law 107-110, better known as the No Child Left Behind Act of 2001. The law concerns educational standards and testing, teacher training and recruitment, English language instruction, school safety, and other matters. The site has an A-Z index and includes information aimed at parents and teachers. It also has policy updates and an e-mail newsletter, *Extra Credit*.
Subjects: Education — Policy; Educational Testing

572. Office of Innovation and Improvement (OII)
http://www.ed.gov/about/offices/list/oii/
Sponsor(s): Education Department — Innovation and Improvement Office
Description: OII administers discretionary grant programs, coordinates public school choice and supplemental educational efforts, works with the non-public education community, and develops guidance for the No Child Left Behind initiative. The

Web site's Non-Public Education section includes a private school locator and statistics on private education in the United States.

Subjects: Elementary and Secondary Education; Education Policy

573. White House Initiative on Educational Excellence for Hispanic Americans

http://www.yic.gov/

Alternate URL(s): http://www.yosipuedo.gov/

Sponsor(s): President's Advisory Commission on Educational Excellence for Hispanic Americans

Description: The White House Initiative on Educational Excellence for Hispanic Americans and the President's Advisory Commission on Educational Excellence for Hispanic Americans were established by executive order in 2001. The Education Department provides the primary support for the initiative. The Web site has information on the Commission and also features a series of toolkits, or online guides, with educational tips relevant to early childhood, elementary and secondary schooling, and postsecondary education. The alternate URL listed above is for a Spanish-language version of the site.

Subjects: Educational Resources; Hispanic Americans

Publications: *From Risk to Opportunity: Fulfilling the Educational Needs of Hispanic Americans . . .*, ED 1.2:

Education Research and Statistics

574. ERIC — Educational Resources Information Center

http://www.eric.ed.gov/

Sponsor(s): Education Department — Institute of Education Sciences

Description: ERIC is a database and information system funded by the Education Department to provide organized access to a wide array of published and unpublished material about education. It references education literature from 1966 to the present. The Web site describes ERIC as "the world's largest digital library of education literature."

The ERIC search interface has basic and advanced versions. Searchable fields include title, author, ERIC number, identifier, ISBN, ISSN, journal name, source institution, sponsoring agency, thesaurus descriptor, and date range. Searches can be limited by type of material cited (e.g., journal article, non-print media, or dissertation). The ERIC Thesaurus is linked to the search interface; users can also browse and search the thesaurus separately. An interface called My ERIC allows for some customization once users register for a My ERIC account.

ERIC is a key resource for research in education and related fields. Although the database was previously handled by a network of academic and nonprofit clearinghouses, the Department of Education established centralized control in late 2004. Since then, new features and content have been phased in. ERIC users should check the ERIC online news for regular updates; however, there is no e-mail or RSS feed subscription for the news.

Subjects: Educational Resources; ERIC

575. Institute of Education Sciences (IES)

http://www.ed.gov/about/offices/list/ies/

Sponsor(s): Education Department — Institute of Education Sciences

Description: IES was set up in 2002 to focus on education research. It includes the National Center for Education Research (NCER), the National Center for Education Statistics (NCES), the National Center for Education Evaluation and Regional

Assistance (NCEE), and The National Center for Special Education Research (NCSER). The Web site has information on IES and its grants and component programs.
Subjects: Education Research

576. International Comparisons in Education
http://nces.ed.gov/surveys/international/
Sponsor(s): Education Department — Institute of Education Sciences — National Center for Education Statistics (NCES)
Description: NCES provides a central page for linking to the international education statistics that the agency collects. The site links to information on the Trends in International Mathematics and Science Study (TIMSS) and Program for International Student Assessment (PISA) assessments, as well as the Progress in International Reading Literacy Study (PIRLS) and Adult Literacy and Lifeskills (ALL) international comparative studies.
Subjects: Educational Assessment — International

577. National Center for Education Statistics
http://nces.ed.gov/
Sponsor(s): Education Department — Institute of Education Sciences — National Center for Education Statistics (NCES)
Description: NCES collects and analyzes data concerning education in the United States and other nations. Its Web site is a primary source for education statistics for all educational levels and for data on educational assessment, libraries, and international educational outcomes. Most data on the site are drawn from major NCES statistical publications, such as *Education Statistics Quarterly*, *The Condition of Education*, and the *Digest of Education Statistics*. The NCES Fast Facts section highlights frequently requested information, such as data on the effects of reading to children and data on average tuition costs at colleges and universities. The site also includes a searchable directory of private and public schools, colleges, and public libraries.

   For users searching for statistics related to any form of education, this site should be the first place to visit.
Subjects: Education Statistics
Publications: *Developments in School Finance*, ED 1.139:
Digest of Education Statistics, ED 1.326:
Directory of Postsecondary Institutions, ED 1.111/4:
Dropout Rates in the United States, ED 1.329:
Education Statistics Quarterly, ED 1.328/13:
Federal Support for Education, ED 1.328/8:
Indicators of School Crime and Safety, ED 1.347:
NAEP Trends in Academic Progress, ED 1.335/4:
Projections of Education Statistics, ED 1.120:
The Condition of Education, ED 1.109:
Youth Indicators, ED 1.327:

Educational Technology

578. Computers for Learning
http://www.computers.fed.gov/School/user.asp
Sponsor(s): General Services Administration (GSA)
Description: The Computers for Learning Web site is designed for public, private, parochial, and home schools serving the K–12 student population, as well as other

nonprofit educational organizations. The service allows these groups of students and nonprofit organizations to request donations of surplus federal computer equipment. The site includes program and eligibility information, and sections on how to give and receive computers.

Subjects: Educational Technology; Surplus Government Property

579. Minority University Space Interdisciplinary Network (MU-SPIN)
http://muspin.gsfc.nasa.gov/

Sponsor(s): National Aeronautics and Space Administration (NASA) — Goddard Space Flight Center (GSFC)

Description: MU-SPIN is designed for Historically Black Colleges and Universities (HBCUs), and Other Minority Universities (OMUs). The program focuses on transferring advanced computer networking technologies to HBCUs and OMUs to help support their multidisciplinary research. The Web site has information about the program and its associated events, conferences, and resources.

For minority colleges and universities, this is an important resource for high technology and computer networking information and training.

Subjects: Computer Networking; Minority Groups; Science Education

580. Office of Educational Technology (OET), Department of Education
http://www.ed.gov/about/offices/list/os/technology/

Sponsor(s): Education Department — Educational Technology Office

Description: OET develops national educational technology policy and works with the educational community and the Department of Education to promote national goals for educational technology. Major sections of the site are Grants Programs, Reports and Research, and Internet Safety. The site also has a directory of state government contacts for educational technology and the online publication *Teacher's Guide to International Collaboration on the Internet.*

Subjects: Distance Learning; Educational Technology — Grants

Publications: *Toward a New Golden Age in American Education*, ED 1.2:

Elementary and Secondary Education

581. Education Resource Organizations Directory (EROD)
http://wdcrobcolp01.ed.gov/Programs/EROD/

Sponsor(s): Education Department — Elementary and Secondary Education Office

Description: EROD is a database of state and regional organizations that provide education-related information. It includes organizations such as state literary resource centers and regional education laboratories. Each organization's entry has complete contact information and a description of its services. The database has simple and advanced search forms.

Subjects: Educational Resources

582. Emergency Planning
http://www.ed.gov/emergencyplan/

Sponsor(s): Education Department — Office of Safe and Drug-Free Schools

Description: The Emergency Planning Web site, launched in March 2003, describes itself as a "one-stop shop that provides school leaders with information they need to plan for any emergency, including natural disasters, violent incidents and terrorist acts" (from the Web site). The site includes crisis planning resources and model emergency response plans. It also links to information on Pandemic Flu preparedness for schools.

Subjects: Disaster Preparedness; School Buildings

583. NSF Division of Elementary, Secondary, and Informal Education (ESIE)

http://www.nsf.gov/div/index.jsp?div=ESIE

Sponsor(s): National Science Foundation (NSF)

Description: As part of the National Science Foundation, ESIE focuses on improving pre-K–12 science, technology, engineering, and mathematics (STEM) education in the United States. Its Web site includes descriptions of the programs and funding opportunities offered by this agency. Program area sections include Advanced Technological Education, Informal Science Education, International Polar Year (2007–2008), and Presidential Awards for Excellence in Mathematics and Science Teaching.

Subjects: Mathematics Education — Grants; Science Education — Grants

584. Office of Elementary and Secondary Education (OESE)

http://www.ed.gov/about/offices/list/oese/

Sponsor(s): Education Department — Elementary and Secondary Education Office

Description: The OESE Web site has information on its programs, office contacts, and reports. The Laws, Regulations, and Guidance section is largely concerned with the No Child Left Behind Act. Both the Standards, Assessment, and Accountability section and the Flexibility and Waivers section also cover areas of No Child Left Behind. The Consolidated State Info section has information on the No Child Left Behind Consolidated State Performance Report for states reporting accomplishments and data. The site is searchable through an A-Z index.

The alphabetical index is useful in uncovering all of the information at this site. Much of the site is intended for elementary and secondary education professionals and officials who need to comply with the No Child Left Behind Act or who are interested in its documents.

Subjects: Education Standards; Educational Assessment; Elementary and Secondary Education

585. Office of Safe and Drug-Free Schools

http://www.ed.gov/about/offices/list/osdfs/

Sponsor(s): Education Department — Office of Safe and Drug-Free Schools

Description: OSDFS's major programs come under the categories of Health, Mental Health, Environmental Health, and Physical Education; Drug-Violence Prevention; and Character and Civic Education. Many of the programs are for the elementary and secondary level, although some programs also apply to higher education. The Web site has information on the grants that fall under these program categories and offers news, publications, and links to related resources on the Internet.

Subjects: Drug Control; School Safety

586. Office of Special Education Programs (OSEP)

http://www.ed.gov/about/offices/list/osers/osep/

Sponsor(s): Education Department — Special Education and Rehabilitative Services Office — Office of Special Education Programs (OSEP)

Description: OSEP has the primary responsibility of administering programs and projects relating to the education of all children, youth, and adults with disabilities, from birth through age 21. Sections describe OSEP's Programs and Projects, Grants and Funding, Legislation and Policy, Publications and Products, and Research and Statistics. It includes extensive information on the Individuals with Disabilities Education Act (IDEA), which authorizes OSEP programs.

Subjects: Special Education — Grants

Publications: *Annual Report to Congress on the Implementation of the Individuals with Disabilities Education Act*, ED 1.32:

587. U.S. Presidential Scholars Program
http://www.ed.gov/programs/psp/
Sponsor(s): Education Department
Description: The U.S. Presidential Scholars Program recognizes up to 141 outstanding high school graduates each year. The Web site has information on eligibility, the application process, and the current year's Presidential Scholars.
Subjects: High Schools — Awards and Honors

588. School District Demographics
http://nces.ed.gov/surveys/sdds/
Sponsor(s): Education Department — Institute of Education Sciences — National Center for Education Statistics (NCES)
Description: This site presents demographic and geographic data for school districts from the 2000 census and 1990 census. The Map Viewer application allows users to view state or individual school district maps. The School District Profiles section can be used to compare Census 2000 demographic information between any school districts. Documentation for the data and the system is in the Library section.

The data from this special census tabulation can be helpful for studying school districts as well as for examining general demographics of children and families with children.
Subjects: Census; Elementary and Secondary Education — Statistics

589. The Nation's Report Card
http://nces.ed.gov/nationsreportcard/
Sponsor(s): Education Department — Institute of Education Sciences — National Center for Education Statistics (NCES)
Description: This is the online home of the National Assessment of Educational Progress (NAEP), an ongoing national assessment for student achievement at grades 4, 8, and 12. It provides background information on the history and current operations of the NAEP. Current results are available in the form of state profiles, or users can construct custom data tables and get reports at the national level or by state, region, or major urban district. The Subject Areas section provides background and reports on assessments in mathematics, reading, science, civics, and other specific subjects.
Subjects: Educational Assessment; Elementary and Secondary Education

Higher Education

590. Air Force Institute of Technology
http://www.afit.edu/
Sponsor(s): Air Force — Air Force Institute of Technology (AFIT)
Description: A component of Air University, AFIT is the Air Force's graduate school of engineering and management and its institution for technical professional continuing education. The Web site provides information on each of AFIT's schools and centers.
Subjects: Air Force; Military Training and Education

591. Air University

http://www.au.af.mil/au/

Sponsor(s): Air Force — Air University

Description: Air University (AU), located at Maxwell Air Force Base, conducts professional military education, graduate education, and professional continuing education for officers, enlisted personnel, and civilians. This site links to each of the component schools that make up AU. It also provides information on the university's history and mission. The Other AU Links section links to the university's course catalogs and publications, the Air University Press, and the Air University Library.

Subjects: Air Force; Military Training and Education

Publications: *Air and Space Power Journal*, D 301.26/24:
Community College of the Air Force Catalog, D 301.80:

592. Army Logistics Management College

http://www.almc.army.mil/

Sponsor(s): Army — Army Logistics Management College (ALMC)

Description: The Army Logistics Management College site features information a course catalog, course schedule, and an online version of *Army Logistician*.

Subjects: Army; Military Training and Education

Publications: *Army Logistician* (bimonthly), D 101.69:

593. Barry M. Goldwater Scholarships

http://www.act.org/goldwater/

Sponsor(s): Goldwater Scholarship and Excellence in Education Foundation

Description: Goldwater Scholarships are awarded for undergraduate education in the fields of mathematics, science, and engineering. The Goldwater Foundation was established by Congress to encourage study in these fields. The Web site has scholarship application information and lists of past awardees.

Subjects: Higher Education; Scholarships

594. Carlisle Barracks and the U.S. Army War College

http://carlisle-www.army.mil/

Sponsor(s): Army — Carlisle Barracks

Description: Carlisle Barracks is the home of the U.S. Army War College, the Center for Strategic Leadership, the Strategic Studies Institute, Peacekeeping and Stability Operations Institute, the Army Physical Fitness Research Institute, Army Heritage and Education Center, and the Military History Institute. This site features information on the Barracks and the resident institutions. The Web site's home page features summaries of timely studies in national defense. The site also carries the quarterly *Parameters*, the Army's senior professional journal; issues are archived online from 1996 onward.

Subjects: Army; Military Training and Education

Publications: *Parameters: U.S. Army War College Quarterly*, D 101.72:
Strategic Studies Institute (General Publications), D 101.146:

595. College Opportunities On-Line

http://www.nces.ed.gov/ipeds/cool/

Sponsor(s): Education Department — Institute of Education Sciences — National Center for Education Statistics (NCES)

Description: This database, also known as COOL, has information about roughly 7,000 colleges, universities, community colleges, technical colleges, and similar institutions. The database can be searched by institution name or by location, type of school, programs offered, or other criteria. For each institution, the database typically supplies phone numbers, a URL, average costs, and basic background information. Up to four colleges can also be compared side-by-side for such factors as estimated student expenses and graduation rates.

The COOL database is a useful reference for college-bound students as well as for those simply looking for a college's phone number or URL. Note that the site states that an institution's inclusion in the database does not constitute a recommendation by the Department of Education.

Subjects: Higher Education

596. Command and General Staff College
http://www-cgsc.army.mil/
Sponsor(s): Army — Army Command and General Staff College
Description: The U.S. Army Command and General Staff College is focused on leadership development within the Army. This site offers information on the college, its training programs, and its organizations.
Subjects: Army; Military Leadership; Military Training and Education
Publications: *Military Review*, D 110.7:
Military Review (Portuguese), D 110.7/3:
Military Review (Spanish), D 110.7/2:

597. Defense Language Institute Foreign Language Center (DLIFLC)
http://www.dliflc.edu/
Sponsor(s): Defense Department — Defense Language Institute (DLI)
Description: DLIFLIC is the primary foreign language training institution within the Department of Defense. Programs are for U.S. military personnel and select agency staff. The Web site has information on the history of the center and its current language programs. The Center's journal, *Applied Language Learning*, is online dating back to 1996.

The site is primarily of interest to those eligible for and interested in DLI language training.
Subjects: Language Education; Military Training and Education
Publications: *Applied Language Learning*, D 1.105:

598. Harry S. Truman Scholarship Foundation
http://www.truman.gov
Sponsor(s): Truman Scholarship Foundation
Description: Truman Scholarships are awarded to outstanding undergraduate students who wish to pursue graduate study and careers in government or public service. This Web site has information about the Truman Foundation and its scholarship program, with sections for candidates, faculty, and current Truman Scholars.
Subjects: Public Policy; Scholarships

599. Marine Corps University
http://www.mcu.usmc.mil/
Sponsor(s): Marine Corps — Training and Education Command
Description: The Marine Corps University's Web site provides information about its schools, including the Expeditionary Warfare School, the Command and Staff College, the School of Advanced Warfighting, and the Marine Corps War College.
Subjects: Military Training and Education

600. NASA Academy

http://academy.nasa.gov/

Sponsor(s): National Aeronautics and Space Administration (NASA) — Goddard Space Flight Center (GSFC)

Description: This is the central page for NASA Academy summer programs for college students in science, math, engineering, or computer science. The site has application forms and detailed program information.

The information on these pages will be of interest to college students interested in careers or further study with NASA and to the advisers of students with pertinent majors.

Subjects: Science Education

601. NASA Office of Higher Education at Goddard Space Flight Center

http://university.gsfc.nasa.gov/

Sponsor(s): National Aeronautics and Space Administration (NASA) — Goddard Space Flight Center (GSFC)

Description: This office manages fellowships, grants, and other higher education programs at NASA's Goddard Space Flight Center in Maryland. The programs target colleges and universities along the eastern seaboard and aerospace-oriented institutions nationwide with programs of mutual interest to Goddard. The site has information about these and other NASA-wide higher education programs.

Subjects: Fellowships; Science Education — Grants

602. National Defense University (NDU)

http://www.ndu.edu/

Sponsor(s): Defense Department — National Defense University (NDU)

Description: The NDU Web site provides an online course catalog and links to the University's component colleges and schools: Joint Forces Staff College, National War College, Industrial College of the Armed Forces, Information Resources Management College, and School for National Security Executive Education. NDU Research Centers online include the Institute for National Strategic Studies and the Center for the Study of Weapons of Mass Destruction. A Professional Military Reading Lists section presents bibliographies of recommended reading from the chiefs of the armed services and others.

Subjects: Military Training and Education; National Defense — Research

Publications: *Defense Horizons*, D 5.420:

Joint Force Quarterly, D 5.20:

McNair Papers, D 5.416:

Security and Defense Studies Review, D 5.419:

Strategic Forum, Institute for National Strategic Studies, D 5.417:

603. Naval Postgraduate School

http://www.nps.edu/

Sponsor(s): Navy — Naval Postgraduate School (NPS)

Description: NPS emphasizes education and research programs relevant to the Navy, defense, and national and international security interests. The Web site links to information from each of the NPS component schools: Business and Public Policy, Engineering and Applied Sciences, Operational and Information Sciences, and International Graduate Studies. The Research section includes archives of technical reports and thesis abstracts.

Subjects: Military Training and Education

604. Naval War College
http://www.nwc.navy.mil/
Sponsor(s): Navy — Naval War College (NWC)
Description: This site offers information about the history and academics of the NWC. At the time this book went to press, access to this site was not available to the public.
Subjects: Military Training and Education; Navy
Publications: *Naval War College Review,* D 208.209:
Newport Papers, D 208.212:

605. NSF Division of Graduate Education
http://www.nsf.gov/div/index.jsp?div=DGE
Sponsor(s): National Science Foundation (NSF)
Description: The programs of the NSF's Division of Graduate Education promote the early career development of scientists and engineers by offering support at critical junctures of their careers. This Web site describes the Division's research and teaching fellowships for graduate students in the sciences. The Publications section includes program guidelines. There is also a page to search for awards.
Subjects: Fellowships; Science Education

606. NSF Division of Undergraduate Education
http://www.nsf.gov/div/index.jsp?div=DUE
Sponsor(s): National Science Foundation (NSF)
Description: The NSF's Division of Undergraduate Education (DUE) focuses on improving undergraduate education in science, technology, mathematics, and engineering. The Division awards funds to scholarship programs at educational institutions; they do not award scholarships directly to students. The Division also funds programs for teacher education and curriculum development. The Web site has information on the programs, deadlines, and awards.
Subjects: Science Education

607. Office of Postsecondary Education (OPE)
http://www.ed.gov/about/offices/list/ope/
Sponsor(s): Education Department — Postsecondary Education Office
Description: In the Programs/Initiatives section, this Web site provides a guide to the more than 40 postsecondary-related education programs administered by the OPE. Initiatives include programs for improving educational institutions, supporting international education, funding teacher training, and reaching out to students from disadvantaged backgrounds. The Reports and Resources section of the site has data on student aid programs such as Pell Grants, Federal Student Loans, and Federal Family Education Loans. The Accreditation section of the site explains the accreditation of educational institutions and has a directory of the numerous accrediting agencies.

This is a very useful site with a substantial body of information sources of interest to students, educators, and financial aid offices.
Subjects: Financial Aid to Students; Higher Education; International Education
Publications: *Fund for the Improvement of Postsecondary Education Program Book,* ED 1.23/2:

Grant Application for the Undergraduate International Studies and Foreign Language Program, ED 1.94/2:

608. Smithsonian Office of Fellowships
http://www.si.edu/ofg/
Sponsor(s): Smithsonian Institution
Description: The Office of Fellowships has applications, lists of fellowship and internship opportunities, and announcements of the current recipients. The publication *Smithsonian Opportunities for Research and Study* is available online in an HTML format.
Subjects: Fellowships

609. U.S. Merchant Marine Academy
http://www.usmma.edu/
Sponsor(s): Transportation Department — Maritime Administration (MARAD)
Description: The Merchant Marine Academy Web site has information about admissions, academics, and other activities. The site also links to the Global Maritime and Transportation School (GMATS) for maritime and transportation industry professionals. Both the Academy and GMATS are operated by the Department of Transportation's Maritime Administration.
Subjects: Military Training and Education; Shipping

610. United States Air Force Academy
http://www.usafa.af.mil/
Sponsor(s): Air Force — Air Force Academy
Description: The United States Air Force Academy Web site provides information for cadets, staff, and faculty. It includes visitor information and sections on admissions, academics, and cadet life. The Academy's libraries are listed in the USAFA Organizations section.
Subjects: Air Force; Military Training and Education

611. United States Military Academy at West Point
http://www.usma.edu/
Sponsor(s): Army — United States Military Academy (USMA)
Description: The West Point Web site has information for prospective and current students, alumni, visitors, and the West Point community. There are sections on Admissions, Cadet Life, and the Academic, Physical, and Military Programs. A brief section on USMA history, found in the About the Academy section, includes a timeline and list of notable graduates.
Subjects: Army; Military Training and Education

612. United States Naval Academy
http://www.usna.edu
Sponsor(s): Navy — United States Naval Academy (USNA)
Description: This site contains information on the Naval Academy, mainly for students, prospective students, and midshipmen. The About USNA section links to information about the Academy's history and notable graduates.
Subjects: Military Training and Education; Navy

613. White House Initiative on Historically Black Colleges and Universities
http://www.ed.gov/about/inits/list/whhbcu/edlite-index.html
Sponsor(s): Education Department — White House Initiative on Historically Black Colleges and Universities
Description: The White House Initiative on Historically Black Colleges and Universities was established by executive order in 1981. This Web site has information

on the Initiative's work, Board of Advisors and staff, and budget. It also has a list of Historically Black Colleges and Universities by state and type of institution, with Web addresses provided for each institution.
Subjects: African Americans; Higher Education
Publications: *Economic Impact of the Nation's Historically Black Colleges and Universities*

614. White House Initiative on Tribal Colleges and Universities

`http://www.ed.gov/about/inits/list/whtc/edlite-index.html`
Sponsor(s): Education Department — White House Initiative on Tribal Colleges and Universities
Description: The President's Board of Advisors on Tribal Colleges and Universities and the White House Initiative on Tribal Colleges and Universities were established by executive order in 2002. In addition to information on the Board, this site has a directory of tribal colleges and universities.
Subjects: Higher Education; American Indians

International Education

615. Bureau of Educational and Cultural Affairs

`http://exchanges.state.gov/`
Sponsor(s): State Department — Educational and Cultural Affairs Bureau
Description: The Bureau of Educational and Cultural Affairs Web site has information about its many international exchange and education programs. For U.S. citizens, the site has information on Fulbright Scholarships, English-language teaching abroad, study abroad, and other opportunities. For the audience abroad, the site has information about studying in the United States, the Fulbright Program, and a range of programs from the high school level up to the scholar and professional level. The site covers a range of other initiatives, such as the National Security Language Initiative, the Global Cultural Initiative, and the Edward R. Murrow Journalism Initiative.
Subjects: Cultural Exchanges; International Education

616. EducationUSA

`http://www.educationusa.state.gov/`
Sponsor(s): State Department — Educational and Cultural Affairs Bureau
Description: EducationUSA is a global network of more than 450 advising and information centers in 170 countries supported by the Department of State's Bureau of Educational and Cultural Affairs. The Web site's About Us section provides contact information for individual centers worldwide. Other sections of the site provide information about finding a school, student visas, and living in the United States. Information is available for all levels of higher education and specialized professional study. Booklets from the department's "If You Want to Study in the United States" series are online in Arabic, Chinese, French, Russian, Spanish, and English.
Subjects: International Education

617. Fulbright Scholar Program

`http://exchanges.state.gov/education/fulbright/`
Alternate URL(s): `http://www.iie.org/fulbright/`
Sponsor(s): State Department — Educational and Cultural Affairs BureauInstitute of International Education (IIE)
Description: The Fulbright Program, sponsored by the United States, is an international education program that provides grants for graduate students, scholars,

professionals, teachers, and administrators from the United States and other countries. This site, geared toward U.S. and non-U.S. applicants, describes the program and links to the Fulbright Commissions around the world.

Much of the program is administered for the Department of State by the Institute of International Education (IIE), an independent nonprofit organization. The alternate URL for this entry leads to the IIE Fulbright Web site. For applicants from the United States, the relevant applications are available online.

Subjects: International Education — Grants

618. Future State

http://www.future.state.gov/
Sponsor(s): State Department
Description: Designed as the student Web site for the Department of State, Future State is largely written for the students at the secondary school level, although it has one section for students in grades K–6. The site explains the work of the department, international education opportunities available to students, and the nature of careers within the Department of State. A section for parents and educators includes lesson plans and online resources.

Future State includes a substantial amount and variety of information relating to diplomacy, U.S. diplomatic history, country information, international exchange programs, and educational outreach activities.

Subjects: Career Information; Diplomacy

619. International Affairs Office

http://www.ed.gov/about/inits/ed/internationaled/
Sponsor(s): Education Department
Description: The International Affairs Office coordinates the Education Department's international programs and works with international agencies such as the United Nations Educational, Scientific, Cultural Organization (UNESCO). The Web site provides a directory to Education Department programs that have an international aspect. It also describes the office's activities, such as International Education Week and the United States Network for Education Information (USNEI) program.

Subjects: International Education

620. U.S. Network for Education Information (USNEI)

http://www.ed.gov/about/offices/list/ous/international/
usnei/edlite-index.html
Sponsor(s): Education Department
Description: USNEI is an interagency and public-private partnership set up to provide official information for anyone seeking information about U.S. education. It also provides U.S. citizens with authoritative information about education in other countries. The site covers all levels of education, with topics including visas, accreditation, professional licensure, and teaching abroad (or in the United States). The site's Foreign Country Database links to Web sites for individual countries' official education agencies and organizations.

Subjects: International Education

621. Worldstudy.gov

http://worldstudy.gov/
Sponsor(s): National Security Education Program
Description: Worldstudy.gov was created by the National Security Education Program (NSEP), a government program that works to strengthen national security by helping educate U.S. citizens about world cultures and languages. NSEP awards

the David L. Boren Scholarships and Fellowships for study relating to global security at the graduate and undergraduate levels. The site provides information on the Boren grants and features accounts of student experiences while studying abroad.
Subjects: International Education; Scholarships

Kids' Pages

622. America's Story from America's Library
http://www.americaslibrary.gov/
Sponsor(s): Library of Congress
Description: This Library of Congress site is designed for children and their families. It uses digitized images from the Library's collection, accompanied by text and graphics, to create educational pages about American history and culture. Sections include Explore the States, Jump Back in Time, and Meet Amazing Americans.
Subjects: History; Kids' Pages

623. BAM! Body and Mind
http://www.bam.gov/
Sponsor(s): Health and Human Services Department — Centers for Disease Control and Prevention (CDC)
Description: BAM!, designed for children ages 9 to 13, has tips on fighting stress and adopting healthy lifestyles. It contains information about fitness, nutrition, safety, and handling peer pressure.
Subjects: Kids' Pages; Child Health and Safety

624. Ben's Guide to U.S. Government for Kids
http://bensguide.gpo.gov/
Sponsor(s): Government Printing Office (GPO) — Superintendent of Documents
Description: With a cartoon version of Benjamin Franklin as a guide, this GPO site for children covers topics such as the U.S. Constitution, how laws are made, the branches of the federal government, and citizenship. It features sections for specific age groups, plus a special section for parents and educators. The major sections are About Ben, K–2, 3–5, 6–8, 9–12, and Parents and Teachers.

Ben's Guide has received numerous accolades. It is useful as a grade school or high school student's homework helper, but may also help older students refresh their basic knowledge of U.S. government and history.
Subjects: Kids' Pages; Civics Education

625. BLM's History Mystery
http://www.blm.gov/heritage/HE_Kids/kid_pg_rev1.htm
Sponsor(s): Interior Department — Bureau of Land Management (BLM)
Description: BLM presents three history mysteries to be solved by students in the upper elementary grades or high school. The mysteries include "Butch Cassidy and The Sundance Kid," "The Mystery of the First Americans," and "The Ghost Town Mysteries."
Subjects: Social Studies Education; Kids' Pages

626. BLS Career Information
`http://www.bls.gov/k12/`
Sponsor(s): Labor Department — Bureau of Labor Statistics (BLS)
Description: The BLS Career Information page for youth uses a graphical interface to match kids' interests with potential careers. It has an alternative text menu. A Teachers' Guide refers teachers to additional information available from BLS.

The site is easy and fun to use. It is most appropriate for upper elementary grades and high school students.
Subjects: Career Information; Kids' Pages

627. CIA Home Page for Kids
`https://www.cia.gov/cia/ciakids/`
Alternate URL(s): `https://www.cia.gov/cia/ciakids/index_2.shtml`
Sponsor(s): Central Intelligence Agency (CIA)
Description: The CIA offers a variety of information targeted towards children. This Web site features sections including Who We Are and What We Do, Operation History, CIA Canine Corps, Aerial Photography Pigeons, Intelligence Book Lists, and Say No to Drugs. The site at the primary URL is for students in grades 6–12. The alternate URL takes users to the corresponding page for students in grades K–5.
Subjects: Intelligence Agencies; Kids' Pages

628. CryptoKids(tm)
`http://www.nsa.gov/kids/intro.htm`
Sponsor(s): Defense Department — National Security Agency (NSA)
Description: This site has games, activities, and background information about NSA's specialty, cryptography. The Student Resources section has NSA career information for high school and college students.
Subjects: Kids' Pages

629. DOI Just For Kids
`http://www.doi.gov/kids/`
Sponsor(s): Interior Department
Description: This central Department of the Interior Web site for children links to more than a dozen pages from related agencies. Linked sites include Endangered Species, Earthquakes for Kids, Web Rangers, and Careers in Science.
Subjects: Environmental Education; Kids' Pages

630. Dr. E's Energy Lab: Energy Efficiency and Renewable Energy Network
`http://www.eere.energy.gov/kids/`
Sponsor(s): Energy Department — Energy Efficiency and Renewable Energy Office
Description: This Department of Energy page for children features links to the following headings: Energy Efficiency Tips, Wind Energy, Solar Energy, Geothermal Energy, Alternative Fuels, and General Renewable Energy.

The main page uses a simple cartoon interface, but many of the linked resources are text-heavy.
Subjects: Renewable Energies; Kids' Pages

631. Energy Department — For Students and Kids
`http://www.energy.gov/forstudentsandkids.htm`
Description: This site centralizes access to Energy Department Web sites for kids and students, including energy glossaries and agency-sponsored contests and

competitions. Linked sites cover a range of topics, from the relationship between garbage and energy to the Virtual Frog Dissection Kit.
Subjects: Science Education; Kids' Pages

632. Energy Kids' Page: What is Energy?
http://www.eia.doe.gov/kids/
Sponsor(s): Energy Department — Energy Information Administration (EIA)
Description: The Department of Energy's Information Administration provides this educational page. Sections include: Energy Facts, Fun and Games, Energy History, Classroom Activities, and Glossary.
Subjects: Energy; Kids' Pages

633. EPA Student Center
http://www.epa.gov/students/
Sponsor(s): Environmental Protection Agency (EPA)
Description: The EPA Student Center Web site serves as a portal to information at a variety of educational levels and offers links to a Kids' Page, a site for high schoolers, and a site for teachers. Sections include Environmental Club Projects, Environmental Youth Awards, Fun Activities, and Environmental Basics.
Subjects: Environmental Education; Kids' Pages

634. FBI Kids' Page
http://www.fbi.gov/fbikids.htm
Sponsor(s): Justice Department — Federal Bureau of Investigation (FBI)
Description: The FBI site provides pages for kids in kindergarten through 5th grade, such as About Our Dogs, and for those in grades 6 through 12, such as How We Investigate.
Subjects: Crime Detection; Kids' Pages

635. FDA Kids' Site
http://www.fda.gov/oc/opacom/kids/
Sponsor(s): Health and Human Services Department — Food and Drug Administration (FDA)
Description: The colorful FDA Web site for children presents health and safety information in several sections, including the Food Safety Quiz and All About Animals. The center box links to a page for teens, which addresses such topics as mononucleosis, tattoos, and birth control. The center box also links to the Parents' Corner with information on child health and safety.
Subjects: Adolescents; Health Promotion; Kids' Pages

636. Federal Reserve Kids Page
http://www.federalreserve.gov/kids/
Sponsor(s): Federal Reserve
Description: This site has answers to twelve questions, ranging from "what is inflation?" to "what is the FOMC, and what does it do?"
   The Federal Reserve has a broader education site with resources for teachers available at ⟨http://www.federalreserveeducation.org/⟩.
Subjects: Kids' Pages

637. FEMA for Kids
http://www.fema.gov/kids/
Sponsor(s): Federal Emergency Management Agency (FEMA)
Description: This FEMA site provides information and resources to help children prepare for and prevent disasters. The Get Ready, Get Set section has information

and activities about preparing for a disaster and the Disaster Area section gives details about 10 kinds of disasters (including hurricanes and tornadoes). The Disaster Connections section has children's artwork, poems, and letters with their thoughts on disasters such as tornadoes and the 9-11 attacks. A section called For the Little Ones has games and coloring pages. The site uses audio and video in appropriate places.

FEMA has done an excellent job pulling together a Web site of resources explaining disasters to children without scaring them.

Subjects: Disaster Preparedness; Kids' Pages

638. FirstGov for Kids
http://www.kids.gov/
Sponsor(s): General Services Administration (GSA)
Description: This FirstGov for Kids Web site is a portal to Web pages designed for children. Annotated Web links are arranged by topic, such as Careers, Geography, History, Homework, Safety, and Space. Each topic features government Web pages but also links to Web sites from commercial, educational, and other sources.

FirstGov for Kids is an easy way for children (as well as teachers and parents) to find kid-friendly information on the Web. It is particularly helpful as an index to government Web pages for children. A few commercial sites require login information or are more appropriate for teachers, but many have appropriate content that is low in advertising.

Subjects: Government Information; Finding Aids; Kids' Pages

639. GirlsHealth.gov
http://girlshealth.gov/
Sponsor(s): Health and Human Services Department
Description: GirlsHealth.gov is designed to help adolescent girls (ages 10–16) learn about the health issues and social situations that they will encounter during the teen years. Sections provide information about fitness, nutrition, the mind, relationships, and other related topics. The site also has sections for parents, caregivers, and teachers.

Subjects: Health Promotion; Kids' Pages

640. HHS Pages for Kids
http://www.hhs.gov/kids/
Sponsor(s): Health and Human Services Department
Description: This page links to various kids' pages offered by agencies related to the Department of Health and Human Services. They distribute information about health, avoiding cigarettes and drugs, food safety, and more.

Subjects: Health Promotion; Kids' Pages

641. Indian Health Service Native American KIDS page
http://www.ihs.gov/PublicInfo/Publications/Kids/
Sponsor(s): Health and Human Services Department — Indian Health Services (IHS)
Description: This site is divided into sections for children's content on health, safety, Native American culture, and Native American stories. Some of the links lead to material developed for the IHS; others lead to kids pages at other federal agencies. The McGruff link to the left of the page leads to the Department of Justice's McGruff® and Scruff's® Drug and Violence Prevention Story and Activity Book Web site, which features Indian Country themes.

Subjects: American Indians; Kids' Pages

642. Justice for Kids and Youth
http://www.usdoj.gov/kidspage/
Sponsor(s): Justice Department
Description: The Department of Justice page for youth provides information about the department and its agencies, primarily the FBI. Information is arranged by category, including Kids (grades K–5), Youth (grades 6–12), Teachers and Parents, and Subjects. Links from the home page lead to special subject sections, such as Inside the Courtroom, Get It Straight (the Facts about Drugs), Civil Rights, and Cyberethics for Kids.
Subjects: Criminal Justice; Kids' Pages

643. Kidd Safety
http://www.cpsc.gov/kids/kidsafety/
Sponsor(s): Consumer Product Safety Commission (CPSC)
Description: The Kidd Safety page uses a cartoon goat named Kidd to guide users through games and information about safety. The site covers topics such as bicycle helmets, riding a scooter, and safety around the house.
Subjects: Safety; Kids' Pages

644. Kids and Families — Social Security
http://www.ssa.gov/kids/
Sponsor(s): Social Security Administration (SSA)
Description: This SSA Web site includes a Kids' Place and a Parents' Place. The Kids' Place offers tales about saving for the future and an introduction to the Social Security card. On the main page, there is also a link to information for the families of youth with disabilities.
Subjects: Social Security; Kids' Pages

645. Kids' Corner, Endangered Species Program
http://endangered.fws.gov/kids/
Sponsor(s): Interior Department — Fish and Wildlife Service (FWS)
Description: This site features a selection of educational activities about endangered species, most designed to be used by a teacher or parent for the benefit of young learners. The "Endangered Means There is Still Time" activity includes slide shows, a quiz, an activity workbook, and teachers' resources. The site also links to related programs from inside and outside the government, such as the Junior Duck Stamp Program and the National Wildlife Federation's Backyard Wildlife Habitats program.
Subjects: Endangered Species; Kids' Pages

646. Kids in the House
http://clerkkids.house.gov/
Sponsor(s): Congress — House of Representatives — Office of the Clerk
Description: The House Clerk's Web site for kids includes material (written primarily for upper grade or high school students) that provides information on House procedures and history. It also discusses how bills are made into law. Features include a cartoon field trip to Capitol Hill, games, and a resource section for parents and teachers.
Subjects: Legislative Procedure; Kids' Pages; Civics Education

647. Kids Next Door
http://www.hud.gov/kids/kids.html
Sponsor(s): Housing and Urban Development (HUD)
Description: HUD's Web site for children is subtitled "Where kids can learn more about being good citizens." The page features sections including Meet Cool People, See Neat Things, and Visit Awesome Places. Within each of these sections are activities and pages such as Help the Homeless, Kids Volunteer, Safe Places to Play, and Build A Community.
Subjects: Kids' Pages

648. Kid's Zone, Pablo's Classroom
http://www.yesicankids.gov
Alternate URL(s): http://www.yosipuedo.gov/kidszone/kidszone3.html
Sponsor(s): President's Advisory Commission on Educational Excellence for Hispanic Americans
Description: Featuring the cartoon character Pablo the Eagle, this kids' page is part of the White House Initiative on Educational Excellence for Hispanic Americans. Reflecting the Initiative's emphasis on reading skills, the site has a collection of bedtime stories with color illustrations. The site also has a Spanish-language version, available at the alternate URL above.
Subjects: Reading; Kids' Pages

649. MyPyramid for Kids
http://www.fns.usda.gov/tn/kids-pyramid.html
Sponsor(s): Agriculture Department (USDA) — Food and Nutrition Service (FNS)
Description: The MyPyramid for Kids Web site provides nutrition education resources for teachers and parents of elementary school children. Resources include a MyPyramid for Kids poster, coloring page, and worksheet in PDF format. Classroom materials on the site include three lesson plans. The site also has a Tips for Families color brochure. The MyPyramid Blast Off game is intended for use by children.
Subjects: Health Promotion; Nutrition

650. NASA Kids
http://www.nasa.gov/audience/forkids/home/
Alternate URL(s): http://www.nasa.gov/audience/forstudents/
Sponsor(s): National Aeronautics and Space Administration (NASA) — Education Office
Description: The NASA Kids page features games, stories, and activities related to space and science.
   The alternate URL above links to the NASA For Students page, which has sections for students in grades K–4, 5–8, 9–12, and postsecondary levels. Both the Kids page and the For Students Page are part of a comprehensive NASA Education Web site at ⟨http://education.nasa.gov/home/⟩.
Subjects: Space; Kids' Pages

651. NCEH Kids' Page
http://www.cdc.gov/nceh/kids/99kidsday/
Sponsor(s): Health and Human Services Department — Centers for Disease Control and Prevention (CDC) — National Center for Environmental Health (NCEH)
Description: Designed for the young reader, the site is based on *Take Your Children to Work Day*, a booklet created by NCEH for its employees' children to introduce them to the work of the agency. It includes sections on Asthma, Cruise Ship Inspection, Disabilities, Emergency Response, Global Health, and Lead Poisoning.

The booklet is available as a PDF version that may be downloaded and printed. It is also available in Spanish.
Subjects: Health Promotion; Kids' Pages

652. NIEHS' Kids Pages
http://www.niehs.nih.gov/kids/home.htm
Sponsor(s): National Institutes of Health (NIH) — National Institute of Environmental Health Sciences (NIEHS)
Description: This Kids Page offering from the NIEHS has both a Spanish-language and a text-only version. It includes sections such as Games and Activities, Color Our World, and Environmental Health Science Education. It also has a page for kids about Pandemic Flu.
Subjects: Environmental Education; Health Promotion; Kids' Pages

653. NROjr.GOV
http://www.nrojr.gov/
Sponsor(s): Defense Department — National Reconnaissance Office (NRO)
Description: The NRO kids' page features games and activities with a satellite and space theme. With content offering simple online coloring pages, stories, and music, it is aimed at the younger set.
Subjects: Kids' Pages

654. Patent and Trademark Office Kids' Page
http://www.uspto.gov/go/kids/
Sponsor(s): Commerce Department — Patent and Trademark Office (PTO)
Description: The PTO Web site offers children's contests, games, and puzzles having to do with creativity, invention, and the operations of the PTO. The site has sections designed for students in grades K–6 and 6–12, as well as information for parents, teachers, and coaches.
Subjects: Inventions; Kids' Pages

655. Peace Corps Kids' World
http://www.peacecorps.gov/kids/
Sponsor(s): Peace Corps
Description: The Peace Corps offers this kids' page, with sections including What is the Peace Corps?; Make a Difference; Explore the World; Tell Me a Story; and Food, Friends, and Fun. This site mainly provides information about the Peace Corps program. Some resources on foreign countries are listed under the Explore the World and Food, Friends, and Fun sections.
Subjects: Geography; Kids' Pages

656. Safety City
http://www.nhtsa.dot.gov/kids/
Sponsor(s): Transportation Department — National Highway Traffic Safety Administration (NHTSA)
Description: Vince and Larry, the NHTSA's crash test dummies, serve as the guides for this children's Web site, which provides information on vehicle safety. The site features sections such as Safety School, Bike Tour, and School Bus Safety.
Subjects: Traffic Safety; Vehicle Safety; Kids' Pages

657. Sci4Kids
http://www.ars.usda.gov/is/kids/
Alternate URL(s): http://www.ars.usda.gov/is/espanol/kids/
Sponsor(s): Agriculture Department (USDA) — Agricultural Research Service (ARS)
Description: Sci4Kids is designed for children between the ages of 8 and 13. With a colorful all-graphics menu, it shows how scientific research affects many areas of life. The site includes information about careers in science. The alternate URL links to the Spanish-language version of the site.
Subjects: Science Education; Kids' Pages

658. ScienceLab
http://www.osti.gov/sciencelab/
Sponsor(s): Energy Department — Scientific and Technical Information Office
Description: ScienceLab links to student resources at government and other Web sites. Major sections for students include Elementary Lab, Middle School Lab, High School Lab, and Experiments. The site also has a Teachers' Lab and sections about science careers, competitions, and summer camps.
Subjects: Science Education

659. Smithsonian Education
http://www.smithsonianeducation.org/students/
Sponsor(s): Smithsonian Institution
Description: The Smithsonian Web site for kids and students includes sections called Mr. President, Walking on the Moon, and Amazing Collections. The section called At the Smithsonian links to pages of interest to kids from many Smithsonian Web sites.

Much of the content will be of interest to students in the upper grades through high school and their parents. The site will be particularly helpful for kids preparing to visit Smithsonian museums.
Subjects: Kids' Pages

660. Space Place
http://spaceplace.jpl.nasa.gov/spacepl.htm
Alternate URL(s): http://spaceplace.jpl.nasa.gov/sp/kids/index.shtml
Sponsor(s): National Aeronautics and Space Administration (NASA) — Jet Propulsion Laboratory (JPL)
Description: Space Place is full of games, projects, and animations relating to earth and space science. The Teachers' Corner has classroom activity articles. The site has a Spanish-language version, which can be linked to from the top of the home page or directly accessed at the alternate URL listed above.
Subjects: Space; Kids' Pages

661. Stop Bullying Now
http://www.stopbullyingnow.hrsa.gov/
Sponsor(s): Health and Human Services Department — Health Resources and Services Administration (HRSA)
Description: This site has information and activities for kids about dealing with bullying behavior. The portion of the site for adults and educators is also available in Spanish.

This site makes extensive use of animation, sound, and features such as webcasts and podcasts. There does not appear to be a text-only version.
Subjects: Kids' Pages

662. Tobacco Information and Prevention Source (TIPS) for Youth
http://www.cdc.gov/tobacco/tips4youth.htm

Sponsor(s): Health and Human Services Department — Centers for Disease Control and Prevention (CDC) — National Center for Chronic Disease Prevention and Health Promotion (NCCDPHP)

Description: TIPS4Youth links to an extensive list of resources providing information to young people about smoking. The resources include content aimed directly at kids as well as material (such as videos and program guides) for adults organizing anti-smoking campaigns for children. The site also features *SGR 4 Kids*, the Surgeon General's Report for Kids about Smoking.

Subjects: Smoking; Tobacco; Kids' Pages

663. ToxMystery
http://toxmystery.nlm.nih.gov/

Sponsor(s): National Institutes of Health (NIH) — National Library of Medicine (NLM)

Description: ToxMystery is an interactive game designed to teach kids about dangerous household substances. The site includes sections for parents and teachers.

Subjects: Kids' Pages; Environmental Health

664. U.S. Army Corps of Engineers Education Center
http://education.usace.army.mil/

Sponsor(s): Army — Army Corps of Engineers

Description: This site provides educational information and activities about ports, waterway navigation, engineering, and related topics.

Subjects: Kids' Pages

665. United States Mint's Site for Kids
http://www.usmint.gov/kids/

Sponsor(s): Treasury Department — United States Mint

Description: This site is alternatively called H.I.P (History in Your Pocket)/Pocket Change. It features games and activities to teach children about the history of coins, coins around the world, and coin collecting. It includes a section for teachers.

Subjects: Coins; Kids' Pages

666. USA Freedom Corps for Kids
http://www.usafreedomcorpskids.gov/

Sponsor(s): USA Freedom Corps

Description: This USA Freedom Corps page has sections for kids, youth, parents, and teachers — all focused on volunteering. The teachers' section has basic information on service-learning.

Subjects: Volunteerism; Kids' Pages

667. USFA Kids
http://www.usfa.fema.gov/kids/flash.shtm

Sponsor(s): Homeland Security Department — Federal Emergency Management Agency (FEMA) — U.S. Fire Administration

Description: USFA Kids has information on home fire safety, smoke alarms, and escaping from fire. It includes coloring pages and a Hazard House game.

Subjects: Fire Prevention; Kids' Pages

668. VA KIDS
http://www.va.gov/kids/
Sponsor(s): Veterans Affairs Department
Description: VA KIDS has sections for grades K–5 and 6–12 and for teachers. The grades 6–12 section includes information about volunteer and scholarship opportunities. The teacher section has resource guides and contacts for finding classroom speakers.
Subjects: Veterans; Kids' Pages

669. WhiteHouseKids.Gov
http://www.whitehouse.gov/kids/
Sponsor(s): White House
Description: The White House Web site for kids features sections on White House history and traditions, tours of the White House, the First Family's pets, White House sports, and patriotism. It also features quizzes and games relating to the White House. A Parents and Teachers Guide outlines educational activities using the site.
Subjects: White House (Mansion); Kids' Pages

670. World Book @ NASA
http://www.nasa.gov/worldbook/
Sponsor(s): National Aeronautics and Space Administration (NASA)
Description: Through a partnership with *World Book*, the NASA Web site is offering a selection of over 40 *World Book* encyclopedia articles concerning space exploration. Entries range from "Armstrong, Neil" to "Weather."

While not strictly a kids' page, World Book @ NASA will certainly be a homework helper.
Subjects: Science Education; Space

Teaching

671. Federal Resources for Educational Excellence (FREE)
http://www.ed.gov/free/
Alternate URL(s): http://www.ed.gov/free/constitution/
Sponsor(s): Education Department
Description: FREE is a central finding aid for the hundreds of Web-based teaching and learning resources supported by 50 agencies across the U.S. federal government. The Searches and Subjects section is the main access point. Recently added materials are listed in the New Resources section. The More for Students page highlights resources particularly appropriate for K–12 students.

This is one of the most comprehensive finding aids for education-related U.S. government Web sites. Its primary focus is on K–12 resources. The special Constitution Resources section (see alternate URL above) will be helpful to educators planning for the annual Constitution Day.
Subjects: Educational Resources; Finding Aids; Kids' Pages

672. James Madison Graduate Fellowships
http://www.jamesmadison.com/
Sponsor(s): James Madison Memorial Fellowship Foundation
Description: James Madison Graduate Fellowships are for teachers at the secondary school level who wish to enhance their knowledge of the U.S. Constitution. The fellowships are for graduate study leading to a master's degree. This Web site has

more about the program and about the James Madison Memorial Fellowship Foundation, an independent agency within the executive branch.
Subjects: Constitution of the United States; Fellowships; Civics Education

673. NCELA — National Clearinghouse for English Language Acquisition
http://www.ncela.gwu.edu/
Sponsor(s): Education Department — English Language Acquisition Office
Description: NCELA, known in full as the National Clearinghouse for English Language Acquisition and Language Instruction Educational Programs and funded by the Department of Education, is concerned with the effective education of linguistically and culturally diverse learners in the United States. The NCELA Web site provides direct access to a wealth of information on research, funding, and technical assistance for teaching English language learners.
Subjects: Language Education

674. What Works Clearinghouse (WWC)
http://www.whatworks.ed.gov/
Sponsor(s): Education Department — Institute of Education Sciences
Description: WWC collects and reviews studies of the effectiveness of educational programs and practices. The studies and reviews are available in the Products section. The site has information about the review process and an open invitation to submit studies or topics.
Subjects: Educational Assessment

CHAPTER 8

Employment

The federal government has a role in employment law, in regulating workplace conditions, in measuring employment and promoting jobs growth, and also—to a degree—in labor-management relations. All of these areas are reflected in this chapter's Web sites. Many of the sites concerning government's role as an employer, however, can be found in the Government and Politics chapter.

Subsections in this chapter are Employment Law, Employment Statistics, Jobs, Labor-Management Relations, and Workplace Conditions.

Employment Law

675. Benefits Review Board (BRB)
http://www.dol.gov/brb/welcome.html
Sponsor(s): Labor Department — Benefits Review Board (BRB)
Description: BRB rules on appeals of worker's compensation claims that arise under the Longshore and Harbor Worker's Compensation Act and the Black Lung Benefits amendments to the Federal Coal Mine Health and Safety Act of 1969. Its Web site has the text of BRB published and unpublished opinions and lists of case citations for Longshore and Black Lung cases.
Subjects: Employment Law

676. Davis-Bacon and Related Acts Home Page
http://www.dol.gov/esa/programs/dbra/
Sponsor(s): Labor Department — Employment Standards Administration (ESA)
Description: This Web site includes information on the forms and surveys relevant to the construction contractors complying with the Davis-Bacon Act. (The Davis-Bacon Act concerns wage rates for laborers working on public buildings or public works projects.) The Web site's Help section explains many of the Davis-Bacon provisions and will help users learn about these regulations. The site also includes regional contact information for Labor's Wage and Hour Division and has a set of links to other related Web sites.

The information on this Web site will be most useful to construction contractors complying with the Davis-Bacon Act. To its credit, the site is specifically designed to be accessible by the disabled.
Subjects: Construction Industry — Regulations; Wages — Regulations

677. Davis-Bacon Wage Determinations
http://www.gpo.gov/davisbacon/
Sponsor(s): Labor Department — Employment Standards Administration (ESA)
Description: The Department of Labor, under the mandates of the Davis-Bacon Act and related legislation, determines prevailing wage rates for construction-related occupations in most counties in the United States. All federal government construction contracts and most contracts for federally assisted construction totaling over $2,000 must contain the wage determinations. With this database (hosted at the GPO Access Web site), users may search all determinations, browse all determinations by state, view wage determinations that will be modified in the next week, or browse the current week's modifications by determination.

As with most GPO Access databases, researchers are advised to check this Web site's Helpful Hints section for tips on constructing a search and interpreting the results. In addition, a Reference Materials section provides useful background information on the Davis-Bacon Act.

Subjects: Construction Industry — Regulations; Wages — Regulations

Publications: *Davis-Bacon Wage Determinations*, L 36.211/2:

678. Department of Labor

http://www.dol.gov/

Sponsor(s): Labor Department

Description: The Department of Labor uses the front page of its Web site to showcase the variety of information contained in its networks. A sidebar called Find It provides quick links to the Topics, Audiences, Top 20 Items Requested, Forms, Services by Location, and Agencies (links to DOL agency Web sites) section. The home page also highlights the latest Labor Department news and economic indicators from the Bureau of Labor Statistics. Other features of the site are labor law compliance information, press releases and speeches, and links to state labor offices. The Research Library section links users to publications and to each of the Labor Department's affiliated agencies. The DOL site also has a search feature and an A-Z index to aid in navigation.

This Web site provides effective access to Department of Labor information and to related Web sites by providing multiple paths for accessing information and by highlighting the most frequently consulted topics.

Subjects: Employment; Labor Law; Labor Statistics; Labor-Management Relations

Publications: *Semiannual Report of the Inspector General*, L 1.74:
Senior Executive Service, Forum Series, L 1.95:
U.S. Department of Labor: Strategic Plan, L 1.2:

679. Elaws — Employment Laws Assistance for Workers and Small Businesses

http://www.dol.gov/elaws/

Sponsor(s): Labor Department

Description: The elaws advisors are interactive tools designed to help employees and employers understand their respective rights and responsibilities under the laws and regulations administered by the Department of Labor. Each elaws advisor provides information about a specific law or regulation. The advisor imitates the interaction that an individual might have with an employment law expert. It asks questions, provides information, and directs the user to the appropriate resolutions based on the user's responses. Featured sections of expertise include Workplace Safety, Employing Veterans, Workplace Poster Requirements, Wage and Hour Issues, and Health Benefits. This central site links to elaws advisors on the Web sites of component agencies.

Subjects: Labor Law

680. Employee Benefits Security Administration (EBSA)

http://www.dol.gov/ebsa/

Sponsor(s): Labor Department

Description: EBSA, formerly the Pension and Welfare Benefits Administration, is concerned with private retirement plans and private health and welfare plans. Its Web site explains pension rights and employer compliance programs. Major sections include Pension Reform, ERISA (Employee Retirement Income Security Act) Enforcement, Technical Guidance, Compliance Assistance, and Consumer Information. The main page highlights news, upcoming compliance assistance seminars, and frequently asked questions. The site also has forms, news updates (available by e-mail), EBSA publications, and links to relevant laws, regulations, and proposed regulations. Some EBSA publications for consumers and employers are available in Spanish.

The EBSA Web site has material for both employee benefit specialists and consumers. The site design makes it easy for each audience to find relevant content.

Subjects: Health Insurance; Pensions

681. Employment Standards Administration
http://www.dol.gov/esa/

Sponsor(s): Labor Department — Employment Standards Administration (ESA)
Description: ESA is responsible for enforcing and administering laws governing legally mandated wages and working conditions, including child labor, minimum wages, overtime, family and medical leave, equal employment opportunity, workers' compensation, internal union democracy and financial integrity, and union elections. Its Web site links to ESA's four component programs: the Office of Federal Contract Compliance Programs, the Office of Labor-Management Standards, the Office of Workers' Compensation Programs, and the Wage and Hour Division. Other main sections are Laws and Regulations, Minimum Wage, Fair Pay (overtime rules), Family and Medical Leave Act, State Labor Laws, Required Posters, and Forms.
Subjects: Labor Law; Minimum Wage

682. Foreign Labor Certification
http://www.foreignlaborcert.doleta.gov/

Sponsor(s): Labor Department — Employment and Training Administration (ETA)
Description: The Office of Foreign Labor Certification (OFLC) in the Department of Labor provides labor certifications to employers seeking to bring foreign workers into the United States. Its Web site currently features a countdown of months remaining before the OFLC backlog of certification cases is cleared. It also provides background information, policies, regulations, and forms. The Frequently Asked Questions section covers questions about permanent, H1-B, H2-A, and other classifications, and about prevailing wages.
Subjects: Immigrant Workers

683. Job Accommodation Network (JAN)
http://www.jan.wvu.edu/

Sponsor(s): Labor Department — Office of Disability Employment Policy
Description: JAN is an Americans with Disabilities Act information service sponsored by the Department of Labor and operated by West Virginia University. The focus of JAN is on its free consulting service, which is accessible through its toll-free 800 number. This Web site provides information on the consulting service and on the employability of people with disabilities. Information is targeted at private employers, government employers, and individuals with disabilities. The "JAN by Disability: A to Z" section provides quick access to JAN fact sheets and other resources. This site is also available in Spanish.
Subjects: Americans with Disabilities Act (ADA)

684. Office of Disability Employment Policy
http://www.dol.gov/odep/

Sponsor(s): Labor Department — Office of Disability Employment Policy
Description: The Department of Labor's Office of Disability Employment Policy (ODEP) manages programs, policies, and grants to further its mission to increase employment opportunities for people with disabilities. Its Web site has audience-specific portals for groups including adults with disabilities, businesses and

employers, youth and family, researchers, service providers, and veterans. The Employment Supports section covers such topics as transportation, health care, and assistive technology. The Initiatives section links to Web sites for specific ODEP programs and provides grant announcements. The Publications section has numerous fact sheets on accommodations, emergency preparedness, employment laws, and related topics.

This Web site offers an excellent overview on many issues related to employment for people with disabilities.

Subjects: Disabilities — Policy; Employment Discrimination — Laws

685. Office of Special Counsel for Immigration-Related Unfair Trade Practices

http://www.usdoj.gov/crt/osc/

Sponsor(s): Justice Department — Civil Rights Division
Description: The Office of Special Counsel for Immigration-Related Unfair Trade Practices investigates employers charged with national origin and citizenship status discrimination under the antidiscrimination provision of the Immigration and Nationality Act. This Web site provides guidance for both employers and employees and links to relevant laws and regulations. The News section includes press releases and announcements of grants awarded to organizations that provide public education on immigration-related discrimination. A Spanish-language version of the site is also available.
Subjects: Employment Discrimination; Immigrant Workers

686. Pension Benefit Guaranty Corporation

http://www.pbgc.gov/

Sponsor(s): Pension Benefit Guaranty Corporation (PBGC)
Description: PBGC is a federal agency that insures and protects pension benefits in certain pension plans. Its Web site explains what PBGC does and does not guarantee, as well as the legal limits on their guarantees. PBGC offers online transactions for tasks, such as applying for pension benefits and designating a beneficiary; instructions for doing these tasks by phone are also provided. Information is presented for three audiences: Workers and Retirees, Practitioners (pension plan professionals), and Media. The Find Your Pension Plan database, under Workers and Retirees, can be searched by company name or plan name; status and guarantee tables are provided for each plan. The Practitioners section includes interest rates, mortality tables, premium filing instructions, the *Pension Insurance Data Book* (under the heading Plan Trends and Statistics), laws, regulations, appeals board decisions, and opinion letters. The Media section includes publications, news releases, and PBGC congressional testimony. The site's Pension Search section is a directory of people known to be entitled to a pension from a company that went out of business or ended its defined benefit pension plan, but who have not yet claimed their pension.

This Web site offers well-organized content and online services. It should prove useful to anyone seeking information on one of the PBGC-insured pension plans.
Subjects: Pensions; Retirement
Publications: *Annual Report/Pension Benefit Guaranty Corporation*, Y 3.P 43:1/
Fact Sheets (Pension Benefit Guaranty Corporation), Y 3.P 38/2:14/
Finding a Lost Pension, Y 3.P 38/2:
Pension Insurance Data Book, Y 3.P 38/2:2 P 38/7
Your Guaranteed Pension, Y 3.P 38/2:2 P 38/5/

687. Railroad Retirement Board
http://www.rrb.gov/
Sponsor(s): Railroad Retirement Board (RRB)
Description: RRB is an independent agency that administers retirement-survivor and unemployment-sickness benefit programs for railroad workers and their families. The setion of the RRB Web site for beneficiaries and employees has forms, publications, and the Benefit Online Services portal called MainLine. The rail and labor employer section has forms, publications, and online services for employers. The section for the general public serves as a central location for RRB legal opinions and decisions, financial statistics, and organizational information. Due to frequent requests, this section also has useful information for people seeking former railroad employee records for genealogical research. The site also has listings of railroad job openings.

This Web site will be of most interest to people involved in the Railroad Retirement program. It offers a considerable amount of useful information about their benefits.
Subjects: Railroads; Retirement
Publications: *Annual Report/Railroad Retirement Board*, RR 1.1:
Quarterly Benefit Statistics Report, RR 1.16:

688. U.S. Equal Employment Opportunity Commission
http://www.eeoc.gov/
Sponsor(s): Equal Employment Opportunity Commission (EEOC)
Description: EEOC coordinates federal equal employment opportunity regulations and investigates charges of employment discrimination. Its Web site provides information for employees, employers, small businesses, attorneys, and the public. The Types of Discrimination section has clear descriptions of laws related to age, disability, race, religion, and other areas. Statistics and additional information sources are provided for each area. A Laws, Regulations, and Guidance section serves as a library for relevant legal documents. Other topics include enforcement and employment statistics, special information for federal agencies and employees, reports on litigation settlements, how to file a discrimination charge, training and outreach programs, publications and posters, news and an RSS newsfeed. Translations of fact sheets and basic information from the site are available in Spanish, Arabic, Russian, Vietnamese, Korean, and Haitian Creole. A Spanish-language version of the Web site is also available.

The EEOC Web site provides a straightforward presentation of important content. The home page has a clean table-of-contents style that makes the lack of a site map much less critical. The site offers adjustable font size and a plain text version, making it even more accessible.
Subjects: Employment Discrimination — Laws
Publications: *Annual Performance Plan*, Y 3.EQ 2:1/
Digest of Equal Opportunity Law, Y 3.EQ 2:22
Enforcement Guidances, Y 3.EQ 2:2

689. Veterans Employment and Training Service (VETS)
http://www.dol.gov/vets/welcome.html
Sponsor(s): Labor Department — Veterans Employment and Training Service (VETS)
Description: VETS advocates for veterans in the employment marketplace. Materials on the VETS Web site include the text of laws and regulations concerning veterans' employment, information about the Veterans Preference for federal jobs, and information about the Uniformed Services Employment and Reemployment Rights Act (USERRA).
Subjects: Veterans

690. Wage and Hour Division (WHD)

http://www.dol.gov/esa/whd/

Sponsor(s): Labor Department — Employment Standards Administration (ESA)

Description: As part of the Department of Labor's Employment Standards Administration, WHD administers some of the best-known labor laws in the United States. These include Fair Labor Standards Act (which concerns minimum wage and overtime), the Family and Medical Leave Act, the Migrant and Seasonal Agricultural Worker Protection Act, worker protections provided in several temporary visa programs, and the prevailing wage requirements of the Davis-Bacon Act. Its Web site provides fact sheets, posters, opinion letters, and compliance information for these laws. It also links to over a dozen charts comparing state labor laws on a variety of topics. The Compliance Assistance section covers topics including wage garnishment, stock options, lie detector tests, and government contracts. In 2006, WHD added a Back Wage Employee Locator tool to the Web site to provide easy and secure access for employees to find and collect back wages due to them.

Subjects: Minimum Wage; Employment Law

691. Wage Determinations OnLine.gov

http://www.wdol.gov/

Sponsor(s): Labor Department — Employment Standards Administration (ESA)

Description: This Web site, intended for federal contracting officials, provides Service Contract Act (SCA) and Davis-Bacon Act (DBA) wage determinations. It is also open to labor organizations, contractor associations, employees, and the general public. SCA determinations can be searched by state and county. Archived SCA wage determinations can be retrieved by number. Users can also browse a list of determinations due to be revised. DBA wage determinations can be browsed by state, searched by number, or searched by a combination of state, county, and construction type. Archived DBA wage determinations and a list of determinations due to be revised are also online. The Library section links to the *Federal Acquisition Regulations* and other Web sites related to federal contracting.

According to its Web site, Wage Determinations OnLine.gov is a collaborative effort of the Office of Management and Budget, the Department of Labor, the Department of Defense, the General Services Administration, the Department of Energy, and the Department of Commerce.

Wage Determinations OnLine.gov was launched in August 2005. GPO Access has long hosted a Davis-Bacon Act Web site for the Department of Labor, and it continues to do so at this time. The GPO Access Web site, described elsewhere in this chapter, does not include Service Contract Act wage determinations.

Subjects: Construction Industry — Regulations; Government Contracts; Wages — Regulations

Publications: *Davis-Bacon Wage Determinations*, L 36.211/2:

Service Contract Act Directory of Occupations, L 36.202:

692. Youth at Work

http://youth.eeoc.gov/

Sponsor(s): Equal Employment Opportunity Commission (EEOC)

Description: Youth at Work is targeted at working teens. It provides straightforward information on employment discrimination, employee rights, and employee responsibilities. The site uses six engaging case studies and an interactive quiz to teach teens about employment discrimination law and the role of the EEOC. The Free Downloads section has a fact sheet in English and Spanish.

Youth at Work is an engaging Web site that provides useful information to its teenage audience in a style that is simple but not patronizing.

Subjects: Adolescents; Employment Discrimination

693. YouthRules!
http://www.youthrules.dol.gov/
Sponsor(s): Labor Department
Description: The Department of Labor's YouthRules! Program seeks to promote safe work experiences for young workers. The Web site has information on federal and state laws and regulations governing child labor. The four main sections are centered on information pertaining to teens, parents, educators, and employers. A Compliance Assistance section has guides, fact sheets, posters, and other resources for employers of teens.
Subjects: Adolescents — Regulations; Labor Law

Employment Statistics

694. Bureau of Labor Statistics
http://www.bls.gov/
Sponsor(s): Labor Department — Bureau of Labor Statistics (BLS)
Description: BLS has made its Web site a major source for employment, economic, and labor statistics. The emphasis is on access to statistics rather than on information about BLS. A box on the home page entitled Latest Numbers presents the latest key economic indicators. Featured statistics include the Consumer Price Index, unemployment rate, payroll employment, average hourly earnings, Producer Price Index, Employment Cost Index, productivity, and U.S. Import Price Index.

The site's topical sections include consistently formatted pages that describe the statistical series and linking to the major tables, economic news releases, publications, and documentation. The Get Detailed Statistics section links to a search form for creating custom tables. The current figures are given for each statistical series. Dinosaur icons on the page indicate a link to historical data. The Publications and Research sections include online access to the *Monthly Labor Review*, research papers, the *Occupational Outlook Handbook*, the BLS publications catalog, and more.

BLS does not try to hide its wealth of statistics. Much of the information is accessible with one or two clicks. BLS assists the researcher with multiple approaches: an A to Z index, lists of the most frequently requested tables, answers to current user questions, and a useful data availability grid (found in the Get Detailed Statistics section). Page layout and navigation have an overall consistency. Data output options are numerous, but the site remains easy to use.
Subjects: Labor Statistics; Wages — Statistics; Employment Statistics
Publications: *Annual Pay Levels in Metropolitan Areas*, L 2.120/2-4:
BLS Handbook of Methods, L 2.3:
Career Guide to Industries, L 2.3/4-3:
Compensation and Working Conditions (quarterly), L 2.44/4:
Consumer Expenditure Survey, L 2.3/18:
CPI Detailed Report (monthly), L 2.38/3:
Employee Benefit Survey Data, L 2.46/6: to L 2.46/9:
Employee Benefits in Medium and Large Private Establishments, L 2.3/10:
Employee Benefits in State and Local Governments, L 2.3/10-2:
Employer Costs for Employee Compensation, L 2.120/2-13:
Employment Characteristics of Families, L 2.118/2:
Employment Cost Index (quarterly), L 2.117:
Extended Mass Layoffs in the . . ., L 2.120/2-14:
Geographic Profile of Employment and Unemployment, L 2.3/12:
International Comparisons of Hourly Compensation Costs for Production Workers in Manufacturing, L 2.130:

695. Current Population Survey (CPS)

http://www.bls.gov/cps/

Sponsor(s): Labor Department — Bureau of Labor Statistics (BLS)Commerce Department — Economics and Statistics Administration (ESA) — Census Bureau

Description: CPS is the primary source of information on the labor force characteristics of the U.S. population. The survey sample of about 60,000 households is conducted by the Census Bureau for BLS. Estimates obtained from the CPS include employment, unemployment, earnings, hours of work, and other indicators. They are available by a variety of demographic characteristics — including by age, sex, race, marital status, and educational attainment — and by occupation, industry, and class of worker. The monthly CPS news release, *The Employment Situation*, is widely quoted for details on the current national unemployment rate.

The CPS Web page displays a range of current employment statistics and links to the past 10 years of each type of data. Under the Economic News Releases section, the page links to *The Employment Situation* release, its e-mail alert service, and a schedule of upcoming releases. Releases are archived back to 1994.

Other CPS products include an array of tables prepared by BLS and special reports on topics such as union membership, volunteer work, and youth summer employment. Researchers can also create simple, customized tables from the labor force data or download a flat file of the entire database.

The CPS Web page follows the BLS standard format while providing quick access to data, reports, documentation, and assistance that will serve a wide range of users.

Subjects: Employment Statistics
Publications: *The Employment Situation,* L 2.53/2:
Women in the Labor Force: A Databook, L 2.71:

696. Income
http://www.census.gov/hhes/www/income/income.html
Sponsor(s): Commerce Department — Economics and Statistics Administration (ESA) — Census Bureau
Description: The Census Bureau's Web page for income data provides reports, briefs, and research in addition to aggregated data and microdata. It links to the income data from the Current Population Survey, American Community Survey, Decennial Census, and Survey of Income and Program Participation programs; it also provides access to other Census programs. The site provides detailed information on the data sources and links to other income data programs on the Internet.
Subjects: Wages — Statistics

697. Longitudinal Employer-Household Dynamics
http://lehd.dsd.census.gov/led/
Sponsor(s): Commerce Department — Economics and Statistics Administration (ESA) — Census Bureau
Description: This Web site describes the Longitudinal Employer-Household Dynamics (LEHD) project and provides access to the data. LEHD involves a Census Bureau partnership with state labor market information agencies wishing to participate. Most of the site is concerned with Local Employment Dynamics (LED), which provide local labor market conditions designed to assist individual states. LED's Quality Workforce Indicators (QWI) include data for employment, job creation, wages, worker turnover, and other factors at state, county, and city levels. The site features research tools such as QWI Online, user guides, tutorials, and details of ongoing research at LEHD.

LEHD provides an extensive library of information, documentation, and research for social scientists and those familiar with the data; others will face a learning curve. Note that not all states participate, so data is not available from all states.
Subjects: Employment Statistics

698. National Longitudinal Surveys (NLS) Annotated Bibliography
http://www.nlsbibliography.org/
Sponsor(s): Labor Department — Bureau of Labor Statistics (BLS)
Description: The NLS Annotated Bibliography is an ongoing effort to provide the public with an up-to-date, searchable record of research based on data from all NLS cohorts. NLS gathers detailed information about the labor market experiences and other aspects of the lives of a sample of men and women. The NLS Bibliography section contains citations and abstracts of NLS-based journal articles, working papers, conference presentations, and dissertations. The last printed version of the bibliography was published in 1995, and this Web site is a continuation of the effort to provide an online bibliography of research based on data from the NLS.
Subjects: Workforce — Research

Jobs

699. America's Job Bank
http://www.ajb.dni.us/
Sponsor(s): Labor Department
Description: The America's Job Bank computerized network links job seekers and their resumes to employers and their job opportunities. Its Web site is divided into sections for job seekers and employers, both of which require users to register. America's Job Bank is part of a suite of Web tools called CareerOneStop (also described in this section), a product of the Department of Labor.
Subjects: Job Openings

700. Career Guide to Industries
http://www.bls.gov/oco/cg/
Sponsor(s): Labor Department — Bureau of Labor Statistics (BLS)
Description: This Web site presents the online version of the *Career Guide to Industries*, which is also available in print form and is updated every two years. The guide includes career information for the jobs that account for most employment in the United States. Each career profile includes sections on training, earnings, opportunities for advancement, occupational outlook, and sources of additional information. It also links to related occupational information in the online edition of the BLS's *Occupational Outlook Handbook*.
Subjects: Career Information
Publications: *Career Guide to Industries*, L 2.3/4-3:

701. Career Voyages
http://www.careervoyages.gov/
Sponsor(s): Education DepartmentLabor Department
Description: The Career Voyages Web site is designed to spotlight high-growth, high-demand career options and identify the education and skills needed for those careers. It includes sections for career changers, career advisers, students, and parents. The site makes use of online videos and provides links to Web sites related to each career.
Subjects: Career Information

702. CareerOneStop
http://www.careeronestop.org/
Sponsor(s): Labor Department
Description: The CareerOneStop portal includes America's Job Bank, America's Career InfoNet, and America's Service Locator. It is a federal-state partnership funded by grants to the states. Its Web site includes a wealth of information and services for job seekers, employers, students, and human resource professionals.
Subjects: Career Information

703. Employment and Training Administration
http://www.doleta.gov/
Sponsor(s): Labor Department — Employment and Training Administration (ETA)
Description: ETA supports workforce training programs and job placement through employment services. The ETA Web site offers information about services for businesses and industry, workers, and for workforce professionals. The site has a Grants and Contracts section as well as an ETA Library section with research studies, laws, and program information. The site also covers foreign labor certifica-

tion and links to workforce-related state government offices and other related Web sites.
Subjects: Job Training
Publications: *ETA Occasional Paper Series*, L 37.27:
Research and Evaluation Report/Monograph Series, L 37.22/2:

704. HireVetsFirst.gov
http://www.hirevetsfirst.gov/
Sponsor(s): Labor Department
Description: HireVetsFirst.gov calls itself "the comprehensive career Web site for hiring veterans of America's military" (from the Web site). It has sections for employers and for veterans seeking employment and promotes the One-Stop Career Centers available for employers and veterans. The site is sponsored by the President's National Hire Veterans Committee, which was established within the Department of Labor in 2002.
Subjects: Veterans

705. O*NET — The Occupational Information Network
http://online.onetcenter.org/
Sponsor(s): Labor Department — Employment and Training Administration (ETA)
Description: O*NET, the Occupational Information Network, is a database system developed by the Department of Labor to replace the *Dictionary of Occupational Titles (DOT)*. O*NET contains comprehensive information on job requirements and worker competencies. It is aligned with the Standard Occupational Classification (SOC) system. The Web site has a Find Occupations section to search the database by keyword and other criteria, and a Skills Search that allows users to select from a list of skills and match them to occupations. It also has a crosswalk search between the O*NET classifications and other classifications, such as the Military Occupation Classification.
Subjects: Job Skills; Occupations; Databases

706. Occupational Outlook Handbook
http://www.bls.gov/oco/
Sponsor(s): Labor Department — Bureau of Labor Statistics (BLS)
Description: The *Occupational Outlook Handbook* profiles job and career options and describes the work involved and the training or education needed for each career. It is updated every two years. The Web version of the *Handbook* features many hypertext links from within the text to definitions of terms; it also provides links to other related occupations. Each entry is available in HTML or PDF format. The *Handbook* is also available for purchase in print or on CD-ROM.

Occupation profiles can be found with a keyword search or through an A to Z index. Occupations can also be browsed by broad category, such as sales or transportation. The Web site links to supporting material, including a teacher's guide, the *Occupational Outlook Quarterly* magazine, and an overview of trends in job opportunities for the future.

This Web site contains an excellent online implementation of a standard reference source. The links to definitions and crosslinks to other occupations make the *Handbook* easy to browse online. The option of PDF files for printing is a great addition to this already useful resource.
Subjects: Career Information; Occupations; Workforce
Publications: *Occupational Outlook Handbook*, L 2.3/4:
Occupational Outlook Quarterly Online, L 2.70/4:

707. Standard Occupational Classification (SOC) System
http://stats.bls.gov/soc/
Sponsor(s): Labor Department — Bureau of Labor Statistics (BLS)
Description: The SOC system is being implemented by all federal statistical agencies to classify workers into occupational categories for the purpose of collecting, calculating, and disseminating data. This Web site allows users to browse or search the classification system, or to order a copy of the printed edition of the *Standard Occupational Classification Manual*. Related reference material is provided, including the *Standard Occupational Classification (SOC) User Guide*.
Subjects: Occupations
Publications: *Standard Occupational Classification (SOC) User Guide*
Standard Occupational Classification Manual, PREX 2.6/3:

708. Studentjobs.gov
http://www.studentjobs.gov
Sponsor(s): Education Department — Federal Student Aid OfficeOffice of Personnel Management (OPM)
Description: Studentjobs.gov is a clearinghouse of information about student employment and internships in the federal government. Users interested in federal jobs can create and post a resume online or search a database of federal job openings. An Agency Information Gateway section facilitates browsing, with direct links to the relevant employment pages at the agencies' Web sites. The e-Scholar section of the site lists apprenticeships, internships, scholarships, and other educational opportunities offered by federal agencies.
Subjects: Internships; Job Openings; Students

709. The Secretary's 21st Century Workforce Office
http://www.dol.gov/21cw/
Sponsor(s): Labor Department
Description: The 21st Century Workforce Office was created in 2001 to support the Secretary of Labor's 21st Century Workforce Initiative. This policy initiative has the goal of ensuring that U.S. workers can continue to find rewarding work in a changing global economy. This Web site has links to current news and events relating to the initiative.
Subjects: Workforce — Policy

710. USAJOBS
http://www.usajobs.opm.gov/
Sponsor(s): Office of Personnel Management (OPM)
Description: USAJOBS identifies itself as "the official job site of the United States federal government" (from the Web site). The core of the site is a database of current federal government employment opportunities. These openings can be searched by keyword or by other criteria, including by agency, occupational grouping, salary, or state. In the My USAJOBS section, users can create and store a resume online for applying for federal jobs and set up a profile to receive automated job alerts.

Other services on USAJOBS include links to federal employment application forms online, veterans employment resources, and selected information in Spanish.
Subjects: Government Employees; Job Openings

711. Women's Bureau
http://www.dol.gov/wb/welcome.html
Sponsor(s): Labor Department — Women's Bureau
Description: The Department of Labor's Women's Bureau was created in 1920 to promote profitable employment opportunities for women. Its Web site describes the bureau's current and past programs. The Resource & Info section includes fact sheets, reports, and a Statistics subsection with data on women in the workforce.
Subjects: Occupations — Statistics; Women — Policy

Labor-Management Relations

712. Federal Mediation & Conciliation Service
http://www.fmcs.gov/internet/
Sponsor(s): Federal Mediation & Conciliation Service (FMCS)
Description: FMCS is an independent agency set up by Congress to promote sound and stable labor-management relations. One of the agency's major responsibilities is to mediate collective bargaining negotiations. The What We Do section on its Web site provides information about collective bargaining, alternative bargaining processes, arbitration, the FMCS grants program, best practices, and other topics. The site also describes the FMCS e-service, which is called Technology Assisted Group Solutions (TAGS); TAGS includes capabilities for online meetings, online voting, and other services. The Resources section has articles by and about FMCS.
Subjects: Labor-Management Relations; Mediation

713. Key Workplace Documents
http://digitalcommons.ilr.cornell.edu/keydocs/
Sponsor(s): Cornell University. Catherwood Library
Description: Cornell University's Catherwood Library offers this online archive of government reports, statistics, and public policy papers from various commissions and task forces. The subject focus is on the workforce and employer-employee relationships. Federal publications in the collection include many reports from the Congressional Research Service and occasional reports from executive branch agencies.
This collection is small but focused. It is a nongovernmental information source but provides an excellent service in maintaining access to government reports that might not otherwise be available on the Internet.
Subjects: Child Labor; Labor-Management Relations — Policy; Workforce — Policy

714. National Labor Relations Board (NLRB)
http://www.nlrb.gov/
Sponsor(s): National Labor Relations Board (NLRB)
Description: NLRB conducts secret-ballot elections to determine whether employees want union representation; it also investigates unfair labor practices by employers and unions. The Workplace Rights section explains the National Labor Relations Act. Under the heading "I Am New to this Website," the section has basic information employee rights, filing a charge, and petitioning to start or dissolve a union. The Research section has NLRB decisions and memos. Research also includes the weekly summary of new documents and the CiteNet database for the *Classified Index of NLRB Board Decisions and Related Court Decisions*. The Publications section includes NLRB manuals, regulations, annual reports, and election reports on union representation votes. The E-Gov section enables electronic filing of case documents, access to a customizable My NLRB portal, and FOIA information.

NLRB redesigned its Web site in late 2006. The new site features the ability to search either the entire site or an individual section.

Subjects: Labor Unions

Publications: *Classified Index of NLRB Board Decisions and Related Court Decisions*, LR 1.8/6:

Decisions and Orders, NLRB, LR 1.8:

Two Languages — One Law (A Bilingual Guide)

Weekly Summary of NLRB Cases, LR 1.15/2:

715. National Mediation Board

http://www.nmb.gov/

Sponsor(s): National Mediation Board (NMB)

Description: NMB is an independent U.S. government agency whose principal role is to foster harmonious labor-management relations in the rail and air transport industries in order to minimize disruptions to the flow of interstate commerce. The NMB Web site's Mediation section includes information on Presidential Emergency Boards. The What's New section contains a weekly report on mediation, representation, and arbitration activity. The Documents and Forms section includes recent NMB determinations by fiscal year, an archive of the weekly reports, and NMB rules.

Subjects: Airlines; Labor Mediation; Railroads

Publications: *Annual Performance Report*, NMB 1.1:

Determinations of the National Mediation Board, NMB 1.9:

716. Office of Labor-Management Standards (OLMS)

http://www.dol.gov/esa/olms_org.htm

Sponsor(s): Labor Department — Employment Standards Administration (ESA)

Description: OLMS administers and enforces certain reporting, disclosure, and operational requirements for labor unions and union officers. The Internet Public Disclosure Room section on its Web site has financial disclosure reports for labor unions, union officers, and union employees, as well as reports for employers and labor relations consultants. The scanned reports can be viewed in PDF format and are generally available from 2000 to the present. Data from the annual financial reports submitted by unions can also be searched by criteria, such as type of union, state or ZIP code, and the dollar range of assets, liabilities, receipts, and disbursements. The site also has information about regulations governing private sector, federal government, and transit employees, as well as information about OLMS civil and criminal enforcement actions.

Subjects: Labor Unions — Regulations

Workplace Conditions

717. Federal Occupational Health (FOH)

http://www.foh.dhhs.gov/

Sponsor(s): Health and Human Services Department — Health Resources and Services Administration (HRSA)

Description: FOH provides occupational health services to federal government managers and their employees. The site includes the following sections: Who We Are, What We Do, Library, and Member Center (for certain subscription content services). The Library section links to more than 75 FOH articles and fact sheets addressing such topics as ergonomics, stress management, and smoking cessation.

Many of the items in the Library section of this Web site may also be useful to managers and employees outside the federal government.
Subjects: Government Employees; Health Promotion

718. Mine Safety and Health Administration
http://www.msha.gov/
Sponsor(s): Labor Department — Mine Safety and Health Administration (MSHA)
Description: MSHA is charged with enforcing mine safety and health standards to prevent accidents and minimize health hazards. Its Web site has extensive information about mine safety laws and regulations and guidance on compliance with the laws. The site also provides statistics on mining accidents, injuries, and fatalities. It contains the Data Retrieval System, a database with mine overviews, accident histories, violation histories, inspection histories, inspector dust samplings, and operator dust samplings and employment/production data.
Subjects: Mining; Workplace Safety — Regulations
Publications: *Fatalgrams*, L 38.15:
Holmes Safety Association Bulletin (monthly), L 38.12:
MSHA Program Information Bulletin, L 38.17/2:

719. Nanotechnology at NIOSH
http://www.cdc.gov/niosh/topics/nanotech/
Sponsor(s): Health and Human Services Department — Centers for Disease Control and Prevention (CDC) — National Institute of Occupational Safety and Health (NIOSH)
Description: This site is concerned with the occupational safety and health implications related to applications of nanotechnology. The site describes NIOSH research and links to the developing NIOSH Nanoparticle Information Library resource on the Web.
Subjects: Nanotechnology; Workplace Safety

720. National Institute of Occupational Safety and Health
http://www.cdc.gov/niosh/homepage.html
Sponsor(s): Health and Human Services Department — Centers for Disease Control and Prevention (CDC) — National Institute of Occupational Safety and Health (NIOSH)
Description: NIOSH is responsible for conducting research and making recommendations for the prevention of work-related injuries and illnesses. Its Web site offers multiple points of access to the agency's publications, databases, program information, and other resources. Information is organized into major sections, including Industries and Occupations, Hazards and Exposures, Diseases and Injuries, Chemicals, Safety and Prevention, Emergency Preparedness and Response, and Data and Statistics. NIOSH databases on the site include the Registry of Toxic Effects of Chemical Substances, the NIOSHTIC-2 bibliographic database, the NIOSH Power Tools Database (noise levels), and the Work-Related Injury Statistics Query System. The Information Resources section links to NIOSH publications and to a Spanish-language version of the site. The site also has an A to Z subject index and a search engine.
Subjects: Workplace Safety
Publications: *Criteria for a Recommended Standard...*, HE 20.7110:
Health Hazard Evaluation Summaries, HE 20.7125:
NIOSH Alerts, HE 20.7123:
NIOSH Certified Equipment List, HE 20.7124:
NIOSH Current Intelligence Bulletins, HE 20.7155:

NIOSH Manual of Analytical Methods, HE 20.7108:994/
NIOSH Pocket Guide to Chemical Hazards, HE 20.7108:
Worker Health Chartbook, HE 20.7302:

721. Occupational Safety and Health Administration
http://www.osha.gov/

Sponsor(s): Labor Department — Occupational Safety and Health Administration (OSHA)

Description: OSHA's mission is to prevent work-related injuries, illnesses, and deaths. The OSHA Web site provides information on the agency and its regulations and educational and enforcement activities. Major sections include Compliance Assistance; Laws and Regulations (including standards, interpretations, directives, and dockets); Enforcement, Newsroom (including publications); Safety and Health Topics; Statistics; and International. The Statistics section provides multiple ways of searching OSHA inspection data and has a tool to find the industries that have the most violations of a specified federal or state OSHA standard. OSHA links to the Bureau of Labor Statistics for workplace injury, illness, and fatality statistics.

This Web site includes a Spanish-language section designed for employers and employees. Other special sections are offered for small businesses, workers, and teenage workers.

Subjects: Workplace Safety — Regulations
Publications: *Fact Sheet* (series), L 35.24:
JS&HQ (Job Safety & Health Quarterly), L 35.9/3:
News, L 1.79:

722. OSHA's Lost Workday Injury and Illness Database
http://www.thememoryhole.org/osha/lwdii.htm

Sponsor(s): The Memory Hole

Description: The Memory Hole, a nongovernment Web site, provides data from OSHA regarding the lost workday injury and illness rates for companies. The data was originally obtained by a *New York Times* reporter using the Freedom of Information Act and from subsequent litigation. The data cover the 1996–2002 period and are presented online in ZIP files. This site includes documentation and warnings about the data from both OSHA and The Memory Hole.

Subjects: Workplace Safety

723. Substance Abuse Information Database (SAID)
http://said.dol.gov/

Sponsor(s): Labor Department

Description: SAID is designed to assist employers in establishing and maintaining programs to address workplace substance abuse. The materials in SAID can be searched or browsed by title, author, topic, or other criteria. Topics include drug and alcohol testing, sample programs and policies, laws and regulations, and training supervisors. The site also has a clickable map that provides workplace substance abuse law information for each of the 50 states and Puerto Rico.

Subjects: Personnel Management; Substance Abuse

CHAPTER 9
Energy

The federal government is both a regulator and producer of energy. The government sets energy policy and plays a role in the development of energy-related technologies. This chapter covers the varied federal Web sites that describe energy use and production, consumer energy issues, and energy statistics. Information about the work of the Department of Energy's laboratories can be found in the Science and Space chapter. Information on some aspects of Energy's defense work can be found in the Defense and Intelligence chapter. The topic of transportation is covered in the Transportation chapter.

Subsections in this chapter are Alternative and Renewable Fuels, Energy Policy and Information, Fossil and Nuclear Fuels, and Utilities.

Alternative and Renewable Fuels

724. Alternative Fuels Data Center
http://www.eere.energy.gov/afdc/
Sponsor(s): Energy Department — Energy Efficiency and Renewable Energy Office
Description: Alternative fuels for vehicles is the singular theme of this Department of Energy Web site. The site describes fuels such as biodiesel, electricity, ethanol, hydrogen, natural gas, and propane. An Alternative Fuel Vehicles section includes buying guides and explanatory material. The site also has an alternative fuel station locator for finding CNG, ethanol/E85, LPG, biodiesel, LNG, and electric refueling stations, with a tally of each type in each state. Another section details state and federal incentives for alternative fuel vehicle owners. The Information Resources section features a documents database, the "Clean Fleet Guide," vehicle and fuels statistics, a glossary, and other relevant resources.
Subjects: Fuels

725. Bioenergy Feedstock Information Network
http://bioenergy.ornl.gov/
Sponsor(s): Energy Department — Oak Ridge National Laboratory (ORNL)
Description: The Bioenergy Feedstock Information Network (BFIN) Web site is a gateway to information resources from the Department of Energy's Oak Ridge National Laboratory, Idaho National Laboratory, and National Renewable Energy Laboratory, and other facilities. The site covers biomass basics and offers details on the related economics, environmental issues, and supply system. It includes fact sheets, reports, databases, a glossary, and other resources.

This is an information-rich site for users interested in renewable energy and biofuels.
Subjects: Renewable Energies

726. Biomass Programs
http://www1.eere.energy.gov/biomass/
Sponsor(s): Energy Department — Energy Efficiency and Renewable Energy Office
Description: The Energy Department's Office of the Biomass Program encourages the development of biomass technologies through its research and development activities. The Web site's About the Program section has information on policy and budget, and a description of Energy's National Bioenergy Center. The Program Areas section describes the initiatives in Biomass Feedback, Sugar Platform, Ther-

mochemical Platform, Biobased Products, and Integrated Biorefineries. The Information Resources section includes publications, state and local program information, and audience-specific pages for industry, researchers, policymakers, consumers, and students.
Subjects: Biomass Fuels — Research

727. Biomass Research
http://www.nrel.gov/biomass/
Sponsor(s): Energy Department — National Renewable Energy Laboratory (NREL)
Description: This Web site describes the biomass research activities of the National Renewable Energy Laboratory, the lead national laboratory for the National Bioenergy Center effort. Capabilities and projects discussed on the site include biochemical conversion, thermochemical conversion, and biobased products. The site offers tools and databases for biomass researchers. It also links to the National Biomass Program Document Database and related Web sites.
Subjects: Biomass Fuels — Research

728. Biomass Research and Development Initiative (BRDI)
http://www.brdisolutions.com/
Sponsor(s): Agriculture Department (USDA); Energy Department
Description: As stated on the Web site, "The Biomass Initiative is the multi-agency effort to coordinate and accelerate all Federal biobased products and bioenergy research and development." Participating agencies include the Department of Energy and the Department of Agriculture. The site's Solicitations section compiles information about funding opportunities from various agencies, and the Calendar section provides links to related workshops and conferences. The About section has information on the Biomass Research and Development Technical Advisory Committee and the Biomass Research and Development Board. The Publications section includes the BRDI's annual report to Congress and meeting minutes from the Technical Advisory Committee.
Subjects: Biomass Fuels — Research
Publications: *Annual Report to Congress on the Biomass Research and Development Initiative*
Fostering the Bioeconomic Revolution in Biobased Products and Bioenergy, E 1.2:

729. Clean Cities
http://www.eere.energy.gov/cleancities/
Sponsor(s): Energy Department — Energy Efficiency and Renewable Energy Office
Description: The Clean Cities Program promotes alternative fuels and vehicles, fuel blends, fuel economy, hybrid vehicles, and a reduction in engine idle time for diesel vehicles. Clean Cities is a voluntary program that involves government, industry, and professional associations. Its Web site provides information about these coalitions and the program's accomplishments. It features a Tools section that links to the Alternative Fuels Data Center (AFDC) document database, information about state and federal incentives and laws, the "Clean Fleet Guide," and funding sources.
Subjects: Alternative Fuel Vehicles

730. Energy Efficiency and Renewable Energy (EERE)
http://www.eere.energy.gov/
Sponsor(s): Energy Department — Energy Efficiency and Renewable Energy Office
Description: EERE's mission is to enhance energy efficiency and productivity and bring clean, reliable, and affordable energy technologies to the marketplace. The EERE Web site links to detailed sections on each of the office's program areas,

including biomass, building technologies, vehicle technologies, solar energy, and wind and hydropower technologies. The site provides a number of approaches to discovering all of the online information offered by EERE, including a subject index, an EERE site name index, a technology portal, quick links to popular topics (such as ethanol and home energy audits), a central page about EERE financial opportunities, and customized pages for consumers and educators. The site's Offices section covers EERE's mission, planning, economic and policy analysis, budget, and structure.

Each EERE program has a separate, in-depth Web site that is worth exploring. The program sites explain the technology behind each program and include Information Resources and Funding Opportunities sections.

Subjects: Energy Conservation; Renewable Energies

731. Hydrogen Portal

http://www.rita.dot.gov/agencies_and_offices/research/hydrogen_portal/

Sponsor(s): Transportation Department — Research and Innovative Technology Administration (RITA)

Description: The Hydrogen Portal aggregates Department of Transportation information about the use of hydrogen fuel cells for transportation applications. The site includes the following sections: Hydrogen-related Regulations; and Safety, Codes, and Standards. It also provides Hydrogen Program information and reports, speeches, and presentations. Additionally, the site offers an online version of the *Research, Development, Demonstration, and Deployment Roadmap for Hydrogen Vehicles & Infrastructure to Support a Transition to a Hydrogen Economy.*

Subjects: Alternative Fuel Vehicles

Publications: *Research, Development, Demonstration, and Deployment Roadmap for Hydrogen Vehicles & Infrastructure to Support a Transition to a Hydrogen Economy*

732. Hydrogen.gov

http://www.hydrogen.gov/

Sponsor(s): White House — National Science and Technology Council (NSTC)

Description: Hydrogen.gov is an interagency Web site for information about hydrogen and fuel cell research and development activities. The Federal Programs section of the site links to information about the Hydrogen Research and Development Task Force. The site also has information about the President's Hydrogen Fuel Initiative.

Subjects: Alternative and Renewable Fuels — Research

733. National Renewable Energy Laboratory

http://www.nrel.gov/

Sponsor(s): Energy Department — National Renewable Energy Laboratory (NREL)

Description: NREL was originally established as a national center for federally sponsored solar energy research and development. It has since expanded into areas of energy efficiency, wind energy, advanced vehicle technologies, geothermal technologies, and other renewable energy fields. This Web site presents detailed information about each of NREL's major research and development areas. An Applying Technologies section covers the laboratory's technology transfer, technical and other assistance to governments, and programs for universities. The Learning About Renewable Energy section includes resources for students and basic information for anyone interested in learning about biomass, hydrogen, and other alternative energy sources. A separate Resources section includes publications, a photo library, and a page with links to relevant maps and data.

The availability of many full-text documents and detailed project descriptions makes this an excellent site for finding information about solar, wind, and other renewable energy topics.

Subjects: Renewable Energies — Research; Research Laboratories

734. Wind and Hydropower Technologies Program
http://www.eere.energy.gov/windandhydro/
Sponsor(s): Energy Department — Energy Efficiency and Renewable Energy Office
Description: This Web site's content is evenly divided between the wind power and hydropower technologies research programs of the Office of Energy Efficiency and Renewable Energy. Each section provides a basic overview of the technology, program information, research and development news, financial opportunities, and an online Information Resources Catalog section for further research.
Subjects: Hydroelectric Power; Wind Power

Energy Policy and Information

735. Building Technologies Program: Building America
http://www.eere.energy.gov/buildings/building_america/
Alternate URL(s): http://www.buildingamerica.gov/
Sponsor(s): Energy Department — Energy Efficiency and Renewable Energy Office
Description: Building America is a partnership program between the Department of Energy and industry to research new solutions for more energy-efficient homes. Its Web site features a national, interactive map/database of homes constructed as a result of participation in Building America research projects. The site reports on building technologies research and includes sections for builders, building scientists, and consumers. Much of the research conducted by the Building Technologies Program is funded through competitive solicitations, and the site provides information in the Financial Opportunities section.
Subjects: Energy Conservation; Home Construction

736. Department of Energy
http://www.energy.gov/
Sponsor(s): Energy Department
Description: The Department of Energy's home page presents news and headlines, with links to major sections including Science and Technology, Energy Sources, Energy Efficiency, Environment, Prices and Trends, National Security, and Safety and Health. Each of these sections provides topical access to department offices and programs. The Offices and Facilities section provides more detailed listings of affiliated organizations. The site also has sections designed for target audiences such as consumers, researchers, educators, and students and kids.

This site makes an excellent starting point for searching for any type of energy-related information, although the Energy Information Administration Web site is also highly recommended.
Subjects: Energy Policy
Publications: *Office of Inspector General Public Reports*, E 1.136:
U.S. Department of Energy National Telephone Directory, E 1.12/3:

737. Directives, Regulations, Policies, and Standards
http://www.directives.doe.gov/
Sponsor(s): Energy Department
Description: The site serves a dual audience: Department of Energy employees and the general public. It is a finding aid for many Energy Department documents.

The general public can use the Read section, which is linked from the site's home page. The site can also be used by Energy Department employees who are writing or commenting on directives. (Directives are meant to guide or instruct employees in the performance of their jobs.) The Regulations section points users to Energy Department regulations online and to government Web sites with information about federal regulations. The Standards section has approved, draft, and archived Energy Department technical standards. The site also has a section for the Energy Department's Secretarial Delegations of Authority, the legal instrument used to transfer authority granted to the secretary of energy to another official within the department.

Subjects: Energy — Regulations

738. Energy Citations Database
http://www.osti.gov/energycitations/
Sponsor(s): Energy Department — Scientific and Technical Information Office
Description: The Energy Citations Database indexes energy and energy-related scientific and technical information from the Department of Energy and its predecessor agencies for material published from 1948 to the present. The citations include bibliographic information and abstracts. For some of the newer works cited, there are direct links to online full-text versions or files in PDF format. The indexed articles, books, papers, dissertations and patents cover such topics as chemistry, climatology, engineering, geology, oceanography, and physics. An advanced search feature allows users to search by title, subject, identifier numbers, and other bibliographic fields. Results can be sorted by relevance, publication date, system entry date, resource/document type, title, research organization, sponsoring organization, or the document's unique OSTI identifier number.
Subjects: Scientific and Technical Information; Databases

739. Energy Information Administration
http://www.eia.doe.gov/
Sponsor(s): Energy Department — Energy Information Administration (EIA)
Description: EIA provides data, forecasts, and analyses regarding energy and its interaction with the economy and the environment. The EIA Web site is divided into major topical areas, including Petroleum; Natural Gas; Electricity; Coal; Nuclear; Renewable and Alternative Fuels; Environment; and Households, Buildings, Industry and Vehicles. Each section has data, reports, analyses, and forecasts. Other major sections focus on international data, historical data, and forecasts and analyses. The About Us section explains EIA's data processes, forecasting methods, analysis activities, and the policy-independent nature of its work.

EIA has an extensive line of statistical publications and datasets, many of which are available on this site. The Publications section includes both current and archival editions. The site also has a section that centralizes all of the e-mail update services that provide users with regular notification of new data releases on petroleum, coal, natural gas, consumption, forecasts, U.S. state and international data, and other topics. In the Announcements & News section, EIA provides lists of new and upcoming reports and data releases.

For highly specialized information beyond the scope of the site, EIA provides a directory of its subject experts on a wide range of topics, including energy taxation, wind energy, and electric power emissions. The site also includes an energy glossary and a reference section called Energy Basics 101.

With its broad scope and multiple access points, the EIA Web site is the place to start when looking for energy-related data. Much of the data are at the national level, but state, regional, and international data are also available.
Subjects: Energy — Statistics; Energy Prices and Costs

Publications: *Annual Coal Report*, E 3.11/7-3:
Annual Energy Outlook, E 3.1/4:
Annual Energy Review, E 3.1/2:
Country Analysis Briefs
Crude Oil Watch, E 3.34/3:
Current EIA Publications, E 3.27/8:
EIA Publications Directory, E 3.27:
Electric Power Annual (Volume 1), E 3.11/17-10:
Electric Power Annual (Volume 2), E 3.11/17-10:
Electric Power Monthly, E 3.11/17-8:
Emissions of Greenhouse Gases in the United States, E 3.59:
Energy Education Resources, Kindergarten through 12th Grade, E 3.27/6:
Energy INFOcard, E 3.2:IN 3
Fuel Oil and Kerosene Sales, E 3.11/11-3:
International Energy Annual, E 3.11/20:
International Energy Outlook, E 3.11/20
International Petroleum Monthly, E 3.11/5-6:
Monthly Energy Review, E 3.9:
Motor Gasoline Watch, E 3.13/6:
Natural Gas Annual, E 3.11/2-2:
Natural Gas Monthly, E 3.11:
Natural Gas Weekly Update, E 3.11/2-12:
Oil and Gas Field Code Master List, E 3.34/2:
Oil and Gas Lease Equipment and Operating Costs, E 3.44/2:
On-Highway Diesel Prices, E 3.13/8:
Performance Profiles of Major Energy Producers, E 3.37:
Petroleum Marketing Annual, E 3.13/4-2:
Petroleum Marketing Monthly, E 3.13/4:
Petroleum Supply Annual, E 3.11/5-5:(year)/V.1
Petroleum Supply Annual, E 3.11/5-5:(year)/V.2
Petroleum Supply Monthly, E 3.11/5:
Propane Watch, E 3.13/7:
Quarterly Coal Report, E 3.11/9:
Renewable Energy Annual, E 3.19/2:
Retail Gasoline Prices, E 3.13/9:
Short Term Energy Outlook, E 3.31:
State Electricity Profiles, E 3.2:ST 2/5
State Energy Data Reports, E 3.42:
State Energy Price and Expenditure Reports, E 3.42/3:
U.S. Crude Oil, Natural Gas, and Natural Gas Liquids Reserves, E 3.34:
Uranium Marketing Annual Report, E 3.46/5:
Voluntary Reporting of Greenhouse Gases, E 3.2:V 88/
Voluntary Reporting of Greenhouses Gases Annual Report, E 3.59/2:
Weekly Petroleum Status Report, E 3.32:

740. Energy Savers
http://www.energysavers.gov/
Sponsor(s): Energy Department — Energy Efficiency and Renewable Energy Office
Description: This Energy Savers Web site has sections with information for home-owners, contractors and builders, building managers, realtors, state agencies, drivers and fleet managers, and industry managers. Each section links to government information about energy efficient technologies and practices. The site also has information about the Partnerships for Home Energy Efficiency, a joint effort by the Department of Energy, the Environmental Protection Agency, and the

Department of Housing and Urban Development to promote home energy efficiency.
Subjects: Energy Conservation

741. Energy Savers: Tips on Saving Energy
http://www.eere.energy.gov/consumer/tips/
Sponsor(s): Energy Department — Energy Efficiency and Renewable Energy Office
Description: Energy Savers provides tips for conserving energy at home, with in-depth information about such topics as water heating, insulation, windows, lighting, and appliances. The information is derived from the 36-page *Energy Savers* booklet, which can be downloaded in PDF format. The full Web version and booklet are also available in Spanish.

At this time, the Department of Energy also has a site at ⟨www.energysavers.gov⟩, also called Energy Savers and described in this section. That site has a broader scope, with information for builders, building managers, state agencies, and other audiences, including homeowners.
Subjects: Energy Conservation
Publications: *Energy Savers*

742. ENERGY STAR
http://www.energystar.gov/
Sponsor(s): Energy DepartmentEnvironmental Protection Agency (EPA)
Description: ENERGY STAR is a voluntary labeling program designed to identify and promote energy-efficient products. The core of this Web site is its extensive and detailed directory of qualified projects. Other sections cover energy-efficient home improvement projects, finding new homes that qualify for ENERGY STAR, and guidelines for businesses trying to save money by conserving energy. In the Partner Resources section, the site has information for organizations such as utilities, home builders, schools, and congregations.

This Web site is well designed, informative, and customer-oriented.
Subjects: Energy Conservation

743. EnergyFiles—Energy Science and Technology Virtual Library
http://www.osti.gov/energyfiles/
Sponsor(s): Energy Department — Scientific and Technical Information Office
Description: EnergyFiles is a portal to "over 500 databases and Web sites containing information and resources pertaining to science and technology of interest to the Department of Energy, with an emphasis on the physical sciences" (from the Web site). The Subject section uses topical pathfinders to guide users to the diverse databases and tools available. Subject subsections include Biology and Medicine, Chemistry, Fission and Nuclear Technologies, Fossil Fuels, Geosciences, Physics, Power Transmission, and Renewable Energy. The OSTI Resources section presents a list of databases that can be searched singly or in any combination.

EnergyFiles is a flexible and user-friendly finding aid. The site continues to add features and resources while maintaining a straightforward interface.
Subjects: Scientific and Technical Information; Finding Aids

744. Federal Energy Regulatory Commission
http://www.ferc.gov/
Sponsor(s): Federal Energy Regulatory Commission (FERC)
Description: FERC is an independent regulatory commission, organized under the Department of Energy, with responsibilities in the areas of electricity, natural gas, oil, and hydroelectric power businesses. The About FERC section of its Web site enumerates the responsibilities that are inside and outside FERC's jurisdic-

tion. The site serves as a central point for parties filing documents with FERC and for researchers seeking FERC documents. A For Citizens section helps users locate FERC documents and filings for energy projects by geographical area. The Legal Resources section has current information about administrative litigation, court cases involving FERC, and the FERC Alternative Dispute Resolution process. Special sections provide guidance to regulated parties and other users on such topics as the Energy Policy Act of 2005 and open access transmission tariff reform.
Subjects: Energy — Regulations
Publications: *Annual Report, Federal Energy Regulatory Commission,* E 2.1:

745. Saving Starts at Home
http://www.ftc.gov/energysavings
Sponsor(s): Federal Trade Commission (FTC)
Description: This consumer-oriented Web site provides tips on reducing energy costs through the use of energy-saving appliances, compact fluorescent bulbs, better gas mileage in cars, and other household strategies. The site is also available in Spanish.
Subjects: Energy Conservation

746. Subject Portals (Energy)
http://www.osti.gov/subjectportals/
Sponsor(s): Energy Department — Scientific and Technical Information Office
Description: The Subject Portals (Energy) Web page includes only two portals at this time: Geothermal Technologies and Wind Energy Technologies. The Geothermal Technologies Portal includes Department of Energy–sponsored reports from the 1970s to the present, as well as citations and reports from other agencies and organizations. The Wind Energy portal also links to reports from the Energy Department and other agencies.
    The subject portals now have an advanced search feature. Unfortunately, the number of portals has declined.
Subjects: Geothermal Power; Wind Power

747. Weatherization and Intergovernmental Program
http://www.eere.energy.gov/wip/
Sponsor(s): Energy Department — Energy Efficiency and Renewable Energy Office
Description: The Weatherization and Intergovernmental Program works with regional and state energy offices to promote energy-efficient technologies and policies. This Web site outlines its major program areas and funding opportunities. Major programs include Weatherization Assistance, the State Energy program, the Tribal Energy program, and the Renewable Energy Production Assistance.
Subjects: Energy Conservation — Grants

Fossil and Nuclear Fuels

748. Department of Energy Office of Health, Safety, and Security
http://hss.energy.gov/
Sponsor(s): Energy Department
Description: This Department of Energy office is responsible for worker and public health and safety at Energy Department sites, including the former nuclear weapons production complex, the national laboratories, and research and testing facilities. The site has information about requirements, guidance, and technical standards for health and safety issues.

The Office of Health, Safety, and Security was established in August 2006, replacing the Office of Environment, Safety, and Health. At the time this book went to press, the office had not fully converted the old Web site into its new Web presence.

Subjects: Nuclear Fuels — Regulations; Radiation Exposure; Workplace Safety

749. Depleted UF6 Management Information Network

http://web.ead.anl.gov/uranium/

Sponsor(s): Energy Department — Argonne National Laboratory (ANL)

Description: The Depleted UF6 Management Information Network is a public information Web site about the Department of Energy's management of its depleted uranium hexafluoride inventory. The material is a product of the uranium enrichment process and must be managed to protect the environment and the safety of workers and the public. This Web site provides information about the material, its uses and risks, and the status of the management program. It includes Environmental Impact Statements, program documents, and answers to frequently asked questions.

Subjects: Nuclear Waste

750. Energy Resources Program

http://energy.usgs.gov/

Sponsor(s): Interior Department — U.S. Geological Survey (USGS)

Description: The USGS Energy Resources Program conducts research and provides scientific information and supply assessments for geologically-based energy resources, such as oil, natural gas, and coal. Information, including maps and images, is organized by energy source and by U.S. region, with notable sections for Alaska and U.S. federal lands. International information includes assessments of petroleum resources and consumption around the globe. Other sections cover environmental and health issues, such as acid mine drainage and mercury emissions from coal, and USGS research in geochemistry and geophysics. The site has an online publications catalog and downloadable spatial and tabular data sets.

Subjects: Fossil Fuels

751. Fuel Economy

http://www.fueleconomy.gov/

Sponsor(s): Energy Department; Environmental Protection Agency (EPA)

Description: The Department of Energy and the Environmental Protection Agency co-sponsor this Web site, which is also known as Fueleconomy.gov. The site features a database that can be used to find and compare gas mileage, greenhouse gas emissions, and air pollution ratings for various car and truck models. The site also has tips for improving gas mileage and explains why miles per gallon (MPG) rates can vary. The Gasoline Prices section of the site links to gas price data from other sources and has information about related topics, such as gasoline taxes and regional variations in retail price. Other sections cover hybrid and alternative fuel vehicles. The annual *Fuel Economy Guide*, available online in PDF format, compiles fuel economy values for the model year for gasoline and alternative fuel cars, as well as light trucks, minivans, and sport utility vehicles.

Subjects: Gasoline; Motor Vehicles — Statistics

Publications: *Fuel Economy Guide*, E 1.8/5:

752. Gas Price Watch Reporting Form
http://gaswatch.energy.gov/
Sponsor(s): Energy Department
Description: The Department of Energy provides this online form for citizens who believe there may be price gouging, or price fixing, in their local area. The site also links to *A Primer on Gasoline Prices* and frequently asked questions about gas pricing.

While not strictly a Web site, this page merits special mention because of the recent publicity it has received due to high gasoline prices.
Subjects: Consumer Information; Energy Prices and Costs; Gasoline
Publications: *A Primer on Gasoline Prices*, E 3.2:

753. Global Nuclear Energy Partnership
http://www.gnep.energy.gov/
Sponsor(s): Energy Department
Description: The Global Nuclear Energy Partnership is a Bush administration initiative to foster safe use of nuclear power. The Web site describes the program and its implementing elements, such as nuclear power expansion, minimized nuclear waste, fuel supply and waste services for countries without advanced nuclear technologies, and international nuclear safeguards.
Subjects: Nuclear Energy

754. Idaho National Laboratory
http://www.inl.gov/
Sponsor(s): Energy Department — Idaho National Laboratory (INL)
Description: The Idaho National Engineering and Environmental Laboratory (INEEL) and the Argonne National Laboratory-West became the new Idaho National Laboratory (INL) in February 2005. This Web site describes INL's research and development work in the nuclear energy, national security, and energy science and technology areas. It includes information about the Center for Advanced Energy Studies, an INL facility established in 2005. The site also links to the Idaho Cleanup Project, which is dismantling former INL nuclear facilities.
Subjects: Nuclear Energy — Research; Scientific Research

755. National Energy Technology Laboratory (NETL)
http://www.netl.doe.gov/
Sponsor(s): Energy Department — Fossil Energy Office
Description: NETL conducts research related to coal, natural gas, and oil. The Web site's Onsite Research section describes NETL's research capabilities in such areas as carbon management, combustion science, fuel cells, geosciences, and methane hydrates. The Technologies section covers topics including oil and natural gas supply, carbon sequestration, and hydrogen as a future energy source. Online publications include *Project Fact Sheets* on NETL projects, conference proceedings, and the *Journal of Energy and Environmental Research*. Information about research grants, acquisitions, and technology transfer is available in the Solicitations and Business section.
Subjects: Fossil Fuels — Research
Publications: *Journal of Energy and Environmental Research*, E 1.90/11:
NETL Project Fact Sheets, E 1.90/8:

756. Nuclear Regulatory Commission
http://www.nrc.gov/

Sponsor(s): Nuclear Regulatory Commission (NRC)

Description: NRC is an independent agency charged with regulating civilian use of nuclear materials. Its Web site highlights current news, public meetings schedules, and current rulemakings. Much of the material explaining NRC regulations and responsibilities can be found under the Nuclear Reactors, Nuclear Materials, and Radioactive Waste headings. Of interest to the general public, the site has a section on public involvement in NRC regulatory activities, information about reporting a safety or security concern, a directory of operating nuclear facilities, a section on radiation protection, and the option to receive e-mail news notices. The Event Reports section gives a daily status of nuclear power reactors, and the For the Record section provides NRC responses to "information on controversial issues or to significant media reports that could be misleading" (from the Web site).

The Electronic Reading Room section organizes access to NRC public documents. It features the Agencywide Documents Access and Management System (ADAMS), a database that provides access to all image and text documents that the NRC has made public since November 1, 1999, as well as bibliographic records that the NRC made public before that date. Other online document collections include NRC Regulations, Commission Papers, Commission Orders, Significant Enforcement Actions, NUREG-Series Publications, and Regulatory Guides.

Subjects: Nuclear Energy — Regulations

Publications: *Brochure Reports (NUREG-BR) Series*, Y 3.N 88:31/
Contractor Reports NUREG/CR (series), Y 3.N 88:25/
Forms, Y 3.N 88:59/
Information Digest, Y 3.N 88:10/1350/
NMSS Licensee Newsletter (quarterly), Y 3.N 88:57/
NRC News Releases, Y 3.N 88:7/
NRC Staff Reports (NUREGs), Y 3.N 88:10
NUREG/CP (series), Y 3.N 88:27/
Rules & Regulations (Title 10 Chapter 1 CFR), Y 3.N 88:6/
Telephone Directory, Y 3.N 88:14/
Weekly Information Report, Y 3.N 88:50/

757. Office of Fossil Energy
http://fossil.energy.gov/

Sponsor(s): Energy Department — Fossil Energy Office

Description: The Department of Energy's Office of Fossil Energy organizes its Web site content into major subject sections, including Coal and Natural Gas Power Systems, Carbon Sequestration, Hydrogen and Other Clean Fuels, Oil and Gas Supply and Delivery, Natural Gas Regulation, and U.S. Petroleum Reserves. Each section links to news, related publications, Energy Department program information, and program contacts. Many of the topical sections also feature a database of Energy Department R&D projects in the specific field. From the main page, users should consult the drop-down menus to locate fossil energy projects by state and to find the Web pages for the various component offices and facilities.

Subjects: Fossil Fuels

Publications: *Clean Coal Today*, E 1.84/4:
Coal and Power Systems: Strategic Plan and Multi-Year Program Plans, E 1.84:
Fossil Energy R&D Project Data Base, E 1.90/9:
Natural Gas Import and Export Regulations, E 1.84/8:

758. Office of Nuclear Energy, Science & Technology
http://www.ne.doe.gov/
Alternate URL(s): http://www.nuclear.gov/
Sponsor(s): Energy Department — Nuclear Energy, Science, and Technology Office
Description: The Office of Nuclear Energy, Science, and Technology is concerned with developing new nuclear energy generation technologies, managing the national nuclear infrastructure, and working to support university nuclear engineering programs. Its Web site has information about the Office and its Nuclear Energy Research Advisory Committee (NERAC). In the Program Offices section, links to program home pages are grouped under such headings as Nuclear Fuel Supply Security, Space and Defense Power Systems, and Advanced Nuclear Research. The Public Information section includes budget information, reports to Congress, and information sheets about major programs.
Subjects: Nuclear Energy — Research
Publications: *University Currents*, E 1.86/11

759. Oil and Gas Industry Initiatives
http://www.ftc.gov/ftc/oilgas/
Sponsor(s): Federal Trade Commission (FTC)
Description: As stated on the Web site, "this Web site describes the FTC's oversight of the petroleum industry, with special sections on our activities related to merger enforcement, anticompetitive nonmerger activity, and gasoline price data." The Competition Policy section provides FTC reports on gasoline pricing and mergers in the petroleum industry.
Subjects: Antitrust Law; Petroleum

760. U.S. Petroleum Reserves
http://www.fe.doe.gov/programs/reserves/
Sponsor(s): Energy Department — Fossil Energy Office
Description: This Web site provides profiles of the Strategic Petroleum Reserve and the much smaller Northeast Home Heating Oil Reserve and Naval Petroleum and Oil Shale Reserves. For the Strategic Petroleum Reserve, the site has data on current inventory, general location of the secure storage sites, and detailed background information about when and why crude oil has been released from the reserve.
Subjects: Petroleum

Utilities

761. Bonneville Power Administration
http://www.bpa.gov/
Sponsor(s): Energy Department — Bonneville Power Administration (BPA)
Description: BPA is a self-financing federal power marketing agency that sells power primarily generated by federally owned dams and by one nuclear power plant in the Pacific Northwest. Major sections of its Web site report on BPA's Power Business Line operations, Transmission Business Line, Energy Efficiency, and Industry Restructuring Programs. A fifth section describes the Environment, Fish, and Wildlife operations that form the environmental component of BPA's Transmission, Power, and Energy Efficiency businesses. The Finance and Rates section has BPA financial reports and rates and tariff information for the Power Business Line and Transmission Business Line. The Publications section points to Power and Transmission rate case information and a variety of BPA reports.

The BPA site has no overall site index to help researchers find content in each of its four major sections. A search engine does allow both whole site and section-specific searches. However, each section is structured differently, and researchers are advised to explore each one by browsing.

Subjects: Hydroelectric Power

Publications: *Annual Report (BPA)*, E 5.1:
Journal, Bonneville Power Administration, E 5.23:

762. Rural Utilities Service
http://www.usda.gov/rus/

Sponsor(s): Agriculture Department (USDA) — Rural Utilities Service (RUS)

Description: RUS supports the expansion and maintenance of electric, telecommunications, water, and waste disposal utilities in rural areas. Information about the RUS Web site is divided into sections covering the Utilities Programs, Electric Program, the Water and Environmental Program, Telecommunications, and Distance Learning and Telemedicine Program. Each major section includes relevant regulations, publications, and contacts.

Subjects: Distance Learning — Grants; Rural Development; Rural Utilities; Telemedicine — Grants; Water Treatment

763. Southeastern Power Administration (SEPA)
http://www.sepa.doe.gov/

Sponsor(s): Energy Department — Southeastern Power Administration

Description: SEPA is responsibile for marketing the electric power and energy generated at reservoirs operated by the U.S. Army Corps of Engineers in Alabama, Florida, Georgia, Kentucky, Mississippi, North Carolina, South Carolina, Tennessee, Virginia, West Virginia, and southern Illinois. Its Web site includes rate schedules, a system map, and information about how hydroelectricity works.

Subjects: Hydroelectric Power

Publications: *Annual Report, Southeastern Power Administration*, E 8.1:

764. Southwestern Power Administration
http://www.swpa.gov/

Sponsor(s): Energy Department — Southwestern Power Administration

Description: The Southwestern Power Administration is responsible for marketing the hydroelectric power produced at 24 Army Corps of Engineers multipurpose dams. Its Web site has information about how the Southwestern Power Administration operates and its rate schedules, estimated power generation, and acquisitions information.

Subjects: Hydroelectric Power

Publications: *Annual Report, Southwestern Power Administration*, E 1.95/2:

765. Tennessee Valley Authority
http://www.tva.gov/

Sponsor(s): Tennessee Valley Authority (TVA)

Description: TVA is a federal corporation and public power company. It operates fossil fuel and nuclear power plants and manages a system of dams. The major sections of the TVA Web site include About TVA, Power System, Environmental Stewardship, River System, Economic Development, Investor Resources, and TVA Newsroom. The Power System section discusses how power is generated at fossil fuel, hydroelectric, and nuclear plants. The River System section includes information about flood control, Tennessee River navigation, water quality, and the regional public recreation areas operated by TVA. The Environmental Stewardship section features the annual *Tennessee Valley Authority Environmental Report*, environmental impact statements, and environmental assessments. The Newsroom section has press releases and background information about topics of current interest. A helpful alphabetical site index can be found under the Site Help link.

Subjects: Electricity; Utilities (Energy)

Publications: *Tennessee Valley Authority Environmental Report* (annual), Y 3.T 25:1

766. Western Area Power Administration

http://www.wapa.gov/

Sponsor(s): Energy Department — Western Area Power Administration (WAPA)

Description: WAPA markets and delivers hydroelectric power in the central and western United States. The Power Marketing and Transmission sections provide detailed background information. The About Western section has financial and statistical data. The Energy Services section is designed for customers. Other sections include information about news, acquisitions, *Federal Register* notices, and each WAPA region.

Subjects: Hydroelectric Power; West (United States)

Publications: *Annual Report, Western Area Power Administration*, E 6.1:
Statistical Appendix, Western Area Power Administration, E 6.1/3:

CHAPTER 10
Engineering and Technology

Engineering and technology Web sites from the federal government cover a broad range of applications and goals, such as aerospace research and development, computer security, telecommunications regulations, technical assistance for manufacturers, industrial standards, and technology transfer and commercialization. Sponsors of these Web sites include the military, NASA, the Department of Energy, and the National Institute of Standards and Technology (NIST). Researchers may also want to check the Science and Space chapter, particularly the Scientific and Technical Information section, for additional sites of interest.

Subsections in this chapter are Communications, Engineering, and Technology.

Communications

767. 911 Services
http://www.fcc.gov/911/
Sponsor(s): Federal Communications Commission (FCC)
Description: This FCC Web site provides general, policy, and technical information on 911, the official national emergency number in the United States and Canada. The site contains consumer information and official reports about the basic 911 service. It also has a section about Enhanced 911, or E911, for wireless services and the technical and regulatory changes needed to bring it about. The State 911 section lists official points of contact for each state's 911 plan and links to related online resources. The site also includes a section on Mobile Satellite 911.
Subjects: Disasters and Emergencies; Telephone Service

768. FCC Enforcement Bureau
http://www.fcc.gov/eb/
Sponsor(s): Federal Communications Commission (FCC) — Enforcement Bureau
Description: The FCC's regulatory enforcement arm focuses on implementing rules regarding consumer protection, local competition enforcement, and public safety/ homeland security. In the What We Do section, the bureau explains its work in areas such as consumer telephone issues, local telephone competition enforcement, indecent or obscene broadcasts, and wireless 911 violations. The bureau's Web site has instructions on filing complaints about amateur radio interference, indecent broadcasts, and other topics. The site also has current news and documents including Public Notices, FCC Orders, and Citations and Notices of Violation issued by the bureau's field offices.
Subjects: Broadcasting — Laws; Telecommunications — Laws

769. FCC International Bureau
http://www.fcc.gov/ib/
Sponsor(s): Federal Communications Commission (FCC) — International Bureau
Description: The International Bureau administers the FCC's international telecommunications policies and obligations. Its Web site includes information about bureau contacts and current FCC actions. The Application section includes Earth Station Licensing information, fee filing guides, and a link to the International Bureau electronic filing system. The Industry Information section contains FCC decisions on submarine cable landing licenses, news related to the World Trade

Organization Basic Telecommunications Agreement, and the annual circuit status reports for U.S. facilities-based international common carriers. The Resources section includes foreign ownership guidelines, international agreements, and a Global Outreach page for international users of the FCC Web site.

Subjects: Telecommunications — International

Publications: *Foreign Ownership Guidelines for FCC Common Carrier and Aeronautical Radio Licenses*

770. FCC Media Bureau

http://www.fcc.gov/mb/

Sponsor(s): Federal Communications Commission (FCC) — Media Bureau

Description: The FCC Media Bureau manages policy and licensing programs relating to electronic media, including cable television, broadcast television, and radio. This Web site carries news on regulatory, licensing, and merger developments. Media Bureau Information Sheets, which are offered on the site, cover such topics as cable TV complaints, children's television, closed captioning, and general reference topics such as the history of television and why FM radio frequencies end in odd numbers. The Official Documents section includes documents from the Media Bureau and from its recent predecessors, the Mass Media Bureau and the Cable Services Bureau. The Media Bureau Reports section includes the bureau's annual reports on cable industry prices and its reports on competition in video programming.

Subjects: Broadcasting — Regulations

771. FCC Office of Engineering and Technology

http://www.fcc.gov/oet/

Sponsor(s): Federal Communications Commission (FCC) — Office of Engineering and Technology

Description: The FCC Office of Engineering and Technology (OET) is concerned with the policies and regulations for frequency allocation, spectrum usage, advanced communications technologies, and other matters related to communications engineering. Major sections of its Web site focus on information about radio frequency safety, radio spectrum allocation, and the authorization of equipment using the radio frequency spectrum. The OET Docket page provides access to FCC orders, notices, and press releases. It also links to mapping resources, technical documents, and a database of equipment authorizations. A Projects and Initiatives section focuses on special topics, such as rural communication technologies and digital television channel allotment.

Subjects: Communications Technology — Regulations

772. FCC Public Safety and Homeland Security Bureau

http://www.fcc.gov/pshs/

Sponsor(s): Federal Communications Commission (FCC) — Public Safety and Homeland Security Bureau

Description: FCC Public Safety and Homeland Security Bureau was newly established in 2006 to coordinate FCC activities related to public safety, homeland security, national security, emergency management and preparedness, and disaster management. The Web site covers topics such as the public safety communications spectrum, the Emergency Alert System, Communications Assistance for Law Enforcement Act (CALEA), 911 services, and the recommendations from the FCC's Independent Panel Reviewing the Impact of Hurricane Katrina on Communications Networks.

Subjects: Communications — Policy; Disaster Preparedness; Homeland Security

773. FCC Wireless Telecommunications Bureau
http://wireless.fcc.gov/
Sponsor(s): Federal Communications Commission (FCC) — Wireless Telecommunications Bureau
Description: The Wireless Telecommunications Bureau handles FCC domestic wireless telecommunications programs and policies for cellular, paging, maritime mobile, and other wireless communications services. Its Web site includes bureau press releases, public notices, commission decisions, and other documents. Other sections within the site include Auctions, Universal Licensing System, Public Safety, Antenna Structure Registration, and Wireless Services. The Wireless Services section links to FCC information for over 30 services, including amateur radio, Citizens Band (CB) radio, and broadband Personal Communications Service (PCS).

Most of the information on this Web site addresses the regulated parties rather than the individual consumer.
Subjects: Wireless Communications — Regulations

774. FCC's Parents' Place
http://www.fcc.gov/parents/
Sponsor(s): Federal Communications Commission (FCC)
Description: The FCC created this Web site to help parents understand and monitor their children's use of communications technology, including television and the Internet. The site includes sections on children's television programming, TV ratings, TV channel blocking, 900 numbers, and Internet access.
Subjects: Communications Technology

775. Federal Communications Commission
http://www.fcc.gov/
Sponsor(s): Federal Communications Commission (FCC)
Description: The FCC Web site provides centralized access to information about the commission and its work, along with biographies of its commissioners and links to the FCC bureaus, offices, and advisory committees. The site's main sections include the Consumer Center, Strategic Goals, and Filing Public Comments. The home page also features current FCC headlines and a link to the Web version of *FCC Daily Digest*, which is also available via e-mail delivery. The *Daily Digest* is a synopsis of commission orders, news releases, speeches, public notices and all other FCC documents released each business day, with links to the full text of each document. From 1994 onward, issues are archived and kept online. The FCC offers a variety of finding aids for its Web site and documents collections. Select the Search link at the top of the home page for a full menu of the search tools available.

For anyone following the telecommunications industry, the FCC Web site can serve as a primary source of information.
Subjects: Telecommunications — Regulations
Publications: *FCC Forms*, CC 1.55/2:
Federal Communications Commission Daily Digest, CC 1.56:
Statistics of Communications Common Carriers, CC 1.35:
Telephone Directory, FCC, CC 1.53:

776. Institute for Telecommunication Sciences (ITS)
http://www.its.bldrdoc.gov/
Sponsor(s): Commerce Department — National Telecommunications and Information Administration (NTIA)
Description: ITS is the research and engineering branch of the National Telecommunications and Information Administration (NTIA). The Web site's Programs and

Projects section links to information on such projects as the Audio Quality Research, Video Quality Research, and Broadband Wireless projects. It also links to information about ITS cooperative research and development agreements (CRADAs). The Publications section offers access to a variety of NTIA reports and a glossary of telecommunications terms.

Subjects: Communications Technology — Research
Publications: *ITS Technical Progress Report*, C 60.14:

777. National Communications System (NCS)
`http://www.ncs.gov/`
Sponsor(s): Homeland Security Department — National Communications System
Description: NCS is concerned with national security and emergency preparedness communications for the federal government. It consists of a 23-member inter-agency group managed by the Department of Homeland Security. This Web site describes NCS's mission, structure, and services. It also describes two closely related organizations, the President's National Security Telecommunications Advisory Committee (NSTAC) and the National Coordinating Center for Telecommunications (NCC). The Library section of the site contains NCS newsletters, technical bulletins, and reports, and relevant Executive Orders and Homeland Security Presidential Directives.

Subjects: Disaster Preparedness; National Security; Communications Technology
Publications: *Annual Report, National Communications System*, PREX 1.17:

778. National Telecommunications and Information Administration
`http://www.ntia.doc.gov/`
Sponsor(s): Commerce Department — National Telecommunications and Information Administration (NTIA)
Description: NTIA, an executive branch agency within the Department of Commerce, is principally responsible for domestic and international telecommunications and information policy issues. The NTIA Web site has information about the administration, its publications, and its press releases. Much of the information on the site is found on the pages for NTIA's component offices, such as the pages for International Affairs and for Spectrum Management. The Grants Programs section of the site links to pages for its major programs — the Technology Opportunities Program (TOP) and the Public Telecommunications Facilities Program (PTFP). The NTIA Web site has also added a section with information about the Digital Television Transition and Public Safety Act of 2005.

Since much of the information is filed under NTIA office names, the site map greatly facilitates information-searches.

Subjects: Internet — Policy; Telecommunications — Policy
Publications: *A Nation Online: How Americans Are Expanding Their Use Of The Internet*, C 60.2:N 19
Manual of Regulations & Procedures for Federal Radio Frequency Management (Redbook), C 60.8:R 11/
United States Frequency Allocations: the Radio Spectrum (Wall Chart), C 60.16:R 11

Engineering

779. Advanced Materials, Manufacturing & Testing Information Analysis Center (AMMTIAC)
http://ammtiac.alionscience.com/
Sponsor(s): Defense Department — Advanced Materials, Manufacturing &Testing Information Analysis Center (AMMTIAC)
Description: AMMTIAC was formed by the merger of the AMPTIAC (Materials), MTIAC (Manufacturing), and NTIAC (Nondestructive Testing) Department of Defense-sponsored Information Analysis Centers (IACs). AMMTIAC is concerned with data and information relating to advanced materials and processes, such as ceramics and alloys. Its Web site offers information under sections entitled About AMPTIAC, Products and Services, Information Resources, and News and Events. Resources on the site include the MatPro database of Web sites, reference books, and other resources relating to advanced materials.
Subjects: Information Analysis Centers; Materials Science; Databases

780. Chemical Propulsion Information Agency
http://www.cpia.jhu.edu/
Sponsor(s): Defense Department — Chemical Propulsion Information Agency (CPIA)
Description: This Department of Defense Information Analysis Center is a clearinghouse for information on chemical, electrical, and nuclear propulsion for missile, space, and gun propulsion systems. In the Products section, the Web site includes the CPIA *Bulletin* and listings of other CPIA publications and databases. Database access is granted only to those that meet the eligibility requirements listed on the site. For the general public, the site offers propulsion news items from non-restricted sources.
Subjects: Information Analysis Centers; Propulsion Technology; Rockets
Publications: *Bulletin*

781. Coastal and Hydraulics Laboratory (CHL)
http://chl.erdc.usace.army.mil/
Sponsor(s): Army — Army Corps of Engineers
Description: The U.S. Army Corps of Engineers Coastal and Hydraulics Laboratory (CHL) conducts research and development in civil engineering related to shorelines, coastal structures, water flow, and waterways navigation. The CHL Web site organizes information on their research, applications, and programs, with links to specialized CHL offices. The site also provides access to research studies, data, and modeling systems.
Subjects: Civil Engineering — Research; Waterways — Research
Publications: *Coastal and Hydraulics Engineering Technical Notes*

782. Cold Regions Science and Technology Information Analysis Center (CRSTIAC)
http://www.crrel.usace.army.mil/library/crstiac/crstiac.html
Sponsor(s): Army — Army Corps of Engineers — Engineer Research and Development Center (ERDC)
Description: CRSTIAC manages information generated by the U.S. Army Corps of Engineer's Cold Regions Research and Engineering Laboratory (CRREL). This area of science and engineering covers winter battlefields, the environment, basic

physical processes, and engineering technology that works in the cold. Its Web site primarily consists of information about the lab and the center's activities and information services.

Subjects: Engineering Research; Information Analysis Centers

783. Construction Engineering Research Laboratory

http://www.cecer.army.mil/

Alternate URL(s): http://www.cecer.army.mil/td/tips/index.cfm

Sponsor(s): Army — Army Corps of Engineers — Engineer Research and Development Center (ERDC)

Description: The Construction Engineering Research Laboratory (CERL) conducts research in civil engineering and environmental quality to support sustainable military installations for the army. The Web site has information about CERL, contracting and employment opportunities, and technology transfer and partnerships. Research areas are organized into sections including Facility Acquisition and Revitalization, Installation Operation, and Military Land Management; each research section links to related publications. The Publications section includes technical reports and other documents produced by CERL.

Subjects: Civil Engineering — Research

Publications: *Construction Engineering Research Laboratory: Technical Reports*, D 103.53:

784. Engineering at LLNL

http://www-eng.llnl.gov/

Sponsor(s): Energy Department — Lawrence Livermore National Laboratory (LLNL)

Description: The Engineering at LLNL Web site highlights the engineering projects underway at the Lawrence Livermore National Laboratory. Designed for potential clients and the general public, the site covers such LLNL specialties as biotechnology, micro- and nanotechnologies, and precision engineering. Special sections include For Students, For Researchers, and For Collaborators.

Subjects: Engineering Research; National Laboratories

785. Manufacturing Engineering Laboratory (MEL)

http://www.mel.nist.gov/

Sponsor(s): Commerce Department — Technology Administration (TA) — National Institute of Standards and Technology (NIST)

Description: The National Institute of Standards and Technology Manufacturing Engineering Laboratory (MEL) focuses on measurements and standards issues in parts manufacturing. The MEL Web site features an interactive organizational chart with profiles of the respective divisions: Precision Engineering, Manufacturing Metrology, Intelligent Systems, Manufacturing Systems Integration, and Fabrication Technology. Background pages on MEL research projects report on staffing, funding, goals, and accomplishments. Research areas include calibration, material removal processes, laser and optics, surface and nanometer-scale manufacturing, and simulation and visualization. The Products and Services section of the site includes information on calibrations and Standards Reference Materials (SRMs) supported by MEL.

Subjects: Manufacturing Technology

786. Manufacturing Extension Partnership (MEP)
http://www.mep.nist.gov/

Sponsor(s): Commerce Department — Technology Administration (TA) — National Institute of Standards and Technology (NIST)

Description: MEP is a network of extension centers and experts who offer technical and business assistance to smaller manufacturers. Its Web site describes the program and offers a directory of participating extension centers.

Subjects: Manufacturing

787. Manufacturing Technology Program (ManTech)
https://www.dodmantech.com/

Sponsor(s): Defense Department

Description: The ManTech Web site offers information on the Department of Defense's Manufacturing Technology Program, which focuses on improved processes in the production of weapons systems. The site describes program activities in such areas as metals, composites, and electronics research. The Publications and Links section offers access to full-text strategy and planning documents, papers, presentations, and the proceedings of the Defense Manufacturing Conference. The site also includes information on the program's funding, relevant legislation, business opportunities, and technology transfer.

Subjects: Manufacturing Technology

788. National Institute of Standards and Technology
http://www.nist.gov/

Sponsor(s): Commerce Department — Technology Administration (TA) — National Institute of Standards and Technology (NIST)

Description: NIST, an agency within the Department of Commerce, seeks to promote economic growth by working with industry to develop and apply technology, measurements, and standards. In addition to general information about NIST (including an overview, budget, organizational chart, and relevent testimony), its Web site hosts extensive information on individual programs. The home page links to sites for each of the eight NIST laboratories: Building and Fire Research, Chemical Science and Technology, Electronics and Electrical Engineering, Information Technology, Manufacturing Engineering, Materials Science and Engineering, Physics, and Technology Services. Other featured sections include Standards, Assistance to Small Manufacturers, Calibrations, Laboratory Accreditations, Publications, R&D Funding, Standard Reference Materials (SRMs), and Weights and Measures.

One section of the home page presents relevant information by user type section; these sections include Industry, Researchers, News Media, General Public, and Kids. The Industry section organizes NIST information by industry sector, such as automotive, computers, and construction. Information for researchers includes descriptions of grants available from NIST, links to free databases and software, and NIST research and reference resources. The News Media section leads to press releases and the *NIST Tech Beat* newsletter. The General Public section includes educational material about NIST history, the everyday applications of NIST's work, the metric system, and time measurement. Another section, NIST Research Library, has the NIST Library's online catalog and Web guides on such topics as biotechnology, engineering, physics, and materials science.

The NIST Web site does an excellent job of communicating information to multiple audiences, from scientific and technical researchers to manufacturing and trade business professionals to the general public and education communities. For any topic covered by NIST, the user will find a wealth of accessible information within several clicks. An A-Z Subject Index assists with navigation.

Subjects: Research and Development; Research Laboratories; Standards and Specifications
Publications: *Checking the Net Contents of Packaged Goods (Handbook 133),* C 13.11:133/4
Directory of NVLAP Accredited Laboratories, C 13.58/7:
Federal Information Processing Standards Publications (FIPS Pubs) Index, C 13.52:58/INDEX
Journal of Research of the National Institute of Standards and Technology, C 13.22:
NIST Conference Calendar, C 13.10/3-2:
NIST Special Publications (800 Series), C 13.10:800
NIST Standard Reference Materials Price List, C 13.48/4-2:
NIST Tech Beat, C 13.46/3:
Specifications, Tolerances, and Other Technical Requirements for Weighing and Measuring Devices (Handbook 44), C 13.11/2:
SRM (Standard Reference Materials), C 13.48/4-3:
Uniform Laws and Regulations in the Areas of Legal Metrology and Engine Fuel Quality (Handbook 130), C 13.11:130/

789. Naval Facilities Engineering Command (NAVFAC)
http://www.navfac.navy.mil/
Sponsor(s): Navy — Naval Facilities Engineering Command
Description: NAVFAC manages the planning, design and construction of shore facilities for U.S. Navy activities around the world. Its Web site contains publications, press releases, descriptions of their products and services, links to contracting and procurement opportunities, and links to all NAVFAC locations worldwide. Official documents include NAVFAC Directives and Chief of Civil Engineers Policy Memos.
Subjects: Military Bases and Installations
Publications: *CEC Biweekly*
SEABEE Magazine

790. Reliability Analysis Center
http://quanterion.com/riac/
Sponsor(s): Defense Department — Reliability Analysis Center (RAC)
Description: Sponsored by the Department of Defense, RAC's mission is to analyze and disseminate data on the reliability and maintainability of manufactured components and systems. The primary sections of its Web site are About RAC, Products and Services, and Information Resources. The Information Resources section includes a directory of Web resources on maintainability, reliability, and structural integrity.
Subjects: Information Analysis Centers; Reliability Engineering

791. U.S. Army Corps of Engineers
http://www.usace.army.mil/
Sponsor(s): Army — Army Corps of Engineers
Description: The U.S. Army Corps of Engineers provides engineering services for military construction and for civil works projects in areas such as flood control and waterway navigation and emergency response. Most of the content on the Army Corps of Engineers Web site can be reached through its Missions section. The links to each of the missions — Water Resources, Environment, Infrastructure, Homeland Security, and Warfighting — lead to detailed information on related programs and activities. The Web site's Who We Are section has links to the Army Corps of Engineers component Web sites. The Related Links section links to the *Corps Points* and *Engineer Update* publications and to the Tribal Affairs and

Initiative Page. Technical documents and other publications can be located by following the home page link entitled "How do I . . . find Corps publications?"

In Fall 2005, the Army Corps of Engineers established a separate Web site for information on their response to Hurricane Katrina at http://www.mvd.usace.army.mil/hurricane/. This information is now located on the Corps' New Orleans District Web site at: http://www.mvn.usace.army.mil/.

The Army Corps of Engineers has an extensive network of Web sites. To discover the full range of content available, use the Topics A-Z index on the main page or the organizational and geographic district links in the Who We Are section.

Subjects: Civil Engineering; Waterways
Publications: *Circulars (EC Series)*, D 103.4:
Corps Points
Engineer Regulations (ER Series), D 103.6/4:
Engineer Update, D 103.69:
Manuals (EM Series), D 103.6/3:
Monthly Bulletin of Lake Levels for the Great Lakes, D 103.116:
Public Works Digest, D 103.122/3:
The Corps Environment
Waterborne Commerce of the United States, D 103.1/2:

792. U.S. Army Corps of Engineers Cold Regions Research and Engineering Laboratory (CRREL)
http://www.crrel.usace.army.mil/
Sponsor(s): Army — Army Corps of Engineers — Engineer Research and Development Center (ERDC)
Description: CRREL conducts scientific and engineering research on cold temperature environments. Its Web site features the following sections: About CRREL, Research and Engineering, Research Facilities, Reports and Products, and Partnering and Business Opportunities. In the Reports and Products section, the site offers access to lists of CRREL technical reports (from 1996 onward and in PDF format), fact sheets, the Cold Regions Bibliography Database, and an Ice Jam Database.
Subjects: Engineering Research; Research Laboratories
Publications: *CRREL Reports*, D 103.33.12:

793. Waterways Experiment Station (WES)
http://www.wes.army.mil/
Sponsor(s): Army — Army Corps of Engineers — Engineer Research and Development Center (ERDC)
Description: A U.S. Army Corps of Engineers facility in Mississippi, WES houses the headquarters of the Engineer Research and Development Center (ERDC) and four of its seven laboratories. The site links to pages for each of the labs: the Coastal and Hydraulics Laboratory, the Geotechnical and Structures Laboratory, the Environmental Laboratory, and the Information Technology Laboratory. The Mission section of the site provides an overview of WES operations.
Subjects: Civil Engineering; Engineering Research

Technology

794. Advanced Technology Program (ATP)
http://www.atp.nist.gov/
Sponsor(s): Commerce Department — Technology Administration (TA) — National Institute of Standards and Technology (NIST)
Description: Through cost-sharing with industry and nonprofit research institutions, ATP works to accelerate the development of innovative technologies that can benefit the national economy. Main sections of its Web site include About ATP, Funded Projects, Impacts of ATP Projects, Partnerships, and Statistics (on ATP Awards).
Subjects: Research and Development — Grants; Technology — Research

795. Aeronautical Systems Center Major Shared Resource Center
http://www.asc.hpc.mil/
Sponsor(s): Defense Department — High Performance Computing Modernization Program (HPCMP)
Description: The Aeronautical Systems Center Major Shared Resource Center (ASC MSRC) is a facility for scientific high-performance computing research and visualization, located at Wright Patterson Air Force Base. This Department of Defense high-performance computing Web site provides information on the center, its services, and its hardware and software resources. The journal *Wright Cycles* is available in the Outreach section of the site.

This site, while primarily of interest to authorized users of the Center's resources, may also be interesting to people active in high-performance computing.
Subjects: High-Performance Computing; Military Computing
Publications: *Wright Cycles*, D 301.121:

796. Biometrics Catalog
http://www.biometricscatalog.org/
Sponsor(s): Justice Department — Federal Bureau of Investigation (FBI)
Description: The Biometrics Catalog, sponsored by a group of interested federal agencies, is a central resource for information about technologies that identify an individual by unique characteristics, such as fingerprints or voice. Major sections of the site are Government Documents, Research Reports, Biometrics Privacy, and Newsroom. In the Additional Resources section, the site has congressional reports, federal solicitations, directories of commercial biometrics products and consultants, and an introduction to biometrics. Government sponsors listed on the site include the FBI, the National Institute of Justice, the Department of Defense, and the Department of Homeland Security.
Subjects: Biometrics

797. Biometrics Resource Center Website
http://www.itl.nist.gov/div893/biometrics/
Sponsor(s): Commerce Department — Technology Administration (TA) — National Institute of Standards and Technology (NIST)
Description: NIST is part of the government's Biometric Consortium. This Web site has information on NIST's biometrics research, development, and programs. Sections include Standards, Publications, and a compilation of links to government, academic, and other relevent biometrics Web sites.
Subjects: Biometrics — Research

798. Biometrics.gov
http://biometrics.gov/
Sponsor(s): White House — National Science and Technology Council (NSTC)
Description: Biometrics.gov serves as the federal government's central Web site for information on biometric technologies and federal biometrics activities. The site features a section for publications and presentations from the NSTC's Subcommittee on Biometrics. It also includes an extensive introduction to the field of biometrics, an inventory of relevant federal programs, and a Media Room with press releases and "Fast Facts" about biometrics.
Subjects: Biometrics

799. DACS and Defense Software Collaborators
http://www.dacs.dtic.mil/
Sponsor(s): Defense Department — Data and Analysis Center for Software (DACS)
Description: DACS is a Department of Defense Information Analysis Center that focuses on software technology and software engineering. Topics addressed on this Web site include data mining, grid computing, knowledge management, and rapid prototyping. Technical reports are available online and cover such areas as formal methods, interoperability, and technology transfer. The DACS newsletter, *Software Tech News*, is online in both HTML and PDF formats.
Subjects: Military Computing; Software
Publications: *Software Tech News*

800. Digital Preservation
http://www.digitalpreservation.gov/
Sponsor(s): Library of Congress
Description: Digital Preservation is the Web site for the National Digital Information Infrastructure and Preservation Program (NDIIPP), a collaborative effort led by the Library of Congress that includes the National Library of Medicine, the National Agricultural Library, and other agencies and organizations. This Web site provides information about the program, its strategic planning, its reports and papers, and its press releases. The News and Events section contains a calendar of digital library conferences scheduled worldwide.
Subjects: Archives; Digital Libraries; Information Technology
Publications: *Preserving Our Digital Heritage: Plan for the National Digital Information Infrastructure and Preservation Program*, LC 1.57:

801. Digital Television (DTV)
http://www.dtv.gov/
Sponsor(s): Federal Communications Commission (FCC)
Description: This special FCC Web site is dedicated to educating consumers about digital television. The site has a shoppers' guide, answers to frequently asked questions, a DTV glossary, and a section dedicated to explaining what DTV is. The site also links to regulatory information at the main FCC Web site. Some information is available in Spanish.
Subjects: Television

802. Energy Science and Technology Software Center
http://www.osti.gov/estsc/
Sponsor(s): Energy Department — Scientific and Technical Information Office
Description: The Energy Science and Technology Software Center (ESTSC) licenses and distributes federally-funded scientific and technical software developed by the national laboratories, Department of Energy contractors, and other developers. This Web site serves as the central catalog and order site. The software available

is highly technical and specialized, with titles such as Unsaturated Groundwater and Heat Transport Model and Building Energy Consumption Analysis.
Subjects: Software; Technology Transfer

803. Energy Sciences Network
http://www.es.net/
Sponsor(s): Energy Department — Lawrence Berkeley National Laboratory (LBL)
Description: The Energy Sciences Network, or ESnet, is a high-speed network funded by the Department of Energy (DOE) that provides network and collaboration services in support of the agency's research missions. ESnet is used by researchers at national laboratories, universities, and other institutions and provides direct connections to all major DOE sites with high performance speeds. Major sections of the Web site are Tools and Services, Network Research and Development, Publications and Presentations, and About ESnet. The About ESnet section includes ESnet brochures, program plans, a staff directory, and network maps.

This Web site is aimed at existing and potential ESnet customers. It is useful for finding descriptive information about the network and its services, along with some general information about network research and development.
Subjects: Computer Networking

804. Environmental Technologies Portal
http://www.epa.gov/etop/
Sponsor(s): Environmental Protection Agency (EPA)
Description: The Environmental Technologies Portal (ETOP) links to resources, funding opportunities, and program information from EPA to support public and private sector efforts to develop and commercialize new environmental technologies.
Subjects: Environmental Engineering; Technology Transfer

805. Federal Smart Card Web Site
http://www.smartcard.gov/
Alternate URL(s): http://www.smart.gov/
Sponsor(s): General Services Administration (GSA)
Description: Smart cards make use of integrated circuits and other technologies to store data. This Web site discusses policies, practices, and standards for the use of smart cards by government agencies. It includes the *Smart Card Handbook* developed to help agencies develop and deploy smart card systems and a multimedia tutorial on smart cards. The site also links to related federal government Web sites.
Subjects: Information Technology
Publications: *Smart Card Handbook*

806. Information Access Division
http://www.itl.nist.gov/iaui/
Sponsor(s): Commerce Department — Technology Administration (TA) — National Institute of Standards and Technology (NIST)
Description: The NIST Information Access Division (IAD) researches measurements and standards to support digital and multimedia information access. Major program areas described on the Web site include human language recognition, biometrics technology, usability and accessibility, multimedia standards, and interactive environments/pervasive computing. The site also links to information on the Text REtrieval Conference (TREC) on information retrieval. IAD publications, reference products, and measurement tools are all available on the site.
Subjects: Information Technology

807. Information Technology Laboratory
http://www.itl.nist.gov/

Sponsor(s): Commerce Department — Technology Administration (TA) — National Institute of Standards and Technology (NIST)

Description: This NIST laboratory develops the tests and test methods used by researchers and scientists to measure, compare, and improve information technology systems. Detailed information is available on its Web site, organized by core competency area: computer security, digital information access, computational modeling and virtual measurements, software conformance, and advanced networking. Specialized resources on the site include a biometrics resource center, the *Engineering Statistics Handbook, and an index of online mathematical and statistical software components.*

The Web site does not have its own search engine or index independent from the NIST site. Researchers will want to browse through each section to discover the tools, publications, and other resources provided for in a wide range of IT specialties.

Subjects: Information Technology — Research

Publications: *Engineering Statistics Handbook*
ITL Bulletin, C 13.76:

808. NASA Advanced Supercomputing Division
http://www.nas.nasa.gov/

Sponsor(s): National Aeronautics and Space Administration (NASA) — Ames Research Center (ARC) — Advanced Supercomputing Division (NAS)

Description: The NASA Advanced Supercomputing Division (NAS) provides research, development, and delivery of high-end computing services and technologies to facilitate NASA mission success. This Web site describes NAS activities and hardware and provides information for authorized users of NAS supercomputers. It also links to NAS technical reports and NASA open source software information.

Subjects: High-Performance Computing

809. NASA Independent Verification and Validation Facility
http://www.ivv.nasa.gov/

Sponsor(s): National Aeronautics and Space Administration (NASA)

Description: The NASA Independent Verification and Validation (IV&V) Facility was established in 1993 to ensure the safety and reliability of the agency's mission-critical software and systems. IV&V is defined on the Web site as "a system engineering process . . . for evaluating the correctness and quality of a software product throughout its life cycle." The site has information about this process in the IV&V Services section. Other sections provide information about the facility's mission, organization, research, and education outreach programs.

Subjects: Software

810. NASA TechFinder
http://technology.nasa.gov/

Sponsor(s): National Aeronautics and Space Administration (NASA)

Description: NASA TechFinder highlights the NASA technologies that have commercial potential. The major sections of this Web site are Licensing Opportunities, Technology Opportunities, and Software Technologies. A Success Stories section describes NASA spinoffs into the commercial sector.

Subjects: Space Technology; Technology Transfer

811. National Coordination Office for Information Technology Research and Development
http://www.nitrd.gov/
Sponsor(s): National Coordination Office for Information Technology Research and Development (NITRD)
Description: The National Coordination Office for Information Technology Research and Development coordinates planning, budget, and assessment activities for the federal IT R&D program. NITRD reports to the White House Office of Science and Technology Policy (OSTP) and the National Science and Technology Council (NSTC). This Web site is intended to provide information about multi-agency information technology research and development. It includes NITRD presentations, publications, and news. The full text of NITRD's annual *Supplement to the President's Budget* (commonly referred to as the *Blue Book*) is available at the site.
Subjects: Information Technology — Research
Publications: *Computational Science: Ensuring America's Competitiveness*
Federal Plan for Cyber Security and Information Assurance Research and Development
Supplement to the President's Budget (Blue Book)

812. National Energy Research Scientific Computing Center
http://www.nersc.gov/
Sponsor(s): Energy Department — Lawrence Berkeley National Laboratory (LBL)
Description: The National Energy Research Scientific Computing Center (NERSC) provides high-performance computing services to scientists supported by the Department of Energy Office of Science. Its Web site provides information on NERSC computing resources, research projects, and publications.

Although the computing resources of NERSC are limited to authorized scientists, the NERSC site provides some information for non-affiliated people interested in computational sciences and high-performance computing.
Subjects: High-Performance Computing; Scientific Research

813. National Nanotechnology Initiative
http://www.nano.gov/
Sponsor(s): White House — National Science and Technology Council (NSTC)
Description: The National Nanotechnology Initiative (NNI) is a multi-agency effort to coordinate federal research and development in nanoscale science, engineering, and technology. The NNI Web site includes information on available funding opportunities for nanotechnology R&D, the areas of research focus for NNI, and current research news. It links to the Web sites for government and academic nanotechnology research centers, as well as to lectures, publications, and educational resources on the topic.
Subjects: Nanotechnology — Research

814. National Vulnerability Database
http://nvd.nist.gov/
Sponsor(s): Homeland Security Department — National Cyber Security Division; Commerce Department — Technology Administration (TA) — National Institute of Standards and Technology (NIST)
Description: The National Vulnerability Database provides current information about threats to computer security. Major sources for the information are the US-CERT Alerts and Vulnerability Notes, and the Common Vulnerabilities and Exposures list maintained by MITRE Corporation for the Department of Homeland

Security. The Web site also has a statistics generation engine to graph and chart vulnerability characteristics.
Subjects: Computer Security

815. NIST Computer Security Resource Clearinghouse
http://csrc.ncsl.nist.gov/
Sponsor(s): Commerce Department — Technology Administration (TA) — National Institute of Standards and Technology (NIST)
Description: The NIST Computer Security Resource Clearinghouse (CSRC) is designed to collect and disseminate computer security information and resources to help users, systems administrators, managers, and security professionals better protect their data and systems. The Web site organizes NIST work in current areas of focus into sections: Cryptographic Standards and Applications, Security Testing, Security Research and Emerging Technologies, and Security Management and Guidance. Publications on the CSRC site include Federal Information Processing Standards (FIPS) information and document and links collected as part of their Practices, Implementation Guides, Security Checklists Program. The site also has a special section regarding their current Federal Information Security Management Act (FISMA) Implementation Project.
Subjects: Computer Security
Publications: *Glossary of Key Information Security Terms*

816. President Bush's Technology Agenda
http://www.whitehouse.gov/infocus/technology/
Sponsor(s): White House
Description: The full title of this White House Web page is "Promoting Innovation and Competitiveness: President Bush's Technology Agenda." The text of the accompanying report, "A New Generation of American Innovation," is available online in HTML and PDF formats.
Subjects: Technology — Policy

817. Robert C. Byrd National Technology Transfer Center
http://www.nttc.edu/
Sponsor(s): National Technology Transfer Center (NTTC)Wheeling Jesuit College
Description: Established by Congress in 1989, the Robert C. Byrd National Technology Transfer Center (NTTC) works to help American businesses find technologies, facilities, and researchers within the federal laboratories and agencies with who they can partner. NTTC itself is not a federal agency. The NTTC Web site provides information on its services and programs.
Subjects: Commercialization; Technology Transfer

818. Section 508
http://www.section508.gov/
Sponsor(s): General Services Administration (GSA)
Description: Section 508 of the Rehabilitation Act requires federal agencies to make their electronic and information technology accessible to people with disabilities. This GSA sponsored Web site provides the guidance and explanations of Section 508 requirements to help both agencies and vendors comply with the law. The Communications/Media section links to articles on Section 508, and the 508 Tools and Resources section points to government and nongovernment information on assistive and accessible technology.
Subjects: World Wide Web — Laws

819. Standards.gov

http://standards.gov/

Sponsor(s): Commerce Department — Technology Administration (TA) — National Institute of Standards and Technology (NIST)

Description: Standards.gov provides background information on standards (including a legal definition of "standards" for the purposes of the Web site) and assistance in locating information about the use of standards in government. The site focuses on federal agency use of standards for regulatory and procurement purposes. The Regulations section explains the use of standards or technical requirements in federal regulations. The Federal Agency Info section links to agency Web sites about standards, the Interagency Committee on Standards Policy (ICSP), and federal standards-related laws, policies, and guidance.

Subjects: Standards and Specifications

820. Technology Administration

http://www.technology.doc.gov/

Sponsor(s): Commerce Department — Technology Administration (TA)

Description: The Department of Commerce Technology Administration (TA) works to maximize technology's contribution to America's economic growth. This Web site links to the three agencies managed by the TA: the National Institute of Standards and Technology (NIST), the National Technical Information Service (NTIS), and the Office of Technology Policy (OTP). The site also provides details on TA leadership, publications, budget information, and grant and fellowship opportunities.

Subjects: Commercialization; Technology Transfer

Publications: *Recycling Technology Products: An Overview of E-Waste Policy Issues*
The Dynamics of Technology-based Economic Development: State Science & Technology Indicators, C 1.202:

821. Usability.gov

http://usability.gov/

Sponsor(s): National Institutes of Health (NIH) — National Cancer Institute (NCI)

Description: The Office of Communications within the National Cancer Institute sought to apply evidence-based practices for Web site usability in its design principles for NCI Web sites. The result of their work is distilled into an online guidebook, which is available on this Web site. The site also has links to information on site design, accessibility, and Internet use statistics, as well as to online newsletters concerning Web site design and usability.

This site is an excellent resource for people learning about or working in the field of Web site design.

Subjects: World Wide Web

822. US-CERT

http://www.us-cert.gov/

Sponsor(s): Homeland Security Department — National Cyber Security Division

Description: US-CERT (United States Computer Emergency Readiness Team) is a partnership between the Department of Homeland Security and the public and private sectors that was established to protect the nation's Internet infrastructure. This Web site provides three gateways (Technical Users, Non-Technical Users, and Government Users) into the US-CERT content. US-CERT runs a National Cyber Alert System and publishes guidance for both technical and non-technical audiences; the applicable alerts and guides are in the Publications section.

Computer security knowledge is important for any home or office computer user. US-CERT provides practical guides for a variety of audiences — from the at-home novice to the enterprise-wide network manager.

Subjects: Computer Security

Publications: *National Strategy to Secure Cyberspace*, PR 43.8:IN 3/

CHAPTER 11
Environment and Nature

The Environmental Protection Agency, the Department of the Interior, and the Department of Commerce's National Oceanic and Atmospheric Administration sponsor public Web sites with data, science, policy, and educational information related to the environment. Sites from these and other agencies are included in this chapter. Outdoor recreation information can be found in the Culture and Recreation chapter. Atmospheric sciences sites can be found in the Science and Space chapter.

Subsections in this chapter are Environmental Law, Environmental Policy, Environmental Protection, Environmental Science, Geography, Natural Resources, Pollutants and Waste, and Weather.

Environmental Law

823. Enforcement and Compliance History Online (ECHO)
http://www.epa.gov/echo/
Sponsor(s): Environmental Protection Agency (EPA)
Description: ECHO is an EPA information system providing violation and enforcement information on roughly 800,000 facilities that are regulated under key environmental statutes. From the home page, users can search by ZIP code to find regulated facilities and display their inspection and enforcement history. More advanced search criteria include facility name, type of industry, EPA region, city, state, and county. Searches can be filtered by a number of characteristics, such as whether the facility has multiple violations, is on Indian land, or has a certain percentage of minority population within a three-mile radius. Specific types of data can also be searched separately; for example, compliance on hazardous waste or compliance with water rules.
Subjects: Environmental Law

824. Environmental Appeals Board
http://www.epa.gov/eab/
Sponsor(s): Environmental Protection Agency (EPA)
Description: The Environmental Appeals Board handles administrative appeals under all major environmental statutes that the EPA administers. The Web site carries published decisions, unpublished final orders, and lists of decisions reviewed by the federal courts or pending federal court review. It includes guidance documents, such as *A Citizens' Guide to EPA's Environmental Appeals Board*.
Subjects: Environmental Law
Publications: *Environmental Appeals Board Practice Manual*, EP 1.8:

825. National Environmental Policy Act
http://www.eh.doe.gov/nepa/
Sponsor(s): Energy Department — Environment, Safety, and Health Office
Description: This Web site summarizes DOE's activities related to the National Environmental Policy Act (NEPA). The Documents section beings with this caveat: "Because of the security sensitivity of some information in [NEPA] documents, the [DOE] is limiting access to NEPA documents on this Web site. Members of the public cannot access most of the environmental impact statements and environmental assessments on this Web site." These documents can be requested

in hard copy form. Documents available on the site include relevant Records of Decision, Notices of Intent, and NEPA Annual Planning Summaries. The site also provides environmental impact statement schedules, a public meeting calendar, and the *Lessons Learned* quarterly report. The site also covers NEPA compliance guidance.

Subjects: Environmental Law

826. NEPAnet CEQ Task Force

http://ceq.eh.doe.gov/nepa/nepanet.htm

Sponsor(s): White House — Council on Environmental Quality (CEQ)

Description: This site includes current and past information from the Council on Environmental Quality (CEQ) related to implementation of the National Environmental Policy Act (NEPA). Sections of the site cover the CEQ NEPA Task Force, regulations and state information related to NEPA, information about Environmental Impact Statements, NEPA litigation, and NEPA case law.

Subjects: Environmental Impact Statements; Environmental Law

Environmental Policy

827. Bureau of Oceans and International Environmental and Scientific Affairs

http://www.state.gov/g/oes/

Sponsor(s): State Department

Description: The Department of State's Bureau of Oceans and International Environmental and Scientific Affairs (OES) coordinates U.S. foreign policy related to science, the environment, and the world's oceans. The Web site presents policy statements, documents, and press releases related to such topics as marine conservation, sustainable development, and global climate change. The site links to Web pages for State's regional environmental hubs located in selected U.S. embassies around the world. It also links to the Web page for State's Office of the Science and Technology Adviser.

Subjects: Oceans — Policy; Science and Technology Policy — International; Environmental Policy — International

828. Climate VISION

http://www.climatevision.gov/

Sponsor(s): Energy Department

Description: Climate VISION is a public-private partnership effort announced as a presidential initiative to reduce greenhouse gas emissions using voluntary measures taken by industry. VISION stands for Voluntary Innovative Sector Initiatives: Opportunities Now. The site has information on the initiative, private sector participants and actions, and relevant technologies.

Subjects: Greenhouse Gases

829. Council on Environmental Quality

http://www.whitehouse.gov/ceq/

Sponsor(s): White House — Council on Environmental Quality (CEQ)

Description: The White House Council on Environmental Quality coordinates federal environmental efforts and oversees federal agency implementation of the environmental impact assessment process. The CEQ Web site provides information on administration environmental policy, initiatives, events, and statements. The site

has information on the National Environmental Policy Act (NEPA) which created the CEQ, and it links to related task forces and agencies.
Subjects: Environmental Protection — Policy; National Environmental Policy Act

830. Defense Environmental Network and Information Exchange (DENIX)
https://www.denix.osd.mil/denix/denix.html
Sponsor(s): Defense Department — Office of the Under Secretary of Defense (Installations and Environment)
Description: DENIX is a centralized resource for environment, safety, and occupational health news, policy, and guidance information for the entire Department of Defense. The publicly accessible sections of DENIX include a Subject Areas section that organizes DENIX resources by topic, such as recycling, noise abatement, military installation cleanups, and conservation. Other sections include Publications, Policy, and Laws and Regulations.
Subjects: Defense Administration; Environmental Protection — Policy
Publications: *Defense Environmental Restoration Program, Annual Report to Congress*, D 1.97:

831. EPA National Center for Environmental Economics
http://yosemite.epa.gov/ee/epa/eed.nsf/pages/homepage
Sponsor(s): Environmental Protection Agency (EPA) — National Center for Environmental Economics
Description: EPA's National Center for Environmental Economics conducts economic research and analysis related to environmental issues, such as economic incentives for protecting the environment and the benefits and costs of environmental policies and regulations. The site has information on NCEE's reports and working papers, seminars and workshops, grants and funding, and an extensive catalog of Web sites concerning environmental economics.
Subjects: Economics; Environmental Protection — Policy

832. FedCenter.gov
http://www.fedcenter.gov/
Sponsor(s): Environmental Protection Agency (EPA)White House — Office of the Federal Environmental Executive (OFEE)
Description: The official tagline for FedCenter.gov is "the federal government's home for comprehensive environmental stewardship and compliance assistance information." The site is meant to help federal environmental officials, particularly in the civilian sector, address environmental regulations and goals. Topics include energy use, green buildings, pollution prevention, and chemical management. Each topic section covers regulatory guidance, lessons learned, training and briefings, and conferences and events.
Subjects: Environmental Protection — Regulations; Federal Government

833. Interagency Ocean Policy Group
http://ocean.ceq.gov/
Sponsor(s): Council on Environmental Quality (CEQ)
Description: Members of the Interagency Ocean Policy Group (IOPG) represent executive branch programs concerned with the management and conservation of U.S. oceans and coasts. IOPG was formed by the White House Council on Environmental Quality to consider recommendations of the U.S. Commission on Ocean Policy (USCOP) and to help formulate the Bush administration's response. The Web site links to the USCOP site, and it features news, summaries, and statements about the Bush administration's ocean and coastal management activities.
Subjects: Coastal Ecology — Policy; Oceans — Policy

834. Morris K. Udall Foundation
http://www.udall.gov/
Sponsor(s): Morris K. Udall Foundation
Description: The Udall Foundation is an executive branch agency created by Congress to honor Congressman Morris Udall's service in the House of Representatives. The foundation provides for internships, scholarships, and fellowships, most with a focus on public service, the environment, and Native Americans. The foundation also runs the U.S. Institute for Environmental Conflict Resolution. The Web site includes information on these and other Udall Foundation programs.
Subjects: Environmental Education; American Indians; Scholarships

835. Office of the Federal Environmental Executive
http://www.ofee.gov/
Sponsor(s): White House — Office of the Federal Environmental Executive (OFEE)
Description: The OFEE promotes environmental practices, such as recycling and procurement of recycled products, in the federal government. This site describes both the Office and the efforts federal agencies can take to further their environmental stewardship.
Subjects: Recycling
Publications: *Closing the Circle News*, PREX 14.15:

Environmental Protection

836. American Heritage Rivers
http://www.epa.gov/rivers/
Sponsor(s): Environmental Protection Agency (EPA) — Water Office — Wetlands, Oceans, and Watersheds Office
Description: The American Heritage Rivers Initiative helps communities restore and revitalize waters and waterfronts. The initiative's Web site offers sections on What is the American Heritage Rivers Initiative; Which Rivers Are Designated?; Your River and Its Watershed; and Services for Your River. A *State of the River Report* is available for each American Heritage River.
Subjects: Rivers and Streams

837. America's National Wildlife Refuge System
http://refuges.fws.gov/
Sponsor(s): Interior Department — Fish and Wildlife Service (FWS)
Description: This Fish and Wildlife Service site has brochures for each of the National Wildlife Refuges online. The Web site also provides information on the National Wildlife Refuge System, current news, budget information, and links to related sites.
Subjects: Conservation (Natural Resources); Wildlife
Publications: *Refuge Update*, I 49.44/6:

838. Beaches
http://www.epa.gov/beaches/
Sponsor(s): Environmental Protection Agency (EPA)
Description: With this site, EPA brings together popular information about beaches that can be found on a number of its Web pages. Major sections include Plan a Trip, Learn about Beaches, and How EPA Protects Beaches. The Where You Live section provides a U.S. map linked to reports from EPA's Beach Advisory and

Closing On-line Notification (BEACON) system. The site also links to information about grants for developing beach monitoring and notification programs.
Subjects: Coastal Ecology

839. Coastal Program
http://www.fws.gov/coastal/CoastalProgram/
Sponsor(s): Interior Department — Fish and Wildlife Service (FWS)
Description: The Coastal Program works to conserve fish and wildlife and their habitats in the bays, estuaries, and watersheds around the U.S. coastline. The site has information about the program, notices of funding availability for coastal communities, and fact sheets on high-priority coastal areas in the United States.
Subjects: Coastal Ecology

840. Coastal Services Center
http://www.csc.noaa.gov/
Sponsor(s): Commerce Department — National Oceanic and Atmospheric Administration (NOAA) — National Ocean Service
Description: The Coastal Services Center helps state and local coastal resource management programs by providing them with data, tools, and training. The Web site describes the major services and program areas, including coastal remote sensing, GIS integration, landscape restoration, and online mapping. The center also has fellowship and funding opportunities. Projects in My State, on the home page, is an index to ongoing or completed projects and funding for each state and the outlying Pacific islands.
Subjects: Coastal Ecology; Remote Sensing
Publications: *Coastal Connections*, C 55.49/7:
Coastal GeoTools Conference Proceedings, C 55.32/8:
Coastal Services (bimonthly), C 55.49/5:

841. Cooperative Conservation
http://cooperativeconservation.gov/
Sponsor(s): Interior Department
Description: The Web site describes cooperative conservation as "the efforts of land-owners, communities, conservation groups, industry, and governmental agencies who join together to conserve our environment." Site content relates to Executive Order 13352 from 2004 on Facilitation of Cooperative Conservation. The site provides examples of successful cooperative conservation projects and related news updates. The Library section has documents from the Federal Cooperative Conservation Task Force, an interagency effort.
Subjects: Conservation (Natural Resources) — Policy

842. Division of Bird Habitat Conservation
http://birdhabitat.fws.gov
Sponsor(s): Interior Department — Fish and Wildlife Service (FWS)
Description: This Fish and Wildlife Service division supports bird habitat conservation partnerships through the North American Wetlands Conservation Act grants program and other programs. The site has sections on the Wetlands Grants Program, the Neotropical Birds Grants Program, and Bird Conservation Plans.
Subjects: Birds; Conservation (Natural Resources) — Grants

843. EarthDay.gov
http://www.earthday.gov/
Description: This site is a portal for government information on Earth Day, celebrated each April 22nd. The site has information on environmental practices and the history of Earth Day.
Subjects: Environmental Education

844. Environmental Protection Agency
http://www.epa.gov/
Sponsor(s): Environmental Protection Agency (EPA)
Description: The central EPA site provides access to information resources about the environment, pollution, hazardous substances, and water quality. Featured sections include EPA Newsroom, Browse EPA Topics, Where You Live, Laws and Regulations, Programs, Information Sources, Educational Resources, About EPA, and Programs. Browse EPA Topics links to agency information by major subject area, such as air, pesticides, research, wastes, and water. The section entitled Where You Live allows users to search for local information by ZIP code as well as link to state environmental agencies. The Laws and Regulations section has EPA's online public docket, major environmental laws, non-binding guidance documents, and other legal materials. The Information Sources section provides access to publications, databases, e-mail lists, and newsletters from the EPA and its offices. The Education Resources section arranges resources by audience, with information for students, teachers, and researchers. The Programs section groups links to EPA program information by type of program, such as Research, Grants, and Programs with a Geographic Focus. It also has an alphabetical list of links to all EPA programs. Under EPA Newsroom, the site offers a variety of e-mail lists and RSS news feeds. The EPA Web site also has a Spanish-language version available.

This is an excellent entry point into a vast quantity of EPA documents and data.
Subjects: Environmental Protection
Publications: *Annual Report, Environmental Protection Agency*, EP 4.1:
CleanupNews, EP 1.119:
Environmental Justice Quarterly, EP 13.15:
EPA National Catalog of Publications, EP 1.21:
EPP (Environmentally Preferable Purchasing) Update, EP 5.28:
Inventory of U.S. Greenhouse Gas Emissions and Sinks, EP 1.115:
Labcert Bulletin, EP 2.3/4:
National Biennial RCRA Hazardous Waste Report, EP 1.104/3:
National Water Quality Inventory Report to Congress, EP 2.17/2:
Office of Pesticides Programs Annual Report, EP 5.1:
Oil DROP, EP 1.122:
Oil Spill Program Update, EP 1.121:
Small Business Ombudsman Update, EP 1.117:
Summary of the Budget, EPA, EP 1.1/4:
Superfund Innovative Technology Program, Annual Report to Congress, EP 1.89/4-4:
Technology Profiles, Superfund Innovative Technology Evaluation Program, EP 1.104:
The Benefits and Costs of the Clean Air Act, EP 4.31:
Toxic Chemical Release Inventory Reporting Form R Instructions, EP 5.22/3:
Toxic Release Inventory, EP 5.22/2:
Tribal Air
WasteWise Annual Report, EP 1.1/10:
WasteWise Updates, EP 1.118

845. Estuaries.gov
http://www.estuaries.gov/
Sponsor(s): Commerce Department — National Oceanic and Atmospheric Administration (NOAA)
Description: This educational Web site focuses on National Estuaries Day, the last Saturday in September. The site explains the environmental importance of estuaries and provides classroom activity guides for teachers.
Subjects: Coastal Ecology; Environmental Education

846. Fisheries and Habitat Conservation
http://fisheries.fws.gov/
Sponsor(s): Interior Department — Fish and Wildlife Service (FWS)
Description: The Fish and Wildlife Service (FWS) maintains this Web site as a portal to FWS division and program Web sites concerned with fisheries and habitat conservation. Topics include invasive species, pollution, restoration, and wildlife. Program links lead to the Web sites for the Division of Fish and Wildlife Management and Habitat Restoration, the National Fish Hatchery System, the Division of Habitat and Resource Conservation (Federal Programs Activities), the Division of Environmental Quality, and the Washington Office staff for Fisheries and Habitat Conservation.
Subjects: Conservation (Natural Resources); Fisheries

847. Great Lakes Environment
http://www.epa.gov/glnpo/
Sponsor(s): Environmental Protection Agency (EPA) — Great Lakes National Program Office (GLNPO)
Description: This site has information on the Great Lakes, the environmental problems of the lakes, and projects to restore the environment. A Policies and Strategies section has information and publications from the EPA's Great Lakes National Program Office. Other sections provide detailed assessments, data, and reports from projects concerning monitoring and indicators, ecosystems, and toxics reduction. The site also has information on related funding opportunities.
Subjects: Lakes; Water Pollution
Publications: *Great Lakes Atlas*

848. Marine Protected Areas of the United States
http://mpa.gov/
Sponsor(s): Commerce Department — National Oceanic and Atmospheric Administration (NOAA)
Description: This site provides a classification system for the various types of marine protected areas, including their conservation focus and levels of environmental protection. Major sections of the site include All About MPAs, National System of MPAs, and Science and Analysis. The Helpful Resources section includes an inventory of Marine Managed Areas and a Virtual Library that is an extensive database of information related to MPAs. The site also has organizational information on the National MPA Center and the MPA Advisory Committee.

The MPA Web site was redesigned in 2006 and now provides multiple approaches to rich content on science, policy, regulation, enforcement and many other topics related to marine protected areas.
Subjects: Coastal Ecology; Marine Life

849. Migratory Bird Conservation Commission
http://www.fws.gov/realty/mbcc.html
Sponsor(s): Migratory Bird Conservation Commission
Description: The Migratory Bird Conservation Commission considers any recommendations by the Secretary of the Interior for the purchase or rental of land for the Fish and Wildlife Service. It also considers the establishment of any new waterfowl refuges. The Web site has information on the commission, its members, its annual report, the Migratory Bird Conservation Fund, and related topics.
Subjects: Birds; Conservation (Natural Resources)

850. National Estuaries Restoration Inventory
https://neri.noaa.gov/
Sponsor(s): Commerce Department — National Oceanic and Atmospheric Administration (NOAA)
Description: The National Estuaries Restoration Inventory collects information on estuary habitat restoration projects across the country. Projects can be searched by location, restoration technique, and other factors. The site also reports summary data, such as total acreage restored by region and number of projects by project status. The About section includes links to other online project inventories.
Subjects: Coastal Ecology

851. National Estuarine Research Reserve System
http://nerrs.noaa.gov/
Sponsor(s): Commerce Department — National Oceanic and Atmospheric Administration (NOAA) — National Ocean Service
Description: Areas in the National Estuarine Research Reserve System are protected for long-term research, water-quality monitoring, education, and coastal zone management. The Web site has profiles of the designated areas and the programs offered under the Reserve System. Featured education programs include the National Estuarine Research Reserve System's Graduate Research Fellowships and the Coastal Training Program.
Subjects: Environmental Education; Environmental Protection; Rivers and Streams

852. National Marine Sanctuaries
http://www.sanctuaries.nos.noaa.gov/
Sponsor(s): Commerce Department — National Oceanic and Atmospheric Administration (NOAA) — National Weather Service
Description: The National Marine Sanctuary System provides resource protection, coordinates scientific research on the sanctuaries, and facilitates multiple uses of the national marine sanctuaries. Its colorful Web site includes sections on Visiting Your Sanctuaries, Education, Science, Maritime Heritage, and Resource Protection. Publications are in the Library section. The multimedia *Encyclopedia of the Sanctuaries* is in the Photos and Videos section.
Subjects: Marine Sanctuaries
Publications: *National Marine Sanctuaries State of the Sanctuary Report*

853. National Park Foundation
http://www.nationalparks.org/
Sponsor(s): National Park Foundation
Description: The National Park Foundation is a private nonprofit organization chartered by Congress to support the national parks. The Web site has sections on children's programs, planning your visit, volunteering, and donating to the foundation.
Subjects: National Parks and Reserves

854. National Wild and Scenic Rivers System
http://www.rivers.gov/
Alternate URL(s): http://www.nps.gov/rivers/
Sponsor(s): Interior Department — National Park Service (NPS)
Description: The Wild and Scenic Rivers Act (Public Law 90-542) is intended to protect selected rivers, keeping them free-flowing and preserving the general character of a river. This site describes the Scenic Rivers program and lists protected rivers. At this time, the site is under renovation. The newest version should be available at the primarily URL above. The alternate URL was used for the previous version.
Subjects: Rivers and Streams

855. Natural Resources Conservation Service
http://www.nrcs.usda.gov/
Sponsor(s): Agriculture Department (USDA) — Natural Resources Conservation Service (NRCS)
Description: The USDA's Natural Resources Conservation Service (NRCS) provides expertise in conserving soil, water, and other natural resources. The site's Technical Resources section points to information, models, and data on such topics as air quality, forestry, nutrient management, soils, and wildlife biology. The site has county-level *Electronic Field Office Technical Guides* with soil and conservation profiles. The Features section links to special sections on topics such as backyard conservation, drought information, education materials for K–12 teachers, and NRCS information available in Spanish. The Programs section has an inventory of financial assistance programs for conservation of wetlands, farm and ranch lands, grasslands, and other purposes. It also includes information on program funding and allocations by state. The News section includes the online newsletter *NRCS This Week*, state program news, and a publications catalog.
Subjects: Conservation (Natural Resources); Environmental Protection
Publications: *Basin Outlook Reports*, A 57.46:
Keys to Soil Taxonomy, A 57.2:

856. Office of Ocean and Coastal Resource Management
http://www.ocrm.nos.noaa.gov/welcome.html
Sponsor(s): Commerce Department — National Oceanic and Atmospheric Administration (NOAA) — National Ocean Service
Description: The Office of Ocean and Coastal Resource Management (OCRM) provides national leadership for state and territory coastal programs and estuarine research reserves. The Web site has information on OCRM programs, funding, and the Coastal Zone Management Act. The site also has information on coastal issues, nationwide initiatives, and educational programs. The My State section describes and links to coastal management programs in each U.S. coastal or island region.
Subjects: Coastal Ecology

857. Office of Protected Resources
http://www.nmfs.noaa.gov/prot_res/prot_res.html
Sponsor(s): Commerce Department — National Oceanic and Atmospheric Administration (NOAA) — National Marine Fisheries
Description: The NOAA Fisheries Office of Protected Resources coordinates the protection, conservation, and restoration of marine mammals, endangered species, their habitats, and marine-protected areas. This Web site provides legal and regulatory information on the Marine Mammals Protection Act and the Endangered Species Act, and a listing of proposed, candidate, and threatened and endangered

species. The site also has program descriptions, permit information, and an Education section.
Subjects: Endangered Species; Marine Life; Marine Mammals

858. Office of Wetlands, Oceans, and Watersheds, EPA
http://www.epa.gov/owow/
Sponsor(s): Environmental Protection Agency (EPA) — Water Office — Wetlands, Oceans, and Watersheds Office
Description: The Office of Wetlands, Oceans, and Watersheds Web site covers their programs for wetlands, rivers and streams, lakes, oceans, coasts, and estuaries. The site has information on laws, databases, publications, and training. The What You Can Do section has an extensive list of links to information on such topics as water conservation, becoming a volunteer water monitor, and preventing storm-water runoff pollution. The site has a significant amount of information on watersheds, including watershed regulations, programs, publications, databases, and funding, and a section on the EPA's Watershed Academy.

This EPA Office Web site provides access to a wealth of information for citizens, resource managers, researchers, and educators. An A-Z index facilitates its use.
Subjects: Water Pollution; Watersheds

859. United States Coral Reef Task Force
http://www.coralreef.gov/
Sponsor(s): Interior Department; Commerce Department — National Oceanic and Atmospheric Administration (NOAA)
Description: The Coral Reef Task Force, established by executive order, is an inter-agency task force co-chaired by the Interior Department and NOAA. This site has information about the responsibilities of the task force, its meetings, documents, and working groups. In addition, the site provides educational information about the role and status of coral reefs.
Subjects: Coral Reefs
Publications: *Implementation of the National Coral Reef Action Strategy: Report to Congress*, C 55.402:
National Action Plan to Conserve Coral Reefs, PR 42.8:

Environmental Science

860. Air Resources Laboratory
http://www.arl.noaa.gov/
Sponsor(s): Commerce Department — National Oceanic and Atmospheric Administration (NOAA) — Office of Oceanic and Atmospheric Research
Description: The Air Resources Laboratory conducts atmospheric research, focusing on air quality and climate. The site describes current research and provides access to ARL climate and meteorological data.

This site will be primarily of interest to atmospheric scientists for the data and information on atmospheric and air quality modeling.
Subjects: Air Quality — Research; Atmospheric Sciences

861. Atlantic Oceanographic and Meteorological Laboratory
http://www.aoml.noaa.gov/
Sponsor(s): Commerce Department — National Oceanic and Atmospheric Administration (NOAA) — Office of Oceanic and Atmospheric Research
Description: AOML conducts research in oceanography, tropical meteorology, atmospheric and oceanic chemistry, and acoustics. The major topical sections of the

lab's Web site are Ocean and Climate, Coastal and Regional, and Hurricanes. The site provides online access to the lab's data sets. The Publications section provides a searchable catalog of AOML-authored publications dating back to 1985.

Subjects: Hurricanes — Research; Meteorology — Research; Oceanography — Research

Publications: *AOML Keynotes*

862. Climate Change

`http://epa.gov/climatechange/`

Sponsor(s): Environmental Protection Agency (EPA)

Description: This EPA Web site provides a non-technical overview of global climate change, its causes and effects, and associated policy issues. The site was formerly named Global Warming; it was updated and renamed in October 2006. Main sections of the site are Science (including State of Knowledge), U.S. Climate Policy, Greenhouse Gas Emissions, Health and Environmental Effects, What You Can Do, and an educational section for kids. The Climate Change site links to related Web sites and EPA resources.

Subjects: Climatology; Global Change

863. Coastal and Marine Geology Program

`http://marine.usgs.gov/`

Sponsor(s): Interior Department — U.S. Geological Survey (USGS)

Description: The Coastal and Marine Geology Program promotes understanding of marine and coastal geologic systems, addressing issues relating to environmental quality, public safety, and natural resources. The online newsletter *Sound Waves* has much of the current program information available at the site. Much of the rest of the content is organized as a database, allowing researchers to specify their topic of interest and region of interest. Searches can also be limited to resource type, including research projects, educational material, photographs, maps, publications, and data. Topics include beaches, sediments, erosion, mapping, remote sensing, minerals, and oil and gas. The site also links to field centers in California, Florida, and Massachusetts.

Subjects: Coastal Ecology; Geology

Publications: *Sound Waves*, I 19.171:

864. CSCOR: Center for Sponsored Coastal Ocean Research

`http://www.cop.noaa.gov/`

Sponsor(s): Commerce Department — National Oceanic and Atmospheric Administration (NOAA)

Description: NOAA's Center for Sponsored Coastal Ocean Research (CSCOR) manages a competitive research program to support understanding of complex coastal systems. CSCOR research focuses on the causes of ecosystem change: climate change, extreme natural events, pollution, invasive species, and land and resources use. The Web site includes grants information and a database of sponsored research summaries. The Publications section includes fact sheets and the *Decision Analysis Series*.

Subjects: Coastal Ecology — Grants

Publications: *NOAA Coastal Ocean Program, Decisions Analysis Series*, C 55.49/3:

865. Earth Observatory
http://earthobservatory.nasa.gov/
Sponsor(s): National Aeronautics and Space Administration (NASA) — Goddard Space Flight Center (GSFC)
Description: The Earth Observatory Web site is a NASA outreach effort to provide satellite imagery and scientific information about Earth to the public. The Data and Images section of the site provides an interactive tool for finding earth observation datasets and customizing a display of the data against views of Earth. Other sections include feature articles, news, and fact sheets about Earth observations, with a focus on the global climate and environmental changes. An Experiments section outlines education activities designed to teach about space-based remote sensing. The entire Web site has an optional "glossary mode" in which terms appearing in a special glossary are highlighted and linked to their definitions.

The Earth Observatory Web site is very well organized and easy to navigate. It is appropriate for the high school through undergraduate science levels, or for any non-specialist interested in the topic. Concerning their Web audience, NASA states on the site: "In particular, we hope our site is useful to public media and educators. Any and all materials published on the Earth Observatory are freely available for re-publication or re-use, except where copyright is indicated. We ask that NASA's Earth Observatory be given credit for its original materials."
Subjects: Environmental Education; Global Change; Remote Sensing

866. Ecological Site Information System
http://esis.sc.egov.usda.gov/
Sponsor(s): Agriculture Department (USDA) — Natural Resources Conservation Service (NRCS)
Description: The Ecological Site Information System (ESIS) is the repository for the data associated with the collection of forestland and rangeland plot data and the development of ecological site descriptions. The Web site provides information on its two components, the Ecological Site Description and the Ecological Site Inventory for forestland and rangeland data.
Subjects: Environmental Science

867. Florida Integrated Science Center
http://fisc.er.usgs.gov/
Sponsor(s): Interior Department — U.S. Geological Survey (USGS)
Description: The Florida Integrated Science Center (FISC) focuses on environmental issues in Florida, the Southeastern States, and the U.S. Caribbean. FISC research covers areas such as coastal geology, fisheries, and water resources. The Web site provides information on these and many other special areas of focus, including manatees, coral reefs, amphibian monitoring, and invasive species.

This site has information for both scientific and educational communities in Florida, including real-time water data for the state and background on popular topics such as manatees and the invasive Asian swamp eel.
Subjects: Environmental Science — Research; Florida — Research

868. Forest Ecosystems Dynamics
http://forest.gsfc.nasa.gov/
Sponsor(s): National Aeronautics and Space Administration (NASA) — Goddard Space Flight Center (GSFC)
Description: "The Forest Ecosystem Dynamics (FED) Project is concerned with modeling and monitoring ecosystem processes and patterns in response to natural and anthropogenic effects" (from the Web site). The FED site disseminates project information, archives spatial and scientific data sets, and demonstrates the linking

of ecosystem and remote sensing models. The site features include: Ecosystem Modeling Interface, Multisensor Aircraft Campaign, Imagery Archive, Interactive Soil Map, and Presentations and Publications.

Subjects: Forests — Research

869. Global Change Master Directory

http://gcmd.gsfc.nasa.gov/

Sponsor(s): National Aeronautics and Space Administration (NASA)

Description: NASA's Global Change Master Directory (GCMD) is a catalog of Earth science datasets and services pertaining to global change research. The GCMD database has over 15,000 descriptions of earth science data sets and services. An interface for browsing the dataset descriptions organizes them by topics such as agriculture, atmosphere, biosphere, climate indicators, oceans, and Sun-Earth interactions. The collection can also be searched by word and has an alert service to notify subscribers of new data sets in their areas of interest. The GCMD offers data set descriptions in a standard format, the Directory Interchange Format (DIF), allowing it to be used to create other Web portals for specialized topics. Under About Us, Metadata Standards, the site explains how DIF has been cross-mapped with other standards. The About Us and FAQ section have additional information on the GCMD project.

This well-constructed directory can assist researchers in finding data sets and serve as a model for similar Web projects.

Subjects: Data Products; Global Change

870. Global Hydrology and Climate Center

http://www.ghcc.msfc.nasa.gov/

Sponsor(s): National Aeronautics and Space Administration (NASA) — Marshall Space Flight Center (MSFC) — Global Hydrology and Climate Center

Description: The Global Hydrology and Climate Center, a joint venture between government and academia, promotes study of the global water cycle and its effect on climate. The Research section of the site includes information on the center's studies of urban heat islands, air quality, climate variability, lightning observations from space, and other topics.

Subjects: Climate Research; Remote Sensing

871. Great Lakes Environmental Research Laboratory

http://www.glerl.noaa.gov/

Sponsor(s): Commerce Department — National Oceanic and Atmospheric Administration (NOAA)

Description: The Great Lakes Lab conducts scientific research of relevance to the Great Lakes and marine coastal environments. This site describes the lab, its mission, and its programs. The Data section has an extensive catalog of datasets. Publications are available under Products and Services. Specific topics addressed on this site include water levels, monitoring, invasive species, and toxic materials. The site also provides information on the outreach and educational activities of the lab.

Subjects: Lakes — Research

872. Land Use History of North America

http://biology.usgs.gov/luhna/

Sponsor(s): Interior Department — U.S. Geological Survey (USGS)

Description: This USGS site provides a historical context for understanding ongoing changes in land cover and land use in North American. It presents papers by

scientific researchers on such topics as urbanization, biodiversity, and forest dynamics as studied over time in specific regions of the continent.
Subjects: Global Change — Research; Land — Research
Publications: *Perspectives on the Land Use History of North America*

873. National Centers for Environmental Prediction
http://www.ncep.noaa.gov/
Sponsor(s): Commerce Department — National Oceanic and Atmospheric Administration (NOAA)
Description: This site links to the Web sites for the component NCEP centers: the Aviation Weather Center, the Climate Prediction Center, the Environmental Modeling Center, the Hydrometeorological Prediction Center, the Ocean Prediction Center, the Space Environment Center, the Storm Prediction Center, the Tropical Prediction Center, and NCEP Central Operations. Each of these publishes images, data, and information related to its specialty.
   Most maps and data presented at the Prediction Center sites may too technical for anyone who is not a professional meteorologist, but some of the sites — such as the Storm and Tropical Prediction Centers — carry information that will be of interest to a broader audience.
Subjects: Meteorology; Weather Forecasts

874. National Environmental Publications Information System
http://nepis.epa.gov/
Sponsor(s): Environmental Protection Agency (EPA)
Description: National Environmental Publications Information System (NEPIS) is a searchable database of EPA publications online. The EPA Frequent Questions Web page (on the main EPA site) describes NEPIS as "EPA's largest electronic documents site which allows you to search, view and print; including full images of all original pages and full text, from a collection of over 15,000 archival and current documents." The database can be searched by word, title, publication number, and date the item was added to the database (not the date of publication).
   The NEPIS site includes a Help section that documents the basic search and retrieve functions. However, the usability of the site could be vastly improved starting with, for example, detailed information on the scope of the database.
Subjects: Environmental Protection; Publication Catalogs

875. National Environmental Satellite, Data, and Information Service
http://www.nesdis.noaa.gov/
Sponsor(s): Commerce Department — National Oceanic and Atmospheric Administration (NOAA) — National Environmental Satellite, Data, and Information Service (NESDIS)
Description: NESDIS manages environmental satellites, disseminates data they collect, and conducts related research. The Satellites section of the Web site has information on satellite operations and development. Imagery and other products in the Satellites section are available under Products and organized in the categories of image servers and atmosphere, land, ocean, and space products. The Data and Information section organizes its vast archives into climate, geophysical, ocean, and coastal data centers. The site also has information on the Emergency Beacon tracking system operated by NOAA.
Subjects: Environmental Science; Satellites

876. National Ocean Service

http://www.nos.noaa.gov/

Sponsor(s): Commerce Department — National Oceanic and Atmospheric Administration (NOAA) — National Ocean Service

Description: National Ocean Service (NOS) is the primary civil agency within the federal government responsible for the health and safety of the nation's coastal and oceanic environment. Information about its work is organized by topic under the broad headings of Oceans, Coasts, and Charting and Navigation. Topics include coral reef conservation, ocean exploration, oil spills, coastal ecosystem science, national estuarine research reserves, global positioning, and tides and currents. The site includes the Data Explorer portal to NOS spatial data, and a searchable publications catalog. The Education section offers online tutorials on corals, tides and water levels, and more.

Subjects: Oceanography

877. National Oceanic and Atmospheric Administration

http://www.noaa.gov/

Sponsor(s): Commerce Department — National Oceanic and Atmospheric Administration (NOAA)

Description: With information on environmental issues such as climate, fisheries, and the ocean, the NOAA Web site is a major resource for the environmental sciences. Beyond providing current news and agency information, the site best serves as a finding tool for the substantive content on the sites of NOAA's component divisions and offices. Subject access is provided by links to Weather, Ocean, Climate, Coasts, Fisheries, Charting and Navigation, Research, and Satellites. In addition, the Storm Watch page provides the latest weather forecasts to track storms through NOAA weather satellites. NOAA offers several RSS news feeds and podcasts via links on the home page.

Given the broad scope of environmental topics that NOAA agencies cover, this site can be used as a finding aid for all environmental information that falls under NOAA's domain.

Subjects: Atmospheric Sciences; Environmental Science; Oceanography

Publications: *NOAA Magazine,* C 55.57:

NOAA Report, C 55.53:

878. National Oceanographic Data Center

http://www.nodc.noaa.gov/

Sponsor(s): Commerce Department — National Oceanic and Atmospheric Administration (NOAA) — National Environmental Satellite, Data, and Information Service (NESDIS)

Description: The National Oceanographic Data Center provides public access to global oceanographic and coastal data, products, and information. Click on Access Data on the home page to reach Archived Data, CD-ROMs, Publications, and an Online Store. Available data sets cover ocean currents, plankton, salinity, sea level, and more. The site includes a popular Coastal Water Temperature Guide, reporting average monthly temperatures for the U.S. coastal regions, including Hawaii.

Subjects: Oceanography

879. National Service Center for Environmental Publications

http://www.epa.gov/ncepihom/

Sponsor(s): Environmental Protection Agency (EPA)

Description: The National Service Center for Environmental Publications (NSCEP) distributes the publications of the Environmental Protection Agency. The site has a searchable publications catalog, from which publications can be ordered online. New Offerings lists newly available publications with an order link or direct Web link if the publication is available online. Other sections highlight foreign language publications and sources for online publications.

Subjects: Environmental Protection; Publication Catalogs

880. National Water and Climate Data Center

http://www.wcc.nrcs.usda.gov/

Sponsor(s): Agriculture Department (USDA) — Natural Resources Conservation Service (NRCS)

Description: The NRCS National Water and Climate Data Center provides water and climate information and technology to support natural resource conservation. The Web site features water supply forecasts, snow data, and climate data and reports. The Conservation Planning Information section of the site includes subsections on Animal Waste Management, Irrigation, Nutrient Management, Salinity Management, and related topics.

Subjects: Agricultural Waste; Climatology; Water Supply

881. National Wetlands Inventory

http://wetlands.fws.gov/

Sponsor(s): Interior Department — Fish and Wildlife Service (FWS)

Description: National Wetlands Inventory Center (NWIC) studies and reports on the nation's wetlands and deepwater habitats. The Web site provides mapping tools, downloadable digitized maps and data files, and publications in PDF format. The site features a national list of wetland plant species and a report on the status and trends of wetlands. It also includes a section for kids and educators.

Subjects: Wetlands

Publications: *Status and Trends of Wetlands in the Conterminous United States*, I 49.2:

882. NOAA Earth System Research Laboratory

http://www.esrl.noaa.gov/

Sponsor(s): Commerce Department — National Oceanic and Atmospheric Administration (NOAA)

Description: NOAA's Earth System Research Laboratory (ESRL) was formed in 2005 through the consolidation of six NOAA research organizations. ESRL focuses on global environmental issues such as understanding the roles of gases and particles that contribute to climate change. The Web site describes ESRL research and education activities. Links just beneath the site search box lead to the ESRL publications catalog and frequently asked questions.

Subjects: Climate Research; Meteorology — Research

883. NOAA Research

http://www.noaa.gov/research.html

Alternate URL(s): http://www.research.noaa.gov/

Sponsor(s): Commerce Department — National Oceanic and Atmospheric Administration (NOAA)

Description: This page links to extensive information on NOAA research activities conducted by in-house laboratories and by extramural programs, primarily through the Office of Oceanic and Atmospheric Research. As described on the page, "the NOAA Research network consists of 12 internal research laboratories, NOAA Office of Ocean Exploration, extramural research, a network of more than 200 institutions participating in the Sea Grant university and research programs, 6 undersea research centers, a research grants program through the NOAA Climate

Program Office, and 13 cooperative institutes with academia." The alternate URL above links to the home page of the Office of Oceanic and Atmospheric Research.
Subjects: Environmental Science — Research

884. Pacific Marine Environmental Laboratory
http://www.pmel.noaa.gov/
Sponsor(s): Commerce Department — National Oceanic and Atmospheric Administration (NOAA) — Office of Oceanic and Atmospheric Research
Description: The Pacific Marine Environmental Laboratory (PMEL) carries out interdisciplinary scientific investigations in oceanography and atmospheric sciences. The site has sections for Research, Publications, Data, Theme Pages, and Infrastructure. Special topics include El Niño and La Niña, tsunami monitoring, 3D visualization of data, and virtual reality presentations. The Publications page offers a search of PMEL publications by year, author, title, citation, abstract, division, and media type.
Subjects: Atmospheric Sciences — Research; Oceanography — Research

885. Physical Oceanography Distributed Active Archive Center
http://podaac.jpl.nasa.gov
Sponsor(s): National Aeronautics and Space Administration (NASA) — Jet Propulsion Laboratory (JPL)
Description: The Physical Oceanography Distributed Active Archive Center is a component of the NASA Earth Observing System Data Information System (EOSDIS). The center is responsible for archiving and distributing satellite data relevant to the physical state of the ocean. The site has a data catalog and information on data tools. Data is organized into the sections Ocean Surface Topography, Ocean Vector Winds, and Sea Surface Temperature.
   While most of the data is for the use of scientists, the site also has links to educational Web sites and products.
Subjects: Oceanography

886. Smithsonian Tropical Research Institute
http://www.stri.org/
Sponsor(s): Smithsonian Institution
Description: The Smithsonian Tropical Research Institute is based in Panama. In addition to its own scientific staff, the Institute hosts visiting scholars and students conducting research on the ecology and behavior of tropical plants and animals, and on man's impact in the tropics. This Web site has information on the institute's research, facilities, academic programs, and opportunities for visiting scientists.
Subjects: Environmental Science — Research

887. Upper Midwest Environmental Sciences Center
http://www.umesc.usgs.gov/
Sponsor(s): Interior Department — U.S. Geological Survey (USGS)
Description: The UMESC is a river-related inventory, monitoring, research, spatial analysis, and information-sharing program. One of its main program areas is the Long-Term Resource Monitoring Program (LTRMP) of the Upper Mississippi River System and adjoining geographic areas. The Data Library includes a variety of environmental datasets, photographs, and maps for the Mississippi River. The Science Programs site is organized into sections for aquatic sciences, river inventory and monitoring, invasive species, and terrestrial sciences. The Teachers and Students section has a variety of educational material on the Mississippi River.
   This site provides access to a substantial amount of information for researchers on fish and wildlife, vegetation, invertebrates, water quality, water levels, sedi-

ments, contaminants, and nutrients, as well as access to aerial and satellite photography, software, scientific publications, and geographic information systems maps, quadrangles, and figures.
Subjects: Rivers and Streams — Research

Geography

888. EarthExplorer
http://earthexplorer.usgs.gov
Alternate URL(s): http://edcsns17.cr.usgs.gov/EarthExplorer/
Sponsor(s): Interior Department — U.S. Geological Survey (USGS)
Description: EarthExplorer is a system for finding and ordering satellite images, cartographic products, and high resolution scanned images from photographs through the U.S. Geological Survey. EarthExplorer provides cross inventory search capabilities, standing request functionality, and secured e-commerce support for product orders. Users may log in as guests or as registered users, who have access to more features than guests do. Users who plan to access EarthExplorer frequently may wish to register.
Subjects: Maps and Mapping

889. EROS Data Center
http://edc.usgs.gov/
Sponsor(s): Interior Department — U.S. Geological Survey (USGS)
Description: The Earth Resources Observation Systems (EROS) Data Center is a data management, systems development, and research center for the USGS National Mapping Division. Sections include Products, Science, Satellite Missions, National Satellite Land Remote Sensing Data Archive, and About EROS. The Products section has links or availability information on aerial photographs, topographic maps, digital raster elevation data, imagery collected from satellites, and land use data sets. The Publications section is under About EROS and includes citations for scientific and technical materials authored or co-authored by the professional staff at the EROS Data Center.
Subjects: Maps and Mapping; Remote Sensing

890. Federal Geographic Data Committee
http://www.fgdc.gov/
Sponsor(s): Federal Geographic Data Committee (FGDC); White House
Description: The Federal Geographic Data Committee is "an interagency committee that promotes the coordinated development, use, sharing, and dissemination of geospatial data on a national basis" (from the Web site). The FGDC coordinates the National Spatial Data Infrastructure (NSDI), which encompasses policies, standards, and procedures for organizations to cooperatively produce and share geospatial data. Web site sections include Metadata, Standards, Policy and Planning, Training, and Grants. The Standards section covers FGDC standards projects, processes, and publications.
Subjects: Geography
Publications: *FGDC (Federal Geographic Data Committee) Newsletter*, I 19.115/4:

891. GeoCommunicator
http://www.geocommunicator.gov/
Sponsor(s): Interior Department — Bureau of Land Management (BLM)
Description: GeoCommunicator disseminates geographic data and information from the National Integrated Land System (NILS) about public lands in the United

States. One component of GeoCommunicator allows users to search, locate, and display the BLM's land and mineral use authorizations and mining claims on public lands. Another component, under Federal Land Stewardship, allows users to search, locate, and display federal land management boundaries and agency information for public lands. The site also links to the Land Survey Information System (LSIS), the official government Web site for the distribution of the Public Land Survey System (PLSS) of the United States.
Subjects: Land Management; Maps and Mapping

892. Geodata.gov
http://www.geodata.gov/
Sponsor(s): Interior Department
Description: Geodata.gov is designed to be the "one stop for federal, state, and local geographic data" (from the Web site). The site has also been called Geospatial One-Stop. It is an interagency effort managed by the Interior Department. In addition to federal contributors, the site solicits content from state, local, and tribal sources. Geospatial data currently cataloged at Geodata.gov can be located under such categories as Atmosphere and Climate, Biology and Ecology, Business and Economic, Cadastral, and Transportation Networks. The available data collections can also be searched by geographic location, time frame, and other criteria.

In addition to its catalog, the Geodata site provides information for the geographic data community. Value is added to the site with information in the Help Center on data and metadata standards, metadata tools, and other topics.
Subjects: Geographic Information Systems (GIS); Maps and Mapping

893. National Atlas of the United States of America
http://www.nationalatlas.gov/
Alternate URL(s): http://memory.loc.gov/ammem/gmdhtml/census3.html
Sponsor(s): Interior Department — U.S. Geological Survey (USGS)
Description: The U.S. Geological Survey and partners created the online National Atlas to supersede a printed version published in 1970. Atlas options include map layers, dynamic maps, printable maps, and wall maps (for sale). Available map layers come from a variety of federal agencies and are organized into categories such as biology, boundaries, geology, and transportation. Each category comes with an overview article. The site also has a section for mapping professionals with downloadable data used in the maps.

See the alternate URL for a digitized copy of the 1970 *National Atlas of the United States of America* available from the Library of Congress American Memory collection.

The National Atlas is an excellent site for educators and those learning about the power of online mapping.
Subjects: Maps and Mapping; United States
Publications: *National Atlas of the United States*, I 19.111:

894. National Geodetic Survey
http://www.ngs.noaa.gov/
Sponsor(s): Commerce Department — National Oceanic and Atmospheric Administration (NOAA) — National Ocean Service
Description: NOAA's National Geodetic Survey (NGS) develops and maintains the National Spatial Reference System (NSRS), a national coordinate system that defines latitude, longitude, height, scale, gravity, and orientation throughout the United States, including how these values change with time. Under What We Do, the Web site has brief descriptions of NGS programs such as Aeronautical Survey Program, GPS Orbit Data, National Shoreline, Mapping The Ionosphere, and the Continually Operating Reference System, a national network of permanent Global

Positioning System (GPS) receivers. The site also has a form for online reporting of damaged or missing USGS geodetic markers.

The technical nature of the material available on this site means that it will be of interest primarily to geodesy and remote sensing professionals. It may also be of interest to the science, transportation, and engineering professionals who can use NGS data and applications. Others may wish to consult the "Geodosy for the Layman" primer available on the What We Do page.

Subjects: Geodesy; Maps and Mapping

895. National Geospatial Programs Office
http://www.usgs.gov/ngpo/
Sponsor(s): Interior Department — U.S. Geological Survey (USGS)
Description: The USGS National Geospatial Programs Office (NGPO), established in 2004, is responsible for all USGS-led geospatial programs, such as *The National Map* and the Federal Geographic Data Committee. NGPO works to promote a National Spatial Data Infrastructure for consistent means to share geographic data between parties. The Web site has news and program information.
Subjects: Maps and Mapping
Publications: *National Geospatial Programs Office: A Plan for Action*

896. National Map
http://nationalmap.gov/
Sponsor(s): Interior Department — U.S. Geological Survey (USGS)
Description: The National Map project aims to create public domain core geographic data about the United States and its territories. The project, led by the USGS, involves a consortium of federal, state, and local partners. The National Map Web site includes a viewer for the data that is available so far, project status information, and sections on partnership projects. It has information on the National Map Corps, private citizens providing mapping information for the project. The site also links to related geospatial data projects, such as the *National Atlas*.
Subjects: Maps and Mapping

897. Office of Coast Survey
http://chartmaker.ncd.noaa.gov/
Sponsor(s): Commerce Department — National Oceanic and Atmospheric Administration (NOAA) — National Ocean Service
Description: The Coast Survey is the official U.S. chart-making agency. It manages nautical chart data collections and information programs. This site offers information on nautical charts and hydrography via links such as Historical Maps and Charts, Wrecks and Obstructions, Navigation Services, and Hydrographic Surveys. There are electronic navigational charts to download, and print-on-demand nautical charts. The site also offers a major online service called NowCOAST. This Web-based GIS tool is designed to allow rapid spatial location of real-time weather, ocean, and river information for coastal areas.
Subjects: Maps and Mapping

898. Seamless Data Distribution System
http://seamless.usgs.gov/
Sponsor(s): Interior Department — U.S. Geological Survey (USGS)
Description: The Seamless Data Distribution System (SDDS) provides geospatial data layers to view and download. Datasets to download include the Landsat Mosaic orthoimagery database, National Elevation Dataset, and National Land-Cover Dataset. The site includes a tutorial and frequently asked questions.
Subjects: Maps and Mapping

899. USGS Geography
http://geography.usgs.gov/
Sponsor(s): Interior Department — U.S. Geological Survey (USGS)
Description: This site brings together geography programs, products, and services information from the Geological Survey. The three central USGS geography programs described are Land Remote Sensing, Geographic Analysis and Mapping, and Science Impact. Other featured programs are AmericaView (to promote the availability of remote sensing data and technology), LANDFIRE (Landscape Fire and Resource Management Planning Tools Project), and the National Hazards Support System for near-real time monitoring of natural hazard events. The Products section links to the geographic maps, digital data, publications, and tools on USGS Web sites. The site also links to USGS geographic science centers.
Subjects: Geography; Maps and Mapping

Natural Resources

900. Alaska Science Center
http://alaska.usgs.gov/science/biology/
Sponsor(s): Interior Department — U.S. Geological Survey (USGS)
Description: The USGS Alaska Science Center conducts monitoring, research, and assessments of natural resources issues and natural hazards in Alaska and the region. Under Science, the site links to relevant information in the areas of biology, geography, geology, and water. The Maps, Products, and Publications section has a publications catalog and a link to the Alaska Geospatial Data Clearinghouse. Specific topics covered on the site include volcanoes, fisheries, wildlife veterinary medicine, bird banding, and polar bears.
Subjects: Wildlife — Research; Alaska — Research

901. Animal Care
http://www.aphis.usda.gov/ac/
Sponsor(s): Agriculture Department (USDA) — Animal and Plant Health Inspection Service (APHIS)
Description: The Animal Care (AC) program of the Animal and Plant Health Inspection Service is concerned with enforcement of the Animal Welfare Act. Under About AC, this site describes the scope of the Animal Welfare Act. It also has a section on the Horse Protection Act. The site provides information on current cases, and new or proposed regulations. The AC Publications section has laws, guides, reports, and enforcement statistics, with special sections on elephants, marine mammals, exotic cats, traveling with your pet, and rats, mice, and birds.
Subjects: Animals — Regulations
Publications: *APHIS Animal Care Report*, A 101.22/3:

902. Animal Welfare Information Center
http://www.nal.usda.gov/awic/
Sponsor(s): Agriculture Department (USDA) — National Agricultural Library (NAL)
Description: The Animal Welfare Information Center compiles links to information about the welfare of farm, lab, circus, and zoo animals, as well as companion animals (pets). The site has information on laws, policies, and guidelines, and links to related databases and Web sites. Linked resources come from both government and nongovernment sources.
Subjects: Animals

903. BLM National Wild Horse and Burro Program
http://www.wildhorseandburro.blm.gov/
Sponsor(s): Interior Department — Bureau of Land Management (BLM)
Description: The Bureau of Land Management manages the wild horses and burros on public lands. In cases of overpopulation, BLM removes horses and burros through an adoption program. The Web site provides information on adopting the removed animals; it includes an adoption schedule and application. The site also provides statistics on the wild horse and burro population for the past 30 years.
Subjects: Wild Horses

904. Bureau of Land Management
http://www.blm.gov/nhp/
Sponsor(s): Interior Department — Bureau of Land Management (BLM)
Description: The Bureau of Land Management administers U.S. public lands, which are primarily in the Western states. The News section of the site includes a compilation of BLM regulations concerning public lands leasing, grazing, minerals management, rights-of-way, and other topics. BLM publications are listed under Information, along with an extensive list of Frequently Asked Questions. The Browse button at the top of the home page provides an alphabetical index of subjects and sites. Along with the What We Do section, Browse helps users to find the extensive information BLM maintains beyond its home page. This includes information on abandoned mines; land and mineral records databases; law enforcement on public lands; National Monuments; forests and woodlands; fire response and aviation support; geographic data; environmental education; public lands leases and permits; and land conservation.

For anyone interested in the Bureau of Land Management, public lands leasing and use, and other aspects of the BLM, this site is a rich resource.
Subjects: Public Lands
Publications: *Annual Report, Bureau of Land Management*, I 53.1:
Public Land Statistics, I 53.1/2:

905. Bureau of Reclamation
http://www.usbr.gov/
Sponsor(s): Interior Department — Bureau of Reclamation (USBR)
Description: The subtitle of this Web site is "Managing Water in the West." The bureau manages dams and reservoirs in the western states and produces hydroelectric power. The Programs and Activities section of the Web site serves as an index to many other Reclamation activities, including desalination, cultural resources management, hydroelectric research, and materials engineering and research. The site's DataWeb provides detailed information on operational or substantially completed Reclamation projects. The Water Operations section links to the Web sites for BLM regional offices representing the Great Plains, Lower Colorado, Upper Colorado, Mid-Pacific, and Pacific Northwest. Each regional site has information on its dams, reservoirs, projects, news, and publications.
Subjects: Hydroelectric Power; Water Supply
Publications: *Bureau of Reclamation Annual Report*, I 27.1:
Bureau of Reclamation FY Annual Performance Plan, I 27.1/5:

906. Dataweb: Dams, Projects and Powerplants
http://www.usbr.gov/dataweb/
Sponsor(s): Interior Department — Bureau of Reclamation (USBR)
Description: Project Dataweb is a directory of Bureau of Reclamation dams, powerplants, and other projects. It is an electronic version of information the bureau has long published as a project data book. The site provides detailed information

on each of the projects, which can be located by name or state. The site also has interactive maps for locating projects.

Project Dataweb is intended for use by reclamation professional, planners, and government and policy officials, as well as the general public.

Subjects: Dams; Hydroelectric Power; Water Supply

907. Department of the Interior
http://www.doi.gov/

Sponsor(s): Interior Department

Description: The Interior Web site serves primarily as a portal to the sites for the department's many component agencies, such as the Bureau of Indian Affairs; National Park Service; U.S. Fish and Wildlife Service; and the U.S. Geological Survey. The main page features news from these agencies and links to administration initiatives such as Healthy Forests, Water 2025, and the National Energy Plan. It also links to a directory of Interior offices and officials and to a Spanish-language version of the site. Teacher Resources and a set of links to Interior's kids' pages are also highlighted on the home page.

The site is well organized, and its multiple access points to various DOI resources make it easy to use.

Subjects: Natural Resources; Public Lands

Publications: *DOI Annual Report,* I 1.1:

908. Endangered Species
http://endangered.fws.gov/

Sponsor(s): Interior Department — Fish and Wildlife Service (FWS)

Description: This Fish and Wildlife Service site provides a broad collection of news and information on endangered species and the Endangered Species Act (ESA). The Endangered Species lists for animals and plants, as well as proposals for changes to the list, are in the Species Information section of the site. The Threatened and Endangered Species System (TESS) can be searched by state, region, and other criteria. Additional sections include Laws, Policies, and *Federal Register* Notices; ESA and What We Do; For the Media; The *Endangered Species Bulletin*; Kid's Corner; and Partners in Conservation. The ESA and What We Do section includes an overview of the project, publications, information for landowners, and information on tribal rights and international agreements.

Subjects: Endangered Species; Native Plants

Publications: *Endangered Species Bulletin,* I 49.77:
Recovery Plans, I 49.2:

909. Fish and Wildlife Service
http://www.fws.gov/

Sponsor(s): Interior Department — Fish and Wildlife Service (FWS)

Description: The Fish and Wildlife Service aims to conserve, protect, and enhance fish, wildlife, plants, and their habitats. The FWS site has current news and, under Portal Links, an alphabetical list of topical links to its Web pages. Portal topics include birds, fishing, grants, hunting, kids/educators, permits, and species. The Index link, in the list below the Portal Links, leads to another site index. This one has an alphabetical index and also groups links by resource type, such as National Programs, Recreation Sites, Maps, and Online Databases. The Library section has online FWS publications. Other sections include Duck Stamps, Law Enforcement, Policies (directives, memorandums) and Science.

The FWS site uses the FirstGov search engine, a significant improvement over its former search feature.

Subjects: Birds; Conservation (Natural Resources) — Laws; Fisheries; Natural Resources Management; Wildlife
Publications: *Fish and Wildlife News*, I 49.88:
National Survey of Fishing, Hunting, and Wildlife-Associated Recreation, I 49.98

910. Fort Collins Science Center Online
http://www.fort.usgs.gov/
Sponsor(s): Interior Department — U.S. Geological Survey (USGS)
Description: Scientists at this USGS biological science center study the ecosystems of the mountain, desert, and semi-arid western United States in support of land managers and natural resource decision makers. Programs described on the Web site include Invasive Species Science, Species and Habitats of Federal Interest, and Policy Analysis and Science Assistance. The Product Library has publications, software and data, including a national bat population database.
Subjects: Environmental Science — Policy; Wildlife — Research; West (United States)

911. Great Lakes Information Network
http://www.great-lakes.net/
Sponsor(s): Environmental Protection Agency (EPA) — Great Lakes National Program Office (GLNPO)
Description: The Great Lakes Information Network (GLIN) is a cooperative project to provide a central place for information relating to the Great Lakes region. Sponsored in part by the Environmental Protection Agency's Great Lakes National Program Office, the site includes topics such as the Economy, Environment, Great Lakes, Education, Maps and GIS, and Tourism. Numerous discussion lists on Great Lake topics are hosted on the e-mail list server. Links to related Web sites are available from the Great Lakes link.
Subjects: Lakes; Midwest (United States)

912. Minerals Management Service
http://www.mms.gov/
Sponsor(s): Interior Department — Minerals Management Service (MMS)
Description: The MMS is charged with managing the nation's natural gas, oil, and other mineral resources of the outer continental shelf. They also collect, verify, and distribute mineral revenues from federal offshore mineral leases and from leases on federal and Indian lands. The MMS site includes information on the two major programs, Offshore Minerals Management and Minerals Revenue Management. The site has mineral commodity and revenue statistics and data on the oil and gas production from the Federal Outer Continental Shelf. Other featured programs include Deepwater Environment, Royalty-in-Kind, Oil Valuation, and Gas Hydrates Research. Publications are listed under Products and Services. A topical index links to Web content under subjects such as Advisory Committees, Atlantic Outer Continental Shelf, Gulf of Mexico Outer Continental Shelf, Pacific Outer Continental Shelf, and Tribal Services.
Subjects: Minerals; Offshore Drilling; Public Lands
Publications: *Mineral Revenues: The Report on Receipts from Federal and American Indian Lands* (annual), I 72.13:
MMS Facts and Figures, I 72.2:
MMS Ocean Science, I 72.20:

913. National Fire Plan
http://www.fireplan.gov/
Sponsor(s): Agriculture Department (USDA) — Forest Service (USFS)Interior Department
Description: The National Fire Plan, developed in 2000, is a cooperative effort between the USDA Forest Service and the Interior Department to address the challenges of wildland fires. The Web site provides an overview of the plan, along with information on grants for local areas, contracting opportunities, and employment opportunities. The Resources section of the site includes National Fire Plan documents, links to related research efforts, a glossary, and links to government and nongovernment Web sites. The site has a Spanish-language version.
Subjects: Fire Prevention; Forest Fires

914. National Interagency Fire Center
http://www.nifc.gov/
Sponsor(s): Agriculture Department (USDA) — Forest Service (USFS)Interior Department
Description: The National Interagency Fire Center (NIFC) in Idaho is the national support center for wildland firefighting. In addition to the Forest Service and relevant Interior Department agencies, Fire Center participants include the National Weather Service, U.S. Fire Administration, and the nongovernmental National Association of State Foresters (NASF). The Web site features current wildland fire news, wildland fire statistics, and prevention and education information. It also links to wildland fire training programs. Information about NIFC is under the NIFC Features heading.
Subjects: Firefighting; Forest Fires

915. National Wildlife Health Center
http://www.nwhc.usgs.gov/
Sponsor(s): Interior Department — U.S. Geological Survey (USGS)
Description: The National Wildlife Health Center (NWHC) provides information, technical assistance, and research on national and international wildlife health issues. The Web site's home page features links to information on current issues, such as Avian Influenza, West Nile Virus, and Chronic Wasting Disease. The Disease Information section discusses major wildlife health concerns, with links to reports and Web resources for each. NWHC publications online include fact sheets and quarterly wildlife mortality reports.
Subjects: Wildlife — Research
Publications: *Disease Emergence and Resurgence: The Wildlife-Human Connection Field Manual of Wildlife Diseases*, I 19.210:

916. NOAA's Coral Reef Information System
http://coris.noaa.gov/
Sponsor(s): Commerce Department — National Oceanic and Atmospheric Administration (NOAA) — National Ocean Service
Description: This portal to NOAA coral reef information and data products has a variety of datasets, reference resources, and information on coral reef biology and environmental threats. A Professional Exchanges section offers access to NOAA's Coral Health and Monitoring Program (CHAMP) electronic discussion list. The Publications section in the online library has citations from papers and reports published as a result of NOAA or NOAA-sponsored coral reef activities.

Subjects: Coral Reefs
Publications: *The State of Coral Reef Ecosystems of the United States and Pacific Freely Associated States*

917. Northern Prairie Wildlife Research Center
http://www.npwrc.usgs.gov/
Sponsor(s): Interior Department — U.S. Geological Survey (USGS)
Description: Part of the USGS Biological Research Division, staff at the Northern Prairie Wildlife Research Center study the species and ecosystems of the Great Plains region. In the Biological Resources section of this site, resources are organized by geography, type (e.g., checklists, identification tools, distribution maps) and taxonomy (e.g., waterfowl, mammals, fish). The site's Publication Database includes abstracts of articles authored at the center from 1965 to present. Some more recent articles are available online in HTML format.

The popular Butterflies of North America feature, previously on this Web site, moved in 2006 to the nongovernmental Big Sky Institute at Montana State University site at ⟨http://www.butterfliesandmoths.org/⟩.
Subjects: Conservation (Natural Resources) — Research; Wildlife — Research; Butterflies

918. NWISWeb Water Data for the Nation
http://waterdata.usgs.gov/nwis/
Sponsor(s): Interior Department — U.S. Geological Survey (USGS)
Description: NWISWeb has current and historic data on the quantity, quality, distribution, and movement of surface and underground waters in the U.S. Use the drop-down menu to view information for a particular state.
Subjects: Water Supply

919. Office of Surface Mining
http://www.osmre.gov/
Sponsor(s): Interior Department — Surface Mining Office
Description: OSM has the responsibility of reclaiming abandoned mines and protecting the environment and people during coal mining and reclamation. The Programs section features Regulation of Active Mines; Abandoned Mine Reclamation; and Research and Technology (including technology transfer). The Reference Center offers statistics, forms, surface mining laws and regulations, and OSM publications. Key Topics highlighted include classroom resources, acid mine drainage, and mountaintop mining. The site offers a number of routes to finding information, such as information organized by state, top 20 Web pages viewed (including the popular "Keep Out: Old Mines are Dangerous" posters and public service announcements), and an A-Z index.

The Office of Surface Mining offers a great deal of legislative and regulatory information for the regulated entities and concerned citizens, as well as news and educational information for those living in areas near active or abandoned mines. It is well organized and focused on the needs of the user.
Subjects: Coal; Mining Reclamation
Publications: *Office of Surface Mining Annual Report*, I 71.1:

920. Office of Water, EPA
http://www.epa.gov/OW/
Sponsor(s): Environmental Protection Agency (EPA) — Water Office
Description: As the primary EPA agency overseeing regulatory issues relating to clean water, the Office of Water's Web site features a variety of resources related to drinking water, water pollution, watersheds, and wastewater management.

Major sections — listed toward the bottom of the home page — are: Ground Water and Drinking Water; Water Science (including beach water quality and fish consumption advisories); Wastewater Management; Wetlands, Oceans, and Watersheds; and the American Indian Environmental Office. The site also includes sections for Laws and Regulations; Funding and Grants; Publications; Databases and Software; and Education Resources.
Subjects: Drinking Water; Water Pollution

921. Patuxent Wildlife Research Center
http://www.pwrc.usgs.gov/
Sponsor(s): Interior Department — U.S. Geological Survey (USGS)
Description: PWRC, located in Maryland, is one of 17 research centers of the U.S. Geological Survey. The center focuses on coastal and wetlands ecology and on migratory birds and waterfowl. The center operates national wildlife inventory and monitoring programs and is responsible for the North American Bird Banding Program. The Web site addresses these topics and includes sections on research and education, and a photo gallery of birds, animals, and habitats.

This site will be useful for anyone getting involved with an inventory and monitoring program as well as for those interested in some of these species for which monitoring programs are available.
Subjects: Wildlife

922. USGS Ground Water Information Pages
http://water.usgs.gov/ogw/
Sponsor(s): Interior Department — U.S. Geological Survey (USGS)
Description: This USGS site consolidates information on the ground water resources of the United States and ground water activities of the USGS. It includes sections on Ground Water Data, Publications, the Ground Water Resources Program, Field Techniques and Ground Water Models, and Water Resources Information by State. Among the publications is an online version of the *Ground Water Atlas of the United States*.
Subjects: Ground Water; Water Supply
Publications: *Advisory Committee on Water Information (ACWI) Summary of Meetings*, I 19.74:
Ground Water Atlas of the United States, I 19.89:

923. USGS Mineral Resources Program
http://minerals.usgs.gov/
Sponsor(s): Interior Department — U.S. Geological Survey (USGS)
Description: This USGS site offers access to minerals information formerly supplied by the now-defunct Bureau of Mines. The site features statistics and information on the worldwide occurrence, quantity, quality, and availability of mineral resources and offers online access to numerous publications such as the *Mineral Industry Surveys* and the *Minerals Yearbook*. The site also has information on grant recipients; the Mineral Resources Program (MRP) introduced an External Research Program in 2004. Other site sections include MRP Spatial Data, News, Programs, and Featured Activities.

This is a very useful site for tracking down statistical information on minerals as commodities.
Subjects: Minerals
Publications: *Fact Sheets*, I 19.127:
Metal Industry Indicators, I 19.129:
Mineral Commodity Summaries (annual), I 19.166:
Mineral Industry Surveys (annual), I 19.161:
Mineral Industry Surveys (quarterly), I 19.160:

Mineral Industry Surveys, Mineral Industry of (Country) Minerals (annual), I 19.163:

Mineral Industry Surveys, Mineral Industry of (State) Minerals (annual), I 19.162:

Minerals Yearbook, I 19.165:

924. Water Resources of the United States

http://water.usgs.gov/

Sponsor(s): Interior Department — U.S. Geological Survey (USGS)

Description: As one of the major subject-oriented USGS Web sites, Water Resources of the United States covers USGS materials related to water use, surface water, ground water, and water quality. It links to the Web sites for USGS water resources programs. The primary divisions of this site include Data, Maps, Software, Publications, and Glossaries. A WaterWatch feature links to current U.S. maps illustrating conditions for floods; drought; daily streamflow; monthly streamflow; and ground water. Information is organized by locale in the site's Water Information by State and Science In Your Watershed features.

Subjects: Water

Pollutants and Waste

925. Agency for Toxic Substances and Disease Registry

http://www.atsdr.cdc.gov/

Sponsor(s): Health and Human Services Department — Centers for Disease Control and Prevention (CDC)

Description: ATSDR's public health mission is to prevent harmful exposures and disease related to toxic substances. The site features ToxFAQs™, a series of summaries about hazardous substances. The Data Resources section includes: the HazDat database, maps of hazardous waste sites, Hazardous Substances Emergency Events Surveillance (HSEES), and the National Exposure Registry (NER). It also links to New York City's World Trade Center Health Registry. The Toxic Substances section includes a list of the top 20 hazardous substances on the ATSDR/EPA Priority List, toxicological profiles, and detailed substance data. Other sections of the site focus on emergency response and environmental health education and training. The Publications section includes "A Citizen's Guide to Risk Assessments and Public Health Assessments."

This is an excellent site for finding toxicological data and information on hazardous substances.

Subjects: Public Health; Toxic Substances

Publications: *Toxicological Profiles (Drafts, Updates and Finals),* HE 20.518:

926. AIRData

http://www.epa.gov/air/data/

Sponsor(s): Environmental Protection Agency (EPA) — Air and Radiation Office

Description: AIRData has annual summaries of U.S. air pollution data, taken from EPA's air pollution databases. The data identify emissions and pollutant levels, and include all 50 states plus the District of Columbia, Puerto Rico, and the U.S. Virgin Islands. Users of AIRData can create their own reports and maps based on the air pollution data.

Subjects: Air Pollution; Databases

927. Chemical Safety and Hazard Investigation Board
http://www.chemsafety.gov/
Sponsor(s): Chemical Safety And Hazard Investigation Board
Description: Chemical Safety and Hazard Investigation Board (CSB) is an independent, scientific investigatory board that works to determine the causes of chemical accidents. CSB also investigates chemical hazards. The CSB Web site features current news and reports of current investigations. It also has reports of completed investigations and recommendations.
Subjects: Chemical Industry; Industrial Accidents
Publications: *Investigations and News,* Y 3.C 42/2:16

928. Chemicals in the Environment: OPPT Chemical Fact Sheets
http://www.epa.gov/opptintr/chemfact/
Sponsor(s): Environmental Protection Agency (EPA) — Prevention, Pesticides and Toxic Substances Office
Description: This site offers *Fact Sheets* and *Chemical Summaries* for selected chemicals. The *Fact Sheets* cover the chemical's identity, production and use, environmental fate, and health and environmental effects. They also include a list of laws under which the chemical is regulated, phone numbers, and the names of EPA offices and other agencies one can call or contact for more information. The *Chemical Summaries* are technical support documents that provide detailed technical information on the chemical named in the fact sheet. The older files are in ASCII; the newer files in PDF.
Subjects: Chemical Information; Toxic Substances

929. Department of Energy Hanford Site
http://www.hanford.gov/
Sponsor(s): Energy Department — River Protection Office
Description: Hanford, formerly a plutonium production complex, is now one of the world's largest environmental cleanup projects. The project is being managed by the DOE as it explores ways of handling Hanford's tank waste retrieval, treatment, and disposal, and restoring the Columbia River Corridor where the plant is located. The Web site includes the plant history, resources for reporters, a list of contractors, a calendar of public meetings, a directory of Hanford Public Information Repositories, and advisory committee information.
Subjects: Environmental Cleanup; Nuclear Waste

930. Enviroene — Common Sense Solutions to Environmental Problems
http://es.epa.gov/
Sponsor(s): Environmental Protection Agency (EPA)
Description: Enviroene provides a single repository for pollution prevention, compliance assurance, and enforcement information and databases. It compiles a number of resources on pollution prevention projects and research. The site sections feature Enviroene Cooperatives (federal, state, and international); Solvent Substitution Data Systems; Contacts, Resources, and Vendors; and Compliance and Enforcement.

At the time it was examined for this book, the EPA had posted a notice that they are in the process of updating the structure of Enviroene.
Subjects: Environmental Law; Pollutants — Regulations

931. Envirofacts Data Warehouse
http://www.epa.gov/enviro/
Sponsor(s): Environmental Protection Agency (EPA)
Description: Envirofacts provides various levels of access to major environmental databases from the EPA. Databases include Toxics Release Inventory (TRI), Safe Drinking Water Information System, Permit Compliance System, Brownfields Management System, Compensation and Liability Information System (CERCLIS), and many others. Researchers can choose individual databases or choose the integrated Envirofacts Multisystem Query.

A Quick Start feature allows users to search by ZIP code or city and state. The resulting profile identifies local data on air, toxics, waste, and water. An interactive map marks such features as Superfund sites, hazardous waste handling facilities, toxic releases, and discharges to water. The Topics option provides the same search capability but for a particular type of data, such as toxics or radiation. More advanced capabilities can be found in the Queries, Maps, and Reports sections.
Subjects: Pollutants; Databases

932. EPA Air and Radiation
http://www.epa.gov/oar/
Sponsor(s): Environmental Protection Agency (EPA) — Air and Radiation Office
Description: The Office of Air and Radiation provides information in the following sections: Indoor Air, Transportation/Fuels, Nonroad Equipment, Acid Rain, Ozone Depletion, Visibility, Toxic Air Pollutants, Climate Change, and Radiation. In addition to detailed information on the above topics, this site offers sections on What You Can Do; Where You Live; Grants and Funding; Publications; and Tools and Technical Info. Publications include *Air Quality Trends Reports, Emissions Trends Report,* numerous brochures and pamphlets, and a "Plain English Guide to the Clean Air Act." The site is also available in Spanish.

This site is an excellent entry point for access to the EPA's technical and educational resources on air quality, air pollution, and the Clean Air Act.
Subjects: Air Pollution; Air Quality; Radiation
Publications: *Air Quality Trends Report,* EP 4.64:
National Air Pollutant Emissions Trends Report, EP 4.24:

933. Federal Remediation Technologies Roundtable
http://www.frtr.gov/
Sponsor(s): Federal Remediation Technologies Roundtable
Description: The Federal Remediation Technologies Roundtable is an interagency working group supporting collaboration among the federal agencies involved in hazardous waste site remediation. The Web site features a section on Remediation System Optimization, and a variety of tools, information, and case studies to help with selecting the best technology for remediation tasks. FRTR meeting information and publications are also online.
Subjects: Environmental Cleanup
Publications: *Abstracts of Remediation Case Studies,* EP 1.2:AB 8

934. Green Vehicle Guide
http://www.epa.gov/greenvehicles/
Sponsor(s): Environmental Protection Agency (EPA) — Air and Radiation Office
Description: This online guide uses emissions and fuel economy scores to rank the environmental performance of recent car models. Users can look up the score for a specific model and make of automobile or browse by type of vehicle, such as pickup or minivan. The site includes explanations of the rankings and informa-

tion on auto emissions. A related links section points to EPA and other agency sites with more information on automobile performance and air quality.
Subjects: Motor Vehicles

935. Hazardous Technical Information Services
http://www.dscr.dla.mil/htis/htis.htm
Sponsor(s): Defense Department — Defense Logistics Agency (DLA)
Description: This site serves the DoD community with information on the compliant management of hazardous materials and wastes. Several HTIS publications are available in full text, including the *HTIS Bulletin* and the *Storage and Handling of Hazardous Materials*, and there is a long list of links to DoD and other Web sites relating to hazardous materials.
Subjects: Hazardous Waste
Publications: *HTIS (Hazardous Technical Information Services) Bulletin*, D 7.2/3: *Storage and Handling of Hazardous Materials*, D 7.6/4:

936. Hazardous Waste Clean-Up Information (CLU-IN)
http://clu-in.org/
Sponsor(s): Environmental Protection Agency (EPA)
Description: The Hazardous Waste Clean-up Information Web site provides information about innovative treatment technologies to the hazardous waste remediation community. The site has databases on Remediation and Characterization and Monitoring, as well as technology descriptions and selection tools in these areas. Users with a professional interest in environmental technology can subscribe to e-mail delivery of several newsletters including *Technology News and Trends* or receive an RSS feed of CLU-IN news.
Subjects: Environmental Cleanup
Publications: *Technology News and Trends*, EP 1.10/3:

937. Mercury
http://www.epa.gov/mercury/
Sponsor(s): Environmental Protection Agency (EPA)
Description: This is an EPA portal Web site for information about mercury and its effects on people and the environment. Topics include power plant emissions, mercury in fish and shellfish, mercury in consumer products, handling mercury spills, proper disposal of mercury, relevant laws and regulations, and international actions for reducing mercury emissions and use. The site has special sections for parents, schools, health care providers, industry, and Spanish-speakers.
Subjects: Pollutants

938. National Center for Environmental Health
http://www.cdc.gov/nceh/
Sponsor(s): Health and Human Services Department — Centers for Disease Control and Prevention (CDC) — National Center for Environmental Health (NCEH)
Description: NCEH promotes research, surveillance, guidance, and communication to improve public environmental health. The Programs and About NCEH sections of the Web site provide further information on their activities. Quick Links cover asthma, lead poisoning, cruise vessel sanitation, and other frequently requested topics. The Emergency Response section discusses emergency preparedness and chemical and radiological exposure emergency response. The Publications section includes lists of publications by NCEH authors, full-text fact sheets and brochures, books, and SABER: Statistical Analysis Battery for Epidemiological Research. The site also links to the third *National Report on Human Exposure to Environmental*

Chemicals, released in 2005. The NCEH site is available in a Spanish-language version.
Subjects: Environmental Health
Publications: *Brochures (National Center for Environmental Health)*, HE 20.7513:
National Report on Human Exposure to Environmental Chemicals, HE 20.7515:

939. Nuclear Waste Technical Review Board
http://www.nwtrb.gov/
Sponsor(s): Nuclear Waste Technical Review Board (NWTRB)
Description: The NWTRB is an independent agency of the U.S. government that provides scientific and technical oversight of the U.S. program for management and disposal of high-level radioactive waste and spent nuclear fuel from civilian nuclear power plants. Its site features Board Mission, Board Members, Reports, Correspondence, Testimony, Plans, Press Releases, and Calendar sections. Much of the content concerns the project to develop a permanent repository for spent nuclear fuel at Yucca Mountain, Nevada.
Subjects: Nuclear Waste

940. Office of Civilian Radioactive Waste Management
http://www.ocrwm.doe.gov/
Sponsor(s): Energy Department — Civilian Radioactive Waste Management Office
Description: The Office of Civilian Radioactive Waste Management is charged with building a system for spent nuclear fuel and high-level radioactive waste disposal. The Web site has sections on Yucca Mountain Project, Transporting Nuclear Waste, Receiving Nuclear Waste, and Advanced Science Studies. Each section includes news and documents. The Information Library has technical documents, fact sheets, videos, photos, maps, press releases and event calendars.
Subjects: Nuclear Waste; Yucca Mountain Project

941. Office of Emergency Management
http://www.epa.gov/swercepp/
Sponsor(s): Environmental Protection Agency (EPA)
Description: The Office of Emergency Management (OEM) was created in 2004. It combines the functions of the Chemical Emergency Preparedness and Prevention Office and the Oil Program Center's Emergency Response and Removal Center. The Web site links to the sites for these two programs and for the Emergency Response Center. The site also has information on laws, regulations, policy, and guidance related to environmental emergencies.
Subjects: Disaster Preparedness; Oil Spills; Environmental Health

942. Office of Environmental Management, Department of Energy
http://www.em.doe.gov/
Sponsor(s): Energy Department
Description: This office manages the cleanup of radioactive, chemical, and other hazardous waste left after years of nuclear weapons production. The Web site's home page has a clickable map of the United States linking to information about each of the office's many remediation sites. The site also links to the budget information, congressional testimony, and publications. A Laws and Regulations section links to relevant legislation, compliance agreements, guidance documents, and regulations. The Public Participation and Interested Audiences sections provide policy and outreach information for groups such as the general public, tribal nations, and state and local governments.
Subjects: Environmental Cleanup; Nuclear Waste
Publications: *Nuclear Age Timeline*, E 1.2:

943. Office of Pollution Prevention and Toxics, EPA
http://www.epa.gov/opptintr/
Sponsor(s): Environmental Protection Agency (EPA) — Prevention, Pesticides and Toxic Substances Office
Description: OPPT has primary responsibility for administering the Toxic Substances Control Act. The Projects and Programs section of the site links to information on OPPT's work in asbestos control, environmental labeling, nanoscale materials, assessment of new chemicals in the marketplace, regulation of Polychlorinated Biphenyls (PCBs), High Production Volume (HPV) chemicals, and many other areas. The Concerned Citizens section presents consumer information on such topics as lead-based paint and consumer product labeling. The Information Sources section links to resources such as hotlines and clearinghouses. The Databases and Software page links to numerous electronic resources.
Subjects: Toxic Substances

944. Office of Prevention, Pesticides, and Toxic Substances, EPA
http://www.epa.gov/opptsmnt/
Sponsor(s): Environmental Protection Agency (EPA) — Prevention, Pesticides and Toxic Substances Office
Description: The EPA Office of Prevention, Pesticides, and Toxic Substances (OPPTS) is involved in protecting public health and the environment from potential risk from toxic chemicals. The office promotes pollution prevention and the public's right to know about chemical risks and evaluates pesticides and chemicals to safeguard children and other vulnerable members of the population, as well as threatened species and ecosystems. Sections on Pollution Prevention, Pesticides, and Chemicals have information for individuals as well as for research centers and regulated entities. The QuickFinder guide links to coverage of asbestos, endocrine disruptors, green chemistry, mercury, tribal programs, and many other topics. The Information Sources section includes information about relevant EPA dockets, hotlines, clearinghouses, and publications. A version of the site is available in Spanish.
Subjects: Pesticides; Toxic Substances
Publications: *Pesticide Industry Sales and Usage*, EP 5.29:
Pesticide Reregistration Eligibility Decisions, EP 5.27:

945. Office of Solid Waste and Emergency Response, EPA
http://www.epa.gov/swerrims/
Sponsor(s): Environmental Protection Agency (EPA) — Solid Waste and Emergency Response Office
Description: OSWER provides policy, guidance, and direction for the EPA solid waste and emergency response programs. The site covers such topics as Superfund and federal facility cleanups, brownfields, landfills, oil and hazardous substance spills, underground storage tanks, safe waste management, and environmental emergencies. The Laws and Regulations section has the text of documents organized by topic. Other topics and programs, linked on the bottom half of the home page, include environmental justice, tribal program, and international activities. Publications are available throughout the site.
Subjects: Environmental Cleanup; Hazardous Waste
Publications: *Catalog of Hazardous And Solid Waste Publications*, EP 1.2:H 33/30
Municipal Solid Waste in the United States, EP 1.17:
National Biennial RCRA Hazardous Waste Report, EP 10.16/7:
Tribal Waste Journal, EP 1.17:530-N/
WasteWise Annual Report, EP 1.1/10:

946. RadTown USA
http://www.epa.gov/radtown/
Sponsor(s): Environmental Protection Agency (EPA)
Description: RadTown USA provides educational information about radiation. It uses an interactive graphic of a town to show everyday sources of radiation. Sections of Radtown discuss personal exposure, use of radioactive materials, radiation-treated materials, radioactive waste, natural radiation, and security applications of radiation.
Subjects: Radiation

947. Savannah River Site
http://www.srs.gov/
Sponsor(s): Energy Department
Description: A former production site for weapons-grade nuclear materials, the Savannah River Site (SRS) is now focused on management of the nuclear stockpile and nuclear materials, and on related environmental issues. The Web site features information under the sections About SRS, Business Opportunities, Outreach, Publications, and Programs.
Subjects: Nuclear Weapons
Publications: *Savannah River Site Environmental Report*, E 1.2:SA 9/3/

948. Superfund Program
http://www.epa.gov/superfund/
Sponsor(s): Environmental Protection Agency (EPA) — Solid Waste and Emergency Response Office
Description: This EPA portal for the Superfund environmental cleanup program covers information about the program, the individual Superfund sites, law and policy documents, community involvement, conferences, regional contacts, databases, and even a Superfund for Kids page. It also links to EnviroMapper for Superfund, a tool that combines interactive maps and aerial photography. The Web site has a version in Spanish.
Subjects: Environmental Cleanup
Publications: *National Priorities List (Superfund)*, EP 1.107/3:

949. Tox Town
http://toxtown.nlm.nih.gov/
Sponsor(s): National Institutes of Health (NIH) — National Library of Medicine (NLM)
Description: Tox Town is an educational site about toxic chemicals, designed for a general audience. The site uses a graphical image of a town and a city to serve as an interface to toxics information from such agencies as the National Institutes of Health and the Environmental Protection Agency. It has similar modules for a farm and for the U.S.-Mexico border. Modified versions of the content are provided in Spanish and in a text-only version. Tox Town also has teacher materials and an alphabetical index to information on the site.
Subjects: Toxic Substances

950. ToxFAQs
http://www.atsdr.cdc.gov/toxfaq.html
Sponsor(s): Health and Human Services Department — Toxic Substances and Disease Registry Agency
Description: ToxFAQs offers fact sheets on hazardous substances and the effects of exposure on human health. There are also links to resources from ATSDR, such as minimal risk levels for hazardous substances and Medical Management Guide-

lines for Acute Chemical Exposures. Much of the core material at the ToxFAQs site is also available in Spanish.
Subjects: Hazardous Waste; Toxic Substances

951. Toxics Release Inventory
http://www.epa.gov/tri/
Sponsor(s): Environmental Protection Agency (EPA)
Description: The Toxics Release Inventory (TRI) is a source of information regarding toxic chemicals that are being used, manufactured, treated, transported, or released into the environment. It contains information concerning waste management activities and the release of toxic chemicals by facilities that manufacture, process, or otherwise use such substances. The home page provides a quick ZIP code search option for TRI data and a link to the TRI Explorer for additional search options. The site also provides information on state and international TRI programs.
Subjects: Toxic Substances; Databases
Publications: *Toxic Release Inventory*, EP 5.22

952. ToxSeek
http://toxseek.nlm.nih.gov/
Sponsor(s): National Institutes of Health (NIH) — National Library of Medicine (NLM)
Description: ToxSeek is a search engine from the National Library of Medicine (NLM). It enables simultaneous searching of environment health information from NLM, the National Institutes of Health, government agencies, and international organizations. Individual and multiple databases can be selected for a search.
ToxSeek is a powerful, fast, and flexible search engine. It also offers search results that can be sorted, selected, and saved in various formats.
Subjects: Toxic Substances; Environmental Health

953. TribalAIR
http://www.epa.gov/oar/tribal/
Sponsor(s): Environmental Protection Agency (EPA) — Air and Radiation Office
Description: This site from the EPA's Office of Air and Radiation provides information about air quality programs in Indian Country. It includes regional contacts, the Tribal Authority Rule concerning the Clean Air Act, and success stories from tribal environmental professionals. *Tribal Air News* is also available in full text.
Subjects: Air Quality; American Indians
Publications: *Tribal Air News*, EP 4.67:

954. TTNWeb Technology Transfer Network
http://www.epa.gov/ttn/
Sponsor(s): Environmental Protection Agency (EPA) — Air and Radiation Office
Description: TTNWeb provides centralized access to the technical information available on the Web from the EPA's Office of Air Quality Planning and Standards. These Web resources concern air pollution science, technology, regulation, measurement, and prevention. Sample resources include the Emissions Test Methods, the Air Quality System, and the National Ambient Air Quality Standards.
Subjects: Air Quality; Databases

Weather

955. AIRNow
http://airnow.gov/
Sponsor(s): Environmental Protection Agency (EPA)
Description: AIRNow offers daily Air Quality Index (AQI) forecasts and real-time AQI conditions for over 300 cities across the United States. AIRNow is an inter-agency Web site sponsored by the Environmental Protection Agency (EPA), the National Oceanic and Atmospheric Administration (NOAA), and the National Park Service (NPS), along with partner agencies in tribal, state, and local governments. Detailed local observations and forecasts on the site come from the partner agencies. The site also has information for health professionals, teachers, and kids.
Subjects: Air Quality

956. Aviation Weather Center
http://aviationweather.gov/
Sponsor(s): Commerce Department — National Oceanic and Atmospheric Administration (NOAA) — National Weather Service
Description: The Aviation Weather Center has forecasts, advisories, and observations for pilots. Observations include Pilot Reports (PIREPs), Meteorological Aviation Reports (METARs), and radar and satellite imagery. An Aviation Links section includes other aviation weather sites and Volcanic Ash Advisory Centers.
Subjects: Aviation; Weather Forecasts

957. Climate Analysis Branch
http://www.cdc.noaa.gov/
Sponsor(s): Commerce Department — National Oceanic and Atmospheric Administration (NOAA)
Description: The Climate Analysis Branch (CAB), within NOAA's Earth System Research Laboratory, studies the causes of observed climate variations in order to improve climate models and forecasts. Major sections of the Climate Analysis Branch site include Climate and Weather, Research, and Data Access and Plotting. The Climate and Weather section has a Map Room and U.S. forecasts. The Research section includes citations and some full-text links to journal articles by the scientists. Data sets, online data analysis and visualization, climate research data access are available under Data Access and Plotting. The site also covers selected topics such as El Niño, Western Water Assessment, and U.S. precipitation anomalies. The CAB was formerly known as the Climate Diagnostics Center.
Subjects: Climate Research

958. Climate Prediction Center
http://www.cpc.ncep.noaa.gov/
Sponsor(s): Commerce Department — National Oceanic and Atmospheric Administration (NOAA) — National Weather Service
Description: The Climate Prediction Center maintains a continuous watch on short-term climate fluctuations and attempts to diagnose and predict them. This Web site provides climatological information, with highlights on U.S. Hazards Assessment; Drought Assessment; and ENSO (El Nino/Southern Oscillation) Diagnostic Discussion. Main sections of the site include an Index of Expert Assessments, an Index of Outlooks (Forecasts), an Index of Monitoring and Data; Crosscutting Themes; and information about the center. The site includes a climate glossary.

Subjects: Climatology; El Nino; Weather Forecasts
Publications: *Climate Diagnostics Bulletin* (monthly), C 55.194:
Proceedings of the Climate Diagnostics and Prediction Workshop, C 55.2:C 61/3/

959. Global Systems Division
http://www.fsl.noaa.gov/
Sponsor(s): Commerce Department — National Oceanic and Atmospheric Administration (NOAA)
Description: Global Systems Division, previously the Forecast Systems Laboratory, conducts research to develop global environmental information and forecast technology products. Clients for the technologies include the National Weather Service, other government agencies, and the commercial and general aviation communities. The Web site describes the Global Systems Division's projects and products.
Subjects: Meteorology — Research
Publications: *FSL In Review*, C 55.602:F 76/

960. Heat Island Effect
http://www.epa.gov/heatislands/
Sponsor(s): Environmental Protection Agency (EPA)
Description: The term "heat island" describes the phenomenon of urban and suburban temperatures that are two to ten degrees Fahrenheit hotter than nearby rural areas. The Web site provides information on the effect, research results, and energy use and health impacts. It also features a section on ameliorative measures, such as installing green roofs and planting trees.
Subjects: Climate Research

961. National Climatic Data Center
http://lwf.ncdc.noaa.gov/oa/ncdc.html
Sponsor(s): Commerce Department — National Oceanic and Atmospheric Administration (NOAA) — National Environmental Satellite, Data, and Information Service (NESDIS)
Description: As the world's largest active archive of weather data, NCDC produces numerous climate publications and datasets and makes a wide variety of information available on this site. Users may search for weather station data for a particular location. Information about climate is available in four categories: research, monitoring, extremes, and global hazards. Information is also grouped in the categories of Land Based, Upper Air, Satellite, Marine, Paleoclimatology, and Weather/Climate Events.

NCDC presents various different catalogs and subsets of its products via links or online purchase. Some of the online data and publications require a paid subscription, with exemptions for education, military, and government use.

NCDC provides an enormous amount of information and data. The Web site manages to make it accessible by offering multiple well-designed approaches to the content.
Subjects: Climatology; Data Products; Weather
Publications: *Climatological Data (various states)*, C 55.214/51:
Hourly Precipitation Data: Various States and Countries, C 55.216/45:
Local Climatological Data: Various States, C 55.286/6-54:
Monthly Climatic Data for the World, C 55.211:
Monthly State, Regional, and National Cooling Degree Days, Weighted by Population, C 55.287/60-3:
Monthly State, Regional, and National Heating Degree Days, Weighted by Population, C 55.287/60-2:
Storm Data (monthly), C 55.212:

962. National Data Buoy Center

http://seaboard.ndbc.noaa.gov/

Sponsor(s): Commerce Department — National Oceanic and Atmospheric Administration (NOAA) — National Weather Service

Description: The National Data Buoy Center site provides buoy-measured environmental data and an overview of the NDBC. Current (Real-Time) Meteorological and Oceanographic Data are available for locations along the coasts of North America, Hawaii, the Caribbean, Brazil, Chile, Congo, France, Great Britain, and the Western Pacific. Historical data are also available, grouped by station ID. Other sections of the site include Station Status and Ship Observations, and information on the Dial-a-Buoy program that provides station information over the telephone.

Subjects: Oceans; Weather Forecasts

963. National Hurricane Center — Tropical Prediction Center

http://www.nhc.noaa.gov/

Sponsor(s): Commerce Department — National Oceanic and Atmospheric Administration (NOAA) — National Weather Service

Description: The Tropical Predication Center Web site features data, graphs, and other information on tropical cyclones and hurricanes. Menu items on the home page include Get Storm Info, Tropical Analysis and Forecasting, Hurricane Awareness (preparedness information and extensive educational background), and Hurricane History. The latest forecasts are featured prominently. The site offers advisories that can be delivered via e-mail, RSS feed, or to mobile devices.

This is the key government site to consult during hurricane season.

Subjects: Hurricanes

964. National Severe Storms Laboratory

http://www.nssl.noaa.gov/

Sponsor(s): Commerce Department — National Oceanic and Atmospheric Administration (NOAA) — Office of Oceanic and Atmospheric Research

Description: The National Severe Storms Laboratory site describes research and development work concerning forecasting, radar, and warnings. The Web site features sections on tornadoes, thunderstorms, damaging winds, lightning, hail, winter weather, and flooding. The Scientific Publications section lists papers, books, and articles by lab personnel along with historical data on deaths, injuries, and damage due to lightning. A section on severe thunderstorms catalogs such events from January 2000 to the present. The Education section includes resources for students and teachers.

Subjects: Tornadoes; Weather — Research

965. National Weather Service

http://www.weather.gov/

Alternate URL(s): http://www.nws.noaa.gov/

Sponsor(s): Commerce Department — National Oceanic and Atmospheric Administration (NOAA) — National Weather Service

Description: The National Weather Service (NWS) collects weather data and provides forecasts for the United States and surrounding waters. The NWS home page features a color-coded map of current weather warnings and advisories in the United States. A city name search box gives quick access to local short-and long-term weather forecasts, current conditions, and radar and satellite images. The Forecasts section links to the forecasts available on NOAA Web sites, including drought, fire, marine, aviation, and river flows. The Weather Safety section takes a similar approach, linking to information on NOAA Weather Radio and to safety information related to storms, heat, lightning, hurricanes, tornadoes, rip currents, and floods. Publications designed for the general public are available online in HTML and PDF formats. The Information Center links to NOAA Web pages on popular weather topics, such as damage/fatality/injury statistics, commercial weather companies, and proper siting for weather instruments.

The Organization section on the top menu bar has links to the Web sites for the many NWS regional offices and centers, each of which provides a wealth of local U.S. data.

While the NWS data repository is vast, their Web site makes the most popular data easily accessible.

Subjects: Meteorology; Weather Forecasts

966. National Weather Service Marine Forecasts
http://www.nws.noaa.gov/om/marine/home.htm
Sponsor(s): Commerce Department — National Oceanic and Atmospheric Administration (NOAA) — National Weather Service
Description: This gateway site links to marine weather forecast information. Shortcuts are provided to marine forecasts in text or graphic formats. Other links are grouped by dissemination method, such as Internet, radio, and phone recordings. Links to publications, contact information, and product release schedules are also listed. For each dissemination type, the site provides a description of the service and links to related sites. Preparedness information on such topics as rip currents and thunderstorms is also provided.
Subjects: Maritime Transportation; Weather Forecasts

967. NOAA Tides and Currents
http://tidesandcurrents.noaa.gov/
Sponsor(s): Commerce Department — National Oceanic and Atmospheric Administration (NOAA) — National Ocean Service
Description: Tides and Currents is the Web site for the Center for Oceanographic Products and Services (CO-OPS). The center collects, analyzes, and distributes historical and real-time observations and predictions of water levels, coastal currents, and other meteorological and oceanographic data. The Web site features a zoomable data retrieval map and station list for finding all CO-OPS information by locale. CO-OPS programs include the Physical Oceanographic Real-Time System (PORTS®) that integrates observed and predicted data for mariners. CO-OPS also manages the National Water Level Program (NWLP) and National Water Level Observation Network (NWLON); tide data and predictions are available on the site.
Subjects: Oceanography

968. NOAA Weather Radio
http://www.nws.noaa.gov/nwr/
Sponsor(s): Commerce Department — National Oceanic and Atmospheric Administration (NOAA) — National Weather Service
Description: NOAA Weather Radio (NWR) is a nationwide network of radio stations broadcasting continuous weather information that can be picked up by special radio receivers. This site has station listings, coverage maps, and consumer information on radio receivers. Other sections explain NWR's role as an "all-hazards" radio network, broadcasting non-weather emergency information when requested by state or local state officials.
Subjects: Disasters and Emergencies; Weather

969. nowCOAST

http://www.nowcoast.noaa.gov/

Sponsor(s): Commerce Department — National Oceanic and Atmospheric Administration (NOAA) — National Ocean Service

Description: The NOAA nowCOAST application provides mapping of real-time coastal observation and forecast data for the continental United States. To map data, users choose from coastal locations, data (current observations, such as water quality, or forecasts of conditions), and variables related to the selected data.

Subjects: Geographic Information Systems (GIS); Meteorology

970. Storm Prediction Center

http://www.spc.noaa.gov/

Sponsor(s): Commerce Department — National Oceanic and Atmospheric Administration (NOAA) — National Weather Service

Description: Storm Prediction Center provides forecasts for severe thunderstorms and tornadoes over the contiguous United States. The SPC also monitors heavy rain, heavy snow, and fire weather events across the United States. Their Web site reports on and maps current storm, tornado, fire, and convective watches. The Education and Outreach section features extensive information about tornadoes. SPC research publications on the site include conference papers and journal articles. The Organization section on the top menu bar links to regional centers with more detailed local information. SPC also provides RSS feeds for tornado and severe thunderstorm watches, fire weather outlooks, and other topics.

Subjects: Tornadoes; Weather Forecasts

971. Tides Online

http://tidesonline.nos.noaa.gov/

Sponsor(s): Commerce Department — National Oceanic and Atmospheric Administration (NOAA) — National Ocean Service

Description: The Tides Online page provides users with near real-time information from water-level stations located along the projected path of severe storms such as hurricanes. Access to the information is available by selecting the Storm Surge Mode data option. The State Maps and Regional List data options provide this information from any active station, not just those in the path of a storm.

Subjects: Hurricanes; Tides

972. Tsunami

http://www.tsunami.noaa.gov/

Sponsor(s): Commerce Department — National Oceanic and Atmospheric Administration (NOAA)

Description: The NOAA Tsunami Web site is largely concerned with the agency's responsibility for the nation's Tsunami Warning System. It also provides detailed background information about how tsunamis occur and about NOAA's role in forecasting tsunamis. The site includes sections on current tsunami observations and data, tsunami preparedness and response, and public education.

Subjects: Oceans

CHAPTER 12

Government and Politics

This chapter covers some of the federal government's most familiar roles, such as tax collector, mail carrier, employer, purchaser, and provider of emergency relief.

Subsections in this chapter are Democracy, Government Administration, Government Business, Government Employees, Government Finance, Government Services, Intergovernmental Relations, and Public Policy.

Democracy

973. Campaign Finance Reports and Data
http://www.fec.gov/disclosure.shtml
Sponsor(s): Federal Election Commission (FEC)
Description: FEC's campaign finance retrieval system includes financial data for candidates, campaign committees, and political action committees (PACs). Data can be viewed online or downloaded. Images of the actual campaign finance disclosure filings are also online. The site provides data on "electioneering communications," a category of political broadcast advertisements that became regulated under the Bipartisan Campaign Reform Act (BCRA) of 2002 (Public Law 107-155), also known as McCain-Feingold.

While the FEC site is easy to use, researchers may also want to try nongovernment Web services that download the FEC data and add value to them, emphasizing current data and newsworthy reports. Two sites to try are Open Secrets at ⟨http://www.opensecrets.org/⟩ and the American University Campaign Finance Web site at ⟨http://www1.soc.american.edu/campfin/index.cfm⟩.
Subjects: Campaign Funds; Elections; Databases

974. Core Documents of U.S. Democracy
http://www.gpoaccess.gov/coredocs.html
Sponsor(s): Government Printing Office (GPO)
Description: With input from government documents librarians, GPO has developed a selective list of very important current and historical government publications to feature as having "free, permanent, public access" on the GPO Access Web site. Although GPO aims to provide the same access to many other documents, these have been selected as being essential to an informed democratic process. The selection includes the Constitution of the United States of America, the Bill of Rights, the Declaration of Independence, Supreme Court decisions, congressional bills and the *Congressional Record*, the *United States Code*, the *Budget of the United States Government*, the *Federal Register*, and the *Code of Federal Regulations*.
Subjects: Government Publications

975. Democratic National Committee
http://www.democrats.org/
Sponsor(s): Democratic National Committee
Description: The Web site for the national Democratic Party features news on politics and policy. Interactive features on the site include online contributions, online voter registration, a blog, and a database of state party information. The site also has a version available in Spanish.
Subjects: Political Parties

976. Electioneering Communications Database

http://gullfoss2.fcc.gov/ecd/

Sponsor(s): Federal Communications Commission (FCC) — Media Bureau

Description: This Web site is intended to help political campaigns comply with a provision of the Federal Election Campaign Act that requires those who spend more than $10,000 on an "electioneering communication" during any calendar year to file a statement with the Federal Election Commission. The database helps users determine if their broadcast qualifies as an electioneering communication.

Subjects: Elections — Regulations

977. Electoral College

http://www.archives.gov/federal_register/
electoral_college/electoral_college.html

Sponsor(s): National Archives and Records Administration (NARA) — Electoral College

Description: The National Archives oversees the Electoral College and provides this Web site to inform the public about how its workings. The site features statistics and summaries of the votes in the Electoral College for every presidential election since the election of George Washington. Other features include the Electoral College Calculator, Frequently Asked Questions, and Teaching Resources.

Subjects: Electoral College

978. Federal Election Commission

http://www.fec.gov/

Sponsor(s): Federal Election Commission (FEC)

Description: FEC is an independent regulatory agency whose mission is to disclose campaign finance information, enforce provisions of the law such as the limits and prohibitions on contributions, and oversee the public funding of presidential elections. Major sections of the site include Campaign Finance Reports and Data, Commission Meetings, Enforcement Matters, Help with Reporting and Compliance, and Laws and Regulations. A section called Quick Answers to Common Questions answers over 50 frequently asked questions that typically come from candidates, state party committees, researchers, and the general public.

Subjects: Campaign Funds — Laws; Voting — Statistics

Publications: *Campaign Guide for Congressional Candidates and Committees*, Y 3.EL 2/3:13 C 76/

Combined Federal/State Disclosure and Election Directory, Y 3.El 2/3:14

FEC Reports on Financial Activity, Y 3.El 2/3:15/

Federal Election Commission Annual Report, Y 3.EL 2/3:

Independent Expenditures, Y 3.El 2/3:2 EX 7/

Record Newsletter, Y 3.EL 2/3:11/

Selected Court Case Abstracts, Y 3.EL 2/3:19

Supporting Federal Candidates: A Guide for Citizens, Y 3.EL 2/3:8 C 16/

979. Federal Voting Assistance Program

http://www.fvap.gov/

Sponsor(s): Defense Department — Federal Voting Assistance Program (FVAP)

Description: FVAP provides U.S. citizens worldwide with a broad range of nonpartisan information and assistance to facilitate their participation in the voting process, regardless of where they work or live. Located within the Department of Defense, FVAP is responsible for serving military personnel, their families, and other U.S. citizens residing outside the United States. Its Web site includes information for local elected officials and for military recruiters, as well as for absentee

voters. There are also state-by-state voting instructions and an online version of the federal postcard application for voter registration and absentee ballots.
Subjects: Voting
Publications: *Voting Assistance Guide*, D 2.14:VAG
Voting Information News, D 1.96:

980. Improving U.S. Voting Systems
http://vote.nist.gov/
Sponsor(s): Commerce Department — Technology Administration (TA) — National Institute of Standards and Technology (NIST)
Description: NIST is advising the Election Assistance Commission on the development of technical guidelines for voting systems. This Web site provides news, background, and documents related to the development of the technical guidelines.
Subjects: Voting

981. Information USA
http://usinfo.state.gov/usa/infousa/
Sponsor(s): State Department — International Information Programs Office
Description: Information USA is designed as a resource for foreign audiences seeking information about official U.S. policies, American society, culture, and political processes. The Web site includes the Facts About the USA, Government and Politics, Economy and Trade, Laws and Treaties, Media, Society and Values, Education in the United States, Geography and Travel, and Arts and Culture sections. Each section links to related Web pages, primarily from the Department of State, but also from academic, commercial, and public interest organizations.
Subjects: United States

982. Republican National Committee
http://www.gop.com
Alternate URL(s): http://www.rnc.org
Sponsor(s): Republican National Committee (RNC)
Description: The RNC Web site has sections on how to become active in supporting the party, how to register to vote online, and how to make contributions online. The News section links to *Rising Tide*, the Republican Party magazine, and to other information sources. The Web site also has a directory of the Republican Party's state offices. A Spanish-language version of the site is available.
Subjects: Political Parties

983. Tax Information for Political Organizations
http://www.irs.gov/charities/political/
Sponsor(s): Treasury Department — Internal Revenue Service (IRS)
Description: This IRS Web page focuses on reporting and disclosure requirements for political parties, campaign committees, and political action committees, which fall under section 527 of the Internal Revenue Code. The page links to a searchable database of the filings of Form 8871 (Political Organization Notice of Section 527 Status) and Form 8872 (Political Organization Report of Contributions and Expenditures).
Subjects: Campaign Funds

984. United States Election Assistance Commission
http://www.eac.gov/
Sponsor(s): United States Election Assistance Commission
Description: The United States Election Assistance Commission (EAC) was established by the Help America Vote Act of 2002 (Public Law 107-252) to provide guidance and funding to improve the administration of federal elections. Its Web site features information about the Voluntary Voting System Guidelines adopted by EAC. The site's Funding for the States section includes background information, state plans, and summaries of funds distributed by state. The News and Communications section includes press releases and EAC congressional testimony. Online publications include best practices reports and reports of the EAC inspector general. The Resources section includes voter turnout statistics from various sources, an explanation of the federal election system, and background on voting systems and administration guidelines.
Subjects: Elections — Regulations

985. Voting and Registration
http://www.census.gov/population/www/socdemo/voting.html
Sponsor(s): Commerce Department — Economics and Statistics Administration (ESA) — Census Bureau
Description: On this Web page, the Census Bureau compiles links to its online information about voting. Much of the data comes from the bureau's Current Population Survey, whose estimates regarding voting and registration are based on responses from a sample of the population. The page also links to historical data and estimates of the voting age population.
Subjects: Voting — Statistics

Government Administration

986. Chief Information Officers Council
http://www.cio.gov/
Sponsor(s): Chief Information Officers Council
Description: The Chief Information Officers (CIO) Council is the principal interagency forum focused on federal agency management of information technology (IT). Sections on this Web site include About the Council (with a membership list and meeting minutes), Calendar of Events, Documents, and Links.
Subjects: Information Technology

987. ExpectMore.gov
http://expectmore.gov
Alternate URL(s): http://www.whitehouse.gov/omb/expectmore/
Sponsor(s): Office of Management and Budget (OMB)
Description: OMB rates the performance of federal programs using a Program Assessment Rating Tool (PART). This Web site explains the assessment process and provides lists of programs that are and are not performing. The programs can also be searched by keyword or browsed by broad topic, such as housing or disaster relief. Each program listing includes a summary of what is working well and what areas need improvement.
Subjects: Government Administration; Government Services

988. Federal Advisory Committee Act (FACA) Database
http://fido.gov/facadatabase/
Sponsor(s): General Services Administration (GSA)
Description: The FACA database tracks information for roughly 1,000 federal advisory committees. Its records contain information about meetings, costs, members, reports, and other aspects of the committees, their status, and their work. The agencies and committee managers input the data, which is centrally hosted by GSA.
Subjects: Government Administration

989. Federal Executive Boards
http://www.feb.gov/
Sponsor(s): Office of Personnel Management (OPM)
Description: Federal Executive Boards (FEBs) coordinate many of the activities carried out by federal agency regional offices, which are located outside the national capital area. Based in over 25 cities with a large federal presence, FEBs operate under the direction of OPM and are concerned with coordination in such areas as management strategies, personnel programs, and community relations. This Web site provides background information about the boards and a directory.
Subjects: Government Administration

990. General Services Administration
http://www.gsa.gov/
Sponsor(s): General Services Administration (GSA)
Description: GSA procures and manages federal office space, vehicles, technology, and supplies. The agency also sells off surplus government property. GSA's role is described in this Web site's Buildings, Products, Services, and Technology sections. The Policy section has information about GSA's role in providing leadership on acquisition policy, regulation, and best practices, and has information about the agency's oversight of Federal Advisory Committees. While GSA mostly works with federal agencies or government contractors, the site includes a section for citizens with information about such programs as the Federal Citizen Information Center and government surplus property sales. Other popularly requested information includes federal per diem rates, the Federal Acquisition Regulations, forms, and information for vendors about getting on the GSA schedule.

The GSA Publications, Resources, and Reports section offers a variety of valuable information sources, such as newsletters and e-mail alerts, the *GSA Acquisition Manual*, GSA fleet reports on government vehicles, and the Federal Acquisition Regulations (FAR).

Because GSA is involved in a wide range of activities, first-time users may wish to browse the site map to become familiar with the variety of information available on the site.
Subjects: Government Administration; Government Procurement; Public Buildings
Publications: *Annual Report, General Services Administration*, GS 1.1:
Federal Supply Schedule (by Group), GS 2.7/4:
Forms, GS 1.13:
Index of Federal Specifications and Standards, GS 2.8/2:
Summary Report on Real Property Owned by United States Throughout the World, GS 1.15:
Worldwide Geographic Location Codes, GS 1.34:

991. IGnet — Federal Inspectors General
http://www.ignet.gov/
Sponsor(s): Office of Government Ethics (OGE)
Description: IGnet is a gateway site that serves the IG community, which consists of the offices of the inspectors general who conduct audits, investigations, and inspections in more than 60 federal agencies. There are two IG councils: the President's Council on Integrity and Efficiency (PCIE) and the Executive Council on Integrity and Efficiency (ECIE). The IGnet Web site features the Inspectors General, Reports and Periodicals, PCIE and ECIE, and Related Sites sections. The IG Directory/Homepages link, which can be found in the Inspectors General section, has contact information for presidentially appointed inspectors general and designated federal entity inspectors general.

IGnet provides a broad range of materials for both IG employees and for whistleblowers interested in contacting one of the IG offices.
Subjects: Inspectors General
Publications: *PCIE/ECIE: A Progress Report to the President*, PREX 2.36/2: *PCIE/ECIE: Reports by Year*, PREX 2.36: *PCIE/ECIE: The Journal of Public Inquiry*, PREX 2.36/3:

992. Laws and Links Related to General Federal Agency Operations
http://www.llsdc.org/sourcebook/laws-links.htm
Sponsor(s): Law Librarians' Society of Washington DC, Inc.
Description: This nongovernmental site provides the citations and Web links for laws governing the administration of government agencies, such as the Federal Information Security Management Act, Federal Register Act, and Fly American Act.
Subjects: Government Administration — Laws

993. Office of Governmentwide Policy
http://www.gsa.gov/Portal/gsa/ep/
channelView.do?pageTypeId=8199&channelId=13313
Sponsor(s): General Services Administration (GSA) — Office of Governmentwide Policy (OGP)
Description: OGP was created to consolidate all of GSA's governmentwide policy-making activities within one central office. These activities include acquisitions, government travel, and internal management systems. The site links to OGP's component offices, such as the Office of Real Property, the Office of Technology Strategy, and the Regulatory Information Service Center, and information about each office.
Subjects: Government Administration — Policy; Government Procurement — Policy

994. Office of Management and Budget
http://www.whitehouse.gov/omb/
Sponsor(s): Office of Management and Budget (OMB)
Description: OMB assists the president in overseeing the preparation of the federal budget and supervises budget administration in executive branch agencies. In addition, OMB oversees the administration's procurement, financial management, information, and regulatory policies. OMB's Web site covers each of these areas of responsibility.

Primary sections of the site include President's Budget, Management, Office of Information and Regulatory Affairs (OIRA), Legislative Information, and Agency Information. This last section includes OMB Circulars, Memoranda, and Bulletins. Documents in the President's Budget section include budget supplementals and amendments. The OIRA section includes information about federal statistical programs and standards, information policy, and e-government.

In addition to the collection of federal budget documents, this well-organized site is useful for the availability of the *OMB Circulars*, such as *OMB Circular A-130*, which establishes administration policy for the management of federal information resources, and *OMB Circular A-76*, which concerns federal policy for the competition of commercial activities. OMB's *Statements of Administration Policy*, in the Legislative Information section, will be helpful to those tracking bills in which the administration has a strong interest.

Subjects: Budget of the U.S. Government; Government Administration
Publications: *Budget of the Unites States Government*, PREX 2.8/8:
Mid-Session Review of the . . . Budget, PREX 2.31:
OMB Bulletin, PREX 2.3:
OMB Circulars, PREX 2.4:
Statements of Administration Policy on Non-Appropriations and Appropriations Bills, PREX 2.2:
The President's Management Agenda, PREX 2.2:
The Statistical Program of the United States Government, PREX 2.10/3:

995. Treasury Inspector General for Tax Administration

http://www.treasury.gov/tigta/
Sponsor(s): Treasury Department — Treasury Inspector General for Tax Administration (TIGTA)
Description: TIGTA was established in 1999 to provide independent oversight of Internal Revenue Service (IRS) activities, serving in effect as an inspector general for the IRS. The TIGTA Web site explains the office's role and posts copies of its audit reports and congressional testimony. The site also has information about the TIGTA hotline and an online form for reporting any knowledge of IRS waste, fraud, or abuse.
Subjects: Inspectors General; Taxation
Publications: *Semiannual Report to Congress (TIGTA)*, T 1.1/6:

996. United States Government Manual

http://www.gpoaccess.gov/gmanual/
Sponsor(s): National Archives and Records Administration (NARA)
Description: The GPO Access system has current and previous editions of *The United States Government Manual*, a descriptive directory of the executive, legislative, and judicial agencies and organizations of the federal government. Editions from 1995 to present can be searched by keyword. Editions from 1997 to the present can be browsed and read by chapter. Text and PDF versions of each chapter are available through the browse interface, but only the PDF version contains the agency organization charts and other graphics.

The strength of the *United States Government Manual* lies in the descriptions of the agencies, how they were established, what they do, and the nature of their primary divisions, as well as in the publication's helpful appendixes. As with the print edition, users of the online version of this reference classic will want to check more frequently updated sources — such as agency Web sites — for current personnel information.
Subjects: Federal Government; Directories
Publications: *United States Government Manual*, AE 2.108/2:

997. United States Office of Government Ethics
http://www.usoge.gov/
Sponsor(s): Office of Government Ethics (OGE)
Description: OGE coordinates activities in the executive branch related to the prevention of conflicts of interest on the part of government employees and the resolution of conflicts of interest that do occur. Its Web site features sections such as Laws and Regulations, Advisory Opinions, Common Ethics Issues, Agency Best Practices, and International Technical Assistance and Cooperation Activities. The site includes public and confidential financial disclosure forms, model trust documents, and related materials. The Laws and Regulations section provides the complete text of applicable executive orders, *Federal Register* issuances, and statutes and regulations related to the executive branch ethics program.

This site will be useful to government employees concerned with possible conflict of interest situations. It is also an excellent starting point for members of the general public who are interested in exploring topics in government ethics.
Subjects: Ethics in Government; Government Employees — Regulations
Publications: *Standards of Ethical Conduct for Employees of the Executive Branch*, Y 3.ET 3:2 ST 2/

Government Business

998. Acquisition Central
http://www.acquisition.gov/
Sponsor(s): General Services Administration (GSA)
Description: The Acquisition Central Web site is a central collection point for the type of news, reference, and regulatory information needed by individuals and organizations involved in government contracting and procurement. It links to the Federal Acquisition Regulations and to Web sites relevant to contract awards, bid protests, individual agency procurement, and professional development for government contracting personnel.

While designed for agencies and contractors, researchers will also find this site to be a convenient one-stop shop for federal acquisitions Web sites.
Subjects: Government Procurement; Military Procurement
Publications: *Federal Acquisition Regulation*, GS 1.6/10:

999. Business Partner Network
http://www.bpn.gov/
Sponsor(s): General Services Administration (GSA)
Description: The Business Partner Network (BPN) is a central system for information about vendors and contractors who do business with the federal government. Information provided by registered vendors must only be provided once for use by all government agencies. It encompasses the Department of Defense's Central Contractor Registration (CCR) system, which is now used government-wide. In addition to CCR, the BPN Web site links to key databases for federal agency contracting officials. These include the Excluded Parties List System and the National Pre-Award Registry of contractors who have been found to be in compliance with the Equal Employment Opportunity (EEO) regulations.
Subjects: Government Contracts

1000. Central Contractor Registration

http://www.ccr.gov/

Sponsor(s): Defense Department

Description: The Central Contractor Registration (CCR) Web site was designed to provide a single point of access and registration for vendors who want to do business with the Department of Defense. It is now used government wide. The site includes the *CCR Handbook* and a special information section for small businesses.

Subjects: Defense Contracting; Government Procurement

1001. Defense Reutilization and Marketing Service, Surplus Property

http://www.drms.dla.mil/

Sponsor(s): Defense Department — Defense Reutilization and Marketing Service (DRMS)

Description: The DRMS Web site features a publicly accessible database of items available at public auctions and sales. DRMS offers this site to help people obtain original U.S. government surplus property. To search the inventory, browse property catalogs, submit requests, or place a bid, the site provides three separate versions: one for private companies or individual users; one for government, nonprofit, and public service agency users; and one for "generator/installation of government excess personal property for turn-in" users.

Subjects: Surplus Government Property

1002. Department of Energy's e-Center

http://e-center.doe.gov/

Sponsor(s): Energy Department

Description: The Department of Energy's e-Center provides information about doing business with the department. Its Web site includes current business opportunities, registration for notification of new business opportunities, and information and guidance on the acquisition and financial assistance award process. The Professionals Homepage section provides regulatory guidance in procurement, financial assistance, personal property, contractor human resources management, professional development, and business practices.

Subjects: Government Contracts

1003. FARSite (Federal Acquisition Regulation Site)

http://farsite.hill.af.mil/

Sponsor(s): Air Force — Hill Air Force Base

Description: This Web site provides access to the Federal Acquisition Regulation, as well as to the Defense FAR Supplement (DFARS). Links to federal regulations for the Navy, Army, Air Force, NASA, and the Department of Energy are also offered. Additionally, the site contains regulation status, manuals, changes, and electronic forms as well as a forum for questions and help.

FARSite is a one-stop site for contracting regulations.

Subjects: Government Procurement — Regulations

Publications: *Air Force Acquisition Regulation Supplement (AFFARS)*, D 301.6/2:
Army Federal Acquisition Regulation Supplement (AFARS), D 101.6:
Defense Federal Acquisition Regulation Supplement (DFARS), D 1.6:
Department of Energy Acquisition Regulations Supplement (DEARS)
Federal Acquisition Regulation, GP 3.38/2:
NASA FAR Supplement, NAS 1.6:
Navy Marine Corp Acquisition Regulation Supplement (NMCARS)

1004. FedBizOpps
http://www.fbo.gov/
Alternate URL(s): http://www.fedbizopps.gov/
Sponsor(s): General Services Administration (GSA)
Description: FedBizOpps (FBO) is the central clearinghouse for information about federal government procurement notices in excess of $25,000. Vendors seeking government business opportunities on FBO can search the full-text versions of notices and limit searches by agency, set-aside code, date range, and other criteria. The Vendor Notification Service provides subscribers with free e-mail notification of procurement announcements.
Subjects: Government Contracts; Government Procurement

1005. Federal Acquisition Jumpstation
http://prod.nais.nasa.gov/pub/fedproc/home.html
Sponsor(s): National Aeronautics and Space Administration (NASA)
Description: The Federal Acquisition Jumpstation provides a simple list of links to federal agency Web pages concerned with procurement, contracts, and grants.
Subjects: Government Procurement

1006. Federal Acquisition Regulation
http://www.acquisition.gov/far/
Sponsor(s): General Services Administration (GSA)
Description: This version of the *Federal Acquisition Regulation (FAR)* provides access to HTML, zipped HTML, and PDF versions of the regulations. It includes PDF files of *Federal Acquisition Circulars*, in both their looseleaf and *Federal Register* printing formats. There are also special sections for proposed rules and for Small Entity Compliance Guidelines. Users can subscribe to a FAR News e-mail service to receive news of *Federal Acquisition Circulars*, proposed rules, public meetings, and other information about FAR-related issues.
Subjects: Government Procurement — Regulations
Publications: *Federal Acquisition Circular*, D 1.6/11-2:
Federal Acquisition Regulation, D 1.6/11:

1007. Federal Acquisition Service
http://www.gsa.gov/Portal/gsa/ep/
channelView.do?pageTypeId=8199&channelId-17545
Sponsor(s): General Services Administration (GSA)
Description: The GSA Federal Acquisition Service (FAS) was formed in late 2006 by combining the Federal Technology Service with the Federal Supply Service. FAS offers procurement services for federal government agencies. Its Web site has information about the new organization and links to its component offices.
   Rather than copy the overly long URL listed above, users should go to the GSA home page at ⟨http://www.gsa.gov⟩. On the home page, users should select "About GSA" and then "Organization." FAS can be found near the top of the list of GSA organizations.
Subjects: Government Procurement

1008. Federal Laboratory Consortium for Technology Transfer
http://www.federallabs.org/
Sponsor(s): Federal Laboratory Consortium (FLC)
Description: The Federal Laboratory Consortium for Technology Transfer (FLC) helps to move the federal laboratories' research and development into the U.S. private sector. On the Web site, the FLC Technology Locator allows users to

request technical assistance and be partnered with the appropriate laboratory. The site also has a searchable directory of FLC laboratories.

Subjects: Technology Transfer

1009. Federal Procurement Data System — Next Generation

https://www.fpds.gov/

Sponsor(s): General Services Administration (GSA)

Description: The Federal Procurement Data System-Next Generation (FPDS-NG) is the central repository of statistical information about federal executive branch contracting. It contains detailed information about contract awards over $3,000. The Important Links section includes a list of agencies submitting data to the FPDS-NG. At this time, FPDS-NG does not include current data for Department of Defense contracts, which are expected to be fully integrated by late 2007.

Free registration is required to search the data, which is also available free of charge. Selected reports and "top requests" (such as Hurricane Katrina contract totals) are available from the main page without requiring users to sign in.

FPDS-NG, launched with fiscal year 2004 data, was designed to meet the need for faster reporting of contract actions. The Federal Funding Accountability and Transparency Act of 2006 (Public Law No. 109-282), calls for a publicly accessible system to be launched by 2008 with improved data on contracts and new information about federal grants. The private advocacy group OMB Watch launched a Web site called FedSpending.org in response to the new law. FedSpending.org provides an easy search interface for spending data that the federal government already reports; the new official system required by law would include additional data that the government does not currently collect or report.

Subjects: Government Contracts

Publications: *Federal Procurement Report*, PREX 2.24/13:

1010. FirstGov Shopping and Auctions

http://www.firstgov.gov/shopping/shopping.shtml

Sponsor(s): General Services Administration (GSA)

Description: The FirstGov.gov Web site section that deals with government sales and auctions uses this tag line: "Buy new, seized, and surplus merchandise from government." This portal to other government Internet resources is divided into the following sections: Federal Government Surplus and Seized Property Sales; State and Local Surplus Property Sales; Government Stores (Souvenirs, Books, Gifts); and Sales by Federal Agency, which serves as an index to the sales-related pages on agency Web sites.

Subjects: Government Auctions; Surplus Government Property

1011. GovSales.gov

http://www.govsales.gov/

Sponsor(s): General Services Administration (GSA)

Description: The tagline for GovSales.gov is "The Official Site to Buy U.S. Government Property." The site has separate sections for each type of good, including houses, buildings and land, computers, and industrial. See the Frequent Questions section for important information about registering and bidding.

Subjects: Government Auctions; Surplus Government Property

1012. GSA Advantage!

https://www.gsaadvantage.gov/advgsa/main_pages/start_page.jsp

Sponsor(s): General Services Administration (GSA)

Description: This GSA Web site, for use by federal government agencies only, is an online shopping and supply site. Authorized users can use government credit

cards to purchase products from the Federal Supply Service. Non-registered users can browse the products catalog.
Subjects: Government Procurement

1013. GSA Board of Contract Appeals
http://www.gsbca.gsa.gov/
Sponsor(s): General Services Administration (GSA) — Board of Contract Appeals
Description: The Board of Contract Appeals hears and decides contract disputes between government contractors and GSA, as well as disputes with other agencies such as the Department of States and the Department of Commerce. The board's Web site provides decisions issued since October 1996, and an archive of decisions issued between October 1992 and September 1996. The site also carries the board's rules of procedure.
Subjects: Government Contracts — Laws

1014. Homeland Security Advanced Research Projects Agency — Solicitations Portal
http://www.hsarpabaa.com/
Sponsor(s): Homeland Security Department — Homeland Security Advanced Research Projects Agency (HSARPA)
Description: HSARPA maintains this official Web site for information about its contracting and teaming opportunities. The site lists current solicitations and past awards. It also lists workshops and provides an e-mail service for meeting and solicitation announcements.
Subjects: Government Contracts; Homeland Security — Research

1015. HUBZone Empowerment Contracting Program
https://eweb1.sba.gov/hubzone/internet/
Sponsor(s): Small Business Administration (SBA)
Description: The HUBZone Empowerment Contracting Program provides federal contracting opportunities for qualified small businesses located in distressed areas. A HUBZone is a Historically Underutilized Business Zone. The HUBZone Web site features sections such as Who We Are; Frequently Asked Questions; Are You in a HUBZone?; and Certified HUBZone Concerns. There is also an online tool for applying for certification as a qualified HUBZone Small Business Concern.
Subjects: Government Contracts; Small Business

1016. Hurricane Contracting Information Center
http://www.rebuildingthegulfcoast.gov/
Sponsor(s): Small Business Administration (SBA)
Description: The Hurricane Contracting Information Center is a clearinghouse of information about contracting and subcontracting opportunities related to Gulf Coast recovery from hurricane damage. Its Web site is intended to assist minority-owned businesses, women-owned businesses, and small- and medium-size enterprises.
Subjects: Government Contracts

1017. Interagency Edison
http://www.iedison.gov/
Sponsor(s): National Institutes of Health (NIH)
Description: Government grantees and contractors are required to report any government-funded inventions to the federal agency that made the award. Interagency Edison is an online system designed to streamline the administrative tasks involved

in complying with this requirement. It can be used to report to a number of agencies, including the Department of Energy and the National Institutes of Health.
Subjects: Intellectual Property

1018. Javits-Wagner-O'Day Program
http://www.jwod.gov/
Sponsor(s): Committee for Purchase From People Who Are Blind or Severely Disabled
Description: Through federal procurement policies, The Javits-Wagner-O'Day (JWOD) Program generates jobs and training opportunities for people who are blind or have other severe disabilities. Its Web site features sections such as About Us, Products and Services (Procurement List), How to Participate, Library (Press Releases, Publications), and Contacts.
Subjects: Disabilities; Government Procurement — Policy
Publications: *Annual Report on the Javits-Wagner-O'Day Program*, Y 3.P 97:1/

1019. NASA Acquisition Internet Service
http://www.nasa.gov/audience/forindustry/procurement/index.html
Sponsor(s): National Aeronautics and Space Administration (NASA)
Description: The NASA Acquisition Internet Service Web site provides a central online point of contact for businesses interested in NASA acquisitions and procurement opportunities. The site includes the annual *NASA Acquisition Forecast* and the NASA Procurement Management System (NPMS). The site also offers an e-mail alert system for news of NASA opportunities.
Subjects: Government Procurement

1020. NASA Innovative Partnership Programs
http://www.nctn.hq.nasa.gov/
Sponsor(s): National Aeronautics and Space Administration (NASA)
Description: The NASA Innovative Partnership Programs (IPP) Web site provides access to NASA information resources for research and development, technology partnering, commercialization opportunities, and related topics. The site includes information about NASA's Small Business Innovation Research and Small Business Technology Transfer programs.
Subjects: Small Business — Grants; Technology Transfer
Publications: *Aerospace Technology Innovation*, NAS 1.95:
Spinoff, Annual Report, NAS 1.1/4:

1021. Procurement Gateway
https://progate.daps.dla.mil/home/
Sponsor(s): Defense Department — Defense Logistics Agency (DLA)
Description: The DLA Procurement Gateway allows prospective government contractors to perform searches by Request for Quotation (RFQ), Request for Proposal (RFP), and contract award documents.
   The Help section links to help pages throughout the Procurement Gateway site; consult these for background information before searching.
Subjects: Government Procurement

1022. SBIR and STTR Programs and Awards
http://www.sbaonline.sba.gov/sbir/indexsbir-sttr.html
Sponsor(s): Small Business Administration (SBA)
Description: The Small Business Innovation Research and Small Business Technology Transfer programs are competitive funding programs that encourage innova-

tive research and development in small businesses and nonprofit research institutions. They are offered by agencies with large research and development budgets and are coordinated by SBA. This site describes the programs, lists past winners, and provides a handbook for preparation of SBIR/STTR proposals.
Subjects: Small Business — Grants

1023. Small and Disadvantaged Business Utilization

http://www.usda.gov/da/smallbus/
Sponsor(s): Agriculture Department (USDA) — Small and Disadvantaged Business Utilization Office (OSDBU)
Description: The mission of OSDBU is to assist small businesses with the Department of Agriculture's contracting process. Its Web site includes a directory of subcontracting opportunities, the USDA Procurement Forecast, and workshop information.
Subjects: Government Procurement; Small Business

1024. SUB-Net

http://web.sba.gov/subnet/
Sponsor(s): Small Business Administration (SBA)
Description: This Web site was designed primarily as a place for large businesses to post solicitations and notices. Prime contractors can use SUB-Net to post subcontracting opportunities. These may or may not be reserved for small business, and they may include either solicitations or other notices, such as, notices of sources sought for teaming partners and subcontractors on future contracts. Small businesses can use this site to identify opportunities in their areas of expertise. The site features About SUB-Net, Search for Solicitation, and Post Solicitation sections.
Subjects: Government Contracts

1025. UNICOR — Federal Prison Industries, Inc.

http://www.unicor.gov/
Sponsor(s): Federal Prison Industries, Inc.
Description: The UNICOR Web site allows the federal government and contractors to buy goods and services from Federal Prison Industries (FPI), Inc., whose primary mission is the productive employment of inmates. The site has an online product catalog with ordering and browsing capabilities. It also features a Fact or Fiction section, which addresses common misunderstandings about FPI.
Subjects: Government Procurement; Prisoners

1026. USDA Procurement

http://www.usda.gov/procurement/
Sponsor(s): Agriculture Department (USDA)
Description: This procurement site from the Department of Agriculture's Departmental Administration features procurement news and the following sections: Business Opportunities, Acquisition Toolkit, USDA Automated Procurement System, Policy and Regulations, and Purchase and Fleet Card.
Subjects: Government Procurement

Government Employees

1027. Federal Labor Relations Authority
http://www.flra.gov/
Sponsor(s): Federal Labor Relations Authority (FLRA)
Description: FLRA is an independent agency responsible for administering the labor-management relations program for federal employees. Its Web site includes information about FLRA, news, decisions, policies, and guidelines. Major sections include Filing a Case, Court Opinions, News and Publications, and Alternative Dispute Resolution.
Subjects: Government Employees; Labor-Management Relations
Publications: *Decisions of the Federal Labor Relations Authority*, Y 3.F 31/21-3:10-4/

1028. Federal Retirement Thrift Investment Board
http://www.frtib.gov/
Sponsor(s): Federal Retirement Thrift Investment Board
Description: The Federal Retirement Thrift Investment Board administers the Thrift Savings Plan (TSP) for federal employees. Its Web site features sections such as the Electronic Reading Room, Procurement Information, and Employment Opportunities. The Electronic Reading Room includes an annual FOIA report and annual audit report. The site also links to TSP forms and publications.
Subjects: Government Employees

1029. FedScope
http://www.fedscope.opm.gov/
Sponsor(s): Office of Personnel Management (OPM)
Description: FedScope is a central access point for data about the federal government's civilian workforce. Its Web site provides flexible retrieval of aggregate statistics extracted from OPM's Central Personnel Data File on topics including length of service, gender and age, pay grades, work schedules, and employment location. The Employment Statistics link on the top menu leads to electronic publications on such topics as employment trends and pay structure of the federal civil service. It also points to a suite of prepared statistical products about retirements. Data products are typically available in PDF and spreadsheet formats.

The About Our Data and Data Definitions sections may be particularly helpful to review before using the FedScope data in analyses.
Subjects: Government Employees — Statistics

1030. Merit Systems Protection Board
http://www.mspb.gov/
Sponsor(s): Merit Systems Protection Board (MSPB)
Description: MSPB serves as guardian of the federal government's merit-based system of employment, primarily by hearing and deciding appeals from federal employees of concerning removals and other major personnel actions. The board also hears and decides other types of civil service cases, reviews significant actions and regulations of the Office of Personnel Management, and conducts studies of the merit systems. Its Web site includes additional descriptive information on about board, along with links to decisions, studies, and information about how to file an appeal.
Subjects: Government Employees; Labor-Management Relations
Publications: *Decisions of U.S. Merit Systems Protection Board*, MS 1.10:
Issues of Merit, MS 1.17:

1031. National Personnel Records Center
http://www.archives.gov/st-louis/
Alternate URL(s): http://www.archives.gov/veterans/evetrecs/
Sponsor(s): National Archives and Records Administration (NARA)
Description: The National Personnel Records Center (NPRC) in St. Louis is a central repository for federal civil service and military personnel records. Its Web site describes the collections and how to request information. The records themselves are not available online. A special site, eVetRecs, allows veterans and the next of kin of a deceased veteran to request records online. The eVetRecs site is available at the alternate URL listed above.
Subjects: Government Employees; Veterans

1032. National Security Personnel System (NSPS)
http://www.cpms.osd.mil/nsps/
Sponsor(s): Defense Department
Description: NSPS is an alternative federal government employee pay and promotion system currently being developed by the Department of Defense. The goal of the new system is to substitute current rules regarding pay for time in service with a practice that is based more on pay for performance. The NSPS Web site includes extensive information about the program, along with news and answers to frequently asked questions.

NSPS will affect hundreds of thousands of government employees in the Defense Department and may affect the development of rules for the rest of the civilian government workforce. Users interested in government management issues can follow developments on this site.
Subjects: Civilian Defense Employees; Pay and Benefits

1033. Office of Compliance
http://www.compliance.gov/
Sponsor(s): Office of Compliance
Description: The Office of Compliance is an independent agency that was established by the Congressional Accountability Act of 1995 to protect the safety, health, and workplace rights of covered employees in the legislative branch. Its Web site includes information about employee rights and the text of *Decisions of the Board of Directors*.

Although the Office of Compliance works only with legislative branch employees, this site can be of general use to others interested in employee rights.
Subjects: Labor Law; Legislative Branch — Regulations
Publications: *Annual Report of the Office of Compliance*, Y 11.1:

1034. Office of Personnel Management
http://www.opm.gov/
Sponsor(s): Office of Personnel Management (OPM)
Description: As the federal government personnel office, OPM is a primary source for information about working for the federal government. The OPM Web site's home page links directly to the most requested pages, including the USAJOBS employment Web site and sections such as Salaries and Wages, Health Insurance, Retirement Benefits, Forms, Publications, and Veterans' Information. The Operating Status link on the home page provides current information about times when the federal government is closed due to holidays or emergencies. The site's Reports Portal section includes reports to the president on such topics as locality pay and Hispanic employment, as well as reports to Congress on such topics as annual cost-of-living allowances and the status of telework in the federal government.

The OPM site has a particularly helpful alphabetical subject index.

Subjects: Government Employees; Personnel Management
Publications: *¿Está pensando en su retiro?*, PM 1.10:RI 83-11 SP/
Beneficios de sobreviviente para los hijos, PM 1.10:RI 25-27 SP/
Court-Ordered Benefits for Former Spouses, PM 1.10:RI 84-1/
CSRS and FERS Handbook for Personnel and Payroll, PM 1.14/3-3:
Demographic Profile of the Federal Workforce, PM 1.10/2-3:
Employment and Trends as of . . . (bimonthly), PM 1.15:
Eventualidades de la vida y sus beneficios de retiro y seguro (para pensionados),
   PM 1.10:RI 38-126 SP/
Federal Employees Retirement System (An Overview of Your Benefits), PM
   1.10:RI 90-1/
Federal Employees Retirement System Transfer Handbook, PM 1.10:RI 90-3/
Federal Equal Opportunity Recruitment Program, Report to Congress, PM 1.42:
Guide to Personnel Data Standards, PM 1.14/3:
Guide to Processing Personnel Actions, PM 1.14/3-4:
Handbook for Attorneys, PM 1.10:RI 83-116/
Información para los pensionados, PM 1.10:RI 20-59 SP/
Información para los sobrevivientes pensionados, PM 1.10:RI 25-26 SP/
Information for Survivor Annuitants, PM 1.10:RI 25-26/
Occupations of Federal White-Collar and Blue-Collar Workers (bienniel), PM
   1.10/2-2:
Pay Structure of the Federal Civil Service, PM 1.10/2-4:
Position Classification Standards, PM 1.30:
Salary Tables, Executive Branch of the Government, PM 1.9:
Survivor Benefits for Children, PM 1.10:RI 25-27/
The Fact Book, PM 1.10/2-5:
Work Years and Personnel Costs, PM 1.10/4:
Work-Related Injuries and Fatalities, PM 1.10:RI 84-2/

1035. Per Diem, Travel, and Transportation Allowance

https://secureapp2.hqda.pentagon.mil/perdiem/
Sponsor(s): Defense Department; General Services Administration (GSA)
Description: Designed for civilian Department of Defense employees, this Web page provides easy access to federal per diem rates, meal rates, and cost-of-living allowances (COLA) and housing allowances for travel and living arrangements within the United States or throughout the world. The Per Diem Rates page includes charts for official federal government rates and divides the charts into Continental United States (CONUS), Outside Continental United States (OCONUS), and Overseas sections. The page also provides Overseas Housing Allowances, Basic Allowance for Housing, and Overseas Cost-of-Living Allowances sections.
Subjects: Civilian Defense Employees

1036. Plum Book

http://www.gpoaccess.gov/plumbook/
Sponsor(s): Congress — Senate
Description: The *United States Government Policy and Supporting Positions*, commonly known as the *Plum Book*, contains data on over 8,000 federal civil service leadership and support positions in the legislative and executive branches of the federal government, as well as positions within departments, independent agencies, and government corporations that may be subject to noncompetitive appointment. It includes positions such as chairpersons, secretaries, department and agency heads (and their immediate subordinates), policy executives and advisers, and aides who report to these officials. The directory is published every four years, following each presidential election, for the Senate Committee on

Governmental Affairs. This online version, which is hosted by the Government Printing Office, is presented in PDF format.

Often used as a reference for individuals seeking government appointments, the *Plum Book* is also a source for finding basic directory information, general salary levels for appointed government officials, and expiration dates for some terms of service.

Subjects: Government Employees; Presidential Appointments
Publications: *United States Government Policy and Supporting Positions (Plum Book)*, Y 4.P 84/10:P 75/

1037. Presidential Management Fellows Program
http://www.pmi.opm.gov/
Sponsor(s): Office of Personnel Management (OPM)
Description: The Presidential Management Fellows Program is designed to recruit for public service a variety of outstanding citizens interested in the leadership and management of public policies and programs. This site provides information on the program and how to apply.
Subjects: Government Employees

1038. Salaries and Wages
http://www.opm.gov/oca/payrates/
Sponsor(s): Office of Personnel Management (OPM)
Description: This official OPM Web site for government-wide pay programs for federal employees has information about the General Schedule (GS), Law Enforcement Pay Schedules, and the Federal Wage System (FWS) and provides a variety of resources. Most of the schedules are presented in PDF format. The following schedules are available: General Schedule and Locality Pay Tables, Law Enforcement Special Salary Rate and Locality Pay Tables, Locality Pay Area Definitions, Executive Schedule, Senior Executive Schedule, Special Salary Rate Tables, Administrative Law Judges, Employees in Senior-Level and Scientific or Professional Positions, and Members of Boards of Contract Appeals. The site also links to the past pay schedules and to information about the Federal Wage System, which includes the Minimum Wage Notice and Wage Schedules section.
Subjects: Government Employees; Pay and Benefits

1039. Thrift Savings Plan
http://www.tsp.gov/
Sponsor(s): Federal Retirement Thrift Investment Board
Description: The Thrift Savings Plan (TSP) is a retirement savings plan for federal civilian employees and for uniformed services members. This site offers basic information about the TSP. Major sections of the site include Account Access, Rates of Return and Share Prices, and Calculators.
Subjects: Government Employees

1040. U.S. Office of Special Counsel
http://www.osc.gov/
Sponsor(s): Office of Special Counsel (OSC)
Description: OSC is an independent federal investigative and prosecutorial agency that is responsible for protecting federal employees and applicants from prohibited personnel practices, especially reprisal for whistleblowing. The agency is also concerned with adherence to the Hatch Act, which restricts political activity by federal government employees. Major sections of its Web site explain prohibited personnel practices, whistleblower procedures and protections, and Hatch Act rules. The site also covers the Uniformed Services Employment and Reemploy-

ment Rights Act (USERRA), which prohibits discrimination against persons because of their service in the Armed Forces Reserve, the National Guard, or other uniformed services.

Subjects: Government Employees — Laws; Hatch Act

Publications: *Annual Reports to Congress from the U.S. Office of Special Counsel,* MS 2.1:

Government Finance

1041. Budget of the United States Government
http://www.whitehouse.gov/omb/budget/
Alternate URL(s): http://www.gpo.gov/usbudget/
Sponsor(s): Office of Management and Budget (OMB)
Description: OMB provides the full-text version of the current U.S. budget and supporting documents online. This Web site includes brief summaries of each budget document, with a link to its PDF version. Selected tables are available in spreadsheet format. The site also links to OMB's Public Budget Database, which provides budget data — sometimes below the level of aggregation published in the official budget documents — in spreadsheet format. It is accompanied by a user's guide.

The GPO site, which can be found at the alternate URL listed above, hosts the budget documents for the current year and for previous years. Most of the files are available in PDF format, with some tables available in spreadsheet format. Using the GPO site, users can also search the budget documents by word(s) and display the retrieved sections in PDF or text format. Additionally, the site provides access to the budget documents back to fiscal year 1996.

Subjects: Budget of the U.S. Government; Government Finance

Publications: *Analytical Perspectives,* PREX 2.8/5:
Budget of the United States Government, PREX 2.8:
Budget of the United States Government, Appendix, PREX 2.8:
Budget System and Concepts of the United States Government, PREX 2.8/12:
Economic Report of the President, Pr 42.9:
Historical Tables, Budget of the United States Government, PREX 2.8/8:
Mid-Session Review of The Budget, PREX 2.31:

1042. Bureau of the Public Debt
http://www.publicdebt.treas.gov/
Sponsor(s): Treasury Department — Bureau of the Public Debt
Description: The Bureau of the Public Debt borrows the money needed to operate the federal government and account for the resulting debt. The bureau sells Treasury bills, notes, and bonds, as well as U.S. Savings Bonds. Major sections of the Web site include Federal Investments, State and Local Government Series (SLGS) Securities, the Treasury's Borrowings Program, Trust Funds Management, and Public Debt. The Public Debt section includes current and historical data on the debt, interest expense on the debt, the *Monthly Statement of the Public Debt,* and current and historical Federal Debt Schedules.

Auction data and information about Treasury securities was moved from this site to the TreasuryDirect.gov Web site in August 2006.

Subjects: National Debt

Publications: *Monthly Statement of the Public Debt of the United States,* T 63.215:

1043. Federal Accounting Standards Advisory Board
http://www.fasab.gov/
Sponsor(s): Federal Accounting Standards Advisory Board (FASAB)
Description: FASAB is a federal advisory committee responsible for establishing generally accepted accounting principles for federal entities. FASAB publishes *Statements of Federal Accounting Concepts and Standards*, interpretations, and technical bulletins. Along with background information, its Web site has news releases, a newsletter reporting board meeting highlights, and an e-mail news service.
Subjects: Accounting
Publications: *Statements of Federal Financial Accounting Concepts and Standards. Current Text.*
Statements of Federal Financial Accounting Concepts and Standards. Original Pronouncements., GA 1.13:AIMD-21.1.1

1044. Federal Financing Bank
http://www.ustreas.gov/ffb/
Sponsor(s): Treasury Department — Federal Financing Bank
Description: The Federal Financing Bank (FFB) is a government corporation that works under the general supervision of the secretary of the treasury. FFB coordinates federal and federally assisted borrowing from the public with the overall financial and economic goals of the government. Its Web site includes information about FFB's operations, press releases, and financial statements.
Subjects: Government Finance

1045. Financial Management Service
http://www.fms.treas.gov/
Sponsor(s): Treasury Department — Financial Management Service (FMS)
Description: The Financial Management Service manages the daily cash flow into and out of federal accounts. The agency collects debt owed to the federal government and issues the Treasury checks for Social Security, veterans' benefits, income tax refunds, and other purposes. The FMS Web site is divided into sections for consumer questions and answers (e.g., "How do I replace a lost Treasury check?"); publications and guidance; information about FMS; and information about FMS programs. The home page also features Rates and Sureties and FMS Forms sections.

FMS issues the *Daily Treasury Statement* and the *Monthly Treasury Statement*, which report the government's receipts, outlays, and deficit or surplus. Current and archival issues are available at this site. Starting with fiscal year 2001, the former *United States Government Annual Report* and *Annual Report Appendix* were combined and renamed the *Combined Statement of Receipts, Outlays, and Balances of the United States Government*. The *Combined Statement* is recognized as the official publication of receipts and outlays of the U.S. government. The current report and annual reports back to 1995 are available at this site. The monthly *Treasury Bulletin*, another important reference publication from FMS, contains statements on federal fiscal operations, the federal debt, U.S. savings bonds, federal securities, U.S. claims and liabilities with foreigners, and the status of federal trust funds. Finally, the site provides current and past issues of the annual *Financial Report of the United States*, with a link to the Government Accountability Office guide to understanding the report.
Subjects: Government Finance
Publications: *Combined Statement of Receipts, Outlays, and Balances of the United States Government*, T 63.101/3:
Daily Treasury Statement, T 63.113/2-2:
Financial Connection, T 63.128:

Financial Reports of the United States Government, T 63.113/3:
Monthly Treasury Statement, T 63.113/2:
Status Report of U.S. Treasury-owned Gold, T 63.131:
Treasury Bulletin (quarterly), T 63.103/2:
Treasury Reporting Rates of Exchange, T 63.121:
United States Government Annual Report, T 63.101/2:

1046. Internal Revenue Service
http://www.irs.gov/
Sponsor(s): Treasury Department — Internal Revenue Service (IRS)
Description: The intended audience for the official Web site of the IRS is the average U.S. taxpayer. Special sections also lead to information for businesses, charities and nonprofits, government entities, tax professionals, and users concerned with retirement plans and tax-exempt bonds. A Spanish-language version of the site is also available. The section for individuals includes instructions, forms and publications, and resources for electronic filing through the IRS e-file program. The site's top menu bar of the IRS site also has links to tax statistics, information about the agency, and a newsroom with press releases and "problem alerts."

The IRS site, one of the most heavily used federal Web sites, is well organized and provides multiple points of access to major sections and resources. The site map can help users find specific information.
Subjects: Income Tax; Tax Forms; Taxation
Publications: *Armed Forces' Tax Guide*, T 22.44/2:3/
Federal Employment Tax Forms, T 22.44/2:
Federal Tax Forms, T 22.51/4:
Internal Revenue Bulletin, T 22.23:
Internal Revenue Manual, T 22.2/15-3:
Publication 78, Cumulative List of Organizations (annual), T 22.2/11:
Taxpayer Information Publications, T 22.44/2:
Your Rights as a Taxpayer, T 22.44/2:1/

1047. Tax Statistics
http://www.irs.gov/taxstats/
Sponsor(s): Treasury Department — Internal Revenue Service (IRS)
Description: The Tax Statistics Web page serves as a central access point for a variety of statistics about IRS operations and aggregated from filings with the IRS. Major sections include Business Tax Statistics, Individual Tax Statistics, Charitable and Tax-Exempt Organization Statistics, Statistics of Income, and Statistics by Form. A special Topics section includes statistics on estate and gift tax returns and research on taxpayer compliance.
Subjects: Taxation — Statistics
Publications: *IRS Annual Data Book*, T 22.1:

1048. Taxpayer Advocate Service
http://www.irs.gov/advocate/
Sponsor(s): Treasury Department — Internal Revenue Service (IRS)
Description: The Taxpayer Advocate Service was created to ensure that taxpayer complaints not resolved through the normal channels could be resolved fairly and efficiently, and to recommend system changes based on the experiences that occur while reviewing these complaints. This Web site provides information about the service and how to use it. The site also has the taxpayer advocate's annual report to Congress, which details the most frequent taxpayer complaints and makes recommendations for improvement.

Subjects: Income Tax
Publications: *National Taxpayer Advocate's Annual Report to Congress,* T 22.44/
2:2104/

1049. Treasury Department
http://www.treasury.gov/
Alternate URL(s): http://www.ustreas.gov/
Sponsor(s): Treasury Department
Description: The Treasury Department's Web site provides current news, links to
the department's component bureaus and offices, and direct links to popular
topics such as seized property auctions and money management information.
The site also provides a subject approach to its activities in the following subsections under Key Topics: Accounting and Budget, Currency and Coins, Enforcement, Financial Markets, Health Savings Accounts, International, Small Business,
Taxes, and Technology. The Press Room section offers access to news releases
and other publications arranged by topic, by date, and by type (news, testimony,
speeches, statements, reports, photographs, and U.S. International Reserve Position statements).
Subjects: Government Finance

1050. TreasuryDirect
http://www.treasurydirect.gov/
Sponsor(s): Treasury Department — Bureau of the Public Debt
Description: TreasuryDirect has three separate sections: Individual/Personal Investing, Corporate Investing, and Government Investing. The section for individuals
allows customers to set up an account with the Department of the Treasury;
purchase Treasury bills, bonds, and notes; participate in Treasury security auctions; convert paper savings bonds to electronic; and otherwise manage their
accounts. Treasury also provides an online guided tour of TreasuryDirect and
information about account security.
    The sections for corporate and government investing include technical informa-
tion and electronic services that require a special account.
Subjects: Treasury Bills; Treasury Bonds; Treasury Notes

1051. U.S. Chief Financial Officers Council
http://www.cfoc.gov/
Sponsor(s): U.S. Chief Financial Officers Council
Description: Members of the U.S. Chief Financial Officers Council (CFOC) are the
chief financial officers of the largest federal agencies and senior officials of the
Office of Management and Budget and the Department of the Treasury. The CFOC
Web site includes current membership and committee lists, council meeting
minutes, and the council history and charter.
Subjects: Government Finance

Government Information

1052. CENDI
http://www.dtic.mil/cendi/
Sponsor(s): CENDI
Description: CENDI is a working group of federal scientific and technical information
(STI) managers. (It is named for the initial four entities that formed the group:
the Department of Commerce, the Department of Energy, NASA, and the Defense
Information Managers Group.) This Web site has CENDI publications, materials

from CENDI workshops, and information from CENDI component working groups. Topics covered include digital libraries, copyright, digital content management, knowledge organization, and current federal STI projects.

Despite CENDI's specialized mission and membership, the content available on this site may also be useful to digital library managers outside the realms of federal and scientific/technical information.

Subjects: Digital Libraries; Government Information

1053. Federal Web Content Managers Toolkit
http://www.webcontent.gov/
Alternate URL(s): http://www.firstgov.gov/webcontent/
Sponsor(s): General Services Administration (GSA)
Description: This site is the product of the Web Content Management Working Group, a group of about 20 federal agency Web content managers who work to promote best practices for federal government Web sites. The site outlines the legal requirements for all federal Web sites and recommends specific "visitor-friendly" practices. Other topics covered include Web site evaluation and metrics, content management, and writing for the Internet.

Although some material on this site relates only to federal Web management, nongovernment Web site managers may find the recommendations and the site's library of online links to be useful.

Subjects: World Wide Web

1054. Government Information Preservation Working Group
http://www.itl.nist.gov/div895/gipwog/
Sponsor(s): Commerce Department — Technology Administration (TA) — National Institute of Standards and Technology (NIST)
Description: The Government Information Preservation Working Group (GIPWoG) is concerned with government use of optical storage technologies and with the preservation of digital government data. Its Web site includes minutes of the GIPWoG meetings.

Subjects: Information Technology

1055. Government Printing Office
http://www.gpo.gov/
Sponsor(s): Government Printing Office (GPO)
Description: As stated on its Web site, GPO "is the federal government's primary centralized resource for gathering, cataloging, producing, providing and preserving published information in all its forms." The site has information about GPO, its print and electronic information services for agencies, and contract opportunities for printing and publishing. The GPO site also links to the agency's major online service, GPO Access, at ⟨http://www.gpoaccess.gov/⟩.

Subjects: Government Publications

1056. GPO Access
http://www.gpoaccess.gov/
Sponsor(s): Government Printing Office (GPO) — Superintendent of Documents
Description: GPO produces, catalogs, and disseminates government information in print and electronic formats. Its GPO Access Web site provides catalogs and sales information for print and other physical forms of publication and carries a number of significant government documents in online database form or as electronic publications. GPO also disseminates government information products through the Federal Depository Library Program; depository libraries are listed and

described on this site. The About section describes the mission of GPO and provides links to press releases and relevant statutes.

The GPO Access home page is divided into sections for GPO services and GPO Access resources. The resources — online government publications and databases — are accessible by topic or by browsing under the branch of government responsible for creating the resource. Services include the U.S. Government Online Bookstore and the Federal Depository Library Program.

As the official source for electronic formats of core U.S. government documents, GPO Access is an essential resource. The site presents excellent finding tools for government information. Due to the number of important GPO Access resources, many are described in separate entries in this directory. GPO also has an agency Web site, which can be found at ⟨http://www.gpo.gov⟩.

Subjects: Government Publications; Databases
Publications: *Budget of the United States Government*, PREX 2.8:
Calendar of United States House of Representatives and History of Legislation, Y 1.2/2:
Code of Federal Regulations, AE 2.106/3:
Congressional Bills, Y 1.6:
Congressional Directory, Y 4.P 93/1:1/
Congressional Record (bound), X 1.1:
Congressional Record (Full-text, Daily Digest, Index), X 1.1/A:
Decisions of the Comptroller General, GA 1.5/A-2:
Economic Indicators, Y 4.EC 7:EC 7/
Economic Report of the President, PR 43.9:
Federal Depository Library Directory (Online), GP 3.36/2-2:
Federal Register, AE 2.106:
GAO Reports, GA 1.5/A:
House Bills, Y 1.4/6:
House Documents, Y 1.1/7:
House Reports, Y 1.1/8:
House Rules and Manual, Y 1.2:R 86/2/
List of CFR Sections Affected (cumulative), AE 2.106/2-2:
LSA, List of CFR Sections Affected, AE 2.106/2:
Privacy Act Issuances, AE 2.106/4:
Public Papers of the President, AE 2.114:
Senate Bills, Y 1.4/1:
Senate Calendar of Business (daily), Y 1.3/3:
Senate Documents, Y 1.1/3:
Senate Reports, Y 1.1/5:
Statutes at Large, AE 2.111:
U.S. Public Laws, AE 2.110:
United States Code, Y 1.2/5:
United States Government Manual, AE 2.108/2:
Weekly Compilation of Presidential Documents, AE 2.109:

1057. Information Security Oversight Office
http://www.archives.gov/isoo/
Sponsor(s): National Archives and Records Administration (NARA)
Description: The Information Security Oversight Office (ISOO) is responsible for policy and operations related to classifying, declassifying, and safeguarding national security information. Its Web site describes the scope of the office's authority and responsibilities. It features the *ISOO Annual Report* and annual declassification reports. Resources include a paper on "Methodology For Determining Appropriateness of an Original Classification Decision" and a link to "a listing of products evaluated by The National Security Agency (NSA) for those who need to sanitize, destroy, or dispose of media containing sensitive or classified

information" (from the Web site). The site also links to information about the National Archives' Interagency Security Classification Appeals Panel (ISCAP), which reviews classification decisions.

Subjects: Information Policy; National Security — Regulations
Publications: *ISOO (Information Security Oversight Office) Annual Reports*, AE 1.101/3:

1058. National Archives and Records Administration
http://www.archives.gov/
Sponsor(s): National Archives and Records Administration (NARA)
Description: NARA oversees the archival records of the executive, congressional, and judicial branches of the federal government. Its Web site describes these holdings and provides online access to selected digitized collections. The Research and Order section of the site offers an introduction to the archives' contents and how to search for materials. The Federal Records section has research guides and collections information organized by branch of government. Due to its popularity, the site also has a Genealogy section with tips on researching census records, military records, immigration records (ship passenger lists), naturalization records, and land records. The site's alphabetical subject index provides quick links to specific collections. Basic information about NARA and its copies of the United States Constitution and Declaration of Independence is available in Spanish.

NARA's Web site explains the agency's varied responsibilities and includes equally varied content. For example, NARA houses the Office of the Federal Register, which is responsible for publishing public laws and the *Federal Register*, and also for coordinating the Electoral College. NARA's Information Security Oversight Office works with security classification policies for government and industry. NARA also oversees the Presidential Libraries.

For archivists, the Records Managers section offers news and information pertaining to federal records management policy. For educators and students, the site provides lesson plans, an introductory research activity, and more. Technologists, archivists, librarians, and others may want to use the site to follow the progress of NARA's Electronic Records Archives initiative to develop methods for preserving and accessing electronic records, independent of any specific hardware or software, into the future.

This site is unusual in the scope of materials available. While very little actual archival material is online, NARA has put selected high-interest items on the site.
Subjects: Archives
Publications: *Citing Records in the National Archives of the United States*, AE 1.113:17/
Guide to Federal Records in the National Archives of the United States, AE 1.108:G 94/
ISOO (Information Security Oversight Office) Annual Reports, AE 1.101/3:
NARA Bulletin, AE 1.103:
National Archives and Records Administration Annual Report, AE 1.101:
National Archives, Calendar of Events, AE 1.129:
Prologue, GS 4.23:
Quarterly Compilation of Periodical Literature Reflecting the Use of Records in the National Archives, AE 1.128:

1059. National Technical Information Service

http://www.ntis.gov/

Sponsor(s): Commerce Department — Technology Administration (TA) — National Technical Information Service (NTIS)

Description: NTIS is one of the major government publishing agencies, featuring hundreds of thousands of publications related to scientific, technical, engineering, and business information that have been produced by or for the U.S. government. However, since NTIS is run on a cost recovery basis, many of its services require payment. Major sections of its Web site include Products, Services, National Audiovisual Center, and Homeland Security Information Center.

The NTIS catalog can be searched via the search library, which is found in the Products section. Searches result in citations and full abstracts. Some publications may be available online free of charge, but most must be ordered for a fee. The National Audiovisual Center is a searchable catalog of videos, audiocassettes, and other media products for education and training. The Homeland Security section the site highlights selected documents, videos, and other material available through NTIS for a broad range of areas related to homeland security.

Subjects: Government Publications; Scientific and Technical Information; Publication Catalogs

1060. Office of Information and Privacy

http://www.usdoj.gov/oip/oip.html

Sponsor(s): Justice Department

Description: The Office of Information and Privacy (OIP) manages the Department of Justice's responsibilities related to the Freedom of Information Act (FOIA) and the Privacy Act. These responsibilities include coordinating and implementing policy development and government-wide compliance for FOIA, compliance by the Justice Department for the Privacy Act, and the decisions on all appeals from denials of access to information under those acts by any component of the Justice Department. Its Web site includes online access to reference documents, including the *DOJ Annual FOIA Report.*

Subjects: Freedom of Information Act

Publications: *DOJ Annual FOIA Report,* J 1.1/11:

FOIA Post, J 1.58/1:

Justice Department Guide to the Freedom of Information Act, J 1.8/2:

Privacy Act Overview, J 1.8/2:F 87/

1061. Office of Information and Regulatory Affairs

http://www.whitehouse.gov/omb/inforeg/

Sponsor(s): Office of Management and Budget (OMB)

Description: In addition to its important responsibilities in the area of regulatory policy, OMB's Office of Information and Regulatory Affairs (OIRA) is concerned with government information collection and management. The Paperwork Requirements section of its Web site includes information about the Small Business Paperwork Relief Act, the Inventory of Approved Information Collections, and the federal budget for information collection. The site also has a section that provides federal government statistical programs and standards, including the schedule of release dates for principal federal economic indicators. The Information Policy, IT & E-Gov section covers e-government initiatives, federal information technology spending, information security, privacy guidance, the Government Paperwork Elimination Act, and the Freedom of Information Act.

OIRA also reviews draft federal regulations from federal agencies and articulates the administration's regulatory policy. Documents related to these activities can be found in the Regulatory Matters section of the OIRA site.

Subjects: Government Information — Policy; Regulatory Policy

1062. Public Interest Declassification Board

http://www.archives.gov/declassification/pidb/

Sponsor(s): National Archives and Records Administration (NARA)

Description: The Public Interest Declassification Board (PIDB) advises the president and executive branch officials on issues related to the review and declassification of national security documents to serve the public interest and contribute to an accurate archival record. Its Web site includes the minutes of PIDB meetings.

Subjects: Government Information — Policy; National Security

1063. U.S. Government Bookstore

http://bookstore.gpo.gov/

Sponsor(s): Government Printing Office (GPO)

Description: GPO's sales catalog can be searched by keyword or browsed by topic on this Web site. Documents can be ordered online. The site also features sections such as New Releases, Best Sellers, and Ordering Information. The New Titles e-mail service provides notifications of new publications by topic (such as business or health care).

Subjects: Government Publications; Publication Catalogs

Publications: *Sales Product Catalog*, GP 3.22/7:

1064. XML.Gov

http://www.xml.gov/

Sponsor(s): Chief Information Officers Council

Description: This Web site is maintained by a federal government staff group in order to facilitate implementation of XML technology in government information systems. (XML is a standard for structured documents and data on the Internet.) In addition to information about government activities in this area, the site also has sections on XML standards, guidelines, and tutorials.

Subjects: World Wide Web

Government Services

1065. Citizens' Stamp Advisory Committee

http://www.usps.com/communications/organization/csac.htm

Sponsor(s): Postal Service (USPS)

Description: The Citizens' Stamp Advisory Committee (CSAC) is the mechanism by which subjects are selected to be featured on U.S. postage stamps. CSAC receives recommendations, evaluates them, and makes recommendations to the postmaster general. This U.S. Postal Service Web site has information about CSAC, a list of current committee members, and the formal criteria for stamp subject selection.

Subjects: Postage Stamps

1066. eStrategy — eGov Strategies

http://www.gsa.gov/estrategy/

Sponsor(s): General Services Administration (GSA)

Description: The GSA Office of Electronic Government and Technology operates the eStrategy Web site as its home page. The site carries major laws, regulations, policy statements, and other documents related to electronic government initiatives. Other sections include Delivery of Government Services and Information, Emerging Technology and Standards, and Securely Doing Business with the Government (which covers encryption and authentication).

The eStrategy site is useful for locating government information policy documents and information about standards and practices in this area. It links to a variety of federal content, but some of these Web pages are more frequently updated than others. The site also refers users to Egov.gov for specific examples of electronic government projects.

Subjects: Government Information — Policy

1067. Federal Emergency Management Agency

http://www.fema.gov/

Sponsor(s): Homeland Security Department — Federal Emergency Management Agency (FEMA)

Description: The FEMA Web site features news and victim assistance information for any current disasters in the United States. In the Get Disaster Info section, the site has lists of declared emergencies and disasters going back to 1953. The site also provides information about how to prepare for emergencies ranging from floods to terrorist threats, how to apply for disaster assistance, and how to keep safe and recover after a disaster. Audience-specific sections provide information and resources for businesses, emergency personnel, kids, Spanish speakers, homeowners, and livestock and pet owners. The About Us section has a leadership directory and directories of grants and training. The site map is an alphabetical index providing quick access to resources such as "FEMA Acronyms, Abbreviations, and Terms" (known as the FAAT List), and FEMA programs such as the National Fire Academy, the National Fire Incident Reporting System, the National Flood Insurance Program, and urban search-and-rescue programs. FEMA publications can be searched in the Library section. The FEMA Web site is also available in Spanish.

FEMA attempts to provide clear, factual information for people preparing for risks or recovering from a disaster. While the home page focuses on current events, the alphabetical site index may help users locate information that otherwise might be missed.

Subjects: Disaster Assistance

Publications: *Are You Ready? A Guide to Citizen Preparedness*, FEM 1.8/3:34/
Emergency Management Institute, Course Listings and Descriptions, FEM 1.17/2:
FEMA News Releases, FEM 1.28:
Flood Insurance Manual, FEM 1.8:
National Flood Insurance Program Community Status Book, FEM 1.210
Recovery Times, FEM 1.26:

1068. Federal Funds Express

http://www.house.gov/ffr/federal_funding_reports.shtml

Sponsor(s): Congress — House of Representatives

Description: This House of Representatives resource has two parts: the weekly *Federal Funds Report* and an extensive list of links to Web sites related to grants and financial assistance from both government and private sources. The *Federal Funds Report* includes a weekly summary of items published in the *Federal Register* that affect federal domestic assistance programs. It highlights grants with upcoming deadlines and lists geographic areas currently eligible for economic injury or disaster loans. Reports from the last two months are kept online for in HTML and Microsoft Word formats.

The House of Representatives has long published the *Federal Funds Report* to support members of Congress in their constituent services role. This online public version will be of interest to other users researching federal assistance for their communities.

Subjects: Disaster Assistance; Grants

1069. FloodSmart.gov
http://www.floodsmart.gov/
Alternate URL(s): http://www.fema.gov/business/nfip/
Sponsor(s): Homeland Security Department — Federal Emergency Management Agency (FEMA)
Description: FloodSmart.gov has consumer information on flood risk, preparing for flooding, and flood insurance. The Web site is sponsored by the National Flood Insurance Program (NFIP). The main NFIP Web page is located at the alternate URL above.
Subjects: Flood Insurance

1070. GovLoans.gov
http://govloans.gov/
Sponsor(s): Labor Department
Description: GovLoans.gov is a central location for information about federal loan programs. Major sections cover topics such as agriculture, business, disaster relief, education, housing, and veterans' loans. The site is a cooperative effort between the Departments of Agriculture, Education, Housing and Urban Development, and Veterans Affairs, and the Small Business Administration. It is hosted by the Department of Labor's GovBenefits.gov Web site. GovLoans.gov also has a version in Spanish.
Subjects: Government Loans

1071. LEP.gov
http://www.lep.gov/
Sponsor(s): Federal Interagency Working Group on Limited English Proficiency
Description: The Let Everyone Participate, or LEP.gov, Web site was created by the Federal Interagency Working Group on Limited English Proficiency. The site offers information and guidance for language access to federal and federally assisted programs, with three major target audiences: federal agencies, recipients of federal funds, and community organizations. Linked resources include federal regulations, directories of translator and interpreter organizations, and demographic data on English speaking ability.
Subjects: Civil Rights — Regulations; Language Groups

1072. Postal Rate Commission
http://www.prc.gov/
Sponsor(s): Postal Rate Commission (PRC)
Description: PRC is an independent regulatory agency that reviews Postal Service requests for changes in postal rates. Its Web site lists current and historical postal rates and has a helpful FAQ section about how postal rates are set. The home page menu includes public notices and PRC reports and testimony for Congress. The Contents section provides the easiest access to docketed and pending cases, opinions and decisions, orders, commission rules, and the *Domestic Mail Classification Schedule*; users should click "Contents" on the top menu to view the document listings in the left menu.
Subjects: Postal Service — Regulations
Publications: *Opinion and Recommended Decision*, Y 3.P 84/4:
Report to the Congress: International Mail Volumes, Costs and Revenues, Y 3.P 84/4:

1073. United States Postal Service
http://www.usps.com/
Sponsor(s): Postal Service (USPS)
Description: The USPS Web site features reference resources and services for the general public and businesses, which are organized into sections including: Find ZIP Codes, Calculate Postage, and Locate Post Offices. The Find ZIP Codes section includes a ZIP + 4 Code Lookup form and the option to find all ZIP codes in a city or all cities in a ZIP code. Help, a small link in the upper right corner, provides quick links to reference information such as acronyms, abbreviations, glossaries, and frequently asked questions. The site also features a Business Mail 101 section, which explains the classes of bulk mail. The site's Forms section, which is accessed through a link at the bottom of the page, has over 100 U.S. postal forms in PDF format.

USPS publications and institutional information are available in the About USPS and News section. This section includes employment information, contracting information, news releases, stamp news, and USPS newsletters and publications. In the Serving the Community subsection, there is a directory of postmasters and information on USPS facilities and the security of the U.S. mail.

Subjects: Postal Service
Publications: *Annual Report of the Postmaster General*, P 1.1:
Comprehensive Statement on Postal Operations, P 1.2:P 84/
Domestic Mail Manual, P 1.12/11:
International Mail Manual, P 1.10/5:
Mailers Companion, P 1.47/2:
Memo to Mailers, P 1.47:
Postal Bulletin, P 1.3:
Postal Facts, P 1.60:
ZIP + 4 State Directory, P 1.10/9:

1074. USA Services/Federal Citizen Information Center
http://www.info.gov/
Sponsor(s): General Services Administration (GSA)
Description: This Web site promotes citizen information services administered by the GSA. The site provides information on the toll-free phone service at 1-800-FED-INFO, an e-mail-based federal government information service, and online answers to frequently asked questions. It also links to the FirstGov.gov service.
Subjects: Government Information

Intergovernmental Relations

1075. Advisory Commission on Intergovernmental Relations
http://www.library.unt.edu/gpo/acir/acir.htm
Sponsor(s): Advisory Commission on Intergovernmental Relations (ACIR); University of North Texas Libraries
Description: The Advisory Commission on Intergovernmental Relations (ACIR) was established by Congress in 1959 to study the relationships between local, state, and federal government. The commission was closed in 1996. The University of North Texas Libraries maintains this Web site to provide permanent public access to the electronic publications that were available on the ACIR Web site. It includes editions of *Significant Features of Fiscal Federalism*, a reference tool for data on state and federal revenues and expenditures and federal spending in the states. All volumes from 1976 through 1994 and Volume I from 1995 are available online.

The ACIR materials are accessible thanks to a partnership between the University of North Texas Libraries and the U.S. Government Printing Office to provide permanent public access to the electronic Web sites and publications of defunct U.S. government agencies and commissions.

Subjects: Intergovernmental Relations
Publications: *Intergovernmental Perspective,* Y 3.AD 9/8:11/
Significant Features of Fiscal Federalism, Y 3.AD 9/8:18/

1076. Bureau of Indian Affairs

http://www.doi.gov/bureau-indian-affairs.html
Sponsor(s): Interior Department — Bureau of Indian Affairs (BIA)
Description: Due to ongoing litigation, the Department of Interior is not permitted — at the time of this writing — to operate its BIA Web site. The current BIA Web page provides a brief description of the agency, notes that the site is unavailable due to the litigation, and provides links for other Interior Department sites. The case in question is *Elouise Pepion Cobell, et al., v. Dirk Kempthorne, Secretary of the Interior* (formerly *Cobell v. Norton*); it concerns the management of the Indian trust fund accounting system.
Subjects: American Indians

1077. Code Talk

http://www.hud.gov/offices/pih/ih/codetalk/
Sponsor(s): Housing and Urban Development (HUD) — Office of Native American Programs (ONAP)
Description: Code Talk is an interagency Web site that was established to deliver electronic information from government agencies and other organizations to Native American communities. The name is based on the Native American Code Talkers, heroes of the two World Wars. The site is hosted on the Department of Housing and Urban Development (HUD) Web site and includes detailed information about American Indian housing programs. Other sections include Current Issues, which discusses protection of sacred sites, and Key Topics, which provides resources for urban Indians. The site also features links to related Web sites.
Subjects: American Indians

1078. DisasterHelp

http://www.disasterhelp.gov/
Sponsor(s): Federal Emergency Management Agency (FEMA)
Description: DisasterHelp is the federal government's portal to information about disaster assistance and services from state and federal government and from nongovernment sources. It is meant to help both the general public and first responders (such as local police, fire, and rescue squads). The site provides both preparedness and assistance information about disasters such as earthquakes, floods, hurricanes, and hazardous materials incidents. Validated emergency professionals can register to gain access to additional features on the Web site.
Subjects: Disaster Assistance

1079. Federal, State, and Local Governments (Census)

http://www.census.gov/govs/www/
Sponsor(s): Commerce Department — Economics and Statistics Administration (ESA) — Census Bureau
Description: This Web site brings together information from Census Bureau programs that cover local, state, and federal governments and their finances. Featured data sources include the *Census of Governments, State Government Tax Collections Survey, Federal Assistance Award Data System,* and *Consolidated Federal*

Funds Reports. The site has survey forms, publications, summary reports, and press releases. Statistics are available under topical headings such as Public Employment and Payroll, Finance, Public Employment Retirement Systems, Tax Collections, and Federal Expenditures. Many of the data series are available back to 1992. There are options to view national or individual state data, and reports can be downloaded in spreadsheet format or as a flat ASCII file.
Subjects: Government Employees — Statistics; Government Finance — Statistics; State Government — Statistics
Publications: *Census of Governments*, GP 3.22/2:
Consolidated Federal Funds Report, C 3.266/3:
Federal Assistance Award Data System
Public Elementary-Secondary Education Finances, C 3.191/2-10:
State Government Tax Collection Data by State, C 3.191/2-8:

1080. Insular Affairs
http://www.doi.gov/oia/
Sponsor(s): Interior Department
Description: The Department of the Interior's Office of Insular Affairs (OIA) has administrative responsibility for coordinating federal policy in the territories of American Samoa, Guam, the U.S. Virgin Islands, and the Commonwealth of the Northern Mariana Islands, as well as oversight of federal programs and funds in the freely associated states of the Federated States of Micronesia, the Republic of the Marshall Islands, and the Republic of Palau. OIA's Web site serves as a central point for information about these islands, including island statistics and economic reports. The site has a directory of the islands' representatives, delegates, and liaison offices in the United States and a list of U.S. embassies in the freely associated states.
Subjects: Intergovernmental Relations

1081. Office of the Special Trustee for American Indians
http://www.ost.doi.gov/
Sponsor(s): Interior Department — Office of Special Trustees for American Indians (OST)
Description: The Office of the Special Trustee for American Indians (OST) was created by law in 1994 to improve the accountability and management of Indian funds held in trust by the federal government. This Web site has background information about OST's mission and a Frequently Asked Questions section about Indian trust management. The site's Trust Reform Document Library provides public documents relating to the OST and its work.
Subjects: American Indians
Publications: *Comprehensive Trust Management Plan*, I 1.2:

1082. Office of Tribal Justice
http://www.usdoj.gov/otj/
Sponsor(s): Justice Department — Tribal Justice Office
Description: The Office of Tribal Justice was established in 1995 with the purpose of increasing the responsiveness of the Department of Justice to the concerns of the American Indian Nations, individual Indians, and others interested in Indian affairs. The About OTJ section has the Department of Justice Sovereignty Policy and related presidential documents. The Press Room includes the White House newsletter *Indian Country Update* and press releases about court judgments. The Resources section links to information about law enforcement assistance grants.
Subjects: American Indians

Public Policy

1083. John C. Stennis Center for Public Service

http://www.stennis.gov/

Sponsor(s): Stennis Center for Public Service

Description: The John C. Stennis Center for Public Service was created by Congress in 1988 to promote public service in the United States at all levels of government. The center is governed by a board of trustees appointed by the Democratic and Republican leaders in the U.S. Senate and House of Representatives. The Web site has information about the center's programs and its namesake. Programs described include the Civil Military Leadership Program, the Emerging Congressional Staff Leadership Program, Congressional Staff Fellows, and the Stennis Student Congress.

Subjects: Fellowships; Civics Education

1084. Woodrow Wilson International Center for Scholars

http://www.wilsoncenter.org/

Sponsor(s): Woodrow Wilson International Center for Scholars

Description: The Wilson Center supports scholarship linked to public policy. The center offers fellowships and special opportunities for research and writing with a focus on history, political science, and international relations. As a public-private partnership, the center receives roughly one-third of its operating funds from a U.S. government appropriation. The Web site has information about current Wilson Center projects and publications, and audio files of its weekly radio program, "Dialogue." The site also carries essays and other items from the center's journal, *The Wilson Quarterly*. In the About section, the site offers information on applying for a fellowship or internship with the center, and a media guide with a directory of the center's subject experts.

Subjects: Fellowships; Public Policy — Research; Social Science Research

Publications: *The Wilson Quarterly*

CHAPTER 13

Health and Safety

Government health sciences Web sites serve everyone from research scientists to clinicians and the general public. Health science professionals have used government Web sites to expand a tradition of disseminating research information. Government information on the Internet has also been a boon to average citizens seeking authoritative medical information written in layman's terms. This chapter includes the full range of information, as well as resources on nutrition, safety, and health care finance.

Subsections in this chapter are Conditions and Treatment, Health Care Finance, Health Occupations, Health Policy and Promotion, Health Research, Medical Information, Medicine and Medical Devices, Nutrition, and Safety.

Conditions and Treatment

1085. AIDS.gov
http://www.aids.gov/
Sponsor(s): Health and Human Services Department
Description: AIDS.gov is a portal to federal, domestic HIV/AIDS information and resources. Major sections include News, Basic HIV/AIDS Information, Prevention, Treatment, Testing, Populations, and Research. A section on funding opportunities has information for both individuals and organizations. The site also links to federal program Web sites, organized by categories such as Housing Initiatives, Minority Initiatives, and Treatment and Care Initiatives.
Subjects: AIDS

1086. AIDSinfo
http://aidsinfo.nih.gov/
Sponsor(s): Health and Human Services Department
Description: AIDSinfo is a user-friendly Web site with well designed sections on drugs, clinical trials, vaccines, and guidelines for prevention and treatment. The Health Topics section is a portal to information from government and a variety of other sources on all of these aspects of AIDS treatment. Health Topics and the AIDSinfo Tools section also helpfully provide information on 800 numbers and other non-Internet sources of information. Some publications are available in Spanish.
Subjects: AIDS

1087. Alzheimer's Disease Education and Referral (ADEAR) Center
http://www.alzheimers.org/
Sponsor(s): National Institutes of Health (NIH) — National Institute on Aging (NIA)
Description: The ADEAR Center is operated as a service of the National Institute on Aging. It is an information clearinghouse for health professionals, people with Alzheimer's, their families, and the public. The site provides information on the disease and news of current research and clinical trials, with links to Alzheimer's research centers. An e-mail service provides free updates.
Subjects: Alzheimer's Disease

1088. Cancer Control PLANET
http://cancercontrolplanet.cancer.gov/
Sponsor(s): Health and Human Services Department
Description: Cancer Control PLANET is designed specifically for professional cancer control planners, program staff, and researchers. Its Web site is a portal to information needed in developing cancer control programs; it links primarily to information compiled by the federal government. The site is sponsored the American Cancer Society and by Department of Health and Human Services agencies, including the National Institutes of Health and the Centers for Disease Control and Prevention.
Subjects: Cancer; Public Health

1089. Cancer Information Service (CIS)
http://cis.nci.nih.gov/
Sponsor(s): National Institutes of Health (NIH) — National Cancer Institute (NCI)
Description: CIS is a free, public service set up to answer individual questions about cancer. This central site links to the Web sites of CIS regional offices throughout the United States. In addition to providing information about CIS, the site links to cancer news, resources, and publications. CIS also operates a toll free number, 1-800-4-CANCER.
Subjects: Cancer

1090. CDC Cancer Prevention and Control
http://www.cdc.gov/cancer/
Sponsor(s): Health and Human Services Department — Centers for Disease Control and Prevention (CDC) — Cancer Prevention and Control Division
Description: The CDC Cancer Prevention and Control Web site provides state and national statistics, fact sheets, and publications related to cancer. The Quick Links section covers seven common types of cancer as well as sections on Comprehensive Cancer Control, Cancer Survivorship, Health Disparities in Cancer, and Cancer Registries/Surveillance. The site has a Spanish-language version.
Subjects: Cancer — Statistics
Publications: *The Cancer Atlas*
The Tobacco Atlas
United States Cancer Statistics, HE 20.7045:

1091. CDC National Prevention Information Network
http://www.cdcnpin.org/
Sponsor(s): Health and Human Services Department — Centers for Disease Control and Prevention (CDC) — National Center for HIV, STD, and TB Prevention (NCHSTP)
Description: The CDC National Prevention Information Network (NPIN) focuses on control and prevention of HIV/AIDS, Sexually Transmitted Diseases (STDs), and Tuberculosis (TB). NPIN has databases of relevant organizations, conferences, and private and government funding opportunities for community-based and HIV/AIDS, STD, and TB service organizations. The site also has current news and information about communities at risk.
Subjects: AIDS; HIV Infections; Sexually Transmitted Diseases; Tuberculosis
Publications: *CDC HIV/STD/TB Prevention News Update*, HE 20.7318:

1092. Centers for Disease Control and Prevention
http://www.cdc.gov/

Sponsor(s): Health and Human Services Department — Centers for Disease Control and Prevention (CDC)

Description: The CDC is concerned with public health, disease prevention and control, environmental health, and health promotion and education. Its main Web site has information about the agency with links to all of CDC's component centers, institutes, and offices (under About CDC, CDC Organization). The site features current public health topics of interest. The Health and Safety Topics section is a gateway to extensive CDC information under categories such as Health Promotion, Diseases and Conditions, and Vaccines and Immunizations. The Publications and Products section includes the *Morbidity and Mortality Weekly Report*, the journals *Emerging Infectious Diseases* and *Preventing Chronic Disease*, and the weekly e-mail newsletter *CDC Public Health Law News*. The Data and Statistics section brings together news and links for CDC's many statistical compilation, including pediatric growth charts. The CDC Web site also has a Spanish-language version.

This main CDC page serves as a starting point for finding extensive information on various diseases, disease statistics, and disease prevention. The information is well organized, and the pages are easy to navigate. An A-Z index also aids navigation.

Subjects: Diseases and Conditions; Epidemiology; Public Health

Publications: *Advance Data from the Vital and Health Statistics*, HE 20.6209/3:
Chronic Disease Notes and Reports, HE 20.7009/6:
Emerging Infectious Diseases, HE 20.7817:
Fact Sheets (NCHSTP-HIV/AIDS Prevention Division), HE 20.7320/3:
Health Information for International Travelers, HE 20.7315:
MMWR Recommendation and Reports, HE 20.7009/2-2:
Morbidity and Mortality Weekly Report, HE 20.7009:
National Vital Statistics Report (monthly), HE 20.6217:
Preventing Chronic Disease, HE 20.7620:
Summary of Sanitation Inspection of International Cruise Ships, HE 20.7511:

1093. Diabetes Public Health Resource
http://www.cdc.gov/diabetes/

Sponsor(s): Health and Human Services Department — Centers for Disease Control and Prevention (CDC) — National Center for Chronic Disease Prevention and Health Promotion (NCCDPHP)

Description: This site communicates practical information on diabetes prevention and control. It includes a diabetes fact sheet, frequently asked questions, diabetes statistics, and information on state-based diabetes prevention and control programs. The Newsroom section has CDC statements, press releases, and congressional testimony related to diabetes. The site also has a Spanish-language version.

Subjects: Diabetes

1094. DoD Global Emerging Infections System (DoD-GEIS)
http://www.geis.fhp.osd.mil/

Sponsor(s): Defense Department

Description: This site, also known as DoD-GEISWeb, is concerned with infectious diseases that threaten either military personnel readiness or national security. The Web site has information about the program and infectious disease news from around the world. Programs featured on the site concern antimicrobial resistance, influenza, malaria, and other topics.

Subjects: Military Medicine

1095. GulfLINK

http://www.gulflink.osd.mil/

Sponsor(s): Defense Department — Office of the Special Assistant for Gulf War Illnesses
Description: GulfLINK has news and information on illnesses reported by veterans of the Persian Gulf War of 1991. The site includes a substantial collection of documents, including Environmental Exposure Reports, congressional testimony, and declassified documents. The declassified documents are in ASCII text and can be searched by keyword and or browsed by release date.

Altogether, these resources create a sizable database about the Gulf War Veterans' Disease that can be useful to veterans, health care workers, and researchers.
Subjects: Gulf War Disease
Publications: *GulfNEWS*, D 1.95/5:

1096. HIV/AIDS Surveillance Reports

http://www.cdc.gov/hiv/stats/hasrlink.htm

Sponsor(s): Health and Human Services Department — Centers for Disease Control and Prevention (CDC) — National Center for HIV, STD, and TB Prevention (NCHSTP)
Description: These annual reports contain detailed statistics on the incidence of HIV and AIDS in the United States, including data by state, metropolitan statistical area, mode of exposure to HIV, sex, race/ethnicity, age group, vital status, and case definition category. Past issues are online back to 1982.
Subjects: AIDS — Statistics; HIV Infections — Statistics
Publications: *HIV/AIDS Surveillance Report*, HE 20.7320:

1097. National Center for HIV, STD, and TB Prevention

http://www.cdc.gov/nchstp/od/nchstp.html

Sponsor(s): Health and Human Services Department — Centers for Disease Control and Prevention (CDC) — National Center for HIV, STD, and TB Prevention (NCHSTP)
Description: The NCHSTP Web site features current research news and data. Each of the Center's components maintains a Web page with in-depth information. Divisions include: HIV/AIDS Prevention; the Global AIDS Program; Division of AIDS, STD, and TB Laboratory Research; Tuberculosis Elimination; and Sexually Transmitted Diseases.

This site is worth a visit for information about any of the areas covered by NCHSTP. It offers resources for researchers, patients, public health professionals, and the public.
Subjects: AIDS; HIV Infections; Sexually Transmitted Diseases
Publications: *HIV/AIDS Surveillance Report*, HE 20.7320:
Reported Tuberculosis in the United States, HE 20.7310:
Sexually Transmitted Disease Surveillance, HE 20.7309/2:
TB Notes, HE 20.7310/2:

1098. National Center for Infectious Diseases

http://www.cdc.gov/ncidod/

Sponsor(s): Health and Human Services Department — Centers for Disease Control and Prevention (CDC) — National Center for Infectious Diseases (NCID)
Description: One major resource on this Web site is the electronic version of the journal *Emerging Infectious Diseases* (*EID*). The goals of this publication and the NCID Web site are to promote the recognition of new and reemerging infectious diseases and to improve the understanding of factors involved in disease emergence, prevention, and elimination. The site features resources for teachers and students along with material for health professionals. More information is available

from NCID's division pages, including Global Migration and Quarantine, Parasitic Diseases, Vector-Borne Diseases, and Viral Hepatitis. The site also has a Infectious Disease Index, with an alphabetical list of diseases and links to information about them.

Especially within the online pages of *EID*, this site contains a great deal of information on the prevention and control of traditional, new, and reemerging infectious diseases both in the United States and around the world. A section called Ahead of Print provides citations and selected text of articles scheduled to appear in future issues of *EID*; it is available as an RSS newsfeed.

Subjects: Diseases and Conditions
Publications: *Emerging Infectious Diseases*, HE 20.7817:
Health Information for International Travel, HE 20.7818:
Summary of Health Information for International Travel, HE 20.7818/2:

1099. National Center for PSTD
http://www.ncptsd.va.gov/
Sponsor(s): Veterans Affairs Department
Description: The VA's National Center for Post-Traumatic Stress Disorder (PTSD) provides this Web site as an educational resource concerning PTSD and other consequences of traumatic stress. Topics covered by the site include combat stress but also cover trauma caused by disasters, refugee status, abuse, sexual assault, and other topics. The site offers free online access to PILOTS, a database indexing the literature on PTSD and other mental-health consequences of exposure to traumatic events.
Subjects: Mental Health; Veterans
Publications: *PTSD Research Quarterly*, VA 1.94:

1100. National Diabetes Education Program
http://www.ndep.nih.gov/
Sponsor(s): National Institutes of Health (NIH)
Description: The National Diabetes Education Program (NDEP) is a partnership of NIH, the Centers for Disease Control and Prevention, and over 200 public and private organizations to promote awareness of diabetes prevention and control. The site has a wealth of background information on diagnosis, prevention, and treatment. It includes resources for health, education, and business professionals. The Awareness Campaign section has public service announcements, fact sheets, brochures, and flyers.
Subjects: Diabetes

1101. National Heart, Lung, and Blood Institute
http://www.nhlbi.nih.gov/
Sponsor(s): National Institutes of Health (NIH) — National Heart, Lung, and Blood Institute (NHLBI)
Description: The Institute organizes resources into sections for the public, patients, health professionals, and researchers. Health Information, a section for the public and patients, covers such topics as Heart and Vascular Diseases, Lung Diseases, Blood Diseases, and Sleep Disorders. The site also links to educational material on cholesterol, high blood pressure, weight control, recipes for healthy eating, and heart attack warning signs. Sections for professionals cover information including clinical practice guidelines, scientific reports, and continuing education. Information for researchers includes technology transfer opportunities and clinical trial news. NHLBI also provides a Research and Policy Update e-mail news service.
Subjects: Heart Disease — Research
Publications: *Morbidity and Mortality: Chartbook on Cardiovascular, Lung, and Blood Diseases*, HE 20.3226:

1102. National HIV Testing Resources
http://www.hivtest.org/
Sponsor(s): Health and Human Services Department — Centers for Disease Control and Prevention (CDC)
Description: The site features of nationwide database of HIV testing locations. It also provides information on the topic in both English and Spanish.
Subjects: HIV Infections

1103. National Kidney Disease Education Program (NKDEP)
http://www.nkdep.nih.gov/
Sponsor(s): National Institutes of Health (NIH) — National Institute of Diabetes and Digestive and Kidney Disease (NIDDK)
Description: The NKDEP site has sections for patients and the public, health professionals, and laboratory professionals. Each section provides detailed information on different aspects of kidney disease diagnosis and care. The site also includes resources for promoting awareness of kidney disease.
Subjects: Kidney Disease

1104. NIH Senior Health
http://nihseniorhealth.gov/
Sponsor(s): National Institutes of Health (NIH) — National Institute on Aging (NIA)
Description: The NIH Senior Health Web site is a joint project of the National Institute on Aging and the National Library of Medicine to produce Web content for seniors that is designed in an age-appropriate style. The site uses large print and breaks content into short segments. Sections include Alzheimer's Disease, Arthritis, Hearing Loss, Prostate Cancer, Taking Medicines, and more. Some sections include short video clips with the option of reading the video transcript.
Subjects: Alzheimer's Disease; Senior Citizens

1105. Office of Cancer Survivorship
http://dccps.nci.nih.gov/ocs/
Alternate URL(s): http://survivorship.cancer.gov
Sponsor(s): National Institutes of Health (NIH) — National Cancer Institute (NCI)
Description: This Web site is designed for researchers, health professionals, advocates, and cancer survivors and their families. Sections include About Cancer Survivorship, Post Treatment Resources, Funding Opportunities, Cancer Control Research, and Research Findings.
   The Post Treatment Resources section is the area that may be of most assistance to cancer survivors and their families.
Subjects: Cancer

1106. Office of Rare Diseases
http://rarediseases.info.nih.gov/
Sponsor(s): National Institutes of Health (NIH) — Office of Rare Diseases
Description: The Office of Rare Diseases is concerned with research on rare, or orphan, diseases, defined as diseases or conditions affecting fewer than 200,000 persons in the United States. The Web site provides resources on research, clinical trials, conferences, patient support groups, and relevant genetics information for rare diseases. It also has information on NIH's Genetic and Rare Diseases Information Center, which handles information requests by mail, phone, fax, or e-mail.
Subjects: Diseases and Conditions — Research

1107. Organ Donation
http://www.organdonor.gov/
Sponsor(s): Health and Human Services Department — Health Resources and Services Administration (HRSA)
Description: This Department of Health and Human Services Web site provides general information on the process of organ and tissue donation and information on how to sign up. It features a downloadable donor card and brochure. Sections include: Organ Donor Registries, Myths and Facts, Data (numbers of waiting list candidates, transplants, and donors), Grants, the Advisory Committee on Organ Transplantation, and the National Marrow Donor Program.
Subjects: Medical Information

1108. Prevention Online (PREVLINE): SAMHSA's National Clearinghouse for Alcohol and Drug Information
http://ncadi.samhsa.gov/
Sponsor(s): Health and Human Services Department — Substance Abuse and Mental Health Services Administration (SAMHSA)
Description: PREVLINE provides a wealth of information resources on substance abuse, prevention, and treatment. It includes pamphlets, a treatment facility locator, and self-help resources. The site also organizes content into sections for Family, Youth, School, Workplace, and Community.
Subjects: Substance Abuse
Publications: *Drug Abuse Warning Network (DAWN)*, HE 20.416/3:
Mind over Matter: The Brain's Response to. . ., HE 20.3965/3:
Substance Abuse Treatment Facility Locator, HE 20.410/3:
Tips for Teens about . . ., HE 20.8002:T 49/

1109. SAMHSA's National Mental Health Information Center
http://www.mentalhealth.samhsa.gov
Sponsor(s): Health and Human Services Department — Substance Abuse and Mental Health Services Administration (SAMHSA)
Description: National Mental Health Information Center serves as a clearinghouse for mental health resources and information for the general public, health professionals, and others. The Web site is divided into sections for mental health topics, program information, news releases and media information, publications, and other resources. Many publications are available online in HTML format; others can be ordered online. The Mental Health Topics section provides, for each condition or topic, links to online publications, related Web sites, and information on organizations concerned with the topic.

Because of the breadth of its coverage, this clearinghouse site can be a good place to start when looking for assistance on mental health topics.
Subjects: Mental Health

1110. West Nile Virus
http://www.cdc.gov/ncidod/dvbid/westnile/
Sponsor(s): Health and Human Services Department — Centers for Disease Control and Prevention (CDC) — National Center for Infectious Diseases (NCID)
Description: This Web site has tips on West Nile Virus prevention for individuals, communities, and health professionals. A questions-and-answers feature covers topics such as insect repellants, testing and treatment, and statistics on human cases. Fact sheets are online in English, Spanish, Russian, Vietnamese, and other languages. More technical sections include Clinical Guidance, Laboratory Guidance, and Ecology/Virology. The site also links to state and local Web sites on West Nile.

Subjects: Mosquitoes
Publications: *Epidemic/Epizootic West Nile Virus in the United States: Revised Guidelines for Surveillance, Prevention, and Control,* HE 20.7808:

Health Care Finance

1111. Centers for Medicare and Medicaid Services (CMS)
http://cms.hhs.gov/
Sponsor(s): Health and Human Services Department — Centers for Medicare and Medicaid Services
Description: CMS runs the Medicare program and oversees the federal portions of Medicaid and the State Children's Health Insurance Program (SCHIP). The CMS Web site has information on the programs it administers, which also include portions of the Health Insurance Portability and Accountability Act and the Clinical Laboratory Improvement Amendments. The Regulations and Guidance section includes CMS program manuals, rulings, transmittals, regulatory updates, and extensive background on major laws. The extensive and varied information in the Research, Statistics, Data and Systems section includes the *Health Care Financing Review* journal (in ZIP, PDF format), Medicare enrollment tables, and the report of the Medicare trustees. Other sections include End Stage Renal Disease (ESRD) Center, Legislative Affairs, the Medicare Coverage policy database, and a glossary of program acronyms.

Much of the information on the CMS site is relevant to health care providers and program administrators. For consumer information on Medicare, see Medicare.gov at http://www.medicare.gov. For consumer information on SCHIP, see Insure Kids Now at http://www.insurekidsnow.gov. Each of these sites is listed elsewhere in this book.
Subjects: Health Care Finance; Medicaid; Medicare
Publications: *Active Projects Report,* HE 22.16/2:
CMS Quarterly Provider Update
CMS Rulings, HE 22.38:
Data Compendium, HE 22.511:
Health Care Financing Review, HE 22.512:
Skilled Nursing Facility Manual, HE 22.8/3:
The CMS Online Manual System, HE 22.8/23:

1112. Citizens' Health Care Working Group
http://www.citizenshealthcare.gov/
Sponsor(s): Health and Human Services Department
Description: The Citizens' Health Care Working Group was established by the Medicare Prescription Drug, Improvement, and Modernization Act of 2003 (Public Law 108-173). The group solicited recommendations from the American public and health care experts regarding policy on health care coverage. The group issued its final report in September 2006. The report, group documents, and background information are online at this site.
Subjects: Health Insurance — Policy
Publications: *Health Care that Works for All Americans*
The Health Report to the American People

1113. Competition in the Health Care Marketplace
http://www.ftc.gov/bc/healthcare/
Sponsor(s): Federal Trade Commission (FTC)
Description: This site covers FTC antitrust actions in the health care and pharmaceuticals services sector and efforts to promote competition in the health care market-

place. The site includes news releases on FTC activities, antitrust case documents, and pharmaceutical agreement filings. The research section links to papers by the FTC Bureau of Economics staff on health care competition issues.
Subjects: Antitrust Law; Health Care — Laws

1114. Health Care Benefits and Services
http://www1.va.gov/health/
Sponsor(s): Veterans Affairs Department — Veterans Health Administration (VHA)
Description: The VHA Web site is part of the larger Veterans Administration site. It provides general information on the agency, VHA forms, publications, links to offices within VHA, and a directory of VHA facilities. The Eligibility section has information on enrollment, applying for care, and covered services. For those receiving VHA benefits, the site offers the HealtheVets portal to VHA health information and to managing personal health records online. The site also covers specialized VHA concerns, such as Gulf War illnesses, Agent Orange, and Post-Traumatic Stress Disorder.
Subjects: Veterans
Publications: *Agent Orange Review*, VA 12.3/5
Annual Report to Congress: Federally Sponsored Research on Gulf War Veterans' Illnesses, VA 1.1/8:

1115. Insure Kids Now
http://www.insurekidsnow.gov/
Sponsor(s): Health and Human Services Department — Health Resources and Services Administration (HRSA)
Description: This site links to information on children's health insurance programs in each state and offers answers to a variety of questions about insurance for children. Sections include Your State's Program, About Insure Kids Now, Help Us Spread the Word, and Immigration Concerns. A Spanish-language version is available.
Subjects: Health Insurance; Child Health and Safety

1116. Medicare Payment Advisory Commission
http://www.medpac.gov/
Sponsor(s): Congress — Medicare Payment Advisory Commission (MedPAC)
Description: MedPAC is a nonpartisan congressional advisory body charged with providing policy advice and technical assistance for Medicare payment policies. Major sections of the Web site are About MedPAC, Meetings, Publications, and Research Areas.

Researchers will find extensive information in the Research Areas section and in the MedPAC *Data Book*.
Subjects: Medicare — Policy
Publications: *Data Book: Healthcare Spending and the Medicare Program*, Y 3.M 46/3:
MedPAC Report to Congress, Y 3.M 46/3:

1117. Medicare.gov
http://www.medicare.gov/
Sponsor(s): Health and Human Services Department — Centers for Medicare and Medicaid Services
Description: This official Medicare site for consumers features Medicare pamphlets and publications, news, and basic explanations of various aspects of Medicare. Sections cover information about Medicare enrollment, the prescription drug plan, long-term care, billing, appeals, and general tips on staying healthy. Under Search

Tools, the site offers Web tools to help consumers find, compare, or evaluate services, such as nursing homes, home health care, prescription drug plans, participating physicians, and useful phone numbers. Medicare publications are also listed under Search Tools.

Medicare.gov has a Spanish-language version, a screen reader version, and a printable version. The site also links to an access screen for MyMedicare.Gov, a personal Medicare beneficiary portal.

Subjects: Medicare; Nursing Homes

Publications: *Choosing a Medigap Policy: Guide To Health Insurance For People With Medicare*, HE 22.8/17:

Choosing Long-Term Care, HE 22.8:

Guide to Choosing a Nursing Home, HE 22.8:N 93/

Medicare and You, HE 22.8/16:

Medicare Hospice Benefits, HE 22.21/5:

1118. State Children's Health Insurance Program (SCHIP)
http://cms.hhs.gov/schip/

Sponsor(s): Health and Human Services Department — Centers for Medicare and Medicaid Services

Description: SCHIP is a state-administered federal program intended to help states expand health care coverage to uninsured children. This site has information on national SCHIP policy and a section on how states may cover dental insurance.

This site is intended for program administrators. Consumer information on the program is available from the federal Web site Insure Kids Now at ⟨http://www.insurekidsnow.gov⟩.

Subjects: Health Insurance; Child Health and Safety

1119. TRICARE, Military Health System
http://www.tricare.osd.mil/

Sponsor(s): Defense Department — TRICARE Management Activity

Description: TRICARE is the health care benefit for the military. This Web site provides information and documents for TRICARE beneficiaries and providers, including a directory of providers. The site has both a graphical and a text-only interface.

Subjects: Health Insurance; Military Medicine

1120. Value-Driven Health Care
http://www.hhs.gov/transparency/

Sponsor(s): Health and Human Services Department

Description: This is a policy-oriented site proposing a more interconnected health system with quality measures, comparable prices, and effective incentives for consumers, health care providers, and insurers. Web site sections include Health IT Standards, Quality Standards, Price Standards, and a resource section for employers. The site features information on Executive Order 13410, "Promoting Quality and Efficient Health Care in Federal Government Administered or Sponsored Health Care Programs."

Subjects: Health Care Finance — Policy

Health Occupations

1121. Bureau of Health Professions
http://bhpr.hrsa.gov/
Sponsor(s): Health and Human Services Department — Health Resources and Services Administration (HRSA) — Health Professions Bureau
Description: The mission of the Bureau of Health Professions is to ensure that health care professionals deliver quality services to all geographic areas and to all segments of society. Topics covered on the site include grants, student financial assistance, support for training programs, the National Health Service Corps, the National Center for Health Workforce Analysis, designated Health Professional Shortage Areas, and the Kids Into Health Careers Initiative. The National Center for Health Workforce Analysis section features data on the U.S. population of physicians, nurses, and other health workers. The site also links to the National Practitioner Data Bank (NPDB), described elsewhere in this book.
Subjects: Health Occupations — Grants; Medical Schools — Grants
Publications: *State Health Workforce Profiles*, HE 20.9302:
United States Health Personnel Factbook, HE 20.9002:

1122. Medical Reserve Corps (MRC)
http://www.medicalreservecorps.gov/
Sponsor(s): Health and Human Services Department — Public Health and Science Office — Surgeon GeneralUSA Freedom Corps
Description: MRC consists of local units of volunteer medical and public health professionals organized to assist their communities during emergencies and to promote public health. The MRC Web site has a directory of MRC units, program news, information on joining or forming a unit, and guidance for existing units. The MRC is a partner program with Citizen Corps, which is part of the USA Freedom Corps. The MRC's program office is headquartered in the Office of the U.S. Surgeon General.
Subjects: Disaster Preparedness; Public Health

1123. National Health Service Corps (NHSC)
http://nhsc.bhpr.hrsa.gov/
Sponsor(s): Health and Human Services Department — Health Resources and Services Administration (HRSA) — Health Professions Bureau
Description: NHSC recruits primary care clinicians for medically underserved areas. It offers financial assistance to medical students who will practice in underserved areas, as well as work experiences and residencies. The site has information about NHSC programs, online applications, and information on current communities with available positions.
Subjects: Health Care

1124. National Practitioner Data Bank
http://www.npdb-hipdb.hrsa.gov/
Sponsor(s): Health and Human Services Department — Health Resources and Services Administration (HRSA) — Health Professions Bureau
Description: In keeping with the full title of its Web site, "National Practitioner Data Bank—Healthcare Integrity and Protection Data Bank," the NPDB compiles records of malpractice and other adverse reports filed against physicians, dentists, and other health care practitioners. The HIPDB compiles reports of fraud and abuse in health insurance and health care delivery. Neither database is available to the general public in its entirety. A modified version of the data bank file,

containing selected information and no identification data, may be downloaded from the site. Under Statistical Information, the site links to annual reports, the publicly accessible file, and summary statistics from NPDB and HIPDB. Under Publications, the guidebooks and numerous fact sheets provide extensive information on both programs.

Subjects: Health Care — Regulations; Health Occupations — Regulations; Databases
Publications: *National Practitioner Data Bank Guidebook*, HE 20.9308:D 26/

1125. Uniformed Services University of the Health Sciences
http://www.usuhs.mil/
Sponsor(s): Defense Department — Uniformed Services University of the Health Sciences (USUHS)
Description: USUHS is a federal health sciences university providing specialized training in military medicine. This Web site provides basic information about the university, its School of Medicine, Graduate School of Nursing, and Armed Forces Radiobiology Research Institute.
Subjects: Medical Schools; Military Medicine

Health Policy and Promotion

1126. Administration on Aging
http://www.aoa.dhhs.gov/
Sponsor(s): Health and Human Services Department — Administration on Aging (AoA)
Description: The AoA Web site features resources for the elderly, their families, and professionals working with the elderly. The main page presents news about programs, conferences, and policy initiatives. The online Eldercare Locator is a nationwide directory assistance service designed to help older persons and caregivers locate local support services. A section for Elders and Families covers such topics as Alzheimer's, Caregivers, Elder Rights, and Nutrition. The AoA Grant Programs section describes current funding opportunities. The Press Room has fact sheets, publications, press releases, and other news services related to the aging.

This site includes a great deal of useful information on aging, the elderly, and health care for the elderly, including local referral to non-AoA organizations and resources.

Subjects: Senior Citizens
Publications: *Administration on Aging Annual Report*, HE 1.201:
Resource Directory for Older People, HE 20.3868:

1127. American Indian Health
http://americanindianhealth.nlm.nih.gov/
Sponsor(s): National Institutes of Health (NIH) — National Library of Medicine (NLM)
Description: This NLM-sponsored Web site calls itself "an information portal for and about the health of Native Peoples of the United States." The site links to Web resources from the federal government, academia, and health profession organizations. Information covered includes health care access, traditional healing, environmental health, and research. A Health Topics section points to similar specialized resources, such as a site focusing on health problems in American Indian and Alaska Native women.
Subjects: Health Promotion; American Indians

1128. Army Center for Health Promotion and Preventive Medicine (USACHPPM)
http://chppm-www.apgea.army.mil/
Sponsor(s): Army — Center for Health Promotion and Preventive Medicine
Description: This site presents information about USACHPPM including its mission, products and services, training and conferences, publications, directorates, and subordinate commands. Topical sections on the main page include Hot Topics, Diseases of Interest, and Safety and Environmental Health. The A-Z index points to specific topics, such as anthrax, camel spiders, nerve agents, oil fires, radiation, stress, and yellowjackets.

The site has a substantial amount of information on health promotion. Though targeted at a military audience, there is useful information for the general public.
Subjects: Preventive Health Care

1129. Asian American Health
http://asianamericanhealth.nlm.nih.gov/
Sponsor(s): National Institutes of Health (NIH) — National Library of Medicine (NLM)
Description: This is a portal to health information on the Internet for the diverse Asian American population. Major sections cover common diseases and conditions, complementary or alternative medicine, and behavioral and mental health issues. Links are also organized by Asian population, such as Korean or Filipino.
Subjects: Asian Americans

1130. Bioethics Resources on the Web
http://www.nih.gov/sigs/bioethics/
Sponsor(s): National Institutes of Health (NIH)
Description: This NIH site links to Web sites, documents, regulations, news, conferences, and other information about bioethics issues. Many of the resources are from NIH itself, but sources also include other federal agencies, universities, and organizations. The topics covered include human subjects research, laboratory animal use, stem cell research, and genetic testing.
Subjects: Bioethics

1131. Bureau of Primary Health Care (BPHC)
http://www.bphc.hrsa.gov/
Sponsor(s): Health and Human Services Department — Health Resources and Services Administration (HRSA) — Primary Health Care Bureau
Description: BPHC's mission is to increase access to comprehensive primary and preventive health care and to improve the health status of underserved and vulnerable populations. Its site features sections including Key Program Areas, Funding, Resources, Databases, Documents, and Find a Health Center. Key program areas include Black Lung Clinics, Community Health Centers, Health Care for the Homeless, Migrant and Farmworker Health, and Public Housing Primary Care. The online databases include one for health centers providing free or low-cost care.
Subjects: Hospitals and Clinics — Grants

1132. Chronic Disease Prevention
http://www.cdc.gov/nccdphp/
Sponsor(s): Health and Human Services Department — Centers for Disease Control and Prevention (CDC) — National Center for Chronic Disease Prevention and Health Promotion (NCCDPHP)
Description: NCCDPHP works to reduce the incidence of such chronic diseases as diabetes, cancer, and heart disease. Chronic disease programs also address topics such as arthritis, tobacco use, nutrition and physical activity, and maternal health. The agency's Web site describes its various programs, grants, research, and public health surveillance. The site has summary facts and graphs derived from its surveillance programs for behavioral risk factors, youth risk behavior, cancer registries, and pregnancy risks. State profiles include statistics and contact information for state chronic disease prevention programs.
Subjects: Health Promotion; Preventive Health Care
Publications: *Chronic Disease Notes and Reports*, HE 20.7617:
Physical Activity and Health: A Report of the Surgeon General. Executive Summary, HE 20.7602:P56

1133. Closing the Health Gap
http://www.omhrc.gov/healthgap/
Sponsor(s): Health and Human Services Department — Public Health and Science Office — Minority Health Office
Description: Closing the Health Gap is an educational campaign addressing the issue of good health for racial and ethnic minority groups. The Web site provides information on serious health conditions more likely to strike some minorities. The site in available in English and Spanish.
Subjects: Health Promotion; Minority Groups

1134. Coordinating Office for Global Health (OGH)
http://www.cdc.gov/ogh/
Sponsor(s): Health and Human Services Department — Centers for Disease Control and Prevention (CDC)
Description: OGH focuses on collaborating with other nations and international organizations to promote healthy lifestyles and to prevent high rates of disease, disability, and death in the global health arena. The site includes a map showing CDC's staffing outside of the United States and information on the U.S. and international organizations partnered with OGH.
Subjects: Health Care — International

1135. Health Resources and Services Administration
http://www.hrsa.gov/
Sponsor(s): Health and Human Services Department — Health Resources and Services Administration (HRSA)
Description: HRSA works to expand health care access for the uninsured, underserved, and special needs populations. HRSA concerns include health care for uninsured people, people living with HIV/AIDS, maternal health, rural health, organ transplants and donations, and emergency preparedness. The site includes information on current and past grants and an online grant application process. Under the heading Data, the HRSA Geospatial Data Warehouse has demographic, health care facility, and HRSA Program data.

Two important pages are linked from the top banner. The Questions? link leads to a knowledgebase of frequently asked questions, and the Order Publications link leads to consumer and federal publications and numerous other information resources.

Subjects: Public Health
Publications: *Funding Opportunities Preview*, HE 20.9018:
HRSA (Health Resources and Services Administration) Key Staff Directory,
  HE 20.9015:

1136. HealthierUS.gov
http://www.healthierus.gov/
Sponsor(s): Health and Human Services Department
Description: The HealthierUS site promotes public health with basic information on
healthy habits. The major sections are Physical Fitness, Nutrition, Prevention,
and Making Healthy Choices. Each section provides a brief narrative and links
to information from federal health agencies.
Subjects: Health Promotion

1137. Healthy People 2010
http://www.healthypeople.gov/
Sponsor(s): Health and Human Services Department
Description: Healthy People 2010 is a national health promotion and disease preven-
tion initiative. The site features the following sections: About Healthy People, Be
A Healthy Person, Leading Health Indicators, Implementation, Publications, and
Data. The Publications page includes *Healthy People 2010 Vols. I and II* and the
Healthy People 2010 Toolkit. The Data section has information about the data
being collected, the sources of the data, progress reviews, and provides access to
the DATA2010 database.
Subjects: Health and Safety — Statistics; Health Promotion
Publications: *Healthy People 2010 Toolkit*, HE 20.2:
Healthy people 2010. Vol. 1, HE 20.2:
Healthy People 2010. Vol. 2, HE 20.2:
Healthy People in Healthy Communities, HE 20.8:

1138. HRSA Telehealth
http://www.hrsa.gov/telehealth/
Sponsor(s): Health and Human Services Department — Health Resources and Services Administration (HRSA)
Description: This site describes telehealth as "the use of electronic information and
telecommunications technologies to support long-distance clinical health care,
patient and professional health-related education, public health and health administration." The site features telehealth-related publications and grants information.
It also has information on the federal interagency group called Joint Working
Group on Telehealth (JWGT). A Links section identifies other federal and private
organizations interested in telehealth topics.
Subjects: Telemedicine

1139. National Committee on Vital and Health Statistics
http://www.ncvhs.hhs.gov/
Sponsor(s): Health and Human Services Department — National Committee on Vital
and Health Statistics
Description: The National Committee on Vital and Health Statistics is concerned
with the quality of the health data and statistics that inform national health policy,
including issues of privacy and confidentiality. The Web site has information from
the Workgroup on National Health Information Infrastructure. Reports, recommendations, and meeting transcripts are also online.
Subjects: Medical Information — Policy

1140. NIDA for Teens: The Science Behind Drug Abuse
http://www.teens.drugabuse.gov/
Sponsor(s): National Institutes of Health (NIH) — National Institute on Drug Abuse (NIDA)
Description: NIDA for Teens is designed to educate adolescents ages 11 through 15 (as well as their parents and teachers) with science-based facts about how drugs affect the brain and body. The site include fact sheets on specific drugs and classes of drugs, an Ask Dr. NIDA section for frequently asked questions, teens' stories, and interactive online activities.
Subjects: Adolescents; Drug Abuse
Publications: *Mind over Matter: The Brain's Response to. . .*, HE 20.3958:

1141. Office of Children's Health Protection
http://yosemite.epa.gov/ochp/ochpweb.nsf/
Sponsor(s): Environmental Protection Agency (EPA) — Children's Health Protection Office
Description: Children face special and increased risks from exposure to environmental pollutants. This site explains the risks and how to minimize them. A section called What You Can Do to Protect Children is available in English, Spanish, and Vietnamese. The site also offers publications, regulatory information, data, international news, and other extensive coverage of the topic. It links to the Toxicity and Exposure Assessment for Children's Health (TEACH) database of summarized scientific literature on childhood exposure and health effects from selected chemicals.
Subjects: Child Health and Safety; Environmental Health
Publications: *America's Children and the Environment*, EP 1.2:

1142. Office of Disease Prevention and Health Promotion
http://odphp.osophs.dhhs.gov/
Sponsor(s): National Institutes of Health (NIH)
Description: The Office of Disease Prevention and Health Promotion works to strengthen the disease prevention and health promotion priorities of the Department of Health and Human Services. Its Web site links to relevant publications online and to current announcements of conferences, initiatives, and news in the disease prevention community.
Subjects: Preventive Health Care

1143. Office of Minority Health (OMH)
http://www.omhrc.gov/
Sponsor(s): Health and Human Services Department — Public Health and Science Office — Minority Health Office
Description: OMH is concerned with public health issues affecting racial and ethnic minorities in the United States. This site features a broad collection of material on minority health issues, including information about conferences, data, publications, and links to helpful Web sites. Some Web pages and publications are available in Spanish.
Subjects: Health Policy; Minority Groups

1144. Office of National AIDS Policy
http://www.whitehouse.gov/onap/aids.html
Sponsor(s): White House
Description: The Web site for the White House Office of National AIDS Policy has basic information on the office and links to further information from both the White House and other government sites.
Subjects: AIDS — Policy

1145. Office of Population Affairs (OPA)
http://opa.osophs.dhhs.gov/
Sponsor(s): Health and Human Services Department — Public Health and Science Office — Population Affairs Office
Description: OPA operates programs concerned with reproductive health, family planning, and adolescent pregnancy. Its Web site offers sections including Grants, Office of Family Planning, Office of Adolescent Pregnancy Programs, Publications, and Legislation. The Legislation section has the full text of the statutes and regulations under which OPA operates.
Subjects: Family Planning; Reproductive Health
Publications: *Healthy People 2010—Reproductive Health*

1146. Office of the Assistant Secretary for Planning and Evaluation (ASPE)
http://aspe.os.dhhs.gov/
Sponsor(s): Health and Human Services Department
Description: ASPE advises the Secretary of the U.S. Department of Health and Human Services on policy development, strategic planning, policy research, and economic analyses. The main portion of the home page is set up to perform canned literature searches on 40 topics of concern to ASPE, such as child welfare, disability, insurance, and substance abuse. The Highlighted Work section covers topics such as Indicators of Welfare Dependence and Estimating the Uninsured. A section called Often Requested links to the HHS Poverty Guidelines.
Subjects: Health Care — Policy; Social Services — Policy
Publications: *PIC Highlights*, HE 1.62:

1147. Office of the Surgeon General
http://www.surgeongeneral.gov/
Sponsor(s): Health and Human Services Department — Public Health and Science Office — Surgeon General
Description: The Surgeon General's Web site has current and historical information on the office, including portraits and biographies of all previous Surgeons General. It contains the Surgeon General's speeches, testimony before Congress, and general information on public health priorities. The site has the full text of reports of the Surgeon General and links to the National Library of Medicine's Reports of the Surgeon General site (described elsewhere in this chapter) for their collection of reports as well.
Subjects: Public Health — Policy
Publications: *Bone Health and Osteoporosis: a Report of the Surgeon General*, HE 20.2:
Mental Health: Culture, Race, and Ethnicity, A Supplement to Mental Health: A Report of the Surgeon General, HE 20.402:
Oral Health in America: A Report of the Surgeon General, HE 20.3402:
Reducing Tobacco Use: A Report of the Surgeon General, HE 20.7602:
Surgeon General's Call to Action to Improve the Health and Wellness of Persons with Disabilities

Surgeon General's Call To Action To Prevent and Decrease Overweight and Obesity, HE 20.2:

Surgeon General's Call To Action To Prevent Suicide, HE 20.2:

Surgeon General's Call To Action to Promote Sexual Health and Responsible Sexual Behavior, HE 1.2:

The Health Consequences of Involuntary Exposure to Tobacco Smoke: A Report of the Surgeon General, HE 20.7002:

The Health Consequences of Smoking: A Report of the Surgeon General, HE 20.7002:

Women and Smoking: A Report of the Surgeon General, HE 20.7615:

Youth Violence: A Report of the Surgeon General, HE 20.2:

1148. Office of the U.S. Global AIDS Coordinator

http://www.state.gov/s/gac/

Sponsor(s): State Department — Office of the U.S. Global AIDS Coordinator
Description: As stated on the Web site, "the U.S. Global AIDS Coordinator's mission is to lead implementation of the U.S. President's Emergency Plan for AIDS Relief." The site provides information on the Emergency Plan and participating countries. The Press Room section includes fact sheets, reports, and a monthly newsletter about the program.
Subjects: AIDS — International
Publications: *The President's Emergency Plan for AIDS Relief*, S 1.2:

1149. President's New Freedom Commission on Mental Health

http://www.mentalhealthcommission.gov/

Sponsor(s): White House — President's New Freedom Commission on Mental Health
Description: The President's New Freedom Commission on Mental Health was charged with studying the U.S. mental health service delivery system and advising the president on methods to improve it. The Commission presented its final report, *Achieving the Promise: Transforming Mental Health Care in America*, in July 2003. The full report is available on this site in HTML and PDF formats. The Web site also has meeting minutes, presentations to the Commission, and subcommittee reports. Versions of the report are available in Spanish, Chinese, Vietnamese, and Korean.
Subjects: Mental Health — Policy
Publications: *Achieving the Promise: Transforming Mental Health Care in America*, PR 43.8:

1150. President's Council on Bioethics

http://www.bioethics.gov/

Sponsor(s): President's Council on Bioethics
Description: Established in 2001, the Council is charged with advising the president on bioethical issues that may emerge as a consequence of advances in biomedical science and technology. The Web site includes a Council meeting schedule, meeting transcripts, and brief biographies of its members. Council working papers (under Background Materials) are available in HTML. The site also has the reports of previous bioethics commissions.
Subjects: Bioethics — Policy; Presidential Advisors

1151. President's Council on Physical Fitness and Sports

http://www.fitness.gov/

Sponsor(s): President's Council on Physical Fitness and Sports
Description: Established by executive order in 1956, the President's Council on Physical Fitness and Sports promotes physical fitness and sports participation for

Americans of all ages. The Web site has information on the history, mission, and membership of the Council under the section About the Council. The President's Challenge section has information on the Council's awards program, including the Presidential Physical Fitness Award. The Publications section has online brochures promoting fitness and health. *PCPFS Research Digest* is a quarterly summary of the latest scientific information on issues relating to physical activity.
Subjects: Physical Fitness; Sports
Publications: *President's Council on Physical Fitness and Sports: Research Digests*, HE 20.114:

1152. President's Emergency Plan for AIDS Relief
http://www.pepfar.gov/
Sponsor(s): White House
Description: The President's Emergency Plan for AIDS Relief (PEPFAR) involves strategic funding to combat HIV/AIDS in over 120 countries. The Web site includes information on participating countries, implementing agencies, policy guidance, and PEPFAR reports.
Subjects: AIDS — International; Foreign Assistance; HIV Infections — International

1153. Reports of the Surgeon General
http://sgreports.nlm.nih.gov/NN/
Sponsor(s): National Institutes of Health (NIH) — National Library of Medicine (NLM)
Description: This site carries the full text of all official Reports of the Surgeon General, beginning with 1964's *Smoking and Health*, the first report given. The National Library of Medicine has digitized these along with conference proceedings, pamphlets, photographs, and brochures from the Office of the Surgeon General. Documents are in PDF format; photographs are in JPEG format. A search engine provides full text or fielded search options, searching for a text string in the scanned images or the metadata. Historical information on the Office and on U.S. public health supplements the reports.
Subjects: Public Health — Policy

1154. Smokefree.gov
http://www.smokefree.gov/
Sponsor(s): National Institutes of Health (NIH) — National Cancer Institute (NCI)
Description: NCI maintains this Web site to help smokers quit and to disseminate free anti-smoking materials. Under Talk to an Expert, the site lists 800 numbers and instant messaging services available for information and advice on quitting.
Subjects: Smoking
Publications: *Clearing the Air: Quit Smoking Today*, HE 20.3152:

1155. Specialized Information Services
http://www.sis.nlm.nih.gov/
Sponsor(s): National Institutes of Health (NIH) — National Library of Medicine (NLM)
Description: The Specialized Information Services (SIS) Division is responsible for information resources and services in toxicology, environmental health, chemistry, HIV/AIDS, and specialized topics in minority health. The Web site includes information from its Office of Outreach and Special Populations, which focuses on improving access to quality health information in underserved and special populations. The site features an online tour of NLM's environmental health and toxicology resources, and links to SIS resources such as TOXNET and ChemIDplus.
Subjects: Health Promotion; Environmental Health

1156. State Cancer Legislative Database Program
http://www.scld-nci.net/
Sponsor(s): National Institutes of Health (NIH) — National Cancer Institute (NCI)
Description: NCI has provided summaries of legislation affecting cancer prevention and control since the early 1980s. Since 1989, NCI has monitored cancer-related state legislation and maintained the State Cancer Legislative Database (SCLD) of cancer-related bills and resolutions enacted or adopted in the United States at the state level. The site also provides fact sheets, newsletters, and presentations on the topic.
Subjects: Cancer — Legislation
Publications: *SCLD (State Cancer Legislative Database) Update*
SCLD Fact Sheets, HE 20.3182/9-3:
SCLD Updates Index (Database), HE 20.3182/9:

1157. Substance Abuse and Mental Health Services Administration
http://www.samhsa.gov/
Sponsor(s): Health and Human Services Department — Substance Abuse and Mental Health Services Administration (SAMHSA)
Description: SAMHSA administers grants, programs, and public education campaigns to assist people with or at risk for substance abuse and mental illness. The home page of SAMHSA's Web site organizes program information into subject areas such as co-occurring disorders, homelessness, older adults, and substance abuse treatment capacity. A menu button on the home page leads to grants information and grant awards by state. The Statistics section offers reports and data from the National Household Survey on Drug Abuse (NHSDA) series, the Drug and Alcohol Services Information System (DASIS) series, and the Drug Abuse Warning Network (DAWN).
Subjects: Mental Health; Substance Abuse
Publications: *Drug Abuse Warning Network (DAWN)*, HE 20.416/3:
Mental Health, United States, HE 20.427/4:
National Household Survey on Drug Abuse, HE 20.417/5:
SAMHSA News (quarterly), HE 20.425:

1158. White House Office of National AIDS Policy
http://www.whitehouse.gov/onap/aids.html
Sponsor(s): White House — National AIDS Policy Office
Description: The White House Office of National AIDS Policy posts its information on a section of the White House Web site. The page links to resources from federal agencies concerning prevention and education, general information, and the global pandemic.
Subjects: AIDS — Policy

1159. www.health.gov
http://www.health.gov/
Sponsor(s): Health and Human Services Department — Public Health and Science Office — Disease Prevention and Health Promotion Office
Description: This health gateway site consists of links to federal health initiatives information, government health agency sites, other, popular government health Web sites, and health news.
Subjects: Health and Safety

Health Research

1160. Agency for Healthcare Research and Quality (AHRQ)
http://www.ahrq.gov/
Sponsor(s): Health and Human Services Department — Healthcare Research and Quality Agency
Description: AHRQ is charged with supporting research designed to improve the quality of health care, reduce its cost, and broaden access to essential services. Its Web site features a wide range of resources in sections including Clinical Information, Consumer and Patients, Data and Surveys, Funding Opportunities, Research Findings, Quality and Patient Safety, and Public Health Preparedness. There are also buttons for information on children's, women's, and minority health. Some consumer publications are available in Spanish.
Subjects: Health Policy
Publications: *AHCPR Research Activities*, HE 20.6512/5:
AHRQ Publications Catalog, HE 20.6509/3:
Evidence Report/Technology Assessment (series), HE 20.6524:
MEPS (Medical Expenditure Panel Survey) Chartbooks, HE 20.6517/7:
MEPS (Medical Expenditure Panel Survey) Highlights, HE 20.6517/6:
MEPS (Medical Expenditure Panel Survey) Methodology Report, HE 20.6517/8:
MEPS (Medical Expenditure Panel Survey) Research Findings, HE 20.6517/9:

1161. Arctic Health
http://arctichealth.org/
Sponsor(s): National Institutes of Health (NIH) — National Library of Medicine (NLM)
Description: NLM's Arctic Health Web site is a central point for information on Arctic health and environment. The site has research and publications databases and covers such topics as chronic diseases, traditional medicine, and telemedicine. Arctic Health, which defines the Arctic as encompassing all or portions of Alaska, Canada, Greenland/Denmark/Faroe Islands, Iceland, Norway, Sweden, Finland and Russia, is built on the premise that the populations of these countries are subject to a unique set of health and environmental challenges. Along with NLM, the site is co-sponsored by University of Alaska Anchorage's Health Sciences Information Service.
Subjects: Arctic Regions

1162. Armed Forces Institute of Pathology
http://www.afip.org/
Sponsor(s): Defense Department — Armed Forces Institute of Pathology (AFIP)
Description: The AFIP Web site has information on the institute's research and consulting in pathology and on its Department of Medical Education. The institute's programs include research in basic science, environmental pathology and toxicology, geographic and infectious disease pathology, oncology, molecular diagnostics, and forensic science.
Subjects: Pathology — Research; Military Medicine
Publications: *Legal Medicine Open File*, D 101.117/7:
The AFIP (Armed Forces Institute of Pathology) Letter, D 101.117:

1163. caBIG
https://cabig.nci.nih.gov/
Sponsor(s): National Institutes of Health (NIH) — National Cancer Institute (NCI)
Description: Cancer Biomedical Informatics Grid (caBIG) is a voluntary information network for cancer researchers to share tools, standards, data, applications, and technologies. The Web site provides information on this large project and its progress.

This site will primarily be of interest to cancer researchers and specialists in bioinformatics.
Subjects: Cancer — Research; Medical Computing

1164. Cancer Control and Population Sciences
http://dccps.nci.nih.gov/
Alternate URL(s): http://cancercontrol.cancer.gov
Sponsor(s): National Institutes of Health (NIH) — National Cancer Institute (NCI)
Description: This division of NCI funds and coordinates cancer research and disseminates the research findings. The Web site organizes a large amount of research program information into several broad sections, including Applied Research, Behavioral Research, Epidemiology and Genetics Research, Surveillance Research, and Survivorship Research. Other sections of the site include Funding Opportunities and Research Findings. Like the rest of the site, the Related Information and Resources section uses a simple menu to lead to a large volume of information. It includes Cancer Control publications and compilations of resources on tobacco control, health disparities, statistics, patient information, and cancer journals.
Subjects: Cancer — Research
Publications: *Researchers' Toolbox*, HE 20.3186/2:

1165. Cancer.gov Clinical Trials
http://www.cancer.gov/clinical_trials
Sponsor(s): National Institutes of Health (NIH) — National Cancer Institute (NCI)
Description: This NCI site provides information on cancer-related clinical trials. A database of trials can be searched by type of cancer, type of trial, and location of trial. Other sections cover: Recent Developments, Introduction to Clinical Trials, Conducting Clinical Trials, and Clinical Trial Results.
Subjects: Cancer; Clinical Trials

1166. ClinicalTrials.gov
http://clinicaltrials.gov/
Sponsor(s): National Institutes of Health (NIH) — National Library of Medicine (NLM)
Description: NLM has developed this site to provide patients, family members, and the public with current information about clinical research studies. ClinicalTrials.gov currently contains over 30,000 clinical studies sponsored primarily by NIH and other federal agencies. Users may search the database by disease or condition, location of the trial, study phase, and other criteria.
Subjects: Clinical Trials

1167. Comprehensive Epidemiologic Data Resource (CDER)
http://cedr.lbl.gov/
Sponsor(s): Energy Department
Description: CEDR is a repository of data from occupational and environmental health studies of workers at Department of Energy facilities and nearby community residents. The core data comes from the Department's epidemiological studies of

workers at nuclear weapons facilities, beginning in the 1960s. CEDR continues to be a repository for data about the facilities workforce. This Web site catalogs resources and provides links to the data sets or to information on obtaining them. In some cases, users must register with CEDR to get the data.
Subjects: Radiation Exposure — Research; Environmental Health — Research
Publications: *CEDR, Comprehensive Epidemiologic Data Resource*, E 1.20/3:0339

1168. CRISP—A Database of Biomedical Research Funded by NIH
http://crisp.cit.nih.gov/
Sponsor(s): National Institutes of Health (NIH)
Description: CRISP (Computer Retrieval of Information on Scientific Projects) is a searchable database of federally funded biomedical research projects. Most are extramural projects, grants, contracts, and cooperative agreements conducted primarily by universities, hospitals, and other research institutions. The database can be searched by keywords, principle investigator name, award type, grant number, institution name, state, and other criteria.
Subjects: Biological Medicine — Research; Databases

1169. Environmental Health Perpectives: EHP Online
http://www.ehponline.org/
Sponsor(s): National Institutes of Health (NIH) — National Institute of Environmental Health Sciences (NIEHS)
Description: The EHP Online site provides free access to the NIEHS peer-reviewed journal *Environmental Health Perspectives*, the EHP Student Edition (with teacher resources), and a Chinese version. Issues of the journal are online from 1972 to the present. E-mail alerts are available to receive the table of contents for each new issue. Paid subscriptions are required for the print version of EHP.
Subjects: Environmental Health
Publications: *Environmental Health Perspectives*, HE 20.3559/2:

1170. Epidemic Intelligence Service (EIS)
http://www.cdc.gov/eis/
Sponsor(s): Health and Human Services Department — Centers for Disease Control and Prevention (CDC)
Description: The CDC's Epidemic Intelligence Service (EIS) is a surveillance and response unit for all types of epidemics in the United States and throughout the world. EIS employs physicians and other health specialists seeking a postgraduate program of service and on-the-job training in the practice of epidemiology. The site includes information about EIS's work and has sample case studies intended for epidemiology training.
Subjects: Epidemiology; Public Health — Research

1171. Fogarty International Center
http://www.fic.nih.gov/
Sponsor(s): National Institutes of Health (NIH) — John E. Fogarty International Center (FIC)
Description: The FIC promotes international cooperation and advanced study in the biomedical sciences. It fosters research partnerships between American scientists and foreign counterparts through research and training grants, fellowships, exchange awards, and international agreements. The Web site provides information on these activities and on FIC programs such as the Forum for International Health and the Multilateral Initiative on Malaria.
Subjects: Biological Medicine — Grants; Medical Research — International

1172. HMO Cancer Research Network

http://crn.cancer.gov/

Sponsor(s): National Institutes of Health (NIH) — National Cancer Institute (NCI)
Description: The HMO Cancer Research Network is a consortium funded by NCI to conduct research on cancer prevention, early detection, treatment, long-term care and surveillance. The Web site identifies the participating health plans and centers and describes the nature of the research. Research areas include behavioral research, screening research, and health services and outcomes research.
Subjects: Cancer — Research

1173. National Cancer Institute

http://cancer.gov/

Sponsor(s): National Institutes of Health (NIH) — National Cancer Institute (NCI)
Description: The NCI Web site includes sections covering research programs, research funding, non-technical explanations of cancer and its treatment, clinical trials information, statistics, news, and free informational booklets to download. Some basic cancer information is available in Spanish. The About NCI section has links to NCI's six main divisions, to its advisory boards, and to information on legislation and funding related to cancer research. The Statistics section has information on the public-use Surveillance, Epidemiology, and End Results (SEER) data program, described elsewhere in this chapter. State cancer profiles, maps and graphs of cancer data, and Web-based interfaces to querying cancer data are also provided.

NCI's Web site is an important and substantial resource for any kind of cancer question.
Subjects: Cancer
Publications: *Atlas of Cancer Mortality in the United States: 1950–94*, HE 20.3152:M 84/4

Cancer Progress Report, HE 20.3172/3:

DCEG (Division of Cancer Epidemiology and Genetics) Linkage, HE 20.3196:

Nation's Investment in Cancer Research, A Budget Proposal for FY . . ., HE 20.3190:

NCI Cancer Bulletin, HE 20.3153/4:

NCI Fact Book, HE 20.3174:

NCI Investigational Drugs, Chemical Information, HE 20.3180/2-2:

Report of the President's Cancer Panel, HE 20.3168/5:

1174. National Center for Complementary and Alternative Medicine (NCCAM)

http://nccam.nih.gov/

Sponsor(s): National Institutes of Health (NIH) — National Center for Complementary and Alternative Medicine
Description: NCCAM is concerned with health care practices that are outside the realm of conventional medicine as practiced in the United States. Its Web site describes research grant opportunities and priorities and the clinical trials it conducts. The Health Information section addresses popular topics, such as acupuncture and homeopathy. It also has information for the consumer on choosing alternative medicines or treatments, along with alerts and advisories.
Subjects: Alternative Medicine
Publications: *CAM at NIH Newsletter*

1175. National Center for Research Resources
http://www.ncrr.nih.gov/
Sponsor(s): National Institutes of Health (NIH) — National Center for Research Resources (NCRR)
Description: The NCRR Web site features a variety of resources for biomedical researchers. The research, grants, and publications of each NCRR division are described in their respective sections: Biomedical Technology, Clinical Research, Comparative Medicine, and Research Infrastructure. The Access to Scientific Resources section links to information on NCRR-supported research resources such as the National Gene Vector Laboratories, cell cultures, and DNA materials. The Publications section has directories, reports, fact sheets on their grant programs, *NCRR Reporter*, and other documents.
Subjects: Biological Medicine — Research; Medical Research — Grants
Publications: *NCRR Reporter*, HE 20.3013/6:

1176. National Center for Toxicological Research
http://www.fda.gov/nctr/
Sponsor(s): Health and Human Services Department — Food and Drug Administration (FDA) — National Center for Toxicological Research (NCTR)
Description: NCTR conducts peer-reviewed scientific research in support and anticipation of the FDA's regulatory needs. Initiatives include programs in food safety, bioterrorism, biotechnology, antimicrobial resistance, and HIV/AIDS. NCTR research divisions include Biochemical Toxicology, Microbiology, Molecular Epidemiology, and Neurotoxicology.
Subjects: Biotechnology — Research; Molecular Biology — Research; Toxicology (Medicine) — Research
Publications: *Regulatory Research Perspectives*, HE 20.4051:

1177. National Center on Minority Health and Health Disparities
http://ncmhd.nih.gov/
Sponsor(s): National Institutes of Health (NIH) — National Center on Minority Health and Health Disparities
Description: NCMHHD supports programs involving basic and clinical research, training, and the dissemination of health information to reduce disparities in health for minority population groups. This site has information about the office, its programs, and funding opportunities.
Subjects: Medical Research — Policy; Minority Groups

1178. National Eye Institute
http://www.nei.nih.gov/
Sponsor(s): National Institutes of Health (NIH) — National Eye Institute (NEI)
Description: NEI supports research to prevent and treat eye diseases and other vision disorders. The Health Information section includes fact sheets and guides written at the consumer level. These cover glaucoma, macular degeneration, diabetic eye disease, eye anatomy, and other topics. Many of the guides are also available in Spanish. The Education section of the site has information on public and professional education campaigns, including "Healthy Vision 2010." The site also has a clinical studies database and statistics on the most common eye diseases.
Subjects: Vision Disorders — Research
Publications: *National Plan for Eye and Vision Research*
Outlook, HE 20.3766:
Progress in Eye and Vision Research 1999-2006

1179. National Institute of Allergy and Infectious Diseases
http://www.niaid.nih.gov/
Sponsor(s): National Institutes of Health (NIH) — National Institute of Allergy and Infectious Diseases (NIAID)
Description: NIAID supports and conducts basic research in immunology, microbiology, and infectious disease. On its Web site, users can explore research on AIDS, allergic and immunologic diseases, asthma, biodefense, global health issues, hepatitis, influenza, malaria, tuberculosis, and more. Agency information on this site includes press releases, grants, publications, and NIAID laboratory profiles. On the research side, the site describes each research activity and related clinical trials, news, and resources such as the "NIH AIDS Research and Reference Reagent Program" catalog.
Subjects: AIDS — Research; Allergies — Research; Diseases and Conditions — Research; Medical Research — Grants
Publications: *Airborne Allergens: Something in the Air*, HE 20.3252:
Minorities and Biomedical Research
NIAID Strategic Plan for Biodefense Research, HE 20.3252:
Understanding the Immune System: How it Works, HE 20.3252:

1180. National Institute of Arthritis and Musculoskeletal and Skin Diseases
http://www.niams.nih.gov/
Sponsor(s): National Institutes of Health (NIH) — National Institute of Arthritis and Musculoskeletal and Skin Diseases (NIAMS)
Description: The NIAMS Web site provides health information, information about basic research, clinical and epidemiologic research, research databases, and grant opportunities in the fields of rheumatology, orthopedics, dermatology, metabolic bone diseases, heritable disorders of bone and cartilage, inherited and inflammatory muscle diseases, and sports medicine. The Health Information section includes pamphlets on such conditions as acne, arthritis, lupus, fibromyalgia, osteoporosis, vitiligo, knee problems, and sport injuries. The site has a Spanish-language version.
Subjects: Arthritis — Research; Diseases and Conditions — Research; Medical Research — Grants

1181. National Institute of Biomedical Imaging and Bioengineering
http://www.nibib.nih.gov/
Sponsor(s): National Institutes of Health (NIH) — National Institute of Biomedical Imaging and Bioengineering (NIBIB)
Description: NIBIB supports research to develop innovative technologies that improve health care. The Web site includes information on funding opportunities, training, and internships. It also has a directory of NIBIB Biomedical Technology Resource Centers throughout the United States. The Health and Education section includes materials for teachers and for a general audience. NIBIB overview information is available in Spanish.
Subjects: Medical Computing

1182. National Institute of Child Health and Human Development
http://www.nichd.nih.gov/
Sponsor(s): National Institutes of Health (NIH) — National Institute of Child Health and Human Development (NICHD)
Description: NICHD conducts research, clinical trials, and epidemiological studies related to the health of the human growth, development, and reproductive processes. The Web site has information about NICHD, its divisions, grants and

contracts, intramural research, and fellowships. The Research Resources section links to both internal and external resources, such as the Cochrane Neonatal Collaborative Review Group page. Publications, news releases, and a referral to the information specialists of NICHD are in the Health Information and Media section.

Subjects: Reproductive Health — Research; Child Health and Safety — Research
Publications: *National Institute of Child Health and Human Development Intramural Research Program: Annual Report of the Scientific Director*, HE 20.3365:

1183. National Institute of Dental and Craniofacial Research
http://www.nidcr.nih.gov/

Sponsor(s): National Institutes of Health (NIH) — National Institute of Dental and Craniofacial Research (NIDCR)
Description: The NIDCR Web site offers a substantial collection of documents and information on dental research. Major sections include Health Information, Funding for Research and Training, Clinical Trials, Research, News and Reports, and About NIDCR. Under Research, the Research Resources subsection links to specialized databases and research centers related to microbiology and immunology and to craniofacial development. The Health Information section links to publications and resources on topics such as fluoride, oral cancer, smokeless tobacco, temporomandibular disorders, and cavity prevention. The Kids and Teachers section has classroom materials to help promote oral health.
Subjects: Dental Health — Research

1184. National Institute of Diabetes and Digestive and Kidney Disease
http://www.niddk.nih.gov/

Sponsor(s): National Institutes of Health (NIH) — National Institute of Diabetes and Digestive and Kidney Disease (NIDDK)
Description: The NIDDK Web site features information on disorders studied by the agency, including diabetes, digestive diseases, endocrine diseases, hematologic diseases, kidney diseases, nutrition and obesity, and urologic diseases. Sections include Health Information, Research Funding Opportunities, Clinical Research, NIDDK Laboratories, and Reports, Testimony, and Plans. Under Health Information, the page lists the various diseases that the institute covers and links to online pamphlets and other publications. Spanish-language pamphlets are also available.
Subjects: Diabetes — Research; Medical Research — Grants; Kidney Disease — Research
Publications: *Kidney Disease Research Updates*, HE 20.3324/2-2:
NIDDK Information Clearinghouses Publications Catalog, HE 20.3316:
Prevent Diabetes Problems, HE 20.3326:
Your Guide to Diabetes: Type 1 and Type 2, HE 20.3308/2:

1185. National Institute of Environmental Health Sciences
http://www.niehs.nih.gov/

Sponsor(s): National Institutes of Health (NIH) — National Institute of Environmental Health Sciences (NIEHS)
Description: NIEHS, an institute for research on environment-related diseases, links to a wide variety of information for health researchers, the general public, and teachers. Sections include Environmental Health Information, News, Intramural and Extramural Research Programs, National Toxicology Program, Environmental Genome Project, and the National Center for Toxicogenomics. NIEHS research publications, pamphlets, and fact sheets are listed in the Library section. For the education community, the site offers two sections: Environmental Health Science Education and Kids' Pages. The NIEHS Web site also offers some information in Spanish.
Subjects: Toxicology (Medicine) — Research; Environmental Health — Research
Publications: *Environmental Health Perspectives*, HE 20.3559/2:

1186. National Institute of Mental Health

http://www.nimh.nih.gov/

Sponsor(s): National Institutes of Health (NIH) — National Institute of Mental Health (NIMH)

Description: NIMH conducts and funds research on mental and behavioral disorders, and works to educate the public on mental health topics. The NIMH home page features current news and quick links to health information for the public and funding information for researchers. The Health Information section has a guide to locating mental health services and simple, well organized Web pages on topics such as depression, bipolar disorder, eating disorders, and schizophrenia. The Publications section of the site includes fact sheets, some of which are available in Spanish. Other sections cover scientific meetings and clinical trials.

Subjects: Brain — Research; Mental Health — Research

Publications: *Research Fact Sheets*, HE 20.8139: *The Numbers Count: Mental Disorders in America*

1187. National Institute of Neurological Disorders and Stroke

http://www.ninds.nih.gov/

Sponsor(s): National Institutes of Health (NIH) — National Institute of Neurological Disorders and Stroke (NINDS)

Description: NINDS supports biomedical research on disorders of the brain and nervous system. For researchers, the site has information on research funding, research plans, and the text of conference proceedings. The Disorders section of the site is an extensive guide to numerous neurological disorders, such as Alzheimer's disease, autism, epilepsy, multiple sclerosis, Parkinson's disease, and stroke. Many of these guides are also available in Spanish.

Subjects: Brain — Research; Neurology — Research

1188. National Institute of Nursing Research

http://www.nih.gov/ninr/

Sponsor(s): National Institutes of Health (NIH) — National Institute of Nursing Research (NINR)

Description: The NINR site features information on the broad range of nursing research. The site includes sections for About NINR, News and Information, and Research Funding and Programs. News and Information has citations to NINR-supported investigator publications and summaries of NINR-supported research, as well as articles and meeting reports. The Research Funding and Programs page has grant information and program announcements. A Links section lists nursing organizations and their Web sites.

Subjects: Nursing — Research

1189. National Institute on Aging

http://www.nia.nih.gov/

Sponsor(s): National Institutes of Health (NIH) — National Institute on Aging (NIA)

Description: NIA provides leadership in aging research (including Alzheimer's research), training, health information dissemination, and other programs related to aging. The site has information on research funding opportunities and research training support. The Research Information section offers further details on NIA research areas and has information from NIA conferences and workshops. The Health Information section has publications and a database of organizations that provide help to older people. Under About NIA, the site also has information on the National Advisory Council on Aging, which reviews applications for funding and training and makes recommendations to NIA regarding research plans.

The Health Information section will be of the most interest to the general public.
Subjects: Medical Research — Grants; Senior Citizens
Publications: *Resource Directory for Older People*, HE 1.1002:

1190. National Institute on Alcohol Abuse and Alcoholism

http://www.niaaa.nih.gov/
Sponsor(s): National Institutes of Health (NIH) — National Institute on Alcohol Abuse and Alcoholism (NIAAA)
Description: NIAAA conducts and supports research and education to reduce alcohol-related problems in the population. The NIAAA site features the sections About NIAAA, Publications, Research Information, Clinical Trials, and Resources. Publications include the full text of the bulletin *Alcohol Alert*, along with pamphlets, research monographs, and other publications. The Database Resources section links to resources including APIS (Alcohol Policy Information System) and NESARC (National Epidemiologic Survey on Alcohol and Related Conditions). The site also has a Frequently Asked Questions sections in English and Spanish for the general public.
Subjects: Alcohol Abuse
Publications: *Alcohol Alert*, HE 20.8322:
Alcohol Research & Health, HE 20.8309:

1191. National Institute on Deafness and Other Communication Disorders

http://www.nidcd.nih.gov/
Sponsor(s): National Institutes of Health (NIH) — National Institute on Deafness and Other Communication Disorders (NIDCD)
Description: NIDCD conducts and supports research about the normal and disordered processes of hearing, balance, smell, taste, voice, speech, and language. The Web site has information on the Institute and its grants programs. A section on NIDCD research describes its research in such areas as the biophysics of sensory cells and gene structure and function. The Research section also lists current clinical trials and studies seeking patients. The Health Information section has resources for the general public on topics such as ear infections, hearing aids, balance disorders, aphagia, and stuttering. Some resources are available in Spanish.
Subjects: Hearing Disorders — Research
Publications: *Directory of Organizations, National Institute on Deafness*, HE 20.3660/2:
Inside NIDCD Information Clearinghouse, HE 20.3666:

1192. National Institute on Disability and Rehabilitation Research

http://www.ed.gov/about/offices/list/osers/nidrr/index.html
Sponsor(s): Education Department — Special Education and Rehabilitative Services Office — National Institute on Disability and Rehabilitation Research (NIDRR)
Description: NIDRR sponsors disability research and works with other federal agencies that conduct disability research through the Interagency Committee on Disability Research (ICDR). The Research and Statistics section of the site includes links to publications and databases including the Traumatic Brain Injury Database and the Spinal Cord Injury Database. The Programs and Projects section lists projects currently funded by NIDRR.
Subjects: Disabilities — Research
Publications: *Program Directory, National Institute on Disability and Rehabilitation Research*, ED 1.215:

1193. National Institute on Drug Abuse
http://www.drugabuse.gov/
Sponsor(s): National Institutes of Health (NIH) — National Institute on Drug Abuse (NIDA)
Description: NIDA supports research and education to reduce drug abuse and addiction. In the Researchers and Health Professionals section, the NIDA Web site has information on grants, funding, ongoing research, and clinical trials. Of more general interest, this section also has statistics related to drug use. The Parents and Teachers and the Students and Young Adults sections have educational materials. The site links to NIDA's specialty Web sites designed for the general public, including sites on abuse of inhalants and steroids. The site provides extensive information in Spanish.

The NIDA Web site is easy to use and a recommended first stop for non-technical information on the science of drug abuse and addiction.
Subjects: Drug Abuse
Publications: *Mind Over Matter*, HE 20.3965/3:
NIDA Notes, HE 20.3967:
NIDA Research Report Series, HE 20.3965/2:

1194. National Institutes of Health
http://www.nih.gov/
Sponsor(s): National Institutes of Health (NIH)
Description: The NIH Web site is one of the principal starting points for finding government-related health sciences information. Sections include Health Information; Grants and Funding Opportunities; News and Events; Research Training and Scientific Resources; Institutes, Centers, and Offices; and About NIH. The About NIH link covers its mission, organization, leadership, staff, and budget. The Institutes, Centers, and Offices section lists the many component NIH organizations. Health Information has resources for the general public on health topics, clinical studies, and drug information, with links to health databases and health hotlines.

The Grants and Funding Opportunities section features NIH funding opportunities and application kits, grants policy, and award data. New funding announcements can be viewed online or sent automatically via an e-mail list. The Research Training and Scientific Resources category covers NIH intramural research news, postdoctoral and clinical training opportunities, and laboratory research resources. The News section has press releases available for e-mail delivery or RSS feed, videocasts, podcasts, NIH Radio (mp3 files), and the NIH Calendar of Events.

The NIH is a significant health sciences and medical research institution. This central NIH site contains excellent information about the NIH and its component organizations. More importantly, the site links to an important body of NIH resources in the health sciences for the general public, health science researchers, and health science professionals.
Subjects: Diseases and Conditions — Research; Medical Research — Grants
Publications: *Medical Staff Handbook*, HE 20.3044:
NIH Almanac, HE 20.3016:
NIH Extramural Data and Trends, HE 20.3055/2:
NIH Guide for Grants and Contracts, HE 20.3008/2:
Summer Research Fellowship Program Catalog, HE 20.3015/2:
Telephone and Service Directory, HE 20.3037:
The NIH News in Health
The NIH Record, HE 20.3007/3:

1195. National Toxicology Program (NTP)

http://ntp.niehs.nih.gov/

Sponsor(s): National Institutes of Health (NIH) — National Institute of Environmental Health Sciences (NIEHS)

Description: NTP is an interagency program conducting toxicity/carcinogenicity studies on agents suspected of posing hazards to human health. Hundreds of chemical studies are on file, and much of this information is available on the NTP Web site. The NTP Study Database is searchable and includes toxicology and carcinogenesis studies.

This site contains a significant amount of toxicological data for researchers and those interested in the scientific basis for the regulation of toxic chemicals.

Subjects: Toxicology (Medicine) — Research

Publications: *NTP Current Directions and Evolving Strategies*
Report on Carcinogens, HE 20.3562:

1196. NCI-Frederick (National Cancer Institute at Frederick)

http://web.ncifcrf.gov/

Sponsor(s): National Institutes of Health (NIH) — National Cancer Institute (NCI)

Description: NCI-Frederick is one of the main NCI cancer research centers. It focuses on direct research to help identify the causes of cancer, AIDS, and related diseases. The NCI-Frederick Web site has an index to the staff researchers and detailed information on the research being conducted. The site also has information on training, fellowships, and employment.

Subjects: Cancer — Research

1197. NIAID Biodefense Research

http://www.niaid.nih.gov/biodefense/

Sponsor(s): National Institutes of Health (NIH) — National Institute of Allergy and Infectious Diseases (NIAID)

Description: NIAID conducts biomedical research on pathogens and immune response to ultimately protect civilians from potential agents of bioterrorism. For prospective researchers, this site provides information on research funding and plans. For the general public and the media, it provides summary information on aspects of biodefense research, facts sheets on topics like anthrax and the plague, news releases, and background information about NIAID's work.

Subjects: Biological Warfare — Research

1198. NIH Center for Scientific Review

http://www.csr.nih.gov/

Sponsor(s): National Institutes of Health (NIH)

Description: The Center for Scientific Review receives all grant applications sent to NIH and organizes the peer review groups for a majority of the research grants. The Web site has a section with resources for grant applicants and a section for those serving in peer review study sections.

Subjects: Grants Management; Health Research — Grants

Publications: *Peer Review Notes*, HE 20.3045:

1199. NIH Clinical Center

http://www.cc.nih.gov/

Sponsor(s): National Institutes of Health (NIH)

Description: The NIH Clinical Center is a specialized research hospital at the National Institutes of Health. It is involved in a variety of clinical studies, and the Web site features a section about participating in these. For researchers and physicians,

the site has information about research opportunities, information for referring physicians, summary information on research activities, and other resources.
Subjects: Clinical Medicine
Publications: *Annual Report of Clinical Research Activities*, HE 20.3052:

1200. NIH Human Embryonic Stem Cell Registry
http://escr.nih.gov
Sponsor(s): National Institutes of Health (NIH)
Description: The Stem Cell Registry lists institutions that have developed human embryonic stem cell lines that meet the criteria necessary for federal funding of stem cell research. For each institution, the site identifies the stem cell lines available and gives complete institutional contact information. The site also has a list of providers that currently do not have stem cell lines available.

An Information Center section offers substantial background information on stem cells and stem cell research, including a glossary and links to external Web sites that cover ethical issues of stem cell research. Another section covers related federal policy, statement, and legislation.
Subjects: Biology — Research

1201. NIH Roadmap
http://nihroadmap.nih.gov
Sponsor(s): National Institutes of Health (NIH)
Description: The NIH Roadmap is an effort by NIH to identify and pursue areas that the agency must address as a whole, rather than leaving them to the individual institutes within NIH. The Web site provides background on the target areas and has information on funding opportunities, workshops, and news within the targeted Roadmap areas.
Subjects: Health Research — Policy

1202. Office of Animal Care and Use
http://oacu.od.nih.gov/
Sponsor(s): National Institutes of Health (NIH)
Description: This office provides oversight of animal care and use at NIH. The site is designed as an informational resource for NIH scientists and others at NIH involved in biomedical research. It includes information on NIH policy, guidelines, regulations, and standards, as well as information on health and safety issues.
Subjects: Animals; Biological Medicine — Research

1203. Office of Disease Prevention (ODP)
http://odp.od.nih.gov
Sponsor(s): National Institutes of Health (NIH)
Description: The NIH Office of Disease Prevention coordinates preventive medical research across NIH centers and with agencies and organizations outside NIH. The Web site has information about ODP, and it links to its component offices: the Office of Dietary Supplements, the Office of Medical Applications of Research, and the Office of Rare Diseases. It also links to the NIH Consensus Development Program, which is managed by the Office of Medical Applications of Research.
Subjects: Preventive Health Care — Research
Publications: *National Institutes of Health Consensus Development Conference Reports*, HE 20.3046:

1204. Profiles in Science

http://profiles.nlm.nih.gov/

Sponsor(s): National Institutes of Health (NIH) — National Library of Medicine (NLM)

Description: NLM's Profiles in Science Web site presents information on twentieth-century leaders in biomedical research and public health. For each profiled person, the site includes biographical information and a collection of digitized materials such as manuscripts, journal articles, photographs, and video clips.

Subjects: Biographies; Health Research — History

Medical Information

1205. CDC Wonder on the Web

http://wonder.cdc.gov/

Sponsor(s): Health and Human Services Department — Centers for Disease Control and Prevention (CDC)

Description: CDC Wonder on the Web provides a single point of access to a variety of CDC reports, guidelines, and numeric public health data. The numeric databases can provide the numbers and rates for many diseases and health occurrences, including sexually transmitted diseases, cancer cases, and types of mortality and births in the United States. Users can request data for any disease and demographic group by submitting special queries against available datasets. CDC Wonder also provides free text search facilities and document retrieval for several important text datasets, including the *Morbidity and Mortality Weekly Report (MMWR)* from 1982 to the present, the *Fatal Accident Reporting System*, and the *CDC Recommends: The Prevention Guidelines System.*

Although CDC Wonder includes numerous resources, they are conveniently organized into broad sections such as Chronic Diseases, Communicable Diseases, and Occupational Health. An alphabetical index of datasets is also available.

Subjects: Public Health — Statistics

1206. Commission on Systemic Interoperability

http://www.nlm.nih.gov/csi/

Alternate URL(s): http://endingthedocumentgame.gov/report.html

Sponsor(s): Health and Human Services Department

Description: The Commission on Systemic Interoperability was authorized by the Medicare Modernization Act of 2003 (Public Law 108-173). As stated on the Web site, "the Commission was charged with developing a strategy to make health care information instantly accessible at all times, by consumers and their health care providers." The Commission released its final report, *Ending the Document Game: Connecting and Transforming Your Healthcare Through Information Technology,* in October 2005; the report is available at the alternate URL provided above.

Subjects: Medical Computing; Medical Records

Publications: *Ending the Document Game: Connecting and Transforming Your Healthcare Through Information Technology,* HE 20.3602:

1207. DIRLINE: Directory of Health Organizations

http://dirline.nlm.nih.gov/

Sponsor(s): National Institutes of Health (NIH) — National Library of Medicine (NLM)

Description: DIRLINE (Directory of Information Resources Online) is the NLM's online database containing location and description information about health and

biomedical resources, including organizations, projects, and databases. DIRLINE can be searched or browsed by topic.
Subjects: Medical Information; Databases

1208. Evaluating Internet Health Information
http://www.nlm.nih.gov/medlineplus/webeval/
Sponsor(s): National Institutes of Health (NIH) — National Library of Medicine (NLM)
Description: This site provides a tutorial on evaluating the health information than can be found on the Web. The tutorial can be viewed online or downloaded for use without an Internet connection.
Subjects: Internet

1209. Genetics Home Reference
http://ghr.nlm.nih.gov/
Sponsor(s): National Institutes of Health (NIH) — National Library of Medicine (NLM)
Description: Genetics Home Reference is the National Library of Medicine's Web site for consumer information about genes and genetic conditions. The site has summary information on genetic conditions, genes, and chromosomes. It includes a glossary, Web links, and a Help Me Understand Genetics section. Wording on the site notes that it is not a substitute for professional medical advice, and a link to the National Society of Genetic Counselors is provided.
Subjects: Diseases and Conditions; Genomics

1210. Health Services/Technology Assessment Text (HSTAT)
http://www.ncbi.nlm.nih.gov/books/bv.fcgi?rid=hstat
Sponsor(s): National Institutes of Health (NIH) — National Library of Medicine (NLM)
Description: HSTAT is a searchable collection of clinical practice guideline documents, technology assessment reports, and other health information. Sample contents include *Reports of the Surgeon General*, the *Guide to Clinical Preventive Services*, and evidence reports and technology assessments from the Agency for Healthcare Research and Quality (AHRQ).

The site identifies the HSTAT audience as consisting of "health care providers, health service researchers, policy makers, payers, consumers and the information professionals who serve these groups." The site is well designed with clear explanations regarding its content and search functions.
Subjects: Clinical Medicine

1211. healthfinder®
http://www.healthfinder.gov/
Sponsor(s): Health and Human Services Department
Description: The healthfinder® Web site is designed to assist consumers in finding government health information on the Internet. It links to selected publications, databases, Web sites, support and self-help groups, and government health agencies. The Health Library section organizes health information by broad topics such as prevention and wellness, diseases and conditions, and alternative medicine. There are also links to special resources such as medical dictionaries and health and medical journals. The Consumer Guides covers topics such as ratings of hospitals and nursing homes, guides to health insurance, how to report fraud or make a complaint, medical errors, and privacy issues. The site has consumer health news available by e-mail or as an RSS newsfeed, in English and Spanish. A version of the site is also available in Spanish.

This site is an excellent starting point for finding health information and information about health services at the consumer's level, rather than the more technical information available elsewhere for medical practitioners and researchers.

Subjects: Health Care; Medical Information; Finding Aids

1212. Lister Hill National Center for Biomedical Communications
http://lhncbc.nlm.nih.gov/

Sponsor(s): National Institutes of Health (NIH) — National Library of Medicine (NLM)

Description: Lister Hill specializes in health care communication, computing, and information sciences. The Web site features their work in medical imagery, multimedia visualization, and natural language processing, and other areas. The site carries related journal articles and technical publications.

Subjects: Information Technology — Research; Medical Computing — Research

1213. MedlinePlus
http://medlineplus.gov/

Sponsor(s): National Institutes of Health (NIH) — National Library of Medicine (NLM)

Description: MedlinePlus, NLM consumer health information Web site, presents information on more than 700 diseases and conditions and a guide to prescription and over-the-counter medications. The core of the site is the Health Topics section, which provides portal pages to a wide range of health issues. MedlinePlus also features more than 160 interactive health tutorials, with pictures and sound, on common conditions, treatment, and wellness strategies, and prerecorded webcasts of surgical procedures. Other sections include Drug Information, Dictionaries (medical terms), Directories (doctors, dentists, and hospitals), Health News, and Other Resources, which includes links to a list of U.S. consumer health libraries that provide services to local residents.

MEDLINEplus is an outstanding resource for current, non-technical information on diseases, health conditions, and other medical topics. The site's design and content are both exemplary.

Subjects: Medical Information; Pharmaceuticals; Databases
Publications: *MEDLINEplus Health Information*, HE 20.3602:

1214. Morbidity and Mortality Weekly Report
http://www.cdc.gov/mmwr/

Sponsor(s): Health and Human Services Department — Centers for Disease Control and Prevention (CDC)

Description: The *Morbidity and Mortality Weekly Report (MMWR)*, along with its associated reports, is a standard and authoritative resource for detailed health statistics. The online version presents the full text of each issue of the *MMWR* dating back to February 1982, volume 31 issue 5. Individual components and issues of the *MMWR* series can be browsed in the *MMWR* Publications section.

The CDC has done a commendable job of converting this essential publication to an online format and organizing the Web site so that it is relatively easy to find current articles and back issues.

Subjects: Diseases and Conditions — Statistics; Vital Statistics
Publications: *MMWR CDC Surveillance Summaries* (quarterly), HE 20.7009/2:
MMWR Recommendation and Reports, HE 20.7009/2-2:
Morbidity and Mortality Weekly Report, HE 20.7009:

1215. National Center for Health Statistics
http://www.cdc.gov/nchs/
Sponsor(s): Health and Human Services Department — Centers for Disease Control and Prevention (CDC) — National Center for Health Statistics (NCHS)
Description: NCHS is the lead agency for U.S. health statistics. The What's New section announces recently released reports, fact sheets, and data. The Publications and Information Products section includes links to published reports, data sets (organized in a Data Warehouse section), NCHS e-mail lists, training materials, and more fact sheets.

The site's FASTATS feature has an alphabetical, topical index to various health and disease facts and conditions. It also links to clickable United States maps for state and territorial data. Under the Surveys and Data Collection Systems, there are links to NHANES (National Health and Nutrition Examination Series), NHIS (National Health Interview Series), and the National Vital Statistics System.

NCHS Web site menus provide a layered access to data and reports—from raw data to prepared fact sheets. The home page makes it easy to find the most frequently used information with sections like Top Ten Links and Information Showcase. It also has sections highlighting resources in the areas of microdata and state data tabulations.
Subjects: Health and Safety — Statistics; Health Care — Statistics; Vital Statistics
Publications: *Health, United States*, HE 20.7042/6:
ICD.9.CM International Classification of Diseases, HE 22.41/2:
Life Tables, HE 20.6215:
National Hospital Discharge Survey, HE 20.6209/7:
National Vital Statistics Report, HE 20.6217:
NCHS Catalog of University Presentations, HE 20.6225:
Vital and Health Statistics, HE 20.6209:
Where to Write for Vital Records, HE 20.6210/2:

1216. National Health Information Center (NHIC)
http://www.health.gov/nhic/
Sponsor(s): Health and Human Services Department — Public Health and Science Office — Disease Prevention and Health Promotion Office
Description: NHIC, a health information referral service, produces this Web site featuring health information for health professionals and consumers. The Health Information Resource Database includes about 1,400 organizations and government offices that provide health information upon request. The Publications area has information on Healthy People 2010, the annual National Health Observances, and a list of toll-free numbers for health information.

NHIC also supports the healthfinder® Web site; health care consumers will want to check that site for additional information.
Publications: *Federal Health Information Centers and Clearinghouses*, HE 20.34/ 2:IN 3/2/
National Health Observances, HE 20.2:H 34/

1217. National Rehabilitation Information Center (NARIC)
http://www.naric.com/
Sponsor(s): Education Department — Special Education and Rehabilitative Services Office — National Institute on Disability and Rehabilitation Research (NIDRR)
Description: Funded by NIDRR, the National Rehabilitation Information Center (NARIC) collects and disseminates the results of federally funded research projects in the area of disability and rehabilitation. The site tailors this information for three audiences: the general public, researchers, and NIDRR grantees. The Researchers section includes REHABDATA, an extensive database of literature abstracts covering physical, mental, and psychiatric disabilities, independent living, vocational

rehabilitation, special education, assistive technology, and other issues related to people with disabilities. REHABDATA also has the full text access of original research documents that are the direct result of government funded research.
Subjects: Disabilities — Research
Publications: *NIDRR Program Directory*, ED 1.215:

1218. National Women's Health Information Center (NWHIC)
http://www.4woman.gov/
Sponsor(s): Health and Human Services Department — Public Health and Science Office — Women's Health Office
Description: NWHIC is designed as a gateway to health information particularly relevant to women. The Web site promotes the NWHIC's Call Center, at 1-800-994-WOMAN (1-800-994-9662) or 1-888-220-5446 for the hearing impaired. The site covers topics such as pregnancy, breast cancer, and menopause, and women's health as it relates to concerns such as heart disease and quitting smoking. Other sections discuss funding opportunities in women's health, women's health statistics, and information for health professionals. Some information is available in Spanish.
Publications: *Healthy Women Today*

1219. NIH LISTSERV
http://list.nih.gov/
Sponsor(s): National Institutes of Health (NIH)
Description: NIH sponsors numerous e-mail lists, covering such topics as NIH funding announcements, rural health research, and specific diseases or conditions. This page provides information on subscribing to them, along with searchable Web-based archives for many of the listservs.
Subjects: Medical Information; E-mail Lists

1220. NLM Gateway
http://gateway.nlm.nih.gov/gw/Cmd
Sponsor(s): National Institutes of Health (NIH) — National Library of Medicine (NLM)
Description: The NLM Gateway provides "one-stop searching" for many of NLM's information resources and databases. Using this site, visitors can simultaneously search multiple retrieval systems. Major databases searched by the Gateway include Medline/PubMed, LocatorPlus (book catalog), ClinicalTrials.gov, DIRLINE (directory of health organizations), MedlinePlus (consumer health information), Meeting Abstracts, Genetics Home Reference, and Health Services Research Projects.
Subjects: Medical Information; Databases

1221. Office of the National Coordinator for Health Information Technology
http://www.hhs.gov/healthit/
Sponsor(s): Health and Human Services Department — Office of the National Coordinator for Health Information Technology (ONCHIT)
Description: ONCHIT was established in 2004 by executive order and is charged with developing a nationwide, interoperable health information technology infrastructure. The ONCHIT Web site links to the executive order and other background information about its organization. The site has information on current federal health IT initiatives and on ONCHIT strategic planning. It also has information on the American Health Information Community, a new commission established to advise the Department of Health and Human Services on how to make health

records digital and interoperable while ensuring that the privacy and security of those records are protected.
Subjects: Medical Computing; Medical Records

1222. PubMed
http://www.ncbi.nlm.nih.gov/PubMed/
Alternate URL(s): http://www.ncbi.nlm.nih.gov/entrez/query.fcgi?db=PubMed
Sponsor(s): National Institutes of Health (NIH) — National Library of Medicine (NLM)
Description: PubMed is part of the Entrez Retrieval System operated by NLM's National Center for Biotechnology Information (NCBI). It searches more than 16 million citations to biomedical literature from the 1950s onward. The citations are from MEDLINE and additional life science sources. PubMed also includes links to sites providing full text articles and other related resources. Other PubMed services include Journal Browser, MeSH (Medical Subject Heading Browser), Citation Matcher, Clinical Queries (for physicians), and LinkOut, which links to a wide variety of relevant Web-accessible online resources.
PubMed is a central resource for searching the life sciences literature.
Subjects: Medical Information; Medline; Databases

1223. PubMed Central
http://www.pubmedcentral.nih.gov/
Sponsor(s): National Institutes of Health (NIH) — National Library of Medicine (NLM)
Description: PubMed Central (PMC) is a free digital archive of biomedical and life sciences journal literature. Participating journals deposit their content with PMC, but copyright is retained by the journal or authors, as appropriate. Articles can be searched by keyword, author, or journal title. The About PMC and For Publishers sections of the site explain the site's content development policies and procedures.
Subjects: Biological Medicine — Research; Life Sciences — Research

1224. Surveillance, Epidemiology, and End Results (SEER) Program
http://seer.cancer.gov/
Sponsor(s): National Institutes of Health (NIH) — National Cancer Institute (NCI)
Description: The SEER program collects and publishes cancer incidence and survival data from a number of population-based cancer registries. Its data and publications are available on this site. The Statistical Resources section links to the SEER Public Use Data, statistical software resources, and supporting materials. The Finding Statistics section provides an introduction to cancer statistics and access to simplified quick reference tools such as FastStats and State Cancer Profiles.
Subjects: Cancer — Statistics
Publications: *SEER Cancer Statistics Review*, HE 20.3186:

1225. TOXNET
http://toxnet.nlm.nih.gov/
Sponsor(s): National Institutes of Health (NIH) — National Cancer Institute (NCI)
Description: TOXNET is a group of databases on toxicology, hazardous chemicals, and related areas. The site allows users to search the databases separately or all together. Hosted databases include the Hazardous Substances Data Bank (HSDB), Chemical Carcinogenesis Research Information Service (CCRIS), Drugs and Lactation Database (LactMed), TOXLINE's Toxicology Bibliographic Information, and the Developmental and Reproductive Toxicology Database (DART). The site also

links to TOXMAP, an NLM service that maps EPA's Toxics Release Inventory (TRI) data.

Subjects: Chemical Information; Toxic Substances

1226. United States Renal Data System (USRDS)

http://www.usrds.org/

Sponsor(s): Health and Human Services Department — Centers for Medicare and Medicaid ServicesNational Institutes of Health (NIH) — National Institute of Diabetes and Digestive and Kidney Disease (NIDDK)

Description: USRDS is a national data system that collects, analyzes, and distributes information about end-stage renal disease (ESRD) in the United States. The organization's work is funded by Department of Health and Human Services agencies—the National Institute of Diabetes and Digestive and Kidney Diseases and the Centers for Medicare and Medicaid Services. The site includes an annual data report on end-stage renal disease in the United States and the Renal Data Extraction and Referencing (RenDER) System database.

Subjects: Kidney Disease — Statistics

Publications: *United States Renal Data System, Annual Data Report*, HE 20.3325:

1227. Visible Human Project®

http://www.nlm.nih.gov/research/visible/visible_human.html

Sponsor(s): National Institutes of Health (NIH) — National Library of Medicine (NLM)

Description: NLM's Visible Human Project® is creating digital image datasets of the normal male and female human body. The site includes detailed information on the project and on other projects based on the visible human data set. It provides information on how to obtain the data, including the license agreement.

Subjects: Human Anatomy and Physiology; Medical Computing

Medicine and Medical Devices

1228. Center for Biologics Evaluation and Research

http://www.fda.gov/cber/

Sponsor(s): Health and Human Services Department — Food and Drug Administration (FDA) — Center for Biologics Evaluation and Research (CBER)

Description: CBER regulates biological and related products, including blood and devices used in the collection, storage, and testing of blood and blood components. The Web site features sections on such topics as vaccines, gene therapy, allergenics, tissue, and medical devices. The Products section of the site includes information on product approvals, recalls and withdrawals, and safety issues. The Consumer and Industry sections provide information relevant to those two groups. An online Reading Room links to all documents posted on the site.

Subjects: Medicine and Medical Devices — Regulations

Publications: *Center for Biologics Evaluation & Research Annual Report*, HE 20.4801:

1229. Center for Devices and Radiological Health

http://www.fda.gov/cdrh/

Sponsor(s): Health and Human Services Department — Food and Drug Administration (FDA) — Center for Devices and Radiological Health (CDRH)

Description: CDRH is concerned with the safety and regulation of medical devices and electronic products that produce radiation. Major sections of the Web site include Health Topics, with consumer information, recalls, and product alerts;

Industry Assistance, with guidance documents and standards; Device Program Areas, with current initiatives and statutory information; and Radiological Health, including facts about cell phones, mammographies, and CT scans. A section on Information Resources includes databases, laws, and regulations. The databases include a listing of medical devices in commercial distribution, a directory of FDA certified mammography facilities, and the searchable text of Title 21 of the *Code of Federal Regulations* covering Food and Drugs.

Subjects: Medical Devices — Regulations; Radiation — Regulations

1230. Center for Drug Evaluation and Research
http://www.fda.gov/cder/
Sponsor(s): Health and Human Services Department — Food and Drug Administration (FDA) — Center for Drug Evaluation and Research (CDER)
Description: The CDER Web site features a number of resources on pharmaceuticals. These include the "Orange Book" of approved drugs, a list of current drug shortages, the Inactive Ingredients Database, and the *National Drug Code Directory*. The Regulatory Guidance section of the site includes relevant laws, regulations, forms, and policies. A Specific Audiences section includes material for consumers and some Spanish-language content.

Subjects: Pharmaceuticals
Publications: *CDER Report to the Nation*, HE 20.4701:
Electronic Orange Book: Approved Drug Products with Therapeutic Equivalence Evaluations, HE 20.4715:
National Drug Code Directory, HE 20.4012:

1231. DailyMed
http://dailymed.nlm.nih.gov/
Sponsor(s): National Institutes of Health (NIH) — National Library of Medicine (NLM)
Description: DailyMed provides FDA-approved labels (package insert information) for over 1400 marketed drugs. Label information can be e-mailed from the site or all drug labels can be downloaded at once. DailyMed also has an RSS feed for notification of updates to the database.

Subjects: Pharmaceuticals

1232. Drugs@FDA
http://www.accessdata.fda.gov/scripts/cder/drugsatfda/
Sponsor(s): Health and Human Services Department — Food and Drug Administration (FDA) — Center for Drug Evaluation and Research (CDER)
Description: Drugs@FDA has information on U.S. approved and tentatively approved prescription and over-the-counter drugs intended for human use. It also has information on drugs removed from the U.S. market for reasons besides safety or effectiveness. Drugs@FDA can be used to find labels for approved drugs, generic drug products for a brand name drug, therapeutically equivalent drug products for a brand name or generic drug product, consumer information for drugs approved from 1998 forward, drugs with a specific active ingredient, and the approval history of a drug. The Web site also offers a downloadable file of the Drugs@FDA database.

Subjects: Over-The-Counter Drugs; Pharmaceuticals

1233. Electronic Orange Book
http://www.fda.gov/cder/ob/
Sponsor(s): Health and Human Services Department — Food and Drug Administration (FDA) — Center for Drug Evaluation and Research (CDER)
Description: This online version of *Approved Drug Products with Therapeutic Equivalence Evaluations*, known as the FDA "Orange Book," includes information on prescription drugs, over-the-counter drugs, and discontinued drugs. Users can search by the following categories: Active Ingredient, Applicant Holder, Proprietary Name, Patent Number, or Application Number. The result categories include Active Ingredient, Dosage Form and Route, Applicant Holder, Proprietary Name, Strength, Application Number, Therapeutic Equivalents, and Reference Listed Drug. The Patent Search page can also display recently added patents and patent delistings.

This is a useful database for verifying FDA approval of a drug and for determining the length of time for which it has been approved. Read the Frequently Asked Questions section for important information about how often the database is updated.
Subjects: Pharmaceuticals; Databases
Publications: *Approved Drug Product With Therapeutic Equivalence Evaluations*, HE 20.4715:

1234. Food and Drug Administration
http://www.fda.gov/
Sponsor(s): Health and Human Services Department — Food and Drug Administration (FDA)
Description: The FDA regulates the quality and safety of food, drugs, cosmetics, medical devices, animal feed, and veterinary drugs. The FDA Web site features news, safety alerts, product recalls, statutes and regulations, and a variety of paths to information on its regulated product areas. The Web site also links to the specialized offices that make up the FDA, FDA field offices, and the FDA advisory committees. The site map organizes links under headings including About FDA, Interacting with FDA, News, Hot Topics, Enforcement Activities, Products Regulated by the FDA, Major Initiatives, and Publications. There are links to Information for Specific Audiences, including AIDS patients, cancer patients, health professionals, industry, and the press. The site map also has a link, Search FDA Databases, which leads to a page of links to all major public FDA databases.

The FDA site is well designed, with multiple paths to find all of the information the agency provides on the Web. Use the A-Z index and the site map to find specific information quickly.
Subjects: Food — Regulations; Pharmaceuticals — Regulations
Publications: *FDA Compliance Program Guidance Manual*, HE 20.4008:
FDA Consumer, HE 20.4010:
FDA Enforcement Reports, HE 20.4039:

1235. MedWatch: FDA Safety Information and Adverse Event Reporting Program
http://www.fda.gov/medwatch/
Sponsor(s): Health and Human Services Department — Food and Drug Administration (FDA)
Description: MedWatch provides information and alerts about the safety of medical products to both health care professionals and the public. MedWatch also allows both of these groups to report problems related to medical products to the FDA. The site includes the sections About MedWatch, Safety Information, Submit a

Report, How To Report, and Download Forms. Users can also subscribe to receive MedWatch alerts by e-mail or RSS feed.
Subjects: Medicine and Medical Devices — Regulations

1236. National Immunization Program
http://www.cdc.gov/nip/
Sponsor(s): Health and Human Services Department — Centers for Disease Control and Prevention (CDC) — National Immunization Program (NIP)
Description: The Web site of the NIP provides information on immunization and vaccine safety. The site includes sections for information on Flu Vaccine, Immunization Registries, Vaccines for Children Program, Clinic Assessment Program, Grantee Assessment, and Advisory Committee on Immunization Practices (ACIP). Other broad categories are Vaccines, Vaccine Safety, Diseases, Resources, and Why Immunize. The Spotlight section highlights current topics of interest, such as an update about flu shots and news about the Human Papillomavirus Virus vaccine. For health professionals, resources include the *Epidemiology and Prevention of Vaccine-Preventable Diseases*, known as "The Pink Book." The site is also available in Spanish version.
Subjects: Immunization
Publications: *Epidemiology and Prevention of Vaccine-Preventable Diseases*, HE 20.7970:

1237. Office of Nonprescription Products
http://www.fda.gov/cder/offices/otc/
Sponsor(s): Health and Human Services Department — Food and Drug Administration (FDA) — Center for Drug Evaluation and Research (CDER)
Description: The FDA's Office of Nonprescription Products site has information for consumers, health professionals, and industry about nonprescription drugs. For consumers, it has educational information about over-the-counter (OTC) medicine, a section called Frequently Asked Questions on the Regulatory Process of OTC Drugs, and important news releases. For industry, it offers regulatory information and the latest "OTC Drug Review Ingredient Status Report." The health professionals' section primarily links to safety information found elsewhere on the FDA Web site.

The upper and side navigation aids on this site are for the FDA Center for Drug Evaluation and Research, making your Web browser's back button the best way to navigate within the Office of Nonprescription Products content.
Subjects: Over-The-Counter Drugs

Nutrition

1238. Center for Food Safety and Applied Nutrition
http://www.cfsan.fda.gov/
Sponsor(s): Health and Human Services Department — Food and Drug Administration (FDA) — Center for Food Safety and Applied Nutrition (CFSAN)
Description: CFSAN is responsible for the safety and proper labeling of food and cosmetics. The site has information on national food safety programs, consumer advice, information for industry, and updates on food and cosmetic laws and regulations. The Program Areas section of the site covers Biotechnology, Cosmetics, Dietary Supplements, Food Labeling and Nutrition, Foodborne Illness, Pesticides and Chemical Contaminants, and more. The site also covers the food safety provisions of the Bioterrorism Preparedness and Response Act of 2002 (Public Law 107-188). Databases include Everything Added to Food in the United States

(EAUFUS)—information on over 2,000 substances directly added to food. Under FDA Documents, the site highlights materials that are available in languages other than English.

The CFAN site provides fresh, relevant, and practical content for consumers, industry, health professionals, legal experts, and others.

Subjects: Food — Regulations; Food Safety
Publications: *Food Code*, HE 20.4002:
Interstate Certified Shellfish Shippers List, HE 20.4014:
Regulatory Fish Encyclopedia, HE 20.4002:
The Bad Bug Book: Foodborne Pathogenic Microorganisms and Natural Toxins Handbook, HE 20.4508:

1239. Center for Nutrition Policy and Promotion
http://www.usda.gov/cnpp/
Sponsor(s): Agriculture Department (USDA) — Center for Nutrition Policy and Promotion (CNPP)
Description: CNPP is the focal point within USDA for scientific research linked with the nutritional needs of the public. Its site offers the About CNPP section, as well as information on projects, publications, and press releases. Project links include *Dietary Guidelines for Americans*, the Health Eating Index, MyPyramid Food Guidance (also available in Spanish), and *Nutrient Content of the U.S. Food Supply*.
Subjects: Dietary Guidelines; Nutrition
Publications: *Cost of Food at Home Estimated for Food Plans at Four Cost Levels*, A 98.19/2:
Dietary Guidelines for Americans, A 1.77:232/
Expenditures on Children by Families: Annual Report, A 1.38:
Family Economics and Nutrition Review, A 98.20:
Nutrient Content of the U.S. Food Supply, A 1.87:55
Nutrition and Your Health: Dietary Guidelines for Americans, A 1.77:232/

1240. Eat 5 to 9 a Day
http://www.5aday.gov/
Sponsor(s): National Institutes of Health (NIH) — National Cancer Institute (NCI)
Description: The 5 A Day for Better Health Program promotes eating 5 to 9 fruits or vegetables a day. The National Cancer Institute is the lead federal agency for the program. The Web site provides extensive information on the nutritional value of fruits, recipes, and advice on how to work them into your daily menu.
Subjects: Fruit; Nutrition; Vegetables

1241. Food and Nutrition Information Center
http://www.nal.usda.gov/fnic/
Sponsor(s): Agriculture Department (USDA) — National Agricultural Library (NAL)
Description: The FNIC Web site provides information to the consumer on the topics of food, food safety, nutrition, food labels, and school meals. Categories include Dietary Guidance, Diet and Disease, Food Composition, and Weight and Obesity. A Databases page allows users to search a suite of FNIC databases simultaneously. Databases include the Food Stamp Nutrition Collection and the Native American Nutrition Education Database. The site also links to resources for nutrition professionals.
Subjects: Nutrition

1242. Food Stamp Nutrition Connection
http://www.nal.usda.gov/fnic/foodstamp/
Sponsor(s): Agriculture Department (USDA) — National Agricultural Library (NAL)
Description: The Food Stamp Nutrition Connection Web site is designed for Food Stamp Program nutrition education providers, but it includes excellent resources for anyone looking for nutrition information. The Resource Library section has Resource Finder database of educational and training materials on topics such as dietary guidelines, meal planning, safe food storage, and weight control. The site also has a Recipe Database of recipes submitted by nutrition and health professionals. Other materials on the site, such as seminar listings and state program links, will be of most interest to the intended audience of Food Stamp Program nutrition educators.
Subjects: Nutrition; Recipes

1243. MyPyramid.gov
http://mypyramid.gov/
Sponsor(s): Agriculture Department (USDA) — Center for Nutrition Policy and Promotion (CNPP)
Description: MyPyramid.gov is the central promotional Web site for the USDA's food guidance system. A colorful pyramid symbol represents the recommended proportion of foods from each food group. The MyPyramid Plan is an interactive tool that provides quick dietary recommendations. MyPyramid Tracker is a more in-depth dietary and physical activity assessment tool. In a section for nutrition education professionals, the site has further information and downloadable charts and brochures in PDF format. The News and Media section has background information and downloadable graphics. The site is also available in Spanish.
Subjects: Nutrition
Publications: *Dietary Guidelines for Americans*, A 1.77:232/

1244. Nutrition.gov
http://www.nutrition.gov/
Sponsor(s): Agriculture Department (USDA)
Description: Nutrition.gov is a portal Web site for government information on nutrition. It organizes links to nutrition information from many federal agencies into sections such as Smart Nutrition 101, Weight Management, Dietary Supplements, and Food Assistance Programs. The News section carries announcements of new publications and events. The site serves consumers, nutrition educators, health providers, and researchers.

This resource is an example of the federal initiative to organize information across agencies. One can locate nutrition information on the Web without first knowing the agency responsible for posting the information.
Subjects: Nutrition

1245. Office of Dietary Supplements (ODS)
http://ods.od.nih.gov/
Sponsor(s): National Institutes of Health (NIH) — Office of Dietary Supplements
Description: ODS promotes scientific research in the area of dietary supplements. The Web site describes ODS programs, research, and funding. ODS does not have granting authority but co-sponsors research with other institutes. In the Research section, the ODS site provides resources such as the Computer Access to Research on Dietary Supplements Database (CARDS) and International Bibliographic Information on Dietary Supplements (IBIDS). The Health Information section has information for the consumer, including information on health claims and labeling.

The site also offers helpful fact sheets on dietary supplements, including botanical supplements, vitamins, and minerals.

This site provides extensive information for health professionals and consumers. The ODS booklet "How To Evaluate Health Information on the Internet: Questions and Answers" should be of assistance to many consumers—even beyond those with an interest in dietary supplements.

Subjects: Dietary Supplements; Nutrition — Research

1246. Recipe of the Week, Navy Environmental Health Center
http://www-nehc.med.navy.mil/hp/nutrit/recipes/
Sponsor(s): Navy — Navy Environmental Health Center
Description: This government Web site offers a new recipe each week and an archive of past recipes. The recipes meet dietary guidelines and contain nutritional information. The recipes are listed under sections including Entrees, Salads, Side Dishes, Soups and Stews, Dips and Such, Desserts, Breakfast, Appetizers, Beverages, Holiday, and Microwave.
Subjects: Recipes

1247. WIC Works Resource System
http://www.nal.usda.gov/wicworks/
Sponsor(s): Agriculture Department (USDA)
Description: This site offers resources for state-based professionals facilitating the USDA's Special Supplemental Nutrition Program for Women, Infants, and Children (known as WIC). WIC Works is a clearinghouse for educational and promotional materials about nutrition for WIC program clients.
Subjects: Nutrition

Safety

1248. Air Force Rescue Coordination Center (AFRCC)
http://www.acc.af.mil/afrcc/
Sponsor(s): Air Force — Air Combat Command (ACC)
Description: The AFRCC is the single federal agency responsible for coordinating search and rescue (SAR) activities in the continental United States. AFRCC also coordinates search and rescue agreements, plans, and policy. This Web site describes their structure and operations. The SAR Links section includes Web links to other federal and private search and rescue organizations. AFRCC annual reports provide detailed reporting and statistics on the previous year's missions.
Subjects: Search and Rescue

1249. CDC Emergency Preparedness and Response
http://www.bt.cdc.gov/
Sponsor(s): Health and Human Services Department — Centers for Disease Control and Prevention (CDC)
Description: This CDC portal site links to a broad range of practical information about health and safety emergencies. Major categories are Bioterrorism, Chemical Emergencies, Radiation Emergencies, Mass Casualties, Natural Disasters and Severe Weather, and Recent Outbreaks and Incidents. The site also links to resources such as the CDC Laboratory Response Network, Disaster Mental Health, Surveillance, and Training and Education for Emergency Preparedness. A Spanish-language version of the site focuses on information for a general audience.
Subjects: Disaster Preparedness

1250. FireSafety.gov
http://www.firesafety.gov/
Sponsor(s): Health and Human Services Department — Centers for Disease Control and Prevention (CDC)Consumer Product Safety Commission (CPSC)Homeland Security Department — Federal Emergency Management Agency (FEMA) — U.S. Fire Administration
Description: FireSafety.gov is the product of an interagency collaboration to increase awareness of fire dangers and fire prevention. The site features current news of product recalls and a Fire Safety Directory. The Directory has information about residential fire safety and prevention, with sections for at-risk populations such as the elderly, the visually impaired, and the hearing impaired. The Reference Materials section includes statistics, information on grants, and a database of fire-related consumer product recalls. Selected information from the site is available in Spanish.
Subjects: Fire Prevention

1251. Food Safety and Inspection Service
http://www.fsis.usda.gov/
Sponsor(s): Agriculture Department (USDA) — Food Safety and Inspection Service (FSIS)
Description: FSIS is the public health regulatory agency in the Department of Agriculture responsible for ensuring that meat, poultry, and egg products are safe, wholesome, and accurately labeled. Major topics covered by the FSIS Web site include food safety education, food safety science, regulations and policies, FSIS recalls, and food defense and emergency response. The Regulations section has information on federal and state inspection programs, compliance assistance, news on food safety issues in the United States, and background on the Codex Alimentarius Commission, the international mechanism for guarding safety in food trade. The FSIS Recalls section lists current food recalls, which are voluntary actions by a manufacturer or distributor. It also has information on how to report a food problem. The site has numerous fact sheets covering topics such as safe food handling, food labeling, and meat, poultry, and egg preparation. Other publications can be found in the FOIA Electronic Reading Room, linked from the bottom of the page. Consumer education material is available in Spanish.
For anyone concerned with food safety issues, this site offers easy access to relevant information.
Subjects: Food Safety
Publications: *Food Safety Educator*, A 110.19:
Food Standards and Labeling Policy Book, A 110.18:

1252. Healthy Homes and Lead Hazard Control
http://www.hud.gov/offices/lead/
Sponsor(s): Housing and Urban Development (HUD) — Office of Healthy Homes and Lead Hazard Control
Description: This HUD office works to eliminate lead-based paint hazards in privately-owned and low-income housing. The site focuses on regulations, enforcement, compliance assistance, grants information, technical training, and technical studies and guidelines. One section explains the Residential Lead-Based Paint Hazard Reduction Act of 1992, requiring the disclosure of known information on lead-based paint and lead-based paint hazards before the sale or lease of most housing built before 1978. The Documents/Reference Library section has a Residential Lead Desktop Reference Library, with links to resources from HUD and other organizations. The site is also available in Spanish,
Subjects: Home Maintenance; Lead Poisoning

1253. Household Products Database
http://householdproducts.nlm.nih.gov
Sponsor(s): National Institutes of Health (NIH) — National Library of Medicine (NLM)
Description: This database of over 6,000 brand-name household products provides information on the chemicals the products contain, any ill effects those chemicals may cause, and what first aid steps should be taken if necessary. It also provides the manufacturer's toll free number, the products' health and flammability ratings, and tips for handling and disposal. The database can be searched by product or ingredient. Product sections include Auto Products, Pesticides, Landscape/Yard, Inside the Home (cleansers, paints, etc.), and more.
Subjects: Chemical Information; Product Safety
Publications: *Material Safety Data Sheets*, D 5.302:

1254. National Center for Injury Prevention and Control
http://www.cdc.gov/ncipc/
Sponsor(s): Health and Human Services Department — Centers for Disease Control and Prevention (CDC) — National Center for Injury Prevention and Control (NCIPC)
Description: NCIPC seeks to reduce morbidity, disability, mortality, and costs associated with injuries outside the workplace. Its Web site features sections for Facts, Data, Publications, and Funding. Topical categories include Injury Care, Violence, and Unintentional Injury. The Resources section has a calendar of injury-related conferences and links to numerous injury-related Web sites. The site also has several online tools: WISQARS (Web-based Injury Statistics Query and Reporting System), a database that provides customized reports of injury-related data; and InjuryMaps, a tool for mapping the geographic distribution of injury-related mortality rates in the United States.
Subjects: Injuries; Safety
Publications: *Injury Fact Book*, HE 20.7952:

1255. U.S. Fire Administration
http://www.usfa.fema.gov/
Sponsor(s): Homeland Security Department — Federal Emergency Management Agency (FEMA) — U.S. Fire Administration
Description: As part of FEMA, the Fire Administration works to reduce life and economic losses due to fire, arson, and related emergencies. For the public, the agency's Web site provides guidance on home fire prevention. A Hotel-Motel Master List offers a searchable database of hotels and motels that meet fire and life federal safety requirements. The site also has information on firefighter fatalities, fire statistics, and the National Fire Department Census Database. The Training section includes information on the National Fire Academy. Other sections cover grants and funding, research projects, the National Fire Incident Reporting System (NFIRS), and a directory of state fire contacts. Selected information is online in Spanish.

The USFA Web site provides resources, data, and practical information for both firefighting professionals and the general public. A subject directory and A-Z index for the site aid in navigation.
Subjects: Fire Prevention; Firefighting — Grants
Publications: *A Profile of Fire in the United States*, FEM 1.117/2:
Fire in the United States, FEM 1.117:
Firefighter Fatalities, FEM 1.116:
Topical Fire Research Series

1256. www.FoodSafety.gov
http://www.foodsafety.gov/

Sponsor(s): Health and Human Services Department — Food and Drug Administration (FDA) — Center for Food Safety and Applied Nutrition (CFSAN)

Description: FoodSafety.gov is a gateway to selected food safety-related information on government Web sites. Information is organized under sections such as Consumer Advice, News and Safety Alerts, Industry Assistance, Report Illnesses and Product Complaints, Foodborne Pathogens, National Food Safety Programs, Federal and State Government Agencies, and Kids, Teens, and Educators. The Language button leads to a page of links to food safety information in languages other than English.

Subjects: Food Safety

CHAPTER 14

International Relations

This chapter includes a number of Web sites from the Department of State and other agencies whose work involves international assistance, immigration control, diplomacy, and other topics related to the role of the United States in the world. The field of international relations often intersects with those of defense and commerce. Researchers may want to check the Defense and Intelligence chapter and the International Trade section of the Business and Economics chapter for additional Web sites of interest. Also, the Education chapter has a section on International Education.

Subsections in this chapter are Arms Control, Country Information, Diplomacy, Foreign Policy, International Migration and Travel, and International Relations.

Arms Control

1257. Bureau of International Security and Nonproliferation
http://www.state.gov/t/isn/
Sponsor(s): State Department — International Security and Nonproliferation Bureau
Description: The Bureau of International Security and Nonproliferation (ISN) is responsible for managing a broad range of nonproliferation, counterproliferation, and arms control functions. ISN was formed in 2005, merging the former Bureau of Arms Control and Bureau of Nonproliferation. ISN has 13 component offices, including the Office of Chemical and Biological Weapons Threat Reduction, the Office of Conventional Arms Threat Reduction, the Office of Missile Threat Reduction, and the Office of Weapons of Mass Destruction Terrorism; all of these offices are described on the Web site. The site also has information about nonproliferation sanctions, export controls, relevant international treaties and agreements, the Nonproliferation and Disarmament Fund, and the Secretary of State's Arms Control and Nonproliferation Advisory Board.
Subjects: Arms Control; Nonproliferation

1258. Bureau of Verification, Compliance, and Implementation
http://www.state.gov/t/vci/
Sponsor(s): State Department — Verification, Compliance, and Implementation Bureau
Description: The Bureau of Verification, Compliance, and Implementation (VCI) works to ensure compliance with international arms control, nonproliferation, and disarmament agreements and commitments. Its Web site includes information about the VCI's Nuclear Risk Reduction Center, the communications channel for formal notifications made between the United States and other countries under the terms of arms control treaties. The site also links to the text of relevant treaties and agreements.
Subjects: Arms Control; Nonproliferation

1259. Nonproliferation and Disarmament Fund
http://www.ndf.org
Sponsor(s): State Department — Nonproliferation Bureau
Description: The Nonproliferation and Disarmament Fund (NDF) was set up to enable quick responses to stop the proliferation of nuclear, biological, and chemical weapons; weapons of mass destruction; and advanced conventional weapons.

The NDF Web site provides information on fund control, legal authority, and management restrictions. NDF project descriptions provide summaries and funding amounts and are displayed in these sections on the NDF Web site: Education/ Training; Destruction/Conversion; Enforcement/Interdiction; Safeguards/Verification; and Administrative.

Subjects: Arms Control; Nonproliferation
Publications: *NDF Annual Report*

1260. U.S. Chemical Weapons Convention Web Site
http://www.cwc.gov/
Sponsor(s): Commerce Department — Bureau of Industry and Security (BIS)
Description: This Web site brings together background information, regulations, documents, and reports related to U.S. compliance with the Chemical Weapons Convention. The treaty affects U.S. private industries that produce, process, consume, import, or export dual-use chemicals that could be used to produce chemical weapons. The site includes handbooks and forms to assist companies with compliance.
Subjects: Chemical Warfare

Country Information

1261. Background Notes
http://www.state.gov/r/pa/ei/bgn/
Sponsor(s): State Department
Description: This popular publication series of brief country profiles comes from the Department of State. Each country edition of *Background Notes* is consistently formatted and contains facts and narrative on aspects of the geography, people, history, government, political conditions, economy, foreign relations, U.S. relations, and travel/business conditions. The site links to the profiles through an alphabetical list of countries; each profile shows the date of its latest revision. Most *Background Notes* have been updated within the past year. For the online version of *Background Notes*, the State Department has added links to additional information. Click on the name of the country at the top of each entry to see a country map, flag, and the additional information (which typically consists of links to major State Department reports and releases about the country).

The *Background Notes* series is useful for bringing together basic historical, political, social, and economic information for each country, and the online version's HTML format makes it easy to link to referenced resources. However, be sure to check the date of the latest revision for each country; there may have been significant changes in a country since the last update.
Subjects: Foreign Countries
Publications: *Background Notes* (various countries), S 1.123:

1262. Country Studies: Area Handbook Series
http://lcweb2.loc.gov/frd/cs/cshome.html
Sponsor(s): Library of Congress
Description: These books, alternatively known as *Country Studies* or Army *Area Handbooks*, are excellent sources of detailed — if dated — information on other countries. Each publication in the series covers a particular foreign country, describing and analyzing its political, economic, social, and national security systems and institutions and examining the interrelationships of those systems and the ways they are shaped by cultural factors. Each study was written by a multidisciplinary team of social scientists. Intended as background material for

the U.S. Army, the series includes such countries as North Korea and Kazakhstan but does not cover Canada, France, or Italy. This site offers full-text search capabilities across all or any combination of the available books. It has recently added the *Country Profiles* series, which consists of summary reports that are typically 20 pages long and much more current than the in-depth *Country Studies*.

Many *Country Studies* have not been updated for at least 10 years because the Army discontinued funding for the project. The Web site's FAQ section notes that funding has been restored and that the series will be updated in the future.

Although these books have not been updated to reflect current events, they remain valuable reference tools for the cultural and historical information they provide. Each study also includes a selective bibliography for further research. Due to the unique publication history of the *Country Studies*, the FAQ section should be consulted as a reference.

Subjects: Foreign Countries
Publications: *Area Handbook Series*, D 101.22:550

1263. Portals to the World

http://www.loc.gov/rr/international/portals.html

Sponsor(s): Library of Congress
Description: This directory of Web sites provides links to information about and from over 200 countries and territories. The links have been selected by regional specialists at the Library of Congress. For each country, links are organized under informational topics such as business, culture, media, libraries, national security, and search engines.

Portals to the World provides a much more efficient path than the general search engines for finding country information on the Internet.

Subjects: Foreign Countries; Finding Aids

1264. World Factbook

https://www.cia.gov/cia/publications/factbook/

Sponsor(s): Central Intelligence Agency (CIA)
Description: The CIA's *World Factbook* is a standard reference for country information. A print version is issued annually; the online version is updated throughout the year. For each country, the online version of the *World Factbook* provides a map, a color image of the national flag, and a profile that includes reference information about the country's geography, population, government, economy, communications, transportation, military, and transnational issues. Each field of information can be displayed for all countries at once using the "field listing" icon. The *World Factbook* also has prepared tables ranking the countries on certain numerical data, such as total population. Appendixes include an extensive list of international organizations and acronyms and a conversion table for weights and measures. The *World Factbook* Web site also links to a low-bandwidth version of the publication and a compressed, downloadable version.

Given its authority and frequent updates, the *World Factbook* Web site is a recommended online reference tool. Consult the Guide to Country Profiles section and the FAQ section to make the best use of the *World Factbook*.

Subjects: Foreign Countries
Publications: *World Factbook*, PREX 3.15:

1265. World News Connection®
http://wnc.fedworld.gov/
Alternate URL(s): http://wnc.dialog.com
Sponsor(s): Commerce Department — Technology Administration (TA) — National Technical Information Service (NTIS); Central Intelligence Agency (CIA) — Open Source Center (OSC)
Description: The World News Connection® is a fee- and subscription-based service that features news and information from thousands of non-U.S. media sources. All items in this service have been translated into English. Content includes newspaper articles, conference proceedings, television and radio broadcasts, periodicals, and non-classified technical reports. The Foreign Broadcast Information Service (FBIS), a U.S. intelligence service, has been translating open-source foreign news reports for over 60 years. FBIS was absorbed into the newly created CIA Open Source Center in 2005. NTIS now secures copyright permission and pays royalty fees to originating news sources in order to make their full-text translations available online through World News Connection®. Access to World News Connection® is available through Dialog, a subsidiary of the Thomson Corporation (see the alternate URL listed above).

This site is a very useful service for a number of audiences, but the cost of subscriptions keeps most of the general public away. The equivalent Web source maintained by the CIA at is not available to the public.
Subjects: News Media — International

Diplomacy

1266. Bureau of Diplomatic Security
http://www.state.gov/m/ds/
Sponsor(s): State Department — Diplomatic Security Bureau
Description: The Bureau of Diplomatic Security (DS) is the security and law enforcement arm of the Department of State. DS manages the security programs that protect the U.S. diplomatic personnel working in U.S. diplomatic missions around the world. DS also assists foreign embassies and consulates in the United States with security and manages immunity issues for foreign diplomats in the United States. They investigate passport and visa fraud and manage the Department of State's personnel security clearance program. The Web site describes each aspect of the DS mission in detail and provides current information about its activities. The News section includes press releases, publications, congressional testimony, photos, and other background information.

Given the current attention to the security of U.S. assets abroad, the Diplomatic Security Service Web site contains timely background information.
Subjects: Terrorism
Publications: *Political Violence Against Americans*, S 1.138/2:
The Antiterrorism Assistance Program: Report to Congress for Fiscal Year . . ., S 1.138/3:

1267. Cultural Programs Division
http://exchanges.state.gov/education/citizens/culture/
Sponsor(s): State Department — Educational and Cultural Affairs Bureau
Description: The Department of State's Cultural Program Division conducts cultural exchange programs in the visual arts, performing arts, film, arts education, arts management, and cultural studies. Its Web site reports on these exchanges and

has information about the program's grants to U.S. nonprofit organizations for carrying out cultural exchanges.

Subjects: Cultural Exchanges

1268. Department of State

http://www.state.gov/

Sponsor(s): State Department

Description: The home page of the Department of State Web site features current news, scrolling headlines, and a video of the "Daily Press Briefing." Information on the Web site is organized into four major sections: Issues and Press; Travel and Business; Youth and Education; and About the State Department. The Issues and Press section links to information by topic, such as foreign assistance, landmines, and Middle East peace. The section also links to State Department's Public Diplomacy and Public Affairs sites and to speeches, briefings, press releases, publications, various e-mail lists, RSS feeds, and podcasts offered by the State Department. The Youth and Education section includes information on educational and cultural exchange programs, State Department and U.S. diplomatic history, and links to resources for teachers. The About State section includes biographies of State Department officials, organizational information, treaty information, and directories such as Key Officers at Foreign Service Posts and U.S. Embassies and Consulates.

This Web site's extensive subject index is helpful for users searching for information on a particular country, service, program, or publication.

Subjects: Diplomacy; Foreign Policy

Publications: *Annual Report on International Religious Freedom*, S 1.151:
Background Notes, S 1.123
Battling International Bribery, S 1.2:B 31/
Country Commercial Guides (annual), S 1.40/7:
Country Reports on Economic Policy and Trade Practices, Y 4.IN 8/16:C 83/
Country Reports on Human Rights Practices (annual), Y 4.IN 8/16-15:
Country Reports on Terrorism, S 1.138:
Diplomatic List, S 1.8:
English Teaching Forum, S 21.15:
Foreign Affairs Manual & Foreign Affairs Handbooks, S 1.40/2:
Foreign Consular Offices in the United States, S 1.69/2:
Foreign Relations of the United States, S 1.1:
Foreign Terrorist Organizations, S 1.2:
International Narcotics Control Strategy Reports, S 1.146:
Key Officers of Foreign Service Posts, S 1.40/5:
Maximum Travel Per Diem Allowances for Foreign Areas, S 1.76/3-2:
Patterns of Global Terrorism, S 1.138:
Semiannual Report to Congress, Office of Inspector General, S 1.1/6:
Standardized Regulations (Government Civilians, Foreign Areas), S 1.76/3:
State (monthly), S 1.118:
Telephone Directory, S 1.21:
Treaties in Force, S 9.14:
Treaty Actions, S 9.14/2:
U.S. Department of State Indexes of Living Costs Abroad, Quarters Allowances and Hardship Differentials, S 1.76/4:
U.S. Refugee Admissions Program for FY (annual), S 1.1/7-2:
United States Participation in the United Nations, S 1.70/8:
Victims of Trafficking and Violence Protection Act: 2000, Trafficking in Persons Report (annual), S 1.152:
Voting Practices in the United Nations, S 1.1/8:

1269. DOSFAN Electronic Research Collection

http://dosfan.lib.uic.edu/ERC/index.html

Sponsor(s): State Department; University of Illinois at Chicago Library

Description: The University of Illinois at Chicago's library, in partnership with the Federal Depository Library Program and the Department of State, has collected archived electronic documents from the State Department. It has also preserved the Web sites of the former U.S. Arms Control and Disarmament Agency and U.S. Information Agency (USIA). The site has a topical and alphabetical index that links to the documents. Highlights include "Daily Press Briefings" going back to 1991, Secretary of State speeches and congressional testimony back to 1993, and issues of the State Department's *Dispatch* magazine from 1990 to its final 1999 issue.

Subjects: Foreign Policy; Government Publications

Publications: *ACDA Annual Report to Congress*, AC 1.1:
Dispatch, S 1.3/5
United States Information Agency: A Commemoration
World Military Expenditures, AC 1.16:

1270. International Broadcasting Bureau

http://www.ibb.gov/

Sponsor(s): International Broadcasting Bureau

Description: The International Broadcasting Bureau's Web site explains the international broadcasting operations of the federal government, which were previously part of the former U.S. Information Agency (USIA). IBB is supervised by the Broadcasting Board of Governors, which was established as an independent federal entity in 1999. The IBB provides support for Voice of America (VOA); Radio Free Europe; Radio Free Asia; Radio Sawa (Arabic language); Radio Farda (Persian language); Alhurra TV (Arabic); and Radio/TV Martí broadcasts. The IBB Web site covers each of these services. Other features include the Engineering section, which discusses such topics as signal interference and monitoring reception of shortwave broadcasts.

Subjects: Broadcasting — International

1271. Japan-US Friendship Commission

http://wwwnew.jusfc.gov/index.asp

Sponsor(s): Japan-United States Friendship Commission

Description: The Japan-United States Friendship Commission (JUSFC) is an independent agency that administers a trust fund for promoting scholarly, cultural, and public affairs activities between the two countries. Its Web site has information on the JUSFC grants, fellowships, and Creative Artists Program.

Subjects: Culture — Grants; International Education — Grants; Japan

1272. Office of the Chief of Protocol

http://www.state.gov/s/cpr/

Sponsor(s): State Department

Description: This Web site details the varied responsibilities of the Department of State's chief of protocol and features information about major diplomatic events both in the United States and abroad. Reference material on the site includes a list of visits to the U.S. by foreign heads of state, from 1874 to present; the Diplomatic List, accredited diplomatic officers of foreign embassies within the United States, a directory of foreign consular offices in the United States, and a Protocol FAQ section that addresses such questions as "What is the order of display for the U.S. flag and a flag of a foreign nation?"

Subjects: Diplomacy
Publications: *Diplomatic List*, S 1.8:
Foreign Consular Offices in the United States, S 1.69/2:

1273. Open World Leadership Center
http://www.openworld.gov/
Sponsor(s): Open World Leadership Center
Description: The Open World Leadership Center enables emerging political and civic leaders from Russia and other Eurasian countries to work with their U.S. counterparts. Open World also sponsors a cultural program. The Open World Leadership Center was established in the Library of Congress and is part of the legislative branch. This Web site provides information about the program and its exchanges.
Subjects: Cultural Exchanges; Russia

1274. Peace Corps
http://www.peacecorps.gov/
Sponsor(s): Peace Corps
Description: The Peace Corps sends volunteers to developing areas of the world to help communities in these areas meet their basic needs and to promote mutual understanding. Its Web site focuses on providing information on the Peace Corps experience for potential volunteers, with information about the application process, benefits, and safety; it also offers an online application kit. Other targeted audiences include family and friends of volunteers, returned volunteers, teachers and students, and donors. For a wider audience, the Online Library section shares the program materials used to train staff in areas such as cultural awareness, teaching English, and community development.

The Peace Corps Web site is well designed and full of accessible information for both applicants and the general public.
Subjects: Foreign Assistance; Volunteerism

1275. U.S. Agency for International Development (USAID)
http://www.usaid.gov/
Sponsor(s): Agency for International Development (USAID)
Description: USAID is an independent agency that provides economic development and humanitarian assistance around the world. The USAID Web site has information about the agency, its work and locations, policy documents, press releases, contracting and acquisition opportunities, and agency employment. Its many program areas include HIV/AIDS treatment and prevention, democracy and governance training, Food for Peace, American Schools and Hospitals Abroad, literacy, microenterprise development, and the Denton Program for transporting humanitarian donations on U.S. military cargo planes. Information about these and other programs is provided under general section headings, such as Agriculture and Health.

Key USAID documents are listed in the About USAID section and include the *U.S. Overseas Loans and Grants, Obligations and Loan Authorizations* (also known as the *Greenbook*). This publication reports all overseas loans and grants authorized by the U.S. government for each fiscal year from 1945 to the present. The *USAID Yellow Book* provides a detailed listing of contracts and assistance awarded during a given fiscal year.
Subjects: Foreign Assistance
Publications: *FrontLines*, S 18.63
OFDA (Office of Foreign Disaster Assistance) Annual Report, S 18.70:

U.S. Overseas Loans & Grants Online (Greenbook)
USAID in Africa, ID 1.17:
USAID Yellow Book: Contracts, Grants and Cooperative Agreements

1276. United States Institute of Peace
http://www.usip.org/
Sponsor(s): United States Institute of Peace (USIP)
Description: USIP is an independent, nonpartisan federal institution created and funded by Congress to strengthen the nation's capacity to promote the peaceful resolution of international conflict. The Our Work section describes each USIP program, including the Center for Conflict Analysis and Prevention, education programs at all levels, the Muslim World Initiative, and the bipartisan Iraq Study Group. Other sections of the site include Grants and Fellowships, the Specialists Directory, Newsroom, Events, Publications, and Library.

For research into peace and the U.S. involvement in peace processes, this Web site can be very useful. For people needing a speaker or an expert to consult, the directory of specialists is accessible by name or topic and is easy to use.
Subjects: International Relations — Research; Peace
Publications: *Peace Watch*, Y 3.P 31:15-2/
Special Reports, Y 3.P 31:20/

1277. United States Mission to International Organizations in Vienna
http://www.usun-vienna.rpo.at/
Sponsor(s): State Department
Description: UNVIE works with the cluster of UN and UN-related agencies headquartered in Vienna. These include the International Atomic Energy Agency (IAEA), the Preparatory Commission for the Comprehensive Nuclear Test-Ban Treaty Organization, and the Wassenaar Arrangement on Export Controls for Conventional Arms and Dual-Use Goods and Technologies. The UNVIE Web site provides a brief description of each organization, links to relevant documents, and UNVIE statements and speeches.
Subjects: International Organizations

1278. United States Mission to the European Union
http://www.useu.be
Sponsor(s): State Department
Description: The United States Mission to the European Union (EU) is based in Brussels and uses its Web site to provide news, policy, and information about the mission for U.S. and international audiences. The site covers a wide array of issue profiles on such topics as biotechnology, data privacy, trade, and U.S. foreign policy.
Subjects: Foreign Policy; International Economic Relations; Europe — Policy

1279. United States Mission to the OECD
http://www.usoecd.org
Sponsor(s): State Department
Description: The Organisation for Economic Co-operation and Development (OECD) in Paris works to foster cooperation among advanced market-based democracies. Along with information about the current ambassador to the OECD, this Web site summarizes U.S. goals and work in current issue areas. Current issues include anti-bribery, cyber-security, corporate governance, and trade.
Subjects: International Economic Relations; International Organizations

1280. United States Mission to the OSCE

http://www.usosce.rpo.at

Description: The Organization for Security and Co-operation in Europe (OSCE) is a regional security organization with 55 participating nations from Europe, Central Asia, and North America. The Web site for the U.S. Mission to the OSCE in Vienna explains the work, history, and structure of the OSCE and the U.S. objectives in the organization. It includes U.S. statements to the OSCE Permanent Council dating back to 1998.

Subjects: International Relations; Europe — Policy; International Organizations

1281. United States Mission to the United Nations

http://www.un.int/usa/

Sponsor(s): State Department

Description: The U.S. Representative to the United Nations, along with several deputies who serve with ambassador rank, represents the United States in meetings with the United Nations. This Web site provides information about the work of the ambassadors and staff in the U.S. mission to the United Nations, which uses the acronym USUN. The site provides official statements, press releases, and background information on a wide range of foreign policy issues.

Subjects: Diplomacy; International Organizations

1282. Vietnam Education Foundation

http://www.vef.gov/

Sponsor(s): Vietnam Education Foundation

Description: The Vietnam Education Foundation (VEF) provides opportunities for Vietnamese nationals to pursue graduate and postgraduate studies in science and technology in the United States and for American citizens to teach in the same fields of study in Vietnam. Its Web site provides news and information about the program.

Subjects: International Education; Vietnam

1283. Voice of America

http://www.voanews.com/

Sponsor(s): International Broadcasting Bureau

Description: The Voice of America (VOA) is an international broadcasting service funded by the U.S. government. VOA programs, which cover U.S. news, information, and culture, are produced and broadcast in English and over 40 other languages through radio, satellite, and the Internet. The VOA Web site highlights daily VOA newswire stories and broadcasts, and provides news via RSS feeds. Current and past VOA programs are available (usually in RealPlayer format) as are the VOA schedules and broadcast frequencies. The VOA also offers VOA Mobile, an all-text version of top stories for use on Web-enabled handheld devices.

Subjects: Broadcasting — International; News Services

Publications: *VOA History*, B 1.2:

VOA Program Guide, B 2.10:

1284. Volunteers for Prosperity

http://www.volunteersforprosperity.gov/

Sponsor(s): USA Freedom Corps

Description: Volunteers for Prosperity is an initiative of the Bush administration to organize skilled American professionals for voluntary service abroad. These professionals join U.S. organizations already working on specific U.S. development

initiatives, such as AIDS relief. The Volunteers for Prosperity Web site explains the nature of the program and has information on finding volunteer opportunities.
Subjects: Volunteerism — International

Foreign Policy

1285. Bureau of African Affairs
http://www.state.gov/p/af/
Sponsor(s): State Department — African Affairs Bureau
Description: The Bureau of African Affairs is concerned with sub-Saharan Africa policy. In the Regional Topics section, the Bureau of African Affairs Web site has press releases and documents on such issues as the African Growth and Opportunity Act and the Malaria Initiative. The site also has biographies of Chiefs of Mission and other senior State Department principals in Africa.
Subjects: Africa — Policy

1286. Bureau of East Asian and Pacific Affairs
http://www.state.gov/p/eap/
Sponsor(s): State Department — East Asian and Pacific Affairs Bureau
Description: The Bureau of East Asian and Pacific Affairs is concerned with policy toward China, Mongolia, Japan, Korea, Vietnam, Indonesia, Malaysia, Australia, New Zealand, and other countries in the East Asia and Pacific region. The Regional Topics section of the site includes information on the Association of Southeast Asian Nations (ASEAN) and the Asia-Pacific Economic Cooperation (APEC). It also links to information about tsunami relief and rebuilding efforts.
Subjects: Asia — Policy

1287. Bureau of Economic and Business Affairs
http://www.state.gov/e/eb/
Sponsor(s): State Department — Economic and Business Affairs Bureau
Description: The Department of State's Bureau of Economic and Business Affairs is responsible for coordinating U.S. foreign economic policy. The bureau's Web site describes its work in supporting U.S. business in foreign markets; negotiating at economic summits and with international organizations; combating bribery in international commerce; coordinating economic sanctions policy; and making recommendations for national energy security. The site also includes reports, fact sheets, speeches, and press releases from the bureau and its component offices.
Subjects: International Economic Relations — Policy

1288. Bureau of European and Eurasian Affairs
http://www.state.gov/p/eur/
Sponsor(s): State Department — European and Eurasian Affairs Bureau
Description: The Bureau of European and Eurasian Affairs is concerned with policy toward the region that extends from Iceland in the northwest to the countries of Cyprus, Turkey, Armenia, and Azerbaijan in the southeast. The Regional Topics section on the bureau's Web site includes information about the G-8 Summits, the Balkans, the European Union, the Northern Ireland peace process, and other issues. The Releases section of the site has news, fact sheets, and reports, such as the annual report on U.S. government assistance to and cooperative activities with Eurasia. It also has the text of the Dayton Peace Accords, formally known as the "General Framework Agreement for Peace in Bosnia and Herzegovina."
Subjects: Eurasia — Policy; Europe — Policy

1289. Bureau of Near Eastern Affairs
http://www.state.gov/p/nea/
Sponsor(s): State Department — Near Eastern Affairs Bureau
Description: The Bureau of Near Eastern Affairs is concerned with policy toward Algeria, Bahrain, Egypt, Iran, Iraq, Israel, Jordan, Kuwait, Lebanon, Libya, Morocco, Oman, Qatar, Saudi Arabia, Syria, Tunisia, the United Arab Emirates, and Yemen. The Regional Topics section of its Web site includes information on Iraq, Middle East peace, and the Middle East Partnership Initiative. The section on Middle East peace includes key documents and official statements and fact sheets.
Subjects: Middle East — Policy

1290. Bureau of South and Central Asian Affairs
http://www.state.gov/p/sca/
Sponsor(s): State Department — South and Central Asian Affairs Bureau
Description: The Bureau of South and Central Asian Affairs is concerned with policy toward the countries of Afghanistan, Bangladesh, Bhutan, India, Kazakhstan, Kyrgyzstan, the Maldives, Nepal, Pakistan, Sri Lanka, Tajikistan, Turkmenistan, and Uzbekistan. The Regional Issues section of the bureau's Web site features information on U.S.-India relations, tsunami relief, Afghanistan reconstruction, and "diplomacy and the global coalition against terrorism."
Subjects: Asia — Policy

1291. Bureau of Western Hemisphere Affairs
http://www.state.gov/p/wha/
Sponsor(s): State Department — Western Hemisphere Affairs Bureau
Description: The Bureau of Western Hemisphere Affairs is concerned with policy toward the region including Canada, Mexico, Central and South America, and the Caribbean island nations. The Web site features sections on Hemispheric Security and the U.S. Mission to the Organization of American States. The Regional Topics section links to information on the Central American Free Trade Agreement (CAFTA) and the Commission for Assistance to a Free Cuba.
Subjects: North America — Policy; South America — Policy; Caribbean — Policy

1292. Foreign Relations of the United States
http://www.state.gov/r/pa/ho/frus/
Alternate URL(s): http://libtext.library.wisc.edu/FRUS/
Sponsor(s): State Department
Description: The *Foreign Relations of the United States (FRUS)* series, published by the Department of State's Office of the Historian, is a compilation of U.S. foreign policy documents beginning with the Lincoln administration in 1861. Documents selected for inclusion come from the State Department and other sources, including the intelligence agencies and private papers. The State Department Web site provides a description of the series, a list of all of its volumes, information about print volumes sold by the Government Printing Office, and the status of their work on the series (now compiled partially through the Nixon-Ford administration). The State Department also provides the full text of volumes starting with the Truman administration; these are available in HTML format. Online volumes from the Eisenhower administration forward can be searched by keyword.

The alternate URL listed above links to a *FRUS* digitization project at the University of Wisconsin–Madison Libraries. This site has scanned copies of the *FRUS* for 1861 through 1960 (with some gaps). The set can be browsed by volume or searched by keyword.
Subjects: Foreign Policy — History

1293. Iraq Study Group

http://www.usip.org/isg/

Sponsor(s): United States Institute of Peace (USIP)

Description: The Iraq Study Group was formed to make a bipartisan, independent assessment of the current and prospective situation in Iraq. The group was facilitated by the Institute of Peace with the support of the Center for Strategic and International Studies (CSIS), the Center for the Study of the Presidency (CSP), and the James A. Baker III Institute for Public Policy at Rice University. The Web site has news, background information, and documents from the group.

Subjects: Iraq

Publications: *Iraq Study Group Report*, Y 3.P 31:

1294. USINFO

http://usinfo.state.gov

Sponsor(s): State Department — International Information Programs Office

Description: The Department of State's Office of International Information Programs (IIP) communicates U.S. policy and government information to individuals and communities abroad. The leaders, citizens, and media of other countries are the principal audience for its USINFO Web site, which is available in English, Spanish, French, Russian, Arabic, Chinese, and Persian. The Web site features foreign policy reports, statements from U.S. leaders, news of diplomatic developments around the world, and articles about U.S. culture. IIP also publishes a number of electronic journals: *Economic Perspectives*, *U.S. Foreign Policy Agenda*, *U.S. Society & Values*, *Global Issues*, and *Issues of Democracy*; all of these publications are available in the Products section. The site also carries a Current Issues news feed that reports on events related to U.S. foreign policy. Formerly known as the Washington File, this news service is available on the Internet in RSS format or as a mobile edition for handheld devices. The site's Resource Tools section includes a page identifying popular misinformation about the U.S. government and an International Events Calendar that notes when State Department leaders are traveling abroad.

Although this Web site was developed for foreign audiences, U.S. readers will find many sections to be of interest.

Subjects: Foreign Policy; International Education; News Services — International

Publications: *Economic Perspectives (various languages)*, S 20.16:

Global Issues (various languages), S 20.18:

Issues of Democracy (various languages), S 20.20:

U.S. Foreign Policy Agenda (various languages), S 20.17:

U.S. Society & Values (various languages), S 20.19:

International Migration and Travel

1295. Bureau of Population, Refugees, and Migration

http://www.state.gov/g/prm/

Sponsor(s): State Department — Population, Refugees, and Migration Bureau

Description: The Bureau of Population, Refugees, and Migration (PRM) has primary responsibility for formulating policies on population, refugees, and migration, and for administering U.S. refugee assistance and admissions programs. The Web site includes background information and news releases. It also has funding information for nongovernmental organizations that carry out relief services overseas and an e-mail list for refugee and resettlement news.

Subjects: Refugees — Policy

1296. CDC Travel Information
http://www.cdc.gov/travel/
Sponsor(s): Health and Human Services Department — Centers for Disease Control and Prevention (CDC)
Description: This Web site provides health risk information by travel destination. It contains information about diseases and disease outbreaks, including avian influenza; vaccine recommendations; safe food and water; insect protection; traveling with children; special needs travelers; and cruise ship and air travel. The site also links to CDC's "Yellow Book" (*Health Information for International Travel*).
Subjects: Diseases and Conditions — International; Tourism
Publications: *Health Information for International Travel*, HE 20.7818:

1297. Citizenship and Immigration Services
http://uscis.gov/
Sponsor(s): Homeland Security Department — Citizenship and Immigration Service (USCIS)
Description: The responsibilities of the U.S. Citizenship and Immigration Service (USCIS) include asylum and refugee processing, naturalization, special immigration status programs, and issuance of immigration documents. The USCIS Web site's Services and Benefit section links to information on permanent residency (green card), citizenship, visiting the United States, employment authorization, and adoption. It also has a directory of USCIS field offices and overseas offices. The site provides immigration forms, laws, regulations, and guides. The Education and Resources section includes citizenship study materials, resources for public libraries, and the immigrant guide *Welcome to the Unites States*, which is available in English and 10 other languages.
Subjects: Citizenship; Immigration Law
Publications: *Guide to Naturalization*, HS 8.8:
Learn About the United States: Quick Civics Lessons, HS 8.2:
USCIS Civics Flash Cards, HS 8.2:
USCIS Today
Welcome to the United States: A Guide for New Immigrants, HS 1.8:

1298. Executive Office for Immigration Review
http://www.justice.gov/eoir/
Sponsor(s): Justice Department — Executive Office for Immigration Review
Description: The Executive Office for Immigration Review (EOIR) conducts immigration court proceedings, appellate reviews, and administrative hearings in individual cases. This Web site contains information about the EOIR, its organization and activities, and its Pro Bono Program. It includes a national directory of immigration courts and statistics on the EOIR caseload. The Virtual Law Library section provides immigration decisions, regulations, and resources for attorneys.
Subjects: Immigration Law
Publications: *Immigration Judge Benchbook*
Statistical Year Book, Executive Office for Immigration Review

1299. Immigration Statistics
http://www.dhs.gov/ximgtn/statistics/
Sponsor(s): Homeland Security Department — Citizenship and Immigration Service (USCIS)
Description: This site compiles links to publications, data tables, and other sources of statistics related to migration to the United States. Statistics cover immigration; naturalization; refugees; asylum seekers; the illegal immigrant population; applications for immigration benefits; and related topics. The format of the data varies

from PDF or HTML to spreadsheet tables, depending on the source and statistic. The site also includes maps showing the relative flow of immigrants, or "Legal Permanent Residents," to each U.S. state.

Subjects: International Migration — Statistics
Publications: *Yearbook of Immigration Statistics*, HS 8.15:

1300. Office of Refugee Resettlement
http://www.acf.hhs.gov/programs/orr/
Sponsor(s): Health and Human Services Department — Administration for Children and Families (ACF)
Description: The Office of Refugee Resettlement (ORR) provides assistance to people fleeing persecution in their homelands. Its Web site describes the programs, policy, and funding of ORR and explains the legal definition of refugee status and who is eligible for benefits. A Data section reports on refugee arrivals by country of origin and by U.S. state.
Subjects: Refugees

1301. Travel.State.Gov
http://travel.state.gov/
Sponsor(s): State Department — Consular Affairs Bureau
Description: The Bureau of Consular Affairs, which maintains this Web site, is concerned with the safety of U.S. citizens in foreign countries. The bureau issues passports for U.S. citizens traveling abroad and visas for foreign citizens traveling to the United States. Travel.State.Gov has practical news, advice, and fact sheets about travel safety, applying for a passport, and U.S. visa programs. In the International Travel section, the site supplies consular information sheets for each country, which summarize entry requirements, local health and safety information, customs regulations, and registering with the local U.S. embassy or consulate. This section also contains official Travel Warnings and Public Announcements for specific countries or regions. The Law and Policy section has clear explanations of legal issues related to Americans abroad (such as those pertaining to death notification, marriage, and divorce), citizenship and nationality, and law enforcement.

The Bureau of Consular Affairs site provides simple, straightforward access to essential travel information. The passport and visa infomation is particularly thorough and includes links to the necessary forms.
Subjects: Passports; Visas
Publications: *Foreign Entry Requirements*, S 1.2:F 76 E/
Passports: Applying for Them the Easy Way, S 1.2:P 26/
Tips for Travelers to. . ., S 1.2:
Visa Bulletin, S 1.3/4:

1302. UnitedStatesVisas.gov
http://www.unitedstatesvisas.gov/
Sponsor(s): State Department
Description: UnitedStatesVisas.gov provides information on U.S. entry visas for citizens of other countries. Major sections include What is a Visa?; U.S. Visa Policy; How to Get a Visa; and Visa News. This Web site is normally available in French, Spanish, Arabic, and Russian versions. At the time of this writing, the non-English language versions were being updated.

UnitedStatesVisas.gov is a clear presentation of what can be a confusing topic. The Visa News section is a valuable service as security, screening, and application processes change and become more automated.
Subjects: Visas

International Relations

1303. Bureau of International Labor Affairs
http://www.dol.gov/ilab/welcome.html
Sponsor(s): Labor Department — International Labor Affairs Bureau (ILAB)
Description: The Bureau of International Labor Affairs (ILAB) coordinates programs, policies, research, and technical assistance related to international labor issues. The ILAB Web site features a list of products that are believed to have been made using forced or indentured child labor; this list is maintained in accordance with Executive Order 13126 and Federal Acquisition Regulations. The Publications section of the site includes *Foreign Labor Trends* reports for about 20 countries and the European Union, as well as various reports on the topic of child labor.
Subjects: Child Labor — International; Labor Law — International
Publications: *Findings on the Worst Forms of Child Labor* (annual), L 29.18: *Foreign Labor Trends Series*, L 29.16:

1304. Commission on Security and Cooperation in Europe
http://www.csce.gov/
Sponsor(s): Commission on Security and Cooperation in Europe (CSCE)
Description: CSCE, better known as the Helsinki Commission, is an independent government agency created by Congress. It monitors and encourages compliance with the Helsinki Final Act and other commitments of the countries participating in the Organization for Security and Cooperation in Europe (OSCE). The commission's Web site includes information about the CSCE and OSCE and the full text of the commission's press releases, hearings, briefings, and its statements in the *Congressional Record*. Documents are organized by country name and by issues including freedom of speech, national minorities, elections, and rule of law.
Subjects: Human Rights

1305. Congressional-Executive Commission on China
http://www.cecc.gov/
Alternate URL(s): http://www.gpoaccess.gov/congress/joint/prccommission/index.html
Sponsor(s): Congressional-Executive Commission on China (CECC)
Description: CECC was established to monitor the human rights situation and development of the rule of law in China. Its Web site has information about the commission and records of their hearings and roundtables. It includes information on Chinese law, a directory of Chinese government Web sites, and a database of prisoners of conscience in China. The alternate URL listed above, located in the GPO Access system, provides CECC documents in text and PDF formats from 2002 to present.
Subjects: Human Rights; China — Policy

1306. Defense Security Cooperation Agency
http://www.dsca.osd.mil/
Sponsor(s): Defense Department — Defense Security Cooperation Agency (DSCA)
Description: DSCA assists U.S. allies through foreign military sales, training, and technical and humanitarian assistance. The DSCA Web site provides background information on the agency and its organizational components and features announcements of major foreign military arms sales. The Publications section provides links to the key policy and legal documents on foreign military assistance. The Data and Statistics section contains current and past editions of the *DSCA*

Facts Book, also known as the *Foreign Military Sales, Foreign Military Construction Sales and Military Assistance*.

While much of the DSCA Web site is technical in nature and written for a very specific audience, researchers will find this to be a valuable source for U.S. security assistance and arms transfer policy and regulatory information.

Subjects: International Relations; National Defense — Policy

Publications: *DSCA Facts Book: Foreign Military Sales, Foreign Military Construction Sales and Military Assistance Facts*, D 1.66:

1307. Famine Early Warning System Network (FEWS NET)
http://www.fews.net/

Sponsor(s): Agency for International Development (USAID)

Description: FEWS NET provides information and analysis on food security conditions in African nations. FEWS NET is funded by USAID and implemented through a partnership with other federal agencies and regional organizations in Africa. Its Web site highlights food emergency announcements and warnings, drought and flood hazard assessments, and remote-sensing imagery of rainfall and vegetation on the African continent.

Subjects: Famine; Africa

Publications: *FEWS (Famine Early Warning System) Bulletin*, S 18.68:
FEWS (Famine Early Warning System) Special Report, S 18.68/2:

1308. Foreign Agents Registration Act (FARA)
http://www.usdoj.gov/criminal/fara/

Sponsor(s): Justice Department — Criminal Division

Description: The Foreign Agents Registration Act (FARA) requires that individuals and organizations lobbying on behalf of foreign business or foreign government interests register with the Department of Justice. The Foreign Agents Registration Unit, within the Criminal Division's Counterespionage Section, has responsibility for administering the act. This Web site has information for those who need to register as well as for those interested in viewing FARA registrations at the public office maintained by the Justice Department for this purpose.

Subjects: Lobbyists — Regulations

Publications: *Report of the Attorney General to the Congress of the United States on the Administration of the Foreign Agents Registration Act . . . (semiannual)*, J 1.30:

1309. House Democracy Assistance Commission
http://hdac.house.gov/

Sponsor(s): Congress — House of Representatives

Description: As stated on the Web site, "the [House Democracy Assistance] Commission's mission is to strengthen democratic institutions by assisting parliaments in emerging democracies." The site includes the commission's annual report and a list of countries participating in parliamentary assistance programs.

Subjects: Democracy — International; Foreign Assistance

1310. Inter-American Foundation
http://www.iaf.gov/

Sponsor(s): Inter-American Foundation (IAF)

Description: IAF is an independent agency that provides assistance to Latin America and the Caribbean by awarding grants directly to local organizations throughout the region. Its Web site features sections entitled About IAF, News and Events, Grants, Fellowships, and Publications. The Grants section has application information and descriptions of awarded grants listed by year and by country. The Publica-

tions section provides links to annual reports and to *Grassroots Development,* the journal of the IAF. Spanish and Portuguese versions of the site are available.
Subjects: Foreign Assistance; South America
Publications: *Grassroots Development,* Y 3.IN 8/25:15
Inter-American Foundation (annual), Y 3.IN 8/25:

1311. Middle East Partnership Initiative
http://www.mepi.state.gov/
Sponsor(s): State Department
Description: The Middle East Partnership Initiative (MEPI) is a Bush administration program that supports reform in the areas of politics, economics, education, and women's issues in the Middle East. Its Web site provides background information and lists the government and nongovernment partners in the initiative. The Countries section lists projects and funds by country.
Subjects: Foreign Assistance; Middle East

1312. Millennium Challenge Corporation
http://www.mcc.gov/
Sponsor(s): Millennium Challenge Corporation
Description: The Millennium Challenge Corporation (MCC), a government corporation, works with countries to promote sustainable economic growth and reduce poverty through investments in areas such as agriculture, education, and private sector development. Countries are selected to receive aid based on their performance in governing justly, investing in their citizens, and encouraging economic freedom. The Web site provides information on MCC, its leadership, and its documents. The Countries section describes the selection criteria and how each participating country meets them.
Subjects: International Economic Development

1313. Office of the Coordinator for Counterterrorism
http://www.state.gov/s/ct/
Sponsor(s): State Department — Counterterrorism Office
Description: The Department of State's Office of the Coordinator for Counterterrorism develops U.S. counterterrorism policy and coordinates U.S. efforts to improve counterterrorism cooperation with foreign governments. Its Web site includes statements on U.S. policy and describes the office's programs. The site also links to the annual publication *Country Reports on Terrorism* and the Foreign Terrorist Organization list, which is maintained by the office.
Subjects: Terrorism — Policy
Publications: *Country Reports on Terrorism,* S 1.138:

1314. Office of War Crime Issues
http://www.state.gov/s/wci/
Sponsor(s): State Department — War Crimes Issues Office
Description: As described on the Web site, the Office of War Crimes "advises the Secretary of State directly and formulates U.S. policy responses to atrocities committed in areas of conflict and elsewhere throughout the world." In the U.S. Releases section, the site provides press releases, testimony, and reports on issues related to war crimes.
Subjects: War Crimes

1315. Overseas Security Advisory Council
http://www.ds-osac.org/
Sponsor(s): Overseas Security Advisory Council
Description: OSAC was established to promote security cooperation and communication between the U.S. government and U.S. private sector companies and organizations that operate abroad. OSAC services are for registered constituent organizations. The OSAC Web site provides unclassified information, such as daily news of foreign events, reports on topics including crime and security trends in foreign countries, a database of Department of State posts, and a database of terrorist organizations. The Country Councils section of the site provides links to the Web pages for each of the over 50 regional OSAC councils. The Resource Library section organizes OSAC reports and external links on topics such as personal security, cargo security, and emergency preparedness.
Subjects: Terrorism; Crime Prevention — International

1316. Security and Prosperity Partnership of North America
http://www.spp.gov/
Sponsor(s): Commerce Department — International Trade Administration (ITA)
Description: This Web site describes the security and economic prosperity agenda agreed to by the leaders of the United States, Canada, and Mexico. It includes SPP fact sheets and information about the various SPP working groups.
Subjects: North America — Policy; Canada ; Mexico

1317. Sustainable Development Partnerships
http://www.sdp.gov/
Sponsor(s): State Department — Public Affairs Bureau
Description: The Sustainable Development Partnerships Web site is managed by the Department of State's Bureau of Public Affairs to demonstrate how the U.S. government has joined with foreign governments, international organizations, and other communities to promote sustainable development for the world's poorer regions. Its Web site provides fact sheets on sustainable development initiatives, organized by country, region, and issue. It also links to other government Web sites on related topics.
Subjects: Foreign Assistance; International Economic Development

1318. U.S.-China Economic and Security Review Commission
http://www.uscc.gov/
Sponsor(s): United States-China Security Review Commission
Description: The U.S.-China Economic and Security Review Commission (USCC) was created to review the national security implications of trade and economic ties between the United States and the People's Republic of China. Major sections of its Web site include Press Releases, Hearing Schedule, and Congressional Testimonies. The site also has directories of the commissioners and staff, and copies of research papers prepared at the request of the commission.
Subjects: International Economic Relations; China — Policy

1319. United States Commission on International Religious Freedom
http://www.uscirf.gov/
Sponsor(s): United States Commission on International Religious Freedom
Description: The Commission on International Religious Freedom is a federal government commission established to monitor the status of religious freedom in other nations and make policy recommendations to the president, secretary of state, and Congress. The commission issues an annual report on religious persecution around the world; current and past reports are available on this Web site. The

site also has additional information about the commission and its hearings, press releases, congressional testimony, and relevant legislation.

Subjects: Human Rights

Publications: *Annual Report of the United States Commission on International Religious Freedom*, Y 3.R 27:1/

1320. United States Mission to NATO

http://nato.usmission.gov/

Sponsor(s): Defense DepartmentState Department

Description: The Department of State and Department of Defense have a combined United States Mission to the North Atlantic Treaty Organization (NATO). This Web site has current speeches and statement from the U.S. ambassador to NATO and current news from the U.S. government on security issues.

Subjects: International Agreements

CHAPTER 15

Law and Law Enforcement

Web sites concerning law and law enforcement are primarily sponsored by the Department of Justice and the federal courts. The Justice Department in particular has a very broad role in legal matters, covering topics from legal practices to community policing to homeland security issues. This chapter has a similarly broad scope. However, some subject-specific Web sites, such as the site concerning environmental law, can be found in the relevant subject chapters in this publication.

Subsections in this chapter are Areas of Law, Courts and the Judicial System, Crime and Enforcement, and Laws and Legal Information.

Areas of Law

1321. Access Board: A Federal Agency Committed to Accessible Design
http://www.access-board.gov/
Sponsor(s): Access Board
Description: The U.S. Access Board, also known as the Architectural and Transportation Barriers Compliance Board, is an independent federal agency whose mission is to promote accessibility for people with disabilities. Its Web site has information on accessibility guidelines and standards and enforcement of the Architectural Barriers Act (ABA). The Guidelines section includes online versions of *ADA Accessibility Guidelines (ADAAG) for Buildings and Facilities, Electronic and Information Technology Accessibility Standards (Section 508)*, and other guidelines. The About the Board section includes information on relevant laws and policies. The Publications section has the full text of publications organized under topics including facilities, public rights-of-way, transportation, and communication.
Subjects: Americans with Disabilities Act (ADA)
Publications: *ADA Accessibility Guidelines for Buildings and Facilities (ADAAG)*, Y 3.B 27:8 AM

1322. ADA Home Page
http://www.ada.gov
Sponsor(s): Justice Department — Civil Rights Division
Description: The Justice Department's central Web site about the Americans with Disabilities Act (ADA) compiles a wide range of information for the general public, businesses, state and local governments, and other audiences. Major sections include a catalog of publications about ADA regulations and technical assistance and information about ADA enforcement actions. The site also refers to Justice's toll-free ADA hotline at 800-514-0301 (voice) and 800-514-0383 (TDD).

This site has a broad scope and will be of interest to anyone concerned with ADA compliance.
Subjects: Americans with Disabilities Act (ADA)
Publications: *Enforcing the ADA, A Status Report from the Department of Justice*, J 1.106:
Guide to Disability Rights Laws, J 1.8:D 63/2

1323. Administrative Decisions and Other Actions
http://www.lib.virginia.edu/govdocs/fed_decisions_agency.html
Sponsor(s): University of Virginia Library
Description: This university Web site is a finding aid for administrative actions that fall outside the usual scope of the *Code of Federal Regulations* and the *Federal Register*. Its lengthy list includes links to items such as the advisory opinions from the Consumer Product Safety Commission, Department of Energy directives, Federal Labor Relations Authority decisions, Food and Drug Administration enforcement reports, and Postal Service administrative decisions. It links to Electronic FOIA Reading Rooms for each agency covered, since these reading rooms often contain such administrative decisions and actions.

Maintained at the University of Virginia Library's Government Information Resources site, this page fills an important niche in finding legal information on the Web.
Subjects: Administrative Law; Finding Aids

1324. Antitrust Division
http://www.usdoj.gov/atr/
Sponsor(s): Justice Department — Antitrust Division
Description: The Antitrust Division uses its Web site to provide full-text cases, information about the division and its activities, and press releases. The Public Documents section links to selected appellate briefs (back to 1993), the division's workload statistics, guidelines, and other publications. The Antitrust Case Filings page includes online cases arranged alphabetically going back to 1994.
Subjects: Antitrust Law

1325. Civil Rights Division
http://www.usdoj.gov/crt/
Sponsor(s): Justice Department — Civil Rights Division
Description: The Civil Rights Division of the Justice Department enforces federal statutes prohibiting discrimination. Pages for each of the division's organizational sections hold most of the content at the site. The organizational sections are Appellate, Coordination and Review, Criminal, Disability Rights, Educational Opportunities, Employment Litigation, Housing and Civil Enforcement, Special Litigation, Voting, and Office of Special Counsel for Immigration Related Unfair Employment Practices. Each section typically includes background material on the relevant area of practice, statutes enforced, and cases or briefs. The Special Topics section has material on a wide range of topics not covered elsewhere on the site, such as the pamphlet "Federal Protections Against National Origin Discrimination" in 16 languages besides English.
Subjects: Civil Rights — Laws
Publications: *Civil Rights Forum*, J 1.104:
Enforcing the ADA, A Status Report from the Department of Justice, J 1.106:

1326. Commission on Civil Rights
http://www.usccr.gov/
Sponsor(s): Civil Rights Commission
Description: The United States Commission on Civil Rights investigates and reports on discrimination because of race, color, religion, sex, age, disability, or national origin. The USCCR Web site includes commission news, meeting transcripts, reports, congressional testimony, and information on filing a complaint. Topics covered on the site include voting rights, federal contracting practices, and health care. A small amount of content is available in Spanish.
Subjects: Civil Rights

Publications: *Civil Rights Directory*, CR 1.10:15
Civil Rights Journal, CR 1.17:
Funding Civil Rights Enforcement

1327. Comptroller General Decisions and Opinions
http://www.gao.gov/legal.htm
Alternate URL(s): http://www.gpoaccess.gov/gaodecisions/
Sponsor(s): Government Accountability Office (GAO) — Comptroller General
Description: The Comptroller General of GAO issues decisions regarding use of federal appropriations, government contract bid protests, and major federal regulations. This site provides access to the full text of recent decisions, in HTML and PDF formats. For older decisions (going back to November 1995), there is a link to the GAO Comptroller General Decisions database on GPO Access, at the alternate URL provided above.

While the decisions are also available as one of the GPO Access databases, this version provides a good explanation of and easy access to the most recent decisions.
Subjects: Government Contracts — Regulations
Publications: *Decisions of the Comptroller General*, GA 1.5/A-2:

1328. Copyright Office
http://lcweb.loc.gov/copyright/
Sponsor(s): Library of Congress — Copyright Office
Description: The U.S. Copyright Office Web site includes information on copyright law, registering a work for copyright protection, and searching existing copyright records. The site also highlights hot topics and provides an RSS feed of copyright news. The Publications section of the site has copies of the office's circulars, brochures, and forms. Circulars include *Copyright Basics*, an overview, in English and Spanish. One-page fact sheets cover specific topics such as fair use, international copyright, and how to register specific types of works, such as books, music, and photographs. The section on registration addresses copyright registration for literary works, visual arts, performing arts, sound recordings, and periodicals. Information about how to register a work is available in Spanish.

Simple in design and organization, this site does an exemplary job of providing frequently requested documents and information in an easy-to-find manner.
Subjects: Copyright Law; Intellectual Property
Publications: *Annual Report of the Register of Copyrights*, LC 3.1:
Catalog of Copyright Entries, LC 3.6/6:
Copyright Basics, LC 3.4/2:
Copyright Information Circulars, LC 3.4/2:
Copyright Law of the United States, LC 3.4/2:
Forms, Copyright Office, LC 3.14:
NewsNet, LC 3.4/3:

1329. Copyright Royalty Board (CRB)
http://www.loc.gov/crb/
Sponsor(s): Library of Congress
Description: CRB was created by the Copyright Royalty and Distribution Reform Act of 2004 (Public Law 108-419). The CRB consists of three permanent copyright royalty judges who were appointed in early January 2006. The Web site has information on rate and distribution proceeding, CRB notices in the *Federal Register*, and forms for filing royalty fee claims for cable, satellite, and digital audio recording devices and media. Several sections of the Web site are still under development at the time of this writing.
Subjects: Copyright Law

1330. Department of Justice

http://www.justice.gov/
Alternate URL(s): http://www.usdoj.gov/
Sponsor(s): Justice Department
Description: The central Web site for the Justice Department links to the department's 50-plus component divisions and programs. Under Resources, the site brings together the department's publications, press releases, grants, acquisitions and procurement operations, and budget information. The Legal Cases and Documents section, also under Resources, compiles links to Justice Department briefs, letters, and other documents under these headings: Antitrust; Bureau of Alcohol, Tobacco, Firearms, and Explosives; Civil; Civil Rights; Criminal; Enron Exhibits; Environment; Executive Office for Immigration Review; Office of Legal Counsel; Office of Solicitor General; Terrorism-Related Documents; U.S. Trustees; and Violence Against Women Program.

The site also has extensive information relating to the Freedom of Information Act (FOIA). The FOIA section includes basic reference material explaining FOIA, a list of principal FOIA contacts at federal agencies, links to other agencies' FOIA sites, and links to the annual FOIA reports submitted by federal departments and agencies. In addition to this government-wide material, the Justice Department also provides links to the online FOIA reading rooms of its component divisions and offices.

The Justice Department Web site provides a clear interface to the numerous components, programs, and publications of the department. Many of the specific component sites are described in separate entries in this book.
Subjects: Freedom of Information Act; Law and Law Enforcement
Publications: *Annual Report of the Attorney General of the United States*, J 1.1:
FY . . . Performance and Accountability Report, Department of Justice, J 1.1:
Office of Inspector General Semiannual Report to Congress, J 1.1/9:
United States Attorneys' Bulletin, J 31.12:
United States Attorneys' Manual, J 1.8:AT

1331. Department of Labor Office of Administrative Law Judges (OALJ)

http://www.oalj.dol.gov/
Sponsor(s): Labor Department — Office of Administrative Law Judges (OALJ)
Description: The Labor Department's administrative law judges preside over cases related to many of the department's programs, such as black lung benefits cases and Fair Labor Standards Act enforcement. The office also includes the Board of Contract Appeals (BCA) and the Board of Alien Labor Certification Appeals (BALCA). Decisions and other online documents are organized in the Library Collections section by program area, including Davis-Bacon Act, Longshore, Black Lung, Whistleblower, and Immigration. They can also be searched by complainant or employer name, date, and OALJ case number.
Subjects: Labor Law
Publications: *Judges' Benchbook of the Black Lung Benefits Act*, L 1.2:

1332. Federal Mine Safety and Health Review Commission

http://www.fmshrc.gov/
Sponsor(s): Federal Mine Safety and Health Review Commission (FMSHRC)
Description: The Federal Mine Safety and Health Review Commission is an independent adjudicative agency that provides administrative trial and appellate review of legal disputes arising under the Federal Mine Safety and Health Amendments Act of 1977. Sections featured at the site include About FMSHRC, Rules, Mine Act and Regulations, Guides and Publications, Recent Decisions, Published Decisions, and FOIA.

Subjects: Mining — Laws
Publications: *Decisions, Federal Mine Safety and Health Review Commission*, Y 3.M 66:9/

1333. Foreign Claims Settlement Commission
http://www.usdoj.gov/fcsc/
Sponsor(s): Justice Department — Foreign Claims Settlement Commission
Description: The Foreign Claims Settlement Commission is a quasi-judicial, independent agency within the Department of Justice. The commission rules on claims of U.S. nationals against foreign governments. The Web site has information on the Commission, special claims programs, and copies of the annual report. Special topics include property claims against Cuba and the U.S.-Albanian Claims Settlement Agreement.
Subjects: International Law
Publications: *Annual Report to Congress, Foreign Claims Settlement Commission*, J 1.1/6:

1334. Historical Publications of the United States Commission on Civil Rights
http://www.law.umaryland.edu/marshall/usccr/index.asp
Sponsor(s): University of Maryland. Thurgood Marshall Law Library
Description: This site provides access to PDF copies of Civil Rights Commission documents that are in the collection of the University of Maryland Thurgood Marshall Law Library. It includes a selection of documents dating back to the Civil Rights Act of 1957, which created the original Civil Rights Commission. Topics covered by the materials include educational opportunity, police-community relations, hate crimes, and the Voting Rights Act.
Subjects: Civil Rights

1335. Judge Advocate General's Corps
http://www.jagcnet.army.mil/
Sponsor(s): Army — Judge Advocate General's Corps
Description: The Judge Advocate General's Corps (JAGC), the Army's lawyers corps, has divided its Web site into two sections. The Visitor section links to public information. The page tab labeled Enter JAGCNet is restricted to authorized users. Public links include information on JAGC leadership, a legal services section for members of the military, and the Web site for the Legal Center and School.
Subjects: Military Justice

1336. Military Legal Resources
http://www.loc.gov/rr/frd/Military_Law/
Sponsor(s): Library of Congress — Federal Research Division (FRD)
Description: This Library of Congress site provides access to a growing collection of historic, digitized military legal resources, including: *Military Law Review*, 1958 to the present; *Uniform Code of Military Justice* legislative history materials; *Manuals for Courts-Martial*; *The Army Lawyer*, from 1971 forward; and the indexed *Enactments and Approved Papers of the Control Council and Coordinating Committee* from the Allied Control Authority in Germany, 1945–1948. The materials are in PDF format. They are selected from the collection of the U.S. Army Judge Advocate General's Legal Center and School Library in Charlottesville, VA.
Subjects: Military History; Military Justice
Publications: *Manual for Courts-Martial, United States*, D 1.15:
Military Law Review, D 101.22:
The Army Lawyer, D 101.22/32:

1337. National Indian Gaming Commission
http://www.nigc.gov/
Sponsor(s): National Indian Gaming Commission
Description: The National Indian Gaming Commission is an independent federal regulatory agency established by the Indian Gaming Regulatory Act of 1988 (Public Law 100-497). The Web site includes an overview of the commission and the laws and regulations with which it is concerned. The Reading Room section includes National Indian Gaming Commission decisions, enforcement actions, approved gaming ordinances, and more. Under Tribal Data, the site has a list of gaming facilities by tribe and data on tribal revenue from gaming operations.
Subjects: Gambling — Regulations; American Indians

1338. Occupational Safety and Health Review Commission
http://www.oshrc.gov/
Sponsor(s): Occupational Safety and Health Review Commission (OSHRC)
Description: OSHRC is an independent federal agency created to decide contests of citations or penalties resulting from OSHA inspections. The commission functions as an administrative court, with established procedures for conducting hearings, receiving evidence, and rendering decisions by its administrative law judges. Its site has recent decisions by the commission and administrative law judges. Other sections include Procedural Rules, Publications, and Budget.
Subjects: Workplace Safety — Laws
Publications: *Guide to Review Commission Procedures*, Y 3.OC 1:8 P
OSHRC decisions. ALJ decisions., Y 3.OC 1:10-5/

1339. Office of Legal Counsel
http://www.justice.gov/olc/
Sponsor(s): Justice Department — Office of Legal Counsel
Description: The Office of Legal Counsel drafts legal opinions of the attorney general and provides legal advice for the White House and executive branch agencies. The office also reviews draft executive orders and proclamations for legality. The Web site has the text of selected opinions and memoranda from the office, from 1992 to present.
Subjects: Legal Issues
Publications: *Opinions of the Office of Legal Counsel*, J 1.5/4:

1340. Privacy and Civil Liberties Office
http://www.usdoj.gov/pclo/
Sponsor(s): Justice Department — Deputy Attorney General
Description: The mission of the Privacy and Civil Liberties Office is to ensure that the Justice Department is compliant with laws and policies regarding personal privacy and the protection of individual civil liberties. The Web site has information on the interagency Privacy and Civil Liberties Board and the Privacy Act of 1974. The Privacy Reports and Resources section has the text of laws and Office of Management and Budget policies regarding privacy.
Subjects: Privacy

1341. USDA Office of the Assistant Secretary for Civil Rights
http://www.usda.gov/cr/
Sponsor(s): Agriculture Department (USDA) — Civil Rights Office
Description: The USDA Office of the Assistant Secretary for Civil Rights handles complaints regarding employment discrimination for USDA staff and program discrimination for those served by USDA programs. The Web site has information on how to file a complaint and has the full text of directives and regulations. The

Outreach section describes programs such as the "USDA/1890 Initiative" to attract minority students into careers in agriculture and related fields. Much of the site is also available in Spanish.

Subjects: Civil Rights; Employment Discrimination

Courts and the Judicial System

1342. Civil Division
http://www.justice.gov/civil/
Sponsor(s): Justice Department — Civil Division
Description: The Civil Division represents the United States, its departments and agencies, members of Congress, Cabinet officers, and other federal employees in litigation. Special sections of the site include Tobacco Litigation, Radiation Exposure Compensation Program, Vaccine Injury Compensation Program, and Office of Immigration Litigation. A Selected Cases section features documents from a handful of cases, such as the *Cobell v. Norton* case involving the Interior Department.
Subjects: Litigation

1343. Court of Appeals. (01) First Circuit
http://www.ca1.uscourts.gov/
Sponsor(s): Court of Appeals. (01) First Circuit
Description: The First Circuit covers Maine, Massachusetts, New Hampshire, Puerto Rico, and Rhode Island. The court's official site has a database of its opinions and dockets. It also features the court calendar, rules and procedures, forms, and links to the Web sites of other courts in the First Circuit.
Subjects: Federal Appellate Courts

1344. Court of Appeals. (02) Second Circuit
http://www.ca2.uscourts.gov/
Sponsor(s): Court of Appeals. (02) Second Circuit
Description: The Second Circuit covers Connecticut, Vermont, and New York. The court's official site has opinions issued within the current and previous month. Opinions can be browsed by date range or searched by case name or docket number. The official site also offers a court directory, forms, and the *Second Circuit Handbook*.
Subjects: Federal Appellate Courts

1345. Court of Appeals. (03) Third Circuit
http://www.ca3.uscourts.gov/
Alternate URL(s): http://vls.law.vill.edu/Locator/3/
Sponsor(s): Court of Appeals. (03) Third Circuit
Description: The Third Circuit covers Delaware, New Jersey, Pennsylvania, and the Virgin Islands. At its official site, the court has its most current opinions, searchable by keyword. A much more comprehensive source is available at the Villanova University School of Law site listed here as the alternate URL. Villanova has the full text of the decisions from the Third Circuit of the federal Court of Appeals from May 1994 to the present.

The court's site also has a Death Penalty Information section, listing the appeals status and history for individuals given a death sentence in courts within the Third Circuit.
Subjects: Federal Appellate Courts

1346. Court of Appeals. (04) Fourth Circuit
http://www.ca4.uscourts.gov/
Sponsor(s): Court of Appeals. (04) Fourth Circuit
Description: The Fourth Circuit covers Maryland, North Carolina, South Carolina, Virginia, and West Virginia. The Court of Appeals site has its opinions online going back to 1996; it also offers an e-mail alert service for new opinions. The Web site's Cases of Public Interest provides updated docket information for recent cases of broad public interest. The Information section of the site includes judge biographies, filing instructions, and a map of the districts within the Fourth Circuit.
Subjects: Federal Appellate Courts

1347. Court of Appeals. (05) Fifth Circuit
http://www.ca5.uscourts.gov/
Sponsor(s): Court of Appeals. (05) Fifth Circuit
Description: The Fifth Circuit covers Louisiana, Mississippi, and Texas. The official Fifth Circuit Court of Appeals Web site includes published and unpublished opinions released from 1992 to the present. The cases can be searched by date, docket number, and keyword. Users can sign up to have opinions sent by e-mail as soon as they are posted on the site. The site also includes dockets, calendars, and biographies of judges.
Subjects: Federal Appellate Courts

1348. Court of Appeals. (06) Sixth Circuit
http://www.ca6.uscourts.gov/
Sponsor(s): Court of Appeals. (06) Sixth Circuit
Description: The Sixth Circuit covers Kentucky, Michigan, Ohio, and Tennessee. The official site of the Sixth Circuit of the federal Court of Appeals has a database of published opinions issued since July 1999 and unpublished opinions issued since October 2004. The site also has dockets, forms, fee information, and links to the Sixth Circuit District Courts.
Subjects: Federal Appellate Courts

1349. Court of Appeals. (07) Seventh Circuit
http://www.ca7.uscourts.gov/
Sponsor(s): Court of Appeals. (07) Seventh Circuit
Description: The Seventh Circuit covers Illinois, Indiana, and Wisconsin. This site has searchable access to its opinions and oral arguments; searching is only by case number or person's name. Under Library, the site lists Seventh Circuit cases since 1997 by name, docket number, and decision date, providing the official citation for each. The Seventh Circuit also has an RSS feed for new opinions and makes oral arguments available as audio files and podcasts.
Subjects: Federal Appellate Courts

1350. Court of Appeals. (08) Eighth Circuit
http://www.ca8.uscourts.gov/
Sponsor(s): Court of Appeals. (08) Eighth Circuit
Description: The Eighth Circuit covers Arkansas, Iowa, Minnesota, Missouri, Nebraska, North Dakota, and South Dakota. Online documents include opinions and oral arguments. The site also has the court calendar, rules, and publications. It links to similar basic information for the Bankruptcy Appellate Panel for the Eighth Circuit.
Subjects: Federal Appellate Courts

1351. Court of Appeals. (09) Ninth Circuit
http://www.ca9.uscourts.gov/
Sponsor(s): Court of Appeals. (09) Ninth Circuit
Description: The Ninth Circuit covers Alaska, Arizona, California, Hawaii, Idaho, Montana, Nevada, Oregon, Washington, Guam, and the Northern Mariana Islands. The Ninth Circuit Court of Appeals Web site has the text of its opinions back to 1995. Opinions can be browsed by date or case number. The site has added audio files of oral arguments before the Ninth Circuit; they are available online the day after the oral argument is made. Other sections of the site include the court calendar, rules, phone directory, and status of pending cases.
Subjects: Federal Appellate Courts
Publications: *Ninth Circuit Capital Punishment Handbook*

1352. Court of Appeals. (10) Tenth Circuit
http://www.ck10.uscourts.gov/
Alternate URL(s): http://www.kscourts.org/ca10/
Sponsor(s): Court of Appeals. (10) Tenth Circuit
Description: The Tenth Circuit covers Colorado, Kansas, New Mexico, Oklahoma, Utah, and Wyoming. This official site features information on the circuit, links to current opinions, and a link to the Bankruptcy Appellate Panel of the Tenth Circuit. Opinions can be browsed back to 1995, but users must know the docket number. Enhanced access to opinions is available at the alternate URL above.
Subjects: Federal Appellate Courts

1353. Court of Appeals. (11) Eleventh Circuit
http://www.ca11.uscourts.gov/
Sponsor(s): Court of Appeals. (11) Eleventh Circuit
Description: The Eleventh Circuit covers Alabama, Florida, and Georgia. On the Web site, published opinions are available from 1995 to the present. Unpublished opinions are online from May 2005 to present. The site also includes a court directory, brief biographies of the justices, court rules, and links to district and bankruptcy court sites within the Eleventh District.
Subjects: Federal Appellate Courts

1354. Court of Appeals. District of Columbia Circuit
http://www.cadc.uscourts.gov/
Alternate URL(s): http://www.ll.georgetown.edu/federal/judicial/cadc.cfm
Description: The D.C. Circuit Court of Appeals hears appeals from the U.S. District Court for the District of Columbia, and also for many federal administrative agencies. The court's Web site carries its opinions going back to September 1997. Georgetown University's Law Library site, the alternate URL provided here, carries the opinions going back to March 1995.

The court's site includes a section with historical information from its special independent counsel division, whose authority to appoint new independent counsels expired in 1999.

Due to the jurisdiction of the court, researchers will find the site useful for documents in high profile cases involving the federal government.
Subjects: Federal Appellate Courts

1355. Court of Appeals. Federal Circuit
http://www.fedcir.gov/
Alternate URL(s): http://www.ll.georgetown.edu/federal/judicial/cafed.cfm
Description: The U.S. Court of Appeals for the Federal Circuit has nationwide jurisdiction to hear appeals in specialized claims cases, including patent cases. The

Federal Circuit Court's Web site carries its opinions online for two years. For earlier opinions, the Federal Circuit site points to the Web site of Georgetown University's Law Library; there, the opinions are available back to August 1995.
Subjects: Federal Appellate Courts

1356. Executive Office for United States Attorneys
http://www.usdoj.gov/usao/eousa/
Sponsor(s): Justice Department — United States Attorneys
Description: This office serves as a liaison between the Department of Justice and the U.S. attorneys located throughout the United States. The Web site features a directory of the U.S. attorneys' offices with links to the office Web sites. The FOIA Electronic Reading Room includes the *United States Attorneys' Annual Statistical Report*.
Subjects: Litigation
Publications: *United States Attorneys' Annual Statistical Report*, J 31.10:
United States Attorneys' Bulletin, J 31.12:

1357. Federal Judicial Center
http://www.fjc.gov/
Sponsor(s): Federal Judicial Center (FJC)
Description: The Federal Judicial Center conducts research on federal court operations and history, and it manages training programs for federal judges and court employees. The FJC publishes research, analysis, and training products on such topics as alternative dispute resolution, court management, federal judges, and probation and pretrial services. Many of these publications are available online. Educational materials online include an introductory overview called "Inside the Federal Courts." The Federal Judicial History section includes biographies of federal judges since 1789 and a history of landmark legislation affecting the courts.
Subjects: Federal Courts
Publications: *Annual Report, Federal Judicial Center*, JU 13.1:
Benchbook for U.S. District Court Judges, JU 13.2:B
Catalog of Publications, Federal Judicial Center, JU 13.11/2:
Federal Courts and What They Do, Ju 13.2:
Federal Securities Law, JU 13.2:SE 2/
Reference Manual on Scientific Evidence, JU 13.8:SCI 2

1358. FindLaw: Cases and Codes: U.S. Circuit Courts
http://www.findlaw.com/casecode/courts/
Sponsor(s): Findlaw, Inc.
Description: FindLaw — a free, nongovernment Web site — offers this section with cases from all the circuit courts. Most cover the past ten years and are searchable by docket number, party name, or words in the text. The cases can also be browsed by date. FindLaw also provides a court directory for each circuit.
   Like their Supreme Court database, FindLaw's Circuit Court site is an easy-to-use tool for searching for recent opinions. In addition, the site functions as a meta-site for the other Web sites about the courts and that also provide cases online.
Subjects: Federal Courts; Finding Aids

1359. FindLaw: Supreme Court Opinions
http://www.findlaw.com/casecode/supreme.html
Sponsor(s): Findlaw, Inc.
Description: FindLaw, a major finding aid for Internet law sources, features Supreme Court opinions in HTML format back to 1893, volume 150 of the *U.S. Reports*.

Browse by year and volume number. The opinions have hypertext links from references to other cases available through FindLaw.

This is an excellent, free source for Supreme Court opinions on the Web.

Publications: *U.S. Reports*
Subjects: Supreme Court

1360. FLITE Supreme Court Decisions
http://www.fedworld.gov/supcourt/
Alternate URL(s): http://www.access.gpo.gov/su_docs/supcrt/
Sponsor(s): Commerce Department — Technology Administration (TA) — National Technical Information Service (NTIS); Government Printing Office (GPO) — Superintendent of Documents
Description: The Federal Legal Information Through Electronics (FLITE) database of Supreme Court opinions provides public access to a formerly limited access database. The file consists of Supreme Court opinions dating from 1937 through 1975, from volumes 300 through 422 of *U.S. Reports*. This database is available through NTIS Fedworld and, at the alternate URL, GPO Access.

FindLaw, a nongovernment site described in this chapter, provides even greater access to Supreme Court cases.
Subjects: Supreme Court

1361. History of the Federal Judiciary
http://www.fjc.gov/history/home.nsf
Sponsor(s): Federal Judicial Center (FJC)
Description: The History of the Federal Judiciary Web site presents basic reference information about the history of the federal courts and the judges who have served on the federal courts since 1789. Major sections on this site include: Judges of the United States Courts, to search for judges by name or by alphabetical listing; Courts of the Federal Judiciary, which contains a legislative history for every court in the system; and Landmark Judicial Legislation, presenting the text of 21 statutes related to the organization and jurisdiction of the federal judiciary.
Subjects: Federal Courts — History; Judges

1362. Legal Services Corporation
http://www.lsc.gov/
Sponsor(s): Legal Services Corporation (LSC)
Description: Legal Services Corporation is a private, nonprofit corporation established by Congress to provide civil legal assistance to low-income people. Its Web site has information about LSC's activities and a clickable map of the United States for finding LSC programs by state. The Government Relations section has LSC's budget documents, reports to Congress, and congressional testimony.
Subjects: Legal Assistance
Publications: *Equal Justice Magazine*, Y 3.L 52:15/
Semiannual Report to the Congress, Legal Services Corporation, Y 3.L 52:1/

1363. LII Supreme Court Collection
http://supct.law.cornell.edu/supct/
Sponsor(s): Legal Information Institute (LII)
Description: The Legal Information Institute at Cornell University has the full text of Supreme Court decisions back to 1990. LII also offers a Historic Collection with approximately 300 selected historic decisions dating back to 1793. All decisions can be searched by keyword or browsed by topic, decision author, or party name. LII also offers an e-mail current awareness service, called LII-bulletin,

which includes syllabi of U.S. Supreme Court decisions in bulletin format within hours after their release.

The LII Supreme Court Collection is not the most comprehensive collection online, but it provides one of the best interfaces and does a good job in documenting the content and context of its collection.

Subjects: Supreme Court

1364. Office of Legal Policy

http://www.justice.gov/olp/

Sponsor(s): Justice Department — Office of Legal Policy

Description: The Office of Legal Policy develops and promotes the legal policy initiatives of the president and the Justice Department. The office also assists with filling certain judicial vacancies. A key section of the Web site is Judicial Nominations; it includes current information and statistics on judicial vacancies and the nominations made to fill them.

Subjects: Judges; Laws — Policy

Publications: *Attorney General's Report on Criminal History Background Checks*

1365. Office of Special Counsel

http://www.usdoj.gov/usao/iln/osc/

Sponsor(s): Justice Department — Deputy Attorney General

Description: This is the Web site for the office of Special Counsel Patrick J. Fitzgerald, appointed to handle the Justice Department's investigation into the alleged unauthorized disclosure of a CIA employee Valerie Plame's identity. The Web site retains documents about the grand jury investigation, which concluded in 2005. Updated information on the legal proceedings is available by following the link "In Re: Special Counsel Investigation."

Subjects: Litigation

1366. PACER Service Center

http://pacer.psc.uscourts.gov/

Sponsor(s): Administrative Office of the U.S. Courts

Description: "Public Access to Court Electronic Records (PACER) is an electronic public access service that allows users to obtain case and docket information from Federal Appellate, District, and Bankruptcy courts, and from the U.S. Party/Case Index" (from the Web site). The service is fee-based and is financed through the collection of these user fees. Registration is required. The type of information available through case dockets on PACER includes listing of all parties and participants in the case, a chronology of case events, appellate court opinions, and judgments or case status. The main sections include PACER Overview, Register for PACER, U.S. Party/Case Index, PACER Documents, and PACER Announcements. U.S. Party/Case Index is a national index for U.S. district, bankruptcy, and appellate courts.

Subjects: Federal Courts; Databases

1367. State Justice Institute

http://www.statejustice.org/

Sponsor(s): State Justice Institute

Description: The State Justice Institute (SJI) is a federally funded organization established by Congress to award grants to improve the state court system. The Web site has information on available grants. The SJI Grant Map links to information on SJI-funded projects in each state.

Subjects: Court Administration — Grants

1368. Supreme Court Nomination Hearings

http://www.gpoaccess.gov/congress/senate/judiciary/
scourt.html

Sponsor(s): Government Printing Office (GPO)

Description: The Senate Judiciary Committee's Supreme Court nomination hearings are online from 1971 forward. They begin with "Hearings on the Nominations of William H. Rehnquist, of Arizona, and Lewis F. Powell, Jr., of Virginia, to be Associate Justices of the Supreme Court of the United States." The hearings are available in PDF format and can be downloaded in a compressed format.

Subjects: Supreme Court

1369. Supreme Court of the United States

http://www.supremecourtus.gov/

Sponsor(s): Supreme Court of the United States

Description: The Supreme Court's official Web site has the full text of its opinions from the present term and back to 1991. Opinions can be browsed by term and are in reverse date order. The Opinions section of the site includes an excellent explanation of the differences between various print and electronic versions in the section Information About Opinions, reminding researchers that "only the bound volumes of the *United States Reports* contain the final, official text of the opinions of the Supreme Court." The Opinions section also carries PDF versions of the bound volumes of *United States Reports*. These include all of the opinions, orders, and other materials issued each term; they are online for the 1991 term forward. Other helpful material in the Opinions section includes a directory of the many print and electronic versions of Supreme Court opinions available from other sources, and a Case Citation Finder with the official citation for published opinions from 1790 forward.

Other sections of the site include About the Supreme Court, Docket, Oral Arguments, Bar Admissions, Court Rules, Case Handling Guides, Orders and Journal, Visiting the Court, and Public Information. The Public Information section includes press releases, media advisories, and the justices' speeches. The section About The Court has PDF copies of fact sheets on the court's operations and history, including a list of justices from 1789 to the present and biographies of the current members.

The official Supreme Court site does not have the best search interface to its opinions, but it is useful for current documents and news from the court. The site is also valuable for information about the history of the court and the documents it generates.

Subjects: Supreme Court

Publications: *Rules of the Supreme Court of the United States*, JU 6.9:
Slip Opinion, JU 6.8/B:
United States Reports, JU 6.8:

1370. U.S. Court of Appeals for the Armed Forces

http://www.armfor.uscourts.gov/

Sponsor(s): Court of Appeals for the Armed Forces

Description: The United States Court of Appeals for the Armed Forces has appellate jurisdiction over members of the armed forces on active duty and others subject to the Uniform Code of Military Justice. This site provides information about the court and access to online opinions. Opinions are available back to 1997; access is by date. The site also has information on court history, jurisdiction, judges, rules, and scheduled hearings.

Subjects: Military Justice

Publications: *Annual Report of the U.S. Court of Appeals for the Armed Forces*, D 1.19:

1371. U.S. Court of Appeals for Veterans Claims
http://www.vetapp.gov/
Sponsor(s): Court of Appeals for Veterans Claims
Description: The court reviews final decisions of the Board of Veterans' Appeals, largely cases concerning entitlement to benefits. The court's Web site has information on how to appeal, court rules, forms, and fees. Court decisions can be searched online or downloaded.
Subjects: Veterans

1372. U.S. Courts: The Federal Judiciary
http://www.uscourts.gov/
Sponsor(s): Administrative Office of the U.S. Courts
Description: The Administrative Office of the U.S. Courts maintains this site, which features sections describing the U.S. Supreme Court, courts of appeals, district courts, and bankruptcy courts. These sections explain the operations of the court, provide caseload statistics and other material, and link to the online site for each court. An Educational Outreach section of the site has lesson plans and classroom resources. The Electronic Access section covers court information systems. For the legal professional, the Federal Rulemaking section covers federal rules of practice, procedure, and evidence. The Judicial Conference section explains the role of the Judicial Conference of the United States, which makes policy regarding court administration, and posts its proceedings. Publications, statistical reports, and court fee schedules are in the Library section. The Newsroom includes press releases and "A Journalist's Guide to the Federal Courts." Finally, a Court Links page has links to federal court Web sites.

The Federal Court System in the U.S., in the site's Publications section, is provided in English, French, Italian, Russian, Serbian, Spanish, and Turkish. It provides an explanation of the U.S. system for foreign audiences.

The U.S. Courts site provides clear explanations of the workings of the federal judiciary. The site itself is an excellent reference tool, addressing popular topics in a succinct manner. The court links pages are conveniently arranged for quickly locating the proper court or for bookmarking for future reference.
Publications: *A Journalist's Guide to the Federal Courts*
Federal Court Management Statistics, JU 10.14:
Federal Probation Journal, JU 10.8:
Judicial Business of the United States Courts, JU 10.1/4:
The Federal Court System in the U.S.
The Third Branch, Bulletin of the Federal Courts, JU 10.3/2:
Understanding the Federal Courts, JU 10.2:
Wiretap Report, JU 10.19:

1373. United States Bankruptcy Courts
http://www.uscourts.gov/bankruptcycourts.html
Sponsor(s): Administrative Office of the U.S. Courts
Description: Federal courts have exclusive jurisdiction over bankruptcy cases. This Web site has information on federal bankruptcy courts and copies of official bankruptcy forms. The Bankruptcy Resources section includes information on credit counseling, bankruptcy statistics, and the Bankruptcy Abuse Prevention and Consumer Protection Act of 2005 (Public Law 109-8).
Subjects: Bankruptcy Court
Publications: *Bankruptcy Basics*, JU 10.2:B 22/3/

1374. United States Court of Federal Claims

http://www.uscfc.uscourts.gov/

Sponsor(s): Court of Federal Claims

Description: The Court of Federal Claims is authorized to hear primarily money claims founded upon the Constitution, federal statutes, executive regulations, or contracts, with the United States. As described on the site, many of the cases before the court concern complex tax refund disputes, government contracts, natural resource issues, civilian and military pay, and Indian tribe and Nation claims. Court decisions are available from July 1997 to the present. The site also has information on rules, forms, fees, and the court's Office of Special Masters which handles claims under the National Vaccine Injury Compensation Program.

Subjects: Federal Courts

1375. United States Court of International Trade

http://www.cit.uscourts.gov/

Sponsor(s): Court of International Trade

Description: The United States Court of International Trade handles litigation rising out of international trade disputes. The court's Web site has sections for the weekly court calendar, court staff directory, rules and forms, and biographies of the judges. Slip opinions are online for 1999 forward.

Subjects: Federal Courts; International Trade — Laws

1376. United States Sentencing Commission

http://www.ussc.gov/

Sponsor(s): Sentencing Commission

Description: The United States Sentencing Commission was created by the Sentencing Reform Act of 1984 to reduce disparities in federal sentences. The commission is an independent agency in the judicial branch. Its Web site carries the *Federal Sentencing Guidelines Manual* and its amendments, and provides federal sentencing statistics by state, district, and circuit. The commission also has information on its training materials for teaching sentencing guidelines applications to judges, attorneys, and others. The site also features a section about the 2005 federal sentencing guidelines decision of the Supreme Court, referred to as "Booker/Fanfan."

Subjects: Sentencing

Publications: *Annual Report*, Y 3.SE 5:1

Guide Lines: News from the U.S. Sentencing Commission, Y 3.SE 5:17/

Guidelines Manual, Y 3.SE 5:8 G 94/

Sourcebook of Federal Sentencing Statistics, Y 3.SE 5:1/

1377. United States Tax Court

http://www.ustaxcourt.gov/

Sponsor(s): Tax Court

Description: The United States Tax Court, a federal court established by Congress under Article I of the Constitution, provides a judicial forum for affected persons to dispute "tax deficiencies" as determined by the Commissioner of Internal Revenue, prior to payment of the disputed amounts. The site has sections for Today's Opinions, Opinions Search, Forms, Rules, Press Releases, and general information about contacts, fees and charges, and frequently asked questions. The Opinions Search section offers a search of past opinions by release date, petitioner's name, judge, and opinion type, and sorted by case name or release date. The Taxpayer Information section is a guide to the process for those who represent themselves before the Tax Court.

Subjects: Federal Courts; Taxation — Laws

Publications: *Rules of Practice and Procedure, U.S. Tax Court*, JU 11.8:

1378. United States Trustee Program
http://www.usdoj.gov/ust/
Sponsor(s): Justice Department
Description: The United States Trustee Program oversees the bankruptcy process to ensure legal and procedural compliance. The Trustee Web site has information on its mission and organization, and a directory of its 21 regional offices. The site also has online brochures explaining such topics as the bankruptcy code and consumer bankruptcy. A Bankruptcy Information Sheet is available in eight languages besides English. The site also has information on the Bankruptcy Abuse Prevention and Consumer Protection Act of 2005 (Public Law 109-8) and instructions on reporting suspected bankruptcy fraud.
Subjects: Bankruptcy

Crime and Enforcement

1379. AMBER Alert
http://www.amberalert.gov/
Sponsor(s): Justice Department — Justice Programs Office
Description: AMBER Alerts are local systems for alerting the public when a child has been abducted. This site includes frequently asked questions about the program and the AMBER Wireless Alert Initiative. Resources include AMBER Alert contacts, and the publications section has guides for parents, law enforcement agencies, and media outlets.
Subjects: Kidnapping

1380. ATF Online — Bureau of Alcohol, Tobacco, Firearms and Explosives
http://www.atf.gov/
Sponsor(s): Justice Department — Bureau of Alcohol, Tobacco, Firearms, and Explosives
Description: As part of the Homeland Security Act of 2002, the Bureau of Alcohol, Tobacco, Firearms and Explosives (ATF) was transferred from the Treasury Department to the Justice Department in early 2003. (Certain functions of the ATF remain with Treasury in the newly created Alcohol and Tobacco Tax and Trade Bureau or TTB. See separate entry for the TTB Web site.)

ATF is a law enforcement organization charged with enforcing federal laws and regulations relating to alcohol, tobacco, firearms, explosives and arson. The ATF Web site features news, organizational information, and major sections for Alcohol and Tobacco Diversion, Firearms, Arson and Explosives, and Laboratories. The Regulations section has current notices of proposed rulemaking in the areas of alcohol, tobacco, and firearms/explosives. The site also has ATF hotline numbers, forms, statistics, and links to the field office Web sites.
Subjects: Law Enforcement; Wanted People
Publications: *ATF Annual Report*, T 70.1:
ATF Explosives Industry Newsletter, J 38.15:
ATF Industry Circulars, T 70.10:
Federal Firearms Licensee Newsletter, T 70.18:
Federal Firearms Regulations Reference Guide, T 70.8:
Firearms Curios or Relics List, T 70.15:
Firearms State Laws and Published Ordinances, T 70.14:

1381. Attorney General

http://www.usdoj.gov/ag/

Sponsor(s): Justice Department — Attorney General

Description: The United States attorney general is head of the Justice Department and chief law enforcement officer of the federal government. This site describes the office and has some biographical information on the current attorney general. It also provides links to speeches, testimony, annual reports, and FOIA.

Subjects: Law Enforcement

Publications: *Annual Report of the Attorney General of the United States*, J 1.1: *Assessment of U.S. Government Activities to Combat Trafficking in Persons*, J 1.2:

1382. Border Patrol

http://www.cbp.gov/xp/cgov/border_security/border_patrol/

Sponsor(s): Homeland Security Department — Customs and Border Protection Bureau

Description: On its Web site, the U.S. Border Patrol describes its priority mission as "preventing terrorists and terrorists weapons, including weapons of mass destruction, from entering the United States." The site carries the *National Border Control Strategy* report and identifies the U.S. Border Patrol geographic sectors. The site also has a section on Border Patrol history.

Subjects: Homeland Security; International Borders

1383. Bureau for International Narcotics and Law Enforcement Affairs

http://www.state.gov/p/inl/

Sponsor(s): State Department — International Narcotics and Law Enforcement Affairs Bureau

Description: The Bureau for International Narcotics and Law Enforcement Affairs assists foreign countries in implementing anti-narcotics strategies. It works with other countries to counter transnational crime, such as alien smuggling. The office also conducts programs fighting official corruption and recruiting civilian police for international peacekeeping missions. Under Narcotics Certification Process, the Web site has the annual presidential announcement listing the major illicit drug producing and drug-transit countries. The annual *International Narcotics Control Strategy Report* is under Releases, along with fact sheets and press releases.

Subjects: International Crimes; International Drug Trade

Publications: *International Narcotics Control Strategy Report*, S 1.146:

1384. Bureau of Justice Assistance

http://www.ojp.usdoj.gov/BJA/

Sponsor(s): Justice Department — Justice Programs Office

Description: The Bureau of Justice Assistance (BJA) supports local criminal justice agencies throughout the United States, offering grants, training, and technical assistance. The BJA Web site includes information on a number of grant programs including the Bulletproof Vest Partnership, the Local Law Enforcement Block Grant Program and the Byrne Formula Grant Program. All major BJA assistance is described in the Programs section. In the Justice Issues section, major areas of BJA focus are described and there are links to related publications, Web sites, and BJA training.

Subjects: Law Enforcement — Grants

Publications: *Local Law Enforcement Block Grants Program*, J 26.33:

1385. Bureau of Justice Statistics
http://www.ojp.usdoj.gov/bjs/
Sponsor(s): Justice Department — Bureau of Justice Statistics (BJS)
Description: The Justice Department's Bureau of Justice Statistics collects and reports data on crime, offenders, victims, and the criminal justice system. Its Web site features quick access to frequently requested statistics on these topics. The site's Press Releases section highlights BJS publications as they are released, and links to the full text of the reports as well as associated spreadsheet files. The Publications section lists reports in alphabetical order and links to the full electronic version when one is available.

BJS also supports grants programs for state, local, and tribal governments to assist with criminal justice statistics programs at those levels. The programs are described under the heading Justice Records Improvement Program.

The BJS site provides well-organized access to its own reports but also links to related statistics from other sites, such as the United Nations or other Justice bureaus including the FBI.

Subjects: Criminal Justice — Statistics; Prisons — Statistics
Publications: *Background Checks for Firearm Transfers*, J 29.11:F
Bureau of Justice Statistics Fiscal Year: At A Glance, J 29.1/2:
Bureau of Justice Statistics Publications Catalog, J 29.14/2:
Capital Punishment, J 29.11/3:
Census of State and Federal Corrections Facilities, J 29.16:
Compendium of Federal Justice Statistics, J 29.20:
Correctional Populations in the United States, J 29.17:
Criminal Victimization (A National Crime Victimization Survey Report), J 29.11/10:
Federal Criminal Case Processing, with Reconciled Data, J 29.2:C 26
Federal Law Enforcement Officers, J 29.11:L
Felony Defendants in Large Urban Counties, J 29.2:F
Felony Sentences in State Courts, J 29.11/11:
Felony Sentences in the United States, J 29.11/11-2:
Guide to the BJS Website, J 29.8:W 39/
HIV in Prisons and Jails, J 29.11:P 93/
Homicide Trends in the United States, J 29.27/2:
Indicators of School Crime and Safety, ED 1.347:
Jails in Indian Country, J 29.11/5-3:
Justice Expenditure and Employment Extracts (annual), J 29.11/2-2:
Justice Expenditure and Employment in the U.S. (annual), J 29.11/2-3:
Law Enforcement Management and Administrative Statistics, J 29.2:L 41/
Local Police Departments, J 29.2:P 75/
National Corrections Reporting Program, J 29.11/13-2:
Presale Handgun Checks, J 29.11:H 19/
Prison and Jail Inmates at Midyear, J 29.11/5-2:
Prisoners, J 29.11/7:
Prosecutors in State Courts, J 29.11/15:
Sheriffs' Offices, J 29.2:SH 5/
Sourcebook of Criminal Justice Statistics, J 29.9/6:
State Court Prosecutors in Large Districts (biennial), J 29.11/16:
State Court Sentencing of Convicted Felons, J 29.11/11-3:
Survey of State Criminal History Information Systems, J 29.9/8:H 62/
Survey of State Procedures Related to Firearm Sales, J 29.2:F

1386. Community Capacity Development Office
http://www.ojp.usdoj.gov/ccdo/
Sponsor(s): Justice Department — Justice Programs Office
Description: The Community Capacity Development Office (CCDO) sponsors programs to help communities reduce crime and improve the local quality of life. The Web site describes their major programs, such as the Weed and Seed Initiative. It also provides information on funding, training, and technical assistance for communities.
Subjects: Crime Prevention

1387. Community Relations Service
http://www.usdoj.gov/crs/
Sponsor(s): Justice Department — Community Relations Service
Description: The Community Relations Service (CRS) was established by the Civil Rights Act of 1964 to help communities resolve serious racial or ethnic conflicts. Major sections of the Web site include Commonly Asked Questions, Publications and Useful Handbooks, and the Map of CRS Regional and Field Offices. Publications cover such topics as hate crime, police use of force, and conflict resolution.
Subjects: Dispute Resolution; Mediation
Publications: *Annual Report of the Community Relations Service,* J 23.1:

1388. Computer Crime & Intellectual Property Section
http://www.cybercrime.gov/
Sponsor(s): Justice Department — Criminal Division
Description: Also known as Cybercrime.gov, the Web site for the Justice Department's Computer Crime and Intellectual Property Section (CCIPS) has policy, cases, guidance, laws, and documents. CCIPS provides information on reporting Internet-related crime, legal issues in electronic commerce, international aspects of computer crime, and related topics. The site also has "cyberethics" information for teachers, parents, and kids.
Subjects: Computer Security; Intellectual Property

1389. Coordinating Council on Juvenile Justice and Delinquency Prevention
http://www.juvenilecouncil.gov/
Sponsor(s): Coordinating Council on Juvenile Justice and Delinquency Prevention
Description: The Coordinating Council on Juvenile Justice and Delinquency Prevention is an independent body within the executive branch. It coordinates federal programs concerning juvenile delinquency prevention, programs and activities that detain or care for unaccompanied juveniles, and programs relating to missing and exploited children. The Web site has information on the council, its members, and its meetings.
Subjects: Child Welfare; Juvenile Delinquency; Juvenile Justice

1390. COPS Office: Grants and Resources for Community Policing
http://www.cops.usdoj.gov/
Sponsor(s): Justice Department — Community Oriented Policing Services
Description: The COPS Office makes grants to state and local law enforcement agencies to advance community policing. The Web site has information on the grants and training available. It also covers community policing topics such as gangs and school safety. Under Congressional Resources, the site has COPS budget information and summaries of COPS funding awarded in each state.
Subjects: Police-Community Relations — Grants

1391. Counter-Terrorism Training and Resources for Law Enforcement
http://www.counterterrorismtraining.gov/
Sponsor(s): Justice Department
Description: This site is a centralized counterterrorism information clearinghouse for law enforcement and local agencies. Linked resources come from both the federal government and private nonprofit and commercial services. Major portal sections link to resources on training and technical assistance, conferences, research, equipment, planning, and victim assistance. A Funding section links to appropriations news and current funding opportunities. The site is sponsored by many federal agencies, including Justice and the Department of Homeland Security.
Subjects: Homeland Security; Law Enforcement

1392. Criminal Division
http://www.usdoj.gov/criminal/
Sponsor(s): Justice Department — Criminal Division
Description: Justice's Criminal Division enforces and prosecutes federal criminal law. Most of the information on the Web site can be reached through the Criminal Division Organizations link. Each organizational unit — such as the Counterterrorism Section, the Fraud Section, and the Organized Crime and Racketeering Section — provides a single-page description and contact information. The site also links to information on topics of special interest, including the Hurricane Katrina Fraud Task Force, the Computer Crime and Intellectual Property, and Victim Notification and Services.
Subjects: Crime; Law Enforcement
Publications: *Report of the Attorney General to the Congress of the United States on the Administration of the Foreign Agents Registration Act*, J 1.30:
Report to Congress on the Activities and Operations of the Public Integrity Section, J 1.1/16:

1393. Cyber Investigations
http://www.fbi.gov/cyberinvest/cyberhome.htm
Sponsor(s): Justice Department — Federal Bureau of Investigation (FBI)
Description: The FBI is concerned with stopping computer network intrusions, online sexual predators, online operations that target U.S. intellectual property, and organized criminal enterprises engaging in Internet fraud. The Cyber Investigations Web site has FBI news and initiatives in these areas. It also carries advice to the public about protection from computer crime, including an alert service on new e-mail-based scams.
Subjects: Computer Security

1394. Drug Enforcement Administration
http://www.usdoj.gov/dea/
Sponsor(s): Justice Department — Drug Enforcement Administration (DEA)
Description: The DEA Web site focuses on information about current illegal drug threats and recent DEA enforcement actions. Topical sections include Drug Information, Law Enforcement (including state fact sheets), Drug Prevention For Young Adults, Drug Policy, and Diversion Control and Prescription Drugs. Under About Us, the Programs and Operations section links to Web pages on specific aspects of DEA work, such as aviation, money laundering, Southwest Border Initiative, and forensic sciences.
Subjects: Drug Control; Law Enforcement
Publications: *Drugs of Abuse*, J 24.2:
Get It Straight: The Facts about Drugs, J 24.2:

Guidelines for the Cleanup of Clandestine Drug Laboratories, J 24.8:
Microgram Bulletin, J 24.31:
Speaking Out Against Drug Legalization, J 24.2:

1395. Federal Bureau of Investigation
http://www.fbi.gov/
Sponsor(s): Justice Department — Federal Bureau of Investigation (FBI)
Description: For an overview of the FBI's work, see this site's What We Investigate section. It links to substantial information on FBI programs in counterterrorism, counterintelligence, public corruption, organized crime, white collar crime, art theft, and other areas. Other sections of the Web site cover crime prevention tips, the FBI's Most Wanted, laboratory services, information technology initiatives, agency history, and directories of FBI field and overseas offices. The site also has an online form for submitting tips about suspected criminal activity.

The Freedom of Information Act section, linked from the bottom of each page, can be accessed directly at ⟨http://foia.fbi.gov⟩. It has an index to the popularly requested FOIA documents in its Washington FOIA reading room, with links to those documents that have been digitized and put online. An Electronic Reading Room section has only online documents, which are organized alphabetically and by topics such as "Gangster Era" and "Famous Persons."

Because information is spread throughout the many sections of this site, first time users may want to consult the site map along with the About Us section.
Subjects: Crime Detection; Law Enforcement; Wanted People
Publications: *Crime in the United States*, J 1.14/7-8:
FBI Laboratory Annual Report, J 1.14/27:
FBI Law Enforcement Bulletin, J 1.14/8:
Financial Institution Fraud and Failure Report, J 1.14/26:
Forensic Science Communications, J 1.14/18-2:
Handbook of Forensic Services, J 1.14/18-3:
Hate Crime Statistics, J 1.14/7-9:
Law Enforcement Officers Killed and Assaulted, J 1.14/7-6:
Uniform Crime Reports, J 1.14/7:

1396. Federal Bureau of Prisons
http://www.bop.gov/
Sponsor(s): Justice Department — Federal Bureau of Prisons
Description: The Bureau of Prisons is responsible for the federal prison system and federal inmates. The BOP Web site has an Inmate Locator database of federal inmates incarcerated from 1982 to present. It also has a Facility Locator and links to Web pages for each of the facilities operated by the Bureau of Prisons. The Inmate Matters section covers topics such as medical care, substance abuse treatment, preparation for release, and the Victim/Witness Notification Program. The site also has information on employment and acquisition opportunities.
Subjects: Prisons
Publications: *State of the Bureau*, J 16.1:
Weekly Population Report, J 16.32:

1397. Federal Law Enforcement Training Center
http://www.fletc.gov/
Sponsor(s): Homeland Security Department — Federal Law Enforcement Training Center (FLETC)
Description: FLETC is the federal government's centralized law enforcement training facility. Its Web site includes the "Catalog of Training Programs," listing programs in such areas as financial fraud investigations, driver training, firearms techniques, and other security and investigative specialties. The site also has information on

FLETC's International Law Enforcement Academies, International Training and Technical Assistance, and Law Enforcement Leadership Institute.

The FLETC site will be of interest primarily to those considering FLETC training.

Subjects: Homeland Security; Law Enforcement

1398. Financial Crimes Enforcement Network (FinCEN)

http://www.fincen.gov/

Sponsor(s): Treasury Department

Description: FinCEN supports law enforcement investigations into domestic and international financial crimes and money laundering. The agency works with the law enforcement (local, national, and international), financial, and regulatory communities on information sharing in the network. The site has regulatory guidance on the Bank Secrecy Act, USA PATRIOT Act, regulations for casinos, and other rules. FinCEN publications, in the Press Room section, include the *SAR Activity Review* of statistical data from the Suspicious Activity Report forms filed by various financial institutions. The *FinCEN Advisory* publications, which often focus on financial transactions with specific countries, are also in the Press Room section.

Much of the information on this site will be of primary interest to regulated financial institutions.

Subjects: Financial Crimes; Money Laundering

Publications: *FinCEN Advisory*, T 22.3/4:

SAR Activity Review

1399. Gang Resistance Education and Training Program

http://www.atf.gov/great/

Sponsor(s): Treasury Department — Bureau of Alcohol, Tobacco, and Firearms (ATF)

Description: The Gang Resistance Education And Training Program (G.R.E.A.T.) is designed to be carried out by local police agencies to educate school-aged children on avoiding gang and crime-related activity. The site includes information on setting up a G.R.E.A.T. program, program guidelines, and other program support information.

This site will be of primary interest to communities seeking to participate in the program.

Subjects: Juvenile Delinquency

1400. Identity Theft

http://www.consumer.gov/idtheft/

Sponsor(s): Federal Trade Commission (FTC)

Description: This site serves as a central point for government information on identity theft, described as when someone appropriates your personal information without your knowledge to commit fraud or other crimes. The FTC provides detailed information for consumers, businesses, law enforcement, and members of the military. The Consumer section is available in Spanish. The Reference Desk section has national and state laws and statistics regarding identity theft.

Subjects: Identity Theft

1401. Immigration and Customs Enforcement

http://www.ice.gov/

Sponsor(s): Homeland Security Department — Immigration and Customs Enforcement (ICE)

Description: Immigration and Customs Enforcement (ICE) has investigation and law enforcement responsibilities within the Department of Homeland Security. ICE is concerned with such areas as illegal shipments, drug trafficking, immigrant smuggling, and air and marine security. Most information about the agency's operations is in the Public Information section under Topics of Interest. Topics include child exploitation, financial and trade investigations, fugitive operations, human smuggling and trafficking, immigration enforcement, intellectual property rights, and worksite enforcement. The Public Information section also includes news releases and numerous fact sheets on ICE programs. The International Students section covers the Student and Exchange Visitor Program (SEVP) and related issues.

Subjects: Customs (Trade); Homeland Security; Immigration Law
Publications: *Inside ICE*, HS 4.215:

1402. Internet Crime Complaint Center
http://www.ic3.gov/
Sponsor(s): Justice Department — Federal Bureau of Investigation (FBI)
Description: The Internet Crime Complaint Center is a partnership between the FBI and the National White Collar Crime Center. The Web site describes current Internet crime schemes and has a form for filing a complaint online. The annual report carries statistics on complaints by state.
Subjects: Fraud

1403. JUSTNET — Justice Technology Information Network
http://www.nlectc.org/
Sponsor(s): Justice Department — National Institute of Justice (NIJ) — National Law Enforcement and Corrections Technology Center (NLECTC)
Description: JUSTNET is the home page for the National Law Enforcement and Corrections Technology Center (NLECTC), which assists state and local law enforcement and corrections personnel with technology, equipment, and information systems. The Web site describes NLECTC programs in technology assistance, equipment testing and evaluation, and training assistance. It also provides a directory of grants for law enforcement from government and nongovernment sources.
Subjects: Law Enforcement — Grants
Publications: *TechBeat*, J 28.37:

1404. MethResources.gov
http://www.methresources.gov/
Sponsor(s): Health and Human Services Department; Justice Department; White House — National Drug Control Policy Office
Description: MethResources.gov is an interagency Web site providing resources and information on battling methamphetamine abuse. The site includes sections on publications, research, conferences, state and local programs, funding, technical assistance, policies, and legislation. Resources are also organized by topic, such as enforcement and treatment, and by audience, such as parents and businesses. Meth in Your State, a clickable map, organizes resources by state.
Subjects: Drug Abuse; Drug Control

1405. National Criminal Justice Reference Service
http://www.ncjrs.org/
Sponsor(s): Justice Department — National Criminal Justice Reference Service (NCJRS)
Description: The National Criminal Justice Reference Service (NCJRS) compiles resource information from a number of federal agencies involved in law enforcement research and policy. It responds to queries from law enforcement and

corrections officials, lawmakers, judges and court personnel, and researchers. The NCJRS site contains a vast number of publications on a wide range of criminal justice and law enforcement topics. It also provides access to the NCJRS Abstracts Database with summaries of more than 180,000 criminal justice publications.

Other topical links on the main page include Corrections, Courts, Crime Prevention, Statistics, Drugs and Crime, International, Juvenile Justice, Law Enforcement, and Victims of Crime. These topic sections include links to the publications, Justice seminars, and related links. The NCJRS site also includes a list of federal grants relating to criminal justice.

The vast number of publications available from the NCJRS site makes it a leading source for criminal justice statistics and reports. Many of the publications are available directly from the authoring agencies, but NCJRS provides the service of centralizing access.

Subjects: Criminal Justice
Publications: *NCJRS Abstracts Database,* J 28.31/2-2:

1406. National Drug Intelligence Center
http://www.usdoj.gov/ndic/
Sponsor(s): Justice Department — National Drug Intelligence Center (NDIC)
Description: The NDIC is the federal government's center for strategic domestic counterdrug intelligence. The Web site provides copies of the annual *National Drug Threat Assessment* and specific *State Drug Threat Assessment* reports. NDIC bulletins and briefs on the site focus on specific drug abuse topics. Some NDIC publications are available in Spanish or French.
Subjects: Drug Control; Intelligence Agencies
Publications: *National Drug Threat Assessment,* J 1.2:D

1407. National Institute of Justice
http://www.ojp.usdoj.gov/nij/
Sponsor(s): Justice Department — National Institute of Justice (NIJ)
Description: NIJ supports research, evaluation, and demonstration programs, development of technology, and both national and international information dissemination in the area of criminal justice. Programs include forensic DNA, crime mapping, and body armor safety. The Web site has information on the institute, its programs, funding opportunities, and publications.
Subjects: Criminal Justice — Research
Publications: *National Institute of Justice Annual Report to Congress,* J 28.1: *National Institute of Justice Journal,* J 28.14/2-2:

1408. National Sex Offender Public Registry
http://www.nsopr.gov/
Sponsor(s): Justice Department
Description: The National Sex Offender Public Registry is a cooperative effort between the state agencies hosting public sexual offender registries and the federal government. It can be searched by name, county, city/town, and ZIP code. The site provides background information that should be consulted before using the database. It covers what, legally, may constitute a sex offense and warns about the differences in registries from state to state. The site also has a lengthy "conditions of use" statement that includes individual states' conditions of use for the information.

The Web site was renamed the Dru Sjodin National Sex Offender Public Registry in October 2006 in memory of Dru Sjodin, a college student who was murdered in North Dakota by a convicted sex offender.
Subjects: Criminals

1409. National Youth Violence Prevention Center

http://www.safeyouth.org/

Sponsor(s): Health and Human Services Department — Centers for Disease Control and Prevention (CDC)

Description: National Youth Violence Prevention Center is a clearinghouse for information about preventing violence committed by and against children and teens. The site is sponsored by the Centers for Disease Control and Prevention in collaboration with a number of other federal agencies. The Order Publications section provides subject access to youth violence-related publications from a variety of federal agencies. The Funding section pulls together information on a number of relevant grants. There are also special sections for parents and guardians, professionals (educators, researchers, and others), teens, and the press. The site provides an extensive directory of resources in Spanish.

Subjects: Juvenile Delinquency

1410. Office for Victims of Crime

http://www.ojp.usdoj.gov/ovc/

Sponsor(s): Justice Department — Justice Programs Office

Description: The Office for Victims of Crime (OVC) was established by the 1984 Victims of Crime Act to oversee grants, training, and other programs that benefit victims of crime. Major sections include Grants and Funding, Help for Victims, Publications, OVC Resource Center, Training and Technical Assistance, Resources for International Victims, and Research and Statistics. The Help for Victims section directs users to resources, especially nongovernmental organizations and their Web sites, that can assist with such areas as child abuse, campus crime, elder abuse, sexual abuse, workplace violence, and terrorism and mass violence. It also features an online directory of crime victim services.

Much of the funding and technical assistance information on the OVC Web site is for professionals and organizations managing victims assistance programs. The Help for Victims section can be of direct interest to individuals.

Subjects: Victims of Crime

Publications: *Directory of International Crime Victim Compensation Programs,* J 34.10:

OVC Fact Sheets, J 34.4:

OVC National Directory of Victim Assistance Funding Opportunities, J 34.10/2:

OVC's Legal Series Bulletins, J 34.3/3:

1411. Office of Child Support Enforcement

http://www.acf.dhhs.gov/programs/cse/

Sponsor(s): Health and Human Services Department — Administration for Children and Families (ACF) — Child Support Enforcement Office

Description: Child support enforcement is conducted primarily at the state level. The Federal Office of Child Support Enforcement (OCSE) supports state and local efforts to locate participants in child support cases, collect child support payments, and enforce of child support orders. The Web site has information on the locator systems it supports, available grants, and publications. It also links to child support offices at the state level. Some materials, such as a handbook for the party seeking child support, are available in Spanish as well as English.

Subjects: Child Support

Publications: *Child Support Enforcement Handbook,* T 22.44/2:

Child Support Report, HE 24.9:

1412. Office of Justice Programs
http://www.ojp.usdoj.gov/
Sponsor(s): Justice Department — Justice Programs Office
Description: The Office of Justice Programs (OJP) provides federal assistance to the nation's justice system. OJP and its program bureaus are responsible for collecting statistical data and conducting analyses, identifying emerging criminal justice issues, providing technical assistance and training, evaluating program results, and disseminating information to state and local governments. Major sections of the Web site include Funding Opportunities, Research, Statistics, and Publications. The Research section highlights upcoming conferences and current research initiatives.
Subjects: Criminal Justice — Research; Law Enforcement — Grants
Publications: *Office of Justice Programs Resource Guide*, J 1.8/2:

1413. Office of Juvenile Justice and Delinquency Prevention (OJJDP)
http://ojjdp.ncjrs.org/
Sponsor(s): Justice Department — Justice Programs Office
Description: The OJDPP supports states and communities in their work to prevent and control juvenile crime. Featured sections of the site include Topics, Funding, Programs, Publications, State Contacts, and Statistics. The Topics section organizes OJJDP publications, programs, funding opportunities, and events by subject. Topics include child protection, courts, delinquency prevention, schools, and victims. The Publications catalog links to full text publications on the NCJRS site.
Subjects: Juvenile Delinquency; Juvenile Justice
Publications: *Juvenile Justice Journal*, J 32.19:
Juvenile Offenders and Victims, J 32.23:J 98/
OJJDP Annual Report, J 32.1:
OJJDP Bulletin, J 32.21/2-2:
OJJDP Fact Sheets, J 32.21:
OJJDP News @ a Glance, J 32.25:

1414. Office of National Drug Control Policy
http://www.whitehousedrugpolicy.gov/
Sponsor(s): White House — National Drug Control Policy Office
Description: This White House office produces the federal drug control strategy with the goal of reducing illicit drug abuse and distribution and its consequences. The site includes the sections About ONDCP, Drug Facts, Publications, Policy, Funding, Prevention, Treatment, Enforcement, State and Local, International, and Science and Technology. The Publications page includes reports and fact sheets from both the ONDCP and other federal agencies. The site also features a blog called "Pushing Back" and a podcast.
Subjects: Drug Policy
Publications: *National Drug Control Policy*, PREX 26.1/2:

1415. Office of Terrorism and Financial Intelligence
http://www.ustreas.gov/offices/eotffc/
Sponsor(s): Treasury Department
Description: The Office of Terrorism and Financial Intelligence (TFI) develops policies, regulations, and strategies in support of statutes such as the National Money Laundering Act, the Bank Secrecy Act, and the USA PATRIOT Act. Topics covered by the Web site include freezing terrorist assets and protecting charities from misuse by terrorist organizations. The site has lists and information on sanctioned countries and "Specially Designated Nationals and Blocked Persons."
Subjects: Financial Crimes; Terrorism
Publications: *National Money Laundering Strategy for . . .*, T 1.67/2:

1416. Office of the Associate Attorney General
http://www.usdoj.gov/aag/
Sponsor(s): Justice Department
Description: This page offers a brief description of the office of the associate attorney general along with FOIA, speeches, and testimony by the associate attorney general.
Subjects: Law Enforcement Policy

1417. Office of the Deputy Attorney General
http://www.usdoj.gov/dag/
Sponsor(s): Justice Department — Deputy Attorney General
Description: This page features the deputy attorney general's speeches, testimony, and publications such as the *Health Care Fraud and Abuse Control Program* and a *Survey of the Federal Death Penalty System*. The site also links to information on President Bush's Corporate Fraud Task Force, which is led by the deputy attorney general.
Subjects: Law Enforcement Policy
Publications: *Health Care Fraud and Abuse Control Program Annual Report*, J 1.1/13:
The Federal Death Penalty System: A Statistical Survey, J 1.2:

1418. Office of the Federal Detention Trustee
http://www.justice.gov/ofdt/
Sponsor(s): Justice Department — Office of the Federal Detention Trustee
Description: Office of the Federal Detention Trustee centrally manages the detention of federal prisoners and aliens awaiting trial or removal from the United States. The office assesses detention space needs and reviews the health, safety, and other conditions of detention space against a set of standards. Along with background information, the Web site includes statistics on the number of people held in federal detention.
Subjects: Prisoners

1419. Office on Violence Against Women
http://www.usdoj.gov/ovw/
Sponsor(s): Justice Department
Description: The Office on Violence Against Women was established as a source for assistance to women victims of violence. The Web site links to resources and publications on help for victims (including hotline numbers), domestic violence, sexual assault, and stalking. The site also has information on grant programs, federal laws, and the National Advisory Committee on Violence Against Women.
Subjects: Domestic Violence; Victims of Crime

1420. Office to Monitor and Combat Trafficking in Persons
http://www.state.gov/g/tip/
Sponsor(s): State Department
Description: The Office to Monitor and Combat Trafficking in Persons is concerned with preventing abusive smuggling of the men, women, and children across international borders. The Web site provides background information on the issue, and has sections about government-funded anti-trafficking programs and U.S. laws on trafficking in persons.
Subjects: International Crimes
Publications: *Trafficking in Persons Report*, S 1.152:

1421. President's DNA Initiative
http://www.dna.gov/
Sponsor(s): Justice Department
Description: The goal of the President's DNA Initiative is to increase the effective use of DNA evidence technology in the criminal justice system through the support of grants, training, and guidance. The Web site has sections on grant funding, training, services for laboratories, publications, and legal information on the use of DNA technology. It also features an overview of forensic DNA and current research. Under Browse by Audience, the site has sections tailored to constituency groups such as forensic scientists, court officers, victim advocates, crime lab managers, and policymakers.
Subjects: Crime Detection; Forensics — Grants

1422. Project Safe Childhood
http://www.projectsafechildhood.gov/
Sponsor(s): Justice Department
Description: Project Safe Childhood is designed to strengthen the investigation and prosecution of sexual exploitation crimes committed against children through the Internet. The Web site provides detailed information on the program, and news and reports related to the online victimization of youth.
Subjects: Children

1423. Project Safe Neighborhoods
http://www.psn.gov/
Sponsor(s): Justice Department
Description: Project Safe Neighborhoods is a national, state, and local effort to reduce gun violence. Federal support comes in the form of funding, grants, law enforcement training, and technology. This Web site provides extensive background information on the project and links to related publications and Web sites.
Subjects: Guns; Crime Prevention

1424. Sourcebook of Criminal Justice Statistics
http://www.albany.edu/sourcebook/
Sponsor(s): Justice Department — Bureau of Justice Statistics (BJS)
Description: The *Sourcebook of Criminal Justice Statistics* is a key Justice Department reference publication presenting over 600 tables of data from over 100 sources. This university site has made the *Sourcebook* available online. While the print counterpart is issued annually, this Web site is more frequently updated to include new data that will appear in the next print edition. Data tables are in PDF and spreadsheet formats. The site also has an archive of past *Sourcebook* editions going back to 1994.

This is an important reference source for criminal justice statistics and can include more recent data than the printed source.
Subjects: Criminal Justice — Statistics
Publications: *Sourcebook of Criminal Justice Statistics*, J 29.9/6:

1425. U.S. Marshals Service
http://www.usdoj.gov/marshals/
Sponsor(s): Justice Department — Marshals Service
Description: The U.S. Marshals Service, in existence since 1789, today has a range of duties including court security, fugitive investigations, and the sale of properties seized and forfeited by federal law enforcement agencies. The Web site emphasizes news of current fugitives and recent captures. Other sections of the site cover the U.S. Marshals duties, the long and eventful history of the service, fugitive

investigations (including the "15 Most Wanted"), the Asset Forfeiture Program (including current asset sales), prisoner transportation and custody issues, court and witness security, and service of process. The site also has career information and a detailed directory of the local district offices.
Subjects: Law Enforcement; Wanted People

1426. U.S. National Central Bureau of Interpol
http://www.usdoj.gov/usncb/
Sponsor(s): Justice Department
Description: The U.S. National Central Bureau of Interpol acts as the U.S. representative to the International Criminal Police Organization (INTERPOL) on behalf of the U.S. attorney general. Among its responsibilities, the bureau distributes INTERPOL notices on fugitives, lost persons, stolen art and cultural objects, organized crime groups, and other matters. The Web site has information on the bureau's mission, organization, and programs.
Subjects: International Crimes

1427. U.S. Postal Inspection Service
http://www.usps.com/postalinspectors/
Sponsor(s): Postal Service (USPS) — Postal Inspection Service
Description: The Postal Inspection Service is a federal law enforcement agency with the security and enforcement responsibilities for the U.S. mail and Postal Service workers. Major sections of the Web site concern mail fraud, mail theft, and prohibited mail. The site also has a list of the Postal Inspection Service's most wanted criminals, with links to their wanted posters.
Subjects: Postal Service; Wanted People

1428. United States Park Police
http://www.nps.gov/uspp/
Sponsor(s): Interior Department — National Park Service (NPS)
Description: This site describes the history, role, and activities of the United States Park Police, law enforcement officers with jurisdiction in National Park Service areas and certain government properties. The site includes United States Park Police Most Wanted List and a phone directory for their offices in New York, San Francisco, and Washington, DC.
Subjects: National Parks and Reserves; Police

1429. United States Parole Commission
http://www.usdoj.gov/uspc/
Sponsor(s): Justice Department — Parole Commission
Description: The United States Parole Commission makes parole determinations in certain federal offender cases, District of Columbia Code violation cases, Uniform Code of Military Justice offender cases, and for certain state probationers and parolees who have been placed in the federal witness protection program. The site describes the commission and its specific jurisdiction. There are links to such sections as Mission, The Victim/Witness Program, Our History, FOIA and Online Reading Room, and Rules and Procedures Manual. Questions such as "How does the commission decide if someone is eligible for parole?" and "What happens at a parole hearing?" are addressed in a section called Answering Your Questions.
Subjects: Prisoners

Laws and Legal Information

1430. Code of Federal Regulations
http://www.gpoaccess.gov/cfr/
Alternate URL(s): http://www.gpoaccess.gov/ecfr/
Sponsor(s): National Archives and Records Administration (NARA) — Federal Register OfficeGovernment Printing Office (GPO)
Description: As described by the Government Printing Office (GPO), The *Code of Federal Regulations* (CFR) "is the codification of the general and permanent rules published in the *Federal Register* by the executive departments and agencies of the federal government. It is divided into 50 titles that represent broad areas subject to federal regulation." The CFR on GPO Access represents an online version of the printed edition. Content is updated as the print volumes are updated, and the content can be browsed by title, part, and section as it would be in print. Past editions, going back to 1997, are kept online. The online CFR can also be searched by word and CFR citation. Results can be viewed in plain text or PDF formats.

GPO has also developed a complementary online version, called e-CFR. The e-CFR is available at the alternate URL listed above. The e-CFR text is continually updated with new federal regulations as they become effective. The text also integrates links to newly finalized regulations that will become effective in the future. Search and browse options are available. Results are in HTML format.

The e-CFR is an important step forward for public access to federal regulations. Researchers using either version of the CFR should read the online background information to learn how the regulations are updated.
Subjects: Legal Information
Publications: *Code of Federal Regulations*, AE 2.106/3:

1431. Global Legal Information Network
http://www.glin.gov/
Sponsor(s): Library of Congress — Law Library
Description: Global Legal Information Network (GLIN) is a searchable database of laws, regulations, judicial decisions, and legal literature contributed by governments and international organizations around the world. Each document is summarized in English, and often in other languages; full text is available depending on the agreement with the contributing agency. Not all countries participate in GLIN. See the Help Center and About GLIN sections for detailed information on the database content.
Subjects: Legal Information — International

1432. Global Legal Monitor
http://www.loc.gov/law/public/glm/
Sponsor(s): Library of Congress — Law Library
Description: The Law Library of Congress introduced the *Global Legal Monitor* (*GLM*), an online publication, in 2006. The Web site states that *GLM* will be updated "frequently"; thus far, it has been published on roughly a bimonthly basis. The publication features legal news by topic and by country.
Subjects: Legal Information — International

1433. Office of the Law Revision Counsel
http://uscode.house.gov/

Sponsor(s): Congress — House of Representatives — Office of the Law Revision Counsel

Description: "The Office of the Law Revision Counsel prepares and publishes the United States Code, which is a consolidation and codification by subject matter of the general and permanent laws of the United States" (from the Web site). The Law Revision Counsel makes the U.S. Code available online for searching, browsing, or downloading. The site also features the office's classification tables, which show where recently enacted laws will appear in the U.S. Code and which sections of the code have been amended by those laws.

Also see the separate entry in this section for the U.S. Code site sponsored by the Legal Information Institute.

Subjects: Laws

1434. Preserving Life and Liberty
http://www.lifeandliberty.gov/

Sponsor(s): Justice Department

Description: This Justice Department Web site has a single purpose: defending the USA PATRIOT Act (Public Law 107-56), which has been a topic of public debate. The site presents speeches from the attorney general and quotes from newspaper editorials supporting the law. It includes supportive quotes from members of Congress and shows the congressional votes in favor of the bill.

This Justice site, dedicated to promoting a single argument, exemplifies a major development in the way the government is using the Internet. It stands in contrast to the original federal agency Web sites that presented basic organizational information and documents.

Subjects: Laws — Policy

1435. Public and Private Laws
http://www.gpoaccess.gov/plaws/

Sponsor(s): Government Printing Office (GPO)

Description: The GPO Access system has a database of public and private laws enacted from 1995 to the present. The database can be searched, or lists of laws can be browsed by congressional session. Laws are in both text and PDF formats. The site also links to the congressional publication *How Our Laws Are Made*.

Subjects: Laws

1436. Public Laws
http://www.archives.gov/federal-register/laws/access.html

Sponsor(s): National Archives and Records Administration (NARA) — Federal Register Office

Description: Public laws are published by the National Archive's Office of the Federal Register. This Web page explains how laws are numbered and printed. Users can view a list of laws from the current session of Congress or sign up to receive automatic e-mail announcements of new public law numbers. The site links to the Government Printing Office database for the text of public laws.

Subjects: Laws

1437. RegInfo.gov
http://reginfo.gov/
Sponsor(s): General Services Administration (GSA); Office of Management and Budget (OMB)
Description: RegInfo.gov is a finding aid for federal regulatory information. It links to online resources such as the *Federal Register* and *Code of Federal Regulations* at GPO Access, Small Business Administration Regulatory Alerts, and the *Unified Agenda of Federal Regulatory and Deregulatory Actions*. The site also features a Reg Map that provides a step-by-step overview of the rulemaking process.
Subjects: Regulatory Policy; Finding Aids

1438. Regulations.gov
http://www.regulations.gov/
Sponsor(s): Environmental Protection Agency (EPA)
Description: Regulations.gov is intended to make it easier for the general public to participate in the federal regulations review process. The site is an interagency effort led by the Environmental Protection Agency. Users can search by agency or word to find proposed and final regulations currently open for comment. Search results include a docket ID, *Federal Register* citation and date for when the regulation was first published, and final date for comments. The results also have links to view the *Federal Register* announcement in text or PDF formats and a link to a Web form for submitting comments.

Regulations.gov is a developing system. Researchers who wish to verify the current status of a proposed or final rule and associated comment requirements can also check the official edition of the *Federal Register*.
Subjects: Regulatory Policy

1439. Statutes at Large
http://www.gpoaccess.gov/statutes/
Sponsor(s): National Archives and Records Administration (NARA) — Federal Register OfficeGovernment Printing Office (GPO)
Description: The *United States Statutes at Large* compiles every public and private law in order of the date enacted into law. It also includes concurrent resolutions, proclamations by the president, any proposed and ratified amendments to the Constitution, and reorganization plans. GPO recently began making a digital version available. At present, only one volume from the 108th Congress is online. It can be searched by keyword. Alternatively, separate indexes by bill number and public law number, and for concurrent resolutions, popular names, and proclamations, can be browsed.
Subjects: Laws

1440. U.S. Code
http://www4.law.cornell.edu/uscode/
Sponsor(s): Legal Information Institute (LII)
Description: Cornell University's Legal Information Institute (LII) offers this popular and free interface for searching the U.S. Code. The code can be searched by word, by title and section number, or browsed. The site also features a table of popular names of laws, such as Voting Rights Act and Railroad Retirement Act. Where these laws can easily be linked to one part of the code, LII does so.

Also see the separate entry in this section for the Office of the Law Revision Counsel Web site.
Subjects: Laws

1441. Unified Agenda

http://www.gpoaccess.gov/ua/

Sponsor(s): Government Printing Office (GPO)

Description: The *Unified Agenda of Federal Regulatory and Deregulatory Actions* is published twice a year in the *Federal Register*. It provides information on federal regulations in development and, in the year's second edition, identifies federal regulatory priorities and major actions expected for the coming year. The content is compiled by the General Services Administration, coordinating with the Office of Management and Budget. This GPO Access site provides keyword searching of *Unified Agenda* documents for 1994 to present. Browse by chapter access is provided for the second half of 2002 forward.

Subjects: Regulatory Policy

Publications: *Unified Agenda of Federal Regulatory and Deregulatory Actions*, GS 1.6/11-2:

CHAPTER 16
Legislative Branch

The United States Congress is comprised of 2 chambers, 535 Member offices, over 40 committees, various legislative and operational offices, and several major congressional support agencies. Most of these entities have their own Web sites. In addition, many private and educational sites help to spread and interpret congressional information. This chapter describes major legislative branch Web sites and other useful finding aids for legislative information. (The Web sites for individual members of Congress and congressional committees are listed in two appendixes at the end of this publication.)

Subsections in this chapter are Congress, Congressional Support Agencies, and Legislative Information.

Congress

1442. Biographical Directory of the United States Congress
http://bioguide.congress.gov/
Sponsor(s): Congress
Description: For over a century, the *Biographical Directory of the United States Congress* has provided valuable information about the more than 13,000 individuals who have served in the national legislature, including in the Continental Congress and in the Senate and the House of Representatives. Congress offers an online version of this invaluable historical resource. The online version goes beyond the scope of the printed *Biographical Directory* to include images and extended information about research collections relating to each member. The online version is also continuously updated. The biographies may be searched by name, position (e.g., senator or Speaker of the House), party, and state.
Subjects: Members of Congress; Biographies
Publications: *Biographical Directory of the United States Congress*

1443. Congressional Directory
http://www.gpoaccess.gov/cdirectory/
Sponsor(s): Congress — Joint Committee on Printing
Description: The *Congressional Directory*, the official directory of Congress, has been published since 1888. The Government Printing Office has made it available online from the 104th Congress (1995–1996) to the present. Each edition of the *Congressional Directory* can be searched by keyword or browsed by section. The online edition is typically updated once before the next edition appears in print.

The publishing schedule of the *Congressional Directory* makes it less valuable as a source of current contact information than as a source of historical reference. Useful reference information updated in each edition includes: a list of joint sessions of Congress for 1789 to present; a list of House impeachments of judges, presidents, and members of Congress; and political divisions in the House and Senate from 1855 forward. The site's browse feature is more helpful than its search feature for finding these sections.
Subjects: Congressional Information
Publications: *Congressional Directory*, GP 3.22/2:228/

1444. Congressional Member and Staff Organizations
http://www.cha.house.gov/oversight/organization_list.aspx
Sponsor(s): Congress — House of Representatives
Description: Congressional Member Organizations and Congressional Staff Organizations must register with the House Administration Committee for each session of Congress. These organizations bring together House members that share a legislative focus, such as the Congressional Black Caucus or the Republican Study Committee. This House Administration Committee Web page provides a directory of registered organizations.
Subjects: House of Representatives

1445. History of the United States Capitol
http://www.access.gpo.gov/congress/senate/capitol/index.html
Sponsor(s): Congress — Architect of the Capitol
Description: The full-text version of the *History of the United States Capitol: A Chronicle of Design, Construction, and Politics*, a book by architectural historian William C. Allen, is available in PDF format on this GPO Access Web site. The book, which was sponsored by Congress and printed as a Senate document, includes numerous illustrations and photographs, as well as a bibliography.
Subjects: Capitol Building — History
Publications: *History of the United States Capitol: A Chronicle of Design, Construction, and Politics*, Y 1.1/2:SERIAL 14620

1446. House of Representatives — Committee Offices
http://www.house.gov/house/CommitteeWWW.html
Sponsor(s): Congress — House of Representatives
Description: This Web page provides links to all House committee Web sites. At the bottom of the page, a series of Committee Quick Links provides direct access to specific types of information that are typically available on the committee sites. This includes information about subcommittees, jurisdiction, hearings, and webcasts. Aside from some expected information (such as a list of members), the content of these Web sites can vary tremendously from one committee to the next. The sites also typically link to a Web site for the committees minority party members.

The House committee Web sites can be useful sources of current legislative information and of information about the programs within their jurisdiction. The majority and minority member sites usually reflect their party's agenda.
Subjects: Congressional Committees

1447. Lobbying Disclosure — House
http://lobbyingdisclosure.house.gov/
Sponsor(s): Congress — House of Representatives — Office of the Clerk
Description: The House provides this Web site for those who must, in compliance with the Lobbying Disclosure Act of 1995, register with the House Clerk's Office and file semiannual reports. The site does not carry the reports, which must be viewed in person at the office.
Subjects: Lobbyists

1448. Lobbying Disclosure — Senate
http://www.senate.gov/pagelayout/legislative/g_three_sections_
with_teasers/lobbyingdisc.htm
Alternate URL(s): http://sopr.senate.gov/
Sponsor(s): Congress — Senate — Secretary of the Senate
Description: For those who wish to lobby the Senate, this Web page provides access
to filing forms and information about compliance with the Lobbying Disclosure
Act of 1995. The alternate URL links to the Web site for the Senate's Office of
Public Records Lobby Filing Disclosure Program, which provides online copies of
lobbyist filings from 1998 onward. The reports can be searched by lobbyist name,
client name, and other criteria.
Subjects: Lobbyists

1449. Majority Whip
http://www.majoritywhip.house.gov/
Sponsor(s): Congress — House of Representatives — Office of the House Majority
Whip
Description: The Majority Whip is responsible for marshalling the votes of members
of the majority party in the House. The whip's Web site is used to keep members
informed about upcoming legislation and floor votes; researchers can also use
it for this purpose. Users can sign up to receive e-mail notices of upcoming
floor schedules.
Subjects: Congress — Policy; Legislation

1450. Office of the Clerk, United States House of Representatives
http://clerk.house.gov/
Sponsor(s): Congress — House of Representatives — Office of the Clerk
Description: The Clerk of the House is charged with a variety of procedural and
administrative duties. The clerk's Web site includes information about the office
itself, along with a wealth of congressional information associated with the clerk's
duties. The site includes directories of members of Congress, leadership offices,
committees, and subcommittees; House legislative activity schedules; legislative
procedure information; roll call vote results; congressional history; congressional
election statistics; and public disclosure information, such as members' financial
disclosure reports and official foreign travel and expenditures reports. It also
carries the official list of congressional office vacancies and current tallies of party
alignment in the House and Senate.
     The Office of the Clerk site serves as a central point for much of the official
information about the House's operations. The site provides a basic site map, but
researchers who wish to take advantage of the full array of information offered
should browse through each section.
Subjects: Congressional Information; Legislative Procedure
Publications: *Election Statistics*, Y 1.2/10:

1451. United States House of Representatives
http://www.house.gov/
Sponsor(s): Congress — House of Representatives
Description: The House of Representatives Web site includes a wealth of current
legislative and policy information. The site provides quick links to House member
and committee Web sites, which vary in coverage but may provide helpful legislative news and documents. Other major sections of the site are Schedule Information, Legislative Information, General Information (which includes the House
directory and employment and contracts information), and Search House Sites.
A sidebar has links to House organizations and offices, such as the Office of the

Chaplain and the Clerk of the House. The clerk's site, described in a separate entry, is particular useful for legislative research.

Current, official information about many of the House's operations and activities is readily available on this site. Its simple home page belies the tremendous amount of information that is available several levels down; this information includes hearings transcripts provided by some committees and historical information from the Clerk of the House.

Subjects: House of Representatives

1452. United States Senate

http://www.senate.gov/

Sponsor(s): Congress — Senate

Description: The United States Senate Web site is a source for both current legislative news and historical Senate information. The major sections of the site are Senators, Committees, Legislation and Records, Art and History, Visitors, and Reference. As with the House site, the content of individual member and committee sites varies, and the committee sites typically carry hearings schedules and some form of testimony.

The Legislation and Records section links to Senate votes, schedules, lobbying disclosure reports, and guides to the legislative process. The Active Legislation section identifies currently active bills and labels them by topic. The Treaties section supplements the THOMAS Treaties database with documents that identify treaties received, approved, receiving action, and reported. The Nominations section performs a similar role and includes lists of nominations by status, nominations withdrawn, and nominations failed or returned.

In the Reference section, the Senate Library offers a Virtual Reference Desk with information about topics including filibusters, Senate traditions, congressional medals and honors, the Senate Page program, and women and minorities in the Senate. This section also has reference statistics and lists (including a list of the longest-serving senators), bibliographies, research guides, and a glossary.

Subjects: Senate

1453. United States Senate: Committees Home

http://www.senate.gov/pagelayout/committees/d_three_sections_with_teasers/committees_home.htm

Sponsor(s): Congress — Senate

Description: The Senate's home page for its committees features direct links to the committees' Web sites, a list of each senator's committee assignments, committee membership lists, and a schedule of upcoming committee hearings and meetings. It also provides background information about the committee system and offers links to related Web sites.

Subjects: Congressional Committees

Congressional Support Agencies

1454. Architect of the Capitol

http://www.aoc.gov/

Sponsor(s): Congress — Architect of the Capitol

Description: The Architect of the Capitol (AOC) is responsible for the maintenance, operation, development, and preservation of the United States Capitol Complex, which includes the Capitol Building and its grounds, the congressional office buildings, the Library of Congress buildings, the Supreme Court building, the

Capitol Power Plant, and other facilities. The major sections of this Web site are About Us, Capitol Complex, Capitol Visitor Center, Projects, and Business Center.

The Capitol Complex section provides extensive information about the history, art, and architecture of the Capitol Building, supplemented by many historic and contemporary photographs and illustrations. The About Us section includes a list of all architects since 1793. The Visitor Center project, the most prominent current project on Capitol Hill, is explained in detail; the information provided includes construction schedules, sketches, and photographs.

The detailed current and historical information on this site makes it a useful resource for reference or research. It may be of interest to tourists as well as students of history, government, art, architecture, and historical preservation.
Subjects: Capitol Building

1455. Congressional Budget Office
http://www.cbo.gov/
Sponsor(s): Congressional Budget Office (CBO)
Description: CBO provides Congress with the analyses needed for economic and budget decisions and with the information and estimates required for the congressional budget process. The CBO Web site has the full-text versions of its many publications, including economic forecasts, budget projections, analysis of the president's budget, CBO testimony before Congress, and cost estimates for bills reported by congressional committees. CBO publications can be searched or browsed by topic. The New-Document Notification e-mail service sends subscribers publication announcements. The About CBO section includes a helpful chart called Timeline for Analyses, which tracks the releases of CBO products throughout the year.

CBO publications provide a wealth of information about the federal budget and on tax and spending proposals. Outside of its regular budget report series, CBO publishes special reports on policy and program topics such as funding for homeland security and the outlook for Social Security.
Subjects: Budget of the U.S. Government; Congressional Support Agencies
Publications: *An Analysis of the President's Budgetary Proposals for Fiscal Year . . .*, Y 10.19:
Budget Options, Y 10.2:
CBO's Economic Forecasting Record
Effective Federal Tax Rates, Y 10.2:T 19/11/
Final Sequestration Report for Fiscal Year . . ., Y 1.1/7:
Monthly Budget Review, Y 10.21/2
The Budget and Economic Outlook: An Update, Y 10.17:
The Budget and Economic Outlook: Fiscal Years . . ., Y 10.13:
Unauthorized Appropriations and Expiring Authorizations, Y 10.22:

1456. Congressional Research Service Employment Opportunities
http://www.loc.gov/crsinfo/
Sponsor(s): Library of Congress — Congressional Research Service (CRS)
Description: The Congressional Research Service is a legislative support agency located within the Library of Congress. Its mission is to provide nonpartisan analysis and research services to Congress. The purpose of its Web site is to provide information about job openings, internships, and other employment options. Basic background information on CRS is also provided. Because CRS works exclusively for Congress, this employment page is its only official public site.
Subjects: Congressional Support Agencies

1457. CRS Reports — LLRX.com
http://www.llrx.com/features/crsreports.htm
Sponsor(s): LLRX.com
Description: Because CRS works solely for Congress, it cannot distribute its reports directly to the public — although citizens can request specific reports from their elected congressional representatives. This Web page, part of a privately published legal information site, provides background information about *CRS Reports* and how to locate them online.
Subjects: Finding Aids; Legislative Information

1458. CRS Reports — Open CRS Network
http://www.opencrs.com/
Sponsor(s): Center for Democracy and Technology
Description: CRS works exclusively for Congress and does not provide direct public access to its reports. This private, nongovernment Web site provides access to *CRS Reports* already in the public domain. Open CRS Network encourages citizens to request *CRS Reports* from their congressional representatives and to contribute them to its growing database of the reports.
Subjects: Legislative Information

1459. CRS Reports — UNT Libraries
http://digital.library.unt.edu/govdocs/crs/
Sponsor(s): University of North Texas Libraries
Description: The goal of the *CRS Reports* project at the University of North Texas Libraries is to provide permanent public access to *CRS Reports* that have been available at a variety of different Web sites since 1990. The reports can be searched or browsed by topic. Subject indexing of the reports uses the CRS Legislative Indexing Vocabulary, supplemented with Library of Congress Subject Headings.

This University of North Texas (UNT) Web site was released at about the same time as the Open CRS Network Web site, also described in this chapter. The Open CRS site is focused on expanding the number of *CRS Reports* in the public domain and lobbying for better public access to these reports. This UNT Libraries Web site brings greater search capabilities, subject indexing, and the goal of permanent public access to current and past *CRS Reports*.
Subjects: Legislative Information

1460. Government Accountability Office
http://www.gao.gov/
Sponsor(s): Government Accountability Office (GAO)
Description: GAO is the investigative arm of Congress. It examines the use of public funds and evaluates federal programs and activities to help the Congress in oversight, policy, and funding decisions. Its Web site features the full-text versions of *GAO Reports and Testimony* and recent comptroller general decisions and opinions. (The full-text versions of these reports and decisions are also available on the GPO Access Web site.) E-mail alert lists are offered to notify subscribers when new reports or decisions are published. GAO's FraudNET service allows the public to report allegations of fraud, waste, abuse, or mismanagement of federal funds; the site provides an online form for reporting such allegations.
Subjects: Congressional Support Agencies; Government Administration
Publications: *Abstracts of Reports and Testimony*, GA 1.16/3-3:
Decisions of the Comptroller General, GA 1.5/A-2:
GAO Reports, GA 1.13:
GAO Strategic Plan, GA 1.1/3:

Government Auditing Standards (Yellow Book), GA 1.2:
Month in Review, GA 1.16/3:
Today's Reports, GA 1.16/7:

1461. Office of Technology Assessment: The OTA Legacy

http://www.wws.princeton.edu/~ota/

Sponsor(s): Office of Technology Assessment (OTA)

Description: After Congress terminated its Office of Technology Assessment (OTA) at the end of 1995, the official OTA Web site ceased. This Princeton University site makes archived OTA information available to the public. It provides the full text of OTA publications arranged by title, year, and topic, as they were on the official OTA site. The Technology Assessment and the Work of Congress section describe the history and operations of OTA, including speeches and news reports about its role.

Through the publications available at this site, OTA provided analyses of the scientific and technical policy issues for Congress. This Princeton University site provides a valuable archive and record of this work.

Subjects: Science and Technology Policy

Publications: *OTA Reports*, Y 3.T 22/2:

Legislative Information

1462. A Century of Lawmaking for a New Nation: U.S. Congressional Documents and Debates, 1774–1875

http://memory.loc.gov/ammem/amlaw/lawhome.html

Sponsor(s): Library of Congress

Description: Congressional documents from the Continental Congress through 1875 are available to search, browse, and display courtesy of the Library of Congress and its Law Library. The digitized collection includes the *Journals of the Continental Congress* (1774–1789); the *Letters of Delegates to Congress* (1774–1789); the *Records of the Federal Convention of 1787*, or *Farrand's Records*, and the *Debates in the Several State Conventions on the Adoption of the Federal Constitution* (1787–1788), or *Elliot's Debates*; the *Journals of the House of Representatives* (1789–1875) and the Senate (1789–1875), including the *Senate Executive Journal* (1789–1875); the *Journal of William Maclay* (1789–1791); the debates of Congress as published in the *Annals of Congress* (1789–1824), the *Register of Debates* (1824–1837), *Congressional Globe* (1833–1873), and *Congressional Record* (1873–1875); the *Statutes at Large* (1789–1875); the *American State Papers* (1789–1838); and congressional bills and resolutions for selected sessions beginning with the 6th Congress (1799) in the House of Representatives and the 16th Congress (1819) in the Senate. It also includes selected documents from the *U.S. Serial Set* from 1833 through 1916.

The site provides tips on using, searching, and viewing the collection. A "Search All Titles" button leads to a search page with many options, including searching one specific title or a combination of several titles. Browse options are also presented on the search page. The title page for each document includes links to a citation guide and some basic historical context for the documents.

This collection makes a substantial contribution toward public access to the documentary history of American democracy.

Subjects: Congress — History; Congressional Documents

1463. Center for Legislative Archives
http://www.archives.gov/records_of_congress/index.html
Sponsor(s): National Archives and Records Administration (NARA)
Description: The Center for Legislative Archives is the repository for historically valuable congressional records at the National Archives and Records Administration. The center, located in Washington, DC, holds more than 170,000 cubic feet of records dating from the first Congress to modern Congresses. The official records from the committees of the House of Representatives and the Senate — the standing, select, special, and joint committees, which Congress uses to accomplish the majority of its work — represent the core holdings of the center. It also holds some collections from legislative support agencies, such as federal government publications from the Government Printing Office. The site provides various online finding guides, which can be searched by keyword.

Most of the holdings are not available online. Some have been digitized and are available in the Featured Documents subsection (under the Resources section). The Other Congressional Collections subsection, also under Resources, links to a directory of congressional members' personal papers collections, most of which are held at archival institutions other than the National Archives.

The Finding Aids to Legislative Records section of this site may be of the most value to researchers unable to travel to Washington to use the center's collections.
Subjects: Congressional Documents

1464. C-SPAN.org
http://www.c-span.org/
Sponsor(s): C-SPAN
Description: The cable television industry created C-SPAN (Cable-Satellite Public Affairs Network) in 1979 to provide live, gavel-to-gavel coverage of the House of Representatives. Senate coverage began in 1986, when the Senate began televising its proceedings. C-SPAN currently offers audio and video of floor proceedings and some hearings over the Internet. Online users can browse the schedules for C-SPAN's cable and radio stations and receive public affairs and congressional programming online.

The C-SPAN Web site offers a number of resources for researchers and users following Congress. The Web Resources section leads to audio of all Senate hearings from CapitolHearings.org, a congressional glossary, The *Capitol Spotlight* congressional news service, and many more linked resources.
Subjects: Congressional Information; Legislative Procedure

1465. GPO Congressional Publications Releases
http://www.llsdc.org/gpo/
Sponsor(s): Law Librarians' Society of Washington DC, Inc.
Description: Members of LLSDC's Legislative Research Special Interest Section transcribe, from twice-daily GPO telephone recordings, the week-by-week listing of newly issued congressional documents for sale by GPO. A link is provided if the publication is available online. Any recently signed laws are noted at the end of each week's document.

While not an official government source, the Law Librarians' Society's list is a helpful tool for tracking new congressional documents.
Subjects: Congressional Documents

1466. How Our Laws Are Made
http://thomas.loc.gov/home/lawsmade.toc.html
Sponsor(s): Congress — House of Representatives; Library of Congress
Description: This classic guide provides a readable and non-technical outline of the numerous steps in the federal lawmaking process. It is available online as either one long ASCII file or as a chapter-divided HTML file.

The HTML version of this classic is organized to make it is relatively easy for users to read the entire work or browse relevant sections.
Subjects: Legislative Procedure
Publications: *How Our Laws are Made,* Y 1.1/7:

1467. Legislative Branch Resources on GPO Access
http://www.gpoaccess.gov/legislative.html
Sponsor(s): Government Printing Office (GPO)
Description: This section of the GPO Access Web site provides centralized access to the site's legislative branch content. Among its many congressional resources are the following documents: House and Senate bills, committee hearings, the *Congressional Directory,* the *Congressional Pictorial Directory,* the *Congressional Record,* public and private laws, and the *United States Code.*
Subjects: Congressional Documents; Databases
Publications: *Calendar of United States House of Representatives and History of Legislation,* Y 1.2/2:
Cannon's Precedents of the House of Representatives
Congressional Directory, Y 4.P 93/1:1
Congressional Pictorial Directory, Y 4.P 93/1:1 P/
Congressional Record, X 1.1/A:
Constitution of the United States of America: Analysis and Interpretation, Y 1.1/3:
Constitution, Jefferson's Manual, and Rules of the House of Representatives, Y 1.1/7:
Deschler's Precedents of the United States House of Representatives, Y 1.1/2:
Economic Indicators, Y 4.EC 7:EC 7/
Hinds' Precedents of the House of Representatives
House Practice: A Guide to the Rules, Precedents, and Procedures of the House (Brown), Y 1.2:
Riddick's Senate Procedure, Y 1.1/3:
Senate Calendar of Business (daily), Y 1.3/3:
Senate Manual, Y 1.1/3:
U.S. Public Laws, AE 2.110:
United States Code, Y 1.2/5-2:

1468. LLSDC's *Legislative Source Book*
http://www.llsdc.org/sourcebook/
Sponsor(s): Law Librarians' Society of Washington DC, Inc.
Description: For this online version of the *Legislative Source Book,* the Legislative Interest Section of the Law Librarians' Society of Washington, DC, has compiled a variety of useful legislative research tools developed by its members. Many are unique to this Web site. They include GPO Congressional Publication Releases, a weekly list of releases; a guide to researching federal legislative histories; an overview of the *Congressional Record* and its predecessor publications; and instructions for finding and establishing direct links to documents online at THOMAS and GPO Access. The link to a "Table of Congressional Publication Volumes and Presidential Issuances (1789-current year)" will be of interest to legislative researchers and librarians. It is a reverse chronological correlation of Congressional session numbers; calendar year; *Congressional Record, Statutes*

at Large, Serial Set, and *Federal Register* volume numbers; presidential administration; and executive order and presidential proclamation numbers.

This site will be of interest to government documents librarians and serious legislative researchers.

Subjects: Congressional Documents; Legislation — Research

1469. THOMAS: Legislative Information on the Internet
http://thomas.loc.gov/

Sponsor(s): Library of Congress

Description: THOMAS, a service of the Library of Congress that acts under the direction of the Congress, makes U.S. legislative information freely available on the Internet. The site is divided into three broad categories: Legislation, *Congressional Record*, and Committee Information. The Bill Summary and Status database is the core THOMAS database; it is available for the 93rd Congress (1973) to the present. It tracks the action on each bill in Congress, provides links to the full-text version of the bill and related debate in the *Congressional Record*, and identifies congressional sponsors or cosponsors, amendments to the bill, and any related bills. The *Congressional Record* section includes the full-text versions of the *Record* (from 1989 onward), its *Index* (from 1995 onward), and current lists of House and Senate roll call votes as provided by those chambers. The Committee Information section features the full-text versions of committee reports (from 1995 onward), and links to current information provided online by the congressional committees themselves. THOMAS also has databases of Presidential Nominations (from 1987 to the present) and Treaties (largely from 1975 to the present), both of which are handled by the Senate.

This is one of the most widely used Internet sources for legislative information. While it does not yet deliver all the information that some users might desire, it does make a significant body of legislative documentation easily available to the public.

Subjects: Legislation; Databases

Publications: *Congressional Record*, X 1.1/A:

House Bills, Y 1.4/6:

House Concurrent Resolutions, Y 1.4/9:

House Joint Resolutions, Y 1.4/8:

House Resolutions, Y 1.4/7:

How Our Laws are Made, Y 1.1/7:

Senate Bills, Y 1.4/1:

Senate Concurrent Resolutions, Y 1.4/4:

Senate Joint Resolutions, Y 1.4/3:

Senate Printed Amendments, Y 1.4/5:

Senate Resolutions, Y 1.4/2:

CHAPTER 17
Presidency

As the second presidential administration on the Internet, the Bush administration continues the practice of posting press releases, radio addresses, and other presidential communications on the White House Web site. Offices that directly support the White House have pages on the White House Web site and closely integrated with this main site. This chapter includes Web sites sponsored by the current presidential administration and finding aids for documents from the current and previous presidential administrations.

Subsections in this chapter are Current Administration, Presidential Information.

Current Administration

1470. Council of Economic Advisers
http://whitehouse.gov/cea/
Sponsor(s): Council of Economic Advisers (CEA)
Description: The CEA, which consists of one chairman and two members, advises the president of the United States on domestic and international economic policy and assists in the preparation of the *Economic Report of the President*. The CEA Web site describes the council's mission and operations of the Council and links to current CEA publications and the text of the chairman's speeches.
Subjects: Economic Statistics; Economic Policy; Presidential Advisers
Publications: *Economic Indicators*, Y 4.EC 7:EC 7/
Economic Report of the President, Pr 42.9:

1471. Domestic Policy Council
http://www.whitehouse.gov/dpc/
Sponsor(s): White House — Domestic Policy Council
Description: The Domestic Policy Council manages the president's domestic policy agenda. Its Web site provides a brief description of the council's history and its work. It links to the pages for the Office of National AIDS Policy, the Office of National Drug Control Policy, the Office of Faith-based and Community Initiatives, and other offices affiliated with the Domestic Policy Council.
Subjects: Presidential Advisers; Public Policy

1472. First Lady Laura Bush
http://www.whitehouse.gov/firstlady/
Sponsor(s): White House — First Lady's Office
Description: The First Lady's Web site links to her biography, the full texts of her speeches and statements, and press releases from the Office of the First Lady. Sections of this site focus on her initiatives, such as Preserve America and Helping America's Youth.
Subjects: First Lady

1473. National Economic Council
http://www.whitehouse.gov/nec/
Sponsor(s): National Economic Council
Description: The National Economic Council coordinates the economic policy advice for the president and ensures that economic policy decisions and programs are

consistent with the president's stated goals. This Web site provides only a brief overview of the council and the name of the current director.
Subjects: Economic Policy; Presidential Advisers

1474. National Security Council
http://www.whitehouse.gov/nsc/
Sponsor(s): National Security Council (NSC)
Description: NSC is the president's forum for considering national security and foreign policy matters with his senior national security advisers and cabinet officials. The NSC Web site describes its establishment, membership, and function, and links to selected White House press releases. The NSC History section gives information about the NSC from the Truman administration to the Clinton administration with an appendix listing the national security affairs assistants to the president during these years.
Subjects: National Security — Policy; Presidential Advisers
Publications: *National Security Strategy of the United States of America*, PR 43.2:

1475. Office of Administration
http://www.whitehouse.gov/oa/
Sponsor(s): White House — White House Office of Administration
Description: The Office of Administration provides administrative support services to all units within the Executive Office of the President. These services include financial management and information technology support, human resources management, library and research assistance, facilities management, and procurement. Its Web site features information about competitive vacancies within the Executive Office of the President, the Freedom of Information Act, and the Preservation Office. The Preservation Office page includes a virtual tour of the Eisenhower Executive Office Building.
Subjects: White House (Mansion)

1476. President's Foreign Intelligence Advisory Board
http://www.whitehouse.gov/pfiab/
Sponsor(s): White House — President's Foreign Intelligence Advisory Board
Description: The President's Foreign Intelligence Advisory Board (PFIAB) provides advice to the president concerning the quality and adequacy of intelligence collection, analysis and estimates, counterintelligence, and other intelligence activities. The PFIAB, through its component Intelligence Oversight Board, also advises the president on the legality of foreign intelligence activities. This Web site includes basic information on the role and history of the PFIAB and a list of past chairpersons.
Subjects: Intelligence; Presidential Advisers

1477. Privacy and Civil Liberties Oversight Board
http://www.privacyboard.gov/
Sponsor(s): White House — Executive Office of the President
Description: The Privacy Board, established within the Executive Office of the President, began its work in 2006. Its Web site states that the board "advises the president and other senior executive branch officials to ensure that concerns with respect to privacy and civil liberties are appropriately considered" in executive branch policies. The site provides background information about the establishment of the board, as well as biographies of its members and news releases.
Subjects: Presidential Advisers; Privacy

1478. Results.gov: Resources for the President's Team
http://www.whitehouse.gov/results/
Sponsor(s): White House — Executive Office of the President
Description: This public Web site is subtitled "Resources for the President's Team." A section on the *President's Management Agenda* features information about the agenda and quarterly scorecards rating departments' progress on the agenda. A section on the president and his leadership team has a directory of Bush administration appointees, along with photographs and brief biographies. The Tools for Success section has information about ethics, records management, the legislative process, and government oversight.
Subjects: Government Administration — Policy
Publications: *The President's Management Agenda*, PREX 2.2:

1479. Vice President Richard B. Cheney
http://www.whitehouse.gov/vicepresident/
Sponsor(s): White House — Vice President's Office
Description: Vice President Richard B. Cheney's Web site includes his biography (also available in Spanish), his speeches and statements, and a biography of his wife, Lynne Cheney. The site has historical information on the Ceremonial Office of the Vice President, located in the Eisenhower Executive Office Building, and a video tour of the official Vice President's Residence.
Subjects: Vice President

1480. White House
http://www.whitehouse.gov/
Sponsor(s): White House
Description: The White House Web site combines current news and policy statements from the administration with historical information relating to both the building and the Executive Office of the Presidency. Principal sections include the following: President; News; Vice President; History and Tours; First Lady; and Mrs. Cheney. The home page is primarily used for news of presidential speeches, events, and initiatives. A section called Issues pulls together background information, speeches, documents, and government links on major topics, such as homeland security and the economy. The Your Government section links to organizations within the Executive Office of the Presidency, such as the National Security Council and the Office of Faith-based and Community Initiatives.

The President section highlights current administration news, the president's biography, and photos. The President section also links to information on the cabinet with photos of the cabinet members and links to their home departments and offices. The News section has the full text of the Press Secretary's press briefings and White House press releases, the president's weekly radio addresses, the president's speeches, proclamations, and executive orders, and a list of nominations made by the president. Also of note, History and Tours section features information on past presidents and an online tour of the White House. The First Lady section provides current news, as well as biographical information on past first ladies.

A Spanish-language version and a text-only version of the site are also available.

The White House Web site should be the first stop online for users seeking current presidential news, statements, and documents; biographies of elected and appointed White House officials; speeches of the vice president and first lady; and other historical information about the White House and its occupants.
Subjects: First Lady; Presidency; White House (Mansion)
Publications: *National Security Strategy of the United States of America*, PR 43.2: *National Strategy for Homeland Security*, PR 43.14:

Reliable, Affordable, and Environmentally Sound Energy for America's Future: Report of the National Energy Policy Development Group, PR 43.2: *Strengthening Social Security for the 21st Century*, PR 43.8:

1481. White House Fellows Program

http://www.whitehouse.gov/fellows/

Sponsor(s): White House
Description: The non-partisan White House Fellows Program was established by President Lyndon B. Johnson in 1964 to provide early-career professionals first-hand experience in governing the nation. Each fellow works full time for one year as a special assistant to a cabinet member or senior presidential adviser. This Web site proveds information about the program, selection criteria, the application process, the current class of fellows, and prominent alumni.
Subjects: Fellowships; Public Policy

1482. White House Military Office

http://www.whitehouse.gov/whmo/

Sponsor(s): White House
Description: This Web site explains the role and responsibilities of the White House Military Office. There are links to pages describing each of the Office's units: the White House Communications Agency; the Presidential Airlift Group (Air Force One); the White House Medical Unit; Camp David; Marine Helicopter Squadron One; the Presidential Food Service; the White House Communications Agency; and the White House Transportation Agency.
Subjects: President

1483. White House Office of Faith-based and Community Initiatives

http://www.whitehouse.gov/government/fbci/

Alternate URL(s): http://www.fbci.gov

Sponsor(s): White House — Faith-based and Community Initiatives Office
Description: The White House Office of Faith-based and Community Initiatives was created by Executive Order in January 2001 to facilitate the involvement of religious and community institutions in federal social services programs. The office's site (hosted at the White House Web site) provides annual data on grants to faith-based organizations along with resources for operational guidance and technical assistance. The site links to the Centers for Faith-based and Community Initiatives in other federal agencies and provides information on conferences and grants.
Subjects: Charities; Social Services — Policy
Publications: *Guidance to Faith-based and Community Organizations on Partnering with the Federal Government*, PR 43.2:

Presidential Information

1484. Codification of Presidential Proclamations and Executive Orders

http://www.archives.gov/federal-register/codification/

Sponsor(s): National Archives and Records Administration (NARA) — Federal Register Office
Description: The Office of the Federal Register presents this online version of the *Codification of Presidential Proclamations and Executive Orders*, which covers proclamations and executive orders issued by the president from April 13, 1945, through January 20, 1989. Documents that had no legal effect on January 20, 1989, are excluded. The Disposition Tables section lists all the documents back to

1945, noting whether the document has been revoked, superseded, or is otherwise obsolete. Earlier proclamations and executive orders are included if they were amended or otherwise affected by documents issued during the 1945–1989 period.
Subjects: Executive Orders; Presidential Documents
Publications: *Codification of Presidential Proclamations and Executive Orders,* AE 2.113:

1485. Executive Orders Disposition Tables
http://www.archives.gov/federal-register/executive-orders/disposition.html
Sponsor(s): National Archives and Records Administration (NARA) — Federal Register Office
Description: This Web site provides citations and status information for executive orders issued by presidents from 1937 through the present. The Disposition Tables include the executive order number, signing date, *Federal Register* citation, title, amendments (if any), and current status (where applicable).
Subjects: Executive Orders; Presidential Documents

1486. First Ladies' Gallery
http://www.whitehouse.gov/history/firstladies/
Sponsor(s): White House
Description: The First Ladies' Gallery presents brief biographies of all first ladies from Martha Washington to the Laura Bush. For many of the first ladies, a portrait is also available. The biographies are taken from the book *The First Ladies* written by Margaret Brown Klapthor and Allida Black (contributing author), which was published by the White House Historical Association with the cooperation of the National Geographic Society.
Subjects: First Lady

1487. Office of the Pardon Attorney
http://www.justice.gov/pardon/
Sponsor(s): Justice Department — Office of the Pardon Attorney
Description: The Office of the Pardon Attorney reviews requests for presidential pardons for federal criminal offenses. Its Web site includes application forms, regulations, and background information relating to clemency petitions. The site also provides clemency statistics from 1900 onward, and lists of clemency recipients from 1989 onward.
Subjects: Pardons

1488. Presidential Directives and Executive Orders
http://www.fas.org/irp/offdocs/direct.htm
Sponsor(s): Federation of American Scientists (FAS)
Description: This Web site, maintained by a nonprofit research organization, focuses on intelligence-related presidential directives and executive orders from the Truman administration onward. Copies of documents that are not still classified are available on this site. The site also links to related sources of information.

The Federation of American Scientists is a private, nonprofit group concerned with public policy. While this Web site is not an official government source of information, the collection is valuable for the ease of access it provides to these documents.
Subjects: Intelligence; Presidential Documents

1489. Presidential Directives and Where to Find Them
http://www.loc.gov/rr/news/directives.html
Sponsor(s): Library of Congress
Description: Although not a source for the directives themselves, this Web site presents a concise guide to finding presidential directives, which are documents issued by the National Security Council that are signed or authorized by the president. It has not been updated in recent years, and covers the period up to the President George H. W. Bush administration.
Subjects: Presidential Documents

1490. Presidential Pardons
http://jurist.law.pitt.edu/pardons.htm
Sponsor(s): University of Pittsburgh School of Law
Description: As part of the University of Pittsburgh School of Law JURIST Web site, the Presidential Pardons site offers a wealth of information on relevant law, history, and statistics. Sections include Constitutional Basis, Administration/Regulations, Cases, Clemency Statistics, and Notable Pardons.
   The content and organization of this site makes it useful as a quick source of reference and as a starting point for more extensive legal or historical research.
Subjects: Pardons

1491. Public Papers of the Presidents of the United States
http://www.gpoaccess.gov/pubpapers/
Sponsor(s): National Archives and Records Administration (NARA) — Federal Register OfficeGovernment Printing Office (GPO)
Description: The *Public Papers of the Presidents of the United States*, a printed volume series that compiles the messages and papers of the presidents, begin with the Hoover administration. GPO Access has put the series online beginning with the 1991 volume in George H. W. Bush administration. Each volume in the series contains the papers and speeches of the president of the United States that were issued by the Office of the Press Secretary during the specified time period.
Subjects: Presidential Documents
Publications: *Public Papers of the President*, AE 2.114:

1492. Public Papers of the Presidents of the United States — University of Michigan
http://www.hti.umich.edu/p/ppotpus/
Sponsor(s): University of Michigan. Library
Description: This Web site from the University of Michigan Digital Library contains the *Public Papers of the Presidents of the United States* from the Hoover administration through the Clinton administration. Volumes will continue to be added in the future. The volumes can be searched or browsed using the standard interface of the University of Michigan collections.
Subjects: Presidential Documents
Publications: *Public Papers of the Presidents of the United States*

1493. The American Presidency Project
http://www.presidency.ucsb.edu/
Sponsor(s): University of California, Santa Barbara
Description: Although it is an unofficial Web site, The American Presidency Project site provides a more complete collection of certain key presidential documents than can be found elsewhere on the publicly accessible Web. In the Documents section, the site contains the following: *Public Papers of the Presidents*, (1929–present); State of the Union addresses, (1789–present); inaugural

addresses (1789–present); transcripts for radio addresses (1982–present) and presidential debates (1960–present); and other related documents.

Subjects: Presidential Documents

1494. Weekly Compilation of Presidential Documents
http://www.gpoaccess.gov/wcomp/

Sponsor(s): National Archives and Records Administration (NARA) — Federal Register Office

Description: The *Weekly Compilation of Presidential Documents*, published every Monday, contains the text of the president's speeches, bill signing statements, executive orders, proclamations, communications to Congress, and other presidential materials released by the White House during the preceding week. *Weekly Compilation* documents from 1993 to the present can be searched by keyword. Beginning with the year 2001, users can also browse the documents by clicking on a weekly table of contents.

Subjects: Presidential Documents

Publications: *Weekly Compilation of Presidential Documents*, AE 2.109:

CHAPTER 18

Science and Space

The federal government is involved in basic and applied science, in helping to disseminate scientific information, and in encouraging scientific research in academia and other research centers. While some Web sites in this chapter present highly specialized and technical information, many of the sites from NASA (which can be found in the Space section) are designed for education and outreach to the general public.

Subsections in this chapter are Life Sciences, National Laboratories, Physical Sciences, Science Agencies and Policy, Scientific and Technical Information, and Space.

Life Sciences

1495. Astrobiology at NASA
http://astrobiology.arc.nasa.gov/
Sponsor(s): National Aeronautics and Space Administration (NASA) — Ames Research Center (ARC)
Description: Astrobiology is the study of the origin, evolution, distribution, and destiny of life in the universe. It uses multiple scientific disciplines and space technologies. This site features a wealth of NASA information on astrobiology, including Science Goals, Technologies, Missions, Education, Societal Issues, and Astrobiology Institute.
Subjects: Astrobiology
Publications: *Astrobiology Magazine*

1496. Biological Resources Division at USGS
http://biology.usgs.gov/
Sponsor(s): Interior Department — U.S. Geological Survey (USGS)
Description: This site links to the Web site for each major USGS biology program. The National Activities section links to information on projects such as the Bird Banding Laboratory and National Biological Information Infrastructure (NBII). The link on Wildlife Diseases leads to the USGS National Wildlife Health Center site. The Features area includes a photo gallery, Learning Room, and links for non-scientists.

With information for children, the general public, and researchers, this site offers one of the best government starting points for general biological information.
Subjects: Natural Resources — Research

1497. Computational Bioscience and Engineering Laboratory
http://cbel.dcrt.nih.gov/
Sponsor(s): National Institutes of Health (NIH)
Description: The work of the Computational Bioscience and Engineering Laboratory (CBEL) addresses areas requiring high-performance computing with projects in areas such as biomedical imaging, human genetic linkage analysis, and computationally intensive statistical applications. Its Web site features links to the lab's divisions and to a bibliography of their published research.
Subjects: Medical Computing — Research

1498. DOE Joint Genome Institute
http://www.jgi.doe.gov/
Sponsor(s): Energy Department — Joint Genome Institute (JGI)
Description: The Joint Genome Institute is a cooperative effort involving the Department of Energy's Lawrence Berkeley, Lawrence Livermore, Los Alamos, Oak Ridge, and Pacific Northwest National Laboratories along with the Stanford Human Genome Center. Operated by the University of California, the institute works on genetic sequencing research with specialties in such areas as computational genomics and evolutionary genomics. The site includes detailed information on their research results and ongoing work, and a portal for JGI genomes and accompanying bioinformatics tools. An Education section includes an introduction to genomics.
Subjects: Genomics — Research

1499. Genomics.energy.gov
http://genomics.energy.gov/
Sponsor(s): Energy Department — Science Office
Description: Genomics.energy.gov consolidates information on the genome programs of the Energy Department's Office of Science. The primary Web sites it links to are: Human Genome Project Information (project completed in 1993); Genomics:GTL (described as a successor to the Human Genome Project); and Microbial Genome Program. The lower half of the home page has sections with information for the media and educators about biofuels, ethical-legal-social issues, and medicine. The Education section features a portal to Spanish-language Web sites about genomics.
Subjects: Genomics — Research

1500. Integrated Taxonomic Information System
http://www.itis.usda.gov/
Sponsor(s): Agriculture Department (USDA)
Description: The Integrated Taxonomic Information System (ITIS) is an excellent tool for looking up taxonomic names and common names of the biota of North America. (Biota refers to all the plant and animal life in an area.) ITIS is a partnership of U.S., Canadian, and Mexican agencies, organizations, and taxonomic specialists cooperating on the development of a scientifically credible list of biological names. The ITIS database can be searched by scientific name, common name, or taxonomic serial number. The records in the database include scientific name, common name, synonym, taxonomic serial number, author, and credibility rating. The full database, or custom reports from it, can be downloaded.
Subjects: Biological Names

1501. Laboratory of Neurosciences
http://www.grc.nia.nih.gov/branches/lns/
Sponsor(s): National Institutes of Health (NIH) — National Institute on Aging (NIA)
Description: The goal of basic research at the Lab of Neurosciences is to establish methods for preventing and treating age-related neurological disorders such as Alzheimer's and Parkinson's diseases. This site offers an overview of the aging nervous system and neurodegenerative disorders. At the bottom of the page are links to the different research areas of the lab and a bibliography of published research.
Subjects: Neurology — Research

1502. Laboratory of Structural Biology
http://dir.niehs.nih.gov/dirlsb/
Sponsor(s): National Institutes of Health (NIH) — National Institute of Environmental Health Sciences (NIEHS)
Description: The lab's mission is to provide insights into the biological processes that impact human environmental health. The site has information on the lab's facilities, principal investigators, and research groups. The research groups specialize in such areas as macromolecular structure and biomolecular crystallography.
Subjects: Molecular Biology — Research

1503. NASA Life Sciences Data Archive
http://lsda.jsc.nasa.gov/
Sponsor(s): National Aeronautics and Space Administration (NASA) — Johnson Space Center (JSC)
Description: The Life Sciences Data Archive is a searchable collection of information and data sets from space flight experiments funded by NASA. The growing archive is to include documentation from the 953 experiments flown since 1961 that include human, animal, or plant studies. The archive can be searched by mission, experiment, research hardware, and other parameters. The Web site has sections for researchers, teachers and students, and general space enthusiasts.
Subjects: Astrobiology — Research; Human Space Exploration — Research

1504. National Biological Information Infrastructure (NBII)
http://www.nbii.gov/
Sponsor(s): Interior Department — U.S. Geological Survey (USGS)
Description: The goal of the National Biological Information Infrastructure (NBII) is to improve access to data and information on biological resources. NBII is a collaborative program involving federal and state government agencies, international organizations, and nongovernment, academic, and private industry partners. Its Web site is maintained by the U.S. Geological Survey Center for Biological Informatics.

The site includes information developed by the NBII program, but also links to other government and nongovernment sites for coverage of many topics. The sections titled Current Biological Issues, Biological Disciplines, and Geographic Perspectives serve as extensive topical portals. A Teacher Resources section links to educational resources on botany, aquatic biology, reptiles, insects, and other topics. The Data and Information section has a variety of links, including conferences, journals, a metadata clearinghouse, and expertise databases.
Subjects: Biology

1505. National Center for Biotechnology Information
http://www.ncbi.nlm.nih.gov/
Sponsor(s): National Institutes of Health (NIH) — National Library of Medicine (NLM)
Description: The National Center for Biotechnology Information (NCBI) conducts basic and applied research in computational molecular biology and maintains a variety of databases related to their work. This site describes and links to the NCBI databases and software tools. Literature databases include PubMed, PubMed Central, and Online Mendelian Inheritance in Man (OMIM). Molecular and genome databases include GenBank, Nucleotide and Protein Sequences, Protein Structures, and Complete Genomes. NCBI's Entrez system enables integrated search and retrieval across the databases. Other sections of the site are About NCBI, Genomic Biology, Research at NCBI, Tools for Data Mining, Software Engineering,

and Education. Under About NCBI, a section called Science Primer has information for non-scientists about genome mapping, molecular genetics, and other topics.

This is an important site for genome and genetic sequence researchers. The site provides access to multiple databases with detailed help files for use in searching the databases. NCBI gives multiple means of accessing the data.

Subjects: Genomics — Research; Molecular Biology — Research; Databases
Publications: *NCBI Newsletter*, HE 20.3624/2:

1506. National Human Genome Research Institute
http://www.genome.gov/
Sponsor(s): National Institutes of Health (NIH) — National Human Genome Research Institute (NHGRI)
Description: NHGRI led the now-completed Human Genome Project, and currently focuses its genomic research on human health and disease issues. This site brings together news, research reports, and educational resources related to the institute's work. The Grants section links to information on current opportunities, funding history, and active research. The Health section has information on genetic and rare diseases. A Policy and Ethics section covers such topics as privacy, discrimination, legal issues, and cultural issues. This section also has a searchable database of legislative, legal, administrative, and regulatory materials concerning genetic issues such as genetic testing and privacy of genetic information.
Subjects: Genomics — Research

1507. National Institute of General Medical Sciences
http://www.nigms.nih.gov/
Sponsor(s): National Institutes of Health (NIH) — National Institute of General Medical Sciences (NIGMS)
Description: NIGMS supports basic biomedical research that is not targeted at specific diseases but lays the foundation for advances in disease diagnosis, treatment, and prevention. The Web site spotlights findings from NIGMS-funded research. Major sections of the site are Research Funding, Training and Careers, Minority Programs, and About NIGMS. The Publications section offers a number of science education booklets aimed at the general public; several are available in Spanish.
Subjects: Biological Medicine — Research
Publications: *Catalog of Cell Cultures and DNA Samples*, HE 20.3464:
Findings, HE 20.3470:
NIGMS Minority Programs Update (annual), HE 20.3469:

1508. PubChem
http://pubchem.ncbi.nlm.nih.gov/
Sponsor(s): National Institutes of Health (NIH) — National Library of Medicine (NLM)
Description: PubChem contains the chemical structures of small organic molecules and information on their biological activities. The PubChem system consists of several information tools: PubChem Substance, PubChem Compound, PubChem BioAssay, and a chemical structure similarity search tool.
Subjects: Molecular Biology

National Laboratories

1509. Argonne National Laboratory
http://www.anl.gov/
Sponsor(s): Energy Department — Argonne National Laboratory (ANL)
Description: The Energy Department's Argonne National Laboratory maintains a Web site with a mix of information on research, technology transfer, and educational opportunities. Major sections include Science/Technology, Community/Environment, Media Center, Administration, and Careers. Research at Argonne concerns basic science, energy resources, environmental management, and national security. Educational opportunities include undergraduate, graduate, and K–12 teacher internships and fellowships. The site's extensive Technology Transfer section identifies commercialization and licensing opportunities.

With a wealth of thoughtfully organized information, the Argonne site is equipped to serve audiences ranging from DOE and university scientists to technology companies, educators, students, and the general public.
Subjects: Nuclear Energy — Research; Research Laboratories; Scientific Research
Publications: *Argonne News*, E 1.86/2:
Explorer Magazine
Frontiers, Argonne National Laboratory, Research Highlights, E 1.86/4:
logos, E 1.86/3:

1510. Brookhaven National Laboratory
http://www.bnl.gov/world/
Sponsor(s): Energy Department — Brookhaven National Laboratory (BNL)
Description: BNL carries out and supports research in a multitude of scientific disciplines including nuclear and high energy physics, the physics and chemistry of materials, environmental and energy research, and nonproliferation. Its Web site serves as a gateway to information on its many research projects, facilities (including the Relativistic Heavy Ion Collider), and divisional sites.

Because the BNL site includes so much information on so many projects and fields of science, the A-Z Site Index can be a very helpful approach to discovering information on the site.
Subjects: Particle Accelerators; Research Laboratories
Publications: *Brookhaven Bulletin*
Discover Brookhaven, E 1.12/2-2

1511. Fermi National Accelerator Laboratory
http://www.fnal.gov/
Sponsor(s): Energy Department — Fermi National Accelerator Laboratory
Description: The Fermi National Accelerator Laboratory (Fermilab) is a research lab with a focus on high energy physics and the fundamental nature of matter and energy. It is known for its particle accelerator, the Tevatron. The About Fermilab section summarizes the lab's major research themes and links to pages on major projects. The Fermilab at Work section provides more detail on research, news, and operations. Fermilab Now pulls together links to current lab news and accelerator status reports. The site also has information on the many education programs offered by the lab.

This site is useful for both researchers and the general public. The sections Education, About Fermilab (with its virtual tour), Public Events (with streaming video lectures), and Inquiring Minds all provide information for the general public, while other sections can provide contact and technical information for researchers.
Subjects: Particle Accelerators; Physics — Research; Research Laboratories

Publications: *Fermilab Today*
FermiNews
Symmetry

1512. Lawrence Berkeley National Laboratory
http://www.lbl.gov/
Sponsor(s): Energy Department — Lawrence Berkeley National Laboratory (LBL)
Description: The Berkeley Lab conducts basic research in a wide range of fields including physical biosciences, earth sciences, materials sciences, computing sciences, nuclear science, life science, chemical science, energy, and information technology. Its Web site includes the sections About Berkeley Lab, Scientific Programs, Technology Transfer, Education Outreach, Publications/Reports, and Visitor Information. The Scientific Programs page links to the Web sites for the Berkeley Lab facilities and scientific divisions. A Search option is available for searching either the main Berkeley Lab Web server or all the lab Web servers, and there is also an index and directory for access to the lab's pages and personnel. Publications include the *Berkeley Lab Research Review*, news releases, and a catalog of scientific reports.

The LBL site is well organized and provides a substantial set of scientific information. The large number of subsidiary sites accessible from the top-level LBL page makes this an important site to search for scientists from many fields.
Subjects: Physics — Research; Research Laboratories
Publications: *Berkeley Lab Research Review*, E 1.53/2:
Berkeley Lab View

1513. Lawrence Livermore National Laboratory
http://www.llnl.gov/
Sponsor(s): Energy Department — Lawrence Livermore National Laboratory (LLNL)
Description: The research areas of LLNL include nuclear science, defense technology, energy, computation, and materials science, to name a few. The Science and Technology section of the Web site provides access to Lawrence Livermore Web pages by research areas and technologies. The site's Publications section includes the lab's published research papers, reports, and periodicals, with issues of *Science and Technology Review* as far back as 1994 (when it appears under its previous title of *Energy and Technology Review*). The site also provides information about job opportunities, educational programs, and visiting the lab.

The LLNL provides a substantial amount of online full-text documents of interest to researchers. The site should be the starting point for anyone seeking more information about the lab's programs or its areas of expertise.
Subjects: Nuclear Weapons — Research; Research Laboratories
Publications: *Science and Technology Review: Lawrence Livermore Laboratory*, E 1.53:

1514. Los Alamos National Laboratory
http://www.lanl.gov/
Sponsor(s): Energy Department — Los Alamos National Laboratory (LANL)
Description: Created to help in the development of nuclear weapons, the central mission of the Los Alamos National Laboratory is national security. It has stewardship of the nation's nuclear stockpile and conducts research related to this role. The lab's Web site describes work in this area; research in the areas of battlefield technologies, nonproliferation, and biothreats; and the Center for Homeland Security. The Strategic Science section of the site has information on its Center for Space Science and Exploration, Institute of Geophysics and Planetary Physics, and Quantum Institute. The Educators/Students page describes programs for high school through graduate levels, and for faculty and teachers. A separate section

covers the lab's Postdoctoral Program. The News section includes lab publications. The site also features an extensive section about the history of Los Alamos National Laboratory and the building of the atomic bomb.
Subjects: Nuclear Weapons; Physics — Research; Research Laboratories
Publications: *Los Alamos Science*, E 1.96:

1515. Oak Ridge National Laboratory
http://www.ornl.gov/
Sponsor(s): Energy Department — Oak Ridge National Laboratory (ORNL)
Description: Oak Ridge National Laboratory is a multiprogram science and technology laboratory. ORNL research areas include neutron sciences, high-performance computing, complex biological systems, materials science, energy, and national security. The Science and Technology section of this Web site describes these and other areas of research and links to the Lab's Education Program and its Publications page. Under Publications, a database called the Comprehensive Publications and Presentations Registry (CPPR) has bibliographic information for ORNL reports from 1985 and the full-text of many reports from the late 1990s on. The About ORNL section has information on organizational structure, leadership, procurement, and ORNL history.
Subjects: Research Laboratories; Scientific Research
Publications: *Oak Ridge National Laboratory Review*, E 1.28/17: *ORNL Reporter*

1516. Pacific Northwest National Laboratory
http://www.pnl.gov/
Sponsor(s): Energy Department — Pacific Northwest National Laboratory (PNNL)
Description: PNNL conducts research in computing and information technology, energy, environment, fundamental science, health and safety, national security, and nuclear technology. Work at the lab is described in the Science and Technology section of its Web site. Other sections describe the lab's facilities, educational opportunities, staffing, business resources, and technology licensing program. The News and Publications section has news releases and fact sheets on PNNL's areas of research.
Subjects: Research Laboratories
Publications: *Breakthroughs*, E 1.53/5:

1517. Sandia National Laboratories
http://www.sandia.gov/
Sponsor(s): Energy Department — Sandia National Laboratories
Description: Sandia focuses on research and development related to national security goals. The Mission Areas section of the Sandia site discusses activities in the areas of nuclear weapons, nonproliferation and assessments, military technologies, energy and infrastructure assurance, and homeland security. The News Center has links to news releases, congressional testimony, and Sandia publications.
Subjects: Research Laboratories; Weapons Research
Publications: *Sandia Technology*, E 1.20/5:

Physical Sciences

1518. Alaska Volcano Observatory
http://www.avo.alaska.edu/
Sponsor(s): Interior Department — U.S. Geological Survey (USGS)
Description: The Alaska Volcano Observatory (AVO) is a federal, state, and university partnership to monitor many of Alaska's volcanoes. The Web site describes the monitoring, hazard assessments, and volcano research conducted by AVO. The Volcano Information section features an interactive map of Alaskan volcanoes and a database of eruption events. The Current Volcanic Activity section includes webcams and volcano activity notifications.

The well-designed AVO site has content for those with general interest in volcanoes and for those in the scientific and Alaskan regional communities.
Subjects: Volcanoes
Publications: *Catalog of Historically Active Volcanoes of Alaska*, I 19.76:
Summary of Events and Response of the Alaska Volcano Observatory, I 19.76:

1519. Cascades Volcano Observatory
http://vulcan.wr.usgs.gov/
Sponsor(s): Interior Department — U.S. Geological Survey (USGS)
Description: The Cascades Volcano Observatory (CVO) watches volcanoes and other natural hazards, including earthquakes, landslides, and debris flows in the western United States. The CVO Web site has current status and other reports on volcanoes in the Cascade Range, including Mount Rainier and Mount St. Helens. The site features maps, photos, hazard assessment reports, and information on living with volcanoes and visiting volcanoes. The Education Outreach and Living With Volcanoes section each include materials that will be of interest to students, teachers, and the general public.

This site is of interest to volcanologists and the general public living near or visiting the areas of volcanic activity in the Cascades. In addition, basic volcano information makes the site useful to anyone searching for background information on this topic.
Subjects: Volcanoes
Publications: *Preparing for the Next Eruption in the Cascades*, I 19.76:

1520. Chandra X-Ray Observatory
http://chandra.harvard.edu/
Sponsor(s): National Aeronautics and Space Administration (NASA) — Marshall Space Flight Center (MSFC)
Description: Chandra X-Ray Observatory is an orbiting space telescope launched in 1999. Chandra captures X-ray images from high-energy regions of the universe, such as the remnants of exploded stars. This Web site, operated for NASA by the Harvard-Smithsonian Center for Astrophysics, serves as an information center for scientific users, the general public, and educators.
Subjects: Astrophysics; Telescopes

1521. Digital Tectonic Activity Map
http://denali.gsfc.nasa.gov/dtam/
Sponsor(s): National Aeronautics and Space Administration (NASA) — Goddard Space Flight Center (GSFC)
Description: This site documents tectonic activity on a map of the globe. It uses global datasets of seismicity, volcanism, and plate motions. The site provides

background information and downloadable versions in JPEG, PDF, TIFF, and GIF formats.
Subjects: Geographic Information Systems (GIS)

1522. Earth Observing System (NASA)
http://eospso.gsfc.nasa.gov/
Sponsor(s): National Aeronautics and Space Administration (NASA) — Goddard Space Flight Center (GSFC) — Earth Observing System (EOS) Project Science Office
Description: EOS consists of a science component and a data system supporting a coordinated series satellites for global observations of the land surface, biosphere, solid Earth, atmosphere, and oceans. The main categories of this Web site are What's New, For Educators, For News Media, For Scientists, Data Services, and Mission Profiles. Data products and program publications, including EOS-related publications and papers, are in the For Scientists category. The For Educators category offers educational materials, an Earth Observing satellite tracking utility, and the Spacecraft Overpass Predictor.
Subjects: Planetary Science

1523. Earth Observing System (NOAA)
http://www.noaa.gov/eos.html
Sponsor(s): Commerce Department — National Oceanic and Atmospheric Administration (NOAA)
Description: This NOAA site provides information about the emerging U.S. and Global Earth Observation Systems. It provides news, documents, and fact sheets, and links to related sites.

The Environmental Protection Agency and NASA also provide Web pages on earth observing systems and the international Global Earth Observation Systems of Systems (GEOSS) plan. Both are also described in this chapter.
Subjects: Planetary Science

1524. Earthquake Hazards Program
http://earthquake.usgs.gov/
Sponsor(s): Interior Department — U.S. Geological Survey (USGS)
Description: The mission of the Earthquake Hazards Program is to understand the characteristics and effects of earthquakes and to apply this knowledge to reduce deaths, injuries, and property damage from earthquakes. The Web site's Earthquake Center page features interactive maps of the latest earthquakes in the United States and the world, as well as historical earthquake information. The site also has regional information, such as earthquakes by state. The Research section covers USGS earthquake monitoring and research, grants for external research, and access to USGS monitoring data. The site's extensive Learning and Education section has something for everyone, including earthquake- and fault-related USGS publications (including an earthquake notification service), earthquake trivia, a visual earthquake glossary, preparedness advice, and sections for students and teachers.

With everything from earthquake shakemaps and photos to research data to science fair project ideas, this USGS site is a good place to start your earthquake information search.
Subjects: Earthquakes

1525. Earthquake Hazards Program — Northern California
http://quake.wr.usgs.gov/
Sponsor(s): Interior Department — U.S. Geological Survey (USGS)
Description: This USGS site focuses specifically on earthquake activity in Northern California. The site features real-time earthquake maps for California-Nevada, real-time shaking maps for California, and maps showing the probability of strong shaking at any location in California within the next 24 hours. The site also includes regional information on the latest quakes, earthquake preparedness, and earthquake research.

For the centennial anniversary of the 1906 San Francisco earthquake, this site highlights information on that historic event, including background information, photos, and eyewitness accounts.

This site provides excellent detail on Northern California seismic conditions.
Subjects: Earthquakes

1526. Frederick/Bethesda Data and Online Services
http://cactus.nci.nih.gov/
Sponsor(s): National Institutes of Health (NIH)
Description: This collaborative Web site includes chemical information databases, software tools, and links to other chemistry-related databases at U.S. government Web sites. It features a Chemical Structure Lookup Service for discovering if a structure occurs in any of the public and commercial databases the service has checked.

The site is open to the general public, however "the information is not geared toward the general public, and will probably be most useful for researchers working with, or interested in, chemical information" (from the Web site).
Subjects: Chemical Information

1527. GEODE — USGS GEO-DATA Explorer
http://geode.usgs.gov/
Sponsor(s): Interior Department — U.S. Geological Survey (USGS)
Description: The GEO-DATA Explorer site is also called GEODE. It displays geologic data from programs such as Coastal and Marine Geology, Earth Surface Dynamics, Earthquake Hazards, and Mineral Resources. GEODE can display the data as world map, a series of North American maps, or maps of other world regions. GEODE has an HTML version and a JAVA version for added functionality.
Subjects: Maps and Mapping

1528. Geology Discipline Home Page
http://geology.usgs.gov/
Sponsor(s): Interior Department — U.S. Geological Survey (USGS)
Description: U.S. Geological Survey Geology Discipline covers natural hazards, earth resources, and geologic processes. The site provides a central point for geology-related publications and for links to all related USGS programs. The programs are grouped into three categories: Resources includes Energy and Minerals programs; Hazards includes Earthquakes, Landslides, Geomagnetism, and Volcanoes; and Landscape has Astrogeology, Earth Surface Dynamics, Geologic Mapping, and Coastal and Marine Geology. Each section leads to detailed information about the program and the science involved.

This site is a useful starting point for finding geology information from the USGS. More geology resources are available on the main USGS server, so researchers will want to check both.
Subjects: Geology

1529. Geophysical Fluid Dynamics Laboratory
http://www.gfdl.gov/
Sponsor(s): Commerce Department — National Oceanic and Atmospheric Administration (NOAA) — Office of Oceanic and Atmospheric Research
Description: GFDL is a research laboratory focusing on the physical processes influencing the behavior of the atmosphere and the oceans as complex fluid systems. Its site features sections for Research, Products and Services, and Reference. The Research topics are Climate Dynamics, Atmospheric Physics and Chemistry, Biospheric Processes, Oceans and Climate, Climate Diagnostics, and Weather and Atmospheric Dynamics. The Reference area provides a GFDL bibliography, seminar information, and a link to the GFDL Library.
Subjects: Atmospheric Sciences — Research; Climatology — Research

1530. Global Earth Observation System of Systems
http://www.epa.gov/geoss/
Sponsor(s): Environmental Protection Agency (EPA)
Description: Sixty-one countries have agreed on an implementation plan for a Global Earth Observation System of Systems (GEOSS) to improve understanding of the Earth environment. EPA's Web site explains the projects and its own role in it. Under Where You Live, the site provides information on how GEOSS could benefit each U.S. state.
Subjects: Planetary Science

1531. Goddard Earth Sciences Data and Information Services Center
http://daac.gsfc.nasa.gov/
Sponsor(s): National Aeronautics and Space Administration (NASA) — Goddard Space Flight Center (GSFC)
Description: The Distributed Active Archive Center (DAAC) is the central feature of this Web site for the NASA Goddard Earth Sciences (GES) Data and Information Services Center (DISC). The DAAC is under the heading Data Access. The DAAC includes data from earth observing satellites for experiments such as Solar Radiation and Climate Experiment and the Tropical Rainfall Measuring Mission. Data sets can be ordered or, in some cases, downloaded directly from the site. The site also links to the EOS Data Gateway, which provides search and order of data sets from other NASA data centers, including GES DISC DAAC data.
Subjects: Atmospheric Sciences; Global Change

1532. Harvard-Smithsonian Center for Astrophysics
http://cfa-www.harvard.edu/
Sponsor(s): Harvard-Smithsonian Center for Astrophysics
Description: The Harvard-Smithsonian Center for Astrophysics is a collaboration between the Smithsonian Astrophysical Observatory and the Harvard College Observatory to study the basic physical processes that determine the nature and evolution of the universe. The Web site has information about the center, its research, and its facilities. The Research section includes information from the center's six scientific divisions: Atomic and Molecular Physics; High Energy Astrophysics; Optical and Infrared Astronomy; Radio and Geoastronomy; Solar, Stellar, and Planetary Sciences; and Theoretical Astrophysics. The center's Science Education Division includes teacher resources and information on professional development programs for teachers.
Subjects: Astrophysics — Research

1533. Hawaiian Volcano Observatory
http://wwwhvo.wr.usgs.gov/
Sponsor(s): Interior Department — U.S. Geological Survey (USGS)
Description: The Hawaiian Volcano Observatory (HVO) conducts research on the volcanoes of Hawaii and works with emergency-response officials to protect people and property from earthquakes and volcano-related hazards. The site has information on current activity, history, and hazards for Mauna Loa and Kilauea volcanoes. Other sections include About HVO, Earthquakes, Other Volcanoes, and Volcanic Hazards. The site also features *Volcano Watch,* a weekly newsletter for the general public that is written by scientists at the HVO.

This site will be of great interest to anyone living on or visiting the Big Island of Hawaii, and it provides educational information for anyone else interested in volcanoes and volcanology.
Subjects: Volcanoes
Publications: *Volcano Watch,* I 19.170:

1534. High Energy Astrophysics Science Archive Research Center
http://heasarc.gsfc.nasa.gov/
Sponsor(s): National Aeronautics and Space Administration (NASA) — Goddard Space Flight Center (GSFC)
Description: The purpose of the High Energy Astrophysics Science Archive Research Center (HEASARC) is to support a multimission archive facility in high-energy astrophysics for scientists all over the world. HEASARC has data from 25 observatories covering 30 years of X-ray and gamma-ray astronomy. The data from spaceborne instruments are provided along with a science-user support staff and tools to analyze multiple datasets. The site links to the other NASA data archives as well. The HEASARC Web site also has astronomy information for kids, students, and teachers.

Primarily intended for professional astronomers and astrophysicists, the HEASARC Web site does offer some content for the general public (such as an Astronomy Picture of the Day, and for the educational community).
Subjects: Astrophysics — Research

1535. Jefferson Lab
http://www.jlab.org/
Sponsor(s): Energy Department — Thomas Jefferson National Accelerator Facility
Description: The Thomas Jefferson National Accelerator Facility (Jefferson Lab) is a nuclear physics research laboratory built to probe the nucleus of the atom to learn more about the quark structure of matter. The Jefferson Lab's Web site features information about its scientific program as well resources for K–12 education. The JLab at Work section includes information on the organization, technology transfer, and JLab publications.
Subjects: Nuclear Physics — Research; Particle Accelerators; Research Laboratories

1536. NASA Astrophysics Data System
http://adswww.harvard.edu/
Sponsor(s): Harvard-Smithsonian Center for Astrophysics; National Aeronautics and Space Administration (NASA)
Description: The Astrophysics Data System (ADS) is a NASA-funded project maintaining three sets of bibliographic databases: Astronomy and Astrophysics, Physics, and preprints in Astronomy (ArXiv e-prints). All are available to search or browse at this site. The site also has a current awareness e-mail service called myADS.

This is an important site for anyone searching for information in the astrophysics field.

Subjects: Astrophysics

1537. NASA Goddard Institute for Space Studies

http://www.giss.nasa.gov/

Sponsor(s): National Aeronautics and Space Administration (NASA) — Goddard Space Flight Center (GSFC) — Goddard Institute for Space Studies (GISS)

Description: GISS is a NASA research institute that emphasizes a broad, interdisciplinary study of global environmental change. A key objective of its research is the prediction of atmospheric and climate changes in the twenty-first century. Its Web site includes sections on Research, Data and Images, Publications, Software, Education, and About GISS.

The news and features on the site explain climate change phenomena for the general public, but most of the site is geared toward research scientists and graduate and postdoctoral students.

Subjects: Global Change

1538. National Earthquake Information Center

http://neic.usgs.gov/

Sponsor(s): Interior Department — U.S. Geological Survey (USGS)

Description: The National Earthquake Information Center (NEIC) identifies its mission as "to rapidly determine location and size of all destructive earthquakes worldwide and to immediately disseminate this information to concerned national and international agencies, scientists, and the general public" (from the Web site). NEIC maintains a recorded phone message with current earthquake information, the Earthquake Information Line at 303-273-8516. NEIC also disseminates more information through this Web site. The site features a searchable catalog of earthquakes with options to report data in various formats, including maps.

Subjects: Earthquakes

Publications: *International Registry of Seismograph Stations*
Routine Mining Seismicity in the United States

1539. National Geophysical Data Center

http://www.ngdc.noaa.gov/

Sponsor(s): Commerce Department — National Oceanic and Atmospheric Administration (NOAA) — National Environmental Satellite, Data, and Information Service (NESDIS)

Description: The mission of the National Geophysical Data Center (NGDC) is to prepare and provide geophysical data sets that are in the public domain. Data groups include bathymetry and topography, marine geology and geophysics, natural hazards, geomagnetic data and models, earth observations from space, and space weather. Much of the data is available online; some data sets can be purchased on DVD-ROM. Other sections of the Web site include Education, News, and Products.

The site contains numerous data products of use to research professionals in the relevant disciplines, and a selection of educational products for the general public.

Subjects: Data Products; Environmental Science

1540. National Radio Astronomy Observatory
http://www.nrao.edu/
Sponsor(s): National Science Foundation (NSF) — National Radio Astronomy Observatory (NRAO)
Description: The NRAO designs, builds, and operates state-of-the-art radio telescope facilities for use by the scientific community. The NRAO Web site has extensive information on each of its telescopes. NRAO's sites in Virginia, West Virginia, Arizona, New Mexico, and Chile also have pages on the site. The Image Gallery includes galaxies, stars, comets, black holes, telescopes, and historical photographs of telescopes and astronomers. Much of the site's material is divided into sections for different audiences: the general public, astronomers, and teachers and students. The section for astronomers includes radio astronomy surveys using NRAO telescopes, software resources, and information on making proposals for use of telescope time. The teachers/students section describes educational opportunities available through NRAO.
Subjects: Astronomy; Observatories

1541. New Brunswick Laboratory
http://www.nbl.doe.gov/
Sponsor(s): Energy Department — Security Office
Description: The New Brunswick Laboratory is a federal lab specializing in the science of measuring nuclear materials. This site describes the mission and programs of the lab. Programs include Nuclear Safeguards and Nonproliferation Support, Measurement Development, Measurement Evaluation, Measurement Services, and Certified Reference Materials.
Subjects: Chemistry Research; Standards and Specifications

1542. NIST Physics Laboratory
http://physics.nist.gov/
Sponsor(s): Commerce Department — Technology Administration (TA) — National Institute of Standards and Technology (NIST)
Description: The Physics Laboratory supports industry by providing measurement services and research for electronic, optical, and radiation technologies. The site links to detailed information from each of the research divisions: Electron and Optical Physics, Atomic Physics, Optical Technology, Ionizing Radiation, Time and Frequency, and Quantum Physics. The Product and Services section of the site features the following sections: Physical Reference Data; Measurement and Calibration; Constants, Units, and Uncertainty; Publications; and General Interest (covering time measurement and NIST's atomic clock).
Subjects: Physics — Research; Standards and Specifications
Publications: *From Sundials to Atomic Clocks: Understanding Time and Frequency*, C 13.44:

1543. Ocean Surface Topography from Space
http://topex-www.jpl.nasa.gov/
Sponsor(s): National Aeronautics and Space Administration (NASA) — Jet Propulsion Laboratory (JPL)
Description: This site describes NASA research and missions related to ocean topography, and provides related educational materials. It has information on the TOPEX/Poseidon Mission, a partnership between the United States and France to monitor global ocean topography, discover the links between the oceans and atmosphere, and improve global climate predictions. The follow-on mission, called Jason-1, is also described in detail.
Subjects: Oceans — Research

1544. Princeton Plasma Physics Laboratory
http://www.pppl.gov/
Sponsor(s): Energy Department — Princeton Plasma Physics Laboratory (PPPL)
Description: Princeton Plasma Physics Laboratory (PPPL) is concerned with fusion energy and plasma physics research. PPPL is managed by Princeton University for the Energy Department. The site features information about the lab, its research, and its equipment. Categories include News at PPPL, Fusion Basics, Research Projects, Education Programs, Publications, Colloquia, and Technology Transfer. The Publications section provides access to abstracts and preprints of technical reports.
Subjects: Plasma Physics — Research
Publications: *PPL News*, E 1.103/2:

1545. SOHO: The Solar and Heliospheric Observatory
http://soho.nascom.nasa.gov/
Sponsor(s): National Aeronautics and Space Administration (NASA)
Description: SOHO is a cooperative project of NASA and the European Space Agency to study the Sun and solar wind. Major sections of the SOHO Web site are The Mission, Science, Data, Resources, and Community. The Data section features an image gallery and access to a variety of data archives. The Resources section includes mission news and educational materials. The Publications page, under Community, includes a SOHO bibliography and publications database, SOHO documentation, and links to privately published online journals that cover solar physics research.
Subjects: Solar-Terrestrial Physics; Sun

1546. Stanford Linear Accelerator Center
http://www.slac.stanford.edu/
Sponsor(s): Energy Department — Stanford Linear Accelerator Center (SLAC)
Description: SLAC, operated by Stanford University for the Energy Department, conducts high-energy physics research. This site provides an introduction to SLAC and its programs. Two major sections are dedicated to photon science and to particle astrophysics. SPIRES, linked under News Sources, is the home of the Stanford Public Information REtrieval System databases of high-energy physics literature and research.
Subjects: Particle Accelerators; Physics — Research; Research Laboratories

1547. T-2 Nuclear Information Service
http://t2.lanl.gov/
Sponsor(s): Energy Department — Los Alamos National Laboratory (LANL)
Description: Run by the Nuclear Physics Group of the Theoretical Division of Los Alamos National Lab, this site covers nuclear modeling, nuclear data, cross sections, nuclear masses, nuclear astrophysics, radioactivity, radiation shielding, data for medical radiotherapy, data for high-energy accelerator applications, and data and codes for fission and fusion systems. Available categories include Tour (educational material, orientation to the site), Data (sets of nuclear data), Codes (for preparing nuclear data tables for various applications), and Publications.
   The very technical nature of this data means that the site will primarily be of interest to nuclear physicists.
Subjects: Nuclear Physics

1548. United States Group on Earth Observations
http://usgeo.gov/
Sponsor(s): United States Group on Earth Observations
Description: The United States Group on Earth Observations (USGEO) is an interagency group that participates in the international planning of the Global Earth Observation System of Systems (GEOSS). USGEO was established in March 2005 as a standing subcommittee of the National Science and Technology Council Committee on Environment and Natural Resources. The Web site provides documents and background information on USGEO and the project.
Subjects: Planetary Science

1549. United States Naval Observatory
http://www.usno.navy.mil/
Sponsor(s): Navy — Naval Observatory (USNO)
Description: The United States Naval Observatory is responsible for measuring the positions and motions of the Earth, Sun, Moon, planets, stars, and other celestial objects; providing astronomical data; determining precise time; measuring the Earth's rotation; and maintaining the Master Clock for the United States. The Web site provides access to USNO departments: Astronomical Applications, Earth Orientation, Time Service, Library, and Flagstaff Station. It also offers such popular links as Sky This Week, Sun Rise/Set, and the official time.
This site is useful for information on the official current time and general information on the Naval Observatory and its programs.
Subjects: Astronomy; Observatories

1550. US Climate Change Science Program
http://www.climatescience.gov/
Sponsor(s): White House
Description: The Climate Change Science Program (CCSP) is a successor to the U.S. Global Change Research Program (USGCRP). The current program is an interagency research effort overseen by four White House agencies: the Office of Science and Technology Policy, the Council on Environmental Quality, the National Economic Council, and the Office of Management and Budget. The Web site includes information by and about the program. CCSP publications are posted throughout the site.
Subjects: Climatology — Research; Global Change
Publications: *Our Changing Planet: The U.S. Climate Change Science Program for Fiscal Years . . .*, PREX 23.14/2:
Strategic Plan for the U.S. Climate Change Science Program, PREX 23.2:
Temperature Trends in the Lower Atmosphere, PREX 23.14:

1551. Volcano Hazards Program
http://volcanoes.usgs.gov/
Sponsor(s): Interior Department — U.S. Geological Survey (USGS)
Description: This central page from the USGS Volcano Hazards Program includes sections on Volcano Updates, Volcano Hazards, Reducing Volcanic Risk, and the U.S. Volcano Disaster Assistance Program for foreign countries. The Web site's Resources section has USGS fact sheets and reports, Volcano FAQs, Volcano Videos, and an Educator's page.
For checking either current activity or historical eruptions, this is a great starting point for finding information on volcanoes.
Subjects: Volcanoes

1552. William R. Wiley Environmental Molecular Sciences Laboratory
http://www.emsl.pnl.gov/
Sponsor(s): Energy Department — Environmental Molecular Sciences Laboratory (EMSL)
Description: The EMSL national research lab conducts fundamental research in molecular and computational sciences, particularly in relation to energy technologies. Its Web site includes sections on Research, Capabilities, People, User Access, and Publications. The Research, Capabilities, and People sections highlight the equipment, facilities, and expertise that this lab has to offer. The Publications section cites science journal articles in which all or part of the research was carried out using EMSL resources. The site also has a virtual tour of the lab facilities.
Subjects: Research Laboratories; Scientific Research

1553. World Data Center System
http://www.ngdc.noaa.gov/wdc/
Sponsor(s): Commerce Department — National Oceanic and Atmospheric Administration (NOAA) — National Environmental Satellite, Data, and Information Service (NESDIS)
Description: According to the Web site, the World Data Center System — sponsored by the nongovernmental International Council for Science — works to guarantee access to solar, geophysical, and related environmental data. There are over 50 World Data Centers (WDCs) around the globe; this NOAA site represents U.S. participation in the project. The Web site provides background information, a directory of WDCs, and information on WDC data sets.
Subjects: Data Storage; Scientific Research — International

Science Agencies and Policy

1554. Federal R&D Project Summaries
http://www.osti.gov/fedrnd/
Sponsor(s): Energy Department — Scientific and Technical Information Office
Description: Federal R&D Project Summaries is a portal to research summary and awards data maintained in separate databases by the Energy Department, the National Institutes of Health, the National Science Foundation, the Environmental Protection Agency, the Small Business Administration, and the Agriculture Department. Users can conduct keyword searches across all databases simultaneously or select individual databases to search.
Subjects: Research and Development; Databases

1555. National Aeronautics and Space Administration (NASA)
http://www.nasa.gov/home/
Sponsor(s): National Aeronautics and Space Administration (NASA)
Description: The central NASA Web site provides information about the agency and links to the numerous other Web sites and resources NASA maintains. Major categories on the front page include About NASA, Latest News (including an RSS newsfeed), Multimedia (images, video, and NASA TV), Missions, MyNASA (a customizable page), and Work for NASA. Links to feature stories on NASA projects are divided into sections entitled Life on Earth, Humans in Space, and Exploring the Universe. The site also has pointers to information for target audiences: kids, students, educators, media, and researchers. The Researchers section includes links to technical reports, data, and research funding opportunities. The About NASA section has information on careers with NASA, business opportunities with the agency, and agency budget information. A drop-down menu at the bottom

of the page provides links to the Web sites for NASA's mission directorates, headquarters, and field centers. Text-only and non-Flash versions of this site are available. A link at the top of the page leads to information on NASA Web sites available in Spanish.

NASA has so many Web sites and resources that it may not be easy to discover them all using this site. Many other NASA Web sites are described in this book, primarily in the Science and the Engineering chapters.
Subjects: Space
Publications: *A Journey to Inspire, Innovate, and Discover: Report of the President's Commission on Implementation of United States Space Exploration Policy,* PR 43.8:
NASA Strategic Plan, NAS 1.15:

1556. National Science Advisory Board for Biosecurity
http://www.biosecurityboard.gov/
Sponsor(s): National Science Advisory Board for Biosecurity (NSABB)
Description: The NSABB is an interagency board chartered with minimizing the risk of misuse of life sciences research technologies, particularly as a threat to public health and national security. The Web site has the NSABB charter, membership list, and meeting schedule and minutes.
Subjects: Scientific Research — Policy; Life Sciences — Policy

1557. National Science and Technology Council
http://www.ostp.gov/nstc/html/nstc.html
Sponsor(s): White House — National Science and Technology Council (NSTC)
Description: This page provides brief information on the National Science and Technology Council (NSTC) and links to council documents. Formed in 1993, the council focuses on coordination of science, space, and technology research and development.
Subjects: Science and Technology Policy
Publications: *Science for the 21st Century,* PREX 23.2:

1558. National Science Board
http://www.nsf.gov/nsb/
Sponsor(s): National Science Foundation (NSF) — National Science Board (NSB)
Description: The National Science Board (NSB) is the governing board for the National Science Foundation and serves as national science policy adviser to the president and Congress. The Web site has information on NSB membership and meetings, and the honorary science awards it bestows. The documents section has NSB reports and congressional testimony.
Subjects: Science — Policy
Publications: *Long-Lived Digital Data Collections: Enabling Research and Education in the 21st Century*

1559. National Science Foundation
http://www.nsf.gov/
Sponsor(s): National Science Foundation (NSF)
Description: As one of the government's major scientific agencies, the NSF promotes science and engineering research and education. NSF, an independent federal agency, is — according to their Web site — the funding source for approximately 20 percent of all federally supported basic research conducted by America's colleges and universities. The Web site has a section customized for the research and education community, with information on funding and links to each NSF program area. The FastLane section of the site is a portal for online interaction

with NSF, such as submitting grant proposals or conducting peer review. A Science and Engineering Statistics section includes a wealth of publications and data from NSF, particularly on science and engineering education, funding, and the workforce. A Discoveries section profiles discoveries and innovations that began with NSF support.

For all those involved with NSF grants or interested in applying for one, this is an essential site to visit. It provides very useful information on grants in the sciences. The NSF provides useful statistics on science and engineering education.

Subjects: Science Education; Scientific Research — Grants

Publications: *Characteristics of Doctoral Scientists and Engineers in the United States*, NS 1.22:

Graduate Students and Postdoctorates in Science and Engineering, NS 1.22/11:

Grant Policy Manual, NS 1.20:G76/2/

Guide to Programs, NS 1.47:

InfoBrief, NS 1.62:

National Patterns of R&D Resources, NS 1.22/2:

NSF Engineering Online News, NS 1.22/10:

Science and Engineering Doctorate Awards, NS 1.44:

Science and Engineering Indicators, NS 1.28/2:

Science and Engineering State Profiles, NS 1.22/12:

Science and Technology Pocket Data Book, NS 1.2:

Science Engineering Research Facilities at Universities and Colleges, NS 1.53:

Women, Minorities, and Persons with Disabilities in Science and Engineering, NS 1.49:

1560. Office of Science and Technology Policy
http://www.ostp.gov/
Sponsor(s): White House — Office of Science and Technology Policy (OSTP)
Description: Established in 1976, the Office of Science and Technology Policy (OSTP) serves as a source of scientific and technological analysis and judgment for the president with respect to major policies, plans, and programs of the federal government. The Web site offers general information on the organization and activities of OSTP. Along with current news, major sections of the site include Science and Technology Policy and Budget and Government Science and Technology.
Subjects: Science and Technology Policy

1561. President's National Medal of Science
http://www.nsf.gov/nsb/awards/nms/medal.htm
Sponsor(s): National Science Foundation (NSF)
Description: The National Medal of Science was established by Congress in 1959 as a Presidential Award to be given to individuals "deserving of special recognition by reason of their outstanding contributions to knowledge in the physical, biological, mathematical, or engineering sciences" (from the Web site). In 1980, Congress expanded this recognition to include the social and behavioral sciences. This site features information on nomination procedures, former medalists, and members of the President's Committee.
Subjects: Science — Awards and Honors

1562. RaDiUS®
https://radius.rand.org/radius/
Sponsor(s): National Science Foundation (NSF); RAND Corporation
Description: RaDiUS is a database of information on the research and development (R&D) activities funded by the federal government. RaDiUS was developed by RAND in cooperation with the National Science Foundation (NSF), and it draws

on over 12 federal data sources. The site is free, but registration is required. The Getting Started section provides instructions for applying for a user account and password. The User Handbook and FAQ section provide vital tips for accessing and searching the database.
Subjects: Research and Development

1563. The National Academies
http://www.nas.edu/
Sponsor(s): National Academies
Description: Chartered by Congress to advise the federal government on matters of science, technology, and medicine, the National Academies are private, nonprofit societies of distinguished scholars. The National Academy of Sciences, along with the National Academy of Engineering and the Institute of Medicine, are supervised by the National Research Council. All groups provide scientific advice to Congress on a variety of topics. The Web site features sections on each organization, their staff and member directories, and a database of current projects. The linked National Academies Press (NAP) Web site includes an extensive catalog of reports; some reports can be downloaded for free in PDF format.
   This site should be of broad interest to the scientific and science policy community.
Subjects: Science and Technology Policy
Publications: *The National Academies In Focus*

1564. U.S. Arctic Research Commission
http://www.arctic.gov/
Sponsor(s): United States Arctic Research Commission
Description: The Arctic Research Commission was established to set the national goals and priorities for the federal basic and applied scientific research plan for the Arctic. This Web site has information on the commission and its reports, including its annual report on research goals.
Subjects: Scientific Research — Policy

1565. U.S. Geological Survey
http://www.usgs.gov/
Sponsor(s): Interior Department — U.S. Geological Survey (USGS)
Description: As one of the government's primary scientific agencies, the USGS offers a broad range of scientific material on its Web site. This central USGS site site features major sections dedicated to information on the agency's focus: biology, geography, geology, geospatial information, and water. USGS provides scientific and safety information concerning natural hazards, such as landslides, earthquakes, and volcanoes. USGS also studies natural resources, such as minerals. Science in Your State links to USGS information — such as flood or drought watches — for each state, the District of Columbia, Puerto Rico, and the U.S. Virgin Islands. The Maps, Products, and Publications section centralizes access to the many USGS Web pages that provide catalogs or collections of USGS information products. A consolidated list of USGS RSS newsfeeds includes earthquake news, avian influenza updates, volcano watches, and more. The Web site also has a substantial science-related Education section.
   The USGS home page provides multiple access points to its rich collection of scientific resources and publications.
Subjects: Geography; Geology; Natural Resources; Scientific Research
Publications: *Contaminant Hazard Reviews*, I 19.167:
Geographic Names Information System, I 19.16/2:
National Elevation Dataset, I 19.127:
National Hydrography Dataset, I 19.127:

National Landcover Data Set, I 19.168:
USGS Bulletins, I 19.3:
USGS Circulars, I 19.4/2:
USGS Digital Spectral Library, I 19.76:
USGS Yearbooks, I 19.1:

Scientific and Technical Information

1566. DOE Information Bridge
http://www.osti.gov/bridge/
Sponsor(s): Energy Department — Scientific and Technical Information Office
Description: The DOE Information Bridge provides free access to full-text DOE research reports in physics, chemistry, materials, biology, environmental sciences, energy technologies, engineering, computer and information science, renewable energy, and other topics. Reports are available in PDF format. Coverage is from 1994 forward. The site has a basic word search option and a fielded search option for more precise searching. Users can register to receive news of new documents in a selected topic area.
Subjects: Scientific and Technical Information; Databases
Publications: *DOE Information Bridge*, E 1.137:

1567. E-print Network
http://www.osti.gov/eprints/
Sponsor(s): Energy Department — Scientific and Technical Information Office
Description: The full, formal title of this site is "E-print Network: Research Communications for Scientists and Engineers." According to the Web site, e-prints include "pre-publication drafts of journal articles (preprints), scholarly papers, technical communications, or similar documents relaying research results among peer groups." Disciplines covered by the site include physics, materials science, chemistry, mathematics, biology, computer science, geosciences, engineering, environmental sciences, fission, fusion, and other areas related to the Energy Department's research interests. They are made available by a variety of sources, including academic institutions, government research laboratories, scientific societies, and individual scientists. The e-prints can be searched by word and topic or browsed by discipline. The site also has an e-mail alert service for notification of new e-prints by topic.
Subjects: Preprints; Scientific and Technical Information

1568. Gov.Research_Center
http://grc.ntis.gov/
Sponsor(s): National Information Services Corporation (NISC); Commerce Department — Technology Administration (TA) — National Technical Information Service (NTIS)
Description: The Gov.Research_Center is a partnership between NTIS and the National Information Services Corporation that provides a single access point to a number of government databases. This is not a free service. Each individual database has its own pricing and subscription plan. Currently available databases include AGRICOLA, AgroBase, Energy Science and Technology, Nuclear Science Abstracts, Federal Research in Progress, NTIS, NIOSHTIC, and the Registry of Toxic Effects of Chemical Substances (RTECS).
Subjects: Scientific and Technical Information; Databases

1569. NASA Scientific and Technical Information (STI)
http://www.sti.nasa.gov/
Sponsor(s): National Aeronautics and Space Administration (NASA)
Description: NASA defines STI as basic and applied research results from the work of scientists, engineers, and others. The NASA Scientific and Technical Information Program disseminates STI from NASA research and other sources to the public. This site offers databases, documents, and new reports announcements. The major asset on the site is the NASA Technical Reports Server (NTRS), which covers NASA materials such as reports, journal articles, conference and meeting papers, and technical videos. As of 2006, NTRS also includes records from the National Advisory Committee for Aeronautics (NACA) database; NACA, NASA's predecessor, was operational from 1917 to 1958. In addition, NTRS includes the NASA Image eXchange (NIX) collection and material from outside organizations, such as Great Britain's Aeronautical Research Council.

Other free STI resources on the site include NASA's *Spinoff* magazine and a database of abstracts for every successfully commercialized NASA technology published in *Spinoff*. The site also offers two current awareness services announcing newly released and newly acquired STI: the *Selected Current Aerospace Notices* (SCAN) service and *Scientific and Technical Aerospace Reports* (STAR). An RSS feed is available for tracking new STI from NASA.

The NTRS is a major bibliographic database of broad interest to the engineering and scientific communities. NTRS and the other services offered by NASA's STI program make this site a key resource for scientific and technical literature.
Subjects: Scientific and Technical Information; Databases
Publications: *NASA Technical Reports Server*
Scientific and Technical Aerospace Reports, NAS 1.9/4:
Spinoff, NAS 1.1/4:

1570. National Science Digital Library
http://nsdl.org/
Sponsor(s): National Science Foundation (NSF)
Description: The National Science Digital Library (NSDL) is a National Science Foundation program. The NSDL goal is to provide "a digital library of exemplary resource collections and services, organized in support of science education at all levels" (from the Web site). NSDL collections focus on science portal sites that provide material for educators or students. The collections can be searched by word and type (text, video, etc.). The site also has an alphabetical list of the collections. In addition to the collections, the NSDL site includes project information and information on NSDL-related grants.
Subjects: Science Education

1571. NIST Data Gateway
http://srdata.nist.gov/gateway/
Sponsor(s): Commerce Department — Technology Administration (TA) — National Institute of Standards and Technology (NIST)
Description: The NIST Data Gateway links to over 70 free, public databases from the National Institute of Standards and Technology. As stated on the site, "these data cover a broad range of substances and properties from many different scientific disciplines." Specific resources include the Atomic Spectra Database (ASD), Engineering Statistics Handbook, Fundamental Physical Constants, HIV Structural Reference Database (HIVSDB), and the NIST Chemistry WebBook. The site also links to NIST databases that are available for purchase.
Subjects: Engineering Research; Scientific and Technical Information; Databases

1572. Office of Energy, Science, and Technical Information
http://www.osti.gov/

Sponsor(s): Energy Department — Scientific and Technical Information Office
Description: The site is the home page for the Energy Department's Office of Scientific and Technical Information (OSTI), and has information on OSTI's mission and leadership. It also serves as a gateway to databases and other information resources for scientific and technical topics relevant to the Energy Department.

To direct researchers to this resource, libraries and schools may wish to reproduce any of the brochures in the "OSTI Flyers" section under Communications.
Subjects: Preprints; Scientific and Technical Information; Databases
Publications: *DOE Information Bridge*, E 1.137:
Energy Citations Database, E 1.137/4:
Federal R&D Project Summaries, E 1.142:
GrayLit Network, E 1.137/3:

1573. Science Conferences
http://www.osti.gov/scienceconferences/

Sponsor(s): Energy Department — Scientific and Technical Information Office
Description: This science conference portal collects information on programs, papers, and proceedings from 16 organizations and Web sources. The sources can be searched all at once or selectively. The About section explains what each source offers.
Subjects: Scientific and Technical Information

1574. Science Inventory
http://cfpub.epa.gov/si/

Sponsor(s): Environmental Protection Agency (EPA)
Description: The EPA's Science Inventory site is a database of EPA scientific and technical projects. Database entries include project descriptions, products produced, types of peer review, links to related work, and contacts for additional information. The database can be searched by word. Researchers can also browse ongoing or recently completed research activities by EPA's geographic regions.
Subjects: Scientific Research; Databases

1575. Science Tracer Bullets Online
http://www.loc.gov/rr/scitech/tracer-bullets/tbs.html

Sponsor(s): Library of Congress
Description: The Library of Congress Science Tracer Bullets are research guides for finding books, journal articles, Internet resources, and other literature on specific science and technology topics. The guides cover such topics as careers in science, earthquakes, introductory physics, global warming and climate change, and science fair projects.

The Tracer Bullets range from one year to over ten years old. Only the newest include Internet resources. While much of the research guidance is still worthwhile, researchers should remember that more current resources are probably available. Link to the home page of Science Reference Services for additional science research guides.
Subjects: Science — Research
Publications: *LC Science Tracer Bullet Series*, LC 33.10:

1576. science.gov

http://www.science.gov/

Sponsor(s): Energy Department — Scientific and Technical Information Office
Description: Science.gov represents a collaborative effort by a group of government agencies to select and share the best of their online science information. Science.gov accesses at least 30 databases and more than 1,700 science Web sites. The Energy Department's Office of Scientific and Technical Information (OSTI), listed here as the sponsor, hosts the site. The science resources can be browsed by topic or searched by word. The search feature allows users to select a combination of government science Web sites and databases to search. Users can also set up e-mail alerts based on search topics. Indexed resources in science.gov include AGRICOLA, National Biological Information Infrastructure, Energy Citations Database, PubMed, ERIC, and National Science Foundation publications.

Science.gov also has special collections of links on topics such as science conferences and internships and fellowships.

Science.gov is an example of the current effort to build agency-independent access to government information through subject-oriented portals. It allows for easy discovery of science and technical information distributed through government Web sites.

Subjects: Scientific and Technical Information; Finding Aids

1577. Scientific and Technical Information Network (STINET)

http://stinet.dtic.mil/

Sponsor(s): Defense Department — Defense Technical Information Center (DTIC)
Description: The scope of the STINET database includes defense research topics, the basic sciences, and specific documents such as conference papers and patent applications. There are two versions of STINET: a public one and a secure, limited-access version. Public STINET is free of charge. It provides access to citations to unclassified unlimited documents entered into DTIC's Technical Reports Collection since December 1974 and to online copies of some of those documents. It also links to related defense resources such as the Air University Library's Index to Military Periodicals. Private STINET is available only to registered DTIC users. It provides access to the same unclassified information contained in Public STINET plus limited special collections and resources, commercial databases, the full text of some unclassified technical reports, and other features.

STINET is an important resource because of its unique scope and inclusion of gray literature. Non-military users should be aware that some of the publications may have access restrictions on them and thus be difficult to obtain.

Subjects: Scientific and Technical Information; Databases

1578. SciTechResources.gov

http://www.scitechresources.gov/

Sponsor(s): Commerce Department — Technology Administration (TA) — National Technical Information Service (NTIS)
Description: For SciTechResources.gov, NTIS reviews government scientific and technical Web sites and selects sites with information deemed relevant to its audience. The audience is identified as scientists, engineers, technologists, and science-aware citizens. The main feature of the site is a searchable catalog of the selected Web sites. Each record has a brief description of the Web site and link to the source. A smaller Science for Citizens database has only those sites selected by database editors as being of general interest. Featured lists extracted from the full database include lists of portals, popular general interest sites, and sources of articles and R&D publications.

Researchers may also wish to check the Science.gov site, to which SciTechResources.gov is a contributor.
Subjects: Scientific and Technical Information; Finding Aids

Space

1579. Aeronautics Research Mission Directorate (ARMD)
http://www.aero-space.nasa.gov/
Sponsor(s): National Aeronautics and Space Administration (NASA) — Aeronautics Research Mission Directorate
Description: ARMD is concerned with cutting-edge aeronautics research. The Programs section of the ARMD Web sites links to NASA Research Announcement information in four areas: Fundamental Aeronautics Program, Airspace Systems Program, Aviation Safety Program, and Aeronautics Test Program. The Reference Materials section has ARMD and related NASA publications. The Education section has resources on aeronautics for all levels of students.
Subjects: Aerospace Engineering — Research

1580. Ames Research Center
http://www.nasa.gov/centers/ames/home/
Sponsor(s): National Aeronautics and Space Administration (NASA) — Ames Research Center (ARC)
Description: NASA's Ames Research Center in California specializes in researching and developing new technologies in such fields as information technology, nanotechnology, fundamental space biology, biotechnology, aerospace and thermal protection systems, and human factors research. The Research section of the site provides information on current projects. The Research section also links to pages on Ames Technology Partnership Division and NASA Research Park, which work on technology development collaboration among academic, industry, and government agencies. A Spanish-language version of the Web site is available.
Subjects: Space Sciences — Research; Space Technology — Research

1581. Asteroid and Comet Impact Hazard
http://impact.arc.nasa.gov/
Sponsor(s): National Aeronautics and Space Administration (NASA) — Ames Research Center (ARC)
Description: This NASA Ames site has news, explanations, and frequently asked questions about possible Earth collision with asteroids and comets (often called Near Earth Objects, or NEOs). The site includes fact sheets, congressional documents, and NASA studies related to impact hazards. The NEO Catalog section has a listing of all known Earth-crossing asteroids and predicted close approaches to the Earth in the near future.

With popular media exploring the concept of the earth being struck by a comet or asteroid, this site should prove interesting to the general public as well as scientists taking a more scholarly interest in the phenomena.
Subjects: Planets

1582. Astrogeology Resource Program
http://astrogeology.usgs.gov/
Sponsor(s): Interior Department — U.S. Geological Survey (USGS)
Description: The USGS Astrogeology Resource Program works closely with NASA and specializes in planetary geologic processes, remote sensing and monitoring, and the mapping of extraterrestrial bodies. The Web site highlights their work on

exploratory missions (such as the Cassini-Huygens Mission to Saturn and Titan, also decribed in this section), and it provides detailed information on each of the program's research areas. The Data and Information section of the site has databases, images, and maps. Databases include the Gazetteer of Planetary Nomenclature, Historical Lunar Data Archive, and Global Land Ice Measurements from Space.
Subjects: Geology — Research; Planetary Science; Remote Sensing
Publications: *Gazetteer of Planetary Nomenclature*, I 19.3:

1583. Astronomy Resources at STScI
http://www.stsci.edu/resources/
Sponsor(s): Space Telescope Science Institute
Description: The Space Telescope Science Institute (STScI) is one of the astronomy centers operated by the Association of Universities for Research in Astronomy, Inc. (AURA) for NASA. It is responsible for the scientific operation of the Hubble Space Telescope and will also be supporting the James Webb Space Telescope (JWST) for NASA; each one is described in detail at this site. Other main categories at this Web site include The Institute, Science Initiatives, Catalogs and Surveys, Publications, Software, Hardware, Picture Gallery, and Educational Activities.
Subjects: Astronomy; Telescopes

1584. Cassini-Huygens Mission to Saturn and Titan
http://saturn.jpl.nasa.gov/home/
Sponsor(s): National Aeronautics and Space Administration (NASA) — Jet Propulsion Laboratory (JPL)
Description: This site provides information and images from the mission of the Cassini orbiter, now in Saturn's orbit, and the Huygens probe to the moon Titan. The site provides detail on the spacecraft, instrumentation, and science involved. It also discusses Saturn and its moons. Special sections are targeted to the news media, planetariums, educators, and kids.
Subjects: Spacecraft; Saturn

1585. CGRO Science Support Center
http://cossc.gsfc.nasa.gov/docs/cgro/
Sponsor(s): National Aeronautics and Space Administration (NASA) — Goddard Space Flight Center (GSFC)
Description: The Compton Gamma Ray Observatory (CGRO), in service from 1991–2000, was the second of NASA's four Great Observatories. The Web site has sections for the CGRO data archive, data analysis, and the CGRO instruments. It also has an education section detailing CGRO discoveries.
Subjects: Astronomy; Telescopes

1586. Columbia Accident Investigation Board
http://caib.nasa.gov/
Alternate URL(s): http://govinfo.library.unt.edu/caib/
Sponsor(s): Columbia Accident Investigation Board
Description: The Columbia Accident Investigation Board (CAIB) was established to determine actual or probable causes of the failure of NASA's Columbia space shuttle on February 1, 2003. The CAIB Web site includes the final report, information on board members, the board charter, press releases, transcripts of press briefings, and minutes of any public meetings.

   The CAIB Web site is also archived at the University of North Texas Libraries' CyberCemetery, at the alternate URL listed above.

Subjects: Space Shuttle
Publications: *Columbia Accident Investigation Board Final Report*, NAS 1.2:C 72/ V.1-6

1587. Cosmicopia
http://helios.gsfc.nasa.gov/
Sponsor(s): National Aeronautics and Space Administration (NASA) — Goddard Space Flight Center (GSFC)
Description: NASA's Cosmicopia Web site is designed to increase people's interest in cosmic and heliospheric science. (It was formerly known as the Cosmic and Heliospheric Learning Center.) The information on the site is aimed at the general public or at about a high school level of science understanding. Cosmicopia features sections for Astrophysics Basics, Cosmic Rays, The Sun, and Space Weather.
Subjects: Science Education; Sun

1588. Crustal Dynamics Data Information System (CDDIS)
http://cddis.gsfc.nasa.gov/
Sponsor(s): National Aeronautics and Space Administration (NASA) — Goddard Space Flight Center (GSFC)
Description: CDDIS supports data archiving and distribution activities for the space geodesy and geodynamics community. This site offers access to CDDIS datasets, documents, programs, and reports.
  This site is primarily of interest to researchers in this field.
Subjects: Geodesy

1589. Eclipse Home Page
http://sunearth.gsfc.nasa.gov/eclipse/eclipse.html
Sponsor(s): National Aeronautics and Space Administration (NASA) — Goddard Space Flight Center (GSFC)
Description: This site provides details on total and partial solar and lunar eclipses around the world. It includes eclipse maps, listings, path coordinates, explanations, and predication information. The site also has information on lunar eclipses and planetary transits across the sun.
  The clear organization of this site makes it an excellent reference source on the topic.
Subjects: Eclipses; Sun

1590. Galileo Legacy Site
http://galileo.jpl.nasa.gov/
Sponsor(s): National Aeronautics and Space Administration (NASA) — Jet Propulsion Laboratory (JPL)
Description: NASA's Galileo mission ended when the spacecraft impacted Jupiter on September 2003 as planned. The Galileo site provides an extensive collection of information on the Galileo spacecraft and the planet Jupiter. The site includes images, mission details, and educational resources.
Subjects: Jupiter; Spacecraft

1591. Glenn Research Center
http://www.nasa.gov/centers/glenn/home/
Sponsor(s): National Aeronautics and Space Administration (NASA) — Glenn Research Center
Description: Formerly known as the Lewis Research Center, the Glenn Research Center was renamed after John H. Glenn, former astronaut and U.S. senator.

Researching aeronautics and aeropropulsion technologies is the center's main focus. All technology projects are profiled in sections titled Aeronautics, Exploration Systems, Space Operations, and Earth and Space Science. Other sections profile Glenn test facilities and its research, including technical reports.
Subjects: Aerospace Engineering — Research; Space Technology — Research

1592. Goddard Space Flight Center
http://www.nasa.gov/centers/goddard/home/
Sponsor(s): National Aeronautics and Space Administration (NASA) — Goddard Space Flight Center (GSFC)
Description: Goddard's overall mission deals with space science, technology, and earth science, with a focus on observations from space. This NASA field center is a major U.S. laboratory for developing and operating unmanned scientific spacecraft. The center manages many of NASA's earth observation, astronomy, and space physics missions, and its Web site has information on each of its space missions. Major topical sections are entitled Earth and Sun, Solar System, and Universe. The site also links to detailed information on educational and University programs sponsored by NASA and Goddard. The GSFC Library page, in the About section, provides an online catalog, links to sources for standards and technical reports, and the Goddard Projects Directory.
Subjects: Space Sciences; Space Technology

1593. GRIN — Great Images in NASA
http://grin.hq.nasa.gov/
Sponsor(s): National Aeronautics and Space Administration (NASA) — History Office
Description: GRIN is a collection of over one thousand photographs of significant historical interest from both NASA and its predecessor, the National Advisory Committee for Aeronautics (NACA). The images, all in JPEG format, can be searched by topic, keyword, or NASA center. While most of the images are not protected by copyright, the Copyright Information section should be reviewed for information on use restrictions.

The emphasis of this selective collection is on NASA history. Researchers looking for a broader collection of images may also wish to check the NASA Image eXchange (NIX) and NASA Multimedia Gallery Web sites. Both are linked from the GRIN home page.
Subjects: Aerospace Engineering — History; Photography; Space — History

1594. Hubble Space Telescope Project
http://hubble.nasa.gov/
Sponsor(s): National Aeronautics and Space Administration (NASA)
Description: The Hubble Space Telescope has been orbiting the Earth since its launch in 1990. This Web site provides extensive project background information and a gallery of images from Hubble. Major sections of the site cover Hubble operations, technology, news, and servicing mission information.
Subjects: Astronomy; Telescopes

1595. International Space Station
http://www.nasa.gov/mission_pages/station/main/
Sponsor(s): National Aeronautics and Space Administration (NASA)
Description: This central Web site for NASA's International Space Station (ISS) has news, mission and crew profiles, images, interactive features, and science information. Separate sections focus on station resupply, station science, and

station structure. The main page links to information on sighting the International Space Station in the night sky.
Subjects: Space Stations

1596. James Webb Space Telescope
http://www.jwst.nasa.gov/
Sponsor(s): National Aeronautics and Space Administration (NASA) — Goddard Space Flight Center (GSFC)
Description: The James Webb Space Telescope (JWST) is the planned successor to the Hubble Space Telescope. This Web site gives an overview of the project, news, science goals, and mission hardware. The section specifically for scientists has information for astronomers who would like to learn more about using JWST for their research programs. Other sections are tailored to the general public and to the media.
Subjects: Astronomy; Telescopes — Research

1597. Jet Propulsion Laboratory
http://www.jpl.nasa.gov/
Sponsor(s): National Aeronautics and Space Administration (NASA) — Jet Propulsion Laboratory (JPL)
Description: JPL is the lead U.S. center for robotic exploration of the solar system. Major subject links on the JPL Web site include Earth, Solar System, Stars and Galaxies, and Technology. The Missions page profiles specific robotic spacecraft, such as Voyager and the Mars Global Surveyor, and the accomplishments of their missions. The Images and Multimedia sections include planetary images and online videos, including slide shows and podcasts related to the Mars Rover. The News section includes press releases, mission fact sheets, and annual reports. The site also has sections on JPL science, research, and education programs.
Subjects: Planets; Space Technology

1598. Johnson Space Center
http://www.nasa.gov/centers/johnson/home/
Sponsor(s): National Aeronautics and Space Administration (NASA) — Johnson Space Center (JSC)
Description: Programs at NASA's Johnson Space Center (JSC) in Texas focus on human spaceflight, the International Space Station (ISS), the Mission Control Center, and astronaut training. Major topical sections of the Web site are Space Station, Space Shuttle, Exploration, and Astronauts. The Astronauts section has astronaut biographies and information on their selection and training. The News section includes status reports for the ISS and Space Shuttle. The Education section provides news and information about JSC education programs and about careers at JSC.

Most of the material on this site is geared toward the public, the press, and business users. It is an excellent site for students and teachers to find material for education related to humans in space, manned space flights, and basic astronomy. It also answers popular questions about how to become an astronaut.
Subjects: Astronauts; Human Space Exploration; Spacecraft
Publications: *Astronaut Fact Book*, NAS 1.74:

1599. Kennedy Space Center

http://www.nasa.gov/centers/kennedy/home/
Sponsor(s): National Aeronautics and Space Administration (NASA) — Kennedy Space Center (KSC)
Description: NASA's Kennedy Space Center in Florida has primary responsibility for ground turnaround, support, and launch of the space shuttle and its payloads, including elements for the International Space Station (ISS). Major sections of the KSC Web site include Shuttle Operations, Launching Rockets, and Station Payloads. The site has launch schedules (under Missions) and information for visitors (under About Kennedy). Other sections include News, Multimedia, and Education.
Subjects: Space Shuttle; Space Stations; Rockets

1600. Mars Exploration

http://mars.jpl.nasa.gov/
Sponsor(s): National Aeronautics and Space Administration (NASA) — Jet Propulsion Laboratory (JPL)
Description: NASA's Mars Exploration Program is the central topic of this Web site, which has special sections for kids, students, educators, and the press. The site has information and images for Mars missions such as the Mars Global Surveyor, Mars Exploration Rover, and Mars Express. The section Mars: Extreme Planet presents information on extreme conditions there and has a digital Martian tour. Another feature focuses on the popular culture interest in Mars.

   Written for the student or non-technical adult, this site offers a substantial collection of current information and imagery related to Mars, as well as fun things to do for kids.
Subjects: Mars

1601. Marshall Space Flight Center

http://www.nasa.gov/centers/marshall/home/
Sponsor(s): National Aeronautics and Space Administration (NASA) — Marshall Space Flight Center (MSFC)
Description: The Marshall Space Flight Center in Alabama develops space transportation and propulsion systems and oversees science and hardware development for the International Space Station. Its Web site provides a broad range of technical and background information on the many projects, scientific disciplines, and specific space flight missions with which the center is involved. Major topical sections include Missions, Science and Technology, Space Shuttle Propulsion, Space Systems, Space Transportation, and Safety and Mission Assurance.
Subjects: Microgravity; Propulsion Technology; Space Technology

1602. NASA Dryden Flight Research Center

http://www.dfrc.nasa.gov/
Sponsor(s): National Aeronautics and Space Administration (NASA) — Dryden Flight Research Center (DFRC)
Description: Dryden Flight Research Center, located on Edwards Air Force Base in California, is responsible for flight research and flight testing. Web site sections include About Dryden, Capabilities and Facilities, Research, Education, History, and Doing Business. The Multimedia section has an archive of digitized photos, movies, and drawings of many of the unique research aircraft flown at the facility from the 1940s to the present. The Web site also has a Spanish-language section with basic information about Dryden.
Subjects: Aerospace Engineering — Research; Aircraft — Research

1603. NASA Exploration Systems Mission Directorate
http://exploration.nasa.gov/
Sponsor(s): National Aeronautics and Space Administration (NASA) — Exploration Systems Mission Directorate
Description: NASA Exploration Systems Mission Directorate (ESMD) leads the agency's human and robotic exploration programs. The Web site has sections for the directorate's acquisitions information and research and technology development programs. The Centennial Challenges section describes NASA's relatively new program of prize contests to stimulate innovation and competition in the technical areas of solar system exploration. The Library section has ESMD documents and meeting reports. The Library's Research and Technology Data section features prepared searches to run in the government's PubMed database for publications reporting space flight experiment results.
Subjects: Human Space Exploration; Space Technology

1604. NASA Headquarters
http://www.nasa.gov/centers/hq/home/
Sponsor(s): National Aeronautics and Space Administration (NASA)
Description: NASA Headquarters in Washington, DC, manages the space flight centers, research centers, and other NASA installations. The Headquarters Web site provides information on its leadership and organization, and on NASA news and initiatives. The Links section includes links to headquarters offices, such as the NASA History Division and the NASA Office of the Inspector General, and to other useful sites, such as the NASA Online Directives Information System (NODIS) and NASA Advisory Council.
Subjects: Space

1605. NASA History Division
http://history.nasa.gov/
Sponsor(s): National Aeronautics and Space Administration (NASA) — History Office
Description: The NASA History Program, dating back to 1959, documents and preserves the agency's history. The site includes a brief history of NASA — including that of its predecessor, NACA — and an extensive topical index to historical information distributed on the many NASA Web sites. The Publications section lists print publications about NASA history, many of which are also available online, and links to NASA's own electronic publications about the agency history.
　The topical index this site provides is very helpful for tracking down historical information on NASA's many Web sites. The online publications provide direct access to some historical reference works otherwise not readily available.
Subjects: Spacecraft — History
Publications: *Apollo by the Numbers: A Statistical Review*, NAS 1.21:
The Problem of Space Travel: The Rocket Motor, NAS 1.21:

1606. NASA Image eXchange (NIX)
http://nix.nasa.gov/
Sponsor(s): National Aeronautics and Space Administration (NASA)
Description: The NASA Image eXchange (NIX) is a central search engine for many of the agency's distributed online multimedia collections. The collections can be searched by word and multimedia type. Images can also be browsed with a hierarchical menu of topics. While NASA images are not generally protected by copyright, users should review the Copyright section for reproduction guidelines.
Subjects: Photography; Space

1607. NASA Langley Research Center

http://www.nasa.gov/centers/langley/home/

Sponsor(s): National Aeronautics and Space Administration (NASA) — Langley Research Center (LaRC)

Description: NASA's Langley Research Center, located in Virginia, has long been a major center for aeronautics research. The Web site provides news, images, and information related to this research, and also highlights Langley contributions to space exploration and science. The Doing Business with Us section has information on procurement and technology transfer.

With a wide collection of aeronautical information, this site is an important resource for researchers in aeronautics.

Subjects: Aerospace Engineering — Research

1608. NASA Multimedia Gallery

http://www.nasa.gov/multimedia/highlights/

Sponsor(s): National Aeronautics and Space Administration (NASA)

Description: The NASA Multimedia Gallery presents a selection of NASA images, video, podcasts, interactive presentations, and space-related art. The gallery highlights timely images, and it links to NASA TV. NASA video is generally not copyrighted, but users will want to check section on Image Use Guidelines for complete information.

This NASA site makes it easy to find images and video recordings tied to recent NASA news. For a more extensive collection, see the NASA Image eXchange (NIX) site also described in this book.

Subjects: Space

1609. NASA Shuttle

http://www.nasa.gov/mission_pages/shuttle/main/

Sponsor(s): National Aeronautics and Space Administration (NASA) — Spaceflight Office

Description: The NASA shuttle site has information on current, past, and planned future missions. The Shuttle Archives section documents the crew, payloads, and timeline for previous missions back to 1981. Other sections include Behind the Scenes, Launch and Landing, and Vehicle Structure.

Subjects: Space Shuttle

1610. NASA Tech Briefs

http://www.nasatech.com/

Sponsor(s): Associated Business Publications

Description: *NASA Tech Briefs* publishes information on any commercially significant technologies developed in the course of NASA research and development. The publication is a joint publishing venture of NASA and Associated Business Publications (ABP); this Web site is run by ABP. The site offers free downloadable Technical Support Packages, which provide in-depth information on the innovations described in the *NASA Tech Briefs*. Qualified individuals are eligible for a free U.S. subscription to *NASA Tech Briefs*. The site offers subscription request forms and renewal forms.

Subjects: Space Technology; Technology Transfer

Publications: *NASA Tech Briefs*, NAS 1.29/3-2:

1611. NASA White Sands Test Facility (WSTF)

http://www.wstf.nasa.gov/

Sponsor(s): National Aeronautics and Space Administration (NASA) — Johnson Space Center (JSC)

Description: NASA's White Sands Test Facility (WSTF) in New Mexico is operationally part of the NASA Johnson Space Center. The facility tests rocket propulsion systems, propellants and hazardous fluids, and materials and components used in spaceflight. It also serves as the primary training area for space shuttle pilots practicing landings. The Web site describes WSTF capabilities in each of these areas.

Subjects: Aerospace Engineering; Propulsion Technology

1612. National Space Science Data Center

http://nssdc.gsfc.nasa.gov/

Sponsor(s): National Aeronautics and Space Administration (NASA) — Goddard Space Flight Center (GSFC)

Description: National Space Science Data Center serves as the permanent archive for data from NASA spaceflight missions. The data are related to the fields of astronomy and astrophysics, solar and space plasma physics, and planetary and lunar science, and earth sciences. The site has an online Master Catalog of available data and resources. Some resources are available online; others must be ordered. The data are intended for use by the professional scientific community. The Space Science Education Outreach section links to educational and general sites from NASA.

Subjects: Space Sciences

Publications: *NSSDC News*, NAS 1.37/2:

SPACEWARN Bulletin, NAS 1.37/3:

1613. NSPIRES — NASA Research Opportunities

http://nspires.nasaprs.com/external/

Sponsor(s): National Aeronautics and Space Administration (NASA)

Description: NSPIRES stands for NASA Solicitation and Proposal Integrated Review and Evaluation System. The Web site is an online service center for each stage in the NASA research solicitation and award process. Users can search for open, closed, past, and future NASA research announcements; and view the list of proposals selected to conduct NASA research, including the principal investigator, institution, and proposal title. A module still under development will enable users to search for and view the results of NASA grantees' research. The site links to related resources, such as the guidebook for responding to NASA Research Announcements.

Subjects: Scientific Research — Grants; Space — Research

1614. Office of Space Commercialization

http://www.nesdis.noaa.gov/space/

Sponsor(s): Commerce Department — National Oceanic and Atmospheric Administration (NOAA) — National Environmental Satellite, Data, and Information Service (NESDIS)

Description: The Commerce Department's Office of Space Commercialization promotes the competitiveness of the U.S. commercial space industry. The site features special sections on satellite navigation, satellite imaging, and space transportation. Other sections cover policy issues and market opportunities. Publications can be found in the Library section.

Subjects: Space Technology
Publications: *Market Opportunities in Space*, C 1.202:
Space Economic Data, C 1.202:

1615. Planetary Data System
http://pds.jpl.nasa.gov/
Sponsor(s): National Aeronautics and Space Administration (NASA) — Space Science Mission Directorate
Description: The Planetary Data System (PDS) is an archive of peer-reviewed data products from NASA planetary missions such as Galileo, Mars Odyssey, Viking, and Voyager. The site includes sections for data services information, tools to manage the downloaded data, and documentation and manuals. PDS is managed by a system of nodes — NASA offices and university consortia — with specialties in the planetary disciplines. Links to each node's specialized Web site are at the bottom of the PDS home page.
    The Planetary Data System was designed by scientists for scientists. The data sets are very large and of a highly technical nature.
Subjects: Planetary Science — Research

1616. Planetary Sciences at the NSSDC
http://nssdc.gsfc.nasa.gov/planetary/
Sponsor(s): National Aeronautics and Space Administration (NASA) — Goddard Space Flight Center (GSFC)
Description: The NSSDC is responsible for the collection and storage and distribution of planetary images and other data to scientists, educators, and the general public. This site offers a separate page for each planet as well as for the moon, asteroids, and comets. Each of these separate pages features fact sheets, images, a Frequently Asked Questions file, other resources, and information on spacecraft missions to that specific astral body. Other links connect to a variety of NSSDC data resources.
    This site offers a substantial body of textual and pictorial information for all the planets in our solar system. Information is available at many levels, from the child to the research scientist. It is definitely worth a visit by anyone looking for basic information or images of the planets, the moon, asteroids, or comets.
Subjects: Planetary Science; Planets

1617. Science@NASA
http://science.hq.nasa.gov/
Sponsor(s): National Aeronautics and Space Administration (NASA) — Space Science Mission Directorate
Description: NASA's Science Mission Directorate offers this Web site with detailed information on the agency's science strategy and science missions. Thematic sections include Earth-Sun System, Solar System, and Universe. The site includes images and videos, amateur astronomer resources, education products, and an extensive section for kids and young adults.
Subjects: Space Sciences

1618. Solar System Exploration
http://sse.jpl.nasa.gov/
Sponsor(s): National Aeronautics and Space Administration (NASA) — Jet Propulsion Laboratory (JPL)
Description: The Jet Propulsion Lab's Solar System Exploration Web site is a public outreach effort with a wealth of information on the Earth's solar system and on planetary science. It profiles current and past planetary missions, and includes

a multimedia section with images. Most of the site is written for the general public of high school or adult age, but it also has sections for kids and for educators.

This is a colorful and well-designed site with fresh content for space enthusiasts and amateur astronomers.

Subjects: Planetary Science

1619. Space Calendar

http://www2.jpl.nasa.gov/calendar/

Sponsor(s): National Aeronautics and Space Administration (NASA) — Jet Propulsion Laboratory (JPL)

Description: JPL's Space Calendar covers space-related activities and historical anniversaries for the coming year, with numerous links to related Web pages. The calendar includes launch dates, conferences, and celestial events such as eclipses. The site also offers calendar archives for the past several years.

This is an excellent resource for amateur astronomers and those interested in the history of space exploration.

Subjects: Space — History

1620. Space Environment Center

http://www.sec.noaa.gov/

Sponsor(s): Commerce Department — National Oceanic and Atmospheric Administration (NOAA) — Office of Oceanic and Atmospheric Research

Description: The Space Environment Center (SEC) is "the official source of space weather alerts and warnings" (from the Web site). SEC provides real-time monitoring and forecasting of solar and geophysical events, conducts research in solar-terrestrial physics, and develops techniques for forecasting solar and geophysical disturbances. Featured sections include Space Weather Now, Data and Products, and About SEC. Space Weather Now has solar wind measurements, reports of any geomagnetic storms or radio blackouts, and the latest alerts and advisories. The Education/Outreach section has classroom materials, brief papers on topics such as the ionosphere and radio wave propagation, and general information on space weather, including a Web page in Spanish.

This site presents a wealth of data for researchers in solar-terrestrial physics and for anyone interested in images and reports on the Sun and its effects on Earth. The SEC's products are of more direct use to those responsible, for example, for satellites, air transportation, and power grids.

Subjects: Space Environment; Sun

Publications: *Space Environment Center*, C 55.2:

1621. Space Operations

http://www.hq.nasa.gov/osf/

Sponsor(s): National Aeronautics and Space Administration (NASA) — Space Operations Mission Directorate

Description: The NASA Space Operations Mission Directorate directs space flight operations, space launches and space communications, and other systems in operation. Major sections of the site include International Space Station, Space Shuttle Program, and Space and Flight Support (space communications and launch services). Each operation is covered in detail. The site also links to the NASA SkyWatch application for determining when to view the space station from selected cities around the world.

Subjects: Human Space Exploration; Space Shuttle; Space Stations

1622. Spitzer Space Telescope
http://www.spitzer.caltech.edu/spitzer/
Alternate URL(s): http://www.spitzer.caltech.edu/espanol/
Sponsor(s): National Aeronautics and Space Administration (NASA) — Jet Propulsion Laboratory (JPL)
Description: The Spitzer Space Telescope is a cryogenically-cooled infrared observatory. It is the final element of what are called NASA's four "Great Observatories," the others being the Hubble Space Telescope, Compton Gamma Ray Telescope, and Chandra X-ray Observatory. The About Spitzer section of the site provides detailed information on project's history, mission, science, and technology. The site also has project news, a large image gallery, and a Features section including podcasts and videos.

The alternate URL has information about the Spitzer Space Telescope in Spanish. A technical site for astronomers is available at: ⟨http://ssc.spitzer.caltech.edu/⟩
Subjects: Astronomy; Telescopes

1623. Stennis Space Center
http://www.nasa.gov/centers/stennis/home/
Sponsor(s): National Aeronautics and Space Administration (NASA) — Stennis Space Center (SSC)
Description: SSC is NASA's primary center for testing large rocket propulsion systems and for developing remote sensing technology. These programs are detailed in the Missions section of the Web site. Under Multimedia, the site has a retrieval system for images and videos related to work at SSC.
Subjects: Propulsion Technology; Remote Sensing; Rockets

1624. Voyager
http://voyager.jpl.nasa.gov/
Sponsor(s): National Aeronautics and Space Administration (NASA) — Jet Propulsion Laboratory (JPL)
Description: This site covers the missions of the Voyager-1 and Voyager-2 spacecraft, both launched in 1977 and now heading out of the solar system. The site has information on the science, spacecraft, and images of the Voyager missions.
Subjects: Spacecraft

1625. Wallops Flight Facility
http://www.wff.nasa.gov/
Sponsor(s): National Aeronautics and Space Administration (NASA) — Wallops Flight Facility
Description: Wallops Flight Facility is responsible for the launch and operation of suborbital and small orbital payloads that support space-based research focused on Earth. It supports NASA's Sounding Rocket and Scientific Balloon Programs. The Web site describes the Wallops programs, facilities, business opportunities, and education outreach.
Subjects: Rockets

1626. World Wind
http://worldwind.arc.nasa.gov/
Sponsor(s): National Aeronautics and Space Administration (NASA) — Ames Research Center (ARC)
Description: NASA's World Wind is downloadable software that allows users to view Earth image data, zooming from satellite altitude into any place on Earth. The Web site includes sample screen shots, a manual, a user forum, and the software.

At this time, the World Wind software is only compatible with newer versions of the Windows operating system. See the site's FAQ for details on system requirements.

Subjects: Imaging Technology

CHAPTER 19
Social Welfare

The federal government develops programs and policies and administers grants in areas such as housing, community development, volunteer services, and welfare. This chapter includes agency Web sites that either serve the customers of these programs or compile information about these programs.

Subsections in this chapter are Child Welfare, Economic Development, Housing, Social Services, and Volunteerism and Charities.

Child Welfare

1627. Administration for Children and Families
http://www.acf.dhhs.gov/
Sponsor(s): Health and Human Services Department — Administration for Children and Families (ACF)
Description: ACF is a federal agency that funds state, local, and tribal organizations to provide family assistance (welfare), child support, child care, Head Start, child welfare, and other services relating to children and families. Its Web site presents program and agency information under sections including Services for Families, Working with ACF, Policy/Planning, and About ACF. Program information and resources organized under Services cover such topics as adoption, child care, energy assistance, Head Start, Healthy Marriage Initiative, and Temporary Assistance for Needy Families (TANF). The Working with ACF section has a full list of ACF program descriptions, information for employers, grant opportunities, and links to relevant state and local resources. Policy/Planning has budget and legislative background information, policy documents, links to program materials and clearinghouse sites, and research, data, and statistics on program areas.

The ACF Web site is a well organized and rich resource for child and family welfare federal programs. The program research, data, and statistics information should be of interest to social service researchers. On the home page, the About ACF and ACF News sections are linked from the bottom of the page and not readily evident.
Subjects: Child Welfare; Early Childhood Education; Families; Welfare

1628. Afterschool.gov
http://www.afterschool.gov/
Sponsor(s): General Services Administration (GSA)
Description: This site is designed to connect visitors to online resources in support of children and youth during after-school hours. It includes information on financing and operating an afterschool program and provides activity ideas for children in such programs.
Subjects: Child Care

1629. Child Care Bureau
http://www.acf.hhs.gov/programs/ccb/
Sponsor(s): Health and Human Services Department — Administration for Children and Families (ACF) — Child Care Bureau
Description: The Child Care Bureau administers federal funds to states, territories, and tribes to help low-income families obtain quality child care. The site has policy and regulatory guidance documents and technical assistance information

for the local governments administering the funds. It links to resources for child care providers and for parents seeking quality child care. Under Research and Data, the site provides statistics on the Child Care and Development Fund.
Subjects: Child Care

1630. Child Welfare Information Gateway
http://www.childwelfare.gov/
Sponsor(s): Health and Human Services Department — Administration for Children and Families (ACF) — Children's Bureau
Description: The Child Welfare Information Gateway is a central resource replacing the Web sites for the National Clearinghouse on Child Abuse and Neglect Information and the National Adoption Information Clearinghouse. The site is a portal to information on such topics as child abuse and neglect, out-of-home care, and adoption. Resources include the National Adoption Directory, statistics on child neglect issues and adoption, summaries of state laws, and links to relevant national organizations. Core information and some publications are available in Spanish.
Subjects: Child Welfare
Publications: *Children's Bureau Express*

1631. Family and Youth Services Bureau (FYSB)
http://www.acf.dhhs.gov/programs/fysb/
Sponsor(s): Health and Human Services Department — Administration for Children and Families (ACF) — Family and Youth Services Bureau (FYSB)
Description: FYSB provides runaway and homeless youth service grants to local communities. It also funds research and demonstration projects. The FYSB divisions described on the Web site are Youth Development, Family Violence, and Abstinence Education. Each division offers funding opportunities and links to resources. The About FYSB section has publications and policy documents.
Subjects: Adolescents; Social Services — Grants
Publications: *Report to Congress on the Youth Programs of the Family and Youth Services Bureau*

1632. Helping America's Youth
http://www.helpingamericasyouth.gov/
Sponsor(s): White House — First Lady's Office
Description: This site describes First Lady Laura Bush's initiative to raise awareness about the challenges facing young people, particularly at-risk boys. The site has information about positive influences for children and the increased risk factors for boys. It also features the online *Community Guide to Helping America's Youth*.
Subjects: Children — Policy

1633. Missing Children Notice Program
http://r6.gsa.gov/pbs/kids/
Sponsor(s): General Services Administration (GSA)
Description: The Missing Children Notice Program uses federal buildings across the country to disseminate notices of missing children. This site provides information about the program and current notices.
Subjects: Children

1634. National Clearinghouse on Families and Youth
http://www.ncfy.com/
Sponsor(s): Health and Human Services Department — Administration for Children and Families (ACF) — Family and Youth Services Bureau (FYSB)
Description: The National Clearinghouse on Families and Youth (NCFY) provides information on youth development, family violence prevention, abstinence education, and mentoring children of prisoners. The site is intended to support Family and Youth Service Bureau grantees and organizations interested in youth programming and policy.
Subjects: Adolescents; Families

1635. National Network for Child Care
http://www.nncc.org/
Sponsor(s): Agriculture Department (USDA) — Cooperative State Research, Education, and Extension Service (CSREES)
Description: The National Network for Child Care is an online resource developed through the CSREES and land grant universities. It includes links to articles, newsletters, reports, and Web sites on the topics of childcare and development. The site also hosts a KIDCARE e-mail forum; users can subscribe via the Web form on the site.
Subjects: Child Care

Economic Development

1636. Administration for Native Americans
http://www.acf.dhhs.gov/programs/ana/
Sponsor(s): Health and Human Services Department — Administration for Children and Families (ACF)
Description: As stated on the Web site, "the Administration for Native Americans (ANA) promotes the goal of social and economic self-sufficiency of American Indians, Alaska Natives, Native Hawaiians, and peoples of Guam, American Samoa, and the Commonwealth of the Northern Mariana Islands." The site has information on grant programs and awards, technical assistance, and training. Special initiatives include the Native American Healthy Marriage Initiative and Native Language Preservation and Maintenance.
Subjects: Indigenous Peoples; Social Welfare; American Indians
Publications: *Native Language Preservation: A Reference Guide for Establishing Archives and Repositories*

1637. Appalachian Regional Commission
http://www.arc.gov/
Sponsor(s): Appalachian Regional Commission (ARC)
Description: ARC supports economic and social development in the Appalachian region. Appalachia is defined as the region that spans the spine of the Appalachian Mountains from southern New York to northern Mississippi. It includes all of West Virginia and parts of 12 other states: Alabama, Georgia, Kentucky, Maryland, Mississippi, New York, North Carolina, Ohio, Pennsylvania, South Carolina, Tennessee, and Virginia. The Web site features news and information about ARC and the Appalachian region, *Appalachia Magazine*, and an Online Resource Center with resources for community planning, funding, and regional data and research.
Subjects: Rural Development
Publications: *Annual Report, Appalachian Regional Commission*, Y 3.AP 4/2:1/ *Appalachia Magazine*, Y 3.AP 4/2:9-2/

1638. Community Development Programs
http://ocdweb.sc.egov.usda.gov/
Sponsor(s): Agriculture Department (USDA) — Rural Development
Description: The Agriculture Department's Office of Community Development (OCD) is part of the Rural Development program. The OCD Web site provides background information and resources reflecting the office's programmatic emphasis on rural community empowerment, a concept described on the site. The Web site's OCD Programs section describes such initiatives as Rural Economic Area Partnership (REAP) Zones, Information Systems Support, and technical assistance.
Subjects: Rural Development

1639. Economic Development Administration (EDA)
http://www.eda.gov/
Sponsor(s): Commerce Department — Economic Development Administration (EDA)
Description: EDA gives grants to local communities for infrastructure and business development. The site provides information on the agency's grant programs, notices of funding availability, and application guidelines. The Research/Tools section has the text of economic development research reports and extensive background information on development practices.
Subjects: Economic Development — Grants

1640. National Rural Development Partnership (NRDP)
http://www.rurdev.usda.gov/nrdp/
Sponsor(s): Agriculture Department (USDA) — Rural Business-Cooperative Service (RBS)
Description: NRDP promotes rural development through partnerships with local, state, tribal, and federal governments, as well as for-profit and nonprofit organizations. This site features information about the NRDP, accomplishments, budget, and congressional updates. It also links to state and national partners and other rural development sites.
Subjects: Rural Development

1641. Rural Development Business and Cooperative Programs
http://www.rurdev.usda.gov/rbs/
Sponsor(s): Agriculture Department (USDA) — Rural Business-Cooperative Service (RBS)
Description: The Rural Development Business and Cooperative Programs support businesses and cooperatives in rural areas through funding and technical assistance. The Web site describes the business programs, cooperative programs, and special initiatives. A special section focuses on the grant and loan program created in Section 9006 of the 2002 Farm Bill to help fund renewable energy and energy efficiency projects in rural America. Some information is available in Spanish.

The site provides an excellent starting point for finding information on the service and its programs. It will be of most interest to businesses and rural community leaders.
Subjects: Rural Development
Publications: *Cooperative Information Reports*, A 109.10/2:
RBS Research Reports, A 109.10:
Rural Cooperatives, A 109.11:

1642. Rural Information Center (RIC)

http://www.nal.usda.gov/ric/

Sponsor(s): Agriculture Department (USDA) — National Agricultural Library (NAL)
Description: RIC is a specialized information and referral service within the National Agricultural Library. The site features links to community development resources, funding resources (including a searchable database), USDA rural development program sites, state and local resources, and Native American programs. RIC also provides a documented definition of "rural."

The RIC Web site is an excellent starting point for those researching rural development topics for grant-writing or other purposes. It can be of assistance to rural governments, grant-seekers, small farms, and nonprofit organizations.
Subjects: Rural Development — Research
Publications: *Rural Information Center Publication Series*, A 17.29:

1643. USDA Rural Development

http://www.rurdev.usda.gov/

Sponsor(s): Agriculture Department (USDA)
Description: The Rural Development Web site links to information on its major programs: Business and Cooperative, Housing and Community Facilities, Utilities, and Community Development. It includes current notices of funding availability and program news. The site also carries regulations, fact sheets, and publications. Some publications are available in Spanish, and a version of the site is also available in Spanish.
Subjects: Rural Development
Publications: *Rural Cooperatives*, A 109.11:

Housing

1644. Community Connections Information Center

http://www.comcon.org/

Sponsor(s): Housing and Urban Development (HUD) — Community Planning and Development Office
Description: The Community Connections Information Center is the clearinghouse for HUD's Office of Community Planning and Development (CPD). Its Web site serves state and local agencies, nonprofit organizations, public interest groups, and others interested in housing and community development. The site has information on CPD's programs and initiatives, including the Brownfields Redevelopment Initiative (BRI), Emergency Shelter Grants, Home Investment Partnerships Program (HOME), and the HUDVet Veteran Resource Center. The Publications section includes a list of publications that can be requested.
Subjects: Community Development

1645. Federal Housing Administration (FHA)

http://www.hud.gov/offices/hsg/fhahistory.cfm

Sponsor(s): Housing and Urban Development (HUD) — Office of Housing
Description: FHA provides mortgage insurance on loans made by FHA-approved lenders. This Web page provides basic information on the FHA, a government agency that operates entirely from its self-generated income.
Subjects: Home Mortgages

1646. Federal Housing Finance Board
http://www.fhfb.gov/
Sponsor(s): Federal Housing Finance Board
Description: The Federal Housing Finance Board regulates the 12 Federal Home Loan Banks that improve the supply of funds to local lenders financing loans for home mortgages. Its Web site features background information on the Federal Housing Finance Board, the system, and its programs; it also links to each of the regional Federal Home Loan Banks. The "Monthly Interest Rate Survey" press release is online in the Reporting section, along with summary tables downloadable in the Excel spreadsheet format. The same information is available for the Adjustable Rate Mortgage Index. The Regulation/Supervision section includes FHFB rules and notices, regulatory guidance, and regulatory actions such as Approval Letters and No-Action Letters.
Subjects: Home Mortgages
Publications: *Monthly Interest Rate Survey and Annual Summary*, FHF 1.15:

1647. Ginnie Mae
http://www.ginniemae.gov/
Sponsor(s): Housing and Urban Development (HUD) — Government National Mortgage Association (Ginnie Mae)
Description: Ginnie Mae, a wholly owned government corporation within HUD, aims to help provide affordable, government-insured mortgages to American families. Its Web site includes sections for investors, homeowners, mortgage-backed securities issuers, as well as information about Ginnie Mae. For prospective homeowners, the site has a Rent vs. Buy Calculator and a Loan Estimator Calculator. Full-text issues of *All Participants Memoranda* and its annual reports are available online.
Subjects: Housing Finance
Publications: *All Participants Memoranda (Ginnie Mae)*, HH 1.37/4:
Annual Report, Government National Mortgage Association, HH 1.37:
Mortgage-Backed Securities Handbook, HH 1.6/6:

1648. Home Loan Guaranty Services
http://www.homeloans.va.gov/
Sponsor(s): Veterans Affairs Department
Description: The VA home loan program helps veterans finance the purchase of homes through favorable loan terms and competitive interest rates. The Web site provides information for home buyers, lenders, loan servicers, and real estate professionals. The Home Loan Information page has online videos, pamphlets, and disaster advice for VA borrowers. The site also has information on grants for specially adapted housing.
Subjects: Housing Finance; Veterans

1649. Housing and Community Facilities Programs
http://www.rurdev.usda.gov/rhs/
Sponsor(s): Agriculture Department (USDA) — Rural Housing Service
Description: The Housing and Community Facilities Programs (HCFP) office provides loans and grants to rural communities and individuals, and works with local organizations and governments to provide technical assistance. Initiatives described on the Web site include a program to fund equipment and services for emergency responders in rural areas. Featured sections include Where to Apply, Nonprofit Opportunities, Public Bodies Opportunities, Lender Opportunities, Developer Opportunities, Individual and Family Opportunities, Regulations, and

Information for Existing Borrowers. The site also has a Spanish-language version available.

Subjects: Housing; Rural Development

1650. Housing and Urban Development — Homes and Community
http://www.hud.gov/

Sponsor(s): Housing and Urban Development (HUD)

Description: HUD's Web site describes the agency's programs in housing and community development. The site offers sections including HUD News, Homes (Buying, Selling, Renting, Improvements, Foreclosure, Homeless, Fair Housing, HUD Homes, FHA Refund, and Foreclosures), Communities, Working with HUD, Resources, and Tools. The Working with HUD page has sections on grants and contracting opportunities with HUD and information about filing a complaint with the agency. Under Resources, the site has an extensive online library of information organized by subjects such as fair housing, congressional activity, legal information, and funding. The Tools section contains webcasts, RSS news feeds, and numerous e-mail lists for interested users.

The site also offers information by audience type under the section "Information For. . . ." The long list of subsections includes first-time Homebuyers, Senior Citizens, Veterans/Military, People With Disabilities, Farmworkers/Colonias, Native Americans, Students, Researchers, Landlords, Lenders, Brokers, Appraisers, Small Businesses, and Grantees/Nonprofits.

This well-designed site offers a great deal of useful information to consumers and businesses. Multiple access points make the site easy to navigate. See the HUD User site for additional HUD documents.

Subjects: Community Development; Housing

Publications: *HOMEfires: Policy Newsletter of the HOME Investment Partnerships Program*, HH 1.114/3:

Labor Relations Letters, HH 1.117:

Legal Opinions of the Office of General Counsel (annual), HH 1.86:

1651. HUD User
http://www.huduser.org/

Sponsor(s): Housing and Urban Development (HUD) — Policy Development and Research Office

Description: HUD User is the primary source for federal government reports and information about housing policy and programs, building technology, economic development, urban planning, and other housing-related topics. The main sections include Publications, Periodicals, Data Sets, Bibliographic Database, Order Online, and Ongoing Research. The HUD User Bibliographic Database offers access to bibliographic information on thousands of reports, articles, case studies, and other research literature related to housing and community development. The Data Sets section includes the original electronic data sets from the *American Housing Survey* and other housing research initiatives. The Regulatory Reform link leads to the Regulatory Barriers Clearinghouse, labeled on the site as "your source for solutions to state and local regulatory barriers to affordable housing."

Subjects: Community Development — Research; Housing — Research; Databases

Publications: *Annual Adjustment Factors*, HH 1.34:

Cityscape — A Journal of Policy Development and Research, HH 1.75/2:

FieldWorks: Ideas Housing and Community Development, HH 1.75/3:

Guide to PD&R Data Sets

Income Limits and Section 8 Fair Market Rents, HH 1.126:

Recent Research Results, HH 1.84:

State of the Cities, HH 1.2:C 49/13/
U.S. Housing Market Conditions (quarterly), HH 1.120/2:
Urban Research Monitor, HH 1.23/8:

1652. HUDCLIPS
http://www.hudclips.org/
Sponsor(s): Housing and Urban Development (HUD)
Description: HUDCLIPS (HUD's Client Information and Policy System) is a searchable online database containing the entire inventory of official HUD policies, procedures, announcements, forms, and other materials. The Short Cuts section provides links to frequently requested documents. The Forms area features official forms in PDF, Excel, and Word template formats. The Library provides search and browse access to the following databases: *Federal Register*, Codes, Laws, *Congressional Record*, Guidebooks, Handbooks and Notices, Letters, Inspector General, Veterans Affairs, Travel Regulations, Housing Waivers, and Legal Opinions.
Subjects: Housing; Publication Catalogs

1653. Interagency Council on Homelessness
http://www.ich.gov/
Sponsor(s): Interagency Council on Homelessness
Description: More than 15 federal departments and agencies are members of the Interagency Council on Homelessness. The council coordinates federal policy and programs on homelessness and employs regional coordinators to work with state and local governments. The Web site provides information on the council's activities, programs to reduce homelessness, and news about funding and technical assistance.
Subjects: Homelessness

1654. Office of Housing
http://www.hud.gov/offices/hsg/
Sponsor(s): Housing and Urban Development (HUD)
Description: HUD's Office of Housing oversees the Federal Housing Administration and includes offices for single-family housing, multiple-family housing, and regulatory programs. These programs, as well as information about financing for hospital construction and the Office of Affordable Housing Preservation (OAHP), are covered on this Web site. The Reading Room section includes homebuying publications in Spanish, new HUD mortgagee letters, HUD handbooks, housing and mortgage glossaries, and a selection of other reports and data. A Spanish-language version of the site is available.
Subjects: Home Mortgages; Housing Finance
Publications: *FHA Outlook*
Housing Today, HH 1.128:
Mortgagee Letters, HH 2.6/4:

1655. OFHEO — Office of Federal Housing Enterprise Oversight
http://www.ofheo.gov/
Sponsor(s): Housing and Urban Development (HUD) — Federal Housing Enterprise Oversight Office
Description: OFHEO oversees the financial condition of two government-sponsored enterprises, the Federal National Mortgage Association (Fannie Mae) and the Federal Home Loan Mortgage Corporation (Freddie Mac). OFHEO makes examinations, sets standards, issues regulations, and takes enforcement actions. OFHEO issues a quarterly House Price Index; the press releases and downloadable data

are available on the site. The site's Consumer Information section includes English- and Spanish-language brochures on shopping for the best mortgage. Other sections include Capital Requirements, Research and Analysis, and Regulations and Policy Guidance. Some publications are available in the News Center section.
Subjects: Home Mortgages; Housing Finance

Social Services

1656. Administration on Developmental Disabilities (ADD)
http://www.acf.hhs.gov/programs/add/
Sponsor(s): Health and Human Services Department — Administration for Children and Families (ACF)
Description: ADD coordinates service programs for those with developmental disabilities (defined as physical or mental impairments that begin before age 22 and restrict a person's ability to perform basic tasks for self-sufficiency). The site provides ADD publications and program guidance, and describes ADD's major programs and program outcomes.
Subjects: Disabilities
Publications: *ADD Update*, HE 23.6015:

1657. Campaign to Rescue and Restore Victims of Human Trafficking
http://www.acf.hhs.gov/trafficking/
Sponsor(s): Health and Human Services Department — Administration for Children and Families (ACF)
Description: Health and Human Services is responsible for helping victims of human trafficking become eligible to receive benefits and services. The Web site provides information on their campaign to locate human trafficking victims. It provides campaign toolkits for social service organizations, health care providers, and law enforcement officers. The site also links to other agency program Web sites concerned with human trafficking.
Subjects: International Crimes; International Migration

1658. Catalog of Federal Domestic Assistance (CFDA)
http://www.cfda.gov/
Alternate URL(s): http://12.46.245.173/cfda/cfda.html
Sponsor(s): General Services Administration (GSA) — Office of Governmentwide Policy (OGP)
Description: This online version of the classic print document, *Catalog of Federal Domestic Assistance* (CFDA), is a searchable version of the catalog with additional information and links. CFDA describes a broad range of federal assistance programs, including formula-based grants, guaranteed loans, insurance, counseling, training, information services, and donation of goods. Most of the programs are not for direct assistance to individuals, but rather for state and local governments, Indian tribal governments, or other organizations that administer the distribution of aid. Catalog entries include a program identifier number, description, eligibility requirements, program contact information, and details on the application and awards process. The CFDA Web site also has information on using the catalog, applying for assistance, and writing grant proposals.
    This resource is highly recommended for governments and others researching federal assistance programs.
Subjects: Government Loans; Grants
Publications: *Catalog of Federal Domestic Assistance*, PREX 2.20:

1659. Center for Faith-based and Community Initiatives (Education)
http://www.ed.gov/about/inits/list/fbci/
Sponsor(s): Education Department
Description: This is one of seven Centers for Faith-based and Community Initiatives in federal agencies, intended to encourage new participation in federal grant programs. The Web site includes a fact sheet and a Frequent Questions section written for interested faith-based and community organizations. It also has a guide to grants and tips for new applicants.
Subjects: Education Funding; Grants

1660. Center for Faith-based and Community Initiatives (HHS)
http://www.hhs.gov/fbci/
Sponsor(s): Health and Human Services Department
Description: The HHS Center for Faith-based and Community Initiatives works to encourage the participation of religious and neighborhood organizations in the department's many service programs for those in need. The site has information on technical assistance and opportunities for faith-based and community organizations.
Subjects: Grants; Social Services

1661. Center for Faith-based and Community Initiatives (Labor)
http://www.dol.gov/cfbci/
Sponsor(s): Labor Department
Description: This is one of seven such agency centers established by a White House initiative. The site carries news on the Labor Department's grants, funding, and regulatory changes to reduce barriers to faith-based organizations' participation in grants programs. It also links to an online training program for grant-seeking organizations called "Touching Lives and Communities."
Subjects: Employment — Policy; Grants

1662. Department of Health and Human Services (HHS)
http://www.hhs.gov/
Sponsor(s): Health and Human Services Department
Description: The HHS Web site is a major resource for all of the health and social services areas overseen by the department. The Web site uses the following sections for access to more detailed information: Diseases and Conditions, Safety and Wellness, Drug and Food Information, Disasters and Emergencies, Families and Children, Aging, and Specific Populations. Other major sections are Grants and Funding, Reference Collections (publications, databases, statistics), Resource Locators, Policies and Regulations, and About HHS. The Web site links to the sites for each HHS agency and highlights the most requested Web pages, such as those about the Health Insurance Portability and Accountability Act (HIPAA) Privacy Rule and the HHS Office of Human Research Protections.
Subjects: Public Health; Social Services

1663. DisabilityInfo.gov
http://www.disabilityinfo.gov/
Sponsor(s): White House
Description: DisabilityInfo.gov is a portal to federal Web sites and programs of concern to persons with disabilities. The site is divided into topical sections, including Employment, Education, Housing, Transportation, Health, Income Support, Technology, Community Life, and Civil Rights. The site is available in a text-only version.
Subjects: Disabilities

1664. Faith-based and Community Initiatives (HUD)
http://www.hud.gov/offices/fbci/
Sponsor(s): Housing and Urban Development (HUD)
Description: The HUD Center for Faith-based and Community Initiatives uses this Web site to help religious and neighborhood organizations find funding, volunteers, and resources. It includes information on finding grants and grantwriting. The information is also available in Spanish.
Subjects: Grants; Social Services

1665. Food and Nutrition Service
http://www.fns.usda.gov/fns/
Sponsor(s): Agriculture Department (USDA) — Food and Nutrition Service (FNS)
Description: FNS manages programs including the Women, Infants, and Children Program; the Food Stamp Program; and the National School Lunch Program. This Web site provides basic information on the programs including information on applying, hotline numbers, links to other relevant USDA sites, and fact sheets. The Data and Statistics section has statistics on the major FNS programs, such as the number of meals served in the National School Lunch Program or the average monthly benefit per person in the Food Stamp Program. A Nutrition Education section highlights federal programs and resources in this area. The Newsroom section includes press releases, publications, and speeches. Other sections cover Grants, Food Safety, and Research. The site also has a Spanish-language version.
Subjects: Food Stamps; Nutrition; School Meal Programs
Publications: *Characteristics of Food Stamp Households*, A 98.21:
School Programs Commodity Update, A 98.19:
Trends in Food Stamp Program Participation Rates, A 98.22:
WIC Program and Participants Characteristics, A 98.17:

1666. GovBenefits.gov
http://www.govbenefits.gov/
Sponsor(s): Labor Department
Description: GovBenefits.gov is a multi-agency effort to provide a single Web site for those with questions about government benefits. The site can help users find benefits information without having to know which agency to contact. The major benefits finding tools are a list of federal programs on the site, a list of state programs on the site, a custom list by type of benefit and type of aid, and a Get Results by Questionnaire section. The Questionnaire section uses your responses to a long series of questions to determine eligibility for specific government benefits. The site never asks for identity information (such as name or Social Security number). A Spanish-language version is available.

Although the site is managed by a multi-agency partnership, the Department of Labor takes the lead role.
Subjects: Social Welfare

1667. GrantsNet
http://www.hhs.gov/grantsnet/
Sponsor(s): Health and Human Services Department — Grants and Acquisition Management Office
Description: GrantsNet is a tool for finding information about Department of Health and Human Services' grant programs. Under the Electronic Roadmap to Grants link, the page is divided into four regions: Introduction to HHS Grants, Application Process, Managing Grants, and Useful Resources. The Application Process section offers information on how to apply and write grant proposals. It also has standard

forms in PDF format available to download. In the Managing Grants section, there are such sections as *Grants Administration Manual*, Grants Policy Statements, and Laws, Executive Orders, and Regulations.

While the focus of this gateway site is on HHS grants, it also has useful general information on the grants process.

Subjects: Grants; Public Health — Grants; Social Services — Grants
Publications: *Grants Administration Manual*, HE 1.6/7:

1668. HIV/AIDS Bureau
http://hab.hrsa.gov/
Sponsor(s): Health and Human Services Department — Health Resources and Services Administration (HRSA) — HIV/AIDS Bureau
Description: The HIV/AIDS Bureau coordinates the federal programs funded under the Ryan White Comprehensive AIDS Resources Emergency (CARE) Act. CARE Act programs are designed to help individuals with HIV who lack the health insurance and financial resources necessary for their care. The programs include health care and support, grants, training, and technical assistance. This site provides detailed information on the CARE Act and on the related policy, programs, and funding. A Reports and Studies section has statistics on clients served by the program and data on funds allocated by service type. The site also offers sections on Grant Opportunities, Education and Training, and Publications. The e-mail newsletter *HRSA Care Action* can be viewed online.
Subjects: AIDS; HIV Infections
Publications: *HRSA Care Action*, HE 20.9516

1669. House Ways and Means Committee Prints
http://www.gpoaccess.gov/wmprints/index.html
Alternate URL(s): http://waysandmeans.house.gov/Documents.asp?section=10
Sponsor(s): Congress — House Committee on Ways and Means
Description: The House Committee on Ways and Means has jurisdiction over most programs authorized by the Social Security Act, and its special publications can be useful sources of information on entitlement and benefits programs. At the primary URL above, the GPO Access system hosts the Ways and Means Committee's publications Web site. The alternate URL is the publications page on the Ways and Means Committee's own Web site. Of particular use for reference and research is the committee print *Background Material and Data on Programs Within the Jurisdiction of the Committee on Ways and Means*, popularly known as the *Green Book*. This document is a unique collection of program descriptions and historical data on a wide variety of social and economic topics, including Social Security, employment, earnings, welfare, child support, health insurance, the elderly, families with children, poverty, and taxation.

Other Ways and Means Committee prints of interest are the *Medicare and Health Care Chart Book*, a statistical guide to issues including Medicare, health insurance, and health care spending, and the *Compilation of the Social Security Laws, Including the Social Security Act, as Amended, and Related Enactments* .

While the *Green Book* and *Medicare Chart Book* prints are often updated, they are not issued every year or even every session of Congress. Browse the Ways and Means Committee site to determine the most recent edition available.
Subjects: Health Insurance — Statistics; Social Security — Statistics; Welfare — Statistics
Publications; *Compilation of the Social Security Laws . . .*, Y 4.W 36:
Green Book, Y 4.W 36:10-4/
Medicare and Health Care Chartbook, Y 4.W 36:

1670. Indian Health Service
http://www.ihs.gov/
Sponsor(s): Health and Human Services Department — Indian Health Services (IHS)
Description: IHS, the primary federal agency responsible for providing health care services to American Indians and Alaska Natives, provides a variety of information resources on its site. Featured sections include Jobs and Scholarships, Press and Public Relations, Area Offices and Facilities, Information Technology Resources, Medical and Professional Programs, Nationwide Programs and Initiatives, and Tribal Leaders. The Resources for IHS Management section includes information on the Health Insurance Portability and Accountability Act (HIPAA), IHS regulations, and the *Indian Health Manual* for policies, procedures, and operating standards
Subjects: Health Care; American Indians
Publications: *Indian Health Manual*
Indian Health Service Circulars
The IHS Primary Care Provider, HE 20.320:

1671. Low Income Home Energy Assistance Program (LIHEAP)
http://www.acf.hhs.gov/programs/liheap/
Alternate URL(s): http://www.liheapch.acf.hhs.gov/
Sponsor(s): Health and Human Services Department — Administration for Children and Families (ACF)
Description: LIHEAP is a federally funded program that helps low-income households with their home energy bills for heating or cooling. Its Web site provides information for consumers who may be eligible for LIHEAP, as well as for professionals who coordinate LIHEAP programs in states, tribal areas, and localities. Sections include Data, Funding, Program Performance, Grantee Forms, and Guidance (for professionals working in the field of low income energy assistance). Instructions on applying are available in Spanish and English.
The alternate URL above links to the LIHEAP Clearinghouse, a network for parties interested in low-income energy issues and a repository for information on the topic.
The LIHEAP Web site and LIHEAP Clearinghouse provide simple access to a wide range of information for those participating in or interested in the program. Its information on household energy issues and data will be of interest to a broader audience.
Subjects: Energy Prices and Costs

1672. Maternal and Child Health Bureau
http://www.mchb.hrsa.gov/
Sponsor(s): Health and Human Services Department — Health Resources and Services Administration (HRSA) — Maternal and Child Health Bureau
Description: The Maternal and Child Health Bureau administers Title V of the Social Security Act, which provides federal support to the states for health services for mothers and children. The Programs section of this Web site explains Title V and the bureau's objectives and programs. The Funding section describes available grants and provides guidance and forms. The Data section reports statistical indicators of women's and children's health.
Subjects: Motherhood; Child Health and Safety
Publications: *Child Health USA*, HE 20.9213:
Health and Well-Being of Children: A Portrait of States and the Nation, HE 20.9002:
Understanding Title V of the Social Security Act, HE 20.9208:
Women's Health USA, HE 20.9216:

1673. Migrant and Seasonal Farm Workers
http://www.doleta.gov/msfw/
Sponsor(s): Labor Department — Employment and Training Administration (ETA)
Description: The Department of Labor maintains this Web site for their National Farmworker Jobs Program (NFJP). The program provides funding to community-based organizations and public agencies that assist migrant and seasonal farmworkers with job skills training, housing, and health care. The Web site has information on the program, grant awards, and state allocations.
Subjects: Farms and Farming; Job Training — Grants

1674. Neighborhood Networks
http://www.hud.gov/nnw/nnwindex.html
Sponsor(s): Housing and Urban Development (HUD)
Description: Neighborhood Networks works to enhance the self-sufficiency, employability, and economic self-reliance of low-income families and the elderly living in HUD properties by providing onsite access to computer and training resources at community technology centers. Major sections of the site include About Neighborhood Networks, Find A Center, Start a New Center, Resources for Centers, Residents' Corner, and Success Stories. Under the Resources for Centers page, the Publications subsection includes fact sheets, guides, and partnership reports, all in PDF format.
Subjects: Computer Literacy
Publications: *Neighborhood Networks Fact Sheet*, HH 13.16/5:
Neighborhood Networks Newsline, HH 13.16/2:

1675. Office of Family Assistance (OFA)
http://www.acf.hhs.gov/programs/ofa/
Sponsor(s): Health and Human Services Department — Administration for Children and Families (ACF)
Description: OFA administers the Temporary Assistance for Needy Families (TANF) welfare program. Along with non-technical overviews of how TANF works, the site provides legislative, regulatory, and financial data, as well as other legal and technical documents related to the program. Other useful information includes the names of state TANF programs and the *Indicators of Welfare Dependence* report.
Subjects: Welfare
Publications: *Annual Report to Congress/Temporary Assistance to Need Families*, HE 25.11:
Indicators of Welfare Dependence, HE 1.1/4:

1676. Office of University Partnerships (OUP)
http://www.oup.org/
Sponsor(s): Housing and Urban Development (HUD)
Description: OUP functions as a national clearinghouse for disseminating information about HUD's Community Outreach Partnership Centers Program. HUD established the OUP in 1994 to encourage university-community partnerships. Its Web site features the following sections: About OUP, Funding, Research Tools, Publications, and Technical Assistance. A grantee database lists current and past grant recipients by state. The Research Tools section includes more information on completed research and links to related Web sites.
Subjects: Community Development — Grants

1677. Partnerships Against Violence Network — Pavnet Online
http://www.pavnet.org/
Sponsor(s): Agriculture Department (USDA) — National Agricultural Library (NAL)
Description: The Partnerships Against Violence Network (Pavnet Online) site brings together information on violence prevention programs, funding sources, and technical assistance from seven different federal agencies. The Research Database section has a catalog of federally funded research on violence. The Programs section includes links to violence prevention programs, curricula and teaching materials, and available technical assistance. Interested users can subscribe to the Pavnet anti-violence e-mail forum by using a Web form on the site.
Subjects: Crime; Victims of Crime

1678. Poverty Guidelines, Research, and Measurement
http://aspe.os.dhhs.gov/poverty/poverty.shtml
Sponsor(s): Health and Human Services Department
Description: This site provides the text of the current HHS poverty guidelines, as published annually in the *Federal Register*. A table lists the actual dollar figures going back to 1982 and links to the guidelines going back to 1996. The site explains the difference between the "poverty threshold" issued by the Census Bureau and the "poverty guidelines" issued by HHS. The site includes papers and articles about how poverty can be measured and how it has been measured over time. It also links to academic research centers studying poverty.

   This is a useful site for checking the current poverty guidelines, especially since it includes additional explanatory information.
Subjects: Poverty

1679. Social Security Advisory Board
http://www.ssab.gov/
Sponsor(s): Social Security Advisory Board
Description: The Social Security Advisory Board is an independent, bipartisan board whose purpose is to advise the president, Congress, and the Commissioner of Social Security on the Social Security and Supplemental Security Income programs. Its Web site has information on the board's authority and operations and has brief biographies of its members. The board's reports are online in full text back to 1998.
Subjects: Social Security
Publications: *A Disability System for the 21st Century*, Y 3.2:
Retirement Security: The Unfolding of a Predictable Surprise, Y 3.2:
Social Security: Why Action Should Be Taken Soon, Y 3.2:

1680. Social Security Online
http://www.socialsecurity.gov/
Alternate URL(s): http://www.ssa.gov/
Sponsor(s): Social Security Administration (SSA)
Description: The SSA's central Web site leads to a wealth of information and online services from the agency. Major categories on the home page include Retirement; Medicare; Disability and SSI; Widows, Widowers, and Other Survivors; and Get Help With Your Situation (marriage, adoption, identity theft, death, etc.). Other sections give information about resources (forms, publications, data, regulations); information by audience type (employers, immigrants, etc.); and news. The site also provides prominent links to information about the Social Security number and card.

   Under Resources, the Publications subsection features publications about benefits, with versions in Spanish; information about the Social Security Statement;

actuarial publications, such as the Trustees Report and SSI Annual Report; and the online *Social Security Handbook*. Under History, Research & Data, the Data section links to the Office of the Chief Actuary and the Policy, Research & Statistics section, both of which have key statistical reports; the Actuary section has cost-of-living adjustment (COLA) figures. Another section, Information for the Press, includes the Facts and Figures series, which has information sheets on frequently requested statistics and program questions.

Other Languages, located on the top menu of the home page, links to the SSA Multilanguage Gateway. Consumer information is available there in 15 languages, including Spanish, Arabic, Chinese, French, Portuguese, Farsi, Korean, and Russian. Each section also has information on interpreter services. A Spanish-language version of the site, though not complete, is available through the Seguro Social link at the top right of the home page.

The design of the SSA's main Web page makes it easy to find information on popular topics. The site also has a search engine and alphabetical site index (the site map). For specific topics, one of the most helpful tools may be the Answers to Your Questions knowledgebase. It can be accessed indirectly from a number of locations on the site or can be accessed directly at http://ssa-custhelp.ssa.gov/.

Subjects: Social Security

Publications: *Actuarial Notes*, SSA 1.25:

Actuarial Studies, SSA 1.25/2:

Annual Report of the Board of Trustees of the OASDI Trust Funds, SSA 1.1/4:

Annual Statistical Supplement to the Social Security Bulletin, SSA 1.22/2

Compilation of Social Security Laws . . ., Y 4.W 36:10-3/

Earnings and Employment Data for Wage and Salary Workers Covered by Social Security, by State and County, SSA 1.17/3:

Fast Facts and Figures About Social Security, SSA 1.26:

Income of the Aged Chartbook, SSA 1.2:IN 2/

Income of the Population 55 or Older, SSA 1.30:

OASDI Beneficiaries by State and County, SSA 1.17/4:

Performance Plan, Fiscal Year. . .and Revised Final Fiscal Year . . . Performance Plan, SSA 1.2:P 41/

Program Operations Manual System (POMS)

Seguro Social, hechos sobre cupones de alimentos, SSA 1.2:F 73/2/

Seguro Social, Seguridad de Ingreso Suplementario Para Extranjeros, SSA 1.2:N 73/

Social Security Bulletin, SSA 1.22:

Social Security Handbook, SSA 1.8/3:

Social Security Programs in the United States, SSA 1.24/2:

Social Security Programs Throughout the World (annual), SSA 1.24:

Social Security Rulings, HE 3.44/2:

SSA's Accountability Report for FY . . ., SSA 1.1/2:

SSI Recipients by State and County, SSA 1.17:

What You Need to Know When You Get Retirement or Survivors Benefits. . ., SSA 1.20:

1681. Social Security Online — For Women

http://www.ssa.gov/women/

Sponsor(s): Social Security Administration (SSA)

Description: This site provides SSA program information on retirement, survivors, disability, and Supplemental Security Income benefits relevant to women. Information is organized into categories that correspond to the various life stages of women: Working Woman, Beneficiary, Bride, New Mother, Divorced Spouse, Caregiver, and Widow.

Subjects: Social Security; Women

1682. Task Force for Faith-based and Community Initiatives (Justice)

http://www.ojp.usdoj.gov/fbci/

Sponsor(s): Justice Department

Description: The Task Force is charged with identifying and eliminating barriers to the participation of faith-based and community-based organizations in grants funded by the Department of Justice. The site highlights opportunities for communities and faith-based organizations to become involved in Justice programs and provides information on competing for grants.

Subjects: Grants

1683. Title V Information System (TVIS)

https://performance.hrsa.gov/mchb/mchreports/Search/search.asp

Sponsor(s): Health and Human Services Department — Health Resources and Services Administration (HRSA) — Maternal and Child Health Bureau

Description: TVIS electronically captures data from annual Title V Block Grant applications and reports. Title V of the Social Security Act covers a major federal block grant program funding health promotion efforts for mothers, infants, and children. Reports available on the site include "Financial Data for the Most Recent Year," "Program Data for the Most Recent Year," and "Measurement and Indicator Data."

Subjects: Reproductive Health — Statistics; Child Health and Safety — Statistics

Publications: *Title V: A Snapshot of Maternal and Child Health*, HE 20.9202:

1684. Unemployment Insurance

http://workforcesecurity.doleta.gov/unemploy/

Sponsor(s): Labor Department — Employment and Training Administration (ETA)

Description: Each state administers a separate unemployment insurance (UI) program within guidelines established by federal law. This Department of Labor Web site provides a centralized location for information on the federal-state program. Major sections cover program information, laws and regulations, statistics, budget, and reemployment services. The site also links to each state office administering unemployment insurance.

Subjects: Unemployment Insurance

1685. United We Ride

http://www.unitedweride.gov/

Sponsor(s): Federal Interagency Coordinating Council on Access and Mobility (CCAM)

Description: The federal United We Ride initiative coordinates grants to states to improve transportation options for groups such as the elderly, low-income individuals, or disabled persons. The site provides program policy and funding information, guidance to the states, and strategies for improving citizens' mobility. Publications and the *United We Ride Newsletter* are in the Resources section of the site.

Subjects: Transportation Funding

1686. USAID: Faith-based and Community Initiatives

http://www.usaid.gov/our_work/global_partnerships/fbci/

Sponsor(s): Agency for International Development (USAID)

Description: The Office of Faith-based and Community Initiatives at USAID uses this page to highlight current funding opportunities and provide resources for interested organizations. The site also has information on the rules governing participation by religious organizations.

Subjects: Foreign Assistance; Grants

1687. USDA Faith-based and Community Initiatives
http://www.usda.gov/fbci/
Sponsor(s): Agriculture Department (USDA)
Description: This USDA site highlights opportunities for faith-based and community organizations in USDA programs. It includes guidance documents and success story examples.
Subjects: Grants; Social Services

Volunteerism and Charities

1688. AmeriCorps
http://www.americorps.org/
Sponsor(s): Corporation for National and Community Service — Americorps
Description: AmeriCorps is a program of the Corporation for National and Community Service. AmeriCorps volunteers serve on education, public safety, health, and environmental assistance projects and are eligible for an education-related stipend. The Web site has information for potential volunteers and for organizations seeking AmeriCorps assistance. Under the Our Programs section, the site describes AmeriCorps*VISTA (Volunteers in Service to America), AmeriCorps*N-CCC (National Civilian Community Corps), and AmeriCorps*State and National.
Subjects: Volunteerism

1689. Citizen Corps
http://www.citizencorps.gov/
Sponsor(s): USA Freedom Corps
Description: Citizen Corps, part of USA Freedom Corps, was created to help coordinate volunteer activities to prepare communities to respond to emergency situations. Its Web site describes the major programs it supports: Neighborhood Watch, CERT (Community Emergency Response Teams), VIPs (Volunteers in Police Service), the Fire Corps, and the Medical Reserve Corps. The site also links to emergency preparedness guidance.
Subjects: Volunteerism

1690. Corporation for National and Community Service (CNCS)
http://www.cns.gov/
Sponsor(s): Corporation for National and Community Service
Description: CNCS is a federal corporation governed by a board of directors. CNCS programs include AmeriCorps, Learn and Serve America, National Senior Service Corps, and a number of special initiatives. The Web site has prominent links to the Web sites for its programs and information about how to volunteer. The About Us section has information on staff and organizational structure, fact sheets, relevant laws and regulations, and the annual report to Congress. Other sections include information about grants, funding, jobs, and internships.
Subjects: Volunteerism
Publications: *National Service News*, Y 3.N 21/29:

1691. Learn and Serve America
http://www.learnandserve.org/
Sponsor(s): Corporation for National and Community Service — Learn and Serve America
Description: Learn and Serve America is a program of the Corporation for National and Community Service that makes grants to governments and organizations for

service-learning projects. The projects are designed to help students learn while working to meet community needs. The site has information on grants and assistance for organizations, and on opportunities for students, educators, and other individuals. Special programs described on the site include the Universities Rebuilding America Partnership and the Presidential Freedom Scholarship.

Subjects: Education — Grants; Volunteerism

1692. Search for Charities

http://www.irs.gov/charities/article/0,,id=96136,00.html

Sponsor(s): Treasury Department — Internal Revenue Service (IRS)

Description: This is an online version of IRS Publication 78 *Cumulative List of Organizations*. It can be searched to see if a particular organization is exempt from federal taxation and if contributions to them are tax deductible. It can be searched by name, city, or state, or by browsing an alphabetical list of organizations. The organization list can also be downloaded in its entirety.

On the search page, be sure to check the Additions to Publication 78 section. It provides a listing of organizations to which contributions are tax deductible, but whose names were not included in the latest online version. The site also has helpful background information that should be consulted before conducting a search or using the information.

Subjects: Charities; Databases

Publications: *Publication 78, Cumulative List of Organizations* (annual), T 22.2/11:

1693. Senior Corps

http://www.seniorcorps.org/

Sponsor(s): Corporation for National and Community Service — Senior Corps

Description: Senior Corps is a program of the Corporation for National and Community Service involving volunteers ages 55 and older. The Web site describes its major projects: Foster Grandparents, Senior Companions, and Retired and Senior Volunteer Program (RSVP). The site has information for potential volunteers and for organizations seeking assistance from Senior Corps.

Subjects: Senior Citizens; Volunteerism

1694. Take Pride in America

http://www.takepride.gov/

Sponsor(s): Interior Department

Description: Take Pride in America is an effort to encourage and recognize volunteers who work to improve public parks, forests, wildlife refuges, local playgrounds, and other public lands areas. The site has a nationwide database of volunteer opportunities and descriptions of such programs as Take Pride Cities and Take Pride Schools.

Subjects: Public Lands; Volunteerism

1695. USA Freedom Corps

http://www.usafreedomcorps.gov/

Sponsor(s): USA Freedom Corps

Description: The USA Freedom Corps came out of a presidential initiative proposed in the wake of the September 11, 2001, terrorist attacks. Its goal is to encourage and support volunteerism and national service. The site has information for potential volunteers, for educators, for organizations and businesses, and for those wishing to donate money or goods.

Subjects: Volunteerism

1696. Volunteer.Gov/Gov
http://www.volunteer.gov/gov/
Sponsor(s): Interior Department
Description: The goal of Volunteer.Gov/Gov is to connect people with public service volunteer opportunities. Users can view descriptions of volunteer opportunities by topic or ZIP code and apply for positions online. Volunteer.Gov/Gov is an interagency effort; the site is managed by the Department of the Interior.
Subjects: Volunteerism

CHAPTER 20

Transportation

While some aspects of transportation are handled at the state and local levels, the federal government still plays a major role in transportation funding, policy, regulation, and research. This chapter covers many modes of transportation and includes Web sites that are intended for consumers, as well as sites intended for transportation operators and makers of transportation policy.

Subsections in this chapter are Aviation, Maritime Transportation, Mass Transit, Surface Transportation, Transportation Policy and Research, and Transportation Safety.

Aviation

1697. Air Transportation Stabilization Board
http://www.ustreas.gov/offices/domestic-finance/atsb/
Sponsor(s): Treasury Department — Office of Domestic Finance
Description: The Air Transportation Stabilization Board was created by Congress to issue federal loan guarantees to air carriers that suffered losses due to the September 11, 2001, terrorist attacks. Its Web site provides information on the board and the Air Transportation Safety and System Stabilization Act (Public Law 107-42). Content includes regulations, press releases, meeting minutes, and highlights of recent activities.
Subjects: Airlines

1698. Federal Aviation Administration
http://www.faa.gov/
Sponsor(s): Transportation Department — Federal Aviation Administration (FAA)
Description: The Federal Aviation Administration (FAA) is responsible for the safety of civil aviation. Major sections of the FAA's Web site include the following: Aircraft; Airports and Air Traffic (with airport status and airline on-time statistics); Data and Statistics (with data on accidents, delays, passengers); Education and Research (with links to aviation schools); Licenses and Certificates (including Airmen and Aircraft Registries); Regulations and Policies; and Safety. The Library section comprises reports, forms, newsletters, handbooks, and other documents from FAA and its offices. The site also has audience-specific sections for travelers, pilots, mechanics, and others.
Subjects: Aviation — Regulations; Aviation Safety — Regulations
Publications: *Administrator's Fact Book*, TD 4.20/2:
Advisory Circular Checklist, TD 4.8/5:
Aeronautical Information Manual, TD 4.12/3:
Air Traffic Publications Library, TD 4.78:
Airplane Flying Handbook, TD 4.8/2:
Aviation Capacity Enhancement Plan, TD 4.77:
Aviation Safety Statistical Handbook
FAA Aviation News, TD 4.9:
Federal Aviation Regulations, TD 4.6:
Index and User Guide Vol. 1, Airworthiness Directives Small Aircraft, TD 4.10/5:
Index and User Guide Vol. 2, Airworthiness Directives Large Aircraft, TD 4.10/5-2:
International Flight Information Manual, TD 4.309:
National Plan Integrated Airport Systems, TD 4.33/3:

Notices to Airmen, TD 4.12/2:
Summary of Airworthiness Directives: Large Aircraft, TD 4.10/3:
Summary of Airworthiness Directives: Small Aircraft, TD 4.10/2:

1699. Flight Standards Service

http://www.faa.gov/about/office_org/headquarters_offices/
avs/offices/afs/

Sponsor(s): Transportation Department — Federal Aviation Administration (FAA)
Description: The FAA's Flight Standards Service maintains this Web site to provide FAA safety-related information for pilots and others regarding flying, airlines, and aircraft. The site has information on its safety programs and the Civil Aviation Registry, which is responsible for the registration of United States civil aircraft and certification of airmen. The site organizes major Flight Standards Service divisions into sections including, Air Transportation, Aircraft Maintenance, Flight Technologies and Procedures, General Aviation and Commercial, and Regulatory Support.
Subjects: Aircraft — Regulations

1700. National Aeronautical Charting Office (NACO)

http://www.naco.faa.gov/

Sponsor(s): Transportation Department — Federal Aviation Administration (FAA) — National Aeronautical Charting Office (NACO)
Description: NACO is charged with the compilation, reproduction, and distribution of aeronautical navigation products and digital databases for the United States and its territories and possessions. The NACO Web site describes the office and provides information about how to order its products. It also includes sections for Catalogs, Free Online Products, Sales Agents Listings, and Special Notices. The Free Online Products section includes the Aeronautical Chart User's Guide and Visual Flight Rule (VFR) Chart Update Bulletins.
Subjects: Aviation; Maps and Mapping
Publications: *Catalog of Aeronautical Charts*, C 55.418/2:

1701. PilotWeb

https://pilotweb.nas.faa.gov/

Sponsor(s): Transportation Department — Federal Aviation Administration (FAA)
Description: The FAA's PilotWeb provides links to airport and flight path condition information for pilots. It links to the FAA's *Notices to Airmen* (NOTAMs), which can be searched by flight path and radius. It also links to information and tools such as a real-time airport arrival demand chart, route management tool, runway visual range database, and NOAA's Aviation Weather Center.
Subjects: Aviation
Publications: *Notices to Airmen*, TD 4.12/2:

1702. William J. Hughes Technical Center

http://www.tc.faa.gov/

Sponsor(s): Transportation Department — Federal Aviation Administration (FAA)
Description: The William J. Hughes Technical Center is an aviation research, development, engineering, testing, and evaluation facility located in New Jersey. Center activities involve testing and evaluation in air traffic control, communications, navigation, airports, and aircraft safety and security, as well as long-range R&D projects. This Web site includes an overview of the center's work and provides links to specific activity information, such as the Transportation Security Laboratory, Airway Operational Support, and Airport/Aircraft Safety Research and Development.
Subjects: Aviation Safety — Research

Maritime Transportation

1703. Federal Maritime Commission
http://www.fmc.gov/
Sponsor(s): Federal Maritime Commission (FMC)
Description: The Federal Maritime Commission is responsible for the regulation of shipping in the foreign trades of the United States. Its Web site is designed for providers and consumers of international shipping services. The site's Electronic Reading Room section has rulemakings, investigations, reports, and the Controlled Carrier List. The Web site also links to SERVCON, the commission's electronic filing system.
Subjects: Shipping — Regulations
Publications: *Commonly Used Commission Forms (Federal Maritime Commission)*, FMC 1.13:
Formal Docket Decisions, FMC 1.10/2:
News Releases, FMC 1.7:
Small Claims Decisions (Informal Dockets) (Federal Maritime Commission), FMC 1.10/3:
Speeches and Remarks (Federal Maritime Commission), FMC 1.9/3:

1704. Maritime Administration
http://marad.dot.gov/
Sponsor(s): Transportation Department — Maritime Administration (MARAD)
Description: The Department of Transportation's Maritime Administration (MARAD) promotes the U.S. merchant marine for both waterborne commerce and as a naval and military auxiliary in time of war or national emergency. The About MARAD section links to information about its programs and initiatives, such as shipbuilding, national security, cargo preference laws, and support for U.S. ports. The Education section features maritime career information, maritime history, and a page for kids. Statistics provided on the site cover fleet inventory, waterborne traffic, shipbuilding, cruise passengers, and related topics. Publications include *Glossary of Shipping Terms* and *Compilation of Maritime Law*.
Subjects: Merchant Marine; Shipping
Publications: *Compilation of Maritime Laws*, TD 11.6:
Glossary of Shipping Terms, TD 11.2:
Introducing the Maritime Administration, TD 11.2:M 33/3
MARAD Update
Maritime Security Report, TD 11.36:
U.S. Domestic Ocean Trades
U.S. Foreign Waterborne Transportation Statistics, TD 11.35:
U.S. Maritime Administration Annual Report, TD 11.1:
Vessel Calls at U.S. and World Ports

1705. Saint Lawrence Seaway Development Corporation
http://www.seaway.dot.gov/
Alternate URL(s): http://www.greatlakes-seaway.com/
Sponsor(s): Transportation Department — Saint Lawrence Seaway Development Corporation (SLSDC)
Description: SLSDC works to ensure the safe transit of vessels through the two U.S. locks and navigation channels of the Saint Lawrence Seaway System. SLSDC works cooperatively with the Canadian Saint Lawrence Seaway Management Corporation, and many of the links on this site lead to a binational Web site run by both corporations (see alternate URL). The Briefing Room section includes press releases, Seaway Notices, and the toll schedule. Annual reports from 1997 onward

are available under a separate heading. Other sections include Port Profiles, Regulations, and the *Seaway Handbook*.
Subjects: Shipping

1706. USCG Navigation Center
http://www.navcen.uscg.gov/
Sponsor(s): Homeland Security Department — Coast Guard
Description: The U.S. Coast Guard Navigation Center provides navigation services that promote safe transportation and support the commerce of the United States. The site features information on Navigation Rules, Maritime Telecommunications, Global Positioning System (GPS), Differential Global Positioning System (DGPS), Notice Advisories to Navstar Users (NANUs), Local Notices to Mariners, and the LORAN-C service.
Subjects: Maritime Transportation
Publications: *Federal Radionavigation Plan*, D 1.84:
Light List, TD 5.9:
Local Notice to Mariners, HS 7.19/6:
Radionavigation Bulletin, TD 5.3/10:

Mass Transit

1707. Federal Transit Administration
http://www.fta.dot.gov/
Sponsor(s): Transportation Department — Federal Transit Administration (FTA)
Description: The Federal Transit Administration assists in the planning, development, and financing of public transportation. Its Web site has major sections on FTA grant programs and research and technical assistance. The site also has a section with information about transit safety and security, with an emphasis on both accident prevention and security threats. The About FTA section has agency budget and contracting information. News and Events section has press releases, procurement news, congressional testimony, and "Dear Colleague" letters to state transportation agencies. The site also provides transit laws and regulations, as well as regulatory guidance. At the bottom of the home page, a U.S. map links to local transit agency Web sites by FTA region.

The FTA Web site provides important content for those people with professional interests in mass transit and transportation funding and policy.
Subjects: Mass Transit; Transportation — Grants
Publications: *Advanced Public Transportation Systems*, TD 10.2:
Annual Report on New Starts: Proposed Allocations of Funds for FY. . ., TD 7.1/2:
Statistical Summaries: FTA Grant Assistance Programs, TD 7.2:G 76/2/
Status of the Nation's Highways, Bridges, and Transit, TD 2.30/5:

1708. National Transit Database
http://www.ntdprogram.com/ntdprogram/
Sponsor(s): Transportation Department — Federal Transit Administration (FTA)
Description: The National Transit Database consists of data submitted by more than 650 transit agencies and collected by the Federal Transit Administration. Information is available in spreadsheet and PDF formats and includes financial data, ridership counts, and safety reports. The data is intended for transit planning purposes and is also used in the formula allocations of federal transit funds.
Subjects: Mass Transit — Statistics
Publications: *National Transit Database*, TD 7.11/2-2:

1709. TransitWeb
http://www.transitweb.its.dot.gov/
Sponsor(s): Transportation Department — Federal Transit Administration (FTA)
Description: Transit agencies are the target audience for this Web site. The site promotes best practices for transit agency Web sites and other methods of communicating with riders. For example, it includes a handbook for making public transit Web sites easier to use and information about bus signage for the visually impaired.
Subjects: Mass Transit

Surface Transportation

1710. Amtrak
http://www.amtrak.com/
Sponsor(s): Amtrak (National Railroad Passenger Corporation)
Description: Passengers can use the Amtrak Web site to plan rail excursions, book trips, and check on train schedules. Main sections include Reservations, Schedules, Routes, and Stations. Amtrak, officially the National Passenger Railroad Corporation, is a federally chartered for-profit public corporation. For information about its operations and finances, see the Inside Amtrak and News and Media sections, which are linked at the bottom of each page. The site is also available in Spanish.
Subjects: Amtrak; Railroads
Publications: *Amtrak Annual Report*
Amtrak Strategic Reform Initiatives

1711. Central Federal Lands Highway Division
http://www.cflhd.gov/
Sponsor(s): Transportation Department — Federal Highway Administration (FHWA)
Description: The Federal Lands Highway Program administers highway programs in cooperation with other federal agencies and provides transportation engineering services for the highways and bridges that are on, or provide access to, federally owned lands. The Central Federal Lands Highway Division has responsibility for most states west of the Mississippi River, excepting those in the far northwestern United States. Its jurisdiction also includes Hawaii and American Samoa. This site contains information about its Projects, Procurement, Design Resources, and Technology Development section. The Projects section lists projects by state and provides links to construction documents.
Subjects: Highways and Roads; West (United States)

1712. Eastern Federal Highway Lands Division
http://www.efl.fhwa.dot.gov/
Sponsor(s): Transportation Department — Federal Highway Administration (FHWA)
Description: The Federal Lands Highway Program administers highway programs in cooperation with other federal agencies and provides transportation engineering services for the highways and bridges that are on, or provide access to, federally owned lands. The Eastern Division serves 31 states east and immediately west of the Mississippi River, Puerto Rico, and the Virgin Islands. The site has sections on Projects, Procurement, Design Resources, and Technology Development. A Planning and Public Involvement section includes National Environmental Policy Act documents and public notices. The Procurement section has information about bid solicitations, results, and awarded contracts.
Subjects: Highways and Roads

1713. Federal Highway Administration
http://www.fhwa.dot.gov/
Sponsor(s): Transportation Department — Federal Highway Administration (FHWA)
Description: The FHWA Web site offers a wide range of information related to the nation's highways and roads. The main page highlights news on topics such as the Highway Trust Fund and the 2005 Safe, Accountable, Flexible, Efficient Transportation Equity Act: A Legacy for Users (SAFETEA-LU). The FHWA Program section of the site serves as an index to the administration's offices, programs, and component Web sites. Major categories include Planning, Environment, and Real Estate Services; Infrastructure; Operations; Safety; Policy; and Research, Development, and Technology. The Policy section contains the Web site for the FHWA Office of Policy, with its numerous statistical reports on highway use, economics, funding, fuel, and related topics.

The Electronic Reading Room links to Freedom of Information Act (FOIA) information, publications, statistics, and legislation and regulations. Other sections include About FHWA, Employee Phone Directories, and Doing Business with FHWA. The site has featured an extensive historical section in commemoration of the fiftieth anniversary of the Eisenhower Interstate System.
Subjects: Highways and Roads
Publications: *Financing Federal-Aid Highways*, TD 2.30/5:
Greener Roadsides, TD 2.30/16-2:
Guide to Reporting Highway Statistics, TD 2.30/5:
Highway Information Quarterly, TD 2.23/4:
Highway Information Updates, TD 2.23/5:
Highway Statistics (annual), TD 2.23:
Highway Taxes & Fees: How They are Collected and Distributed, TD 2.64:
Innovative Finance Quarterly, TD 2.75:
National Household Travel Survey
Our Nation's Highways: Selected Facts & Figures, TD 2.23/6:
Toll Facilities in the United States, TD 2.2:T 57/
Traffic Volume Trends, TD 2.50:
Women in Transportation, TD 2.30/5

1714. Federal Railroad Administration
http://www.fra.dot.gov/
Sponsor(s): Transportation Department — Federal Railroad Administration (FRA)
Description: The Federal Railroad Administration consolidates government support of railroad activities and provides regulation and research for improved railroad safety. The site includes the following sections: Safety; Freight Railroading; Passenger Rail; Research and Development; Regulations, Legislation, and Litigation; and Press Room. An Issue Briefs section features a number of background papers on such topics as highway-rail crossings, intercity passenger rail, and U.S. rail export opportunities.
Subjects: Railroad Safety; Railroads — Regulations

1715. FreedomCAR and Vehicle Technologies Program
http://www.eere.energy.gov/vehiclesandfuels/
Sponsor(s): Energy Department — Energy Efficiency and Renewable Energy Office
Description: The goal of the FreedomCAR program is "more energy efficient and environmentally friendly highway transportation technologies that will enable America to use less petroleum" (from the Web site). The CAR in FreedomCAR stands for Cooperative Automotive Research; partners in the program include major U.S. car manufacturers and oil companies. The Web site has information about the program, financial opportunities, and related information resources.

Special sections cover the key program areas, such as hybrid and vehicle systems, energy storage, and advanced combustion engines.
Subjects: Motor Vehicles — Research

1716. National Traffic and Road Closure Information
http://www.fhwa.dot.gov/trafficinfo/
Sponsor(s): Transportation Department — Federal Highway Administration (FHWA)
Description: This FHWA site centralizes access to government and commercial road condition and traffic information Web sites nationwide.
Subjects: Highways and Roads

1717. Surface Transportation Board
http://www.stb.dot.gov/
Sponsor(s): Transportation Department — Surface Transportation Board (STB)
Description: The Surface Transportation Board (STB) is an independent adjudicatory body within the Department of Transportation. The Board is responsible for the economic regulation of interstate surface transportation, primarily railroads. The Web site features sections including: Rail Consumers (shippers, receivers, rail car owners, rail car manufacturers); Industry Data (economic and merger data); and Environmental Matters (regulations, cases, correspondence). An E-Library section has STB decisions and notices, transcripts and statements from STB hearings, and relevant statutes, rules, and legislation.
Subjects: Railroads
Publications: *Surface Transportation Board Reports: Decisions of the Surface Transportation Board*, TD 13.6/2:

1718. Turner Fairbank Highway Research Center (TFHRC)
http://www.tfhrc.gov/
Sponsor(s): Transportation Department — Federal Highway Administration (FHWA)
Description: TFHRC is the applied research facility of the Federal Highway Administration. The center is charged with researching preservation and improvement of national highways, especially in areas such as safety, intelligent transportation systems, pavements, and materials and structural technologies. The center's Web site has information on its products and research. Online versions of three periodicals are available: *Research & Technology Transporter*, *Focus*, and *Public Roads*.
Subjects: Highways and Roads — Research; Pavements — Research
Publications: *Focus*, TD 2.30/13-2:
Public Roads, TD 2.19:
Research & Technology Transporter, TD 2.70:

1719. Western Federal Lands Highway Division
http://www.wfl.fhwa.dot.gov/
Sponsor(s): Transportation Department — Federal Highway Administration (FHWA)
Description: The Federal Lands Highway Program administers highway programs in cooperation with other federal agencies and provides transportation engineering services for the highways and bridges that are on, or provide access to, federally owned lands. The Western Federal Lands Highway Division serves Oregon, Washington, Idaho, Montana, Wyoming and Alaska. This site has information organized into sections including Projects, Procurement, and Design Resources. It also has information on the Forest Highway Program and links to information on any road construction or closures for the states served by the division.
Subjects: Highways and Roads; West (United States)

Transportation Policy and Research

1720. Best Workplaces for Commuters
http://www.bwc.gov/
Sponsor(s): Environmental Protection Agency (EPA)Transportation Department
Description: Best Workplaces for Commuters is a public-private sector voluntary program that advocates for employee commuter benefits. Its Web site provides information on commuting trends and information for employers who wish to set up a commuter benefits program. The site identifies the companies with the best programs and provides information for the media to promote the campaign.
Subjects: Commuting; Workplace Conditions

1721. Bureau of Transportation Statistics
http://www.bts.gov/
Sponsor(s): Transportation Department — Bureau of Transportation Statistics (BTS)
Description: The BTS Web site is a central source for U.S. transportation data collected by BTS and other agencies. The home page features current news and data releases. Many BTS publications can be ordered for free online, in either print or in a another physical format through the Bookstore section. Many publications are also available for free online viewing; these publications typically are offered in a variety of file formats, including PDF, HTML, and — for data tables — spreadsheet format. The BTS publication *The Journal of Transportation and Statistics* has been discontinued by BTS because of budget constraints; as stated on the Web site, "BTS hopes to bring the *Journal* back as a virtual publication in the future." *Journal* issues from 1998 to 2005 are still available online. In 2005, BTS became a part of the Department of Transportation's Research and Innovative Technology Administration (RITA). The About BTS section explains their funding and organizational status, mission, and goals.

The Data section, called TranStats, is described in elsewhere in this chapter.

The strong points of the BTS Web site include detailed airline on-time statistics, summary reports on U.S. transportation, and insight into the government statistical programs on this topic.
Subjects: Transportation — Statistics
Publications: *Estimated Impacts of September 11th on US Travel*
Freight in America
Journal of Transportation and Statistics, TD 12.18:
National Transportation Statistics, TD 12.1/2:
Pocket Guide to Transportation, TD 12.8/2:
State Transportation Statistics
Strategic Plan for Transportation Statistics
The Changing Face of Transportation, TD 12.2:
Transportation Statistics Annual Report, TD 12.1:
TranStats, TD 12.19:
U.S. International Trade and Freight Transportation Trends, TD 12.2:
U.S. International Travel and Transportation Trends, TD 12.2:

1722. Center for Transportation Analysis
http://cta.ornl.gov/cta/
Sponsor(s): Energy Department — Oak Ridge National Laboratory (ORNL)
Description: The Center for Transportation Analysis (CTA) conducts research and development for many aspects of transportation. The Research Areas section on the CTA Web site includes the following subsections on Aviation Safety, Defense Transportation, Energy and Environmental Policy Analysis, Intelligent Transpor-

tation Systems, and many other topics. The site also has a publications directory and an extensive list of links to related Web sites.
Subjects: Energy Consumption — Research; Transportation — Research

1723. Department of Transportation
http://www.dot.gov/
Sponsor(s): Transportation Department
Description: The Department of Transportation divides its Web content into categories for different audiences, with sections for Citizens, Businesses, and Governments. The Citizens section has a wealth of material to meet frequent information needs. It addresses topics such as air travel, vehicle safety, commuter issues, recreational boating, aircraft certification, and cruise ship travel. The Business section has information about contracting opportunities, acquisitions, and grants, and a section for truckers/motor carriers. The Government Services section has information about programs that regulate, provide grants for, and otherwise affect state governments. Highlighted programs include the Transportation Equity Act for the 21st Century, the Surface Transportation Reauthorization, the Transportation Safety Institute, and the New Starts grant program. The site also includes general information about the department, with links to the Web sites for Transportation Department agencies, relevant regulations and legislation, and the docket management system.
Subjects: Transportation
Publications: *Air Travel Consumer Report*, TD 1.54:
Inspector General Audit Reports, TD 1.1/3-2:
Office of the Inspector General: Semiannual Report to Congress, TD 1.1/3:
SPE News, TD 1.59:
Transportation Acquisition Circular (TAC), TD 1.6/3:
Transportation Acquisition Manual, TD 1.8:

1724. Federal Highway Administration Education Pages
http://www.fhwa.dot.gov/education/
Sponsor(s): Transportation Department — Federal Highway Administration (FHWA)
Description: The central education page from FHWA provides educational information and resources on the administration and its Garrett A. Morgan Technology and Transportation Futures Program. Featured sections include Kindergarten through Fifth Grade, Sixth Grade through Eighth Grade, Ninth Grade through Twelfth Grade, Life-Long Learning, Instructional Aids for Teachers, and Colleges, Universities, and Trade Schools.
Subjects: Transportation; Kids' Pages

1725. John A. Volpe National Transportation Center
http://www.volpe.dot.gov/
Sponsor(s): Transportation Department
Description: The John A. Volpe National Transportation Systems Center conducts research and development, engineering, and analysis on transportation and logistics topics. The Our Work section of the site covers the projects and technical expertise of the center in detail. The center's expertise includes environmental issues, safety engineering, noise and vibration, and Global Positioning Systems (GPS). The Information Resources section includes reports, technical papers, and articles published by Volpe Center staff. The Volpe Center receives no federal appropriations and works on a fee-for-service basis. Its site also has information about doing business with the center for clients and for vendors.
Subjects: Engineering Research; Transportation — Research
Publications: *Volpe Journal*, TD 10.15:

1726. Research and Innovative Technology Administration
http://www.rita.dot.gov/
Sponsor(s): Transportation Department — Research and Innovative Technology Administration (RITA)
Description: RITA is charged with coordinating Department of Transportation research programs and advancing the use of innovative transportation technologies. Its Web site includes links to RITA's component offices, such as the Bureau of Transportation Statistics and the University Transportation Centers.
Subjects: Transportation — Research

1727. TranStats: the Intermodal Transportation Database
http://transtats.bts.gov/
Sponsor(s): Transportation Department — Bureau of Transportation Statistics (BTS)
Description: TranStats offers organized access to over 100 transportation-related databases, as well as the social and demographic data sets commonly used in transportation analysis. The data comes from federal agencies and several transportation-related organizations. The data sets are packaged with basic documentation. The TranStats Web site offers downloading in comma-separated file format and provides some interactive mapping applications. Transportation modes covered by the data sets include aviation, highway, mass transit, rail, bike/pedestrian, pipeline, and others.
Subjects: Transportation — Statistics; Databases
Publications: *Directory of Transportation Data Sources*, TD 1.9/4:

1728. University Transportation Centers (UTC) Program
http://utc.dot.gov/
Sponsor(s): Transportation Department — Research and Innovative Technology Administration (RITA)
Description: The UTC Program funds grants for up to 60 multidisciplinary, university-based centers with transportation research themes. Its Web site includes a directory of the centers and their themes, information about grant competitions, and a catalog of university research reports.
Subjects: Transportation — Grants

Transportation Safety

1729. Boating Safety
http://www.uscgboating.org/
Sponsor(s): Homeland Security Department — Coast Guard
Description: This Coast Guard Web site for the recreational boater has safety tips, news of product defects and recalls, boating accident statistics, and a guide to federal and state boating laws and regulations. It also provides information about grant programs designed to promote boating safety.
Subjects: Boating Safety

1730. BoosterSeat.gov
http://www.boosterseat.gov/
Sponsor(s): Transportation Department — National Highway Traffic Safety Administration (NHTSA)
Description: BoosterSeat.gov promotes public awareness of the value of using proper car safety seats for children who have outgrown toddler seats but are not yet tall

enough for safety belts. The site provides information about seat regulations and a guide to help choose the right seat for the child's size.

Subjects: Child Health and Safety

1731. Fatality Analysis Reporting System (FARS) Web-based Encyclopedia

http://www-fars.nhtsa.dot.gov/

Sponsor(s): Transportation Department — National Highway Traffic Safety Administration (NHTSA)

Description: The Fatality Analysis Reporting System (FARS) presents data from motor vehicle crashes in the United States that result in the death of an occupant of a vehicle or a nonmotorist within 30 days of the crash. This site is designed to make the FARS data easily accessible through the Web. Fact sheets that report trends in the data are listed towards the bottom of the Web site's home page and include fatal crash statistics relating to alcohol, school buses, speeding, pedestrians, children, and other topics.

Users can create their own queries and simple maps of the data. The query system allows users to choose multiple variables concerning the crashes and characteristics of the persons, vehicles, or drivers involved. Data can be reported in text, spreadsheet, or chart formats.

Subjects: Accidents (Motor Vehicles) — Statistics

1732. Federal Motor Carrier Safety Administration

http://www.fmcsa.dot.gov/

Sponsor(s): Transportation Department — Federal Motor Carrier Safety Administration

Description: FMCSA's mission is to "reduce crashes, injuries, and fatalities involving large trucks and buses" (from the Web site). For regulated carriers, the site has online registration for USDOT Numbers, Operating Authority, and Cargo Tank Numbers. The site also carries the text of the FMCSRs — the Federal Motor Carrier Safety Regulations. The Safety Programs section has background information on topics such as cargo securement and hazardous material security. The Facts and Research section has a variety of motor carrier safety statistics, including a table relating the costs of accidents. The Cross Border section includes information on U.S. Commercial Zones and on entering the United States as a commercial truck driver. The site is also available in Spanish.

Subjects: Trucking; Transportation Safety

1733. FHWA Safety

http://safety.fhwa.dot.gov/

Sponsor(s): Transportation Department — Federal Highway Administration (FHWA)

Description: FHWA's Office of Safety focuses on highway engineering to promote road safety. The Web site covers road design research and other topics, such as public education, accident statistics, laws and guidelines, and safety technologies. Special sections discuss the safety of pedestrians, bicyclists, older drivers, intersections, railroad crossings, and routes to school. The site also links to resources for states and localities.

Subjects: Accidents (Motor Vehicles); Highways and Roads; Safety

1734. Hazmat Safety

http://hazmat.dot.gov/

Sponsor(s): Transportation Department

Description: This site offers extensive information resources on the transportation of hazardous materials. The site includes the sections Who and Where We Are,

e-Hazmat Online Services, Rules and Regulations, Training Information, OHM Publications and Reports, Available Files and Documents, Incidents, Emergency Response Guidebook, Risk Management, International Standards, Enforcement, HMT Security, and FOIA.
Subjects: Toxic Substances — Regulations; Transportation Security
Publications: *Biennial Report on Hazardous Materials Transportation*, TD 10.2:M 41/
Emergency Response Guidebook, TD 9.8:
Penalty Actions Taken by the Department of Transportation for Violations of the Hazardous Materials Transportation Regulations, TD 10.2:H 33/

1735. National Highway Traffic Safety Administration
http://www.nhtsa.dot.gov/
Sponsor(s): Transportation Department — National Highway Traffic Safety Administration (NHTSA)
Description: NHTSA sets and enforces safety performance standards for motor vehicles and assists state and local governments with grants for local highway safety programs. The NHTSA Web site has information about product recalls, crash test results, consumer complaints, technical service bulletins, and defects investigations for cars, child seats, tires, and auto equipment. There are car and tire safety tips, as well as regulatory information on such topics as fuel economy, child seats, safety standards, and air bags. The Traffic Safety section covers topics such as aggressive driving, alcohol, child passengers, school buses, and pedestrian and bicycle safety. It also includes state legislative fact sheets on open container laws, motorcycle helmet use, driver's blood alcohol level, and related topics. The Laws and Regulations section covers both state and federal matters. Popular links on the site's side panel include Docket Management System, Grants, and Traffic Safety Materials Catalog.
This site offers a substantial collection of information about the government's testing of vehicles and its auto safety ratings and makes it accessible for consumers. The site also brings together grants, regulatory, and state and national legislative information concerning motor vehicle standards and traffic safety.
Subjects: Motor Vehicles — Regulations; Traffic Safety; Vehicle Safety
Publications: *Automotive Fuel Economy Program*, TD 8.26:
Buying a Safer Car for Child Passengers, TD 8.66:
NHTSA Now
State Legislative Fact Sheets, TD 8.65:
State Traffic Safety Information, TD 8.62:
Traffic Safety Materials Catalog, TD 8.27/3:
Traffic Techs, TD 8.63:

1736. National Transportation Safety Board
http://www.ntsb.gov/
Sponsor(s): National Transportation Safety Board (NTSB)
Description: The National Transportation Safety Board site features information about its programs and the primary areas of safety on which the NTSB works. These programs include Aviation, Highway, Marine, Railroad, Pipeline and Hazardous Material, and Transportation Disaster Assistance. Each program area has a Web page with further details and publications. The NTSB Most Wanted section links to information about safety improvements recommended by the Board. Other major sections are News and Events, Data and Information Products, and Information Sources and Contacts. The News and Events section includes documents from recent major investigations and information about board meetings and public hearings. The Data and Information Products section provides accident statistics, legal documents, and Safety Recommendation Letters. The Information Sources

and Contacts section contains phone numbers and helpful instructions on how to obtain different types of information from NTSB. The Transportation Disaster Assistance section explains the role of NTSB in coordinating responses from federal, state, and local governments and the airlines to meet the needs of aviation disaster victims and their families.

Subjects: Accidents (Motor Vehicles) — Statistics; Safety; Transportation
Publications: *Aircraft Accident Reports*, TD 1.112:
Hazardous Materials Accident Briefs, TD 1.128/2:
Hazardous Materials Accident Reports, TD 1.129:
Highway Accident Briefs, NTSB-HAB (series), TD 1.117/2:
Highway Accident Reports, TD 1.117:
Marine Accident Reports, TD 1.116:
Pipeline Accident Briefs, NTSB-PAB (series), TD 1.118/3:
Pipeline Accident Reports, TD 1.118:
Railroad Accident Briefs, NTSB-RAB (series), TD 1.112/5:
Railroad Accident Reports, TD 1.112/3:

1737. Pipeline and Hazardous Materials Safety Administration
http://www.phmsa.dot.gov/
Sponsor(s): Transportation Department — Pipeline and Hazardous Materials Safety Administration (PHMSA)
Description: PHMSA is responsible for the safe and secure movement of hazardous materials shipments by all modes of transportation, including through pipeline infrastructure. The PHMSA Web site provides detailed information, statistics, and research in its Safety section. Other sections include Regulations, News, and Education and Training. Publications, data, and documents can be found in the Reference section.
Subjects: Toxic Substances; Transportation Safety

1738. SaferCar.gov
http://www.safercar.gov/
Sponsor(s): Transportation Department — National Highway Traffic Safety Administration (NHTSA)
Description: SaferCar.gov provides information about vehicle safety for drivers and car shoppers. Topics covered include tires, air bags, and rollover prevention. The site features a searchable database of results from the New Car Assessment Program, which provide the "government 5-star ratings." It also has information about reported defects and recalls and links for further information on evaluating auto safety.
Subjects: Motor Vehicles

1739. Transportation Safety Institute
http://www.tsi.dot.gov/
Sponsor(s): Transportation Department — Research and Innovative Technology Administration (RITA)
Description: The Transportation Safety Institute is a self-funding federal agency that provides safety and security training to both the public and private sectors. The institute provides training related to mass transit, aviation, pipelines, motor carriers, highway safety, hazardous materials transportation, and risk management. Its Web site provides a course catalog and detailed information about each of its program areas.
Subjects: Transportation Security; Transportation Safety

Members of Congress

This appendix lists the members of the 110th Congress by state and U.S. territory.

Alabama

Sen. Jeff Sessions (R)
http://sessions.senate.gov/
E-mail: http://senate.sessions.gov/email/contact.cfm

Sen. Richard C. Shelby (R)
http://shelby.senate.gov/
E-mail: senator@shelby.senate.gov

Rep. Jo Bonner (R), District: 01
http://bonner.house.gov
E-mail: http://www.house.gov/HoR/AL01/Contact + Us

Rep. Terry Everett (R), District: 02
http://www.everett.house.gov
E-mail: http://www.everett.house.gov/
index.php?option = com_content&task = view&id = 26&Itemid = 32

Rep. Mike Rogers (R), District: 03
http://www.house.gov/mike-rogers/
E-mail: http://www.house.gov/mike-rogers/contact/index.shtml

Rep. Robert B. Aderholt (R), District: 04
http://aderholt.house.gov/
E-mail: http://aderholt.house.gov/IQ_email.shtml

Rep. Bud Cramer (D), District: 05
http://cramer.house.gov
E-mail: budmail@mail.house.gov

Rep. Spencer Bachus (R), District: 06
http://bachus.house.gov
E-mail: http://bachus.house.gov/HoR/AL06/Contact + Me/

Rep. Artur Davis (D), District: 07
http://www.house.gov/arturdavis/
E-mail: http://www.house.gov/arturdavis/zipauth.shtml

Alaska

Sen. Lisa Murkowski (R)
http://murkowski.senate.gov/
E-mail: http://murkowski.senate.gov/contact.cfm

Sen. Ted Stevens (R)
http://stevens.senate.gov/
E-mail: http://stevens.senate.gov/constituents.cfm

Rep. Don Young (R), District: At-Large
http://donyoung.house.gov/
E-mail: http://donyoung.house.gov/contact.htm

American Samoa

Del. Eni F. H. Faleomavaega (D), District: At-Large
http://www.house.gov/faleomavaega/
E-mail: faleomavaega@mail.house.gov

Arizona

Sen. Jon Kyl (R)
http://kyl.senate.gov/
E-mail: http://kyl.senate.gov/contact.cfm

Sen. John McCain (R)
http://mccain.senate.gov/
E-mail: http://mccain.senate.gov/index.cfm?fuseaction = Contact.Home

Rep. Rick Renzi (R), District: 01
http://www.house.gov/renzi/
E-mail: http://www.house.gov/renzi/email.shtml

Rep. Trent Franks (R), District: 02
http://www.house.gov/franks/
E-mail: http://www.house.gov/franks/contact.shtml

Rep. John Shadegg (R), District: 03
http://johnshadegg.house.gov/
E-mail: http://www.house.gov/formshadegg/emailtemplate.htm

Rep. Ed Pastor (D), District: 04
http://www.house.gov/pastor/

Rep. J. D. Hayworth (R), District: 05
http:// hayworth.house.gov/
E-mail: http://hayworth.house.gov/jdcontent/contact/index.shtml
Rep. Hayworth lost his bid for re-election. Harry Mitchell (D) was elected to the House to represent the 5th district of Arizona.

Rep. Jeff Flake (R), District: 06
http://www.house.gov/flake/
E-mail: jeff.flake@mail.house.gov

Rep. Raúl Grijalva (D), District: 07
http://www.house.gov/grijalva/
E-mail: http://www.house.gov/grijalva/contact.html

Rep. Jim Kolbe (R), District: 08
http://www.house.gov/kolbe/
E-mail: http://www.house.gov/kolbe/IMA/issue.htm
Rep. Kolbe did not seek re-election in 2006. Gabrielle Giffords (D) was elected to the House to represent the 8th district of Arizona.

Arkansas

Sen. Blanche Lincoln (D)
http://lincoln.senate.gov/
E-mail: http://lincoln.senate.gov/html/webform.html

Sen. Mark Pryor (D)
http://pryor.senate.gov/
E-mail: http://pryor.senate.gov/contact/

Rep. Marion Berry (D), District: 01
http://www.house.gov/berry/
E-mail: http://www.house.gov/berry/zipauth.shtml

Rep. Vic Snyder (D), District: 02
http://www.house.gov/snyder/
E-mail: http://www.house.gov/snyder/contact/index.htm

Rep. John Boozman (R), District: 03
http://www.boozman.house.gov/
E-mail: http://www.boozman.house.gov/contactform/

Rep. Mike Ross (D), District: 04
http://www.house.gov/ross/
E-mail: http://www.house.gov/ross/contact.shtml

California

Sen. Barbara Boxer (D)
http://boxer.senate.gov/
E-mail: http://boxer.senate.gov/contact/intermediate.cfm

Sen. Dianne Feinstein (D)
http://feinstein.senate.gov/
E-mail: http://feinstein.senate.gov/email.html

Rep. Mike Thompson (D), District: 01
http://mikethompson.house.gov/
E-mail: http://mikethompson.house.gov/contact/email.asp

Rep. Wally Herger (R), District: 02
http://www.house.gov/herger/
E-mail: http://www.house.gov/herger/contactNEW.htm

Rep. Daniel Lungren (R), District: 03
http://www.house.gov/lungren/
E-mail: http://www.lungren.house.gov/feedback.shtml

Rep. John Doolittle (R), District: 04
http://doolittle.house.gov/
E-mail: http://doolittle.house.gov/email/

Rep. Doris O. Matsui (D), District: 05
http://matsui.house.gov/
E-mail: http://matsui.house.gov/email.asp

Rep. Lynn Woolsey (D), District: 06
http://woolsey.house.gov/
E-mail: http://woolsey.house.gov/contactemailform.asp

Rep. George Miller (D), District: 07
http://www.house.gov/georgemiller/
E-mail: george.miller@mail.house.gov

Rep. Nancy Pelosi (D), District: 08
http://www.house.gov/pelosi/
E-mail: sf.nancy@mail.house.gov

Rep. Barbara Lee (D), District: 09
http://lee.house.gov
E-mail: barbara.lee@mail.house.gov

Rep. Ellen Tauscher (D), District: 10
http://www.house.gov/tauscher/
E-mail: http://www.house.gov/tauscher/IMA/get_address.htm

Rep. Richard Pombo (R), District: 11
http://pombo.house.gov
E-mail: http://www.house.gov/pombo/contact/commentsform.htm
Rep. Pombo lost his bid for re-election. Jerry McNerney (D) was elected to the House to represent the 11th district of California.

Rep. Tom Lantos (D), District: 12
http://lantos.house.gov
E-mail: http://lantos.house.gov/HoR/CA12/Contact + Tom/

Rep. Fortney "Pete" Stark (D), District: 13
http://www.house.gov/stark/
E-mail: http://www.house.gov/stark/contact/index.htm

Rep. Anna Eshoo (D), District: 14
http://eshoo.house.gov/
E-mail: http://eshoo.house.gov/
index.php?option = com_content&task = view&id = 6&Itemid = 15

Rep. Michael Honda (D), District: 15
http://www.honda.house.gov/
E-mail: http://www.honda.house.gov/contactmike.shtml

Rep. Zoe Lofgren (D), District: 16
http://zoelofgren.house.gov
E-mail: zoe.lofgren@mail.house.gov

Rep. Sam Farr (D), District: 17
http://www.farr.house.gov/
E-mail: http://www.farr.house.gov/feedback.cfm

Rep. Dennis Cardoza (D), District: 18
http://www.house.gov/cardoza/
E-mail: http://www.house.gov/cardoza/contact.shtml

Rep. George Radanovich (R), District: 19
http://radanovich.house.gov/
E-mail: http://www.house.gov/radanovich/IMA/issue.htm

Rep. Jim Costa (D), District: 20
http://www.house.gov/costa/
E-mail: http://www.house.gov/costa/IMA/issue_subscribe.htm

Rep. Devin Nunes (R), District: 21
http://www.nunes.house.gov/
E-mail: http://www.nunes.house.gov/contact.htm

Rep. Bill Thomas (R), District: 22
http://billthomas.house.gov/
E-mail: http://billthomas.house.gov/Contact.asp
*Rep. Thomas did not seek re-election in 2006. Kevin McCarthy (R) was
elected to the House to represent the 22nd district of California.*

Rep. Lois Capps (D), District: 23
http://www.house.gov/capps/
E-mail: http://www.house.gov/capps/contact/send_an_email.shtml

Rep. Elton Gallegly (R), District: 24
http://www.house.gov/gallegly/
E-mail: http://www.house.gov/gallegly/contact.htm

Rep. Howard "Buck" McKeon (R), District: 25
http://mckeon.house.gov/
E-mail: http://mckeon.house.gov/lets_talk.html

Rep. David Dreier (R), District: 26
http://dreier.house.gov
E-mail: http://dreier.house.gov/talkto.htm

Rep. Brad Sherman (D), District: 27
http://www.house.gov/sherman/
E-mail: http://www.house.gov/sherman/contact/

Rep. Howard L. Berman (D), District: 28
http://www.house.gov/berman/
E-mail: http://www.house.gov/berman/contact/

Rep. Adam Schiff (D), District: 29
http://schiff.house.gov/
E-mail: http://schiff.house.gov/HoR/CA29/Contact + Information/
Contact + Form.htm

Rep. Henry Waxman (D), District: 30
http://www.house.gov/waxman/
E-mail: http://www.house.gov/waxman/contact.htm

Rep. Xavier Becerra (D), District: 31
http://www.becerra.house.gov/HoR/ca31/

Rep. Hilda Solis (D), District: 32
http://solis.house.gov/
E-mail: http://solis.house.gov/Mail_Rep_Solis.htm

Rep. Diane E. Watson (D), District: 33
http://www.house.gov/watson/
E-mail: http://www.house.gov/watson/contact.shtml

Rep. Lucille Roybal-Allard (D), District: 34
http://www.house.gov/roybal-allard/
E-mail: http://www.house.gov/roybal-allard/contact.htm

Rep. Maxine Waters (D), District: 35
http://www.house.gov/waters/
E-mail: http://www.house.gov/waters/IMA/issue.htm

Rep. Jane Harman (D), District: 36
http://www.house.gov/harman/
E-mail: http://www.house.gov/harman/emailJane.html

Rep. Juanita Millender-McDonald (D), District: 37
http://www.house.gov/millender-mcdonald/
E-mail: http://millender-mcdonald.house.gov/HoR/CA37/Contact + Information/
Contact + Form.htm

Rep. Grace Napolitano (D), District: 38
http://www.napolitano.house.gov
E-mail: http://www.napolitano.house.gov/feedback.htm

Rep. Linda Sánchez (D), District: 39
http://www.lindasanchez.house.gov/
E-mail: http://www.lindasanchez.house.gov/index.cfm?section = contact

Rep. Edward R. Royce (R), District: 40
http://www.royce.house.gov/
E-mail: http://www.royce.house.gov/Contact/

Rep. Jerry Lewis (R), District: 41
http://www.house.gov/jerrylewis/
E-mail: http://www.house.gov/jerrylewis/WritetoRepresentativeLewis.htm

Rep. Gary Miller (R), District: 42
http://www.house.gov/garymiller/
E-mail: gary.miller@mail.house.gov

Rep. Joe Baca (D), District: 43
http://www.house.gov/baca/
E-mail: http://www.house.gov/baca/zipauth.shtml

Rep. Ken Calvert (R), District: 44
http://www.calvert.house.gov/
E-mail: http://calvert.house.gov/email.asp

Rep. Mary Bono (R), District: 45
http://bono.house.gov/
E-mail: http://bono.house.gov/Contact_Mary/

Rep. Dana Rohrabacher (R), District: 46
http://rohrabacher.house.gov/
E-mail: dana@mail.house.gov

Rep. Loretta Sanchez (D), District: 47
http://www.lorettasanchez.house.gov/
Email:http://www.lorettasanchez.house.gov/forms/contact.html

Rep. John Campbell (R), District: 48
http://campbell.house.gov/
Rep. Christopher Cox was appointed Chairman of the Securities and Exchange
Commission, effective August 2, 2005.

Rep. Darrell Issa (R), District: 49
http://www.issa.house.gov/
E-mail: http://issa.house.gov/
index.cfm?FuseAction = ContactInformation.ContactForm&CFID = 917943&
CFTOKEN = 26544993

Rep. Brian Bilbray (R), District: 50
http://www.house.gov/bilbray/
E-mail: http://www.house.gov/bilbray/contact.shtml

Rep. Bob Filner (D), District: 51
http://www.house.gov/filner/
E-mail: http://www.house.gov/filner/email.htm

Rep. Duncan Hunter (R), District: 52
http://www.house.gov/hunter/
E-mail: http://www.house.gov/hunter/contact.shtml

Rep. Susan A. Davis (D), District: 53
http://www.house.gov/susandavis/
E-mail: http://www.house.gov/susandavis/IMA/contact.html

Colorado

Sen. Wayne Allard (R)
http://allard.senate.gov/public/
E-mail: http://allard.senate.gov/public/index.cfm?FuseAction = Contact.Home

Sen. Ken Salazar (D)
http://salazar.senate.gov/
E-mail: http://salazar.senate.gov/contact/email.cfm

Rep. Diana DeGette (D), District: 01
http://www.house.gov/degette/
E-mail: http://www.house.gov/degette/comment.shtml

Rep. Mark Udall (D), District: 02
http://markudall.house.gov/
E-mail: http://markudall.house.gov/HoR/CO02/Contact + Mark/

Rep. John T. Salazar (D), District: 03
http://www.house.gov/salazar/
E-mail: http://www.house.gov/salazar/contact.shtml

Rep. Marilyn Musgrave (R), District: 04
http://musgrave.house.gov/
E-mail: http://musgrave.house.gov/contactform/

Rep. Joel Hefley (R), District: 05
http://www.house.gov/hefley/
E-mail: http://www.house.gov/hefley/contact.shtm#dc
*Rep. Hefley did not seek re-election in 2006. Doug Lamborn (R) was elected to
the House to represent the 5th district of Colorado.*

Rep. Thomas Tancredo (R), District: 06
http://tancredo.house.gov/
E-mail: http://tancredo.house.gov/contact/contact_contacttom.shtml

Rep. Bob Beauprez (R), District: 07
http://www.house.gov/beauprez/
E-mail: http://www.house.gov/beauprez/contact.shtml
*Rep. Beauprez did not seek re-election in 2006; instead, he ran unsuccessfully
for governor of Colorado. Edwin Perlmutter (D) was elected to the House to
represent the 7th district of Colorado.*

Connecticut

Sen. Chris Dodd (D)
http://dodd.senate.gov/
E-mail: http://dodd.senate.gov/webmail/

Sen. Joe Lieberman (I/D)
http://lieberman.senate.gov/
E-mail: http://lieberman.senate.gov/contact/index.cfm?regarding = issue
Sen. Lieberman switched his party affiliation from Democrat to Independent
Democrat in 2006.

Rep. John Larson (D), District: 01
http://www.house.gov/larson/
E-mail: http://www.house.gov/larson/emailaddress.htm

Rep. Rob Simmons (R), District: 02
http://simmons.house.gov/
E-mail: http://www.house.gov/formsimmons/ima/send_email.html
*Rep. Simmons lost his bid for re-election. Joseph Courtney (D) was elected to
the House to represent the 2nd district of Connecticut.*

Rep. Rosa DeLauro (D), District: 03
http://www.house.gov/delauro/
E-mail: http://www.house.gov/delauro/IMA/issue.htm

Rep. Christopher Shays (R), District: 04
http://www.house.gov/shays/
E-mail: http://www.house.gov/shays/contact/index.htm

Rep. Nancy Johnson (R), District: 05
http://www.house.gov/nancyjohnson/
E-mail: http://www.house.gov/nancyjohnson/zipauth.htm
Rep. Johnson lost her bid for re-election. Chris Murphy (D) was elected to the House to represent the 5th district of Connecticut.

Delaware

Sen. Joseph R. Biden (D)
http://biden.senate.gov/
E-mail: http://biden.senate.gov/contact/emailjoe.cfm

Sen. Thomas R. Carper (D)
http://carper.senate.gov/
E-mail: http://carper.senate.gov/email-form.html

Rep. Michael N. Castle (R), District: At-Large
http://www.house.gov/castle/

District of Columbia

Del. Eleanor Holmes Norton (D), District: At-Large
http://www.norton.house.gov/
E-mail: http://www.norton.house.gov/forms/contact.html

Florida

Sen. Mel Martinez (R)
http://martinez.senate.gov/public/
E-mail: http://martinez.senate.gov/public/
index.cfm?FuseAction = ContactInformation.ContactForm

Sen. Bill Nelson (D)
http://billnelson.senate.gov/
E-mail: http://billnelson.senate.gov/contact/index.cfm#email

Rep. Jeff Miller (R), District: 01
http://jeffmiller.house.gov/
E-mail: http://jeffmiller.house.gov/index.cfm?FuseAction = Contact.Home

Rep. Allen Boyd (D), District: 02
http://www.house.gov/boyd/

Rep. Corrine Brown (D), District: 03
http://www.house.gov/corrinebrown/
E-mail: http://www.house.gov/corrinebrown/IMA/issue.shtml

Rep. Ander Crenshaw (R), District: 04
http://crenshaw.house.gov/
E-mail: http://crenshaw.house.gov/
index.cfm?FuseAction = ContactInformation.OfficeLocations

Rep. Virginia Brown-Waite (R), District: 05
http://brown-waite.house.gov/
E-mail: http://www.house.gov/formbrown-waite/IMA/issue_subscribe.htm

Rep. Cliff Stearns (R), District: 06
http://www.house.gov/stearns/
E-mail: http://www.house.gov/stearns/Contact.html

Rep. John Mica (R), District: 07
http://www.house.gov/mica/
E-mail: http://www.house.gov/mica/messageform.htm

Rep. Ric Keller (R), District: 08
http://keller.house.gov/
E-mail: http://keller.house.gov/Contact/

Rep. Mike Bilirakis (R), District: 09
http://www.house.gov/bilirakis/
*Rep. Bilirakis did not seek re-election in 2006. Gus Bilirakis (R) was elected
to the House to represent the 9th district of Florida.*

Rep. C.W. Bill Young (R), District: 10
http://www.house.gov/young/
E-mail: bill.young@mail.house.gov

Rep. Jim Davis (D), District: 11
http://www.house.gov/jimdavis/
E-mail: http://www.house.gov/jimdavis/message.html
*Rep. Davis did not seek re-election in 2006; instead, he ran unsuccessfully for
governor of Florida. Katherine Castor (D) was elected to the House to
represent the 11th district of Florida.*

Rep. Adam Putnam (R), District: 12
http://www.house.gov/putnam/
E-mail: http://www.adamputnam.house.gov/pages/contact.html

Rep. Katherine Harris (R), District: 13
http://harris.house.gov/
E-mail: http://www.house.gov/formharris/issue.htm
*Rep. Harris did not seek re-election in 2006; instead, she ran unsuccessfully
for U.S. Senate. Vern Buchanan (R) was elected to the House to represent the
13th district of Florida. At the time this publication went to press, his
opponent, Christine Jennings (D), was challenging the results of the election.*

Rep. Connie Mack (R), District: 14
http://mack.house.gov/
E-mail: http://mack.house.gov/
index.cfm?FuseAction = ContactConnie.ContactForm

Rep. Dave Weldon M.D. (R), District: 15
http://weldon.house.gov/
E-mail: http://weldon.house.gov/Contact/

Rep. Mark Foley (R), District: 16
http://www.house.gov/foley/home.shtml
E-mail: http://www.house.gov/foley/mail.htm
Rep. Foley resigned from the House in September 2006. Timothy Mahoney (D) was elected to the House to represent the 16th district of Florida.

Rep. Kendrick Meek (D), District: 17
http://kendrickmeek.house.gov/
E-mail: http://kendrickmeek.house.gov/contact1.shtml

Rep. Ileana Ros-Lehtinen (R), District: 18
http://www.house.gov/ros-lehtinen/
E-mail: http://www.house.gov/ros-lehtinen/contact.shtml

Rep. Robert Wexler (D), District: 19
http://wexler.house.gov/
E-mail: http://wexler.house.gov/contact.php

Rep. Debbie Wasserman Schultz (D), District: 20
http://www.house.gov/schultz/
E-mail: http://www.house.gov/schultz/zipauth.htm

Rep. Lincoln Diaz-Balart (R), District: 21
http://diaz-balart.house.gov/
E-mail: http://diaz-balart.house.gov/index.cfm?FuseAction = Offices.Contact

Rep. E. Clay Shaw Jr. (R), District: 22
http://shaw.house.gov/
E-mail: http://shaw.house.gov/Contact/
Rep. Shaw lost his bid for re-election. Ronald Klein (D) was elected to the House to represent the 22nd district of Florida.

Rep. Alcee L. Hastings (D), District: 23
http://alceehastings.house.gov/
E-mail: http://alceehastings.house.gov/IMA/issue.htm

Rep. Tom Feeney (R), District: 24
http://www.house.gov/feeney/
E-mail: http://www.house.gov/feeney/contact.htm

Rep. Mario Diaz-Balart (R), District: 25
http://www.house.gov/mariodiaz-balart/
E-mail: http://www.house.gov/mariodiaz-balart/contact.htm

Georgia

Note: Georgia underwent redistricting prior to the November 2006 election.

Sen. Saxby Chambliss (R)
http://chambliss.senate.gov/
E-mail: http://chambliss.senate.gov/public/
index.cfm?FuseAction=ContactUs.ContactForm

Sen. Johnny Isakson (R)
http://isakson.senate.gov
E-mail: http://isakson.senate.gov/contact.cfm

Rep. Jack Kingston (R), District: 01
http://www.house.gov/kingston/
E-mail: jack.kingston@mail.house.gov

Rep. Sanford D. Bishop Jr. (D), District: 02
http://www.house.gov/bishop/
E-mail: http://bishop.house.gov/display.cfm?content_id=229

Rep. Lynn A. Westmoreland (R), District: 03
http://westmoreland.house.gov/
E-mail: http://westmoreland.house.gov/contact/

Rep. Cynthia McKinney (D), District: 04
http://www.house.gov/mckinney/
E-mail: http://www.house.gov/mckinney/guest.htm
*Rep. McKinney was defeated for re-nomination in 2006. Hank Johnson (D)
was elected to the House to represent the 4th district of Georgia.*

Rep. John Lewis (D), District: 05
http://www.house.gov/johnlewis/index.shtml
E-mail: http://www.house.gov/johnlewis/contact.html

Rep. Tom Price (R), District: 06
http://tomprice.house.gov/
E-mail: http://tomprice.house.gov/html/contact_form_email.cfm

Rep. John Linder (R), District: 07
http://linder.house.gov/
E-mail: http://linder.house.gov/index.cfm?FuseAction=Contact.Home

Rep. Jim Marshall (D), District: 08
http://www.house.gov/marshall/
E-mail: http://www.house.gov/marshall/contact.html

Rep. Nathan Deal (R), District: 09
http://www.house.gov/deal/
E-mail: http://www.house.gov/deal/contact/default.shtml

Rep. Charlie Norwood (R), District: 10
http://www.house.gov/norwood/
E-mail: http://www.house.gov/norwood/contact.shtml

Rep. Phil Gingrey M.D. (R), District: 11
http://gingrey.house.gov/
E-mail: http://www.house.gov/formgingrey/IMA/issue.htm

Rep. John Barrow (D), District: 12
http://barrow.house.gov/
E-mail: http://barrow.house.gov/contactemail.asp

Rep. David Scott (D), District: 13
http://davidscott.house.gov/
E-mail: http://davidscott.house.gov/Contact/

Guam

Del. Madeleine Bordallo (D)
http://www.house.gov/bordallo/
E-mail: http://www.house.gov/bordallo/IMA/issue.htm

Hawaii

Sen. Daniel Kahikina Akaka (D)
http://akaka.senate.gov/
E-mail: http://akaka.senate.gov/public/index.cfm?FuseAction = Contact.Home

Sen. Daniel K. Inouye (D)
http://inouye.senate.gov/
E-mail: http://inouye.senate.gov/abtform.html

Rep. Neil Abercrombie (D), District: 01
http://www.house.gov/abercrombie/
E-mail: neil.abercrombie@mail.house.gov

Rep. Ed Case (D), District: 02
http://wwwa.house.gov/case/
E-mail: ed.case@mail.house.gov
Rep. Case lost his bid for the Democratic nomination to the U.S. Senate in 2006. Mazie Hirono (D) was elected to the House to represent the 2nd district of Hawaii.

Idaho

Sen. Larry Craig (R)
http://craig.senate.gov/
E-mail: http://craig.senate.gov/contact.cfm

Sen. Mike Crapo (R)
http://crapo.senate.gov/
E-mail: http://crapo.senate.gov/contact/email.cfm

Rep. C. L. "Butch" Otter (R), District: 01
http://www.house.gov/otter/
E-mail: http://otter.house.gov/contact_information.aspx
Rep. Otter did not seek re-election in 2006; instead, he was elected governor of Idaho. William Sali (R) was elected to the House to represent the 1st district of Idaho.

Rep. Mike Simpson (R), District: 02
http://www.house.gov/simpson/
E-mail: http://www.house.gov/simpson/emailme.shtml

Illinois

Sen. Richard Durbin (D)
http://durbin.senate.gov/
E-mail: http://durbin.senate.gov/contact.cfm

Sen. Barack Obama (D)
http://obama.senate.gov/
E-mail: http://obama.senate.gov/contact/

Rep. Bobby L. Rush (D), District: 01
http://www.house.gov/rush/
E-mail: http://www.house.gov/rush/zipauth.shtml

Rep. Jesse Jackson Jr. (D), District: 02
http://www.house.gov/jackson/
E-mail: http://www.house.gov/jackson/ContactByEMail.shtml

Rep. Daniel Lipinski (D), District: 03
http://www.house.gov/lipinski/

Rep. Luis V. Gutierrez (D), District: 04
http://luisgutierrez.house.gov/
E-mail: http://luisgutierrez.house.gov/feedback.cfm

Rep. Rahm Emanuel (D), District: 05
http://www.house.gov/emanuel/
E-mail: http://www.house.gov/emanuel/IMA/issue.htm

Rep. Henry Hyde (R), District: 06
http://www.house.gov/hyde/
E-mail: http://www.house.gov/hyde/get_address2.htm
Rep. Hyde did not seek re-election in 2006. Peter Roskam (R) was elected to the House to represent the 6th district of Illinois.

Rep. Danny K. Davis (D), District: 07
http://www.house.gov/davis/
E-mail: http://www.house.gov/davis/zipauth.htm

Rep. Melissa L. Bean (D), District: 08
http://www.house.gov/bean/
E-mail: http://www.house.gov/bean/issue_subscribe.htm

Rep. Jan Schakowsky (D), District: 09
http://www.house.gov/schakowsky/
E-mail: http://www.house.gov/schakowsky/contact.html

Rep. Mark Steven Kirk (R), District: 10
http://www.house.gov/kirk/
E-mail: http://www.house.gov/kirk/zipauth.shtml

Rep. Jerry Weller (R), District: 11
http://weller.house.gov/
E-mail: http://www.house.gov/formweller/formweller/zipauth.htm

Rep. Jerry Costello (D), District: 12
http://www.house.gov/costello/

Rep. Judy Biggert (R), District: 13
http://judybiggert.house.gov/
E-mail: http://judybiggert.house.gov/contact.asp

Rep. J. Dennis Hastert (R), District: 14
http://www.house.gov/hastert/
http://speaker.house.gov/
E-mail: http://www.house.gov/hastert/write1.shtml

Rep. Timothy Johnson (R), District: 15
http://www.house.gov/timjohnson/
E-mail: http://www.house.gov/timjohnson/contact/index.shtml

Rep. Don Manzullo (R), District: 16
http://manzullo.house.gov/
E-mail: http://manzullo.house.gov/HoR/IL16/Contact + Info.htm

Rep. Lane Evans (D), District: 17
http://www.house.gov/evans/
E-mail: http://www.house.gov/evans/IMA/issue.htm
*Rep. Evans did not seek re-election in 2006. Philip Hare (D) was elected to
the House to represent the 17th district of Illinois.*

Rep. Ray LaHood (R), District: 18
http://www.house.gov/lahood/
E-mail: http://www.house.gov/lahood/emailray.htm

Rep. John Shimkus (R), District: 19
http://www.house.gov/shimkus/
E-mail: http://www.house.gov/shimkus/emailme.shtml

Indiana

Sen. Evan Bayh (D)
http://bayh.senate.gov/index1.html
E-mail: http://bayh.senate.gov/WebMail1.htm

Sen. Richard G. Lugar (R)
http://lugar.senate.gov/
E-mail: senator_lugar@lugar.senate.gov

Rep. Pete Visclosky (D), District: 01
http://www.house.gov/visclosky/
E-mail: http://www.house.gov/visclosky/contact.htm

Rep. Chris Chocola (R), District: 02
http://chocola.house.gov/
E-mail: http://www.house.gov/formchocola/IMA/chocemailform.htm
Rep. Chocola lost his bid for re-election. Joseph Donnelly (D) was elected to the House to represent the 2nd district of Indiana.

Rep. Mark E. Souder (R), District: 03
http://souder.house.gov/
E-mail: souder@mail.house.gov

Rep. Steve Buyer (R), District: 04
http://stevebuyer.house.gov/
E-mail: http://stevebuyer.house.gov/guest.htm

Rep. Dan Burton (R), District: 05
http://www.house.gov/burton/
E-mail: http://www.house.gov/burton/zipauth.htm

Rep. Mike Pence (R), District: 06
http://mikepence.house.gov/
E-mail: http://www.house.gov/formpence/IMA/contact.htm

Rep. Julia Carson (D), District: 07
http://www.juliacarson.house.gov/
E-mail: http://www.juliacarson.house.gov/contact.me.shtml

Rep. John Hostettler (R), District: 08
http://www.house.gov/hostettler/
E-mail: john.hostettler@mail.house.gov
Rep. Hostettler lost his bid for re-election. Brad Ellsworth (D) was elected to the House to represent the 8th district of Indiana.

Rep. Michael E. Sodrel (R), District: 09
http://sodrel.house.gov/
E-mail: http://www.house.gov/formsodrel/IMA/issue_subscribe.htm
Rep. Sodrel lost his bid for re-election. Baron Hill (D) was elected to the House to represent the 9th district of Indiana.

Iowa

Sen. Chuck Grassley (R)
http://grassley.senate.gov/
E-mail: http://grassley.senate.gov/webform.htm

Sen. Tom Harkin (D)
http://harkin.senate.gov/
E-mail: http://harkin.senate.gov/contact/contact.cfm

Rep. Jim Nussle (R), District: 01
http://nussle.house.gov
E-mail: http://nussle.house.gov/email.htm
Rep. Nussle did not seek re-election in 2006; instead, he ran unsuccessfully for governor of Iowa. Bruce Braley (D) was elected to the House to represent the 1st district of Iowa.

Rep. Jim Leach (R), District: 02
http://www.house.gov/leach/
E-mail: http://leach.house.gov/intermediate.asp?link = http://www.house.gov/writerep/
Rep. Leach lost his bid for re-election. Dave Loebsack (D) was elected to the House to represent the 2nd district of Iowa.

Rep. Leonard Boswell (D), District: 03
http://boswell.house.gov/
E-mail: http://boswell.house.gov/messageform.htm

Rep. Tom Latham (R), District: 04
http://www.tomlatham.house.gov/
E-mail: tom.latham@mail.house.gov

Rep. Steve King (R), District: 05
http://www.house.gov/steveking/
E-mail: http://www.house.gov/steveking/email.shtm

Kansas

Sen. Sam Brownback (R)
http://brownback.senate.gov/
E-mail: http://brownback.senate.gov/CMEmailMe.cfm

Sen. Pat Roberts (R)
http://roberts.senate.gov/
E-mail: http://roberts.senate.gov/e-mail_pat.html

Rep. Jerry Moran (R), District: 01
http://www.jerrymoran.house.gov/
E-mail: http://www.jerrymoran.house.gov/
index.php?option = com_content&task = view&id = 117&Itemid = 86

Rep. Jim Ryun (R), District: 02
http://www.ryun.house.gov/
Rep. Ryun lost his bid for re-election. Nancy Boyda (D) was elected to the House to represent the 2nd district of Kansas.

Rep. Dennis Moore (D), District: 03
http://moore.house.gov/
E-mail: http://www.moore.house.gov/contact.htm

Rep. Todd Tiahrt (R), District: 04
http://www.house.gov/tiahrt/
E-mail: http://www.house.gov/tiahrt/e-mail_todd.htm

Kentucky

Sen. Jim Bunning (R)
http://bunning.senate.gov/
E-mail: http://bunning.senate.gov/index.cfm?FuseAction = Contact.Email

Sen. Mitch McConnell (R)
http://mcconnell.senate.gov/
E-mail: http://mcconnell.senate.gov/contact_form.cfm

Rep. Ed Whitfield (R), District: 01
http://whitfield.house.gov/
E-mail: http://whitfield.house.gov/contact/index.shtml

Rep. Ron Lewis (R), District: 02
http://www.house.gov/ronlewis/
E-mail: http://www.house.gov/ronlewis/contact.shtml

Rep. Anne Northup (R), District: 03
http://northup.house.gov/index.asp
E-mail: http://northup.house.gov/Contact.asp
Rep. Northup lost her bid for re-election. John Yarmuth (D) was elected to the House to represent the 3rd district of Kentucky.

Rep. Geoff Davis (R), District: 04
http://geoffdavis.house.gov/
E-mail: http://geoffdavis.house.gov/Contact.aspx

Rep. Hal Rogers (R), District: 05
http://halrogers.house.gov
E-mail: http://halrogers.house.gov/Contact.aspx

Rep. Ben Chandler (D), District: 06
http://chandler.house.gov/

Louisiana

Sen. David Vitter (R)
http://vitter.senate.gov/
E-mail: http://vitter.senate.gov/?module = webformiqv1

Sen. Mary L. Landrieu (D)
http://landrieu.senate.gov/
E-mail: http://landrieu.senate.gov/contact/index.cfm

Rep. Bobby Jindal (R), District: 01
http://jindal.house.gov
E-mail: http://www.house.gov/formjindal/issue.htm

Rep. William J. Jefferson (D), District: 02
http://www.house.gov/jefferson/
Rep. Charlie Melancon (D), District: 03
http://melancon.house.gov/
E-mail: http://www.melancon.house.gov/emailcharlie.asp

Rep. Jim McCrery (R), District: 04
http://mccrery.house.gov/
E-mail: http://mccrery.house.gov/contact.asp

Rep. Rodney Alexander (D), District: 05
http://www.house.gov/alexander/
E-mail: http://www.house.gov/alexander/contact.html

Rep. Richard Baker (R), District: 06
http://baker.house.gov/
E-mail: http://baker.house.gov/html/contact_form_email.cfm

Rep. Charles W. Boustany (R), District: 07
http://boustany.house.gov/
E-mail: http://boustany.house.gov/ContactCharles.asp

Maine

Sen. Susan Collins (R)
http://collins.senate.gov/
E-mail: http://collins.senate.gov/public/
continue.cfm?FuseAction = ContactSenatorCollins.Email

Sen. Olympia J. Snowe (R)
http://snowe.senate.gov/
E-mail: http://snowe.senate.gov/public/
index.cfm?FuseAction = ContactSenatorSnowe.Email

Rep. Tom Allen (D), District: 01
http://tomallen.house.gov/
E-mail: rep.tomallen@mail.house.gov

Rep. Michael Michaud (D), District: 02
http://michaud.house.gov/
E-mail: rep.mikemichaud@mail.house.gov

Maryland

Sen. Barbara A. Mikulski (D)
http://mikulski.senate.gov/
E-mail: http://mikulski.senate.gov/mailform.html

Sen. Paul S. Sarbanes (D)
http://sarbanes.senate.gov/
E-mail: http://sarbanes.senate.gov/pages/email.html
Sen. Sarbanes did not seek re-election in 2006. Benjamin Cardin (D) was elected to fill Sen. Sarbanes's Senate seat.

Rep. Wayne Gilchrest (R), District: 01
http://gilchrest.house.gov/
E-mail: http://gilchrest.house.gov/contact.asp?ContactType=Form

Rep. C.A. Dutch Ruppersberger (D), District: 02
http://dutch.house.gov/
E-mail: http://dutch.house.gov/writedutch_za.shtml

Rep. Ben Cardin (D), District: 03
http://www.cardin.house.gov/
E-mail: rep.cardin@mail.house.gov
Rep. Cardin did not seek re-election in 2006; instead, he ran successfully for U.S. Senate. John Sarbanes (D) was elected to the House to represent the 3rd district of Maryland.

Rep. Albert R. Wynn (D), District: 04
http://www.wynn.house.gov/
E-mail: http://www.wynn.house.gov/feedback.cfm

Rep. Steny Hoyer (D), District: 05
http://www.hoyer.house.gov/
E-mail: http://www.hoyer.house.gov/contact/email.asp

Rep. Roscoe Bartlett (R), District: 06
http://www.bartlett.house.gov
E-mail: http://www.bartlett.house.gov/Email_Roscoe/

Rep. Elijah E. Cummings (D), District: 07
http://www.house.gov/cummings/
E-mail: http://www.house.gov/cummings/contact.htm

Rep. Chris Van Hollen (D), District: 08
http://www.house.gov/vanhollen/
E-mail: http://www.house.gov/vanhollen/contact.htm

Massachusetts

Sen. Ted Kennedy (D)
http://kennedy.senate.gov/
E-mail: http://kennedy.senate.gov/senator/contact.cfm

Sen. John Kerry (D)
http://kerry.senate.gov/
E-mail: kerry.senate.gov/v3/contact/email.html

Rep. John Olver (D), District: 01
http://www.house.gov/olver/
E-mail: http://www.house.gov/olver/contact/index.html

Rep. Richard E. Neal (D), District: 02
http://www.house.gov/neal/

Rep. Jim McGovern (D), District: 03
http://www.house.gov/mcgovern/
E-mail: http://www.house.gov/mcgovern/emailredirect.html

Rep. Barney Frank (D), District: 04
http://www.house.gov/frank/
E-mail: http://www.house.gov/frank/contact.html

Rep. Martin T. Meehan (D), District: 05
http://www.house.gov/meehan/
E-mail: martin.meehan@mail.house.gov

Rep. John Tierney (D), District: 06
http://www.house.gov/tierney/
E-mail: http://www.house.gov/tierney/IMA/email.shtml

Rep. Edward Markey (D), District: 07
http://www.house.gov/markey/
E-mail: http://markey.house.gov/
index.php?option=com_email_form&Itemid=124

Rep. Mike Capuano (D), District: 08
http://www.house.gov/capuano/
Email http://www.house.gov/capuano/contact/email.shtml

Rep. Stephen F. Lynch (D), District: 09
http://www.house.gov/lynch/
E-mail: stephen.lynch@mail.house.gov

Rep. Bill Delahunt (D), District: 10
http://www.house.gov/delahunt/
E-mail: william.delahunt@mail.house.gov

Michigan

Sen. Carl Levin (D)
http://levin.senate.gov/
E-mail: http://levin.senate.gov/contact/index.cfm

Sen. Debbie Stabenow (D)
http://stabenow.senate.gov/
E-mail: http://stabenow.senate.gov/email.htm

Rep. Bart Stupak (D), District: 01
http://www.house.gov/stupak/
E-mail: http://www.house.gov/stupak/IMA/issue2.htm

Rep. Peter Hoekstra (R), District: 02
http://hoekstra.house.gov/
E-mail: http://www.house.gov/formhoekstra/IMA/email.htm

Rep. Vernon J. Ehlers (R), District: 03
http://www.house.gov/ehlers/
E-mail: http://www.house.gov/ehlers/contact.html

Rep. Dave Camp (R), District: 04
http://camp.house.gov/
E-mail: http://camp.house.gov/WriteRep.aspx

Rep. Dale E. Kildee (D), District: 05
http://www.house.gov/kildee/
E-mail: http://www.house.gov/kildee/contact.shtml

Rep. Fred Upton (R), District: 06
http://www.house.gov/upton/
E-mail: http://www.house.gov/upton/contact.html

Rep. Joe Schwarz (R), District: 07
http://schwarz.house.gov/
E-mail: http://schwarz.house.gov/contact
Rep. Schwarz was defeated for re-nomination in 2006. Tim Walberg (R) was elected to the House to represent the 7th district of Michigan.

Rep. Mike Rogers (R), District: 08
http://mikerogers.house.gov/
E-mail: http://www.mikerogers.house.gov/contact.aspx

Rep. Joe Knollenberg (R), District: 09
http://www.house.gov/knollenberg/
E-mail: http://www.house.gov/knollenberg/contact/zipcode.htm

Rep. Candice Miller (R), District: 10
http://candicemiller.house.gov/
E-mail: http://candicemiller.house.gov/Contact.aspx

Rep. Thaddeus McCotter (R), District: 11
http://mccotter.house.gov/
E-mail: http://mccotter.house.gov/HoR/MI11/Contact/
Office + Contact + Information/Zipcode + Authentication + Page.htm

Rep. Sander Levin (D), District: 12
http://www.house.gov/levin/
E-mail: http://www.house.gov/levin/zipauth.htm

Rep. Carolyn Cheeks Kilpatrick (D), District: 13
http://www.house.gov/kilpatrick/
E-mail: http://www.house.gov/kilpatrick/contact.shtml

Rep. John Conyers Jr. (D), District: 14
http://www.house.gov/conyers/
E-mail: John.Conyers@mail.house.gov

Rep. John D. Dingell (D), District: 15
http://www.house.gov/dingell/
E-mail: http://www.house.gov/dingell/contact.htm

Minnesota

Sen. Norm Coleman (R)
http://coleman.senate.gov/
E-mail: http://coleman.senate.gov/index.cfm?FuseAction = Contact.ContactForm

Sen. Mark Dayton (D)
http://dayton.senate.gov/
E-mail: http://dayton.senate.gov/contact/email.cfm
Sen. Dayton did not seek re-election in 2006. Amy Klobuchar (D) was elected to fill Sen. Dayton's Senate seat.

Rep. Gil Gutknecht (R), District: 01
http://www.house.gov/gutknecht/
E-mail: http://www.house.gov/gutknecht/Contact/form_email.htm
Rep. Gutknecht lost his bid for re-election. Timothy Walz (D) was elected to the House to represent the 1st district of Minnesota.

Rep. John Kline (R), District: 02
http://kline.house.gov/
E-mail: http://kline.house.gov/
index.cfm?FuseAction = ContactInformation.ContactForm&To = mn02hwyr@
housemail.house.gov

Rep. Jim Ramstad (R), District: 03
http://www.house.gov/ramstad/
E-mail: mn03@mail.house.gov

Rep. Betty McCollum (D), District: 04
http://mccollum.house.gov/
E-mail: http://mccollum.house.gov/index.asp?Type = NONE&SEC = {AC61FD79-AD5F-440D-A7F0-555B12349E5B}

Rep. Martin Olav Sabo (D), District: 05
http://sabo.house.gov/
E-mail: http://www.house.gov/formsabo/IMA/issue.htm
Rep. Sabo did not seek re-election in 2006. Keith Ellison (D) was elected to the House to represent the 5th district of Minnesota.

Rep. Mark Kennedy (R), District: 06
http://markkennedy.house.gov/
E-mail: http://markkennedy.house.gov/kennedycontents/contact/
Rep. Kennedy did not seek re-election in 2006; instead, he ran unsuccessfully for governor of Minnesota. Michele Bachmann (R) was elected to the House to represent the 6th district of Minnesota.

Rep. Collin C. Peterson (D), District: 07
http://collinpeterson.house.gov/
E-mail: http://collinpeterson.house.gov/email.html

Rep. James L. Oberstar (D), District: 08
http://oberstar.house.gov/
E-mail: http://wwwc.house.gov/oberstar/zipauth.htm

Mississippi

Sen. Thad Cochran (R)
http://cochran.senate.gov/
E-mail: http://cochran.senate.gov/contact.htm

Sen. Trent Lott (R)
http://lott.senate.gov/
E-mail: http://lott.senate.gov/index.cfm?FuseAction = Contact.Email

Rep. Roger Wicker (R), District: 01
http://www.house.gov/wicker/
E-mail: http://www.house.gov/wicker/Message.htm

Rep. Bennie G. Thompson (D), District: 02
http://benniethompson.house.gov/hor/ms02/
E-mail: http://benniethompson.house.gov/HoR/MS02/Contact + Bennie/

Rep. Charles W. "Chip" Pickering (R), District: 03
http://www.house.gov/pickering/
E-mail: http://www.house.gov/pickering/contact/

Rep. Gene Taylor (D), District: 04
http://www.house.gov/genetaylor/
E-mail: http://www.house.gov/genetaylor/zipauth.htm

Missouri

Sen. Christopher Bond (R)
http://bond.senate.gov/
E-mail: http://bond.senate.gov/contact/contactme.cfm

Sen. James Talent (R)
http://talent.senate.gov/
E-mail: http://talent.senate.gov/Contact/default.cfm
*Sen. Talent lost his bid for re-election. Claire McCaskill (D) was elected to fill
Sen. Talent's Senate seat.*

Rep. William Lacy Clay Jr. (D), District: 01
http://www.house.gov/clay/
E-mail: http://www.house.gov/clay/contact.htm

Rep. Todd Akin (R), District: 02
http://www.house.gov/akin/
E-mail: http://www.house.gov/akin/contact.html#email

Rep. Russ Carnahan (D), District: 03
http://www.house.gov/carnahan/
E-mail: http://www.house.gov/carnahan/contact.shtml

Rep. Ike Skelton (D), District: 04
http://www.house.gov/skelton/
E-mail: http://www.house.gov/skelton/zipauth.htm

Rep. Emanuel Cleaver II (D), District: 05
http://www.house.gov/cleaver/
E-mail: http://www.house.gov/cleaver/IMA/issue.htm

Rep. Sam Graves (R), District: 06
http://www.house.gov/graves/
E-mail: http://www.house.gov/graves/email.htm

Rep. Roy Blunt (R), District: 07
http://www.blunt.house.gov/
E-mail: http://www.blunt.house.gov/Contact.aspx

Rep. Jo Ann Emerson (R), District: 08
http://www.house.gov/emerson/
E-mail: http://www.house.gov/emerson/contact/

Rep. Kenny Hulshof (R), District: 09
http://hulshof.house.gov/
E-mail: http://hulshof.house.gov/Contact.aspx

Montana

Sen. Max Baucus (D)
http://baucus.senate.gov/
E-mail: http://baucus.senate.gov/contact/emailForm.cfm?subj = issue

Sen. Conrad Burns (R)
http://burns.senate.gov/
E-mail: http://burns.senate.gov/public/
index.cfm?FuseAction = ContactInfo.EmailMe
Sen. Burns lost his bid for re-election. Jon Tester (D) was elected to fill Sen. Burns's Senate seat.

Rep. Dennis Rehberg (R), District: At-Large
http://www.house.gov/rehberg/
E-mail: http://www.house.gov/rehberg/contact.shtml

Nebraska

Sen. Chuck Hagel (R)
http://hagel.senate.gov/
E-mail: http://hagel.senate.gov/index.cfm?FuseAction = Contact.Home

Sen. Ben Nelson (D)
http://bennelson.senate.gov/
E-mail: http://bennelson.senate.gov/contact/email.cfm

Rep. Jeff Fortenberry (R), District: 01
http://fortenberry.house.gov/
E-mail: http://fortenberry.house.gov/feedback.shtml

Rep. Lee Terry (R), District: 02
http://leeterry.house.gov/
E-mail: http://www.house.gov/formleeterry/IMA/issue.htm

Rep. Tom Osborne (R), District: 03
http://www.house.gov/osborne/
E-mail: http://www.house.gov/osborne/contact.htm
Rep. Osborne did not seek re-election in 2006; instead, he unsuccessfully sought the Republican nomination for governor of Nebraska. Adrian Smith (R) was elected to the House to represent the 3rd district of Nebraska.

Nevada

Sen. John Ensign (R)
http://ensign.senate.gov/
E-mail: http://ensign.senate.gov/forms/email_form.cfm

Sen. Harry Reid (D)
http://reid.senate.gov/
E-mail: http://reid.senate.gov/contact/email_form.cfm

Rep. Shelley Berkley (D), District: 01
http://berkley.house.gov/
E-mail: http://berkley.house.gov/contact/email.html

Rep. Jim Gibbons (R), District: 02
http://wwwc.house.gov/gibbons/
E-mail: http://wwwc.house.gov/gibbons/contact_feedback.asp
Rep. Gibbons did not seek re-election in 2006; instead, he was elected governor of Nevada. Dean Heller (R) was elected to the House to represent the 2nd district of Nevada.

Rep. Jon Porter (R), District: 03
http://www.house.gov/porter
E-mail: http://porter.house.gov/
index.cfm?SectionID = 8&ParentID = 0&SectionTypeID = 5&SectionTree = 8

New Hampshire

Sen. Judd Gregg (R)
http://gregg.senate.gov/
E-mail: http://gregg.senate.gov/sitepages/contact.cfm

Sen. John E. Sununu (R)
http://sununu.senate.gov/
E-mail: http://sununu.senate.gov/webform.html

Rep. Jeb Bradley (R), District: 01
http://www.house.gov/bradley
E-mail: http://www.house.gov/bradley/contact.html
Rep. Bradley lost his bid for re-election. Carol Shea-Porter (D) was elected to the House to represent the 1st district of New Hampshire.

Rep. Charlie Bass (R), District: 02
http://www.house.gov/bass/
E-mail: cbass@mail.house.gov
Rep. Bass lost his bid for re-election. Paul Hodes (D) was elected to the House to represent the 2nd district of New Hampshire.

New Jersey

Sen. Robert Menendez (D)
http://menendez.senate.gov/
E-mail: http://menendez.senate.gov/contact/contact.cfm

Sen. Frank Lautenberg (D)
http://lautenberg.senate.gov/
E-mail: http://lautenberg.senate.gov/contact/

Rep. Robert E. Andrews (D), District: 01
http://www.house.gov/andrews/
E-mail: http://www.house.gov/andrews/contact_form_za.shtml

Rep. Frank A. LoBiondo (R), District: 02
http://www.house.gov/lobiondo/
E-mail: http://www.house.gov/lobiondo/IMA/issue.htm

Rep. Jim Saxton (R), District: 03
http://www.house.gov/saxton/
E-mail: http://www.house.gov/saxton/contact.htm

Rep. Chris Smith (R), District: 04
http://www.house.gov/chrissmith/

Rep. Scott Garrett (R), District: 05
http://garrett.house.gov/
E-mail: http://www.house.gov/formgarrett/contact.shtml

Rep. Frank Pallone Jr. (D), District: 06
http://www.house.gov/pallone/
E-mail: http://www.house.gov/pallone/contact.shtml

Rep. Mike Ferguson (R), District: 07
http://www.house.gov/ferguson/
E-mail: http://www.house.gov/ferguson/get_address2.shtml

Rep. Bill Pascrell Jr. (D), District: 08
http://www.pascrell.house.gov
E-mail: http://www.pascrell.house.gov/feedback.cfm

Rep. Steve Rothman (D), District: 09
http://rothman.house.gov/
E-mail: http://www.house.gov/rothman/contact_steve.htm

Rep. Donald M. Payne (D), District: 10
http://www.house.gov/payne/
E-mail: http://www.house.gov/payne/IMA/issue.htm

Rep. Rodney Frelinghuysen (R), District: 11
http://frelinghuysen.house.gov/
E-mail: http://frelinghuysen.house.gov/IMA/zip_verify.htm

Rep. Rush Holt (D), District: 12
http://holt.house.gov/
E-mail: http://holt.house.gov/contact.shtml

Rep. Robert Menendez (D), District: 13
http://menendez.house.gov/
*Rep. Menendez was appointed to the U.S. Senate in 2005. Albio Sires (D) was
elected to the House to represent the 13th district of New Jersey.*

New Mexico

Sen. Jeff Bingaman (D)
http://bingaman.senate.gov/
E-mail: senator_bingaman@bingaman.senate.gov

Sen. Pete V. Domenici (R)
http://domenici.senate.gov/
E-mail: http://domenici.senate.gov/contact/contactform.cfm

Rep. Heather Wilson (R), District: 01
http://wilson.house.gov/
E-mail: http://wilson.house.gov/Contact.asp

Rep. Steve Pearce (R), District: 02
http://pearce.house.gov/
E-mail: http://www.house.gov/formpearce/email.htm

Rep. Tom Udall (D), District: 03
http://www.tomudall.house.gov/
E-mail: http://www.tomudall.house.gov/feedback.cfm

New York

Sen. Hillary Rodham Clinton (D)
http://clinton.senate.gov/
E-mail: http://clinton.senate.gov/email_form.html

Sen. Charles E. Schumer (D)
http://schumer.senate.gov/
E-mail: http://schumer.senate.gov/SchumerWebsite/contact/webform.cfm

Rep. Timothy Bishop (D), District: 01
http://wwwc.house.gov/timbishop/
E-mail: http://wwwc.house.gov/timbishop/zipauth.htm

Rep. Steve Israel (D), District: 02
http://www.house.gov/israel/
E-mail: http://www.house.gov/israel/contact/index.htm

Rep. Peter King (R), District: 03
http://peteking.house.gov/
E-mail: http://peteking.house.gov/
index.cfm?SectionID = 3&ParentID = 0&SectionTree = 3&SectionTypeID = 2

Rep. Carolyn McCarthy (D), District: 04
http://carolynmccarthy.house.gov/

Rep. Gary Ackerman (D), District: 05
http://www.house.gov/ackerman/
E-mail: http://www.house.gov/ackerman/pages/contact.html

Rep. Gregory W. Meeks (D), District: 06
http://www.house.gov/meeks/
E-mail: http://www.house.gov/meeks/zipauth.htm

Rep. Joseph Crowley (D), District: 07
http://crowley.house.gov/
E-mail: write2joecrowley@mail.house.gov

Rep. Jerrold Nadler (D), District: 08
http://www.house.gov/nadler/
E-mail: http://www.house.gov/nadler/emailform.shtml

Rep. Anthony D. Weiner (D), District: 09
http://www.house.gov/weiner/
E-mail: weiner@mail.house.gov

Rep. Edolphus Towns (D), District: 10
http://www.house.gov/towns/
E-mail: http://www.house.gov/towns/offices.shtm

Rep. Major Owens (D), District: 11
http://www.house.gov/owens/
E-mail: http://www.house.gov/owens/contact.htm
*Rep. Owens did not seek re-election in 2006. Yvette Clarke (D) was elected to
the House to represent the 11th district of New York.*

Rep. Nydia M. Velázquez (D), District: 12
http://www.house.gov/velazquez/
E-mail: http://www.house.gov/velazquez/contact.htm

Rep. Vito Fossella (R), District: 13
http://www.house.gov/fossella/
E-mail: http://www.house.gov/fossella/email/

Rep. Carolyn Maloney (D), District: 14
http://www.house.gov/maloney/
E-mail: http://maloney.house.gov/
index.php?option = com_email_form&Itemid = 73

Rep. Charles B. Rangel (D), District: 15
http://www.house.gov/rangel/
E-mail: http://www.house.gov/rangel/contact.shtml

Rep. José E. Serrano (D), District: 16
http://www.house.gov/serrano/
E-mail: jserrano@mail.house.gov

Rep. Eliot L. Engel (D), District: 17
http://www.house.gov/engel/
E-mail: http://engel.house.gov/
index.cfm?SectionID = 3&ParentID = 0&SectionTypeID = 5&SectionTree = 3

Rep. Nita M. Lowey (D), District: 18
http://www.house.gov/lowey/
E-mail: http://www.house.gov/lowey/get_address.htm

Rep. Sue Kelly (R), District: 19
http://suekelly.house.gov/
E-mail: http://suekelly.house.gov/ContactInformation.asp
*Rep. Kelly lost her bid for re-election. John Hall (D) was elected to the House
to represent the 19th district of New York.*

Rep. John Sweeney (R), District: 20
http://www.house.gov/sweeney/
E-mail: http://www.house.gov/sweeney/contact/
*Rep. Sweeney lost his bid for re-election. Kirsten Gillibrand (D) was elected
to the House to represent the 20th district of New York.*

Rep. Michael McNulty (D), District: 21
http://www.house.gov/mcnulty/
E-mail: mike.mcnulty@mail.house.gov

Rep. Maurice Hinchey (D), District: 22
http://www.house.gov/hinchey/
E-mail: http://www.house.gov/hinchey/contact/

Rep. John M. McHugh (R), District: 23
http://mchugh.house.gov/
E-mail: http://mchugh.house.gov/zipauth.htm

Rep. Sherwood Boehlert (R), District: 24
http://www.house.gov/boehlert/
E-mail: http://www.house.gov/boehlert/contact.shtml
*Rep. Boehlert did not seek re-election in 2006. Michael Arcuri (D) was elected
to the House to represent the 24th district of New York.*

Rep. James T. Walsh (R), District: 25
http://www.house.gov/walsh/
E-mail: http://www.house.gov/walsh/contact.shtml

Rep. Tom Reynolds (R), District: 26
http://reynolds.house.gov/
E-mail: http://www.house.gov/formreynolds/zipauth.html

Rep. Brian M. Higgins (D), District: 27
http://higgins.house.gov/
E-mail: http://higgins.house.gov/email.asp

Rep. Louise M. Slaughter (D), District: 28
http://www.louise.house.gov/
E-mail: http://www.louise.house.gov/
index.php?option = com_content&task = view&id = 506&Itemid = 150

Rep. John R. "Randy" Kuhl (R), District: 29
http://kuhl.house.gov/
E-mail: http://www.house.gov/formkuhl/IMA/issue.htm

North Carolina

Sen. Elizabeth Dole (R)
http://dole.senate.gov/
E-mail: http://dole.senate.gov/
index.cfm?FuseAction = ContactInformation.ContactForm

Sen. Richard Burr (R)
http://burr.senate.gov/
E-mail: http://burr.senate.gov/index.cfm?FuseAction = Contact.Home

Rep. G.K. Butterfield (D), District: 01
http://www.house.gov/butterfield
E-mail: http://www.house.gov/butterfield/contact.shtml

Rep. Bob Etheridge (D), District: 02
http://www.house.gov/etheridge/
E-mail: http://www.house.gov/etheridge/contactbob.htm

Rep. Walter B. Jones (R), District: 03
http://jones.house.gov/
E-mail: http://jones.house.gov/html/contact_form_email.cfm

Rep. David Price (D), District: 04
http://price.house.gov/
E-mail: http://www.house.gov/formprice/email.htm

Rep. Virginia Foxx (R), District: 05
http://www.foxx.house.gov/
E-mail: http://www.foxx.house.gov/
index.cfm?SectionID = 22&ParentID = 0&SectionTypeID = 5&SectionTree = 22

Rep. Howard Coble (R), District: 06
http://coble.house.gov/
E-mail: howard.coble@mail.house.gov

Rep. Mike McIntyre (D), District: 07
http://www.house.gov/mcintyre/
E-mail: http://www.house.gov/mcintyre/IMA/issue.htm

Rep. Robin Hayes (R), District: 08
http://www.hayes.house.gov/
E-mail: http://www.hayes.house.gov/ContactCongHayes.asp

Rep. Sue Myrick (R), District: 09
http://myrick.house.gov/
E-mail: http://myrick.house.gov/contact_Myrick.shtml

Rep. Patrick McHenry (R), District: 10
http://mchenry.house.gov
E-mail: http://mchenry.house.gov/WriteRep/

Rep. Charles H. Taylor (R), District: 11
http://charlestaylor.house.gov/
E-mail: http://charlestaylor.house.gov/WriteMe/write.htm
Rep. Taylor lost his bid for re-election. Heath Shuler (D) was elected to the House to represent the 11th district of North Carolina.

Rep. Melvin L. Watt (D), District: 12
http://www.house.gov/watt/
E-mail: http://www.house.gov/watt/Tools/contact.htm

Rep. Brad Miller (D), District: 13
http://www.house.gov/bradmiller/

North Dakota

Sen. Kent Conrad (D)
http://conrad.senate.gov/
E-mail: http://conrad.senate.gov/webform.html

Sen. Byron Dorgan (D)
http://dorgan.senate.gov/
E-mail: senator@dorgan.senate.gov

Rep. Earl Pomeroy (D), District: At-Large
http://www.pomeroy.house.gov/
E-mail: http://www.house.gov/formpomeroy/zipauth.htm

Ohio

Sen. Mike DeWine (R)
http://dewine.senate.gov/
Email:
Sen. DeWine lost his bid for re-election. Sherrod Brown (D) was elected to fill Sen. DeWine's Senate seat.

Sen. George V. Voinovich (R)
http://voinovich.senate.gov/
E-mail: http://voinovich.senate.gov/contact/index.htm

Rep. Steve Chabot (R), District: 01
http://www.house.gov/chabot/
E-mail: http://www.house.gov/chabot/contacts.html

Rep. Jean Schmidt (R), District: 02
http://www.house.gov/schmidt/
E-mail: http://www.house.gov/schmidt/contact.shtml

Rep. Michael Turner (R), District: 03
http://www.house.gov/miketurner/
E-mail: http://www.house.gov/miketurner/contact.shtml

Rep. Michael G. Oxley (R), District: 04
http://oxley.house.gov/
E-mail: http://oxley.house.gov/contact.asp
Rep. Oxley did not seek re-election in 2006. Jim Jordan (R) was elected to the House to represent the 4th district of Ohio.

Rep. Paul E. Gillmor (R), District: 05
http://www.house.gov/gillmor/
E-mail: http://www.house.gov/gillmor/mail.htm

Rep. Ted Strickland (D), District: 06
http://www.house.gov/strickland/
E-mail: http://www.house.gov/strickland/contact.htm
Rep. Strickland did not seek re-election in 2006; instead, he ran successfully for governor of Ohio. Charles Wilson (D) was elected to the House to represent the 6th district of Ohio.

Rep. Dave Hobson (R), District: 07
http://www.house.gov/hobson/
E-mail: http://www.house.gov/hobson/formmail.htm

Rep. John Boehner (R), District: 08
http://johnboehner.house.gov
E-mail: http://johnboehner.house.gov/contact.asp

Rep. Marcy Kaptur (D), District: 09
http://www.kaptur.house.gov/
E-mail: http://www.kaptur.house.gov/library/contact.aspx

Rep. Dennis J. Kucinich (D), District: 10
http://kucinich.house.gov/
E-mail: http://kucinich.house.gov/Contact/

Rep. Stephanie Tubbs Jones (D), District: 11
http://www.house.gov/tubbsjones/
E-mail: http://www.house.gov/tubbsjones/contact.htm

Rep. Patrick Tiberi (R), District: 12
http://tiberi.house.gov/
E-mail: http://tiberi.house.gov/Contact/

Rep. Sherrod Brown (D), District: 13
http://www.house.gov/sherrodbrown/
E-mail: http://www.house.gov/sherrodbrown/email.htm
Rep. Brown did not seek re-election in 2006; instead, he ran successfully for U.S. Senate. Betty Sutton (D) was elected to the House to represent the 13th district of Ohio.

Rep. Steven C. LaTourette (R), District: 14
http://www.house.gov/latourette/
E-mail: http://www.house.gov/latourette/zipauth.htm

Rep. Deborah Pryce (R), District: 15
http://www.house.gov/pryce/
E-mail: http://www.house.gov/pryce/IMA/write.html

Rep. Ralph Regula (R), District: 16
http://wwwc.house.gov/regula/
E-mail: http://wwwc.house.gov/regula/zipauth.htm

Rep. Timothy Ryan (D), District: 17
http://timryan.house.gov/
E-mail: http://timryan.house.gov/HoR/OH17/Contact + Me.htm

Rep. Bob Ney (R), District: 18
http://ney.house.gov/
E-mail: http://ney.house.gov/contact.aspx
Rep. Ney did not seek re-election in 2006. Zachary Space (D) was elected to the House to represent the 18th district of Ohio.

Oklahoma

Sen. James M. Inhofe (R)
http://inhofe.senate.gov/
E-mail: http://inhofe.senate.gov/contactus.htm

Sen. Tom Coburn (R)
http://coburn.senate.gov/
E-mail: http://coburn.senate.gov/public/
index.cfm?FuseAction = ContactSenatorCoburn.Home

Rep. John Sullivan (R), District: 01
http://sullivan.house.gov/
E-mail: http://sullivan.house.gov/contact.shtml

Rep. Dan Boren (D), District: 02
http://www.house.gov/boren/index.shtml
E-mail: http://www.house.gov/boren/emailsignup.shtml

Rep. Frank Lucas (R), District: 03
http://www.house.gov/lucas/
E-mail: http://www.house.gov/lucas/zipauth.htm

Rep. Tom Cole (R), District: 04
http://www.house.gov/cole/
E-mail: http://www.house.gov/cole/contact.htm

Rep. Ernest J. Istook (R), District: 05
http://www.house.gov/istook/
E-mail: http://www.house.gov/istook/contact/
*Rep. Istook did not seek re-election in 2006; instead, he ran unsuccessfully
for governor of Oklahoma. Mary Fallin (R) was elected to the House to
represent the 5th district of Oklahoma.*

Oregon

Sen. Gordon H. Smith (R)
http://gsmith.senate.gov/public/
E-mail: http://gsmith.senate.gov/public/index.cfm?FuseAction = Contact.Home

Sen. Ron Wyden (D)
http://wyden.senate.gov/
E-mail: http://wyden.senate.gov/contact/

Rep. David Wu (D), District: 01
http://www.house.gov/wu/
E-mail: http://www.house.gov/wu/contact.htm

Rep. Gregory Walden (R), District: 02
http://walden.house.gov/
E-mail: http://walden.house.gov/index.cfm?FuseAction = ContactGreg.Home

Rep. Earl Blumenauer (D), District: 03
http://blumenauer.house.gov/
E-mail: http://blumenauer.house.gov/about/Contact.shtml

Rep. Peter DeFazio (D), District: 04
http://defazio.house.gov/
E-mail: http://defazio.house.gov/emailme.shtml

Rep. Darlene Hooley (D), District: 05
http://hooley.house.gov/
E-mail: http://hooley.house.gov/
index.asp?Type = DYNAFORM&SEC = {9BDA1E4D-2430-4E7D-B7AB-
236B60C42F5A}

Pennsylvania

Sen. Rick Santorum (R)
http://santorum.senate.gov/public/
E-mail: http://santorum.senate.gov/contactform.cfm
*Sen. Santorum lost his bid for re-election. Robert Casey Jr. (D) was elected to
fill Sen. Santorum's Senate seat.*

Sen. Arlen Specter (R)
http://specter.senate.gov/
E-mail: http://specter.senate.gov/index.cfm?FuseAction = ContactInfo.Home

Rep. Robert A. Brady (D), District: 01
http://www.house.gov/robertbrady/
E-mail: http://www.house.gov/robertbrady/IMA/issue.htm

Rep. Chaka Fattah (D), District: 02
http://www.house.gov/fattah/
E-mail: http://www.house.gov/fattah/functions/contact.htm

Rep. Phil English (R), District: 03
http://www.house.gov/english/
E-mail: http://www.house.gov/english/zipauth.shtml

Rep. Melissa Hart (R), District: 04
http://hart.house.gov
E-mail: http://hart.house.gov/contact.asp
Rep. Hart lost her bid for re-election. Jason Altmire (D) was elected to the House to represent the 4th district of Pennsylvania.

Rep. John E. Peterson (R), District: 05
http://www.house.gov/johnpeterson/
E-mail: http://www.house.gov/johnpeterson/contact.htm

Rep. Jim Gerlach (R), District: 06
http://gerlach.house.gov/
E-mail: http://gerlach.house.gov/Contact/

Rep. Curt Weldon (R), District: 07
http://curtweldon.house.gov/
E-mail: curtpa07@mail.house.gov
Rep. Weldon lost his bid for re-election. Joe Sestak (D) was elected to the House to represent the 7th district of Pennsylvania.

Rep. Michael G. Fitzpatrick (R), District: 08
http://fitzpatrick.house.gov/
E-mail: http://fitzpatrick.house.gov/writeme/write.htm
Rep. Fitzpatrick lost his bid for re-election. Patrick Murphy (D) was elected to the House to represent the 8th district of Pennsylvania.

Rep. Bill Shuster (R), District: 09
http://www.house.gov/shuster/
E-mail: http://www.house.gov/shuster/zipauth.htm

Rep. Don Sherwood (R), District: 10
http://www.house.gov/sherwood/
E-mail: http://www.house.gov/sherwood/contact_email.shtml
Rep. Sherwood lost his bid for re-election. Christopher Carney (D) was elected to the House to represent the 10th district of Pennsylvania.

Rep. Paul E. Kanjorski (D), District: 11
http://kanjorski.house.gov/
E-mail: http://kanjorski.house.gov/HoR/PA11/Hidden + Content/
Contact + Form.htm

Rep. John Murtha (D), District: 12
http://www.house.gov/murtha/
E-mail: http://www.house.gov/murtha/write.shtml

Rep. Allyson Y. Schwartz (D), District: 13
http://schwartz.house.gov/
E-mail: http://schwartz.house.gov/issue_subscribe.shtml

Rep. Mike Doyle (D), District: 14
http://www.house.gov/doyle/
E-mail: http://www.house.gov/doyle/email_mike.shtml

Rep. Charles W. Dent (R), District: 15
http://dent.house.gov/
E-mail: http://dent.house.gov/verifyemail.shtml

Rep. Joe Pitts (R), District: 16
http://www.house.gov/pitts/
E-mail: http://www.house.gov/pitts/service/correspond.htm

Rep. Tim Holden (D), District: 17
http://www.holden.house.gov/
E-mail: http://www.holden.house.gov/feedback-holden.cfm

Rep. Tim Murphy (R), District: 18
http://murphy.house.gov/
E-mail: http://murphy.house.gov/Contact/

Rep. Todd Platts (R), District: 19
http://www.house.gov/platts/
E-mail: http://www.house.gov/platts/email.html

Puerto Rico

Res. Commissioner Luis G. Fortuño (R), District: At-Large
http://www.house.gov/fortuno/
E-mail: http://www.house.gov/fortuno/contact.htm

Rhode Island

Sen. Lincoln Chafee (R)
http://chafee.senate.gov/
E-mail: http://chafee.senate.gov/webform.htm
Sen. Chafee lost his bid for re-election. Sheldon Whitehouse (D) was elected to fill Sen. Chafee's Senate seat.

Sen. Jack Reed (D)
http://reed.senate.gov/
E-mail: http://reed.senate.gov/contact/thoughts.cfm

Rep. Patrick J. Kennedy (D), District: 01
http://www.patrickkennedy.house.gov/
E-mail: Patrick.Kennedy@mail.house.gov

Rep. Jim Langevin (D), District: 02
http://www.house.gov/langevin/
E-mail: http://www.house.gov/langevin/comments.html

South Carolina

Sen. Lindsey Graham (R)
http://lgraham.senate.gov/
E-mail: http://lgraham.senate.gov/index.cfm?mode = contactform

Sen. Jim DeMint (R)
http://demint.senate.gov/
E-mail: http://demint.senate.gov/index.cfm?FuseAction = Contact.Home

Rep. Henry Brown (R), District: 01
http://brown.house.gov/
E-mail: http://brown.house.gov/writebrown/

Rep. Joe Wilson (R), District: 02
http://joewilson.house.gov/
E-mail: http://www.house.gov/formwilson/IMA/issue.htm

Rep. J. Gresham Barrett (R), District: 03
http://www.house.gov/barrett/
E-mail: http://www.house.gov/barrett/writebarrett.shtml

Rep. Bob Inglis (R), District: 04
http://www.house.gov/inglis/
E-mail: http://inglis.house.gov/contact.asp?content = sections/contact/
write_inglis

Rep. John Spratt (D), District: 05
http://www.house.gov/spratt/
E-mail: http://www.house.gov/spratt/email_john.shtml

Rep. James E. Clyburn (D), District: 06
http://www.house.gov/clyburn/
E-mail: http://clyburn.house.gov/
contact.cfm?CFID = 917943&CFTOKEN = 26544993

South Dakota

Sen. John R. Thune (R)
http://thune.senate.gov/
E-mail: http://thune.senate.gov/public/index.cfm?FuseAction = Contact.Email

Sen. Tim Johnson (D)
http://johnson.senate.gov/
E-mail: http://johnson.senate.gov/emailform.cfm

Rep. Stephanie Herseth (D), District: At-Large
http://www.house.gov/herseth/
E-mail: stephanie.herseth@mail.house.gov

Tennessee

Sen. Lamar Alexander (R)
http://alexander.senate.gov/
E-mail: http://alexander.senate.gov/index.cfm?FuseAction = Contact.Home

Sen. Bill Frist M.D. (R)
http://frist.senate.gov/
E-mail: http://frist.senate.gov/
index.cfm?FuseAction = AboutSenatorFrist.ContactForm
Sen. Frist did not seek re-election in 2006. Bob Corker (R) was elected to fill Sen. Frist's Senate seat.

Rep. William L. Jenkins (R), District: 01
http://www.house.gov/jenkins/
E-mail: http://www.house.gov/jenkins/contact.shtml
Rep. Jenkins did not seek re-election in 2006. David Davis (R) was elected to the House to represent the 1st district of Tennessee.

Rep. John J. Duncan Jr. (R), District: 02
http://www.house.gov/duncan/
E-mail: http://www.house.gov/duncan/contact.htm

Rep. Zach Wamp (R), District: 03
http://www.house.gov/wamp/
E-mail: http://www.house.gov/wamp/contact_email.shtm

Rep. Lincoln Davis (D), District: 04
http://www.house.gov/lincolndavis/
E-mail: http://www.house.gov/lincolndavis/emaillincoln.htm

Rep. Jim Cooper (D), District: 05
http://www.cooper.house.gov/
E-mail: http://cooper.house.gov/email.htm

Rep. Bart Gordon (D), District: 06
http://gordon.house.gov/
E-mail: http://gordon.house.gov/contact/index.shtml#onlineform

Rep. Marsha Blackburn (R), District: 07
http://www.house.gov/blackburn/

Rep. John Tanner (D), District: 08
http://www.house.gov/tanner/
E-mail: http://www.house.gov/tanner/contact.htm

Rep. Harold Ford Jr. (D), District: 09
http://www.house.gov/ford/
E-mail: http://www.house.gov/ford/contact/
Rep. Ford did not seek re-election in 2006; instead, he ran unsuccessfully for U.S. Senate. Stephen Cohen (D) was elected to the House to represent the 9th district of Tennessee.

Texas

Sen. John Cornyn (R)
http://cornyn.senate.gov/
E-mail: http://cornyn.senate.gov/index.asp?f = contact&lid = 1#contact

Sen. Kay Bailey Hutchison (R)
http://hutchison.senate.gov
E-mail: http://hutchison.senate.gov/e-mail.htm

Rep. Louie Gohmert (R), District: 01
http://gohmert.house.gov/
E-mail: http://gohmert.house.gov/contact_louie.htm

Rep. Ted Poe (R), District: 02
http://www.house.gov/poe/
E-mail: http://www.house.gov/poe/writeyourrep.htm

Rep. Sam Johnson (R), District: 03
http://www.samjohnson.house.gov/
E-mail: http://www.house.gov/formsamjohnson/IMA/issue.htm

Rep. Ralph Hall (R), District: 04
http://www.house.gov/ralphhall/
E-mail: http://www.house.gov/ralphhall/IMA/zipauth.htm

Rep. Jeb Hensarling (R), District: 05
http://www.house.gov/hensarling/
E-mail: http://www.house.gov/hensarling/contact_web.shtml

Rep. Joe Barton (R), District: 06
http://joebarton.house.gov/
E-mail: http://joebarton.house.gov/contact.asp

Rep. John Culberson (R), District: 07
http://www.culberson.house.gov/
E-mail: http://www.culberson.house.gov/contactinfo.aspx

Rep. Kevin Brady (R), District: 08
http://www.house.gov/brady/
E-mail: rep.brady@mail.house.gov

Rep. Al Green (D), District: 09
http://www.house.gov/algreen/
E-mail: http://www.house.gov/algreen/contact.shtml

Rep. Michael McCaul (R), District: 10
http://www.house.gov/mccaul/
E-mail: http://www.house.gov/mccaul/email.shtml

Rep. Mike Conaway (R), District: 11
http://conaway.house.gov/
E-mail: http://conaway.house.gov/IMA/contact.asp

Rep. Kay Granger (R), District: 12
http://kaygranger.house.gov/
E-mail: http://kaygranger.house.gov/contact.asp

Rep. Mac Thornberry (R), District: 13
http://www.house.gov/thornberry/
E-mail: http://www.house.gov/thornberry/contact_info.htm

Rep. Ron Paul (R), District: 14
http://www.house.gov/paul/
E-mail: http://www.house.gov/paul/contact.shtml

Rep. Rubén Hinojosa (D), District: 15
http://hinojosa.house.gov/
E-mail: http://hinojosa.house.gov/const_services/contact.cfm

Rep. Silvestre Reyes (D), District: 16
http://wwwc.house.gov/reyes/
E-mail: http://wwwc.house.gov/reyes/voice_your_opinion.asp

Rep. Chet Edwards (D), District: 17
http://edwards.house.gov/
E-mail: http://edwards.house.gov/html/contact_form_email.cfm

Rep. Sheila Jackson Lee (D), District: 18
http://www.jacksonlee.house.gov/
E-mail: http://www.jacksonlee.house.gov/feedback.cfm

Rep. Randy Neugebauer (R), District: 19
http://www.randy.house.gov/
E-mail: http://www.randy.house.gov/contact/

Rep. Charles A. Gonzalez (D), District: 20
http://gonzalez.house.gov/
E-mail: http://gonzalez.house.gov/
feedback.cfm?campaign = gonzalez&type = Contact%20Me

Rep. Lamar Smith (R), District: 21
http://lamarsmith.house.gov/
E-mail: http://lamarsmith.house.gov/contact.asp

Vacant, District: 22
Rep. Tom DeLay resigned in June 2006. Nicholas Lampson (D) was elected to the House to represent the 22nd district of Texas.

Rep. Henry Bonilla (R), District: 23
http://bonilla.house.gov/
E-mail: http://bonilla.house.gov/Default.aspx?section = contacts&page = contacts
At the time this publication went to press, the outcome of the election in this district was still being determined.

Rep. Kenny Marchant (R), District: 24
http://www.marchant.house.gov/
E-mail: http://www.marchant.house.gov/contact.shtml

Rep. Lloyd Doggett (D), District: 25
http://www.house.gov/doggett/
E-mail: http://www.house.gov/doggett/doggett_ima/doggett_get_address_test.htm

Rep. Michael Burgess (R), District: 26
http://burgess.house.gov/
E-mail: http://burgess.house.gov/Contact/

Rep. Solomon P. Ortiz (D), District: 27
http://www.house.gov/ortiz/
E-mail: http://www.house.gov/ortiz/email_me.shtml

Rep. Henry Cuellar (D), District: 28
http://www.house.gov/cuellar/
E-mail: http://www.house.gov/cuellar/zipauth.htm

Rep. Gene Green (D), District: 29
http://www.house.gov/green/
E-mail: http://www.house.gov/green/contact/

Rep. Eddie Bernice Johnson (D), District: 30
http://www.house.gov/ebjohnson/
E-mail: http://www.house.gov/ebjohnson/contact_ebj/index.shtml

Rep. John Carter (R), District: 31
http://www.house.gov/carter/
E-mail: http://carter.house.gov/Contact/

Rep. Pete Sessions (R), District: 32
http://sessions.house.gov/
E-mail: http://www.house.gov/sessionsform/emailform.htm

Utah

Sen. Robert Bennett (R)
http://bennett.senate.gov/
E-mail: http://bennett.senate.gov/contact/emailmain.html

Sen. Orrin Hatch (R)
http://hatch.senate.gov/
E-mail: http://hatch.senate.gov/index.cfm?Fuseaction = Offices.Contact

Rep. Rob Bishop (R), District: 01
http://www.house.gov/robbishop/
E-mail: http://www.house.gov/robbishop/contact/

Rep. Jim Matheson (D), District: 02
http://www.house.gov/matheson/
E-mail: http://www.house.gov/matheson/contact.shtml

Rep. Chris Cannon (R), District: 03
http://chriscannon.house.gov/
E-mail: http://chriscannon.house.gov/email.htm

Vermont

Sen. Jim Jeffords (I)
http://jeffords.senate.gov/
E-mail: http://jeffords.senate.gov/contact.html
Sen. Jeffords did not seek re-election in 2006. Bernie Sanders (I) was elected to fill Sen. Jeffords's Senate seat.

Sen. Patrick Leahy (D)
http://leahy.senate.gov/
E-mail: senator_leahy@leahy.senate.gov

Rep. Bernie Sanders (I), District: At-Large
http://bernie.house.gov/
E-mail: http://bernie.house.gov/const_serv/comments.asp
Rep. Sanders did not seek re-election in 2006; instead, he ran successfully for U.S. Senate. Peter Welch (D) was elected to the House to represent the state of Vermont.

Virginia

Sen. George Allen (R)
http://allen.senate.gov/
E-mail: http://allen.senate.gov/public/
index.cfm?FuseAction=AboutGeorgeAllen.SendAnEmail&EmailContactForm=
Type+your+e-mail&x=13&y=10
Sen. Allen lost his bid for re-election. Jim Webb (D) was elected to fill Sen. Allen's Senate seat.

Sen. John Warner (R)
http://warner.senate.gov/
E-mail: http://warner.senate.gov/contact/contactme.cfm

Rep. Jo Ann Davis (R), District: 01
http://joanndavis.house.gov/
E-mail: http://joanndavis.house.gov/HoR/VA01/Contact+Information/

Rep. Thelma D. Drake (R), District: 02
http://drake.house.gov/
E-mail: http://www.house.gov/formdrake/IMA/issue_subscribe.htm

Rep. Robert C. "Bobby" Scott (D), District: 03
http://www.house.gov/scott/
E-mail: http://www.house.gov/scott/contact/index.html

Rep. J. Randy Forbes (R), District: 04
http://www.house.gov/forbes/
E-mail: http://www.house.gov/forbes/zipauth.htm

Rep. Virgil H. Goode Jr. (R), District: 05
http://www.house.gov/goode/
E-mail: http://www.house.gov/goode/contact.shtml

Rep. Bob Goodlatte (R), District: 06
http://www.house.gov/goodlatte/
E-mail: http://www.house.gov/goodlatte/emailbob.htm

Rep. Eric Cantor (R), District: 07
http://cantor.house.gov/
E-mail: http://cantor.house.gov/contact/index.htm

Rep. Jim Moran (D), District: 08
http://moran.house.gov/
E-mail: http://moran.house.gov/feedback.moran.cfm

Rep. Rick Boucher (D), District: 09
http://www.house.gov/boucher/
E-mail: http://www.boucher.house.gov/
index.php?option = com_content&task = view&id = 645&Itemid =

Rep. Frank Wolf (R), District: 10
http://www.house.gov/wolf/
E-mail: http://www.house.gov/wolf/email/email.html

Rep. Tom Davis (R), District: 11
http://tomdavis.house.gov/
E-mail: http://tomdavis.house.gov/davis_contents/center/feedback/

Virgin Islands

Del. Donna Christian-Christensen (D), District: At-Large
http://www.house.gov/christian-christensen/

Washington

Sen. Maria Cantwell (D)
http://cantwell.senate.gov/
E-mail: http://cantwell.senate.gov/contact/index.html

Sen. Patty Murray (D)
http://murray.senate.gov/
E-mail: http://murray.senate.gov/email/index.cfm

Rep. Jay Inslee (D), District: 01
http://www.house.gov/inslee/
E-mail: http://www.house.gov/inslee/contact/email.html

Rep. Rick Larsen (D), District: 02
http://www.house.gov/larsen/
E-mail: rick.larsen@mail.house.gov

Rep. Brian Baird (D), District: 03
http://www.house.gov/baird/
E-mail: http://www.house.gov/baird/IMA/email.shtml

Rep. Doc Hastings (R), District: 04
http://hastings.house.gov/
E-mail: http://hastings.house.gov/ContactForm.aspx

Rep. Cathy McMorris (R), District: 05
http://www.mcmorris.house.gov/
E-mail: http://www.mcmorris.house.gov/IMA/issue_subscribe.htm

Rep. Norm Dicks (D), District: 06
http://www.house.gov/dicks/
E-mail: http://www.house.gov/dicks/contact.html

Rep. Jim McDermott (D), District: 07
http://www.house.gov/mcdermott/
E-mail: http://www.house.gov/mcdermott/contact.shtml

Rep. David Reichert (R), District: 08
http://www.house.gov/reichert/
E-mail: http://www.house.gov/reichert/IMA/issue_subscribe.htm

Rep. Adam Smith (D), District: 09
http://www.house.gov/adamsmith/
E-mail: http://www.house.gov/adamsmith/IMA/email.shtml

West Virginia

Sen. Robert C. Byrd (D)
http://byrd.senate.gov/
E-mail: http://byrd.senate.gov/byrd_email.html

Sen. Jay Rockefeller (D)
http://rockefeller.senate.gov/
E-mail: http://rockefeller.senate.gov/services/email.cfm

Rep. Alan B. Mollohan (D), District: 01
http://www.house.gov/mollohan/

Rep. Shelley Moore Capito (R), District: 02
http://capito.house.gov/

Rep. Nick Rahall (D), District: 03
http://www.rahall.house.gov/
E-mail: http://www.rahall.house.gov/
index.php?option = com_content&task = view&id = 521&Itemid = 162

Wisconsin

Sen. Russell Feingold (D)
http://feingold.senate.gov/
E-mail: http://feingold.senate.gov/contact_opinion.html

Sen. Herbert Kohl (D)
http://kohl.senate.gov/
E-mail: http://kohl.senate.gov/gen_contact.html

Rep. Paul Ryan (R), District: 01
http://www.house.gov/ryan/
E-mail: http://www.house.gov/ryan/email.htm

Rep. Tammy Baldwin (D), District: 02
http://tammybaldwin.house.gov/
E-mail: http://www.house.gov/formbaldwin/IMA/get_address.htm

Rep. Ron Kind (D), District: 03
http://www.house.gov/kind/
E-mail: http://www.house.gov/kind/contact.shtml

Rep. Gwen Moore (D), District: 04
http://www.house.gov/gwenmoore/
E-mail: http://www.house.gov/gwenmoore/contact.shtml

Rep. F. James Sensenbrenner Jr. (R), District: 05
http://www.house.gov/sensenbrenner/
E-mail: sensenbrenner@mail.house.gov

Rep. Tom Petri (R), District: 06
http://www.house.gov/petri/

Rep. Dave Obey (D), District: 07
http://obey.house.gov/
E-mail: http://obey.house.gov/HoR/WI07/Miscellaneous + Information/
email + sign + up + form.htm

Rep. Mark Green (R), District: 08
http://www.house.gov/markgreen/
E-mail: mark.green@mail.house.gov
*Rep. Green did not seek re-election in 2006; instead, he ran unsuccessfully
for governor of Wisconsin. Steve Kagen (D) was elected to the House to
represent the 8th district of Wisconsin.*

Wyoming

Sen. Mike Enzi (R)
http://enzi.senate.gov/
E-mail: http://enzi.senate.gov/email.htm

Sen. Craig Thomas (R)
http://thomas.senate.gov/
E-mail: http://thomas.senate.gov/index.cfm?FuseAction = Contact.Home

Rep. Barbara Cubin (R), District: At-Large
http://www.house.gov/cubin/
E-mail: http://www.house.gov/cubin/zip_auth.html

Congressional Committees

This appendix lists the committees and committee Web sites of the House, Senate, and Joint committees for the 110th Congress. At the time this publication went to press, both Republicans and Democrats were in the process of choosing their committee leaders for the 110th Congress. Democrats, having taken the majorities in the House and the Senate, will chair the committees in both chambers; Republicans will serve as ranking minority members.

United States House of Representatives

Standing Committees:

Committee on Agriculture
http://agriculture.house.gov/

Committee on Appropriations
http://appropriations.house.gov/

Committee on Armed Services
http://armedservices.house.gov/

Committee on the Budget
http://www.house.gov/budget/

Committee on Education and the Workforce
http://edworkforce.house.gov/

Committee on Energy and Commerce
http://energycommerce.house.gov/

Committee on Financial Services
http://financialservices.house.gov/

Committee on Government Reform
http://reform.house.gov/

Committee on Homeland Security
http://hsc.house.gov/

Committee on House Administration
http://www.house.gov/cha/

Committee on International Relations
http://wwwa.house.gov/international_relations/

Committee on the Judiciary
http://judiciary.house.gov/

Committee on Resources
http://resourcescommittee.house.gov/

Committee on Rules
http://www.house.gov/rules/

Committee on Science
http://www.house.gov/science/

Committee on Small Business
http://wwwc.house.gov/smbiz/

Committee on Standards of Official Conduct
http://www.house.gov/ethics/

Committee on Transportation and Infrastructure
http://www.house.gov/transportation/

Committee on Veterans Affairs
http://veterans.house.gov/

Committee on Ways and Means
http://waysandmeans.house.gov/

Special and Select Committees:

House Permanent Select Committee on Intelligence
http://intelligence.house.gov/

United States Senate

Standing Committees:

Agriculture, Nutrition, and Forestry
http://agriculture.senate.gov/

Appropriations
http://appropriations.senate.gov/

Armed Services
http://armed-services.senate.gov/

Banking, Housing, and Urban Affairs
http://banking.senate.gov/

Budget
http://budget.senate.gov/

Commerce, Science, and Transportation
http://commerce.senate.gov/

Energy and Natural Resources
http://energy.senate.gov/public/

Environment and Public Works
http://epw.senate.gov/

Finance
http://finance.senate.gov/

Foreign Relations
http://foreign.senate.gov/

Health, Education, Labor, and Pensions
http://help.senate.gov/

Homeland Security and Governmental Affairs
http://hsgac.senate.gov/

Judiciary
http://judiciary.senate.gov/

Rules and Administration
http://rules.senate.gov/

Small Business and Entrepreneurship
http://sbc.senate.gov/

Veterans Affairs
http://veterans.senate.gov/

Special and Select Committees:

Indian Affairs
http://indian.senate.gov/

Select Committee on Ethics
http://ethics.senate.gov/

Select Committee on Intelligence
http://intelligence.senate.gov/

Special Committee on Aging
http://aging.senate.gov/public/

Joint Committees

Joint Committee on Printing
http://www.house.gov/jcp/

Joint Committee on Taxation
http://www.house.gov/jct/

Joint Committee on the Library
http://www.senate.gov/general/committee_membership/
committee_memberships_JSLC.htm

Note: The Joint Committee on the Library consists only of members of the Senate. Additionally, the committee does not have a vice chairman.

Joint Economic Committee
http://jec.senate.gov/

Sponsor Name/Site Name Index

This index lists Web site names by the sponsoring government department, company, or organization. The numbers refer to entry numbers. Excluded from this index are entries for the Web sites of members of Congress. Please see Appendix A for a list of representatives and senators.

Sponsor/Site Name	Entry Number

Defense Nuclear Facilities Safety Board

Democratic National Committee

Duke University. Perkins Library

Education Department

Publication Index

This index covers many of the online publications available from the sites listed in this book. This index lists the documents by their publication title. Note that the numbers refer to entry numbers and not to page numbers.

Spanish Web Site Index

This index lists Web site names containing Spanish-language content and is grouped by chapter names. The numbers refer to entry numbers and not page numbers.

Master Index: Subjects, Sponsors, and Titles

This index includes entries for the Subjects, Sponsors, and Titles listed in this directory. Where the Title duplicates a Sponsor, the index entries are merged. Note that the numbers refer to entry numbers and not to page numbers.

Entry Number

Entry Number

Entry Number

Entry Number

Entry Number

Entry Number